THE SELF-CONCEPT

REVISED EDITION

VOLUME TWO

Theory and Research on Selected Topics

by

Ruth C. Wylie

in collaboration with

. Peggy J. Miller

Susan S. Cowles

Alice W. Wilson

UNIVERSITY OF NEBRASKA PRESS • LINCOLN/LONDON

To the Memory of
Katherine E. Baker

Contents

Preface

Many of the points made in the Preface to volume 1 are pertinent to this volume as well and therefore are not repeated here. Volume 2 is devoted to critical evaluations of substantive studies of self-concept variables in selected topic areas. For each topical area, a brief theoretical background is given, and published reports are critically evaluated in the light of methodological standards discussed in volume 1 and in each research chapter of volume 2. To the extent that the results permit, provisional generalizations or hypotheses are stated. I hope this volume will give students, researchers, and professional persons some idea of the range of questions which have been considered, the current state of the evidence on selected topics, and the important questions which have not as yet been addressed. It should also provide a sobering view of theoretical and methodological problems which must be taken into account before generalizing about self-concept variables on the basis of past research or laying plans for future work in the area.

One of my greatest sources of enjoyment in preparing this volume has been working with my collaborators. Peggy Miller is the author of chapter 5. Alice Wilson had primary responsibility for preparing chapter 6. Susan Cowles drafted evaluative summaries of a substantial number of the studies in chapters 3 and 7. Both Peggy Miller and Susan Cowles were also involved in all other aspects of the preparation of this volume.

Correspondence with a number of authors whose work is cited in this volume clarified certain questions I had about their theoretical ideas or empirical work. In some cases, correspondents provided enlightening unpublished data. Barbara Long has been helpful in suggesting useful references and giving some items of general background information pertinent to the chapters on developmental and social-psychological topics.

I am much indebted to my mother, Georgiana Wylie, for her unstinting encouragement and professionally informed appreciation of the goals and exacting requirements of my work. My friend and colleague, the late Katherine E. Baker, gave especially valuable support and helpful methodological advice in the earliest phases of preparing this volume.

Every portion of the manuscript has been read by at least one of these persons: Mary Evans Collins, Susan Cowles (who read and made very helpful comments on successive drafts of every chapter), Margaret Crull, Howard Friedman, William McGuire, Kathy Miller, Peggy Miller, Ellen Piers, Olive Westbrooke Quinn, Mark Reutter, Milton Rokeach, Morris Rosenberg, David Rosenthal, Charles Schaefer, Sally Wall, Alice Wilson, Robert Wilson, Lawrence Wrightsman, and Marian Yarrow. The clarity, accuracy, coherence, and comprehensiveness of the work were greatly improved by taking their helpful suggestions into account.

In regard to the technical aspects of preparation of this volume, I am particularly indebted to Kathy Miller for typing and bibliographic search; Philip Cowles, Mary Finn, Peggy Miller, Mary Vancura, and Alice Wilson for typing; and Teresa Perella of the Goucher College Library for obtaining innumerable interlibrary loans.

Goucher College provided a half-year leave of absence and some funds for typing and bibliographic search, greatly facilitating the completion of this volume.

The publisher and the author wish to express their gratitude to the copyright owners listed below for permission to quote from their publications: *Acta Sociologica*, American Psychological Association, Inc., Appleton-Century-Crofts, Inc., Basic Books, Duke University Press, D. Van Nostrand Co., Inc., *Educational and Psychological Measurement*, Houghton Mifflin Co., Inc., *Human Relations, Journal of Clinical Psychology, Journal of Counseling Psychology, Journal of Projective Techniques*, Journal Press, *Journal of Social Issues*, Ohio State University Press, *Personnel and Guidance Journal*, the Ronald Press Co., School of Aviation Medicine, United States Air Force, University of Chicago Press, and Yale University Press.

Preface to Volume 1

A number of considerations entered into my decision to undertake the revision of my 1961 book, *The Self Concept: A Critical Survey of Pertinent Research Literature*. First, it is obvious that interest in the self-concept or some aspect of it has been high and widespread in a number of fields, probably even increasing during the twelve years since the 1961 book went to press. I infer this interest level from the innumerable allusions to the self-concept in many psychology, education, and sociology books, and from the overwhelming volume of research output indexed in the *Psychological Abstracts*.

A second consideration was the increase in methodological publications which presented ideas that self-concept researchers should know about and use. These ideas include critiques of once commonly employed methods, suggestions for improved methods, and current controversies about these more recently suggested methods. Third, an enormous number of substantive research studies has appeared; and it seemed that these need to be summarized, evaluated critically, and synthesized insofar as possible in order to be maximally available and useful to researchers and theorists. Finally, quite a few colleagues and friends encouraged me to undertake this revision because they shared my opinion that the above considerations imply that such a revision will be useful.

It is my hope that this volume will make three kinds of contributions. First and foremost, it may play a part in improving the quality of self-concept research in the future. Although methodological guidelines and critiques are available in many journal articles and books, these ideas are widely scattered. It requires considerable time and effort to find, evaluate, and synthesize them; and it is often not obvious from such sources just how the various methodological considerations are conceptually relevant and practically applicable to the particular problems with which the self-concept researcher wishes to deal. Perhaps the present overview and synthesis will be helpful along these lines. Moreover, I hope that my specific critiques of particular studies and lines of research may prove to be a helpful supplement to general methodological discussions, in that the more specific critiques may alert future self-concept researchers to the characteristic pitfalls they should avoid. Additionally, a quick entrée into what is available by way of instruments and what has been done thus far on given substantive topics may enable future self-concept researchers to choose their next steps more expeditiously and wisely.

Secondly, although the focus of this work is the self-concept, I hope that the methodological sections especially may make a valuable contribution to students of other aspects of personality, helping them to evaluate and improve research in their respective areas. Many of the methodological references brought together here and the methodological issues evaluated in this work are relevant to measurement of a variety of personality constructs and to testing a variety of propositions regarding personality.

The two potential contributions already mentioned could be rather briefly described, but clarifying the third requires somewhat more explanation—an exposition which is longer than the relative importance I assign it among the three potential contributions. I hope that this work may indirectly bring about an improvement in the education of beginning students of psychology. I have been deeply concerned about the possibility that unfortunate educational effects are being created by the way in which ideas about the self-concept have been presented in introductory psychology texts and in texts purporting to be intermediate-level treatments of personality psychology. For example, I looked at 15 introductory books published between 1968 and 1972. Of these, 4 did not index *self-concept* or any apparently related term, and with the omission of the topic I have no quarrel. Although the remaining 11 texts indicated in title and/or preface the intent to present a scientific approach to psychology, all made broad, unsupported, uncriticized generalizations about the self-concept. That is, the sections about the self-concept had one or more of the following failings which could seriously mislead the student and interfere with his acquiring a scientific attitude toward this topic: (a) No indication was given that the statements were intended to be theoretical propositions, as opposed to known relationships. The impression created is that these are obvious truths which may be validated by a reader's experiences, when in fact they are assertions from a most complex, inadequately explored area of psychology. (b) Either no study relevant to any of the general assertions was even mentioned, or one or two were briefly cited. (Sometimes even these were not actually self-concept studies!) (c) No doubts were expressed about the methodological adequacy of the cited study or studies. (d) No inkling was given that a large volume of research has been published and that serious controversy remains, partly because of unresolved methodological problems. Of course I do not believe that an introductory text should be a miniature critical exegesis of research literature and related methodology. But I do believe that such extreme departures from the scientific approach as those listed above can quite probably have one or more unfortunate effects: (a) Widespread credence is lent to unsupported common-sense statements and to the idea that making such assertions in the name of scientific psychology is acceptable among experts. (b) Brighter, more discerning students will develop a disrespect for psychologists' approach to this topic (thus alienating some of them from going on to learn more about the field and to make their own contributions). (c) The future psychologist beginning his exposure to the field by reading such texts will have to unlearn erroneous ideas before he can go on to attain an accurate picture of the field and perhaps to make a scientific contribution; or if he does not unlearn these ideas before undertaking his own research, the volume of uninterpretable research will be further increased.

The situation with regard to intermediate-level personality texts is much the same as with the introductory texts. Excluding those purporting only to present theories and those specializing in personality assessment, I examined eight personality texts published between 1962 and 1972. The seven of these which purported to represent a scientific approach and which discussed the self-concept gave more extensive treatment to the topic than was the case in the introductory books. Only two, however, cited an appreciable number of substantive and methodological research publications; and even here, critical evaluation of the studies themselves or their merits for supporting or refuting the stated generalizations was often superficial, sparse, or missing altogether. All in all, then, even the student who proceeds to the intermediate level of personality study is plausibly liable to suffer many of the same unfortunate educational effects as I suggested might result from his reading about the self-concept in introductory texts.

I am not, of course, suggesting that the present book should be read by beginning students. Rather, I should like to believe that authors of introductory or intermediate texts might be helped by this work to improve the educational effectiveness of their presentations of self-concept materials to introductory students, and that the state of contemporary texts being what it is, instructors may find this book a useful source for correcting or supplementing textual materials.

Every portion of the manuscript has been read by at least one of the following persons; and the clarity, accuracy, and comprehensiveness of the work were much improved by following their helpful suggestions: Katherine E. Baker, Peter Bentler, Robert Bills, Donald T. Campbell, Donald Fiske, David Hamilton, Kristina Pritchard, Barbara Long, Peggy J. Miller, Ellen Piers, Morris Rosenberg, Franklin Shontz, Julian Stanley, Susan Stevenson, and Alice W. Wilson. I am especially indebted to my friend and professional colleague Katherine E. Baker, with whom I have spent many profitable and enjoyable hours discussing psychology in general and the issues in this book in particular. Of course I take responsibility for whatever flaws remain in this manuscript despite all the help which has so generously been given me.

In regard to technical aspects of the preparation of this volume, I wish to thank Catherine Borland and Judith Parker for typing assistance; Stephanie Bernstein and Margaret Weigel for aid in various phases of reading and correcting proof; Mary Coughlin for assistance in bibliographic search; and Peggy J. Miller for aid in all these technical phases of the work as well as for intelligent and thorough aid in categorizing and excerpting the bibliographic references. Teresa Perella and Penelope Partlow of the Goucher College Library have been especially helpful in obtaining interlibrary loans.

Goucher College provided a half-year's leave and some financial support for early phases of the bibliographic search. Without these, this volume could not have been completed.

RUTH C. WYLIE
Goucher College

THE SELF-CONCEPT

1
Introduction

A. General Scope and Purpose of this Book

This is the second of two volumes, the first of which is concerned with a conceptual treatment of methodology relevant to self-concept research and an evaluation of extant designs, procedures, and measurement techniques.

This volume considers selected topical clusters of substantive research studies. Each such cluster is examined from the standpoints of possibly relevant theory, methodological adequacy according to the criteria presented in volume 1, and conclusiveness in light of the methodological adequacy and the range of potential questions which were actually covered by the studies within the cluster.

As was true in volume 1, the domain to be surveyed is broadly conceived to include research publications of pertinence to a wide variety of theories which accord an important or even central role to self-referent constructs, including over-all self-evaluation and more specific cognitions and evaluations of self (e.g., Adler [Ansbacher and Ansbacher, 1956]; Allport, 1961; Angyal, 1941; Aronson, 1969; Byrne, 1971; Cattell, 1966; Erickson, 1959, 1963; Fromm, 1939; Horney, 1937, 1967; E. E. Jones, 1964; Jung [Progoff, 1953]; Lecky, 1945; Lynd, 1958; Maslow, 1954; McClelland, 1951; Mead, 1934; Rogers, 1951, 1959; Snygg & Combs, 1949; Sullivan, 1953). Some of these writers have been called phenomenological theorists because of their stress on the role of the conscious self-concept in determining a person's behavior. Although volume 1 gives some attention to nonphenomenal constructs in the chapters on operational definitions of the nonphenomenal self and insightfulness of the self-concept, this volume includes only studies which appear to be dealing at least partly with the conscious self-concept. This limitation is imposed because I concluded in volume 1 that there are no methodologically defensible ways presently available to measure the unconscious self-concept and insightfulness of the self-concept.

I have construed the term self-concept to include the following: (a) cognitions and evaluations regarding relatively specific aspects of self, e.g., mathematics ability, predispositional anxiety in interpersonal situations, family status such as being a parent, racial identity, gender identity, class membership; (b) ideal self, which I see as comprising not only the person's ideals about specific self-aspects such as being scholastically able, having a sense of humor, being well liked by peers, but also such phenomenal goals as wishing to be a well-educated

3

person or to attain a particular career status; (c) over-all self-regard — my generic term to cover such "global" constructs as self-esteem, self-acceptance, self-favorability, and self-ideal discrepancies which are presumably determined by some combination of cognitions and evaluations of many attributes of self.

Thus, from one viewpoint, any investigation which asks the subject to make a cognitive or evaluative report about any relatively enduring aspect of self might be construed to be a self-concept study. It follows that all researches using personality inventories or interviews referring to self-characteristics might have been included. However, in collecting materials on each topic, I began by examining those studies in which the researcher's avowed purpose was to index self-concept, or whose avowed inspiration came at least partly from self theory. Other investigations with techniques operationally comparable to these were then included, whether or not their authors had called them self-concept researches.

B. Methods and Dates of Search for Titles

As a point of departure, the *Psychological Abstracts* from January, 1960, through June, 1975, were searched by hand and, for some months, by computer. (Interestingly, the two methods yielded somewhat different sets of titles.) The *Annual Reviews of Psychology* from 1960 through 1976 were also examined. In several large university and medical school libraries we looked at the tables of contents of all plausibly appropriate journals for 1973, 1974, and the first seven months of 1975. From the reference lists of the initially collected publications, additional titles were located. Finally, critics of preliminary chapter drafts suggested still other titles.

The tremendous proliferation of journals and books within the last decade is striking. Moreover, a fair number of them are, for practical purposes, inaccessible, even when one uses interlibrary loan or searches directly in such places as large university libraries, the National Library of Medicine, or the Library of Congress. One cannot help wondering of what value to science such publications can be.

Generally speaking, this volume is based on titles which are dated through mid-1975. A few more recent references are cited. Most references from the 1961 edition of the book are also included here.

C. Criteria for Title Inclusion

To be considered for inclusion, a reference (with rare exceptions) had to be published, as opposed to being mimeographed for private circulation, and to be written in the English language. Because publications in *Dissertation Abstracts* typically provide too little information for proper methodological evaluation, they were excluded.

Of course the reference list on any topic in this book is not exhaustive. Some titles which otherwise met the criteria for inclusion are not referred to because reprints or Xerox copies were obtained too late for thorough examination and redrafting of the text. Also, our method of search did not assure us that we turned up every title which might have met our criteria for inclusion.

D. Criteria for Selection of Topics

Since the publication of the first edition of this book in 1961, there has been an overwhelming outpouring of publications avowedly or implicitly directed toward some aspect of self-concept. I estimate that, in the course of preparing this revised edition, I have examined about 4,500 references closely enough to classify them into one or more topical areas. (This figure does not include several hundred which were judged to be irrelevant.)

The only way to get inclusive coverage would be to reduce volume 2 to a large, cumbersome set of very briefly annotated reference lists. This would contribute little to understanding the methodological and substantive status of any topic. Therefore, I selected for relatively thorough consideration a limited number of topics, according to one or more of the following criteria: (a) the intrinsic importance of the variable(s) in personality and social-psychological theories which stress self-referent constructs; (b) the number of research references found in my literature search; (c) the possible relevance of the topic to understanding contemporary society and social action. During the preparation of volume 2, it became obvious that limitations of time and money precluded dealing with every topic which fulfills these criteria. Moreover, such limitations have even precluded dealing with all aspects of each topic within the main ones chosen. This was most strikingly the case with respect to sex differences in self-conceptions, where at least 500 references were examined, although only about 200 could be dealt with in this volume.

E. Criteria for Giving Studies Substantive Attention as Opposed to Simple Listing

The "box score" approach to literature reviewing was deemed indefensible since methodological scope and adequacy vary so widely among publications. Instead, for each chapter, a list of specifically relevant methodological criteria was prepared, and each research report was closely scrutinized in the light of these standards. Those giving too little information for adequate methodological evaluation or those which seemed to be especially inadequate according to the criteria stated in the chapter are usually simply listed. Some references that are little, if any, more adequate than the listed ones are nevertheless dealt with substantively for one or more of the following reasons:

1. They were judged to be of historical importance.
2. They were part of a larger piece of research or series of investigations, which seemed to augment their value.
3. They are widely cited publications which do not seem to warrant the conclusions which are frequently drawn from them in secondary sources, and some detailed criticism seems therefore to be in order.
4. They present detailed descriptions of data which may be useful even if the author's data analysis is inappropriate or unclearly reported.
5. They illustrate methodological faults which should not be repeated.
6. They suggest new techniques which may be worth developing.

The reader may wonder why some studies are simply listed in connection with one topic or point and dealt with substantively in connection with another. Usually when this occurs it is because one part of the results seems to be relatively interpretable whereas another part may be less fully explained or may appear to be uninterpretable.

Obviously, there is great fallibility in such decisions to consider references substantively or simply to list them. However, limitations of time and money precluded making any large-scale systematic attempt to pool judgments or to look at interjudge agreement on these decisions. One reason for listing studies rather than simply omitting them altogether is to enable readers to locate these items and make their own judgments in the light of the methodological criteria set forth in each chapter.

There are two other reasons for listing these references: it seemed that a knowledge of their existence might prove helpful to the reader, and the listings give some idea of the extent to which seriously flawed studies are published in the respective areas.

2

Developmental Studies of Self-Concept

A. General Theoretical and Methodological Introduction

There is a huge volume of rather diffuse theorizing about self-concept characteristics as a function of age and developmental level, e.g., Allport (1961), Back and Gergen (1968), Baldwin (1899), J. H. Block (1973), Buhler (1962), Busse (1969), Cooley (1902), Erikson (1959, 1963), Kohlberg (1969), Kuhlen (1959), M. Lewis and Brooks (1975), Mead (1934), Neugarten (1968), Piaget and Inhelder (1969), Reichard, Livson, and Petersen (1962), Rogers (1951), and Sullivan (1953). To some extent these theories pertain to particular aspects of the self-concept which are allegedly characteristic of specific age levels. For example, theorizing about the young child focuses on an emergence of a sense of self as a separate person and development of gender identity; theorizing about adolescents centers around development of a stable sense of identity; theorizing about middle age emphasizes the sense of autonomy and power, as well as changes in self-perceived body competence; and the sense of being old has particularly drawn the attention of those dealing with self-concepts of elderly persons. But, in addition to specific aspects of self-concept, one finds in this theoretical literature the general assumption that the person throughout the life span attempts to maintain or enhance the level of his or her self-regard and that both the development of standards for self-evaluation and the current self-evaluations are a function of social interaction.

The theorists who have written most extensively on the development of the self-concept in children are those who espouse some variety of interactional, cognitive, and developmental viewpoint (e.g., Baldwin, Cooley, Kohlberg, Mead, Piaget, Sullivan). Of these, Kohlberg (1969) compares Baldwin's and Mead's theories before elaborating on his own views which stem from Piaget. He also compares cognitive-developmental views of "identification" with psychoanalytic and social-learning views of this process.

Denzin (1972) presents a comparative analysis of the views of Mead, Cooley, and Piaget, summarizing their agreements as follows:

> These three theorists agree with each other on five major points. First, they emphasize the importance of affective and cognitive processes in self-development. Second, they view each stage of development as qualitatively different from the previous stage. Third, they emphasize the role of interactional processes in cognitive development and in early self-hood. Fourth, they reject associationist and stimulus-response theories of learning.

9

To them, the organism progressively acquires the ability to stimulate its own conduct and to formulate its own plans of action: objects and stimuli carry no intrinsic meaning. (According to Kohlberg [1969: 347–361], Piaget treats learning as a complex process of differentiation and assimilation, which is in itself contingent on the development of language acquisition.) Fifth, they emphasize comparable empirical methods for the study of self. Each used a variation on the ethnographic, case-study method. . . . Each emphasized the importance of linguistic utterances as central indicators of self-hood. . . . Each attended to gestures, to performances, and to non-verbal actions as self-indicators. [Pp. 293–294]

Denzin sees their chief point of difference in Piaget's tendency to set more definite age levels than do Mead and Cooley for successive stages of cognitive development.

Although, as Denzin pointed out, some empirical observations were made by these three theorists, rigorous scientific work aimed at testing their theoretical propositions is extremely limited or nonexistent. Kohlberg (1969) remarks, "In spite of the obvious scope and suggestiveness of Baldwin's and Mead's theories of the role of imitation and role-taking in the function of the social self, these theories have been almost completely neglected by research child psychologists" (p. 423).

Kohlberg (1969) presents a strongly pessimistic view of most of the extant research in that it attempted to use a naturalistic, cross-sectional method (correlating variables in cultural or parental treatment with variables in children's motivational behavior), and it has yielded only low, inconsistently replicated correlations.

What is needed, of course, is (a) quantifiable description of age-related behaviors observed under controlled conditions—behaviors which would possibly indicate whether the child does pass through the stages of self-concept development postulated by theorists; and (b) functional relationships between such behaviors and their alleged antecedents and consequents established under controlled conditions.

Except for Erikson (1959, 1963), no well-known personality theorist has written systematically about middle-aged and old persons, and even Erikson's treatment of these ages is short and incomplete. Although a few psychologists and sociologists (e.g., Back & Gergen, 1968; Neugarten, 1968) have theorized very briefly about personality in the middle years, this age range has been virtually untouched, theoretically. Most of the numerous publications about old age have come from sociologists and physicians. Accordingly, theorizing about old age, while sparse and unsystematic, tends to emphasize such fac-tors as the reflection of the social stereotype of age in the old person's self-concept, the effects of role loss and role ambiguity in determining self-concept changes, and the effects of declining health and physical powers upon the old person's self-concept.

More specific theoretical statements relevant to each age level are given below where research methods and findings concerning the respective age levels are presented.

B. Studies of Children through Five Years of Age

With reference to quantification of self-concept variables and their relationship to age, there is a considerable body of descriptive research involving subjects older than five years, which I describe and evaluate in section C of this chapter. However, the empirical study of the "sense of self" or aspects of self-evaluation in younger children has barely been touched, and I cite these studies now before going on to the main body of available research.

In their discussions of self-concept development during the infant's first two years, M. Lewis and Brooks (1974 and in 1975) differentiate the more primitive "existential self. . . . the basic notion of existence separate from other" and the "categorical self which refers to the categories by which the infant defines itself vis-á-vis the external world" (M. Lewis and Brooks, 1975, p. 120). After some speculation about factors which may determine the existential self, they suggest, "If [research has demonstrated that 8-month-old] infants have the cognition available to preserve memory of objects no longer present, how can we deny them the ability to have self-permanence? Indeed, is it reasonable to talk of object-permanence capacity without self-permanence capacity?" (M. Lewis and Brooks, 1974, p. 216). They conclude, however, that "the question of the existential self is not open to confirmation or refutation and is, as such, metascientific" (M. Lewis and Brooks, 1975, p. 118).

Self-recognition, however, they view as an aspect of the categorical self which, as such, is open to empirical exploration. The studies from which they infer self-recognition deal with reactions to mirror images and pictures. Although the mirror studies done by Lewis and Brooks and others have showed some variations in developmental sequences of mirror reactions, they have yielded considerable agreement on the age of eventual self-recognition. At one year, the infants studied by Dixon

(1957) directed their behaviors to themselves rather than to their images, whereas in Amsterdam's (1972) study, infants began to withdraw from the image at one year, and not until 18 months were they responding to themselves rather than to the mirror image. Adapting a technique developed independently by Amsterdam (1972) and by Gallup (1970) (who studied self-recognition in chimpanzees), M. Lewis and Brooks (1975) observed the reactions of 23 infants ranging from 16 to 22 months when rouge was put on their noses by their mothers while supposedly wiping the infants' faces. If the infants reacted to their own noses rather than to the mirror, self-recognition was inferred. In the Lewis and Brooks study, none of the 6 16-month-old infants touched his nose, whereas all 8 of the 22-month-old infants did so. This finding coincides well with Amsterdam's observations that mark-directed behaviors first occurred at 18 months and were common by 20 months.

M. Lewis and Brooks's (1975) second technique for exploring self-recognition involved the infants' affective reactions and recorded fixation times directed toward colored pictures of the heads of (a) the infant's mother, (b) the infant himself/herself, (c) a female infant the same age as the subject, (d) a male infant the same age as the subject, (e) a female 5-year-old, (f) a male 5-year-old, (g) a female 10-year-old, (h) a male 10-year-old, (i) a female adult, (j) a male adult. Failing to support their hypothesis, Lewis and Brooks obtained no differences in either affective responses or fixation times to the self picture as opposed to the pictures of other infants. These null findings were obtained in each of the 4 groups, aged 10, 12, 16, and 18 months. (Total $N = 28$ male and 25 female Caucasian infants.) In any event, even if fixation times and affective reactions had differed, such differences would seem only to indicate discrimination and possibly preference, but not necessarily self-recognition.

More convincing evidence of self-recognition comes from the labeling reactions elicited from 11 19-month-old infants and 12 21-month-old infants by asking "Who is that?" when presenting each of 6 slides: (a) infant's mother, (b) infant himself/herself, (c) 9-month-old male infant, (d) baby same age and sex as subject, (e) adult female, (f) adult male.

The 19- and 21-month-olds did *not* label themselves "baby"; either the proper name was uttered or no label was produced. Moreover 11 of the 12 infants who labeled self and/or same age baby labeled them differentially.

The labeling of the self condition provides the strongest evidence for the existence of self-recognition; 7 of the seventeen 19- and 21-month-olds who verbalized in the elicited condition recognized themselves and gave a proper verbal label; they did not mislabel a same-age and same-sex infant. [M. Lewis and Brooks, 1975, p. 42]

Turning now to research concerning the self-concepts of children aged 2 to 5, one finds few studies, most of which used very primitive methods. Since so little in this important area is available, however, I describe below some of the pioneering efforts for their suggestive value, even though they do not report conclusive results.

Ames's (1952) report on nursery school children presents a summary of "data in regard to the growing sense of self such as can be derived from verbalizations to self or to others . . . data are objective in that they consist of actual statements and behaviors of (approximately 100–150) subjects. They are, however, selective. Behaviors and verbalizations considered most pertinent by the observer were recorded and from these records most pertinent data were further selected" (Ames, 1952, p. 194). "From these observations we have built up a developmental picture of the sense of self as it appears to change from age to age" [from one month through 3-1/2 years] (p. 229). The usual procedures for standardizing recording conditions, exploring interobserver reliability, and demonstrating construct validity of behavior categories as indices of "sense of self" were not followed, since the investigator evidently felt they were inappropriate or unfeasible for exploratory work. Thus, this study is only suggestive.

Denzin's (1972) reported method of observing three- and four-year-olds in a nursery school was also apparently very informal and uncontrolled:

My strategy, as an observer, was to sit, play, eat, and drink juice with the children. I often took notes on the spot; to assess my reactive effect in the situation, I also gathered observations from behind a one-way screen. . . . As I developed hypotheses and hunches about the children's conduct, I employed teachers as resources so that I might check my account of a child's behavior against their interpretation. . . . The evidence that I present reflects what I regard (from my field notes) as *representative* cases, types, or examples of the behavior that I describe. I distinguish representative cases from *anecdotal* cases by their frequency of appearance in the field experience. [Pp. 298–299]

He then gives a few examples of language use patterns, especially the use of personal pronouns, self-conduct, and self-other interactions

in play (e.g., role-taking, cooperative and reciprocal play), and indications of uncertainty regarding one's own name.

Possibly more interpretable will be the outcomes of applying a
Piaget-type technique developed by Guardo and Beebe (described by
Guardo, 1968). In their effort to operationalize the "sense of self-
identity," they developed a semi-structured interview in which the
child is

> allowed to respond in his own way and then, depending on his answers, he
> is branched to another set of questions aimed at another facet of self-
> identity. . . . An attempt is made to ascertain: (1) if the child recognizes or
> realizes that he is a singular individual, in a physical, social and/or psycho-
> logical way, (2) if he senses his own humanness and can distinguish himself
> from the lower animals, (3) if he identifies his sex, distinguishes himself from
> the opposite sex, and how or why he does so, and (4) if he perceives his
> present self as continuous with what he has been in the past and will be in
> the future. [Pp. 139–140]

(An exploratory study using this technique with children of six to nine
years of age is evaluated in section C–4 below.)

One of Guardo's aspects of sense of social identity is the child's
concept of his sexual identity, usually called his gender identity. In a
review of theory and research on this topic, Kohlberg (1966) notes that
"gender identity is perhaps the most stable of all social identities" (p.
92), and "from the cognitive-developmental point of view, the stability
of gender-identity concepts is only one aspect of the general
stabilization of constancies of physical objects that takes place between
the years three and seven. The development of such conceptual
constancies has been discussed by Piaget in terms of the conservation
of physical-object properties under apparent changes" (p. 96). Fur-
thermore, "the cognitive-developmental view holds that the child's
difficulties in establishing gender definition closely parallel his difficulties in establishing stable definitions of physical concepts in
general, and that the former are resolved as the latter are" (p. 94).

An early step in the acquisition of one's gender identity involves
learning one's own gender label, which, according to Gesell (cited in
Kohlberg, 1966), usually occurs some time late in the second year of
life. Correct generalization of gender labeling of self and of clothed
doll figures is virtually complete by 48 months of age, according to
Rabban's results from asking children "Which doll looks most like
you?" and "Is it a boy or girl?" (cited in Kohlberg, 1966). However,
Kohlberg argues that constancy of gender identity is not complete
before the age of five to seven. In one unpublished study, he asked

"whether a pictured girl could be a boy if she wanted to, or if she played boy games, or if she wore a boy's haircut or clothes. Most four-year-olds said that she could be a boy if she wanted to, or if she wore the appropriate haircut or clothes. By ages six-seven most children were quite certain that a girl could not be a boy regardless of changes in appearance or behavior" (p. 95).

While these trends are suggestive and theoretically important, we should reserve judgment as to whether the shift in the children's answers reflects solely or entirely a shift in gender identity or whether a change in their understanding of the questions may account at least in part for their changing responses. This is a particularly important caution to keep in mind when interpreting developmental findings in this age range. However, Katcher's (1955) results using a different method reinforce Kohlberg's interpretation that constancy in gender identity is not complete until ages five to seven. In Katcher's task, children were asked to discriminate which was the boy or girl (man or woman) in pairs of segments of human figures, identical except for a single variable: clothing, breasts, hair, or external genitals.

(Chapter 4 considers in detail the many studies of development of a sense of racial/ethnic identity, including investigations involving children in the two to five year age range. Chapter 3 considers the question of a sense of social class identity. However, the few research publications on that topic deal with children no younger than seven or eight.)

Dreyer and Haupt's (1966) study involving self-appraised competence in kindergarten children is uninterpretable because of a number of methodological flaws including the use of uninterpretable discrepancy scores (between child-appraised and teacher-appraised competence of each child), use of an idiosyncratic instrument on which insufficient psychometric information is available, and making of multiple significance tests with no way to evaluate how many were significant by chance alone. Their instrument for revealing a child's self-appraised competence suggests an interesting way to approach the indexing of this construct, however.

Sweet and Thornburg's (1971) study gives somewhat more definite information about procedure and quantitative analysis than do the preceding three. They found that only 8 out of 120 3-, 4-, and 5-year-olds failed to identify their own pictures in a set of 5 pictures of children of the same sex and race. In a second set of pictures of 6 males and 6 females equally divided into 3 ethnic groups (black, white, and Oriental), black and white children of all three ages chose as the picture which looked most like them a picture of a child of their own sex and race. Using three-dimensional abstract figures in graduated sizes, the subject was asked to make his "very own family" and was then asked to point out the various members to the examiner. Of the 120 subjects, only 60 included themselves in the family group. There was a steady increase with age in the tendency to include the self as part of the family.

The interpretation of this frequent exclusion of self from the family is ambiguous. It could mean that the child's self-concept does not as yet include his role as a family member. But a plausible alternative interpretation is that the wording of the instructions might have suggested to the child that he, as an actually present member of his family, was to use the artificial figures to represent the remaining absent family members.

To my knowledge, the most fully described and quantified attempt to measure self-concept variables in young children is that of Weiner (1964). In each of 2 groups of 11 nursery school children (aged 47 to 62 months) he asked each child individually to compare himself or herself with each other child regarding a variety of characteristics. This method of paired comparisons enabled Weiner to infer the child's self-perceived rank order with respect to each characteristic. The items about which he inquired were drawing skill, skill in dressing self, climbing skill, size, friendliness, strength, intelligence, frequency of fighting, and how well each teacher liked the child. Before interviewing the children and asking the paired-comparison questions, he worked with the teachers to develop understandable and appropriate wording. With the possible exception of friendliness, he felt that the children seemed to understand the questions and the idea of the paired-comparison task. Test-retest reliability coefficients were computed, with the result that only teacher preference ($r = .72$) and drawing ($r = .66$) could be considered high. Four of the categories (climbing, size, intelligence, and frequency of fighting) yielded coefficients not significantly different from zero. Weiner suggests that the low coefficients are not necessarily indicative of random responding at this age level but rather might stem from one or more of the following: changes in group structure (more or less accurately reflected in changes of response), changes in relationship to the experimenter, limited range of possible error scores, and homogeneity of the group of subjects. Since all children in Weiner's study were 4-year-olds, no age trends could be obtained. Weiner's correlations between child self-rankings and teacher ratings are subject to methodological criticisms fully described in Wylie (1974, chap. 6). His findings regarding children's self favorability biases in their self-rankings are reported on page 678 of this book.

Because most theoreticians assume that esteem from others is a key factor in development of self-regard, E. P. Kirchner and Vondracek (1975) thought it relevant to look at perceived sources of esteem in 3-, 4-, and 5-year-old children in a day-care center. They asked each of their 282 subjects: "Tell me who likes you. Tell me as many people as you can who really like you." They also conducted "an inquiry subsequent to S's response to permit maximum identification of the sources cited" (pp. 170–171). Although one might suppose that response totals to *any* question might increase as a function of age, no age effect was found in number of esteem sources mentioned. Moreover, no age differences were found in the frequency of mention of the most commonly given esteem sources: child friend, sibling, mother, father.

It is apparent that published studies of self-concept development in young children are rare, and over-all conclusions based on them cannot justifiably be attempted.

One of the amazing and dismaying things is that, despite the existence of at least 18 scales which purport to test some aspect(s) of self-concept in preschool and kindergarten children, none was used in any published article I examined. These scales, along with 28 others purportedly suitable for older children, are listed and classified in a mimeographed document prepared for ERIC/TM by Coller (1970). With very few exceptions, even the older children's self-concept tests have not been used in published research either, nor, with rare exceptions, has anything approximating proper validation research been done on any of these 46 instruments.

C. Studies of Persons Six through Fifty Years of Age

In contrast to the first three studies described above, the reports involving subjects older than five years give some basis for evaluation of their methodological adequacy in terms of conventional standards.

1. Methodological Criteria

Before examining these studies for substantive trends in reported results, I set up some methodological and reporting criteria which, if not met, would render the reported results uninterpretable. Every study excluded from substantive summary fell seriously short on several of these criteria. Had more rigorous criteria been set, scarcely any report would have remained to form the basis for possible psychological interpretations.

1. *Was the self-concept instrument used in the study sufficiently well known through other publications to enable one to evaluate its characteristics as they might affect alternate interpretations of reported findings? Or, if an idiosyncratic or little-known instrument was used, is sufficient information given regarding its content and psychometric properties to enable one to evaluate alternate interpretations of the reported findings?* More than half the studies reported results based on such idiosyncratic, specially devised instruments about which very little or no information was given. Thus, if studies seem to report different results, one cannot even speculatively evaluate the relative contributions of the respectively used instruments.

2. *Were results based on scores which are uninterpretable?* For example, were discrepancy scores used without furnishing information about the relative contributions made by the components to the discrepancy score?

3. *Were the age groups large enough?* Arbitrarily, in view of the probably large number of influences on the dependent variable which would need to be equated through selection of comparison groups, I chose 40 per age group as the minimum number. Virtually every study exceeded this number, especially if sex groups were combined at each age.

4. *If a cross-sectional design was used, is there any information given about whether the different age groups are comparable with respect to other variables which have been shown to be correlated with self-concept?* Few reports gave evidence of recognizing the existence of such a problem. *Were testing, interviewing, or data-collection methods and conditions reported to be comparable across groups?* Many studies gave little or no information on this point.

5. *If a longitudinal study was made, is any information given about the possible effects of subject attrition upon the findings?* Perhaps the trend obtained with the "remainers" is not generalizable to the different age levels per se. *Were testing conditions comparable at successive testings?* Some studies used mail follow-up after individual or group administration of the first test, a procedure which clearly diminishes interpretability. Many studies gave no information to support the argument that there had been reasonable control of these kinds of variables.

6. *Did the study use one of the more modern designs which is more adequate than either the conventional cross-sectional or conventional longitudinal design?* It has long been recognized that both conventional cross-sectional and conventional longitudinal designs are intrinsically limited (e.g., Birren, 1959). For example, in the cross-sectional method, age of subject is confounded with date of birth. This means that different cultural changes could have occurred within the life spans of the groups differing in age. If such different cultural changes have occurred within the life spans of groups born at the different dates (and hence of different ages at the time of study), age-group differences obviously cannot clearly be interpreted as being a function of age with cultural conditions held constant. Or, in the conventional longitudinal method using repeated measures of the same subjects, one introduces the uncontrolled effects of testing upon the outcomes of subsequent tests. Schaie (1965, 1967), among others, has analyzed these problems in considerable detail and has suggested models which would be appropriate to evaluate developmental effects more accurately than does either the conventional cross-sectional or conventional longitudinal method. None of the researches summarized in this section used any of Schaie's suggestions, however.

7. *Is it possible that, on the instrument used in the study, "low self-regard" scores could be attained by two kinds of subjects: those who intentionally wish to report low self-regard, and those who are unreliable reporters due to poor ability or motivation to read or follow directions?* Elsewhere I have discussed in detail this type of contamination between low self-regard and unreliability (Wylie, 1974, pp.119-121). Any upward trend in the self-regard scores as a function of age, especially when the lowest age involves young children, should be viewed skeptically until this sort of artifactual explanation of the upward trend can be ruled out. No report showed recognition of this problem. Many did not give enough information for the skeptical reader to speculate independently about the plausibility of such an artifactual explanation.

8. *Were significance tests properly applied and interpreted? Were many comparisons made between groups without regard for the fact that some such comparisons will be "significant" by chance alone? Were such outcomes of multiple comparisons cross-validated with fresh groups?* An appreciable number of studies gave no significance tests at all, and they gave no justification for omitting them. This was especially true in some of the large-scale sociological studies, where visual trends displayed in numerous tables were simply verbally

described and speculatively interpreted. While one must recognize (Feldman & Coleman, 1962) that significance testing is a complex and expensive matter in large-scale studies involving stratified, multistage sampling, this does not justify a researcher's ignoring the whole question of significance in presenting and especially in interpreting results. Not only the studies which presented no significance tests but also many others were inadequate in regard to the matter of evaluating the significance of multiple comparisons and the need for cross-validation.

The studies selected for substantive summary concerning subjects 6 through 50 years of age involve either verbal report measures of "overall self-regard," self-scores evaluated by judges, self-ideal discrepancies or rs, self-acceptance scores or verbal report measures of over-all ideal self, a nonverbal measure of social self-esteem, the connotative factor structure of a verbal self-concept instrument, or measures of ego identity. The selected studies are presented later on in the order just listed. (I have omitted the few available studies purporting to deal with the nonphenomenal self because of presently unsurmounted problems of construct validity fully discussed in Wylie [1974, chap. 5]).

2. Relevant Theorizing

Theorizing relevant to the predicted outcome of studies of over-all self-regard is sparse, imprecise, and undeveloped.

Some writers (e.g., Adler [in Ansbacher & Ansbacher, 1956]; Long, Henderson, & Ziller, 1967a) have supposed that increased size and competence in childhood should lead to increased self-regard as a function of age.

Others have offered various reasons why self-regard, whether measured by self-ideal discrepancies, "real self" scores, or self-acceptance scores, might decrease in one age range or another. For example, Jorgensen and Howell (1969) have postulated that the increasing importance of superego processes would produce larger self-ideal discrepancies in the latency years as compared to earlier years. Zigler, Balla, and Watson (1972) have argued that "the growth and development of an individual must invariably be accompanied by an increasing disparity between his assessment of his real self and of his ideal self" (p. 81). This is so because of an increase in the individual's capacity to experience guilt and because of an increasing cognitive capacity to employ a greater number of categories which "should increase the probability of a greater disparity between any two complex judgments, including those regarding real and ideal-self images" (p. 82). On page 666 of this book, I suggest that perhaps increasing experience with realistic standards and objective competition with others might lead the older child to have a somewhat lower level of self-regard than does the young child. After reviewing the ideas of a number of psychologists, psychoanalysts, and sociologists, R. Simmons, M. Rosenberg, and F. Rosenberg (1973) state "it is small wonder that social theorists assume that . . . (adolescence) is difficult for the child's self-image" (p. 554). They point out that puberty is typically viewed as the trigger for the assumed self-image disturbance, but that it may be aspects of the social environment which are at work.

Back and Gergen (1968) suggest that the value a person places upon himself will depend on the relationship between two phenomenological factors: perceived bodily capacities and "life space extensity" (by which they mean the extent of space and time in which the person sees himself as acting or being acted upon). They hypothesize

> that the value a person places upon himself will be partially dependent on the relationship between these trajectories. More explicitly, a person will value himself or possess high morale when his physical capacities are capable of matching the life space extensity. Either a very extensive life space accompanied by a physical deficit, or physical vitality accompanied by an impoverished life space should engender low morale. [P. 247]

They plot the hypothetical trajectories for these two variables to show some disparity from the late teens until about 20; minimum disparity in the twenties (where self-value, therefore, should presumably be high); maximum disparity in the fifties (where life space extensity greatly exceeds the sense of bodily well-being, with presumably concomitant low feelings of self-value); and minimum disparity again in old age (where the two trajectories, although both low, are close to one another).

3. Studies of Over-all Self-Regard

Whatever the state of theorizing about over-all self-regard as a function of age, the bulk of the studies summarized below show no association of age and self-regard scores between the ages of 8 and ≥ 23 years (the range jointly covered by the reports). These studies used the conventional cross-sectional method unless otherwise indicated.

a. COMMONLY USED SELF-REPORT INSTRUMENTS

The manuals or published studies involving some of the better known self-concept tests provide the first source of evidence concerning the relationship between age and self-regard scores. I have examined the manuals and published materials concerning Bills's Index of Adjustment and Values (the forms pertaining to elementary schools through adult ages), the Piers-Harris Children's Self-Concept Scale, the Coopersmith Self-Esteem Inventory, the Lipsitt Self-Concept Scale for Children, Rosenberg's Self-Esteem Scale, Gough and Heilbrun's Adjective Check List, LaForge and Suczek's Interpersonal Check List, and the Tennessee Self-Concept Scale. Of these, I could find no information about the age variable and scores on the Adjective Check List or the Interpersonal Check List.

Bills's Index of Adjustment and Values

The manual for Bills's Index of Adjustment and Values (undated) shows that his high school and college student groups obtained highly similar means on all types of self-regard scores, and Dales and Keller (1972) similarly report no age differences in IAV Self scores in their cross-sectional and longitudinal study of eighth-grade through twelfth-grade white subjects. (Black subjects showed some trend toward higher scores in higher grades, but no appropriate analysis of the significance of this trend is given.) It should be noted that the effects of attrition and repeated testing could not be evaluated and that increased reading skills (hence more reliable responding) also might have entered into the upward black "trend."

Piers-Harris Children's Self-Concept Scale

Piers (1969) reports that an earlier relationship of the Piers-Harris self-concept scores to age was not replicated, and, on the basis of a number of studies cited in their manual, she concludes, "It has not so far been demonstrated that consistent differences between grade levels can be expected on the Piers-Harris Scale" (p. 13). However, F. W. Black (1974) found that scores on the Piers-Harris self-concept test were significantly and negatively related to age and grade among a group of elementary school children designated by their schools as having significant learning problems in regular public school classes.

Half of the students were called "normal" readers and half "retarded" readers, according to their scores on the Wide Range Achievement Test. The mean age and mean grade placements were 11.17 years and 3.94 for the normal readers and 11.66 years and 4.22 for the retarded readers. The range of age and grade levels was not given. Mean IQs did not differ between groups, and IQ was uncorrelated with PH scores. Correlations between age and self-concept scores were −.584 for retarded readers and −.499 for normal readers. The generalizability of these significant negative correlations between age and self-concept is limited because of Black's specialized sample. The author speculates that the relationship between self-concept and age could differ in learning-disabled and normal students because learning disabilities and self-concept problems could interact circularly over time.

Coopersmith's Self-Esteem Inventory

Although Coopersmith (1967) gives no information in his book about the relationship of age to scores on his Self-Esteem Inventory, several other investigators have used SEI scores in developmental studies of self-regard. Purkey, Graves, and Zellner (1970) found no main effect of age from third through sixth grade, but their graph shows subjects in an innovative school having higher self-regard scores than students in a traditional school (who showed an inverse relationship between self-regard scores and age). No significance test is given of this visually suggested interaction. Trowbridge (1972a, 1972b), in a study involving 3,789 children from fourth through eighth grades, found a very slight decline in mean SEI scores with increasing age, but concluded that "age is an insignificant factor" (1972a, p. 535). Frerichs (1973), using an insufficiently described modification of the Coopersmith Self-Esteem Inventory, found no difference between 712 female nursing students who were 22 years old or younger as compared to 723 female nursing students who were 23 or older.

Lipsitt's Self-Concept Scale for Children

Lipsitt (1958) also reported essentially no differences in scores on his Self-Concept Scale for Children among fourth-, fifth-, and sixth-graders.

Rosenberg's Self-Esteem Scale

In Rosenberg's (1965) book, no information about the age variable is given. In a multiple-regression study by Hulbary (1975), using a small, admittedly nonrandom sample of black and white adolescents, Grades 8 through 12, no association between age and Rosenberg Self-Esteem scores was observed.

A self-derogation factor score derived from Rosenberg's Self-Esteem Scale was used by Kaplan and Pokorny (1970) in their study of a probability sample of 500 Harris County, Texas, adults. Dividing the subjects into those aged 29 or younger, 30–39, 40–49, 50–59, and 60 and above, they found no relationship between age and self-derogation scores. However, they found 4 subgroups in which the older subjects were significantly *less* likely to be self-derogatory: those reporting no recent life experiences, such as the death of a close friend, which would require "behavioral adaptation"; those reporting no disparity between current and hoped-for standard of living; those reporting no childhood fear of being left alone; and those whose households consisted solely of the subject and his (her) spouse. The latter findings regarding variables which may interact with age in determining relationships between self-regard and age may suggest lines for future research. However, they do not seem to be interpretable as such, for several reasons: (a) The mentioned factors constitute but a few out of many covered by the 23-page interview schedule; so their "significance" needs to be established by cross-validational research. (b) The number of cases in each group became small in some of these subgroup breakdowns. (c) There is no way of evaluating whether the selected subgroups are varying with respect to other biasing factors as well as the one supposedly being varied. Consequently, I conclude that the burden of proof is on the person who wishes to say that any kind of Rosenberg scores vary as a function of age.

Tennessee Self-Concept Scale

So far as the Tennessee Self-Concept Scale is concerned, Fitts (1965) stated in the manual that "the evidence so far suggests that there is no need to establish separate norms by age, sex, race, or other variables" (p. 13). However, W. Thompson (1972) argues that, so far as age is concerned, this statement is in error. To support his argument, he cites 20 studies (18 of which are unpublished, hence unavailable for the reader's independent evaluation). Elsewhere (Wylie, 1974, pp. 230-236) I have criticized the Tennessee Self-Concept Scale (TSCS) in detail, pointing out the indefensibility of interpreting the many separate scores from subscales which contain overlapping items and which are intercorrelated. Accordingly, I consider here only the information Thompson gives on the Total Positive score, based on all items (although Thompson gives information on many of the subscales). I also pointed out earlier (Wylie, 1974) that the TSCS is an instrument in which poor self-regard scores can be obtained in two ways: by unreliable responding or by intention to report poor self-regard. The TSCS calls for at least a sixth-grade reading level, and the procedure of responding is rather complex. Accordingly, one could expect considerable unreliable responding in the younger groups reported on by Thompson, i.e., in the junior and senior high groups. (See Wylie, 1974, pp. 119-121, for a full explanation of this source of artifact in determining "poor self-regard" scores.) Finally, one should note that Thompson makes his age comparisons between studies, as opposed to making age comparisons within a study especially planned so as to hold relevant variables constant between age groups. To counteract this objection, Thompson cites the great similarity between studies involving any one age group, for example, among the 7 studies of junior high school students. While this similarity is important and interesting, it does not guarantee between-age-group equality with respect to relevant variables when the age groups come from different studies. The adult groups consisted very largely of college students or graduates. Finally, I note that the total number of elderly persons (60 or over) was only 116. With all these reservations in mind, one must question Thompson's summary statement that "inspection of the P-Score profiles seems to indicate that self-esteem increases with age. Junior high and high school Ss have below-average P Scores, college and adult Ss earn average P Scores, and elderly people score above average on most P Scores. It seems likely that the higher level of P Scores earned by elderly Ss is in part a result of defensiveness and a disinclination to make negative statements about themselves" (p. 18).

I suggest that the higher P Scores of adults as compared to junior high school and senior high school students may plausibly be indicative of the adults' greater ability to read and follow directions, or it may have been associated with the adults' higher socioeconomic level (since they were almost all college students and graduates). Since we are told nothing about various relevant characteristics of the elderly groups (for example, their educational levels) and nothing about the conditions under which the elderly subjects were tested, their results, too, seem not clearly attributable to age factors.

Summary

In short, then, there is no clear evidence of any association (within the age range from 6 to 50) between chronological age and scores on any of these well-known verbal self-regard scales, when other relevant variables are properly controlled. For some of these scales, there is no information. For others, age trends were not obtained. The numbers of studies, sizes of *N*s, and the consistency among the more methodologically adequate studies suggest that these null trends represent a true lack of association in the age range studied between any one of these types of self-regard scores and age.

b. Studies Using Idiosyncratic Verbal Report Instruments

Studies Showing No Age Trends

With the exception of one part of one study, the following 5 investigations using inadequately described, idiosyncratic verbal report instruments also yielded no relationships between age and self-regard scores: Attenborough and Zdep (1973) tested a national probability sample of 1,684 girls aged 9–17; Lively, Dinitz, and Reckless (1962) tested 1,171 subjects from sixth through ninth grades with 2 instruments aimed respectively at socialization during adolescence and concept of self in relation to the law. Zigler, Balla, and Watson (1972) (whose work is more fully described under the next subhead) found no main effect of age on questionnaire ratings regarding "real self," and no age effect in retarded children on either their questionnaire ratings or their adjective check list score on "real self." This is of some interest when contrasted to F. W. Black's (1974) findings, cited earlier, that age correlates negatively with Piers-Harris self-esteem scores among learning-disabled children who obtained IQ scores within the normal range. Yamamoto, E. C. Thomas, and Karns (1969), using a "merit" factor score from a specially devised semantic differential scale, present means for "Myself" for grades six through nine which appear to show no age trend.

Muller and Leonetti (1974) used the idiosyncratic Primary Self-

Concept Scale to measure self-concepts of low socioeconomic level Chicano and Anglo children from kindergarten through the fourth grade in Las Cruces, New Mexico, public schools. An analysis of variance showed insignificant main effects for grade in school or ethnicity. A significant interaction between grade and ethnicity is uninterpretable, partly because of shifts in teaching approaches relevant to the Chicanos.

Studies Showing Decreasing Self-Regard with Age

The following six studies obtained some (but not entirely consistent) trends for the "real self" evaluation to decrease as a function of age.

To measure self-concepts in 40 first graders and 40 fifth graders, half black and half white, all from father-absent welfare families, Carpenter and Busse (1969) individually administered an idiosyncratic instrument. For black boys, white boys, white girls, and all subjects, fifth-grade mean self-concept scores were significantly lower. Small Ns, lack of information about subject comparability between ages, and lack of psychometric information severely limit the interpretability of these results, however.

Neale and Proshek (1967) used an idiosyncratic semantic differential scale with 350 children in fourth, fifth, and sixth grades from schools characterized as low and medium in socioeconomic level. An evaluative score based on their own factor analysis was obtained for the concept me and 14 other concepts, including specific other persons, aspects of school and schoolwork, and aspects of behavior, such as stealing. The evaluation of me declined consistently and significantly as grade levels increased. This trend is not a discriminantly valid indicator of decline in self-regard, however, because the evaluative score for 13 of the 14 other concepts showed a similar unpredicted, inexplicable decline. (See Wylie, 1974, for a critical discussion of the semantic differential technique.)

P. Katz and Zigler (1967) and Zigler, Balla, and Watson (1972) used the same two incompletely described idiosyncratic measures of over-all self-regard: a specially devised, idiosyncratic questionnaire based partly on Coopersmith's Self-Esteem Inventory, and a specially devised idiosyncratic adjective check list. In the P. Katz and Zigler (1967) study, subjects were enrolled in Grades 5, 8, and 11; whereas in the Zigler et al. (1972) research, 10-year-olds were compared to 16-year-olds. In the P. Katz and Zigler study, "real self" questionnaire ratings of normal children were found to be more negative at Grades 11 and 8 than at Grade 5 (the P value of obtained $F < .01$), and similar results were reported for their adjective check list. However, the Zigler et al. (1972) study found no difference in real-self image for the questionnaire ratings, whereas the younger normal children again had the more favorable real-self ratings on the adjective check list. So far as the ideal-self ratings were concerned, P. Katz and Zigler (1967) report higher ideal-self ratings for older subjects on both their questionnaire and their adjective check list, but Zigler et al. (1972) report significantly higher ideal self for older subjects on the questionnaire only. There are no apparent reasons for this mixed pattern of replication and discrepancy in the findings of the two studies using the same instruments and subjects of approximately the same age range. Zigler et. al. feel that the increasing self-minus-ideal disparities which they found support their idea that self-ideal discrepancies are a mark of maturity, not, as Rogers would have it, an indicator of maladjustment.

L. Soares and A. Soares (1970), using an inadequately described trait-rating scale, report that the mean self-regard score of 373 elementary school students was more favorable than the mean self-regard score of 288 secondary school students. Groups were comparable with respect to proportions of "advantaged" and "disadvantaged" children.

R. Simmons, M. Rosenberg, and F. Rosenberg (1973) studied 1,917 children aged 8 to 18 in a large, urban school system. Schools were selected on the basis of proportion of nonwhite students and income level, and, within each school, students were selected at random. Three self-concept Guttman scales were developed for the purposes of the study: self-consciousness, stability of self-concept, and global self-esteem. Although they are idiosyncratic, each is published verbatim along with psychometric information regarding reproducibility, scalability, and a little evidence for construct validity. Also used were questions about content of self-image (which yielded a self-favorability score); questions about subjects' perceptions of how their teachers, parents, and peers viewed them; and a depressive affect scale. Each of the latter is published verbatim. All subject responses were obtained by individual interview. Consonant with the authors' theoretical expectations, early adolescents (particularly those between 12 and 13 years of age) showed heightened self-consciousness, greater instability of self-image, slightly lower self-esteem, and a less favorable view of the opinions held of them by significant others as compared to children in the 8 to 11 age group. However, they went on to examine the hypothesis that transition to junior high school, rather than the subjects' ages per se, was the effective factor in lowering self-favorability among the 12- to 13-year-old subjects. Scores of 12-year-old children in sixth and seventh grades were compared when race, socioeconomic level, and marks in school were held constant. Also examined were scores of children in the same sixth grade who had recently moved in versus scores of those who had been there for some time. They concluded that the evidence suggested that the child's environment may have a stronger effect than his age in producing their observed age differences in self-regard. It should be noted that improvements in self-concept stability and global self-esteem were reported for subjects beyond the age of 13.

Studies Showing Increasing Self-Regard with Age

In contrast to the preceding six reports, the next six studies, each employing a different idiosyncratic instrument, yielded some evidence of an upward trend in over-all verbal self-regard scores with age: H. V. Perkins (1958a, 1958b), Bowman (1974), Kaplan (1975a), Engel (1959), Bachman and O'Malley (1977), and Gurin, Verhoff, and Feld (1960). They are presented in order of ages of subjects.

Using an idiosyncratic Q-sort set based on Jersild's ideas and fourth- and sixth-grade children as subjects, H. V. Perkins (1958b) obtained a significant increase in self-ideal congruence over a 6-month period. He also found that the sixth-grade children showed greater self-ideal congruence than did the fourth-grade subjects. At least two interpretations of these findings are possible: (a) They represent developmental changes of some kind in self-ideal congruence. (b) They may reflect the greater reliability in sorting which would come with greater familiarity with the instrument and improved reading skills. (The 2-day test-retest reliability of the self-sort was nonsignificantly greater in the sixth-grade group.)

Bowman (1974) obtained significant increments in real self and ideal self upon retesting fourth graders and sixth graders two years later in the sixth and eighth grades, respectively. On the other hand, his tables show that the grade groups did not differ on original testing (i.e., the cross-sectional grade comparison yielded null findings). (At least those parts of the original groups who were later available for retesting did not differ on their original test results. Data from the entire original groups are not presented.) Since one has no way to evaluate the effects of the considerable differential dropout on the longitudinal effects reported by Bowman, the meaning of the grade effects which were obtained remains unclear.

In a longitudinal study of 3,148 seventh graders from one school district, Kaplan (1975a) found that scores on a self-derogation test decreased significantly each year over a 2-year period (3 annual tests). This suggests an increase in students' self-esteem as they progress from the seventh to the ninth grade. Self-derogation was inferred from 7 items from Rosenberg's Self-Esteem Scale — items previously shown by Kaplan and Pokorny (1969) to load on one factor. However, Kaplan's (1975a) longitudinal results are difficult to evaluate. For one thing, of 9,459 students initially tested, only 7,168 returned usable questionnaires the first time, and only 3,148 of these were present for all three testing sessions. Even among the latter, occasional missing bits of data necessitated using varying Ns for different comparisons. Moreover, multiple significance tests impair interpretability of significance levels. He divided his subjects into those with initially low self-derogation scores (N = about 1,200); medium self-derogation scores (N = about 1,000); and high self-derogation scores (N = about 860). Differences between Tests 1 and 2 and between Tests 2 and 3 were tested for the entire group and for each of the above-described subgroups, using t for correlated samples. Additionally, it is difficult to evaluate the possible role of statistical regression artifacts in the findings. A large decrease in self-derogation score (increase in self-esteem) was found in the group with the initially lowest self-derogation mean. This decrease might be attributed, at least in part, to the regression artifact, and perhaps partly to the reliability artifact (see Wylie, 1974, pp. 119–121). However, students with medium self-derogation scores also showed some decreases in self-derogation mean over time, a finding less plausibly attributable to these artifacts. But, to complicate the interpretation, those with originally low self-derogation actually showed a significant increase in self-derogation between first and second testing. This might, of course, be due in part to the statistical regression artifact. If the trends validly represent increases in self-esteem in the medium and low self-esteem seventh graders, one might speculatively attempt to look at them in the light of Simmons, Rosenberg, and Rosenberg's (1973) suggestion mentioned in the immediately preceding section. That is, if self-esteem is degraded by transition to a new school (junior high school), then the improvement between seventh and ninth grades might be a function of adapting to the new environment as opposed to anything having to do with age per se.

Engel (1959) explored the test-retest stability of the self-concept in 172 subjects over a 2-year period. One group of boys and girls was tested in the eighth and tenth grades, whereas the second group was tested in the tenth and twelfth grades. The subjects Q-sorted an idiosyncratic set of items which had been prejudged for positive or negative tone. Results were given in terms of r values which correspond to mean self-self correlations. For 23 of the subjects, the average self-self correlation over a 10-day period was .68. By comparison, the average self-self r over a 2-year period was .53. There was no significant difference between the older and younger groups with respect to self-self correlations over the 2-year period. This confirmed the author's hypothesis which was based on the assumption that "crystallization of the self-concept is achieved earlier in development" (Engel, 1959, p. 121). Self sorts were then scored according to the prejudged favorability values of the items. Over the 2-year period there was an unpredicted increase in mean favorability of the self-concept, significant beyond the .05 level in the case of the older group. This finding could possibly indicate either (a) changes in the self-concept toward favorability values endorsed by adults, or (b) greater reliability of sorting behavior among older subjects, which would lead to their placing the self-items in judged favorable piles more often, or (c) differences between the remaining subjects and those lost through attrition. Engel says that "certain important personality differences may have existed between those who left and those who remained in the school" (p. 212).

In a longitudinal analysis of the impact of educational and occupational attainment on self-esteem, Bachman and O'Malley (1977) used a multistage probability sample of all tenth-grade boys attending public high schools in the 48 contiguous states in 1966. The boys responded to an idiosyncratic, 10-item self-esteem index similar to the Rosenberg Self-Esteem Scale once each year during the tenth, eleventh, and twelfth grades, and then again in 1974, 5 years after most had completed high school. This last testing differed from the others in that it was completed by mail rather than by interview. Of the 2,277 boys originally selected, 2,213 participated in the study in 1966. Attrition narrowed the number to 1,608 who completed all 4 phases of the testing. First-test self-esteem of the lost subjects did not differ significantly from the 1,608 used in the present longitudinal analysis, however.

Bachman and O'Malley report a gradual and substantial increase in the self-esteem scores of these young men from 1966 to 1974. The 1974 mean is one standard deviation level higher than the 1966 mean. Each item showed a similar increase over time. In examining the self-esteem scores for subjects in six different categories of educational attainment ranging from those who were high school dropouts to those attaining postgraduate education in 1974, one sees that the mean scores of each of the six groups increased over time from 1966 to 1974. The same increases in self-esteem over the eight-year period were found in subjects in six different categories of occupational status.

Can these strong, atypical findings be a result of method artifacts? For example, without data to counteract such an interpretation, one might wonder whether the original self-esteem scores were lower due to unreliability, then higher as increasing familiarity with the instrument eliminated this irrelevant influence. If so, what appear to be increases in self-esteem might actually represent the influence of the reliability artifact (see Wylie 1974, pp. 119–121). However, Bachman and O'Malley do counter such an interpretation by presenting the 1970 self-esteem mean from a sample of 115 control subjects drawn in 1966 but not interviewed until 1970. Their mean was virtually identical to that of the repeatedly tested group.

This study is impressive in that its results run counter to those of most developmental research on self-regard, and the method is superior to that of most other studies. One of its strengths is its longitudinal approach. On the other hand, as the authors point out, only one cohort was involved. Thus, it is possible that the observed trend is a function of what was happening in our society between 1966 and 1974 as opposed to being a developmental trend in United States males in the eight years following their enrollment in tenth grade.

In an interview study of a large probability sample of subjects older than those in the preceding three studies, Gurin, Veroff, and Feld (1960) included three idiosyncratic questions concerning "self-perception": (a) "What are some of the ways in which you are different from other people?" (b) "If you had a son (daughter for women), how would you like him to be different from you?" (c) "How about your good points? What would you say were your strongest points?" (p. 53).

The authors coded these questions respectively for positive or negative affect, statement of weaknesses, and denial of strong points. Grouping their subjects into three age groups (21–34, 35–54, 55 and over), they found no age trends in tendency to perceive selves as different from others or to perceive strong points in themselves. Older age groups were less likely to see shortcomings in themselves, however. No significance tests are presented for the tabular data, procedures for coding are vaguely specified, and comparability between age groups is not discussed, so the results are not clearly interpretable.

It is clear that the majority of the relatively more adequate studies report no age differences in over-all verbal self-regard scores, and this majority involves repeated use of well-known instruments as opposed to "one-shot" use of idiosyncratic instruments. It is primarily from the latter that any kind of age trends have resulted. However, the studies using idiosyncratic instruments are divided almost equally among those yielding no trends, upward trends, and downward trends. Moreover, in these studies using idiosyncratic instruments, we found a number of troublesome sources of artifact, especially the possible confounding of unreliability with low self-regard, the inability to account for the effects of loss through attrition in longitudinal studies, and the possible operation of the regression artifact. The most adequate research yielding change as a function of age is the longitudinal one by Bachman and O'Malley (1977). Even here, the use of a single cohort limits the interpretability of reported increases in self-esteem as a function of age.

Therefore, I conclude that the burden of proof still lies upon anyone who claims to find an age difference in over-all self-regard between ages 6 and 50. When such differences are found, they need to be replicated and possible sources of them other than age per se should be explored, as Simmons, M. Rosenberg, and F. Rosenberg, (1973) have done.

c. Nonverbal Self-Esteem

I turn now to the age trends reported for the Self-Social Symbols Test of Long and her colleagues, a widely used nonverbal measure which purports to yield a "social self-esteem" score, among other scores. (See Wylie, 1974, pp. 190–200, for an evaluative review of this instrument.) The self-esteem score from this test typically does not correlate with verbal measures purporting to index over-all self-regard. Accordingly, it is interesting to see whether, in contrast to the verbal self-regard measures, Long et al. obtained age trends in their self-esteem score. They hypothesized that, because physical size and intellectual, motor, and social skills increase with age, the child's conception of his own importance (and hence his self-esteem) will increase as he grows older. In Grades 1–6, Long, Henderson, and Ziller (1967a) found an irregular relationship, with first-grade scores being higher, then a sharp drop from first to second grade, a moderate rise for two grades, and then a moderate decline for two grades. Although this yielded a significant age effect, it was not their predicted systematic upward trend. In Grades 6–12, Long, Ziller, and Henderson (1968) found another significant main effect of grade level on self-esteem scores, but two out of six of the grade-to-grade transitions went against a consistently upward trend. These age effects are not clearly interpretable, for several reasons: (a) The self-esteem score is but one among several overlapping scores to which they applied significance tests. (b) Insufficient information is given to enable one to evaluate comparability of groups and administrative procedures across grades. This is especially true since the second study involved a different version of the test from that used in the first study, precluding a comparison across Grades 1–12. (c) Also, this test is open to confounding between self-regard and unreliable responding in the attainment of a poor self-regard score. This factor might conceivably be operating as a cause in such upward trends as did occur in these two studies. Therefore, I conclude that it remains to be shown that there are valid, consistently upward age trends in the social–self-esteem purportedly measured by Long et al.'s instrument.

4. Studies of Separate Aspects of Self-Concept

If further research sustains the provisional conclusion that there are no age trends in verbal reports regarding over-all self-esteem, it might still be true that different specific aspects of self-evaluation might change in some way with age. Accordingly, it is interesting to examine some studies which attemped to look at separate aspects of self-concept as a function of age.

a. FACTOR SCORES

In his famous 19-year longitudinal study of engaged couples, E. L. Kelly (1955) looked at many personality variables including the

Flanagan Sociability and Self-Confidence factor scores from the Bernreuter Personality Inventory and 10 factorially selected scores from 36 personality self-ratings idiosyncratic to this research. Insufficient information is given to enable one to evaluate the method according to all the criteria listed in section C-1 above, but the comparability of administration between age groups and the making of multiple significance tests must clearly be questioned. The author himself is very cautious about the effects of the sampling procedures, the amount and kinds of attrition, and the psychological interpretability of the obtained results. He reports that females significantly increased in Bernreuter self-confidence; whereas on the 10 factorially established self-rating scores, both sexes significantly moved away from describing themselves as being peppy, neat, and good-natured and as having extremely wide interests. No differences between ages were obtained on the other six factorially established personality self-rating scores or on the Bernreuter factor scores.

In a more recent study, using an idiosyncratic set of semantic differential scales, Monge (1973) tested the hypothesis that there would be a "discontinuity in self-concept in the circumpubescent years" (p. 382). (See Wylie, 1974, pp. 224-230, for critical evaluation of the semantic differential technique in self-concept measurement.) Results of six factor analyses, for boys and for girls in Grades 6, 9, and 12, were compared. Four factors of self-concept were highly consistent across grades within each sex, with two of the four being highly consistent across sexes as well (p. 385). These results failed to support Monge's discontinuity hypothesis. Trends in mean factor scores for four factors (Achievement/Leadership; Congeniality/Sociability; Adjustment; Sex Appropriateness of Self-Concept) were then plotted across grade for each sex, and the significance of the grade effect was evaluated for each factor. In general, the trends across grades were not linear, and no one set of factor score curves followed the same trend. The mean factor scores for Achievement/Leadership show an increase for boys across grades whereas Congeniality/Sociability factor scores increase for both sexes through Grade 10. Both sexes declined with age on Adjustment and became more masculine (less feminine) with increasing age. As I said immediately above, the over-all self-regard scores from other instruments seem preponderantly to show no change with age. In view of Monge's grade trends for the separate factors, one wonders whether the null grade trends from the over-all self-regard scales could be the net result of some aspects of the self-concept becoming more favorable while others become less favorable as a function of age. These different aspects are, of course, all added together in determining the typical over-all self-regard score, so their separate trends, if present, could be obscured in the over-all self-regard score.

b. ERIKSON "SOLUTIONS"

Constantinople's (1969) design included both cross-sectional and longitudinal comparisons of college freshmen, sophomores, juniors, and seniors on a set of self-rating scales adapted from a Q-sort instrument which was devised by Wessman and Ricks (1966) to represent successful and unsuccessful resolutions of each of the first six of Erikson's developmental crises. Supposedly, self-esteem depends in part upon successful resolution of each crisis. The instrument Constantinople used is idiosyncratic; the reliabilities of the respective subscales vary considerably, and, as she points out, no validity estimates have been made for the subscales. It was, of course, expected that older subjects in the cross-sectional comparisons would score higher on successful and lower on unsuccessful resolutions of the crises, especially those immediately preceding or characterizing adolescence (i.e., industry vs. inferiority, identity vs. identity diffusion, and intimacy vs. isolation). Also predicted was a set of trends over time within the same individual toward more successful and fewer unsuccessful resolutions of the last three mentioned Eriksonian crises. The longitudinal data are uninterpretable for two reasons: (a) there was an extremely high rate of attrition, with no way of evaluating the differences, if any, between lost and remaining subjects; (b) the follow-up procedure was completely different from the original data collection process, mail questionnaires being used, as opposed to in-class responding. From the cross-sectional data, Constantinople obtained significant class effects for successful resolutions of the industry-inferiority and identity-identity diffusion crises and for unsuccessful resolutions of the industry-inferiority crisis. (She also found sex differences, and sex × age interactions.)

While the conception of this study seems theoretically relevant and worthy of further development, no generalizations can be reached without further work on the instrument, replication of the findings, and more direct tests of the relationships between reported status of crisis resolution and self-regard.

So far as the need for instrument development is concerned, it is relevant to note that Olczak and Goldman (1975) obtained numerous highly significant rs between subscales of Shostrom's Personal Orientation Inventory and subscales of their idiosyncratic version of Wessman and Ricks's Eriksonian instrument. Obviously, the discriminant validity of the respective Eriksonian scores must be questioned in the light of these findings.

c. SENSE OF SELF-IDENTITY

Guardo and Bohan (1971) used a Piagetian theory and interview technique in their exploratory work on children's development of the "sense of self-identity" which these authors treated conceptually as an "identity involving qualitative constancies" (p. 1920). Developing Guardo's (1968) ideas mentioned in section B above on children up to five years of age, their interview schedule probed four of the allegedly crucial dimensions of this sense of unique identity of self: the child's sense of his humanity (as opposed to his being an animal), sexuality, individuality, and continuity in time from the past through the present into the future. Their groups, aged six, seven, eight, nine were small, and multiple significance tests were made without information regarding the degree of correlation between the responses on which the separate significance tests were made. Therefore, their results are not conclusive, but their work is suggestive of a novel, potentially worthwhile approach to the study of an important aspect of self-concept in children. Their data suggest that even at the earlier ages, considerable sense of self-identity had developed. No clear quantitative age trends were found, but they report that an examination of the responses showed that the older subjects gave qualitatively different, more fully developed rationales in support of their answers to each of the basic identity questions.

Turner's (1975) conception of "identity" was essentially undefined in that he left it up to his respondents to interpret what was meant by the question "Do *you* often, sometimes, or never ask yourself 'Who am I really?'" (p. 150). Thus, there is no way to know whether the question was interpreted in a manner which would make the findings relevant to Erikson's theory, or even to know whether the age differences he obtained might have depended upon differences in the meaning of the question to the different generations. Turner hypothesized that concern with identity would be strongest in his youngest group (aged

18–29) and that transition from adult to elderly status might be associated with renewed preoccupation with identity. The interviewed subjects ($N = 1,008$) were a multistage probability sample of adults in households in Los Angeles County, while 4 university student groups were randomly drawn from registrars' records and tested by written questionnaire: 355 from the University of California at Los Angeles; 402 from Surrey, England; 434 from Australian National University; and 449 from LaTrobe University in Melbourne, Australia.

In the Los Angeles (nonuniversity) sample, high school- and college-educated subjects (but not grade school-educated subjects) showed a strong inverse relationship between age and expressed concern with the identity question. No increase in such concern was manifested among the elderly subjects, failing to support his hunch that renewed preoccupation with identity might occur at that age level. The author concludes that "an overwhelming majority of university students acknowledge a personal quest for identity, in striking contrast to an equally overwhelming majority of the general adult population who deny any such quest" (p. 153). This difference between the enrolled students and the general population is *not* a function of age, since those in university "are almost as different from a general community sample of college-exposed young people as the young people are from adults over fifty" (p. 153).

Subjects were also asked how much they agreed that each of the following was a way to find out who one "really is": help someone who needs your assistance; work hard at a really difficult and challenging task; tell your deepest feelings to someone you trust; forget duties and inhibitions and do just whatever you feel like doing. "Both adults and students endorse altruism most frequently, impulse-release least frequently, and intimacy with intermediate frequency. . . . They differ most in their evaluation of work as a medium for self discovery," with 64.3% of the general Los Angeles sample favoring this route, but only 36.2% to 40.1% of the various university samples favoring it.

While this study addresses itself to a timely and theoretically relevant issue, the definitional problem limits its interpretability, as I have already said. One wishes that the author had tried to find out how the subjects interpreted the question, if he was disinclined to define it more precisely for them. Moreover, the comparability of age groups in the Los Angeles sample with respect to variables other than educational level has not been controlled, so far as we are told. This leaves open the question of what may be accounting for the "age" differences. It would be risky to generalize from this cross-sectional study to within-subject developmental trends of concern with identity and how to attain it.

d. Summary

Obviously, since the above studies of separate aspects of the self-concept are so diverse and respectively inconclusive, they will sustain no integrated, substantive summary. Several of the methods appear to merit further development and application.

5. Studies Not Substantively Summarized

The following studies were not referred to in the substantive summaries of empirical findings concerning age trends in self-concepts of subjects 6 through 50 years of age because they (as well as some of those already mentioned) were judged to be so seriously flawed and/or so incompletely reported as to preclude interpretations: Ahammer (1971); Amatora (1957); K. G. Bailey and Gibby (1971); Bloom (1961); Botwinick (1970); R. E. Boyd (1975); Brozek (1952); Carlson (1965); Cratty (1970); deJung and Gardner (1962); Drummond and McIntire (1975); Fein, O'Neill, Frank, and Velit (1975); Gadzella and Fournet (1975); C. H. Grant (1969); S. W. Gray (1959); Grupp, Ramseyer, and Richardson (1968); Havighurst, Robinson, and Dorr (1946); A. L. Hess and Bradshaw (1970); Homall, S. Juhasz, and J. Juhasz (1975); Jorgensen and Howell (1969); Kagan and Moss (1962); Klaff and Docherty (1975); Kuhn (1960); Lefley (1974); Martin (1969); McConville, Boag, and Purohit (1973); Mullener and Laird (1971); Pannes (1963); B. N. Phillips (1963); Plutchik, Conte, and Weiner (1972); Plutchik, Weiner, and Conte (1971); Rabinowitz (1966); Rizzo and Vinacke (1975); Saleh and Grygier (1966); Schofield and Caple (1971); Schroeder (1973); Schwab, Clemmons, and Marder (1966); Sharan (1974); Sieka (1974); Tyler (1957); Van den Daele (1968); Ward (1971); A. S. Waterman, Geary, and C. K. Waterman (1974); W. F. White, H. E. Anderson, and Cryder (1967); J. D. Williams and Beebe (1973); Ziller and Grossman (1967).

D. Studies of Persons above Fifty Years of Age

Although this section is concerned primarily with subjects above 50 years of age, it also includes researches in which younger age groups are compared with those over 50.

Two secondary sources (G. R. Peters, 1971; Riley & Foner, 1968) give many bibliographic references of use to researchers studying old persons, and one of these (Riley & Foner, 1968) presents tables and other quantitative information from some of the studies referred to in this section. Although Riley and Foner provide a convenient source for detailed information from a variety of publications, neither their book nor Peters's article subjects the primary sources to systematic, close methodological scrutiny before making general statements.

1. Methodological Criteria

In selecting studies for substantive summaries, I used the methodological criteria already given in section C-1 above. As is true in section C, I have excluded from consideration the few available studies purporting to deal with the nonphenomenal self, in view of the presently unsolved problems of construct validity of measures of the nonphenomenal self. (See Wylie, 1974, chap. 5, for a full discussion of these problems.)

In addition, Reichard, Livson, and Petersen (1962) suggest a point which seems especially relevant to evaluating cross-sectional comparisons of self-concept data from old persons as opposed to middle-aged or young persons. To these authors it seems reasonable to suppose that those who survive into old age may be psychologically healthier, inasmuch as psychological stress reactions may often be involved in fatal diseases. If this is so, it perhaps implies that one should find more favorable self-evaluations among surviving aged persons, as compared to younger groups. According to their argument, if such a difference were to be found, it could not properly be interpreted as indicating that self-regard improves with age in the longitudinal development of any person or group.

Still another methodological suggestion particularly pertinent to studies of old persons is Donahue's (1965) idea that the age of the interviewer or tester may introduce unwanted effects on old persons' self-reports or on the interviewers' interpretations of these reports. If it is true that younger persons hold negative views of oldsters, these biases could conceivably have either of these effects. One wonders also whether simply the old person's belief that the interviewer is biased against oldsters might not be a determinant of the oldster's responses, regardless of the actual ideas of the interviewer. These problems are quite analogous, of course, to those seen in studies of race and sex differences.

2. Relevant Theorizing

Although Erikson (1959, 1963) has written about personality development in old age, none of the studies I examined was explicitly based on his views. Adler (in Ansbacher & Ansbacher, 1956) theorized about the probable decline in self-regard in old age, but to my knowledge no study explicitly purports to test his rationale. Contrary to Adler and many common-sense views that self-regard will be low in old age, Back and Gergen (1968) offer theoretical reasons for expecting "self-value" to be minimal in the fifties, but to be improved with age beyond the fifties. (See section C-2 above for their rationale.) To my knowledge, no study has been set up in order to measure their theoretical constructs and arguments, although some researches have been addressed to descriptive age comparisons on self-regard variables. Like Back and Gergen (1968), Reichard, Livson, and Petersen (1962) suggest several reasons why "self-acceptance" might be expected to increase after retirement, e.g., the retiree experiences more "relaxed requirements" in that it becomes socially acceptable for him or her to be more passive and dependent, or he may retrospectively redefine earlier goals to match achievements. Again, no extant research has been addressed to their particular reasons for predicting increasing self-regard in old age.

More generally, the studies I examined either were not based on any particular theory, or they concerned certain supposedly relevant sociological and physical variables.

The sociological analyses relevant to self-conceptions of old persons may be summarized under two major, interrelated categories: the effects of society's views and the effects of role change.

a. EFFECTS OF SOCIETY'S VIEWS

Many persons assume that younger segments of society hold stereotypic views about specific characteristics of older persons and that, as Cooley, Mead, or Rogers might have predicted, the older person's self-concepts come to reflect these views. According to this line of thought, the social stereotypes of old persons are not only characterized by particular traits, but these imputed traits are, to a large degree, pejorative. Thus, if the old person's self-concept is a function of society's stereotypes, his self-regard might be lower than that of other age groups. For example, Rose (1965) argues that "most of the changes associated with the assumption of the role and self-conception of being elderly are negatively evaluated in American culture, and . . . there is no compensatory attribution of prestige as in other societies" (p. 12). Hickey and Kalish (1968) have speculated that the old person's "view of himself is learned not only by the way others see him, but also by his early and prior learning of his contemporary role" (p. 216).

Other social-influence factors which could lead to lowered self-regard among the old are the widely accepted ideas that the old constitute an unwanted economic and personal burden for the young and that young persons tend to avoid associating with old persons because of the unwelcome thoughts of deterioration and dying aroused by their presence.

However, one can say only that self-regard *might* be lower among old persons, because several factors may conceivably operate against the influences mentioned above. For one thing, it is possible that the old person may protect his self-regard by excepting himself from the unfavorable stereotype, as seems to happen in the case of other socially disparaged groups such as women, blacks, and persons from lower socioeconomic levels. Then, too, self-regard of the aged may be based on a sense of accomplishment throughout life (Erikson, 1959, 1963), or being relatively immune to current influences which are construed by the old as beyond their control. Alternately, self-regard may be based upon a person's estimate of how well he or she is doing in comparison with age peers, the most relevant and frequently encountered reference group. As Rose (1965) has argued, various social factors including increases in numbers, health status, and segregation of older persons may be operating to create a "subculture of the aged." This affords opportunities for "group identification, . . . expressions of group pride, and corollary expressions of dismay concerning . . . the younger generations. With this group pride has come self-acceptance as a member of an esteemed group" (p. 14). And, as mentioned earlier, Back and Gergen (1968) and Reichard, Livson, and Petersen (1962) suggest still other reasons why self-regard might not decline or might even increase with old age.

Theorists who espouse the "reflective" view of self-concept development in the aged have been particularly concerned with "age identification," the sense of being young, middle-aged, old, or very old.

This is by far the commonest self-concept variable studied in subjects over 50. One may argue theoretically that, since old age is devalued by society, persons will tend to stave off these sociological influences on their self-concepts by seeing themselves as not yet in the socially disparaged age group. (Of course not wanting to see oneself as old might also depend, in part, on the wish to deny the implications of physical decline associated with age.)

b. THE EFFECTS OF ROLE CHANGE

Sociologists (e.g., Cavan, 1962; Rosow, 1967; Simpson, Back, & McKinney, 1966) have also stressed the fact that certain role changes typically occur as a function of age and that these changes may have important consequences for the self-concepts of older persons. For example, theorists have noted the plausible importance of shifts away from such roles as employed person, parent, and married person. Downward income shifts, typical among aged persons, may also effect role losses, and roles associated with friendship or social groups may also be lost. Deterioration in physical capacities or health may attenuate or eliminate certain important roles while simultaneously putting the old person in the devalued "sick role."

Rosow (1967) and Cavan (1962) have pointed out that role losses characteristic of age are especially damaging in that our society provides the old person no clearly defined new role. Whereas the younger person usually gains a definite new role when losing a previous one, e.g., in moving from a student role to a role as employed person, the role losses of the old person leave him in a very ambiguous position, in a "basically empty" role, according to Rosow's and Cavan's view. Insofar as clarity of self-concept and level of self-evaluation depend on society's provision of relatively clear and well-evaluated roles, the old person's self-concept may be expected to be unclear and/or self-derogatory.

3. Studies of Stereotypes about Old Persons

There is some evidence to suggest that members of our society do hold stereotypes regarding specific characteristics and general favorability of old persons' characteristics and that these stereotypes may be shared to some degree (but not entirely) by persons of widely varying ages (Hickey & Kalish, 1968; Lane, 1964; Lorge, Tuckman, &

Abrams, 1954; National Council on the Aging, 1975; Rosencranz & McNevin, 1969; Tuckman & Lorge, 1953; Tuckman, Lorge, & Spooner, 1953).

By far the most extensive study is a poll conducted by Louis Harris and Associates for the National Council on the Aging (1975). By multistage, random cluster sampling, they obtained a national cross-section which purportedly reflects accurately the population of United States civilians 18 years of age or older, living in private households. "The sample was drawn to allow analysis of the findings by three key age groups: (1) persons aged 18-54, (2) persons aged 55-64, and (3) persons aged 65 and over. An additional black national sample was used to oversample blacks 65 and over" (1975, p. 241).

Although the sampling techniques appear to be appropriate to the researchers' purposes and "trained interviewers" were used, the published report tells nothing about the psychometric characteristics of the sets of questions used to operationalize such psychological constructs as "self image"; nor are problems and procedures of significance testing and the outcomes of such tests dealt with explicitly. Only very occasionally is a reference made to a "significant difference"; such references imply that testing of this sort must have been done, but no systematic information is given about the obtained results. Unfortunately, therefore, the psychological interpretability of this potentially valuable mass of data is severely curtailed, and the summary below must be read with these reservations in mind.

On 7 evaluative variables the investigators compared the "image of most people over 65" held by (a) respondents aged 18-64 and (b) respondents 65 and older. These variables are: friendly and warm, wise from experience, physically active, good at getting things done, bright and alert, open-minded and adaptable, and sexually active. The respondents 65 and older seemed to share the opinions of those under 65 that "most people over 65" are very wise from experience, but are not very bright and alert, not very open-minded and adaptable, not very good at getting things done, not very physically active, and not very sexually active. The older respondents were more favorable to their peers than were the younger regarding open-mindedness and adaptability, and they were somewhat less favorable to their peers regarding whether most people over 65 are very wise from experience. The most striking difference is in respect to the percentages of younger and older respondents seeing most people over 65 as "very friendly and warm." Only 25% of the older respondents as opposed to 82% of the younger ones held this view of most people over 65.

Omitting the "sexually active" dimension, the researchers created a favorability scale by combining responses to the remaining 6 items, weighting answers according to the degree of favorability each answer showed (e.g., "very," "somewhat"). The medians of this over-all favorability score toward "most people over 65" were almost identical between the 2 groups of respondents: those aged 18 to 64, and those 65 and over. More detailed age breakdowns showed favorability to be lowest among respondents aged 18-24, increasing as a function of age up to ages 40-64, then decreasing. However, the only age group whose favorability toward "most people over 65" differed significantly from the public at large was the 18-24 age group.

In reply to a question about usefulness to the community, 86% of both younger and older respondents saw most persons over 65 as either very or somewhat useful to the community. However, more of the older as opposed to the younger respondents tended to see those over 65 as "very useful."

One may take the results pertaining to characteristics imputed to "most people over 65" as an operational definition of part of a stereotype about old persons and argue that a fair degree of agreement regarding this stereotype occurred across age groups. At the same time, however, one cannot know that this is a distinctive stereotype of old-age characteristics because no information is given concerning the public's views about "most people" at some of the younger age ranges. This limitation does not characterize Hickey and Kalish's (1968) much smaller study which compared 4 ratings assigned to hypothetical groups of 4 ages (25, 45, 65, 85) by raters of 4 age groups (median ages = 8, 12, 15.5, 19.5). They found that raters of all ages saw ratees as being more mean or unkind, more lonely, less likely to like children and young persons, and less busy as a function of the ratees' age.

Of the studies about stereotypes mentioned at the beginning of this section, only the National Council on the Aging study may permit comparisons of the "self-images" of the older respondents with the stereotypes held by either older or younger respondents. Even in this study, one can compare only descriptive distributions of percentages of respondents giving various answers to each question, i.e., *one cannot tell for each older individual to what degree, if any, the self-image corresponds to any group's stereotype of most people over 65.*

Nevertheless, a comparison of the percentages leads to the conclusion that the self-descriptions of respondents 65 years of age or older are much more favorable than are their views of most people over 65. The differences between these percents are as follows: very friendly and warm +47%; very wise from experience +13%; very bright and alert +35%; very open-minded and adaptable +29%; very good at getting things done +17%; very physically active +5%; very sexually active +5%.

If one compares the percents for "self-image" reports of respondents of 65 or over with the percents of respondents aged 18-24 attributing each quality to most people over 65, the differences between these percents are as follows: very friendly and warm −10%; very wise from experience +3%; very bright and alert +39%; very open-minded and adaptable +44%; very good at getting things done +20%; very physically active +7%; very sexually active +6%.

Thus using either the younger group's "stereotype" or the older group's "stereotype" about most people over 65, it would appear that, as with other disadvantaged groups such as women and blacks, there is a tendency to accept the validity of a stereotype of one's group more than to agree that the stereotype is descriptive of oneself.

None of the available data permits us to say whether older persons' self-conceptions have been influenced in any way by any stereotypes concerning their age group's characteristics.

4. Studies of Self-Conceptions of One's Age

Of all the theoretically relevant variables cited in section D-2 above, the self-concept of one's age-role status has been examined by far the most often. Twenty reports on this topic have come to my attention, some of them reporting on the same data. Of these, some were looking for "age denial," while others were concerned with relating self-conceived age to other variables, such as actual age or various role statuses.

a. Evidence Relevant to "Denial of Age"

It is unfortunately true that these researches involve a wide variety of ways of posing the question about self-conception of age. Accordingly, firm syntheses and generalizations from various studies may not be made. Even more troublesome is the fact that, within one method, one cannot be sure the subjects are interpreting the wording as the researchers intended. For example, Jeffers, Eisdorfer, and Busse (1962) first asked their 168 subjects aged 60–94 to answer the question used by Burgess, Cavan, and Havighurst (1948), "Do you feel that you are now: Young, Middle-Aged, Elderly, Old, or Aged?" An hour later they asked the subjects to sort cards containing these age labels from earliest to latest period of life and to assign chronological age ranges to each label. Finally, subjects were asked to state again their own self-conceptions of age, this time in terms of their own rank ordering of the age labels, The first point of methodological interest is that comparisons of subjects' rank orders of the age-label categories showed considerable disagreement with the rank orders assumed by Burgess et al. (1948). Second, 55% of the subjects shifted their expressed self-conceptions of age to an older age label as measured in terms of their own ordering of the age-group labels, whereas only 4% shifted to a younger label.

Not only do age-denial studies involve problems of interpretability of wording, but statistical significance tests are lacking in a large number of these reports. These methodological limitations have their worst effects on the possibility of generalizing about the relationships of self-conceived age to other variables. However, it is of some interest to examine the strictly descriptive findings regarding percents of older persons who consider themselves to be old, regardless of variations among studies in respect to subject variables and the way the question was posed to and interpreted by the subjects.

Incidentally, out of the 20 publications involving self-conceived age, distributions of subjects' responses to the question of whether they conceived themselves to be young, middle-aged, or old were reported for only 9 different sets of subjects. Most of these researchers who provided distributions of the responses about self-conceived age have interpreted their descriptive results as indicating personal "age denial" on the part of their chronologically old subjects. But to say that an individual is refusing to admit he belongs in a disparaged category, one must be able to define that category. That is, one can suggest the occurrence of *personal* "age denial" only when the age self-conceptions of chronologically older persons are evaluated against a baseline of the general public's opinion as to when a person may appropriately be considered old in our society. For a rough baseline of society's views on this point, one may look at a large-scale study involving an area-probability sample of 1,452 persons under 45 years of age and 1,115 persons 45 years old or older in which Shanas (1962) asked "At what age do you think a man or woman is old?" Concerning when a man may be considered old, 41.7% of the younger respondents and 31.1% of the older ones thought a man to be old by the time he reached 64 years of age, whereas 85.9% of the younger and 78.4% of the older respondents thought a man was old by the time he reached age 74. Concerning when a woman may be considered old 47.6% of the younger respondents and 41.1% of the older respondents thought a woman old by the time she had reached age 64, whereas 85.4% and 78.7% thought a woman to be old by age 74. (No significance tests are given for any of the above comparisons.)

The National Council on the Aging (1975) study cited above also involved a question concerning the age at which the average man or woman would become old. Almost half the respondents did not name a particular age, giving other criteria or miscellaneous answers. Since the exact question is not published in the report, interpretative comparisons between their data and the Shanas results are impossible. However, of those in the National Council on Aging Study who did cite a particular age at which the "average man or woman would become old," about half thought this would occur by age 64, whereas about 9 out of 10 thought it would occur by age 74. These figures appear to be fairly similar to the more detailed ones from the Shanas study.

In all but one of the studies cited immediately below (Zola, 1962), the distributions of personally applicable self-conceptions of age were obtained from subjects having chronological ages of at least 60; so the above-listed percent values may be relevant to evaluating the distributions of percentages of expressed age-self-conceptions in these studies. The percentages of subjects saying they usually or unqualifiedly felt or considered themselves to be old (including elderly, very old) were as follows: Aisenberg (1964), 18%; Blau (1956), 38%; (apparently this is the same Elmira sample as that reported on by B. S. Phillips, 1957, below); Guptill (1969), 35%; Kastenbaum and Durkee (1964), 49%; Messer (1968) for white subjects, 24.4% of those 62-69 years old; 36.7% of those 70-79 years old; 47.6% for those 80 and over; for black subjects, 51.8, 77.1, and 88 were the percents for the corresponding age ranges; B. S. Phillips (1957) for Elmira subjects, 11% of respondents aged 60-69; 47% of respondents 70 and over (26% of the total Elmira sample, according to Guptill, 1969); B. S. Phillips (1957) for Kips Bay subjects, 27% of respondents aged 60-69: 55% of respondents 70 and over (42% of total Kips Bay sample, according to Kutner, Fanshel, Togo, & Langner [1956] who reported originally on these data); Tuckman and Lorge (1954), 17% of respondents aged 60–69; 38% of respondents aged 70–79; 53% of respondents aged 80 or over; Zola (1962), 21% of men, 20% of women respondents.

Comparative inspection of (a) the Shanas and National Council on Aging data, and (b) the above-cited data concerning self-concept of age suggest the *very tentative statement that some personal denial of old-age status occurred in the subject groups used in the above studies.* We must remember, however, that one cannot tell whether the subjects reporting their self-conceived ages can legitimately be compared with the subjects in the Shanas or National Council on Aging samples regarding such possibly relevant variables as race and socioeconomic level. Thus, we are on uncertain ground in assuming that chronologically older subjects reporting their self-conceived age are excepting themselves by denial from the age-role status attributed to them by that segment of society from which their "reflective self-evaluations" might reasonably be expected to have arisen. Moreover, as Jeffers, Eisdorfer, and Busse (1962) point out in their article:

> It seems that the necessity for the subjects to consider specific chronological periods in relation to age categories [as was done in this study] served to remind them of their own aging and hence to adopt a more realistic attitude in regard to the relationship between their chronological age and the age categories. [P. 439]

This implies that "age denial," to the extent to which it is found, may often be fairly superficial, if it can be lessened by such a minor experimental manipulation.

b. Variables Associated with Individual Differences
   in Self-Conceptions of Age

In addition to the possible influence of individuals' denial of an unwanted old-person status, it seems highly plausible that other variables should determine, or at least be associated with individual differences in self-conceptions of age. In the reports I examined, the variables listed at the end of this section were considered to be plausibly related to self-conception of age, and quite a few researchers reported obtaining associations between self-conceptions of age and the other variables they examined. But when one scrutinizes their reports closely, one finds a number of problems which prevent interpreting their results in the way they propose. First, either significance tests are not reported or insufficient information is given to enable the reader to evaluate the significance of what appear by inspection to be marked trends in the case of some of the studies. But even more important, many of the researches fell short on several of the other minimum methodological criteria (listed in section D-1) which must be fulfilled if one may justifiably conclude that self-conception of age is associated with the researcher's designated variable with other variables held constant.

To the extent that any of the variables below are related to self-conceptions of age, those variables must be held constant when looking at the relationship of any particular variable and self-conception of age, and this has not been accomplished in the listed studies. Accordingly, in the light of all of the above severe methodological limitations, I do not feel that substantive generalizations should be made on the basis of these studies, and they are merely listed for the reader's convenience.

Perhaps the reader will think that at least chronological age must be associated with age self-conceptions. This seems commonsensible and almost inevitable, and several studies have reported such an association (e.g., B. S Phillips, 1957, 1961; Blau, 1956; Messer, 1968; Tuckman & Lorge, 1954). Kastenbaum and Durkee (1964), however, did not find such a relationship within a very old group. But even with respect to the variable, chronological age, one must note that significance tests between age self-conceptions of younger and older groups were not usually given; and the age groups compared were not shown to be comparable with respect to other variables such as socioeconomic status, health, race, and institutional status, which might plausibly be expected to determine or be associated with age conceptions. The plausibility that socioeconomic status should be controlled when comparing self-conceptions of chronological age groups is suggested indirectly by one part of the National Council on Aging report: (a) income level (under or over $7,000 within each of 3 age groups [18-54, 55-64, 65 and over]) tended to be directly related to the percentages reporting self-conceptions of being very good at getting things done, very bright and alert, very physically active, and very sexually active; and (b) educational level within the oldest group was directly related to self-conceptions of being very bright and alert, very good at getting things done, and very physically active.

The reader will remember, however, that this report, although involving superior sampling techniques, does not provide adequate information regarding statistical significance and certain other points; so one must emphasize the suggestive and indirect nature of the above statement concerning the need to hold socioeconomic level constant when comparing groups on self-conceptions of age.

Below is a list of the inconclusive studies in which possible relationships between self-concept of age and other variables have been examined.

1. *Activities, level and type* (Tuckman & Lavell, 1957).

2. *Adjustment, attitudes toward life, morale* (Havighurst & Albrecht, 1953; Kutner, Fanshel, Togo, & Langner, 1956; Perlin & R. N. Butler, no date; Tuckman & Lavell, 1957).

3. *Chronological age* (Aisenberg, 1964; Blau, 1956; Kastenbaum & Durkee, 1964; Messer, 1968; Rosow, 1967; Tuckman & Lorge, 1954; Tuckman & Lavell, 1957).

4. *Employed as opposed to retired and/or unemployed status* (M. L. Barron, 1961; Blau, 1956; B. S. Phillips, 1957).

5. *Interests of elderly patients in institutions* (Tuckman & Lavell, 1957).

6. *Mental, i.e., intellectual status* (Kastenbaum & Durkee, 1964; Tuckman & Lavell, 1957).

7. *Others' view and/or treatment of one* (Aisenberg, 1964; Blau, 1956; R. W. Davis, 1962; B. S. Phillips, 1961).

8. *Perceived changes in self* (Blau, 1956; L. W. Jones, 1935).

9. *Physical illness or handicaps* (Friedsam & Martin, 1963; Suchman, B. S. Phillips, & Streib, 1957–58).

10. *Race* (Messer, 1968).

11. *Role changes, including retirement as cited above; but also widowhood, income-shifts, and health-related roles* (Blau, 1956; B. S. Phillips, 1957, 1961; Rosow, 1967).

12. *Seeing one's parents as elderly* (Zola, 1962).

13. *Self-regard* (Guptill, 1969).

14. *Self-reported health* (Aisenberg, 1964; Friedsam & Martin, 1963; L. W. Jones, 1935; Kutner et al., 1956; Suchman, B. S. Phillips, & Streib, 1957–58; Tuckman & Lavell, 1957).

15. *Social class* (Rosow, 1967).

16. *Social involvement (formal and informal), and family involvement* (G. D. Bell, 1967; Blau, 1956).

5. *Studies of Variables Associated with Self-Regard in Old Persons*

Thus far I have considered whether self-conceptions of old persons coincide with stereotypes held concerning their age group, and whether old persons' self-conceptions of age might be indicative of denial of an unwanted status or might be related to other variables.

Other topics to which I now turn include the over-all self-regard of the aged, their self-evaluations on separate characteristics, and possible relationships of self-evaluative statements to other variables.

One might imagine that over-all self-regard and/or self-evaluation on separate traits as a function of chronological age or some other variables would be a popular research topic, but relatively few relevant publications have appeared. Almost all of the studies they report fall so far short of fulfilling the important methodological criteria discussed in section D-1 above that they do not seem to warrant substantive summary, and they are therefore simply identified or listed at the end of this section.

The study which seems relatively most adequate methodologically is that by the National Council on the Aging (1975) mentioned several times above. Despite its methodological limitations already pointed out, a few tentative substantive statements may be made on the basis of the descriptive information provided.

Without giving a significance test or details about the question asked, the report states, "The public 65 and over have a relatively high self-image in terms of being useful members of the community. . . . The self-image in this area held by the public 65 and over is, in fact, more positive than that held by the public 18-64" (p. 63).

Regarding the results from the seven self-evaluative variables mentioned earlier, the National Council on the Aging (1975) report states: "A striking finding of this study is the fact that age does not appear to influence significantly the way individuals tend to view themselves: The public 65 and over tend to see themselves as less physically active and less sexually active than do those under 65 . . . . [while seeing] itself [sic] as somewhat more friendly and warm . . . , and as wiser from experience. The public's view in both these areas tends to increase continually with age" (p. 54). Small differences were observed regarding percentages of old and young respondents calling themselves very bright and alert, very open-minded and adaptable, and very good at getting things done. The above descriptive statements tend to be fairly applicable within each of three income groups, according to a table presenting responses by age × income (p. 148); and visual inspection of the table does not suggest the possibility of interaction between age and income level in determining responses to the seven variables, although (as mentioned earlier) income is associated with self-regard variables within each age group, showing the necessity for controlling income when comparing age groups.

In a table breaking down answers of the oldest respondents by race, one sees that on every variable except very sexually active, the old blacks' self-images are less favorable than those of the old whites (p. 149). Although the authors of the report claim that such race differences are smaller among younger respondents, they present relevant information about only three of the seven variables (p. 150). Thus one cannot estimate even descriptively the possible interactions between age and race in determining each of the self-image variables. In any case, the data presented suggest the possible importance of holding race constant when making age comparisons on self-image variables.

Within the oldest group, three of the self-image variables appear to be a linearly increasing function of education: very bright and alert, very good at getting things done, and very physically active (pp. 151-152). Unfortunately, only one of these variables (very bright and alert) is analyzed simultaneously by age and educational level: The descriptive information suggests that education probably did not interact with age in determining responses to this question.

The reader will remember that these researchers developed an overall favorability-of-image score for the first six self-evaluative variables combined. Unfortunately, they report nothing about age differences on such a favorability score derived from applying this scoring scheme to self-images.

6. Sense of Identity

In section C-4 above, I summarized and evaluated a study by Turner (1975) which involved responses from subjects aged 18 through 60 + to the question "Do *you* often, sometimes, or never ask yourself 'Who am I really?' " (p. 150). Failing to support Turner's expectations, there was no indication that those above 50 showed a renewed preoccupation with this question. (See section C-4 for details.)

7. Studies Not Substantively Summarized

Below is a list of studies on variables associated with self-regard in old persons which seem sufficiently flawed to preclude substantive interpretation.

Anderson, N. (1967), regarding self-esteem and institutionalization as opposed to institutional-applicant status

Back and Guptill (1966), regarding morale, job deprivation, occupational status and interests

Barron, M. L. (1961), regarding self-ratings of health and occupational status of the aged

Brim, Neulinger, and Glass (1965), regarding self-perceived intelligence

Brozek (1955), regarding self-confidence

Butler, R. N. (1967), regarding self-view, sense of continued usefulness, and survival; use of mirror-image experience as measure of body and self-image

Dodge (1961), regarding feelings of intellectual adequacy in five different age groups and three levels of training in nursing

Gergen and Back (1966), regarding satisfaction with present body weight

Gordon, S. K., and Vinacke (1971), regarding comparisons of self-esteem as a function of dependency and as differing between young and old groups

Gurin, Veroff, and Feld (1960), regarding self-regard as a function of age (See section C-3 above)

Havighurst (1963), regarding associations between positivity of self-concept and zest, resolution, and fortitude, goodness of fit, and mood tone (all five variables rated from the same interviews)

Kaplan and Pokorny (1970), regarding self-derogation in five different age groupings

Kleemeier (1965), Kogan and Wallach (1961), regarding self-regard in young and old groups

Lieberman, Prock, and Tobin (1968), regarding Leary's Interpersonal Check List variables and Cattell's Sixteen Personality Factors of institutionalized residents versus community residents on the waiting list

Markson and Grevert (1972), regarding self-perceptions of incapacity among old people referred for psychiatric care

Mason (1954a, 1954b), regarding feelings of self-worth as a function of age and institutionalization

Miskimins and Simmons (1966), regarding the development of a scale of age-related ideal-self-concept (goals)

Pollack, E. Karp, R. L. Kahn, and Goldfarb (1962), regarding high rates of self-derogation in response to one's mirror image

Reichard, Livson, and Petersen (1962), regarding open rejection of self as a function of retirement status

Rizzo and Vinacke (1975), Schwab, Clemmons, and Marder (1966), regarding self-regard as a function of age

Saleh and Grygier (1966), regarding self-perception of productivity before retirement

Sieka (1974), regarding correlations between age and sex-role esteem in disfigured and not disfigured persons

Simpson, Back, and McKinney (1966), regarding self-regard ("morale") as a function of job deprivation

J. Smith (1966a, 1966b), J. Smith and Turk (1966), regarding feelings of importance to the community

Ziller and Grossman (1967), regarding self-esteem as a function of age

The reader is reminded that section D-4 (variables associated with individual differences in self-conceptions of age) ends with a listing of inconclusive studies on that topic.

Additional studies involving persons over 50 years of age which were characterized by serious methodological flaws and limitations and/or insufficient information to permit evaluation are listed immediately below. The asterisk after the reference indicates it was also listed in section C-5 above as uninterpretable regarding self-concept variables in persons 6 through 50 years old. Ahammer (1971)*; Bloom (1961)*; Botwinick (1970)*; R. M. Coe (1965); Grant (1969)*; Hess and Bradshaw (1970)*; Kahana and Coe (1969); C. N. Lewis (1971); Plutchik, Conte, and R. Weiner (1972)*; Plutchik, R. Weiner and Conte (1971)*; Sharan (1974)*.

3
Socioeconomic Class and Self-Concept Variables

A. General Theoretical and Methodological Considerations

1. Rationales for Possible Associations between Socioeconomic Class and Self-Concept Variables

Why is it plausible to hypothesize that various aspects of self-concept, such as sense of self-identity, components of ideal self (self values), views of one's particular personality attributes, and over-all self-regard, are a function of socioeconomic differences? If any such functional relations obtain, may they depend upon the immediate impact of parental values and child-rearing practices, upon the child's personal experience with significant others outside the home, or upon both? To what extent, if any, do the hypothesized associations between socioeconomic class and self-concept depend on the person's having developed a sense of social-class identity? This section is addressed to a general, hypothetical consideration of such questions. Empirical evidence relevant to some of these questions is given in section B below.

a. Effects Which Depend Mainly or Entirely on Parent-Child Interactions

Differential Parental Values

It has been hypothesized (e.g., by Langner & Michael, 1963; by M. L. Kohn, 1963; and by Pearlin & Kohn, 1966) that parents from different socioeconomic classes hold different values for themselves and their children. For example, M. L. Kohn (1963) proposes that middle-class parents value self-direction and self-control in their children, whereas the working-class parent places more emphasis on conformity to external rules and standards and is less concerned with the child's internal feelings than is the middle-class parent. Therefore, it is conceivable that the parents will convey these values to their children and will differentially reinforce the children's behavior in accordance with their value system. This sequence might reasonably be expected to result in differing value systems (and possibly different behaviors) among children as a function of their parents' socioeconomic class. Insofar as value systems are really part of the ideal self, one might then

---

Susan S. Cowles drafted evaluative summaries of a substantial number of the studies considered in this chapter.

hypothesize that certain ideal-self concept differences are a function of social-class difference.

Different Child-Rearing Techniques

It has also frequently been hypothesized that parents from differing socioeconomic classes use different techniques of child rearing, e.g., more or less reliance on physical punishment, reasoning, or withdrawal of love as reinforcement. Such variations in approach might conceivably result in differences in personality characteristics among children as a function of the parents' socioeconomic class, and, to the extent that the children come eventually to recognize such aspects of their own personalities, their self-concepts concerning specific personality traits might plausibly be expected to differ.

Regarding one particular aspect of self-concept, Langner and Michael (1963) have hypothesized that certain aspects of child-rearing techniques may affect the child's "sense of individuality and identity" (p. 444). For instance, middle- and upper-class children are more apt to experience "identity training through scrapbooks, baby books, family albums, birthday parties. Individuality [is] emphasized — in clothing, love, school work, possession of own toys rather than sharing, [whereas in the lower-class home] interchangeability of function [is] emphasized, clothes and toys (if any) handed down" (pp. 469–470).

Parental Feelings of Over-all Self-Regard

If the child identifies with the parents, and they in turn feel superior or inferior, it is plausible to suppose that the child may develop an over-all level of self-regard which is a function of the parents' level of self-regard. Some theorists have assumed that parents of the lower class are more likely to feel inferior, while those of the middle and upper classes are likely to feel more adequate or superior, with the result that parental socioeconomic class will determine children's over-all level of self-regard. Langner and Michael (1963) state that "the self-esteem of a child is based, to a large degree, on the status of the parents and the parents' self-esteem. The son of a laborer is more likely to internalize a self-rejecting father, a father who judges himself in the same way society judges him. This lowers the self-esteem of the son" (p. 455). It is conceivable that parents who feel that members of their class are typically inferior or superior persons may, accordingly, convey a sense of inferiority or superiority to their children before, and apart from, the child's development of a sense of his own socioeconomic level.

b. Effects which May or May Not Depend upon Persons' Having a Sense of Their Own Socioeconomic-Class Status

Stereotypes Accepted as Self-Descriptive

Sociologists, beginning with Warner and Lunt (1941), have assumed that there are socially shared stereotypes of specific personality traits respectively descriptive of members of differing socioeconomic classes. Unfortunately for clear theorizing and research, they have not resolved the 50-year-old question as to how the concept "stereotype" should be defined, especially whether the trait attributions included in it must be considered to be unjustified by a presumably knowledgeable observer (Brigham, 1974). In any event, it seems to be implicitly assumed that, to the extent that justified or unjustified trait attributions are assigned to a group (e.g., to a socioeconomic level), and to the extent that children develop a sense of socioeconomic-class identity, children may become aware of the stereotypes and accept them as applicable to themselves as individual members of their class. If this chain of events occurs, then it is reasonable to hypothesize that self-concept reports of specific aspects of personality will vary as a function of socioeconomic class and will correspond more or less accurately to the stereotype about personality characteristics supposedly attributed to members of each class.

Over-all Self-Regard as a Function of Nonparental Influences

In addition to the possible class-related parental influences on children's over-all self-regard which I mentioned above, one needs also to consider other class-related factors which might affect over-all self-regard of both children and adults.

Alternate arguments can be developed, predicting a variety of functional relationships between socioeconomic status and self-regard. The two most widely espoused are a strong positive or a minimal (perhaps null) association between these variables.

On the one hand, if one belongs to a socioeconomic class which is

generally held in high (or low) regard, one may (a) be treated with
more (or less) regard by others, and/or have (b) more (or less) access to
financial resources and educational resources with which to develop
oneself. (That the members of different classes are treated unequally
and have varying access to resources has been documented by a
number of studies cited by K. B. Mayer [1955, pp. 34–40].) Both (a)
and (b) could operate on self-regard by way of the adoption of
reflected self-appraisals (as postulated by Mead [1934] and Cooley
[1902], for example). Or they could affect self-regard by determining
feelings of self-potency, which assumedly determine level of self-
regard.

Typical of the numerous strong theoretical statements along these
lines are the following:

> The groups to which a person belongs serve as primary determiners of his
> self-esteem. To a considerable extent *personal* feelings of worth depend
> upon the social evaluation of the *groups* with which a person is identified.
> Self-hatred and feelings of worthlessness tend to arise from membership in
> under-privileged or outcast groups. [D. Cartwright, 1950, p. 440]
>
> In a highly competitive society, it is inevitable that self-esteem will derive
> in part from an individual's perception of his ranking and prestige within
> relevant groups. To the extent that the symbols and realities of
> socioeconomic status, membership in a minority group, and other in-
> dicators of social structure carry such implication of status, they may be
> expected to affect the development of self-regard and identity. [R. D.
> Hess, 1970, p. 482] One of the consequences of lower-class life is a cluster
> of attitudes that express *low self-esteem, a sense of inefficacy and passivity.*
> [P. 467]

Langner and Michael (1963) hypothesize that the low-status person
will have a "negative self-image due to acceptance of negative
stereotypes of the low status person or to internalization of low status
parent" whereas the higher status person will have "generally a more
positive self-image" (p. 471). McKinley (1964) states, "Our view is that
individuals who hold low social status in society (or in any behavior
system), particularly in an urban and industrial society, experience
greater *external* restraint, greater frustration in material comfort and
in feelings of self-esteem" (p. 80).

Kasl and French (1962) argue:

> Occupants of high status jobs will have . . . high objective public esteem.
> Objective public esteem largely determines subjective public esteem which

in turn strongly affects self-esteem. The occupant of a high status job will also tend to have a favorable self-concept; that is, he will have high self-esteem. . . . the above presentation holds primarily for the occupational subidentity rather than for the total self-concept. [P. 76]

Self-regard as a reflection of regard received from society could conceivably come about with or without children's having developed a recognition of their own socioeconomic status, i.e., without their having developed a sense of socioeconomic-class identity comparable to a sense of gender identity, racial identity, or age identity. In other words, a child could realize that he or she was being highly or poorly regarded without necessarily realizing that this has to do with socioeconomic status. However, the tone of most writings seems to imply that a sense of one's socioeconomic identity is, at least in part, a mediator of the effects of social appraisal upon self-regard (e.g., Rosenberg and Simmons, 1972).

On the other hand, one can stay within Meadian theory of reflected self-appraisal but develop an alternate argument to the effect that socioeconomic status as such should be minimally related to self-regard, perhaps even unrelated to it. Rosenberg (1973) has made several points relevant to the development of this argument: Are putative significant others real significant others in the sense that their opinions of us are valued and credible? For what differing kinds of self-appraisals are others' appraisals significant? (For example, parents may be more important than teachers with respect to reflected lovability or reflected congruency of the child's characteristics with parentally valued characteristics, whereas teachers may be more important significant others than are parents with respect to reflected appraisals of the child's schoolwork ability.) How does the individual's location in the social structure determine who will be his/her significant others? The individual's, especially the child's, most in-timate and frequent interactions are with the family, the peer group, and the neighbors, who will convey their appraisals of the person's acceptability according to their standards. Therefore, these groups (not society at large) may comprise the most significant others, especially for a child, and the regard that the larger society holds for a child's class may have little effect upon the development of his/her self-regard. Moreover, since there is considerable segregation by social class, the views of one's class held by members of a wide range of other classes may be encountered quite rarely. In segregated situations such as occur in large cities or isolated rural areas, society at large would be even less expected to be included among significant others than would be the case in a small town in which every child would interact at first hand with a wide range of socioeconomic classes, at least in school. Luck and Heiss (1972) have argued that "significant others" usually come from one's own class, hence self-regard should not be expected to be significantly related to socioeconomic class. A. Soares and L. Soares (1972) also stress the importance of reinforcement received from significant persons in the children's immediate environment. Of course, two implicit assumptions underlie this view: (1) lower-class parents' self-regard has not been damaged by their low-prestige status in society, so they can love their children and serve as credible and valued significant others; (2) lower-class parents are not evaluating their children against inappropriate, unattainable standards which are valued by the larger society.

To my knowledge, no writer has posited any kind of nonlinear relationship or a negative linear relationship between socioeconomic level and self-regard; but one could argue for such possibilities, depending on one's guesses as to how the various possible socioeconomic-level factors might be operating. As an example, it seems plausible that the members of the lowest socioeconomic level are not presented with as severe demands as those of the middle classes, and they have more valid reasons to blame the system for their individual shortcomings, whereas members of the upper classes can obtain vicarious self-esteem simply by virtue of being in the elite group. If these conditions are of overriding importance, a U-shaped association between socioeconomic level and self-regard might occur.

Alternately, the upper-class persons might feel that there is little they can do to go beyond their parents or to prove that their individual characteristics are indicative of their own personal worth, so their self-esteem might be depressed. In such a case their self-regard might even be below that of the middle-class child. Then, if the middle-class children's self-regard level exceeds that of the lower class (for any of the variety of already posited reasons), an inverted U-shaped function could result. Or, if the middle-class children's self-regard is depressed relative to that of the lower class, owing to the unusually high demands which can never be fulfilled, a negative linear function could be expected.

In short, we know so little about what all the relevant, class-linked factors might be, their relative importance, and their possible ways of interacting that no single functional relationship is clearly implied by extant theoretical suggestions.

2. Methodological Problems of Measuring Socioeconomic Class

a. PROBLEMS IN DEFINING SOCIOECONOMIC CLASS

The problems of defining this demographic variable and classifying subjects according to it are more complex than the problems of defining other demographic statuses such as sex, race, or religious affiliation. Although the existence of a class society is assumed by social scientists, the defining criteria of the concept, socioeconomic status, have not been agreed upon, in contrast to agreement in research practice concerning criteria for classifying persons into categories of age, sex, racial, minority group, or religious affiliation. As Kahl and Davis (1965) point out:

> This variable has been conceived of in different ways: as a unidimensional attribute that could be directly measured if we had adequate tools; as a unidimensional attribute, but one that must be measured indirectly; as a unidimensional composite that cannot be directly measured, made up of several interrelated attributes that are measurable and can be combined in an index; as a complex of attributes that are interrelated, but do not form a single dimension and thus should not be measured, directly or indirectly, as a totality. Many researchers have avoided the logical and definitional problems. [P. 317]

It is conceivable that socioeconomic status will never be measurable with reference to any ordinal scale that is applicable to any "society as a whole," such as United States society. For example, what might be agreed upon within a small town as comprising the specific attributes defining top socioeconomic status could be short of, or different from, the attributes defining top status in a large city. Moreover, when one considers that the prestige value of each class may have an especially strong impact on individuals' self-esteem, one realizes how important it is that this aspect of the socioeconomic-class concept, too, may not be quantifiable on a scale equally applicable to small, stable towns and rapidly changing large cities (Mayer, 1955, p. 66; National Opinion Research Center, 1953). As another example, a separate class system within the black group (parallel to, but not exactly corresponding to that within the white group) may be emerging (Mayer, 1955, p. 52).

Billingsley (1968, pp. 145-146) describes a "highly differentiated socioeconomic structure" within the black community, including two upper-class levels, three middle-class levels, and three lower-class levels. And Pettigrew (1964b) cautions against using socioeconomic scales developed for an all-white population on black populations. Parker and Kleiner (1964) developed a new socioeconomic scale for blacks based on several criteria of socioeconomic status which 1,489 members of a Philadelphia black community, aged 20-60, indicated were important indices of socioeconomic status to them. The problem of the possible relativity of the classification system to a local geographical region or to a particular physically defined group has not arisen with reference to other demographic variables such as sex, race, religious affiliation, or chronological age.

Without theoretical clarity about a concept, development and construct validation of measuring instruments for that construct cannot proceed fruitfully, as becomes apparent in the next section.

b. MEASURES OF SOCIOECONOMIC CLASS USED IN SELF-CONCEPT RESEARCH

Variety of Extant Indices

Probably as a consequence of the conceptual problems discussed above, a variety of available indices have been used in self-concept research, e.g., the Hollingshead and Redlich (1958) two-factor index, the Index of Status Characteristics and Evaluated Participation of Warner, Meeker, and Eells (1949), the North-Hatt Scale (National Opinion Research Center, 1953), the Sims Socioeconomic Score Card (Sims, 1927), the American Home Scale (Kerr and Remmers, 1942), and several more idiosyncratic measures. Pfautz (1953) has systematically listed, categorized, and evaluated the many different approaches used up to the time of his publication, and Kahl and Davis (1955) applied 19 different indices to the same subjects, as described below.

Reliability and Validity

The interjudge coding reliability for any one measure has only occasionally been reported in the studies I examined as a basis for this chapter, and the convergent validity among some of these measures has been explored to some extent. Pfautz (1953) reports that Warner found an "extremely high" relationship between his two alternate indices (Index of Status Characteristics and Evaluated Participation), and, according to Pfautz, Hollingshead found a "close agreement between the results of his ranking method and Warner's EP" (p. 398). M. L. Kohn and Schooler (1969) reported a correlation of .89 between Hollingshead and Redlich's (1958) and Duncan's (1961) occupational classifications, as applied to a random sample of 90 out of 3,100 men interviewed in their study. For a sample of 55 college students, Gough (1949a) reports correlations among the American Home Scale (Kerr and Remmers, 1942), Sims Socioeconomic Score Card (Sims, 1927), and Gough's Home Index (Gough, 1949a) ranging from .77 to .88.

Kahl and Davis (1955), who mentioned several early studies of relationships between indices of socioeconomic status, made the only relatively large-scale convergent validity study which came to my attention. They intercorrelated and factor analyzed 19 different indices of socioeconomic status assigned to 219 white male interviewees, aged 30-49. Unfortunately, the authors excluded the Hollingshead and Redlich scale (often used in self-concept studies); they used dichotomized data (precluding a search for nonlinear relationships), and their unreplicated factor analysis is based on relatively few subjects for the purpose. Accordingly, this study provides only a beginning (albeit an important one), not a developed and complete basis, for comparing and synthesizing studies which use a variety of instruments to look at relationships between self-concept variables and socioeconomic status.

The preceding discussion makes clear that there are neither rational nor empirical grounds for using the measure of socioeconomic level as the basis for classifying the available studies about socioeconomic status and self-concept. I have therefore chosen to organize that part of this chapter according to categories of self-concept variables.

c. CATEGORY WIDTH

The preceding sections imply that the most refined level of scaling which a purported measure of socioeconomic class is likely to achieve is ordinal, not interval. Even so, it is relevant to consider the empirical implications of possibly gross variations in category widths between scale points. Actually, little or nothing seems to be known about the width of the steps of any extant scale, but it appears intuitively probable that the steps are quite unequal. For example, the Hollingshead and Redlich occupational Class 1 appears to cover an enormous range of wealth, influence, and education as compared to that covered by occupational Class 5 (skilled blue-collar workers), and persons whose social status is at the very top of Class 1 are probably not discriminated as finely from other members of Class 1 as might be theoretically and predictively useful.

One thing which affects category width and ensuing interpretability of results is the decision which the researcher makes about how to collapse categories, as is sometimes done in data analyses. Researchers who use any one purported measure of socioeconomic class vary with respect to how crudely they categorize their subjects. For example, one could look at seven occupational levels on the Hollingshead and Redlich scale, or one could (for a priori or theoretical reasons or because of a small number of available subjects) dichotomize the subjects into (1-4) and (5-7), the division point being between white-collar and blue-collar workers. Or some other arbitrary set of collapsed categories could be used. This has two unfortunate methodological ramifications. First, when different authors choose different cutoff points (even completely excluding one part of the socioeconomic range in some studies), comparisons among studies and syntheses of their results are precluded. Second, dichotomizing may mask possible nonlinear relationships, which conceivably could be expected on both theoretical and empirical grounds. The theoretical arguments have been developed above. Empirical examples of curvilinear relationships between socioeconomic level and self-regard may be found in studies by Bachman (1970) and M. L. Kohn (1969) which are discussed substantively below.

d. CONFUSIONS BETWEEN SOCIOECONOMIC-CLASS STATUS AND "ADVANTAGED-DISADVANTAGED" STATUS

A number of authors have appeared to equate or hold to be highly similar "low socioeconomic class status" and "disadvantaged status." Their results are often mentioned along with those based only on socioeconomic class when a question of the personality characteristics or self-concept characteristics is under review. This is true for example, in studies by A. Soares and L. Soares (1969, 1971, 1972), Long and Henderson (1968), and Whiteman and Deutsch (1968), where the advantaged and disadvantaged groups vary in race and sometimes in other respects such as urbanness of residence, as well as in socioeconomic status. However, we know enough about associations between race and self-concept variables to know that they differ from the relationships between socioeconomic level and self-concept variables (e.g., Rosenberg and Simmons, 1972; Wylie, 1963; Wylie and Hutchins, 1967). Accordingly, studies of "disadvantaged" status should not be compared with studies concerning socioeconomic class, and the variables involved in defining *disadvantaged* should be analyzed separately for their independent effects and interactions.

e. INDIVIDUAL vs. GROUP CLASSIFICATION WITH RESPECT TO SOCIOECONOMIC CLASS

Some studies manipulate the socioeconomic variable by choosing intact groups from economically poor, middle, and affluent neighborhoods or institutions as opposed to assigning individual socioeconomic classifications to each subject in a heterogeneous neighborhood (e.g., Neale & Proshek, 1967; Preston & Gudiksen, 1966; Trowbridge, 1974; A. Soares & L. Soares, 1969.) It may well be true that the groups are essentially homogeneous with respect to socioeconomic class, so that results cannot be assigned to errors in classifying the subjects. Nevertheless, the following interpretative problem is introduced: In intact groups which are homogeneous regarding socioeconomic standing, invidious comparisons to which the lower-class persons would be subjected may be minimized, and it would make keener competition for achievement and favorable appraisals among persons of the middle group and among persons of the homogeneous affluent group. That is, each person in each of the latter two groups would have fewer persons to look down upon as a help in bolstering self-regard. In such a situation, direct, strong relationships between self-regard and socioeconomic status might be least expected. (Rosenberg & Simmons, 1972, make this point in connection with their study.)

f. OBJECTIVE AND SUBJECTIVE SOCIOECONOMIC STATUS

Is objectively measured socioeconomic status the only appropriate variable to be measured in studies relating socioeconomic status and self-concept variables? On both theoretical and empirical grounds, the answer to this question must be no.

Even if one could get more agreement among social scientists about the conceptual and operational meaning(s) of objective socioeconomic status, one could still argue that phenomenological theories such as self theories must concern themselves partly with this development of the subjective sense of class status and its relationship to other aspects of the self-concept.

Empirically, objective and subjective socioeconomic status do not correlate perfectly, as I discuss more fully below, indicating the need to look at each of these types of measures separately in relationship to self-concept variables. In fact, as Gross (1953) has shown, several alternate measures of subjective social class yield very different results when applied to the same subjects.

g. MISCELLANEOUS MEASUREMENT SHORTCOMINGS IN EXTANT STUDIES

In addition to the above-mentioned conceptual difficulties and/or questionable practices in the measurement of socioeconomic class, published reports often show the following limitations:

1. Little or no information is given about the measure used to classify the subjects with respect to socioeconomic class.
2. The data source used for classifying subjects is unspecified (e.g., we are not told whether the subjects themselves described or classified their fathers' jobs, whether school records were used, or whether an evaluation was made on the basis of the interviewer's impression during a home interview.)
3. The number of unclassifiable subjects and the possible bias introduced by their necessary exclusion is not reported and/or considered in a number of publications.

3. Methodological Problems in Measuring Self-Concept Variables

I cannot review in detail all the methodological problems and requirements in this area. (See Wylie, 1974). Instead, I mention here the major criteria used in classifying and evaluating studies reviewed in this chapter.

1. What reliability and validity information is given concerning measures of subjective socioeconomic status?

2. Have the studies of over-all self-regard or of specific aspects of self-concept (e.g., self-concept of schoolwork ability) used some of the better-known, more fully explored and developed instruments, or have idiosyncratic measures been used? If the latter, is sufficient information given regarding content, procedure used in collecting the subjects' self-reports, scoring, validity, and reliability to render the findings interpretable?

3. Have uninterpretable discrepancy scores been used?

4. Could purported direct associations between socioeconomic class standing and self-concept scores be plausibly interpreted as the result of the reliability artifact? That is, since lower-class children tend to be poorer readers and are assumed by educators to have less motivation for schoollike tasks, could their responses on self-regard tests be determined more by chance than is the case with middle- or upper-class children? If so, as I have fully explained elsewhere (Wylie, 1974, pp. 119–121), some self-regard scales will yield "low self-esteem" scores simply from unreliable responding, not from a valid expression of low self-esteem.

4. Methodological Problems in Relating Socioeconomic Class Measures to Self-Concept Measures

a. PROBLEMS ASSOCIATED WITH THE SIZE OF N

For two sorts of reasons, the Ns in studies relating socioeconomic class to self-concept measures should be large. First, as fully discussed above, social class is not a conceptually homogeneous variable in itself or in the way(s) it could conceivably be related to self-concept variables. Accordingly, large Ns might well be necessary to bring out any "net" trends, with other variables adequately controlled. Second, the empirical trends obtained thus far have been small, and it appears that statistical significance will be reached only if large Ns are used.

On the other hand, there are dangers in the use of very large Ns, since almost any result, no matter how small in absolute terms turns out to be statistically significant. In such instances, psychological interpretation must remain moot.

Empirically, both race and sex interact with socioeconomic level in determining at least some relationships to self-concept reports. Accordingly, these variables must be held constant, if an effect is to be attributed to socioeconomic level.

In short, what is needed is multivariate studies which would enable one to separate the effects of the above three variables and look at their interactions in relationship to self-concept reports.

b. MULTIPLE SIGNIFICANCE TESTS WITHOUT CROSS-VALIDATION

Unfortunately, many of the studies I examined for possible inclusion in this chapter reported numerous significance tests without regard to how many would be expected to be significant by chance alone when many are made within a single study. This practice becomes particularly troublesome when the variables involved in the multiple significance tests are themselves intercorrelated and when very large Ns are involved (as is the case with a number of the available survey-type studies).

c. LACK OF SIGNIFICANCE TESTS

A number of studies make little or no attempt to present significance tests. While it is admittedly difficult or impossible to evaluate significance levels in large-scale studies involving many measurements, one treads on uncertain ground in trying to interpret the many "trends" reported and interpreted by authors of such studies.

d. NEED TO LOOK FOR NONLINEAR RELATIONSHIPS

As already explained above, both a priori and empirical consideration make it necessary to include enough scale steps and a wide enough range on each variable to enable one to look for nonlinear relationships.

e. NEED TO HOLD CERTAIN VARIABLES CONSTANT WHILE LOOKING AT SOCIOECONOMIC CLASS

IQ and achievement indices are well known to be associated with socioeconomic level. IQ and achievement indices are also known to be associated with self-regard measures, especially self-concept of schoolwork ability, ideals for educational and occupational levels to be achieved, and certain specific self-reported personality characteristics (see chapter 7 of this book). Also, even if ability per se is not associated with self-regard, there may be an artifactual relationship between the two, as explained under section 3-4 immediately above. Therefore, if one wishes to conclude that socioeconomic level is related to self-concept measures, one must hold IQ and grade-point average (GPA) constant. More often than not, this important precaution has not been taken.

B. RESEARCH RESULTS

1. Parental Practices and Values as a Function of Socioeconomic Class

a. CHILD-REARING PRACTICES

As pointed out in section A-1, it has been frequently hypothesized that parents from different socioeconomic classes use different techniques of child rearing which could conceivably lead to personality differences in the children as a function of socioeconomic class, which in turn could lead to differences in self-description and self-evaluation as a function of class. Unfortunately, my search for studies relevant to this theoretical sequence has not been especially fruitful.

Concerning the first steps in the hypothesized sequence, many studies have been published, and several reviews of these publications have led to disappointing conclusions. For example, Sewell concludes his 1961 review:

> The studies of child rearing in relation to social class, made since the publication of the Chicago studies, have found fewer class-related differences in infant training than might have been expected and those differences that have been found tend to indicate greater permissiveness in feeding and toilet training on the part of middle-class mothers rather than lower-class mothers. The findings in relation to early childhood training indicate less impulse control, less punitiveness, less reliance on strict regime, less restrictiveness in sex behavior and less restriction on aggression—in other words, generally greater permissiveness on the part of middle-class mothers. [P. 350]

However, he also concludes that "with a few notable exceptions, the level of research and theoretical sophistication in this area has been appallingly low. Some of the most influential work has had little or no acceptable empirical basis" (p. 350).

One possibly relevant study is Rosen's (1959) work with 427 pairs of mothers and sons of various ethnic groups and from varying Hollingshead and Redlich categories. Mean age of independence training (as defined by Winterbottom's scale) varied significantly as a function of socioeconomic status, with earlier independence training characterizing the upper-class mothers. (Ethnicity and the interaction between socioeconomic level and ethnicity were also significant showing the importance of controlling for ethnicity when studying socioeconomic class.) Since the sons (aged 8–14) responded to projective techniques rather than to self-report instruments, no associations between self-concept and independence training by class can be made.

Hess (1970), in his more recent review, including both parental behaviors and researchers' direct observations of parental behaviors states that

> in view of the effort devoted to studies of parental socializing behavior, the predictive power of the data gathered about parents has been disappointingly low or uneven. Results of studies attempting to relate parental values or reports of child-rearing behavior of parents to outcomes in their children show uneven and often contradictory results. [P. 481]

To my knowledge, nothing has been published since Hess's review which would enable us to make definite empirical statements regarding associations between child-rearing practices by parents of differing socioeconomic classes and children's behaviors or personality characteristics. Thus one cannot trace out the hypothetical sequence outlined above.

Of course one might look for studies which attempted to examine associations between parental practices and children's self-concept reports, as these may depend on socioeconomic level. So far as I know, however, no such studies are available.

b. PARENTAL VALUES

As stated in section A-1 above, it has been hypothesized that parents' value systems may vary as a function of socioeconomic class, with possible effects on their children's value systems (ideals for self) and behaviors.

Perhaps some items of the Parent Attitude Research Instrument (PARI) might be considered to involve parental values. If so, the correlations reported between educational or occupational levels and certain PARI scores might be interpreted as support for the first part of the above-stated hypothesis. However, W. Becker and Krug in their 1965 review of PARI research, conclude that "some evidence suggests that the association [of authoritarian attitudes on PARI] with educational level is, at least in part, an artifact of question style" (p. 329). "This does not imply that in a more heterogeneous sample, there might not still be a strong, meaningful relationship to educational level, even with potential artifacts controlled" (p. 343).

In any event, Becker and Krug's evaluation of PARI makes clear that one cannot turn to PARI research for a relevant, methodologically adequate test of the hypothesis regarding parents' and children's value systems.

In a cross-national interview study, Pearlin and Kohn (1966) studied parental values as a function of social class and occupation, using samples of 861 Italian parents from Turin and 421 United States parents from Washington, D.C. Interviewees were asked to choose and rank 3 out of 17 listed qualities which they would say were the most desirable for a boy/girl of their child's age. Pearlin and Kohn report that

> the rank-order of middle-class parents' value choices did not differ greatly from that of working-class parents in either country; the difference between the proportions of middle-class and working-class parents who value any given characteristics is never very large. . . . Self-control and obedience . . . seem to us to embody most clearly the essential difference between the middle-class emphasis on self-direction and the working-class emphasis on conformity to external proscription. [Pp. 470–471]

Inkeles (1960) reports on data provided by International Research Associates concerning the child-rearing values of the upper, middle, and lower classes in 11 countries, including Australia, Austria, Brazil, Britain, Denmark, Germany, Italy, Japan, the Netherlands, Norway, and Sweden. No information is given about the socioeconomic measure used to categorize the three classes. The values examined included stress on ambitiousness, obedience to parents, decency and honesty, trust in God, and enjoyment of self. The differences among the three classes in the percents of respondents stressing each value were usually very slight. With one exception, there were no clear patterns in the responses. In the case of the value of obedience to parents, the lower class had the highest percentage stressing obedience in 8 out of 11 countries. This lack of clear differences among classes in most child-rearing values, along with the one exception being the stress on the value of obedience by the lower class parents, strongly supports the results of Pearlin and Kohn (1966) reported above.

In brief, such evidence as is available does not support the conclusion that numerous strong differences in parental values occur in different social classes. However, the very limited evidence, based as it is on a restricted range of instruments, does not warrant a firm conclusion that such class-related value differences are negligible.

2. Self-Concept of Socioeconomic Class Membership

As I said in section A, it is theoretically possible that objectively indexed socioeconomic status may in some way(s) determine, or at least be predictive of, a number of behaviors and self-concept reports, whether or not the person has developed a sense of belonging to a particular socioeconomic class. Thus, one needs to know the role of objectively indexed socioeconomic status in predicting various aspects of self-concept and behaviors related thereto. I also pointed out that it is important to study the phenomenal sense of socioeconomic status as well as objectively indexed socioeconomic status because such an approach is theoretically appropriate to phenomenological self-concept theories and because the sense of one's socioeconomic status may disagree with objective measures to some extent and be separately predictive of certain self-concept variables. This section is devoted to looking at some empirical findings relevant to these general issues.

To what extent do individuals in the United States develop a sense of socioeconomic class identity (self-concept of socioeconomic class) analogous to their development of a sense of age, race, or gender identity? Is the development of a sense of class identity affected by the degree of awareness the individual has that the United States is stratified into socioeconomic categories? What other variables may affect development of this aspect of the self-concept?

What means have been used to attempt to index the socioeconomic self-concept? Do these alternate indices yield highly similar results when applied to the same sample? If not, what are the implications of this? What do subjects use as a basis for making class distinctions and, by implication, for deciding their own socioeconomic status? How well do the objective indices of socioeconomic status agree with subjects' self-conceived socioeconomic class? If the two disagree, does each index add an increment to the prediction of other self-concept variables, such as self-regard, self-ideals, or self-concepts about specific personality characteristics as schoolwork ability?

Is there evidence that different favorability is accorded to different classes? Does this lead to increasing or decreasing one's self-regard, according to one's perception of the favorability accorded the class to which one subjectively assigns oneself? Or does the perception that different classes are differently evaluated perhaps lead to "class inflation" so far as one's own socioeconomic self-concept is concerned? Evidence is at hand relevant to at least some of these questions.

a. Class Consciousness and Development of Self-Concept of Socioeconomic Class

Popular opinion and the democratic ethos suggest that awareness of the existence of socioeconomic class stratification in the United States may be somewhat limited and/or of low salience to United States residents. Supporting this idea from the sociologist's viewpoint, Rosenberg (1953) has suggested that a number of characteristics of our society act to blur and distort "consciousness of kind" based on socioeconomic stratification, viz., the structure of large-scale industry, territorial rather than class-based political structure, multiple-group membership, and similarities in style of life so far as consumption and mass communication are concerned. If class consciousness is low or not salient, one might expect interview respondents to be unable (not just reluctant) to name classes and to place themselves into a class framework.

It is true that a certain percent of subjects seems unwilling or unable to reply in terms of the concept of socioeconomic class, at least when the interviewer asks an open-ended question. In the *Fortune* poll (1940), for example, about a third of the respondents gave miscellaneous or "don't know" replies as opposed to mentioning the usual class labels when asked to classify themselves according to social class. Also using an open-ended question, Gross (1953) found at least 30% unwilling or unable to use the usual class labels. When Kahl and Davis (1955) began their class-related queries with a series of open-ended questions, the coded replies revealed that

> 12 percent of our respondents had no conception of a class order; 6 per cent understood the questions well enough to explicitly deny that a class order existed in the U.S.; 5 per cent recognized a class order, but either disapproved of it so strongly that they did not want to describe it, or said it was too complex to describe. [P. 324]

When D. R. Segal, M. W. Segal, and Knoke (1970) asked their interviewees whether they believed there were social classes in the United States, only 950 out of 1,571 replied positively. R. Jones (1972) asked 7,252 children in Grades 4, 6, 8, 9, and 10 "Do you see yourself as

middle class? Do you see yourself as lower class?" Not giving details of
his quantitative analysis of results, Jones says only, "most students at
all grade and socioeconomic levels rejected the labels as descriptive of
themselves" (p. 555). It appears that his results depended in part on
the subjects' inability to define the terms used in the question.

However, one cannot conclude from an overview of the above results
that class consciousness is low. One must note that Cantril (1944),
Centers (1949), Kahl and Davis (1955), Gross (1953), and D. R. Segal,
M. W. Segal, and Knoke (1970) all found that only 1% to 6% of
respondents could not or would not choose a class label for themselves
when the labels were supplied by the interviewer. Similarly, although
the majority of Rosenberg and Simmons's (1972) 1,917 black and
white urban children in Grades 3–12 said they had never heard of the
term social class, they had no trouble rating their fathers' jobs on a
pictorial ladder from worst to best or in expressing their views of their
parents' "social position in the community" or how well their parents
"have done in life" (p. 61). Results on this same group of subjects are
reported in Simmons and Rosenberg (1971) and reveal that, although
only 15% of the elementary level children knew what the term "social
class" meant, 39% of the junior high school students and 75% of the
senior high school students understood the term. Also, even though the
younger children were not familiar with the term "social class," a very
high correlation was obtained between their ranking of the "goodness"
of 15 occupations and the ranking of these same occupations by adults
in another study (Hodge, Siegel, and Rossi, 1964). Thus, children do
seem to be aware at a very early age of the relative differences in
prestige attributed to various occupations. And in a sample of 49 black
children Grades 3–6 (R. Jones, 1972), only about 3% to 4% of
respondents were unable to reply to the question "If someone called
you upper/middle/lower class, would that be good or bad?" It is clear
from the distribution of "good" responses that the children were
differentiating among these labels even though one must infer from
other parts of Jones's report that the subjects could not define the
socioeconomic levels.

It seems clear, then, that some kind of socioeconomic class
awareness is quite widespread, even though unwillingness and/or
inability to express it in response to open-ended questions characterized at least one-third of the respondents in some of the studies
mentioned above. At the same time, the frequency distributions
obtained from responses to different types of questions asking for the
respondents' concepts of their own socioeconomic classification vary

markedly as a function of the way the question is framed. Gross (1953) interprets these findings plausibly, if pessimistically, by his statement:

> If class consciousness is a part of a man's ego, a feeling on his part of belongingness to something, then it might be argued that as a minimum condition for its existence one should expect some kind of reasonable consistency in an individual's answers when replying to open-ended and closed type questions in regard to his class affiliation or identification. [P. 403]

Whether or not Gross's interpretation is correct, the lack of agreement among purported indices of self-concept of socioeconomic status implies that relationships between self-concept of socioeconomic status and other variables may well depend at least partly on the method used to index that aspect of the self-concept.

b. Subjects' Criteria for Defining Socioeconomic Classes

What do subjects use as a basis for deciding on their self-concept of socioeconomic status? Centers (1949) looked at this question rather extensively, separating the criteria used by members of four classes to define membership in each of the four classes, respectively. Hammond (1954a, 1954b) examined the same issue with a smaller, Australian sample and a less detailed class breakdown among respondents. From both studies it is apparent that criteria for defining classes (and, presumably, therefore, for establishing one's own self-concept of socioeconomic status) vary according to one's own self-conceived class. This, of course, is relevant to psychological interpretations of any relationships which may be obtained between self-conceived socioeconomic class and other self-concept variables or other behaviors.

c. Relationships of Self-Conceived Socioeconomic Class to Objectively Defined Socioeconomic Class

Even though different methods of questioning may elicit different results regarding distributions of self-conception of socioeconomic class, perhaps one of the subjective measures yields results closely similar to one or more of the objective indices of socioeconomic status when both are applied to the same subjects. This question cannot be answered directly with available data, even though the *Fortune* (1940) study, Cantril (1944), Centers (1949), Gross (1953), Hammond (1954a), Kahl and Davis (1955), Schneider and Lysgaard (1953), D. R. Segal, M. W. Segal, and Knoke (1970), Simmons and Rosenberg

(1971), and Sims (1952)—all looked at the relationship between subjectively and objectively indexed socioeconomic status. The inconclusiveness of the results stems from the facts that various measures of subjective and objective class were used and that some researchers employed only one objective indicator, whereas some used several. Although some degree of correspondence between subjective and objective indices is often apparent, it also appears that there remains considerable lack of correspondence between objective indices and the subjects' self-concepts of socioeconomic class.

Kahl and Davis's (1955) work which compared Centers's subjective class index to each of 18 objective indices is the most extensive research on this topic. The tetrachoric *r*s between Centers's subjective index and the objective indices—(a) Warner's occupational classification, (b) educational level, (c) census occupational category, (d) the North-Hatt Scale, (e) interviewer's impressionistic rating of the subject's standing on Warner's scale, and (f) Warner's "source of income"—fell between .60 and .75. By contrast, the tetrachoric *r*s between each pair of the above objective indices fell between .53 and .93, with 5 out of 12 values ≥ .75.

Rosenberg and Simmons (1972), in the large-scale study of black and white children mentioned above, obtained the association between Hollingshead scale values and each of various measures of self-concept of socioeconomic class. These associations were extremely low among the blacks but varied from "moderate to quite powerful" among the whites. The highest *gamma* (.61) was obtained for the relationship between Hollingshead class status and perceived social class position among subjects 11 years of age and older who had ever heard of the term "social classes." In another analysis of the data from the same subjects, Simmons and Rosenberg (1971) classified the children as being either middle class, i.e., having Hollingshead socioeconomic scores (SES) of 1-3, or working class, i.e., having scores of 4-5. When asked to designate whether they belonged in the upper, middle, working, or lower class, the percentage of those having a social-class identification in agreement with their objective social class increased with age. No significance tests are given for these results.

d. STEREOTYPING AND DIFFERENTIAL FAVORABILITY OF REACTIONS TO DIFFERENT SOCIOECONOMIC CLASSES

As discussed in section A above, it is widely taken for granted that socioeconomic class and self-esteem are directly related and that part of this relationship comes from individuals' personal identifications with the degree of esteem attributed to their respective socioeconomic classes. Since such confident assertions are commonplace, one might suppose that some empirical information would be available regarding the characteristics differentially attributed to members of the various socioeconomic classes and regarding the favorability of these attributions. Actually, however, such information is scanty.

Although Warner and Lunt's (1941) informal reports of their interviews suggest that people do agree about characteristics applicable to different social classes, the generality of occurrence and the content of such stereotypes remain to be evaluated by adequate empirical approaches. We also know nothing about when, if ever, children become aware of the existence and/or specific contents of the stereotypic personality characteristics supposedly descriptive of members of their class.

We have no information concerning the degree to which children have accepted such stereotypic traits as individually applicable to themselves. Although offering no significance tests, Neugarten's (1946) study of elementary and high school students suggests that children of these ages may differentially impute to peers of varying socioeconomic class such characteristics as clean, well-dressed, good-looking, fights a lot, popular, likes school, always has a good time, has good manners, and plays fair. However, Neugarten's method does not permit us to infer that the child raters realized that their nominations varied with respect to the nominees' socioeconomic level.

In R. Jones's (1972) study of 49 black children in Grades 3-6, mentioned above, 92% thought it would be "bad" if someone called them lower class, 30% thought it would be bad if someone called them middle class, whereas only 4% thought it would be bad if someone called them upper class.

Centers (1949), after examining the replies to the questions "What puts a person in upper/middle/working/lower class?" states that

> a surprisingly large proportion of people appear to think of the lower class as a rather despicable group. Poor character and low morals, drink, crime, lack of ability, low intelligence, shiftlessness, laziness, lack of ambition or motivation, menial labor, etc. all indicate the disesteem in which this group is held. . . . [For both the middle and working classes] the term lower class frequently connotes a despised or *declassé* group. [P. 95]

In their research on the race-class stereotypes of 92 white and 180 black college students from segregated colleges, Bayton, McAlister, and Hamer (1956) asked their subjects to select from a list of 85 adjectives 5 which they considered the most typical of upper-class white Americans, upper-class Negroes, lower-class white Americans, and lower-class Negroes. Although many details of the procedure are omitted, the authors report that certain characteristics were attributed to each class, regardless of race, i.e., the upper class, whether black or white, was viewed as being intelligent, ambitious, industrious, neat, and progressive, whereas the lower class, whether black or white, was viewed as being ignorant, lazy, loud, and physically dirty. Thus the results of this study reveal not only the subjects' stereotypes of different classes, but also the prepotency of class over race in these stereotypes.

Hodge, Siegel, and Rossi (1964), among others, have reviewed the literature concerning occupational prestige ratings; it seems that the public's attributions of relative prestige are quite stable across time and countries, although the National Opinion Research Center (1953) report claimed, without giving full supporting data, that such ratings varied somewhat by section of the country, economic level of the respondents, age, and sex. In any event, many objective socioeconomic class indices are comprised of a combination of several factors in addition to occupation; and, to my knowledge, no studies have been made of the degrees of prestige accorded by the public to each of the various classes defined by these composite indices. (Hammond's [1954c] study of Australians' attitudes toward class is too small to be useful.)

In short, although there is some evidence that different characteristics and different degrees of esteem are attributed to members of varying socioeconomic levels, it remains to be seen whether members of those classes accept the attributed traits and over-all favorability levels as applicable to themselves as individuals.

e. Relationships between Self-Concepts of Socioeconomic Class and Other Aspects of Self-Concept

From all that has been said thus far in this chapter, it is clear that self-conceptions of social class (a) have been purportedly indexed in a variety of ways in a number of studies involving many subjects who varied in sex, race, age, nationality, and objectively measured socioeconomic class; (b) are neither theoretically nor empirically the same as objectively indexed socioeconomic class; (c) are widely assumed to be important in determining individuals' behaviors and their levels of self-regard and other aspects of their self-concepts. Accordingly, one might expect to find a fair number of empirical tests of the assumed relationships between self-conceived socioeconomic class and other variables. But such an expectation is not fulfilled.

In their study of United States parents, Kohn and Schooler (1969) used a list of values (characteristics the parents would most like to see in their children's behavior), an analogous list of parents' values for self, and an idiosyncratic questionnaire which purported to measure "social orientation" and "self-conception" (evaluation). Without giving any precise results as a basis for their statement, they say "subjective class identification bear[s] only a small relationship to values and orientation when social class (as we have indexed it) is controlled. On the other hand, class is nearly as strongly related to values and orientation when income and subjective class identification are controlled as when they are not" (p. 669). On this basis of published information it is impossible to say whether this statement is based on acceptable method. No information is given about self-conception and self-concept of socioeconomic status.

In a study of occupational "values" (which one could perhaps construe as relevant to self-ideals), Centers (1949) presented his subjects with a list of 10 job characteristics and asked them to give their first, second, and third choices in response to the question "If you had a choice of one of these kinds of jobs, which would you choose?" The only significant differences in the first choices of subjects who classified themselves as middle or working class were as follows: Within the urban and within the rural groups, the middle-class subjects more often chose "a job where you could express your feelings, ideas, talent, or skill"; and within the urban group, the working-class subjects more often chose "a job which you were absolutely sure of keeping." Unfortunately, 10 comparisons were made in the urban group and 10 in the rural group, so one cannot evaluate the 3 out of 20 differences which were significant at the .05 level.

3. Over-all Self-Regard as a Function of Socioeconomic Status

a. SELF-REGARD INDEXED BY RELATIVELY WELL-KNOWN INSTRUMENTS

The reader will remember from section A-1 above that confident assertions have frequently been made that self-regard is a direct function of socioeconomic status. The research considered immediately below calls those assertions into serious question.

Rosenberg's Self-Esteem Scale (RSE) and Modifications Thereof

Among the better known self-regard indices, Rosenberg's (1965) Self-Esteem score (RSE) or modifications thereof have been most frequently studied in relation to socioeconomic class. (See Wylie, 1974, pp. 180–189 for an evaluation of this instrument.)

In Rosenberg's own study involving 5,024 high school students in New York State, a significant positive association was found between RSE and socioeconomic status measured by an idiosyncratic combination of father's occupation, education, and primary source of income. When separate analyses were made for each sex, a significant association was obtained for boys, but not for girls (although the girls' trend was in the expected direction). Rosenberg argued that the obtained association for boys is not simply a function of reflected self-appraisal of the valuation society gives to the separate socioeconomic classes, but also is a function of factors internal to the family, i.e., that upper-class boys tend to have closer relationships with their fathers. He supports this interpretation indirectly by reference to findings on social class and paternal supportiveness reported by himself and others and by his findings of associations between self-esteem and closeness of relationships with the father.

Herman, Sadofsky, Bensman, Lilienfeld, and Manos (1967) compared RSE scores of 601 black male enrollees in two New York City job-training programs with 196 black male freshmen and sophomores at Howard University. However, socioeconomic level was only one of a number of potentially relevant variables which differentiated these groups. Therefore the extremely low RSE scores of the job-training applicants cannot be safely interpreted as a function of their very low socioeconomic level.

As a measure of self-esteem in his study of a representative sample of 2,213 tenth-grade boys from 87 United States public high schools, Bachman (1970) used 6 RSE items plus 4 items proposed by Cobb. The raw *eta* between this self-esteem score and an idiosyncratic measure of socioeconomic level based on 6 components = .15 (with a conservatively estimated standard error = .03). To estimate the unique predictive effect of socioeconomic level, he used *beta*, (a statistic analogous to *eta*) but adjusted for the effects of IQ and 7 background factors. *Beta* for the unique association of self-esteem and socioeconomic level = .10 (with a conservatively estimated standard error = .03). The author recognizes the questionable interpretability of multiple significance tests, but nevertheless believes that his statistical analysis revealed a weak, significant, positive relationship between socioeconomic level and self-esteem. In evaluating the psychological importance of this result, however, one must also emphasize the extremely small size of both obtained *eta* and obtained *beta* and the fact that, among the 1,043 follow-up subjects discussed immediately below, a partial *r* between these two variables was insignificant.

Bachman and O'Malley (1977) analyzed data from some of the subjects used in the above-mentioned survey by Bachman (1970). Their follow-up results are based on the 1,608 young men for whom longitudinal data were available through the fifth year after their graduation from high school. The family socioeconomic measure was obtained when the respondents were in the tenth grade. The high school self-esteem measure used in the present analysis was a mean of three scores gotten from administrations of the self-esteem measure during tenth, eleventh, and twelfth grades, and the self-esteem measure was repeated in 1974. The subjects' 1974 educational attainments were measured on a 6-point scale ranging from high school dropout to completion of graduate work, and their 1974 occupational status was indexed according to Duncan's scales. Standardized partial regression coefficients based on a series of multiple regression analyses including ability and achievement measures were computed for a subsample of 1,043 subjects who were in the civilian work force in 1974. The partial correlations between family socioeconomic level and high school self-esteem and between family socioeconomic level and 1974 self-esteem were both insignificant. Also, the partial correlations between the subjects' 1974 educational attainment and their high school self-esteem and between their 1974 educational attainment and 1974 self-esteem were also not significant. In one of their path analyses, when family socioeconomic level, high school academic ability, high school academic performance, high school self-esteem, and 1974 educational attainment were taken into account, a standardized partial regression coefficient of .143 ($p < .05$) was obtained between 1974 occupational status and 1974 self-esteem. Following their reasoning underlying the path analysis, the authors consider this coefficient to be indicative of a "direct positive impact" of 1974 oc-

cupational status on 1974 self-esteem. They point out, however, that
path analysis cannot "prove" the validity of the causal assumptions
built into the path model. Rather, it provides a way of estimating the
strengths of different possible causal connections, if one is willing to
accept the assumptions built into the model.

As part of a more comprehensive longitudinal study, D. W. Edwards (1974) examined the relationship between self-esteem and
socioeconomic status in 750 black and white eighth-grade boys in
several Detroit area schools. Bachman's measure of self-esteem was
used, and the socioeconomic status for each boy was determined by
classifying the occupation of each head of household according to
Duncan's socioeconomic status levels. No significant correlations
between self-esteem and socioeconomic status were obtained for boys in
any of the individual schools or in the entire group from all schools
combined.

Hulbary (1975) had only 186 adolescent subjects and an incompletely described, idiosyncratic index of socioeconomic status.
Using a multiple regression technique involving race, socioeconomic
level, exposure to political/social information, age, and racial isolation, Hulbary obtained nonsignificant *beta* weights for socioeconomic
level on RSE scores.

In yet another large-scale investigation involving a modification of
the RSE scale, Epps (1969) studied 966 black males and females in 2
northern segregated and 2 northern biracial high schools and 1,572
black males and females in 4 southern segregated high schools. His
self-esteem measure consisted of 5 items from RSE, chosen on the basis
of factor analysis, and yielding an r with the original RSE $= .66$. Six
rs were computed between this modified RSE score and a
socioeconomic-level index consisting of the mother's educational level
in all groups except northern males, for whom father's occupation was
used: one r was computed for each region and sex; then two rs were
computed by combining regions, but keeping sex separate. The rs
ranged from $-.07$ to $.08$, none being significant. The idiosyncratic
measures of both self-esteem and socioeconomic level, the variation
from group to group in the index of socioeconomic level, the lack of
information about administrative conditions, and the lack of
multivariate analyses make it impossible to make meaningful
speculations about these reported findings. In any event, no support is
given to the hypothesis that self-regard is directly related to
socioeconomic level.

Wegner (1973) studied 1,588 undergraduates, a random sample of the student body at the University of Hawaii. The U.S. Census categories were used to classify the fathers' occupations and the RSE to index self-regard levels. Various ways of subdividing the total sample were used, viz., Caucasians versus Japanese; freshmen versus seniors; living with family versus not living with family. Within any one of these subgroups, subjects were further subdivided into 4 different socioeconomic levels. RSE scores were not a function of socioeconomic level within any subgroup. In fact only one of the numerous possible pair comparisons was "significant." Quantitative results are published only for males, but results for females are said to be comparable.

In Kaplan's (1971) interview study of 500 Houston, Texas, adults, no relationship was obtained between Factor I (Self-derogation) scores from RSE and Hollingshead's two-factor, five-level measure of socioeconomic status. Kaplan hypothesized that his null results were due to his not having taken account of particular conditions under which the predicted relationship would plausibly be found. An ad hoc reanalysis of his data gave obliquely relevant, suggestive support for his "conditional" hypothesis, but that analysis is not described here since it remains to be cross-validated.

In an interview study which involved 3,100 adult males, Kohn (1969) included a self-confidence factor score (comprised of three RSE items plus two others) and a self-deprecation factor score (comprised of three RSE items plus two others). Kohn's graphical presentations show that the relationships between socioeconomic status and self-regard scores are curvilinear or tend toward curvilinearity; so his use of *eta* is appropriate. *Eta* between socioeconomic status and self-confidence = .10, and *eta* between socioeconomic status and self-deprecation = .10. Given the large *N*s, these *etas* are statistically significant even though extremely small. When correlations were computed controlling for such occupational conditions as the subject's report of the degree of self-direction characterizing his occupation, the *etas* were drastically reduced, suggesting that occupational self-direction accounts largely for the *etas* between socioeconomic status and self-regard. (These data are also reported to some extent in Kohn and Schooler, 1969.)

Yancey, Rigsby, and McCarthy (1972) interviewed 1,179 adults from Nashville, Tennessee, and Philadelphia, Pennsylvania, with an equal number of blacks and whites in the sample from each city. The RSE was used as the measure of self-esteem, while the measures of socioeconomic status were work-force participation (either working or not working at present) and level of education (0-2, 3-7, 8, 9-11, or 12 years of school completed, some college completed, or graduation from college). According to a multiple-classification analysis of the data, the variance added by educational level to 6 predictor variables for self-esteem was found to be statistically significant in both samples, whereas the variance added by work-force participation was significant only in the Philadelphia sample. When the data were analyzed separately for each race in the two cities, the variance added by level of education was statistically significant for both blacks and whites in each city, whereas the variance added by work-force participation was significant for whites in both cities, but not significant for blacks in either city. However, since level of education seems to be a more appropriate measure of socioeconomic status than working versus not working, one might expect the results concerning the effects of the former to be more consistent than the latter. These results support the view that adults with higher educational levels have higher self-esteem when the variables of marital status, work-force participation, sex, race, and age are all held constant.

In summary, I have just considered 11 studies which looked for possible associations between some measure of socioeconomic status and the Rosenberg Self-Esteem Scale (RSE) or some modification of it. All but one used extremely large samples. Subjects were adolescents in 5 studies, undergraduates or college age persons in 2 studies, and adults in 3 studies. Adequacy of administrative conditions, instrumentation, data analysis, control of other variables possibly related to self-esteem, and completeness of reporting varied widely among these researches; but a number used multivariate techniques in an attempt to control for other variables while looking for the contribution of socioeconomic level to variance in self-esteem scores. The great majority of these investigators report null findings, and the absolute sizes of partial correlations reported to be significant in the multivariate studies were extremely small. Rosenberg (1965) and M. L. Kohn (1969) both suggest that their significant findings might actually be a function of some class-related variable, as opposed to being dependent on the valuation society accords different socioeconomic groups. Kaplan (1971), in discussing his null findings, suggests that perhaps only under certain conditions would any relationship between self-esteem and socioeconomic level be expected to appear.

Thus, no clear, consistent support is given by this group of 11 studies to the hypothesis that a significant, let alone strong relationship obtains between socioeconomic status and self-regard.

Coopersmith's Self-Esteem Inventory (SEI)

Although Coopersmith's (1967) insignificant association between SEI scores and socioeconomic status is not interpretable, partly because of his use of only 80 subjects and a vaguely described, idiosyncratic index of socioeconomic level, Trowbridge (1972a, 1974) has provided somewhat more interpretable information about SEI scores and socioeconomic class. She obtained SEI scores for 3,789 children in Grades 3–8. Unfortunately, socioeconomic status was varied by using "lower-class" and "middle-class" schools, rather than by classifying each subject. A lower-class school was defined as one which was eligible for Title I federal funding and which was "known" to have very few middle-class children in attendance. A school was categorized as middle class if 90% of the home evaluations in its populated area translated into market values of $12,000–$24,000. The Warner Index of Social Status, determined from information in the school records, confirmed the middle-class school's classification.

In each of 10 IQ-decile groups, the mean SEI score of the lower socioeconomic group was higher than that of the higher socioeconomic group. The over-all mean difference (74.1 − 68.4) was significant. Interactions with race and population density were not significant (Trowbridge, 1972a). In her 1972 report, Trowbridge goes into descriptive detail about subscales and individual items which differentiate the 2 socioeconomic groups, but significance tests are not given.

In an earlier study, Trowbridge (1970, 1972b) had obtained similar trends, but the significantly higher SEI mean for low socioeconomic schools is not so interpretable as in the 1974 study since much less information is given about the criteria used to divide the schools into socioeconomic categories and about race, and no information is given about Ns or about interactions.

Getsinger, Kunce, Miller, and Weinberg (1972) and W. F. White and Richmond (1970) both used the SEI, but their methods were too flawed to warrant substantive comment on their results.

It is clear that studies with the SEI give no support to the proposition that a strong positive relationship between self-regard and socioeconomic status will occur, and, in fact, the trends from the most defensible study are in the direction opposite to this hypothesis. (Wylie, 1974, pp. 169–174 has given an evaluation of the SEI.)

Piers-Harris (PH) and Lipsitt Scales

In C. L. Mayer's (1967) study involving both the Piers-Harris (PH) and Lipsitt scales for children, the subjects were between 12 and 17 years old, with Binet or WISC IQs between 50 and 75 and with no "observable physical, sensory, or emotional disabilities." Three socioeconomic groups were formed on the basis of Warner's Index of Status Characteristics, enabling one to look for curvilinearity of relationship between self-regard and socioeconomic level. To promote subjects' understanding and honesty in replying, small-group administration was used and confidentiality was guaranteed the subjects. No trend was observed for Lipsitt's scale means to vary with socioeconomic level. The consistent trend for self-regard means from the PH scale to be a positive function of socioeconomic level was insignificant. However, the small size of Mayer's Ns (27, 39, 32 in the low, medium, and high socioeconomic groups) was plausibly a factor in his obtaining an insignificant F for this trend.

In the PH test manual, Piers (1969) reports that fourth, fifth, and sixth graders from "economically deprived schools" actually exceeded the self-regard means of the normative group. Of course, no significance tests are warranted, since the deprived and normative groups were not intended to be directly compared; but, in any case, no support is given here for the occurrence of an inverse relationship between socioeconomic level and PH self-regard scores.

Harris and Braun's (1971) report is based on only 60 black children, aged 7–8, and no definition of lower class or middle class is offered. The "upper-class school" was also suburban and had a smaller percentage of black pupils, whereas the "lower-class school" was in the inner city and had a larger percentage of black pupils. Accordingly, the significantly higher mean PH score of the upper-class group cannot possibly be interpreted as indicating a relationship between socioeconomic level per se and self-regard as indexed by the PH scale.

Obviously, the above studies give no support to the hypothesis that self-regard scores from the Piers-Harris or Lipsitt scales are positively related to socioeconomic level. (Wylie, 1974, pp. 169–180, has evaluated the Piers-Harris and Lipsitt Scales.)

Long, Henderson, and Ziller's Self-Social Esteem Score (SSE)

One study which used the SSE score involved only 72 subjects and confounded socioeconomic level with race (Long & Henderson, 1968). Accordingly, no conclusions can be drawn. In a later investigation (Long & Henderson, 1970), data regarding socioeconomic level are presented separately by race and sex for 192 first graders in 13 schools in 2 rural southern counties. The scores on the Hollingshead Occupational Scale were dichotomized into 1–5 vs. 6–7 (precluding the search for curvilinearity). No tendency was observed for SSE score means to vary as a function of socioeconomic level. F ratios for socioeconomic level, for socioeconomic level $\times$ race, and for socioeconomic level $\times$ sex were insignificant. Ziller, Hagey, Smith, and Long (1969) report a reanalysis of the results of a study by Long, Ziller, and Henderson (1967a) in which the 6-item student form of the SSE was administered to 295 white boys and girls in Grades 6–12 in 4 schools located in a rural area of Maryland. The socioeconomic status of the students was determined by classifying their fathers' occupations as follows: professional, business, office worker, and salesman composed Class 1; skilled labor constituted Class 2; farmers constituted Class 3; and semiskilled or unskilled labor composed Class 4. The mean scores on the SSE of the students classified from Class 1 through Class 4 were 23.0, 22.4, 20.4, and 20.5, respectively. An ANOVA showed the differences among these means to be at slightly greater than the .05 level of significance. Accordingly, these results are said by the authors to support the positive association of self-esteem and socioeconomic status. The study by Getsinger, Kunce, Miller, and Weinberg (1972) involved not only Coopersmith's SEI score but also the SSE. However, as stated in the section on the SEI, this study is too flawed to sustain interpretation. (This scale has been evaluated in Wylie, 1974, pp. 190–200.)

Interpersonal Check List (ICL)

Preston and Gudiksen (1966) used "empirically derived [positive and negative] social desirability connotations" to compute self-regard scores from the ICL adjectives endorsed by 242 subjects older than 65 years of age. Subjects were divided into 5 groups: 2 groups of residents of affluent retirement homes, residents of a modest retirement home, members of a modest retirement club, and indigents in a county hospital. Educational, occupational, and financial items obtained by interview supported the authors' contention that the groups represented discriminably different socioeconomic levels. The only significant difference in self-regard was between the indigent group mean and the mean of the other groups, with the indigents showing greater self-derogation. Vagueness about method and control of relevant variables makes the results difficult to evaluate, however. (See Wylie, 1974, pp. 213–223, for an evaluation of ICL scales.)

Phillips Self- and Other-Acceptance Scales

In T. J. Hill's (1957) study, 180 subjects in ninth, tenth, and twelfth grades were divided into bottom and top halves with respect to Warner's Index of Status Characteristics. (See Wylie, 1961, pp. 66–67, for information on the Phillips Questionnaire.) In the ninth and tenth grades, the low-status group obtained a slightly higher mean score on the Phillips questionnaire, whereas the reverse was true in the twelfth grade. Since no information about significance tests is given and since consistent trends were not obtained in all 3 grades, it seems safe to assume that this study offers no support to the hypothesis that self-regard is a direct function of socioeconomic level.

Tennessee Self-Concept Scales

In a methodological study which attempted to find noncognitive measures appropriate for research with "disadvantaged adults," A. B. Moore (1972) found that the Total Positive Score yielded analysis-of-variance reliability coefficients of .87 and .91 on pre- and posttests given to 343 disadvantaged adults. Although Moore did not attempt to compare the group's mean scores to the norms given in the TSCS manual, nor did he attempt to isolate socioeconomic level from other aspects of "disadvantaged status," the results imply that the Total Positive score is sufficiently reliable to warrant using it if one wished to make comparisons of adults of varying socioeconomic levels.

Healey and deBlassie (1974) found no significant association between socioeconomic level as measured by Hollingshead's Two-Factor Index of Social Position and Total Positive Scores on the TSCS for 630 ninth graders in south central New Mexico. (See Wylie, 1974, pp. 230–236, for an evaluation of the TSCS.)

Janis-Field Scales

Schwendiman, Larsen, and Dunn's (1970) study involving an unspecified version of the Janis-Field Scales is so flawed and incompletely
reported as not to merit substantive comment.

Summary

The alleged positive association of socioeconomic level and over-all
self-regard is not supported by available investigations involving the
better known tests of self-regard and modifications thereof. If methods
were improved in such ways as using a wide range and several steps on
the socioeconomic dimension, unconfounding of socioeconomic level
and other factors, and looking for interactions between socioeconomic
level and other possibly relevant variables, some substantive conclusions might emerge. However, nothing in the literature reviewed
above strongly suggests that such a refined search will be particularly
fruitful or enlightening.

b. SELF-REGARD INDEXED BY IDIOSYNCRATIC INSTRUMENTS

I have examined 23 studies which related idiosyncratic self-regard
measures to indices of socioeconomic level. Of course the use of such
idiosyncratic instruments makes the results of these researches even
more difficult to interpret and synthesize than is the case when some
background information is available about the psychometric properties
of the self-regard instrument. In addition to this problem, 15 of these
investigations are so incompletely or vaguely reported (at least with
respect to the relationship between socioeconomic level and self-
regard), and/or they are so seriously flawed methodologically that they
appear to me not to warrant substantive summary. Accordingly, these
15 are simply listed at the end of this section. The substantively
summarized publications discussed immediately below are ordered
according to the ages of the subjects on which they are based.

In her study of 434 kindergartners and second graders, G. Baker
(1973) used an inadequately described, idiosyncratic Pictorial Self-
Concept Scale, about which no published psychometric information
seems to be available. Socioeconomic level was varied according to
school, not by classifying individual subjects, i.e., schools qualifying for

federal funding under Title I were compared to those not qualifying, the assumption being made that students in Title I schools came from lower socioeconomic level. The F for socioeconomic level of school was significant, with higher self-regard being associated with higher socioeconomic level. Without more knowledge of the characteristics of the self-regard index it is hard to know whether this finding could be attributed to the reliability artifact. (See Wylie, 1974, pp. 119–121.) Moreover, as is always the case in studies varying socioeconomic level by intact group, one needs to know how well-grounded the assumption is that the socioeconomic levels of the children in the 2 groups differed, and what variables other than socioeconomic level might be varying between the 2 kinds of schools.

By far the most extensive investigation involving an idiosyncratic self-regard instrument in relationship to socioeconomic level is the one reported by Rosenberg and Simmons (1972). Modeling after the cluster sampling method of the U.S. Census Bureau, the authors drew a sample of 2,625 third- through twelfth-grade pupils from the records of 26 schools in Baltimore City, Maryland. Of those drawn, 1,917 were available to be interviewed. Because the RSE which Rosenberg (1965) had developed for use in his New York State study was deemed unsuitable for the wider age range of the Baltimore subjects, a new 6-item Guttman scale was developed to index self-esteem levels in the Baltimore research. Considerable information about the development of this scale and its psychometric properties is given in Rosenberg and Simmons (1972, pp. 11–20).

A table is presented which groups subjects into three levels of self-esteem and four socioeconomic levels, the latter being formed from Hollingshead's two-factor scale as follows: Classes 1 and 2 combined, Class 3, Class 4, Class 5. Inspection of the table shows no relationship between self-esteem and socioeconomic level among blacks but an apparent positive association within the white sample. The latter trend is most clearly evidenced in the differences in distributions of self-esteem scores between Classes 1–2 and Class 5. No trend toward curvilinear relationships is apparent. These findings of a positive relationship between socioeconomic level and self-esteem are said to hold when age is controlled. No significance tests are given.

Rosenberg and Simmons (1972) proposed that the discrepancy between the findings in the black and white groups might plausibly be explained by two facts: (a) the blacks were much more apt to live in homogeneous socioeconomic environments where their low status was less likely to be brought to their attention; (b) the blacks were much more likely than corresponding whites to inflate their status on a specially devised index of self-perceived socioeconomic status.

The reader may remember that Rosenberg's New York State study of high school pupils revealed a significant positive association between socioeconomic level and self-regard among boys but not girls. No breakdowns of the Baltimore data by sex are published in Rosenberg and Simmons (1972), but in data furnished to me by Rosenberg, this trend was also apparent among the Baltimore subjects, i.e., there was a significant association between socioeconomic level and self-regard among boys but not among girls.

Two researches by A. Soares and L. Soares (1969, 1972) may be considered together because they used the same idiosyncratic self-regard instrument (a 20-scale semantic differential about which insufficient information is given) and the same criteria for defining "advantaged" and "disadvantaged," namely income level and type of residence. In the 1969 study, involving 514 urban children from Grades 4 through 8, the advantaged and disadvantaged samples were formed by taking groups from schools located in advantaged and disadvantaged areas; the procedure is not fully explained in the 1972 report based on 1,379 elementary and 1,033 high school pupils. In at least the 1969 study, and possibly in the 1972 one, degree of advantage is contaminated by urbanness, race, and perhaps characteristics of the respective schools.

Results from both studies were entirely consistent: disadvantaged groups always had higher self-regard. Although this contradicts the usual assumptions made in this area (see section A–1 above), it is empirically consistent with Trowbridge's (1972a) findings cited in section B–3 above. Clear interpretation of these "paradoxical" findings is impossible, however. A. Soares and L. Soares suggest that the disadvantaged groups come from more homogeneous socioeconomic backgrounds where the teachers' expectations for them are met, whereas the advantaged groups are subjected to more pressures, depressing their self-regard. Rosenberg and Simmons (1972) might add that the greater homogeneity of the backgrounds of the disadvantaged subjects would prevent them from becoming aware of their low status. One must also note that blacks were much more numerous in the disadvantaged groups, and they typically have been found not to have low self-regard. (See chapter 4 of this book.) Long (1969) has suggested an artifactual interpretation of A. Soares and L. Soares results, viz., an alleged extremity response set among disadvantaged subjects could be inflating the self-regard means. Her statement is based on an inference from relationships between IQ and extremity set on the one hand and between IQ and socioeconomic level on the other. However, A. Soares and L. Soares (1970c) argue against Long's points. Obviously, the interpretation of these studies must remain moot.

St. John's (1971) 957 sixth graders responded to an idiosyncratic "general self-concept" measure comprised of 10 adjective pairs published in the article. This self-regard measure, about which virtually no psychometric information is given, was not significantly correlated with family socioeconomic level as indexed by "Hollingshead's 7-point scale." In a multiple-regression analysis, family socioeconomic level was not used as one of the predictors of the self-regard scores.

Davidson and Lang (1960) looked for relationships between socioeconomic level and one aspect of children's social self-concepts among 204 fourth, fifth, and sixth graders. The children used an idiosyncratic adjective check list to describe "How My Teacher Thinks I Am," and they were classed into one of 3 socioeconomic levels on the basis of father's and mother's occupation. Mean perception of teacher's feelings toward self declined from upper through lower socioeconomic levels, with a significantly higher mean perception of teacher's feelings for the upper and middle socioeconomic-level children as compared to the lower level ones. These differences also hold regardless of the child's achievement level.

With 420 married, white adults between the ages of 18 and 45, Weidman, Phelan, and Sullivan (1972) looked for relationships between self-evaluated competence and (a) two levels of educational attainment; (b) occupational prestige, defined in terms of the census classifications; (c) two levels of income. The idiosyncratic "self-competence" scale, about which no psychometric information is given, appears from the published questions to be broad enough in coverage to qualify as an over-all self-regard scale. Zero-order relationships using dichotomized variables appear to follow the hypothesized trend that higher self-regard goes with higher education, higher income, and higher occupational prestige. The relationship was strongest for educational attainment, and this relationship remained after "controlling [in an unspecified manner] for these other status indicators" (p. 310). Unfortunately "the simultaneous effects of all three status indicators on competence self-evaluation were not examined. The sample size was too small to use the method of weighted net percentage differences; . . . budgetary considerations precluded the use of multiple regression techniques" (p. 311). Despite the obvious limitations of this study, I summarize it here because it may imply the common-sense suggestion that self-regard scores based on items especially relevant to competence may be related positively to socioeconomic level even if very "broad spectrum" self-regard scores turn out to be only weakly related or unrelated to socioeconomic level.

Parker and Kleiner's (1966) subjects included 1,400 mentally ill and 1,464 community male and female adults, aged 20-60. All subjects were black and were divided into differing occupational status levels according to a specially devised index thought to be particularly appropriate to the black population. Self-esteem was inferred from a mean [Self-Ideal] discrepancy score based on 17 statements comprising an idiosyncratic self-regard index. Self-esteem so measured was apparently unrelated to occupational status position. Interpretation of these null findings is not possible, partly because of lack of information about the psychometric properties of the unrelated variables.

In their study of 1,651 adult northern blacks, aged 21-45, Crain and Weisman (1972) compared educational and income level to scores on a 10-item idiosyncratic self-esteem test. Controlling on sex and region of birth, they found partial correlations of .19 between self-esteem and level of education and .10 between self-esteem and level of income.

Summary

For obvious reasons, the studies I have chosen to discuss immediately above cannot be conclusively interpreted or synthesized. Positive, negative, and null relationships have been reported between self-regard and socioeconomic level. The A. Soares and L. Soares (1969, 1972) studies discussed immediately above and the Trowbridge research (1972a) discussed in section B-3 are the only ones finding "paradoxical" effects, i.e., an inverse relationship between self-regard and socioeconomic level. It is suggestive that in both A. Soares and L. Soares's and Trowbridge's work, socioeconomic level was varied by school, not by classifying each individual's characteristics as a basis for placement into a socioeconomic group. However, not too much should be made of this suggestive point since G. Baker (1973), who also varied socioeconomic level by school rather than by individual classification, did not report "paradoxical" findings; in fact her trend was a positive one. In any event, we need explorations of what factors other than socioeconomic level are varying between groups when this intact-group method is used, and we need more investigation of the possible relevance of such confounding variables to self-regard and to the conditions under which socioeconomic level is or is not related to self-regard.

Excluded Studies

For reasons already mentioned, the following studies are simply listed rather than discussed substantively: L. A. Bennett, Sorensen, and Forshay (1971); Cohen and Miller (1969); Getsinger, Kunce, Miller, and Weinberg (1972); Healy (1973); Kasl and French (1962); Lessing [in Reece, 1974]; Luck and Heiss (1972); Miskimins and R. B. Baker (1973); Nahinsky (1966); Neale and Proshek (1967); Paschal (1968); Rabinowitz (1966); Samuels (1973); W. F. White, H. E. Anderson, and Cryder (1966, 1967), the same data are published in both references; Whiteman and Deutsch (1968).

4. Specific Aspects of Self-Concept as a Function of Socioeconomic Level

a. SELF-CONCEPT OF ABILITY

So far as self-concept of schoolwork ability is concerned, an appreciable amount of published information about scale development, psychometric properties, and relationships of scale scores to other variables is available only for the scales presented by Brookover and his associates: the Self-Concept of Schoolwork Ability—General (SCA); and Self-Concept of Ability in Mathematics, English, Social Studies, and Science. Paterson (1967) has summarized some of the relevant methodological information about these scales, and the questions themselves appear in Brookover, Paterson, and Thomas (1962).

When one wishes to look at possible relationships between self-concept of schoolwork ability and socioeconomic levels, it is especially important to hold ability constant, since, as is frequently reported, there are significant correlations between IQ scores and socioeconomic levels and between grade-point averages or achievement tests and socioeconomic levels. For example, Brookover, LePere, Hamachek, Thomas, and Erickson (1965, p. 182) report significant rs from .25 to .32 between grade-point average (GPA) and socioeconomic status and (on p. 335) a correlation of .26 between IQ and socioeconomic status for subjects from seventh to tenth grades.

So far as socioeconomic level is concerned, Brookover et al. used an idiosyncratic measure described on pages 20 ff. of Brookover, Paterson, and Thomas (1962). On the basis of GPA, R. J. Morse (1967) formed extreme groups of high and low Brookover subjects and published Self-Concept of Ability—General scores by socioeconomic level within each GPA group. In each comparison, with GPA constant, the SCA of the high socioeconomic group significantly exeeded that of the low socioeconomic group. Relationships of socioeconomic level to scores on Self-Concept of Ability in various separate subject areas are given in Brookover, Paterson, and Thomas (1962) and Brookover et al. (1965), but neither IQ nor achievement was held constant.

Epps (1969) used an idiosyncratic modification of the Brookover SCA and an idiosyncratic socioeconomic indicator in his study of black adolescents summarized in section B-3 above. He reports 4 zero-order rs ranging from .09 to .16 for southern males, southern females, northern males, and northern females. Apparently no attempt was made to control for the possible roles of IQ and/or achievement in determining the sizes of these correlations.

Bachman's (1970) study of 2,213 tenth-grade boys (described in section B-3 above) used an idiosyncratic 3-question measure of self-concept of schoolwork ability and an idiosyncratic index of socio-economic level. Zero-order *eta* between socioeconomic level and self-concept of schoolwork ability = .33. *Beta* (analogous to *eta*) was computed to estimate the relationship between socioeconomic level and self-concept of schoolwork ability with 7 family background factors and Quick Test IQ controlled. The value of this *beta* = .16, and no estimate of its statistical significance level is given. The regression line appears to depart somewhat from linearity.

Wylie (1963) and Wylie and Hutchins (1967) used idiosyncratic questions to index self-concept of schoolwork ability in 5 main groups of subjects totaling 4,245: 2 junior high school groups (taken from the same school, in 1959 and in 1965); and 3 different high school groups. In each of 3 of these school groups, subjects were divided into ability subgroups according to 10-unit IQ levels (e.g., 60–69, 70–79), whereas

2 of the school groups were trichotomized on the basis of the Differential Aptitude Test (deciles 7-8-9; 3-4-5-6; 0-1-2). Then, on the basis of Hollingshead's Occupational Scale, each IQ (or DAT) subgroup was divided into high [Classes 1-4] versus low [Classes 5-7] socioeconomic levels.

In four schools, each student was told "by ability we don't mean necessarily how well you actually do your schoolwork, but rather how well you *could* do schoolwork if you tried your best. . . . decide whether you would probably belong in the top half of the students in your homeroom, or . . . somewhere below the top half." They were also asked, "[Assuming parental approval, your desire to attend college, and enough money] do you feel right now that, so far as your ability to do the work is concerned, you will be able to go through college?" (Answers to this question were dichotomized.) In one group (a high school), students were asked only the following question about their ability: "Please indicate the kind of mental ability you think you have: Well above average, above average, average, below average, well below average." (Answers were dichotomized, splitting the answers between above average and average.)

To look for relationships between socioeconomic level and self-concepts of schoolwork ability with ability controlled, 20 pairs of comparison subgroups of white students were formed from the 5 schools in the following way: the 2 subgroups in each pair were equated with respect to ability scores, varied with respect to socioeconomic level, and comprised of at least 10 subjects per subgroup. Each of the 20 comparisons between subgroups was, of course, independent of each other. In 17 out of 20 of these comparisons, a larger proportion of high-socioeconomic-level subjects classified their ability level as "top half," (or, in the fifth school, as "above average"). Each of 7 of these 17 differences between proportions was significant at $\leq .05$ level. Only 4 of the schools were asked the question about college ability; and from these schools, 17 pairs of comparison groups could be formed, each equated with respect to ability scores, varied with respect to socioeconomic level, and comprised of at least 10 subjects per subgroup. Of these 17 subgroup pair comparisons, 16 showed a larger proportion of high socioeconomic level subjects reporting that they had the ability to go through college, and 3 of these 16 differences in proportions were individually significant at $\leq .05$ level. (There were not enough black students in Hollingshead categories 1-4 to permit analyses within the black group parallel to those just described for the whites.)

Among the limitations of this study are two of special relevance to the present topic: (a) the indices of self-concept of schoolwork ability are idiosyncratic, and no psychometric information on them is available; (b) the subjects were dichotomized with respect to socio-economic level, precluding the search for nonlinear relationships. Within these limitations, these data appear to support the contention that self-concept of schoolwork ability among white students in grades 7-12 is a function of socioeconomic level when ability measures are closely controlled.

Wellman's (1971) groups of 938 white and 1,212 black ninth graders responded to the "Who Am I?" test which was scored for "intellectual ability, positively evaluated" and "intellectual ability, negatively evaluated" by applying the General Inquirer content analysis system described in Stone, Dunphy, M. S. Smith, and Ogilvie (1966). Five socioeconomic levels were differentiated according to Duncan's (1961) Index, and data analyses were performed separately within each racial group. While some positive associations between socioeconomic level and self-evaluations of ability seem to be present in Wellman's data tables, only one *gamma* out of four was significant. In any event, there was no control for the correlation between ability scores and socio-economic level, so even significant associations between these variables would be uninterpretable. (See Wylie, 1974, pp. 240-247, for an evaluation of the "Who Am I?" test.)

Attenborough and Zdep's (1973) national sample of 1,884 black and white girls aged 7-17 were classified according to a modification of Hollingshead's 2-factor index. Socioeconomic level was not found to be significantly related to self-descriptions on the scale "quick to learn." Had a significant relationship been found, it would be uninterpretable since ability and achievement were not controlled.

St. John's (1971) study of the relationships of socioeconomic level as indicated by Hollingshead's occupational scales to academic self-concept as indexed by an idiosyncratic instrument yielded zero-order rs of .07 among whites and .02 among blacks. All 957 subjects were sixth graders. Her study as a whole used multiple-regression analysis, but this analysis did not include socioeconomic level versus self-concept of ability with other variables controlled. For obvious reasons, her null findings regarding these 2 variables must remain inconclusive.

Brim, Neulinger, and Glass (1965) asked respondents, a national sample of 1,021 persons ≥ 21 years old, "How do you think you compare to other people in intelligence?" They were asked to make the comparisons with father, mother, brother, sister, spouse, their children, the average person in the U.S. today, people in the same kind of work, people they went to high school with, most of their friends today. Although the authors obtained strong tendencies for favorable self-concepts of ability to go with higher Hollingshead socioeconomic level, the method they used afforded no control for the role of the subjects' actual ability differences in determining the reported trends.

A different sort of self-concept of ability ("Myself as a Teacher") was studied by Walberg (1967), who related an idiosyncratic semantic differential index to a vaguely described socioeconomic index among 965 undergraduate women preparing to become teachers. No relationship was found between the two variables, but gaps in needed information and lack of control of relevant variables leave this null finding even more ambiguous than must be the case with any null outcome.

In summary, all nine studies which came to my attention used different instruments to measure self-concept of ability, and six of them did not attempt to control for actual ability and/or achievement when looking for relationships between socioeconomic level and self-concept of ability. In three large-scale investigations which did try to control for ability and/or achievement, positive relationships emerged between socioeconomic level and self-concept of ability. There is some possibility that the relationship may be nonlinear. These three studies included both males and females from Grades 7 through 12.

None of the controlled studies yielded null findings, although several uncontrolled ones did so. No researcher has reported finding a significant inverse relationship between socioeconomic level and self-concept of schoolwork ability. Therefore, the trend of the results is toward a positive association between self-concept of ability and socioeconomic level, with IQ and/or GPA controlled.

b. SELF-CONCEPTIONS OF OTHER
   SPECIFIC PERSONALITY CHARACTERISTICS

Besides the researches involving self-concept of ability, a few studies have looked at other specific, self-reported personality characteristics as a function of socioeconomic level, using well-known self-report personality tests. These investigations are scattered across tests, with no within-test replication, and many are characterized by serious short-comings of method and/or reporting.

California Psychological Inventory

In Ageton and Elliott's (1974) study of 2,308 males and females, subjects were divided into upper and lower socioeconomic classes by unspecified criteria and procedure and were interviewed annually from ninth to twelfth grade. Three-way ANOVAs (sex × race × socioeconomic level) showed no significant effect of socioeconomic class on the scores from the Socialization Scale (SO) of the California Psychological Inventory (Gough, 1969) on either the initial or final testing.

In a longitudinal study by Haan (1964), childhood and adult social status ratings were compared to adult scores on the CPI. The socioeconomic status of the subjects was determined by using A. Edwards's (1933) scale of 6 occupational levels. The 1934 socioeconomic classification of the subjects was made on the basis of the occupational status of their families when the subjects were in junior high school. Then, in 1958, socioeconomic classifications were again made for each subject on the basis of his or her own occupation, or, in the case of the married women, the occupations of their husbands. For the sample of 45 men and 45 women there were no significant correlations between the 1934 social status rating and any of the 18 CPI scales for the women and only 3 significant correlations for the men. Significant correlations were obtained between the 1958 social status ratings and 7 CPI scales each for the men and the women, but the self-acceptance scale was not among them. The increase in the number of significant correlations could be a result of the greater salience of social status ratings based on one's own occupation rather than on the occupation of one's parent. It could also be that CPI results from 1958 would tend to correlate more highly with 1958 social status ratings because both were made in the same year. Multiple significance testing without cross-validation limits interpretability.

Edwards Personal Preference Scale

In Klett's (1957) study of 1,633 high school students, socioeconomic class (as indexed by the U.S. Census Bureau classification of fathers' occupations), yielded rs with EPPS scales ranging from $-.14$ to $+.08$, the highest rs being $-.12$ for Achievement and $-.14$ for Dominance. In view of the serious objections to the forced choice format of the EPPS (see Wylie, 1974, pp. 76–80) and the lack of cross-validation, it seems safe to say that Klett's findings offer no support to the idea that there is an association between socioeconomic level and any of the self-reported personality dimensions of the EPPS.

Mehlman and Fleming's (1963) and Brazziel's (1964) reports on EPPS scores and socioeconomic class are too flawed to warrant substantive summary.

Interpersonal Check List

Two studies have come to my attention which attempted to look at Dom and Lov scales of the Interpersonal Check List in relationship to socioeconomic class (Bieri & Lobeck, 1961; and McDonald, 1968). Each was severely flawed in several ways, and the reported results seem not to agree, although method differences preclude a firm comparative statement or a speculative analysis of why outcomes may have differed. (See Wylie, 1974, pp. 213–223, for an evaluation of the Interpersonal Check List.)

Minnesota Multiphasic Personality Inventory (MMPI)

In a study involving sex, race, and socioeconomic level (as crudely indexed by the Schneider-Lysgaard classification), McDonald and Gynther (1963) performed 11 3-way ANOVAs, one for each of 11 MMPI scales. No scale yielded a significant F value for socioeconomic level, and only one F (out of 22 possible Fs) was significant for interactions between socioeconomic level and race or interactions between socioeconomic level and sex. Although the ANOVA controlled for race, there was no control between socioeconomic groups for different types of schools attended, since all subjects were enrolled in segregated schools, with unknown implications for other school characteristics.

Other Well-Known Self-Report Personality Measures

The following studies involving other well-known self-report personality instruments seem too flawed and/or inadequately reported to warrant substantive summary: Haller and S. Thomas (1962), California Test of Personality and Cattell's sixteen PF Test; Healey and deBlassie (1974), Tennessee Self-Concept Scales; McPartland and Cumming (1958), Twenty Sentences Test; Sims (1952), Bell Adjustment Inventory; Schwab, Clemmons, and Marder (1966), Tennessee Self-Concept Scale.

Summary Regarding Studies Using Well-Known Tests

Apparently few investigators have attempted to look for possible associations between socioeconomic level and self-concepts of specific personality characteristics (other than ability) as indexed by well-known self-report instruments. Serious methodological shortcomings characterize these studies, and no intepretable, statistically significant findings have emerged.

Idiosyncratic Measures

Rather than testing an hypothesis about specific self-conceptions as a function of socioeconomic level, Gough (1948) sought specific personality-descriptive MMPI items which might empirically differentiate two extreme groups of 38 high school students each, whose socioeconomic status was high or low on the Sims (1927) Score Card. The 34 discriminating MMPI items (published in the article) were administered to a new sample, this time using the American Home Scale (Kerr and Remmers, 1942) as the socioeconomic indicator. For this group, $r = .50$ between the Status self-report scale and the American Home Scale. In a later study of 55 college students (Gough, 1949a) the Status personality scores correlated .28 with an idiosyncratic Home Scale, .11 with the American Home Scale, .25 with the Sims Score Card, and .20 with father's occupation. Only the $rs \geq .25$ were significant. Generalizability of these results is limited by the very small Ns and the fact that all but the college subjects came from one small Minnesota town. However, it does not appear that self-report personality differences associated with socioeconomic status have been brought to light by this approach.

In a study already considered in section B-3 above, Kohn and Schooler (1969) and Kohn (1969) purported to index not only self-regard (as already discussed), but also three other factorially determined self-concept scores based on interview questions: attribution of responsibility, anxiety, and idea conformity. (The exact questions are given in both publications.) The rs between each of these variables and socioeconomic level determined by Hollingshead's Two-Factor Index

= .12 for attribution of responsibility; .06 for anxiety; and .13 for idea conformity. Although very small, these rs are statistically significant since the total $N = 3,100$. These already low zero-order rs are reduced still more by controlling for reported occupational self-direction. Accordingly, no basis is presented for concluding that a psychologically important relationship obtains between socioeconomic level and these aspects of self-conception.

I have examined 11 additional studies which purport to relate socioeconomic status and idiosyncratically measured specific aspects of self-conception other than self-concept of ability. Some of these publications have been mentioned in preceding sections in connection with other variables with which they were also concerned. In any event, no purpose can be served by summarizing here those parts of them which might supposedly be relevant to the present topic because, at least so far as this type of relevance is concerned, they are extremely flawed and/or inadequately reported. Accordingly, I simply list them: Attenborough and Zdep (1973); Bieri and Lobeck (1961); Cohen and Miller (1969); Fannin and Clinard (1965); Gough (1946, 1949b); Klausner (1953); Kosa, Rachiele, and Schommer (1962); National Council on the Aging (1975); Wegner (1973); W. F. White, H. E. Anderson, and Cryder (1967).

5. Values and Ideals for Self as a Function of Socioeconomic Level

As is true in all areas of self-concept research, relatively few investigators who looked at socioeconomic level have been concerned with individuals' conceptions of "ideal self" as opposed to their conceptions of "actual self" or their levels of self-regard. However, it seems to me that one can justifiably assume that persons' reported educational and occupational aspirations constitute a kind of statement about ideal self. Accordingly, I include this kind of report in the first section below. A few studies which dealt with explicit statements about ideal self or with miscellaneous "self values" (which I construe as self-ideals) are in the second section below.

a. EDUCATIONAL AND OCCUPATIONAL ASPIRATIONS

Since, as shown above, IQ and educational achievement tend to vary directly with socioeconomic level, it is necessary to control for ability and achievement when looking for associations between socio-economic level and educational or occupational aspirations. Because grading standards vary so widely within and between schools, either standardized achievement tests or standardized IQ tests or both are preferable ways of trying to control for ability and achievement.

In four of the five large-scale studies of junior and/or senior high school students described below, this type of control has been attempted, in each case by the use of IQ scores. Unfortunately, each study used a different idiosyncratic set of questions, and one may legitimately question whether the wording of some of these queries is suited to eliciting responses which indicate ideals for self. In fact, the authors did not purport to index the ideal self; so this interpretive caution should not be construed as implying a shortcoming from the authors' goals.

In Bachman's (1970) national interview study of 2,213 tenth-grade boys (described in section B-3 above), two idiosyncratic questions were asked: "What do you think you might do for a living?" and "How do you plan to get this sort of work?" (or, for the 15% who gave no codable answer to the first question, "What do you plan to do after high school?") The occupations mentioned in reply to the first question were coded according to the Duncan (1961) Socioeconomic Index. *Eta* between socioeconomic level and level of occupational aspirations = .37. *Beta*, analogous to *eta*, but adjusted for the effects of 7 other background factors and Quick Test IQ = .20. *Eta* between socioeconomic level and whether or not subjects stated a plan for post-high school education = .30. *Beta*, adjusted for the effects of 7 other background factors and Quick Test IQ = .20.

Clearly, the form of Bachman's questions is not entirely suited to getting expressions of "ideal self" uncontaminated by considerations of realistic financial and geographical constraints, and these interesting findings must be viewed with that qualification in mind. (It should be noted that it was not Bachman's purpose to index an aspect of ideal self.)

As in Bachman's (1970) study, the form of the questions asked by Sewell, Haller, and Straus (1957) is not clearly directed to getting expressions of "ideal self," since they concerned the respondents' plans for a college education and a particular vocation. Again, realistic financial and geographical restraints might affect the answers. A one-sixth random sample of all Wisconsin high school seniors in 1947–48 (N = 4,167) was divided into 5 socioeconomic levels according to the

North-Hatt occupational prestige values of their fathers' occupations and into 5 Hemnon-Nelson IQ levels. Occupational aspirations were dichotomized into "high" and "low." Within each of 5 IQ levels, the percent of students expressing high-level occupational aspirations was a direct function of the prestige level of the parent's occupation. This trend was significant for males but not for females. Educational aspirations were dichotomized into those definitely planning to attend a 4-year college and others. Within each of 5 IQ levels, the percent of students expressing 4-year college plans was a decreasing function of the prestige level of the parent's occupation, the trend being significant for both male and female subjects.

In their study of 4,245 subjects described in section B-4 above, Wylie (1963) and Wylie and Hutchins (1967) framed one of their questions about college in terms of aspirations rather than in terms of plans, thus: (Assuming parental approval, enough money, and enough ability, do you) "feel right now that you would be interested in going to college after graduating from high school?" Answers were dichotomized into (a) "wish I could go to college" versus (b) "don't care whether or not I go to college" or "would rather *not* go to college." Answers to the question about career aspirations could, as in the studies already considered, involve both realistic and ideal considerations: "Please describe . . . the career you are thinking about for yourself." Answers to this question were coded and dichotomized into 1-2 and 3-7 on the Hollingshead and Redlich scales.

Out of 17 pairs of groups of white subjects ($N \geq 10$ per group), closely matched regarding IQ but varying regarding Hollingshead and Redlich ratings of fathers' occupations, 16 pairs showed a higher percent of high socioeconomic-level subjects expressing a desire for college. Eight of these comparisons were individually significant at $\leq .05$ level. Out of 15 pairs of groups of white subjects ($N \geq 10$ per group), closely matched regarding IQ but varying regarding Hollingshead and Redlich levels of fathers' occupation, 13 showed a higher percent of high socioeconomic-level subjects "thinking of" a high-level occupation (i.e., levels 1 or 2). Of these 13 group comparisons, 3 were individually significant at $\leq .05$ level. (There were not enough black students in Hollingshead levels 1-4 to permit an analysis of the blacks' responses parallel to the one just described for whites.)

In part of his study of 1,355 California high school boys, A. B. Wilson (1959) varied socioeconomic level according to census data applicable to each of three schools, rather than by classifying each individual. Within each of 4 IQ levels, a strong trend is apparent for percents of subjects planning to attend college to depend directly upon the socioeconomic level of the school. In a fifth group with IQs ≤ 89, no trend is evident. No significance tests are given. Wilson infers that statements about plans indicate aspirations, since junior colleges with open admission to all high school graduates were geographically available to all subjects. However, lower-class subjects might not be financially able to attend. Wilson's tables also show professional-level career aspirations as a joint function of father's occupation and school socioeconomic level, but, unfortunately, no control for IQ is provided in this analysis.

J. H. Davis (1964) looked at the relationship between the educational postgraduate plans and the socioeconomic level of 33,982 June, 1961, graduates from 135 colleges and universities. Students were dichotomized into high or low socioeconomic levels according to the Index of Socio-Economic Status, which is based on family income, father's education, and parental occupation. A measure of intellectual performance called Academic Performance Index (API) was also obtained for each student. This measure was based primarily on the student's cumulative grade-point average but was also weighted to reflect the differing standards of grading in different institutions. Among male respondents, a greater percent of those with high socio-economic status were found to be making plans for immediate graduate study, regardless of their scores on the API, size of their hometown, or field of their career. However, this analysis of plans does not take into account the financial situation of the students. A greater percentage of males with low socioeconomic status claimed they were postponing graduate study or not planning to attend because of financial obstacles. There were no consistent differences between the two socioeconomic levels in the percentages of males who cited lack of motivation as the reason for postponing graduate study. There seemed to be no consistent effect of socioeconomic status among the females except that a greater percentage of high socioeconomic status females cited a lack of motivation as a reason for postponing or not planning to attend graduate school, regardless of API, size of hometown, or type of career. Thus, if motivation to attend graduate school is considered a better measure of educational aspiration than actual plans to attend, then Davis's results support the view that high socioeconomic status is either not consistently related to educational aspirations (in the case of the males) or that high socioeconomic status may be associated with lower motivation (in the case of females).

Heyns's (1974) analysis of J. S. Coleman et al.'s (1966) data examined the relationship between various measures of socioeconomic status (including father's occupation, father's education, and number of siblings) and educational aspirations, measured in terms of number of years of schooling aspired to by high school students. The students were from 48 urban, nonsouthern high schools with a grade span of 4 years and are not claimed by Heyns to constitute a truly random sample. For 15,384 twelfth graders, zero-order correlations of .2399 between aspirations and father's occupation and .2785 between aspirations and father's education were obtained when ability level was not held constant. In a path diagram concerning the determination of aspirations and several other variables, curriculum placement is the main determinant of aspirations, and verbal ability is the strongest determinant of curriculum placement, the unique effects of socioeconomic class on curriculum placement explaining only 3.20% of the variance. One might argue that the positive relationship between socioeconomic status and aspirations found in some other studies is a result of the placement of higher socioeconomic level students in better curricular "tracks." However, Heyns's findings do not support this viewpoint. If the correlation between socioeconomic status and aspirations found in these studies cannot be explained as the result of biased class placement, perhaps there is some other explanation. Two such possibilities might be the students' strong identification with the parental socioeconomic level or, in the case of low socioeconomic level students, financial limitations becoming so ingrained that even aspirations become expressions of what is financially feasible.

In Parker and Kleiner's (1964) survey of 1,489 Philadelphia blacks, aged 20-60 (referred to above), the investigators compared the subjects' socioeconomic levels to occupational and income aspirations for self and occupational and educational aspirations for a hypothetical son. In all 4 of the above comparisons they found that the percentage of those aspiring to a high level, (i.e. professional level in occupation, graduate school in education, and high income) increases from the lowest socioeconomic level to the highest level. Conversely, the percentage of those displaying low aspirations (i.e., unskilled or semiskilled level in occupation, only some high school education, and low income) decreases from the lowest to the highest level of socioeconomic status. However, these results remain uninterpretable since no significance tests are reported and, more importantly, neither ability nor achievement was controlled in this set of comparisons.

In their study of a nationally representative sample of 2,500 high school students, Schneider and Lysgaard (1953) are the only investigators who attempted to relate educational and career aspirations to both objectively defined socioeconomic level and the subjects' self-conceptions of their socioeconomic level. Published tables show clear positive trends which are said to be significant for both socioeconomic indicators, but, unfortunately, no attempt was made to control for ability or achievement.

The reader may wonder whether information relevant to the present topic was published by Rosenberg (1965) or by Rosenberg and Simmons (1972) in their reports of their large-scale investigations in New York State and Baltimore City. Unfortunately, although Rosenberg (1965, chap. 12) asked several questions about respondents' ideas concerning an "ideal job," no information is given about the association of the replies with the respondents' socioeconomic levels. However, Simmons and Rosenberg (1971), reporting on the same group of Baltimore subjects as Rosenberg and Simmons (1972), related socioeconomic level to several measures of occupational aspirations in elementary, junior high, and senior high students. Children were classified as being either middle class, i.e., having Hollingshead SES scores of 1-3, or working class, i.e., having scores of 4-5. However, there was no control for achievement or ability in any of their analyses.

b. IDEAL-SELF-CONCEPTIONS OF MISCELLANEOUS PERSONALITY TRAITS

A few publications report findings purportedly relevant to associations between socioeconomic level and ideal-self statements concerning miscellaneous personality traits.

Although it is well known that mean Social Desirability ratings for self-report items are not necessarily indicative of individuals' ideals for self (see Wylie, 1974, pp. 54-55), it is of some oblique relevance to the present topic that Klett's (1957) mean Social Desirability judgments of Edwards Personal Preference Schedule items did not differ as a function of the socioeconomic level of the high school student judges. (The socioeconomic level was inferred from the U.S. Census Bureau classifications of their fathers' occupations.)

In McDonald's (1968) 3-way ANOVA (2 sexes, 4 socioeconomic

levels, 2 races), Ideal Self responses on the Dom dimension of the Interpersonal Check List showed no significant relationship to socioeconomic class, but a significant race × class interaction appeared. Ideal Self responses on the Lov dimension were significantly inversely related to socioeconomic level, but no interactions were significant. Interpretation of these findings remains moot, however, since McDonald performed 8 ANOVAs involving predicted variables which could not have been uncorrelated with each other, and no cross-validational information is available to help us to evaluate the significance of the reported findings.

In Kohn's (1969) and Kohn and Schooler's (1969) study of a national sample of 3,100 men (described more fully above), 12 idiosyncratic questions were included regarding "self values." From the context, I infer that these questions may be considered to have yielded "ideal self" statements. Such self-ideals as interest in why things happen, good sense and judgment, responsibility, self-reliance, and ability to face facts squarely showed positive relationships with socioeconomic class. *Etas* for the values just mentioned were significant, albeit extremely small (.06 to .10). Self-ideals for ability to do many things well and for being successful were inversely related to socioeconomic level (*etas* = .16 and .06, both significant). The authors wish to infer that "conformity is more valued at lower class levels," but they concede that evidence for this comes from only one value scale, respectability, and the trend for respectability across the 5 socioeconomic classes is not entirely consistent (*eta* = .13).

Since the authors obtained two factors from the entire set of value choices, it is evident that each of the above *etas* cannot be considered to be independent of the other when evaluating their significance levels. The two factors (self direction—conformity; and self-direction—competence) yielded significant *etas* of .17 and .14 with socioeconomic class. More psychometric information about the properties of these value scales (ideal self scales) and cross-validation of the factor analysis and the associations of scales/factors with socioeconomic class are needed before psychological interpretations are warranted.

In Rosenberg's (1965) large-scale research described above, some of the high school subjects were presented with an idiosyncratic list of 44 characteristics, and each subject was "instructed to indicate how much he cared about each of them. Through a series of filtering questions, we obtained the nine qualities which were of outstanding importance, and from these nine, the top three" (p. 246). Data analyses were made separately for boys and girls, and somewhat different results were obtained.

Rosenberg tabulated for each of 4 social-class groupings the percents of boys who considered certain traits to be among the top 9 in importance. The following ideal characteristics showed a direct relationship to socioeconomic level: a good student in school; intelligent, a good mind; logical, reasonable type; imaginative and original; well-respected, looked up to by others. The visually apparent trends are strong, and the relationships significant. The following traits showed an inverse relationship to social-class groupings: tough, not afraid to fight; good at fighting or wrestling; good at working with hands. These inverse trends are also visually clear and significant. Obviously, the first 5 traits must be intercorrelated, as must the latter 3. Accordingly, separate significance tests cannot be properly evaluated. In an additional analysis of the boys' data, *rho* was computed between the means of the importance ranks assigned to the 44 characteristics by the upper and lower socioeconomic groups. *Rho* = .71, indicating some lack of correspondence in self ideals between boys in the 2 extreme socioeconomic levels.

In contrast to the results from the boys, "the self-values of girls in the various social classes are strikingly similar. . . . The relationship of social class to self-values attains statistical significance with regard to only one quality ('good students at school'), and even here the relationship is not completely linear" (pp. 260–261). The *rho* across 44 characteristics between means of the importance ranks assigned the characteristics by the upper and lower socioeconomic levels was .91 for the girls, as contrasted to the .71 reported immediately above for the boys. Rosenberg notes that these results may depend in some unknown way upon the particular 44 characteristics he chose for this study, but he also develops a speculative argument that there are real interactions between sex and socioeconomic influences on self-ideals.

Finally, I mention the inconclusive study of A. Soares and L. Soares (1969), who found significantly "higher" Ideal Self among "disadvantaged" students, when an idiosyncratic 20-trait semantic differential instrument was used. Because subjects responded in 5 ways (Self, Ideal, Reflected Self–Classmates, Reflected Self–Teacher, Reflected Self–Parents) and 5 corresponding 3-way ANOVAs were performed (2 school socioeconomic levels, 2 sexes, 5 grades), there is no way of evaluating the significance levels of the findings. Moreover, socioeconomic level is confounded with other school characteristics and with race in the method used to define "disadvantaged" in this study.

All in all, this small group of publications forms an inadequate basis for any conclusions about the relationship of socioeconomic level to ideal self values concerning a variety of personality characteristics. The study by Kohn (1969) and Kohn and Schooler (1969) and the one by Rosenberg (1965) suggest that further search for some such relationships might yield at least weak positive replicable relationships for certain personality variables, and that interactions between sex and socioeconomic level might be found. It is unfortunate that each study reported above used a different instrument to measure the ideal self. The two better-known instruments (EPPS and ICL) are open to serious criticism (see Wylie, 1974, pp. 76–80; 213–223) and not enough information is offered about the idiosyncratic ones.

C. SUMMARY

What emerges from this examination of the relationships between socioeconomic level and self-concept variables?

First, it is clear that research has proceeded without enough systematic analysis or without any resolution of the theoretical and empirical problems of defining and measuring socioeconomic class, and that most of the studies have used idiosyncratic indexes of self-concept variables about which little or no psychometric information is available. This situation, coupled with numerous serious but avoidable method flaws, greatly diminishes the value of the great amount of effort which has been expended by researchers on the topic of socio-economic level and self-concept variables.

Quite a few studies have examined various ways of indexing self-conceptions of socioeconomic level (subjective social class) and their relationships to one another and to objective indices of socioeconomic class. Clearly, objective and subjective measures of socioeconomic status are not identical. Unfortunately, practically none of the research on socioeconomic status and self-concept variables has been directed toward looking for associations between self-conceptions of socio-economic class and other self-concept variables. This sort of work would be especialy relevant to phenomenological theorizing. The development of a sense of socioeconomic-class identity (analogous to the development of racial, gender, or age identity) has yet to be investigated.

Psychologists, sociologists, and educators have unhestitatingly and prematurely assumed that socioeconomic level would be a powerful variable in affecting the self-concept — especially over-all self-regard, but also persons' ideal-self conceptions and actual-self conceptions about their specific personality characteristics. These socioeconomic effects supposedly are mediated via the parents' over-all self-regard, the parents' value systems, and the parents' child-rearing techniques (all of these assumedly being a function of the parents' socioeconomic level) and also by way of the impact of extrafamily influences on the child and the child's development of a sense of his/her socioeconomic level.

However, firm evidence is not at hand that objectively indexed socioeconomic class is strongly associated with parental self-regard, with most parental values for themselves or their children, or with child-rearing practices. Some of the lack of evidence may be due to the use of insensitive or otherwise inappropriate methods.

Perhaps the most striking thing about the research reviewed in this chapter is that 48 studies involving both well-known and idiosyncratic instruments to index over-all self-regard have yielded contradictory, weak, mostly null results regarding the relationship of socioeconomic level and over-all self-regard. Certainly no support is given to the extreme, but typical, views quoted at the outset concerning the unfavorable impact of lower-class status on self-regard.

Studies of specific self-conceptions as a function of socioeconomic level are relatively rare. Only self-concepts of schoolwork ability or "intelligence" have been looked at in an appreciable number of researches, and this is the only kind of specific self-conception which thus far has been shown in the relatively well-controlled studies to be a function of socioeconomic level.

So far as the ideal-self concept is concerned, virtually no researchers have looked at this category of variables in relationship to socioeconomic level. However, some publications concerned with aspirations and self-values may be construed as relevant to the topic. There appears to be a trend for both educational and occupational aspirations to be a positive function of the family socioeconomic level of young persons even when IQ is held constant, as it should be.

One gets the impression that, so far as a wide variety of personality characteristics is concerned, the similarities in ideal-self concepts between socioeconomic levels greatly exceed the differences, but much remains to be done to provide a firm basis for such a statement. There is some suggestion that socioeconomic level may affect boys' ideal-self-conceptions more than it affects ideal-self-conceptions of girls.

If and when socioeconomic differences in self-conceptions or ideal-self-conceptions are found, it is important to look for ways in which these differences are mediated. Rather than being associated with society's differential evaluation or treatment of the different socioeconomic levels, the effects could conceivably be a function of some aspect of family structure which happens to be associated with socioeconomic class, or they may operate only in special situations encountered by one sex or race.

4

Racial/Ethnic Status, Integration/Segregation, and Self-Concept Variables

117

A. General Theoretical and Methodological Considerations

1. Rationale for Possible Associations between Racial/Ethnic Status and Self-Concept Variables

Why is it plausible to hypothesize that various aspects of self-concept such as sense of self-identity, components of ideal self (self values), views of one's particular personality attributes, and over-all self-regard are a function of racial/ethnic differences? If any such functional relationships obtain, may they depend upon the immediate impact of parental values and child-rearing practices, or upon the child's personal experience with significant others outside the home, or both? To what extent, if any, do the hypothesized associations between racial/ethnic status and self-concept depend on the person's having developed a sense of racial/ethnic identity? This section is addressed to a general, hypothetical consideration of such questions. Empirical evidence relevant to some of these questions is given in section B below.

The reader will recognize that these questions exactly parallel those asked at the beginning of the chapter regarding the functional relationships of socioeconomic status and self-concept variables. To a great extent, the assumed answers to the present set of questions are similar. Moreover, some of the alleged influences of racial/ethnic status are parallel precisely because most minority racial/ethnic groups tend to occupy lower socioeconomic levels. Nevertheless, over and above the possible influences of class status, special problems characterize racial/ethnic minorities, especially those who are most denigrated by the dominant culture, and whose physical appearance precludes their moving out of their ascribed racial/ethnic status.

a. Effects Which Depend Mainly or Entirely on Parent-Child Interactions

The reader is referred to the discussion in chapter 3 regarding hypothetical influences on self-concept and ideal self which could come from (a) differing parental values, (b) differing child-rearing techniques, and (c) differing parental self-regard in various socioeconomic groups. As many writers have explicitly assumed, these arguments are plausibly applicable to differently valued racial/ethnic groups as well as to groups of varying *socioeconomic status*.

119

Below I add some theoretical assertions which have been made specifically about racial/ethnic groups, especially black Americans.

The psychiatrist Dai (1953), one of the first to use Sullivanian theory to speculate about self-concept development in blacks, tries roughly to dichotomize obstacles to development of a "secure self system" into those shared by both blacks and whites and those more or less peculiar to black children. The first or basic self-concept development in both blacks and whites supposedly depends on relationships with parents and parent substitutes, and presumably both blacks and whites could encounter both favorable and unfavorable factors in such relationships. However, like many others, Dai attaches special significance for the black children to the facts that they more frequently live in broken and/or mother-dominated homes, which can harm the child's self-esteem or the development of a sense of gender identity and pride therein. Also, Dai asserts that preoccupation with skin color and other racial features (supposedly mediated mostly in the early primary group), and extraordinary stress on social status, presumably also characterize the black more than the white group, with undesirable influences on black self-concept development.

Seward in her book on psychotherapy and culture conflict (1956) states:

> The argument is frequently advanced that it is the child's relationship with the significant adults in the home that is the important thing for his conception of self, rather than cultural factors. There is, of course, no question about the important role played by the individuals around the child, but . . . the [Negro parent's] very capacity for loving has been impaired by the crippling deprivations which he has experienced throughout his own lifetime. Before the child is conscious of being a Negro himself, he is affected by the tensions in his parents over *their* being Negroes. [P. 130]

Rainwater's (1966) view of the family influence on self-concept development in lower-class black ghetto children is even more pessimistic than Seward's.

> It is important to note that, at least in the urban North, the initial development of racial identity in these terms has very little directly to do with relations with whites. A child experiences these identity placements in the context of the family and in the neighborhood peer group. . . . In this way, one of the effects of ghettoization is to mask the ultimate enemy so that the understanding of the fact of victimization by a caste system comes as a late acquisition laid over conceptions of self and of other Negroes derived from intimate, and to the child often traumatic, experience within

the ghetto community. . . . To those living in the heart of a ghetto, black comes to mean not just "stay back" but also membership in a community of persons who think poorly of each other, who attack and manipulate each other, who give each other small comfort in a desperate world. Black comes to stand for a sense of identity as no better than these destructive others. The individual feels he must embrace an unattractive self in order to function at all. [P. 205]

M. L. Kohn (1969) hypothesized that black fathers would value conformity to external standards more than do whites of similar class position.

b. Effects Which May or May Not Depend upon Persons' Having a Sense of Their Own Racial/Ethnic Status

Stereotypes Accepted as Self-Descriptive

Again parallel to the analysis of socioeconomic influences on self-concept variables, I note that it is commonly assumed that stereotypes of racial/ethnic groups are widely held and that these justified or unjustified attributions may be accepted as individually self-descriptive to the extent that the child develops an awareness of the stereotypes and a sense of racial/ethnic identity. If these assumptions are correct, self-concept reports will vary as a function of racial/ethnic status and will correspond more or less accurately to the stereotype about personality characteristics supposedly attributed to members of each racial/ethnic group.

Over-All Self-Regard as a Function of Nonparental Influences

In still another parallel to the theoretical analysis of the influences of socioeconomic status on self-regard, one must consider whether, in addition to possible racial/ethnic influences mediated by parents, there may also be other racial/ethnic factors which might affect over-all self-regard of both children and adults.

As with socioeconomic class, Mead's, Sullivan's, Cooley's, and other reference-group theories have been used to develop alternate arguments, making the following predictions. Compared to the advantaged, white majority group: (a) lower self-regard will be found among blacks (or other disparaged or disadvantaged minorities); (b) about the same level of self-regard will be found among blacks (or other disparaged or disadvantaged minorities); (c) somewhat higher self-regard will be found among blacks (or other disparaged or disadvantaged minorities).

In support of the first prediction, one can argue that, if one's racial or ethnic group is generally held in high (or low) regard, one may (a) be treated with more or less regard by others, and/or have (b) more or less access to financial resources and educational resources with which to develop oneself. Both (a) and (b) could operate on self-regard by way of the adoption of reflected appraisals, as postulated by Mead (1934) and Cooley (1902), for example. Or they could affect self-regard by determining feelings of self-potency which assumedly determine level of self-regard. The opinions of Cartwright (1950), Langner and Michael (1963), McKinley (1964), and Kasl and French (1962), quoted in chater 3 on socioeconomic level, are all in agreement with this argument.

Others extend these assertions more specifically to racial status and the peculiar sources of negative or confused self-conception associated with it. These theorists include social psychologists, educators, and psychiatrists.

Lewin (1948) was one of the first to maintain that self-hatred is one outcome of membership in an underprivileged group, especially one which is "kept together not only by cohesive forces among its members but also by the boundary which the majority erects against the crossing of an individual from the minority to the majority group" (p. 164). Lewin went on to say, "There also seems to exist in every underprivileged group a tendency to accept the values of the more privileged group in a given society" (p. 177), and "frequently it is the more privileged people within the underprivileged group, or those people whose open or secret intent it is to pass the line . . . [who experience] uncertainty, . . . instability, and often self-hate" (pp. 179–180). "One of the better known and most extreme cases of self-hatred can be found among American Negroes" (p. 189).

Note that Lewin remarks not only on the "self-hatred" generated by enforced membership in a group which was derogated and could not satisfy one's needs, but also on the "typically ambivalent attitude on the part of members of an underprivileged group toward their own group" (p. 177) which, presumably, can lead to confusion and ambivalence in self-attitudes.

K. B. Clark (1959) seems essentially to agree with Lewin in that "the cohesion and strength of the sub-culture [may well be] a direct function of the discrepancy between its values and the values of the larger, rejecting culture" (p. 248), but, nevertheless, the Negro is characterized by "self hatred" and by "confusion about self and his group" (p. 248), since he is not successful in rejecting the standards of the dominant culture and evaluating himself according to the standards of the subculture.

Erikson (1966) remarks, "There is ample evidence of 'inferiority' feelings and of morbid self-hate in all minority groups" (p. 155).

Another concurring psychiatric opinion is expressed in Kardiner and Ovesy's (1951) oft-cited book about 25 black case histories, based on psychoanalytic interviews and, in some instances, Rorschach and Thematic Apperception Test (TAT) protocols. Purportedly finding evidence of self-hatred in all 25 cases, Kardiner and Ovesy strongly assert that social discrimination leading to low self-esteem is at the heart of blacks' psychodynamics. (However, when Rohrer and Edmondson [1960] reexamined the case records, they reported finding evidence for self-hatred in only 7 of the 25 case histories, 5 of these from patients in therapy.)

Ausubel (1958) states,

> Being a Negro, however, has many implications for the ego development of young children that are not inherent in lower-class membership. The Negro child inherits an inferior caste status and almost inevitably acquires the negative self-esteem that is the realistic ego reflection of such status. . . . Having no compelling reasons for not accepting this officially sanctioned, negative evaluation of himself, he develops deeply ingrained feelings of inferiority. [P. 364]

Even though documenting the scarcity and methodological inadequacy of the research available at the time of their 1960 review, Dreger and Miller stated, "Differences in self-concepts are marked, however, in that being a white person in a white society appears to mean little in respect to the development of self-concepts, whereas being a Negro in a white society seems to be one of the most important factors in such development" (p. 386). Moreover, they said, "Self-concepts seem to suffer in the Negro subculture in contrast to those of whites" (p. 394).

Even later, in their 1968 review, after commenting on the severe methodological flaws in the research they examined, Dreger and Miller (1968) nevertheless conclude, "Even with the recognition of [methodological] deficiencies, however, there still seems to be little doubt that the American Negro holds relatively negative self-valuations" (p. 33).

K. B. Clark (1963) asserts, "As minority-group children learn the inferior status to which they are assigned and observe that they are usually segregated and isolated from the more privileged members of their society, they react with deep feelings of inferiority and with a sense of personal humiliation. Many of them become confused about their own personal worth" (p. 63). And again, in 1965, he maintains, "By the age of seven most Negro children have accepted the reality that they are, after all, dark skinned. But the stigma remains; they have been forced to recognize themselves as inferior. Few if any Negroes fully lose that sense of shame and self-hatred" (p. 65).

Pettigrew (1964a), in his landmark book, *Profile of the Negro American,* outlines the many assaults on Negro self-identity and self-esteem, concluding:

> For years, Negro Americans have had little else by which to judge themselves than the second-class status assigned them in America . . . many Negroes, consciously or unconsciously, accept in part these assertions of their inferiority. In addition, they accept the American emphases on "status" and "success." But when they employ these standards for judging their own worth, their lowly positions and their relative lack of success lead to further self-disparagement. [P. 9]

In an oft-cited article, Proshansky and Newton (1973) aver, "There are obvious differences in schools, housing, employment, and income; less visible, but equally serious, are the heavy psychological costs of low self-esteem, feeling of helplessness, and basic identity conflict" (p. 176).

But recently, alternate hypothetical arguments have been developed from Meadian, Sullivanian, and more modern reference-group theories. According to these arguments, racial/ethnic status should either be minimally related to over-all self-regard, or perhaps the self-regard of blacks might be expected to exceed that of whites.

While the earlier theories took for granted that the dominant white majority comprised the "significant others" whose values and reflected appraisals determined the self-regard and other aspects of self-concept in racial/ethnic groups, several recent writers have thought this assumption simplistic.

Rosenberg (1973), among others, implicitly argues against Seward (1956) and Rainwater (1966), contending that the parents of black children are highly valued significant others, capable of building strong self-regard in black children in the early years. Moreover, as Baughman and Dahlstrom (1968), Baughman (1971), J. McCarthy and Yancey (1971), Rosenberg (1973), and Yancey, Rigsby, and McCarthy (1972) point out, de facto segregation means that black children do not have much opportunity to compare their family members, neighbors, peers, or selves with the dominant group culture. Therefore, their self-regard is based mainly on feedback from significant others in their own group. Even in adulthood this protective effect of de facto segregation may continue to some extent. Extending this more positive view, Barnes (1972) asserts,

it is possible for a black child to have or develop a positive, actualizing self-concept in this society, under . . . [the] conditions that the black community containing the child and family be characterized by a sense of peoplehood, group identification, or black consciousness, or pride, and that the family be identified with or experience a sense of belonging to the community. It is postulated that when these conditions prevail, the black community, interposed between the family and white community, serves as a filter against the harmful inputs from the latter. In social system terms, the black community either rejects such messages as input or in its transformations of them renders them innocuous. [P. 178]

These authors evidently do not share Rainwater's (1966) view that there is a substantial possibility that a ghetto black child will attend a school "where his Negro teachers either overtly or by implication reinforce his community's negative conceptions of what it means to be black [so that] the child has little opportunity to develop a more realistic image of himself and other Negroes as being damaged by whites and not by themselves" (p. 205).

In fact, J. McCarthy and Yancey (1971) and Yancey, Rigsby, and McCarthy (1972) believe that "lower status blacks are more likely to be members of a distinctive subculture which provides alternative and achievable criteria of success" (p. 345). In this vein, Hannerz (1968) argues that adoption of the label *soul* among lower-class blacks is, in effect, a method for "proclaiming one's own achievements to be the ideals . . . one's own way of life to be superior, . . . [and] reduc[ing] self-doubt by persuading 'soul brothers' that they are successful . . . [and] belong to a select group" (p. 462). According to Hannerz, clear definition of the term *soul* is to be avoided, as admission of the actual nature of the shared experiences underlying it would not produce ethnic pride, nor could one get such a sense of belonging to a group which shares one's views if one looked carefully at the different meanings the term has to different persons.

Also assigning importance to the black reference group, Wolkon (1971) points out that some writers feel the newly emphasized identification of self as African will improve the level of black self-regard, perhaps because it provides a unique source of ethnic pride in the African heritage, or perhaps because rejecting the American identity frees the black from adopting American values and criteria for performance. Contrariwise, such identification of one's self as African may create more of the sort of ambiguity and confusion detrimental to the self-concept to which Lewin (1948) and K. B. Clark (1959) have alluded. Thus, no definite prediction about associations between self-regard and racial status are implied by this line of thinking.

The reference-group situation as W. S. Hall, Cross, and Freedle (1972) have hypothesized it, is complex, involving a transition through four stages. In the so-called *preencounter stage,* "behavior and basic attitudes towards self are determined by the 'oppressor's logic' " (p. 159). Upon entering the *encounter stage,* the black begins to believe, "the world should be interpreted from a black perspective" (p. 159). Carrying this to extremes, he enters the *immersion stage* in which "everything of value must be relevant to blackness"; and, finally, in the *internalization stage,* "the person focuses on things other than himself and his own ethnic or racial group" and "behaves as if he has an inner security and satisfaction with himself" (albeit keeping his strong commitment to his own and other oppressed groups). It is not clear how many blacks are assumed by the authors to pass through these stages; at what ages, or under what conditions transitions would be expected; or what transitional associated variations in self-esteem might be expected. On the whole, however, it appears to me that their argument points toward a favorable level of self-esteem being found among blacks after the preencounter stage.

In a comprehensive overview of the convergences and applications of modern social evaluation theories, Pettigrew (1967) emphasizes that most of these theories assume that persons engage in a certain amount of "choice" of reference persons and reference groups. Thus, these general theories imply what the above-cited authors have asserted, that blacks would not necessarily be expected to adopt white standards and evaluate themselves by these standards, even if there were more in-tergroup contact than is presently the case.

Although, as Pettigrew (1967) points out, we do not as yet know "under what conditions . . . groups and social categories come to be regarded as referent" (p. 252), some of the determining factors may include various kinds of similarities between self and members of the chosen reference group as well as protection of self-esteem and feelings of power by avoiding comparison with groups or individuals who would set unrealistically high standards. As one possible specific example of this, I note Lorenz's (1972) point that the very same ob-jective factors, e.g., residency in a particular housing project, may have different meaning for the self-esteem of blacks and whites, because for the former, this is a step upward with reference to their own group while for the latter it can represent failure compared to what is expected in their group.

A possibility suggested by Heiss and Owens (1972) is that blacks use different reference groups as bases for their reflected self-appraisals according to the specific kind of self-evaluative area involved. For example, they assume that blacks will use the black group as their self-evaluative standard regarding those particular "traits which are (1) of little concern to the whites with whom a black interacts, (2) relatively irrelevant for success in the larger society" [e.g., self-evaluation as a parent or self-evaluation of attractiveness to the opposite sex] (p. 362).

A possible implication of this view is that blacks may protectively experience such traits as more salient for their over-all self-regard than is the case for traits on which they are more or less forced to evalu-ate themselves relative to whites or "the larger society." Favorable evaluations on the more salient traits could counteract, to some degree at least, less favorable standings on the less salient ones. Thus, perhaps hypotheses about racial/ethnic differences in self-evaluations involving the more and less salient classes of traits may be more fruitful than is the traditional hypothesis that black status in a white society affects blacks' over-all self-regard level.

Agreeing with those who question whether blacks typically feel self-hatred as a result of their status, Baughman (1971) raises "the possibility that the black resisted the white's definition of him more effectively than most observers have usually estimated" (p. 41). He also makes an important methodological point relevant to this alleged observational error, namely "the fact that so many blacks learned to *act* subservient or inferior in the presence of whites cannot be taken as conclusive evidence that they actually *felt* this way about themselves" (p. 41).

But even if blacks adopt the goals of the dominant white majority and they recognize that they have fallen short of these adopted standards, they can use various mechanisms to protect their self-regard. One of these, discussed by Baughman (1971), Hannerz (1968), J. McCarthy and Yancey (1971), Pettigrew (1964b), and Yancey, Rigsby, and McCarthy (1972) is "system blame." Another protective mechanism is implied by Lewin (1948) and made more explicit by Noel (1964), namely that group "self-hatred" is not necessarily personal—one may except one's own segment of the group (e.g., lower-class blacks), or perhaps except one's self and a few of one's intimate associates from the devaluated appraisal one agrees is applicable to one's group.

Thus, the upshot of the entire line of argument summarized immediately above is that (a) over-all self-regard could be minimally, if at all, associated with racial/ethnic status; or (b) depending upon selection of reference groups and operation of certain mechanisms such as system blame, the self-regard of blacks could even be higher than that of whites.

In section B, evidence relevant to all these alternate arguments is presented.

2. Methodological Problems in Defining Racial/Ethnic Status

So far as the assignment of persons to black or white categories is concerned, there has apparently been relatively little problem in comparison to that of classifying persons according to their socioeconomic status. Of course the variations in characteristics such as color and hair texture form continua between the so-called black and white groups; so no clear-cut physical dichotomy exists. Accordingly, status as a white or black person is at least partly socially determined or even self determined in borderline cases. In any event, the subjects involved in the black-white research described in this chapter seem to have been relatively easily assigned to one of the two categories.

Deciding how to classify persons as Chicano or Puerto Rican (the two other groups most frequently studied) presents more problems because vague or changeable criteria may be involved (e.g., surname or language spoken at home).

In practice, the most common flaw in defining supposedly racial/ethnic group differences is the confounding of degree of "advantage" or socioeconomic level with the racial/ethnic classification.

A second avoidable method flaw is the formation of black and white groups simply on the basis of knowledge that particular subject pools (e.g., schools) are predominantly black or predominantly white. This practice not only assigns some subjects to inappropriate racial/ethnic categories but it confounds racial/ethnic status of individual subjects with racial/ethnic context, a variable which can be important in determining self-esteem, as Rosenberg (1975) has shown.

3. Methodological Problems in Measuring Self-Concept Variables

I cannot review in detail all the methodological problems and requirements in this area. (See Wylie, 1974.) Instead, I mention here the major criteria used in classifying and evaluating studies reviewed in this chapter.

1. What reliability and validity information is given concerning measures of sense of racial or ethnic identity (i.e., self-concept of racial or ethnic status)?

2. Have the studies of over-all self-regard or of specific aspects of self-concept (e.g., self-concept of schoolwork ability) used some of the better known, more fully explored and developed instruments; or have idiosyncratic measures been used? If the latter, is sufficient information given regarding content, procedure used in collecting the subjects' self-reports, scoring, validity, and reliability to render the findings interpretable?

3. Have uninterpretable discrepancy scores been used?

4. Could purported direct associations between racial/ethnic standing and self-concept scores be plausibly interpreted as the result of the reliability artifact? That is, since children of certain ethnic minority groups such as blacks and Chicanos tend to be poorer readers and are assumed by educators to have less motivation for schoollike tasks, could their responses on self-regard tests be determined more by chance than is the case with children of the white, English-speaking majority group? If so, as I have fully explained elsewhere (Wylie, 1974, pp. 119–121), some self-regard scales will yield "low self-esteem" scores

simply from unreliable responding, not from a valid expression of low self-esteem.

5. Has the possibility of experimenter effect been accounted for or even considered in interpreting the self-concept reports involved in any given study?

Citing an old Negro folksong which says, "Got one mind for white folks to see, 'nother for what I know is me," Pettigrew (1964b) remarks that "the race of the interviewer is a complicating and not as yet understood factor" (p. 7). In a stronger, more tendentious statement, Nobles (1973) argues:

> It is evident that the data collected by these [white] researchers reflects not the reality of African (black) self-conception but rather the research-ers' natural selective (mis)perception of it. We note that the definitional significance of Africa to black self-conception has not been considered, even though Africa has been critically important in the lives of the great majority of black people. It is possible and highly probable that these researchers are unable to take into account the "African reality" of black people living in America. . . . Because of this, not only is the rejection of all previous research called for, but we must also question whether or not the researchers' actual presence in the black community is at all warranted. [Pp. 26–27]

Sattler's (1970, 1973) reviews of the effects of experimenter's race on various subject responses show that there are virtually no studies in-volving subjects' self-concept reports and that the few possibly relevant ones are severely limited methodologically. Some of them suggest that the experimenter's race may be an influential variable in self-concept research, perhaps interacting with the experimenters' sex and with the subjects' sex and race. Pettigrew (1964a), referring to an unpublished study of North Carolina subjects by Price and Searles, says, "When questioned by a Negro rather than by a white interrogator, Negroes mentioned higher educational aspirations for their children" (p. 50).

On the other hand, three self-concept studies not considered by Sattler found no effect of experimenter's race. Baughman (1971) states that Bridgette's unpublished investigation of eleventh-grade rural North Carolina youth yielded no effect of examiner race on Coopersmith's Self-Esteem Inventory scores. However, only one ex-perimenter of each race was used. Rosenberg and Simmons (1972) report no trend for self-esteem scores of secondary-school subjects to vary according to interviewer race or degree of congruity between the race of interviewer and interviewee. Yancey, Rigsby, and McCarthy

(1972) found that race of interviewer was unrelated to Rosenberg's self-esteem scores (RSE) in their black, adult subjects. Nevertheless, these studies were not specifically planned to test for experimenter effects. This fact in combination with Sattler's reviews and the strong a priori arguments for experimenter effects cited above imply that, until more systematic research is at hand to evaluate this methodological factor, one should at least keep it in mind when suggesting alternate interpretations of reported results. Certainly information about the experimenter's race and sex should be routinely published.

4. Methodological Problems in Relating Racial/Ethnic Status to Self-Concept Measures

a. PROBLEMS ASSOCIATED WITH THE SIZE OF N

For two sorts of reasons, the Ns in studies relating racial/ethnic status to self-concept measures should be large: First, any racial or ethnic group is extremely heterogeneous with respect to a number of variables such as family relationships, social class, or academic achievement levels which are themselves conceptually and empirically associated with certain self-concept variables. Accordingly, large Ns might well be necessary to bring out any main racial/ethnic effects with other variables adequately controlled, or to study interaction between one or more of these variables and racial/ethnic status in affecting self-concept reports. Second, only small empirical trends have thus far been obtained between racial/ethnic variables and most self-concept measures; so it appears that statistical significance will be reached only if large Ns are used.

On the other hand, there are dangers in the use of very large Ns, since almost any result, no matter how small in absolute terms, turns out to be statistically significant. In such instances, psychological interpretation must remain moot.

Of course one cannot specify precise boundaries for acceptable sizes of N for all racial/ethnic studies since this depends in part on such considerations as the homogeneity of the groups with respect to nonracial variables which might affect the self-concept, or the purpose of the study (e.g., an item factor analysis of a new, multiitem self-report instrument would require a much larger N than a comparison of two groups of eight-year-olds on an instrument of known high reliability and factorial characteristics). I have therefore used my judgment in evaluating the methodological adequacy of studies on the grounds of number of cases, and I have pointed out cautionary implications of N size where it seemed appropriate to do so in the evaluation of a particular summarized study.

b. Lack of Significance Tests

A number of studies make little or no attempt to present significance tests. While it is admittedly difficult or impossible to evaluate significance levels in large-scale studies involving many measurements, one treads on uncertain grounds in trying to interpret the many "trends" reported and interpreted by authors of such studies.

c. Multiple Significance Tests without Cross-Validation

Unfortunately, many of the studies I examined for possible inclusion in this chapter reported numerous significance tests without regard to how many would be expected to be significant by chance alone when many are made within a single study. This practice becomes particularly troublesome when the variables involved in the multiple significance tests are themselves intercorrelated, and when very large Ns are involved (as is the case with a number of the available survey-type studies).

d. Need to Hold Certain Variables Constant While Looking at Racial/Ethnic Relationships to Self-Concept Variables

IQ and grade-point average (GPA) are known to be associated with racial/ethnic status. IQ and GPA are also known to be associated with self-concept measures, especially self-concept of schoolwork ability, ideals for educational and occupational levels to be achieved, and certain specific self-reported personality characteristics. Also, even if ability per se is not associated with self-regard, there may be an artificial relationship between the two, as explained in section A-3 immediately above. Therefore, if one wishes to conclude that racial/ethnic status is related to self-concept measures, one must hold IQ and GPA constant. More often than not this important precaution has not been taken.

As pointed out earlier, what is needed are multivariate studies which would enable one to separate the effects of race, sex, and socioeconomic level and to look at their interactions.

Empirically, both sex and socioeconomic level interact with racial/ethnic status in determining at least some self-concept reports. Accordingly, these variables must be held constant if an effect is to be attributed to racial/ethnic variation.

As several authors (e.g., Billingsley, 1968; Pettigrew, 1964b) note, controlling for socioeconomic level is extremely difficult to do because the status implications of occupational, residential, and educational components of commonly applied socioeconomic-level indices differ between black and white groups. Billingsley (1968) points out, "To refer to the masses of Negro families as lower class obscures rather than clarifies much of the variety of status and behavior in that group" (p. 123). If one is working only within black groups, an especially appropriate index might be prepared, as Parker and Kleiner (1964, 1966) did. But this would provide no answer to the question as to how to control for socioeconomic level between racial groups. Pettigrew (1964b) and Billingsley (1968) both stress the need to control for subculture as well as social class, e.g., by not assuming that a white northern lower-class group can be compared to a black southern one in order to discover racial differences with socioeconomic level controlled.

Even if there is no completely acceptable solution to the problem of controlling for socioeconomic level in making racial/ethnic comparisons, some attempts to approach this should be made, and all results should be examined skeptically for possible sources of artifact coming from whatever lack of control of socioeconomic levels remains.

I have already pointed out in section A-2 above the importance of controlling for context when varying racial/ethnic status.

B. RESEARCH

Christmas's (1973) review of some of the research on self-concepts of blacks and whites, and Dreger's (1973) review of some studies of temperament in blacks and whites allude to several *Dissertation Abstracts* and unpublished dissertations which I do not include below. The reader may wish to refer to Christmas's and Dreger's bibliographies for these items and to their substantive summaries and evaluations of these research areas.

1. Parental Practices and Values as a Function
of Racial/Ethnic Status

In *Children of Bondage*, A. Davis and Dollard (1940) are concerned with child-rearing and family influences among New Orleans and Natchez, Mississippi, blacks of varying socioeconomic levels; and Rohrer and Edmondson (1960), also working in New Orleans, interviewed 105 Negro women householders of varying socioeconomic levels concerning their practices and values with respect to a hypothetical adopted child. However, neither of these studies afforded any comparisons with white respondents. Both are suggestive of considerable variety among black New Orleanians with respect to parental practices and values, especially as a function of socioeconomic class.

a. CHILD-REARING TECHNIQUES

As pointed out in section A-1, it has been frequently hypothesized that parents from different racial/ethnic groups use different techniques of child rearing which could conceivably lead to personality differences in the children as a function of racial/ethnic classification, which in turn could lead to differences in self-description and self-evaluation as a function of racial/ethnic classification. As is true in the case of socioeconomic class, discussed in chapter 3, my search has not been fruitful for racial/ethnic studies relevant to this hypothesized sequence. In the case of socioeconomic level, a good many studies are available, but they were judged by reviewers to be so flawed or limited as to warrant no firm conclusions about socioeconomic class differences in parental practices, let alone influences of these differences on self-conceptions. There are even fewer studies available concerning racial/ethnic differences in child-rearing practices with socioeconomic level controlled, and, to my knowledge, no studies about associations between such parental differences and children's self-concepts with other variables adequately controlled.

A possibly relevant study is one by Rosen (1959) which is also mentioned in chapter 3 of this book. In this research, interviews with 427 mothers of sons aged 8–14 included 9 items from Winterbottom's scale to index training in independence and mastery. In an ANOVA involving 6 different ethnic groups and 3 categories of socioeconomic level, ethnicity, socioeconomic level, and their interaction were all significant. From inspection of the data, however, it seems clear that the blacks did not significantly differ from whites (i.e., from the remaining 5 ethnic groups combined). Rosen did not purport to look at associations between these reported parental training practices and the children's self-concepts, but it seems intuitively plausible that such differences, where they occur, could be relevant to self-conceptions.

b. FAMILY ORGANIZATION

Most published writings of possible relevance to family influences on racial/ethnic self-concept differences focus on family organization in the black group. Greatest emphasis has been placed on the alleged matriarchal organization of the black family (with its supposedly detrimental influences on self-concept development in boys), the frequency of broken homes and illegitimacy, and the higher incidence of extended as opposed to nuclear family structure. Writers have traced these and other supposed characteristics to various historical and contemporary social influences (see Billingsley, 1968, for example).

However, J. J. Jackson (1973) in her review of research on family organization and ideology concludes:

> Evidence suggests that social class differences (as usually defined), rather than race, influence patterns of dominance in the family. Other variables contributing toward those patterns include employment of wife and sources of power. Variation, perhaps by race, may well exist in spouses' control over decisions made in particular areas. . . . Although some investigators . . . still tend to cling to distinctive subcultures among family patterns of blacks and whites, the studies under review indicate anew the inappropriateness of that concept. Family patterns among blacks do not represent a distinct subculture. There is considerable variation in family patterns among blacks. Within similar socioeconomic positions, blacks and whites tend to resemble each other more so than those of the same race in different socioeconomic positions. However, to reiterate, inasmuch as race is still one of the significant determinants of socioeconomic and social class positions within these United States, it [race] is quite difficult to ferret out in any meaningful comparison concerned with socialization practices related to developing self-concepts and certainly to familial attitudes and behaviors. [P. 438]

Billingsley's (1968) views agree with those of Jackson concerning variations in family patterns and the lack of distinct subcultural family pattern among blacks.

But even if oversimplified statements about black family life are too commonly encountered, it seems to be true that black children, particularly in northern urban ghettos, are more likely to grow up in a broken family than are white children of comparable socioeconomic level (Rosenberg and Simmons, 1972). In their stratified cluster sample of 1,988 school children in Grades 3-12 of Baltimore City, Maryland, they found substantial racial differences on the following family variables, the percent values indicating the association between family variable and race with the relationship standardized on socioeconomic level:

Intact families	59% blacks	73% whites
Divorced families	7% blacks	13% whites
Separated or never-married parents	27% blacks	7% whites
Broken by death	7% blacks	7% whites

A broken family could hypothetically affect a child's self-esteem either by way of intrafamily influences or by way of the child's treatment outside the home. In the latter case, for example, children might feel stigmatized because of their family backgrounds, especially if they are illegitimate and/or deserted children. However, if the separated or never-married category is relatively more common among blacks than whites, two things could happen: (a) black children might encounter less stigmatization than whites would encounter if they come from that type of broken family; (b) black children could realize that their family background was not especially unusual, therefore this aspect of their background would not be especially salient for self-esteem.

Dividing each racial group into those coming from two types of family background (separated or never-married vs. all others), Rosenberg and Simmons (1972) found a substantial association between self-esteem and family background among whites but not among blacks. To support their idea that this finding could be attributed to the fact that black children from separated or never-married parents experience less stigma than do white children from such backgrounds, Rosenberg and Simmons (1972) showed that

> black children from separated or never-married families are virtually no more likely than other black children to say they have often or sometimes been teased about their family; but white children from such families are considerably more likely than other white children to report this type of teasing. [P. 81]

Assuming that white stigmatization of the separated or never-married family is greater than black and that unusualness of this kind of background might be relevant to degree of stigmatization, Rosenberg and Simmons (1972) predicted, "if he were in a white school, the self-esteem of the black child from a separated or never-married family would clearly be affected, but not if he were in a black school" (p. 81).

Supporting this prediction they found,

In the predominantly black schools [where separated or never-married families were very highly represented], . . . it apparently makes no difference to the child's self-esteem whether or not he comes from a separated or never-married family. In the mixed or predominantly white school, on the other hand, a substantial impact is observed: 42 percent of the black children from separated or never-married families have low self-esteem, compared with only 19 percent of the other black children [$p \leq .01$]. [P. 81]

c. PARENTAL VALUES

In a large, complex study more fully described in section B-3-a of chapter 3, M. L. Kohn (1969) looked at fathers' values for their children as a function of socioeconomic level and racial category. Racial analyses were based on a subsample (1,324 whites, 154 blacks) of a larger representative sample of United States males $\geq$ 16 years old and employed in civilian occupations. Socioeconomic level was indexed by Hollingshead's method; a set of 12 "value choices" (standards parents would most like to see embodied in their children's behavior) was factored, yielding two factors: (a) self-direction . . . conformity and (b) self-direction . . . competence. With socioeconomic and religious background controlled (but with none of the other variables held constant in the way in which they were controlled in Kohn's earlier-described analyses of social class), *eta* for race vs. the self-direction . . . conformity factor = .07, $p < .01$. Kohn (1969) concludes,

Assuming our index of class to be roughly comparable [between races], we conclude that black fathers value conformity to external standards more than do whites of similar class position. . . . Nevertheless, the relationship of social class to fathers' valuation of self-direction or conformity is nearly as strong for blacks as for whites.

Thus, the relationships of class and race to fathers' values would appear to be essentially independent and additive. Of the two, class is by far the more important, its correlation with fathers' valuation of self-direction being more than four times as large as that of race. [Pp. 59-60]

One should note not only the small absolute size of *eta* mentioned above, but also the lack of reported association between racial category and the self-direction . . . competence factor.

2. Sense of Identity as a Member of a Racial/Ethnic Group (Self-Concept of Race)

a. ASPECTS OF DEVELOPMENT OF SENSE OF RACIAL IDENTITY

Conceptually, at least, one can distinguish among a number of interrelated aspects of the development of a sense of racial identity: (a) development of racial/ethnic awareness, i.e., that persons in general may be classified according to a cluster of characteristics into groups which are labeled by society with racial/ethnic names; (b) the development of a sense of belonging to a particular racial/ethnic group; (c) the development of an evaluative attitude toward any particular racial/ethnic status, especially one's own; (d) the development of a favorable or unfavorable self-concept based on one's attitude toward one's racial status. Most of the extant writing about these processes has been devoted to the development of black-white differentiations, not to such other possible differentiations as Jewish/non-Jewish, Anglo/Chicano. Accordingly, discussion in this section is restricted to research on the development of black-white differences in regard to the above aspects. Studies concerning other ethnic differentiations are listed at the end.

b. METHODS USED TO STUDY DEVELOPMENT OF RACIAL AWARENESS, ATTITUDES, AND IDENTITY

As was made clear in Pushkin and Veness's (1973) review, few studies are available regarding the development of cognitive awareness of race as a general social category, although many researches which emphasized the emotional attitudes of children toward their race or toward their personal racial status have, of course, implied a development of cognitive awareness of the general category, race, as a basis for the attitudes purportedly revealed.

Although the above aspects are inevitably intertwined in the child's development, it is both desirable and necessary to attempt to tease them apart operationally so that the temporal sequences of each aspect may be studied and the cognitive developments looked at in their own right as well as in respect to their relationships to the evaluative attitudes which become associated with increasing knowledge. Unfortunately, the spate of studies concerned with these aspects have not used methods which enable one to evaluate the separate aspects with any degree of confidence. In other words, assumptions have been made about the interpretability of children's responses which have not been grounded in instruments of sufficient discriminant validity.

The methodological analysis immediately below examines these issues further, and the studies are considered according to their purported emphases and related interpretability of results.

Children's Misidentification or Mismatching of Pictures or Dolls

The earliest investigations (R. Horowitz, 1939; K. B. Clark & M. K. Clark, 1939) used pictures including black and white children and irrelevant objects such as lion, clown, and chicken and asked "Which one is you?" If the number of "correct" choices exceeded chance, one could plausibly infer both general racial cognitive awareness and some degree of a personal sense of racial identity. However, a correct choice per se warrants no particular inference about the chooser's evaluative feelings toward his/her race or own racial identity, although the latter has often been assumed by researchers. Moreover, *in*correct choices are very ambiguous in that they could be attributed to one or more of the following: (a) undeveloped discriminative capacities in general; (b) inability to understand the task; (c) the availability of only two colors (black or white), neither of which resembles the subject; (d) among more intellectually developed children, a recognition that *none* of those pictured *is* the subject (as Goodman, 1946, pointed out); and (e) rejection of one's recognition of racial identity, and/or unwillingness to express one's correct understanding. The latter influence is commonly but gratuitously inferred from "incorrect" choices.

The children's interest and understanding of the task, and their opportunities to make "correct" responses (and hence to increase the validity of their responses as indicators of their cognitive development) would seem to be improved by the following methodological innovations: (a) use of dolls as opposed to pictures (e.g., K. B. Clark & M. K. Clark, 1947; Goodman, 1946, 1964; Gregor & McPherson,

1966; Radke & Trager, 1950; Simon, 1974); (b) use of several shades (e.g., dark, medium, white) as opposed to black and white (e.g., Greenwald & Oppenheim, 1968; Gitter & Satow, 1969; R. J. Simon, 1974); (c) the use of the question form "Which one looks more (most) like you (your brother, etc.)?" as opposed to "Which one *is* you?" (e.g., K. B. Clark & M. K. Clark, 1947; Goodman, 1946).

Also, increasing the number of response opportunities (picture choices or doll choices) should increase the reliability of the choice scores, which, if other aspects of methodology are properly handled, should also increase their validity for inferring the level of the children's cognitive development.

To help in determining the meaning of *in*correct personal racial identification responses, the task should include some items requiring similar kinds of discrimination (e.g., boy-girl; tall child-short child; adult-child). If comparable percentages and developmental trends were obtained from these nonracial choices, the case would be seriously weakened for inferring own-race rejection and self-rejection from incorrect racial identification responses. In other words, the discriminant validity of incorrect personal racial identification choices would be even more questionable than at present. But if the children chose with high accuracy when making other personal identification choices, while making inaccurate racial ones, the case would be a bit stronger for inferring that their incorrect personal racial identification choices may indicate their negative attitudes toward their race and/or toward their own racial self-identities. Also relevant to the interpretation of personal racial misidentifications would be information as to whether the same children who labeled the colored doll not nice, bad color, etc. were the ones who chose the white doll as looking like them.

(Butts [1963] attempted to show that a child's accuracy in choosing a shade to color a picture representing himself was associated with self-esteem level, but his method was too flawed to warrant substantive consideration here.)

Similar problems of discriminant validity also plague other techniques. For example, Landreth and Johnson (1953) used a specially devised matching task in which each picture was of either a dark, medium, or white color; and three possible insets were constructed to complete the picture, the insets being dark, medium, or white. (Only two of the three insets were presented on any one trial.)

The tester said, "Here is a picture of two _____. Which of these (insets) would you like to put in?" Even though a large number of responses were taken from each child and considerable care was used to control for a variety of irrelevant presentation factors, the authors are still left with the question whether at least some of the children's choices had been affected by their assumption that the task was a matching task as opposed to a racial cognition or racial preference task.

As another example, Goodman (1964) used miniature toys and a doll house and looked at the child's mixing of black and white dolls within the house. Again, whereas nonmixing suggests cognitive differentiation according to color, it could imply either (a) the child construed the task as a matching task, (b) he/she had favorable attitudes toward segregation, or hostility toward the other race or toward racial mixing. Conversely, mixing could indicate either (a) a lower level of cognitive discrimination (of racial differences), (b) carelessness in responding, (c) low emotional salience of a well-developed cognitive appreciation of racial differences, (d) a positive attitude toward racial mixing.

The same type of discriminant validity problem occurs in Morland's (1958) study in which, after a picture identification task involving pointing to a white (or colored) person in each of eight photographs, each child was asked, "Are you white or are you colored?" Looking only at the children who had made $\geq$ 94% correct *picture* identifications, he found 99.5% of whites *said* they personally were white whereas only 52% of blacks said they personally were colored. It seems safe to assume that near-perfect picture discrimination out of 16 possibilities indicates a high level of general color awareness in this particular subgroup. But what do the incorrect *personal* identifications of these black children mean? As the author points out, either they have not yet learned their own racial self-identity (perhaps self-identification follows acquisition of general racial differentiation), or they are "identifying themselves with the dominant privileged race." Although the latter interpretation is plausible, the responses do not have the discriminant validity necessary to ensure its correctness.

Incidentally, since Morland used photographs for the first part of his inquiry, one cannot tell what bases were used by children who correctly identified colored and white persons. That is, skin color and physiognomy simultaneously varied. This is in contrast to some studies which used line drawings or dolls varying only the skin color. Gitter and Satow (1969), in a study to be considered again below, varied these attributes independently.

Most investigators have been interested in racial comparisons of development of awareness of racial categories, a sense of racial identity, and associated evaluative attitudes toward one's race and self because of their concern with the unfavorable social conditions experienced by blacks. The reader will have already discerned that interpretations of such racial comparisons are hazardous unless certain variables are controlled. For example, if blacks are less accurate in racial classification of pictures or in choosing stimulus pictures or dolls most like themselves, such a finding per se cannot be used to infer relatively more negative attitudes among blacks toward race or self. This caution follows from a number of considerations: (a) Level of conceptual attainment of any particular kind varies as a function of cognitive development, and unless black and white subjects are equated in the latter respect, nothing specifically relevant to racial concept attainment can be assumed. One reason this variable has been uncontrolled in some studies is that socioeconomic level (associated with ability and achievement scores) has not been equated between groups. (b) It is possible that young black children have had less reason to begin to differentiate between races owing to more extreme segregation or to parental protectiveness and unwillingness to talk about such differentiations.

Children's Evaluations of Dolls and Pictured Situations

Recognizing some of the above points, researchers have invented a number of other ways of trying to infer children's emotional attitudes toward their own race and themselves as members of that racial group. The Clarks (1947) used such methods of asking questions as: give me the doll that you like to play with best, you don't want to play with, is a good doll, is a bad doll, is a nice color, is not a nice color. An essentially similar approach has been used by Aptowitz (in Freyberg & Shapiro, 1966), Greenwald and Oppenheim (1968), Goodman (1964), Simon (1974), and Stevenson and Stewart (1958). So far as I know, there is only one study (Harris & Braun, 1971) which tried to test directly the assumption that expressed preferences for the black doll might indicate the subject's own self-esteem level. In this research involving 60 7-8-year-old black boys and girls, the median Piers-Harris self-esteem score was significantly higher among those expressing preference for the black doll on 3/4 or 4/4 opportunities to choose. The Piers-Harris test was read to the subjects (presumably helping to control for effects of IQ and cognitive level differences), and the tester was black. Although suggestive, these results do not of course, tell us anything refined about the meaning of doll preferences for inferring individuals' self-esteem levels.

Nevertheless, reactions obtained from doll-evaluation or picture-interpretation techniques certainly seem plausibly more valid indicants of racial attitudes than are the misidentification errors discussed earlier. A number of cautions should be noted, however. In some of the earlier studies, black dolls were not available; so white dolls were painted. While literally equating everything except skin color, this approach creates an anomalous doll, one which might correctly be regarded as "strange" by both black and white children. Moreover, limiting choices to black and white as was done in some studies, may present a less appropriate choice for light-skinned black children than when several shades are available, leading to more cross-race choices among black children.

A more psychometrically sophisticated test of children's racial attitudes was developed by J. E. Williams and Roberson (1967). They note that among adults, "semantic differential E [valuative] scores for the word Negro were found to correlate above .80 with scores obtained on Thurstone's scale of attitude toward the Negro [and] the test-retest reliabilities of the measures were .87 in both cases" (p. 672). Accordingly, they decided to use Osgood adjectives to design two sets of materials to assess evaluative "connotative meanings" of the colors, black and white, and the racial categories, Negro and Caucasian. Their aim was to create a children's instrument which would tap the same attitudes as indexed by adult attitude scales and would also provide some psychometric refinements such as presenting a variety of colors, objects, and animals, as "filler items," allowing a larger number of opportunities to associate favorable or unfavorable connotative adjectives with black/white (in set 1 of their materials) or Negro/Caucasian (in set 2). They also wished to be able to compare development of attitudes toward the abstract concepts black and white with those toward pictured members of Negro and Caucasian groups.

Each of 6 pairs of black/white animals in set 1 was shown twice, a different 2- or 3-sentence story was told, and the child was asked, "Which one is _____?" (one of the evaluative adjectives). Interspersed with the black/white pairs, each of 6 pairs of differently colored objects was shown twice and, following a 2- or 3-sentence story, other kinds of questions were asked, e.g., "Which plane would fly the fastest? Which plane got caught up in the tree?" In the second set, 6 pairs of same-race persons of opposite sex were shown twice, and 6 pairs of same-sex persons of Negro and Caucasian race were shown twice, in an interspersed order. Sex-role questions were asked about the same-race pairs while the evaluative-adjective questions were asked about the different-race pairs. The black-white attitude score, the Negro-Caucasian score, and the sex-role score were based on 12 responses each, potentially increasing the reliability above that obtainable from earlier, shorter instruments. Moreover, developmental trends in consistency of black/white connotative meaning could be compared to developmental trends of Negro-Caucasian connotative meaning and sex-role stereotyping. These authors did not purport to index indirectly the respondents' self-evaluations associated with their own racial identities.

Alternate, more elaborate ways of trying to elicit evaluative reactions have involved the use of pictures of social situations about which the child was questioned. For example, Stevenson and Stewart (1958) showed eight cards and asked such questions as: Who was very mean and pushed the little boy down? Who would come to see if he is all right? Who is the bad man? Which little boy will be chosen as a friend to go home from school?

Among other pictures, Radke, Trager, and Davis (1949) used a drawing of a black child on the periphery of a playgroup comprised entirely of white children. The tester asked such questions as: Why isn't he [the peripheral child] playing? Why don't they ask him to play? Is this little boy glad he is colored? Would he sometimes want to be a white boy? Why?

As I said earlier, such queries concerning dolls and pictured social situations plausibly reveal the respondents' emotional evaluations of their racial group better than does the number of correct responses on a racial identification task. However, over and above the great variations in adequacy of design and method among the studies using this approach, one must question the usual assumption that children's responses about "this little boy" reveal the respondents' own respective attitudes toward their racial groups and toward themselves. The problems in this assumption are typically ignored.

First, one should note that cognitive ability will to some extent determine the choices made in this situation. That is, children who do not understand the question or grasp the vocabulary will tend to reply or choose randomly or choose on the basis of variables irrelevant to the intent of the question. Thus, if the black subjects are not at the same cognitive level as the whites, the greater randomness in their choosing could operate to increase the number of choices not representing their feelings. This could lead artifactually to an inconsistency in favoring their own race—an inconsistency greater than that of the whites. Secondly, as said above, the choices or statements made on behalf of the pictured child are assumed to be valid projections of the child's own feelings about self or race. While this assumption could be correct, a large literature on projective techniques casts very serious doubts on such assumptions. Researchers in this particular area evidently have not realized that they must assume the burden of presenting some research support for the construct validity of their projective techniques as indicative of the respondents' own feelings toward race and especially toward self as a member of that race.

To buttress their assumptions that their quantitative data index blacks' rejection of their own race and selves, many authors offer qualitative comments about their respondents' spontaneous remarks, gestures, facial expressions, or voice tones. These observations are certainly suggestive, but they have not been presented systematically enough, within a design which equated racial cognitive levels, to make up for the basic lack of study of the construct validity of their indices.

Other Possible Approaches

What other ways are there, then, to try to study development of individuals' concepts of racial classifications and personal racial identity and the development of attitudes toward various races and their own racial identity? Extensive observations in natural settings, including observing naturally occurring verbalizations, play behaviors, social interactions, reactions to more or less structured situations, and interviews with parents have been attempted with children. The development of this approach is still in the embryonic stage, so far as putting it on a scientific footing is concerned.

In an exploratory study which has not been followed up, Grossack (1956) proposed the use of qualitative coding of older children's and adults' answers to four open-ended questions such as "What does being a Negro mean to you? What are some of the good things about being a

Negro? What are some of the bad things about being a Negro?" (p. 172).

c. RESEARCH RESULTS AND INTERPRETATIONS

Doll and Picture Identification Studies

Regarding misidentification or mismatching scores, the trends in earlier studies were for errors to be a decreasing function of age, to be more common among blacks, and perhaps to be a function of black respondents' skin color. However, for methodological reasons already analyzed in detail, these results are not clearly interpretable with respect to racial awareness or racial self-identification and evaluation. (The preceding statements are based on the following references: K. B. Clark & M. K. Clark, 1939, 1940, 1947; Goodman, 1946; R. Horowitz, 1939; Landreth & Johnson, 1953; Morland, 1958).

More recent publications have, with one exception, yielded no racial differences in misidentification.

Gregor and McPherson (1966) used the Clarks' doll technique to compare 83 white middle-class children and 92 black, lower-class children from segregated schools in the deep South. Testers were of the same race as the respondents, and the subjects (aged 6 and 7) were older than those in most of the racial identification studies. Even though the socioeconomic level was uncontrolled, hence the black sample's cognitive functioning level might have been lower, virtually no errors were made in either group when it came to choosing the white child, the colored child, the Negro child, and the child that "looks like you."

Greenwald and Oppenheim (1968), using the Clarks' technique, but including 3 instead of 2 shades of doll, report either higher white misidentification or no racial difference in misidentification, according to alternate methods of data analysis. Their subjects were 39 black and 36 white children, mostly 4 or 5 years old, in integrated and segregated nursery schools in New York City and New Rochelle (a suburb of New York City). Experimenters were white.

Simon (1974), also using 3 shades of doll and a modification of the Clarks' technique, found no racial differences in misidentification. Her unusual group of subjects, aged 3–8, included 42 whites and 120 blacks adopted by white families, mostly professionals, and 167 white children born to those families.

Sweet and Thornburg (1971) studied 3-, 4-, and 5-year-old nursery-school and kindergarten children from lower and middle-class socioeconomic levels, using a 3 × 4 matrix of colored photographs of 6 males and 6 females, divided into black, white, and Oriental. Having demonstrated first that only 8 of the 120 subjects failed to identify their own pictures from another card, Sweet and Thornburg asked each child to choose from the 12-picture matrix the one that looked most like him or her. This question was repeated to obtain 12 responses or until the child refused to choose. The authors state, "For all ages and both races the selection pattern for responses 1 and 2 [to the 12-picture matrix] was similar in that children identified with pictures of their own sex and race. This tendency was separately significant within each sex and race group" (p. 24). On later responses the children tended to select a picture of their own sex and another race rather than a picture of their own race and the opposite sex. Of course one cannot infer from this whether sex accuracy was more important than race accuracy to the children or whether race awareness was less developed than gender identity among these respondents.

In the only recent publication reporting racial differences in misidentification, Gitter and Satow (1969) varied both color and physiognomy in their racial identification pictures. To do so, they prepared color slides, each picturing 3 dolls. In each slide, either the dolls were identically colored (all white, all medium, all dark) while physiognomy varied among them (one Caucasian, one mulatto, one Negroid); or the dolls had identical physiognomy (all Caucasian, all mulatto, all Negroid) while color varied among the 3 (one white, one medium, one dark). Photographs of the subjects holding the color samples were used to rate the subjects' own colors and physiognomies. Accuracy of identification was judged according to the discrepancy between the child's actual color and the color of his or her chosen doll, and between the child's judged actual physiognomy and the physiognomy of his or her chosen doll. Each child was also asked, "Are you white or are you Negro, colored, or black?" Among the 80 Headstart-program subjects between 4 and 6 years of age, blacks misidentified significantly more frequently on all 3 measures. Although the refinement in stimulus materials is commendable, there is no way to evaluate whether the general cognitive level of the 2 racial samples had been equated. Also, it might appear that medium black, mulatto-physiognomy subjects could err in 2 "nearby" ways, while whites with Caucasian physiognomies would not actually be equidistant from 2 wrong choices, therefore standing a better chance of discriminating (identifying) correctly. In other words, this could make the task intrinsically more difficult for the blacks. Somewhat counteracting this conjecture, Gitter and Satow (1969) report that the darker Negro subjects misidentified more than the lighter ones, on both the color and the physiognomic measures, though not on verbal self-identification.

In summary, failing to support earlier reports of greater racial misidentification among blacks, four out of five recent publications reported no racial differences in misidentification of racial pictures or dolls. Whether this trend toward null findings is a function of methodological refinements, of changing racial awareness or attitudes on the part of blacks, or of some other unknown factor cannot be discerned by a comparative examination of these publications. Still with us is the need for comparisons of this kind of conceptual development with other kinds of conceptual development (e.g., gender identity, age identity), in order to see whether any racial misidentifications are unique to the respondents' concept development regarding race per se.

None of the reported misidentification data warrants any inferences that correct choices indicate positive attitudes and incorrect ones indicate negative attitudes toward a race or one's own racial identity.

Even in the adult mind, the concept of the social classification currently labeled black versus white is a complex notion, with vague and fluctuating boundaries. Naturally, then, one would not expect children to have a clear and complete concept of racial distinctions. Almost all the identification studies dealt with only one attribute of the concept of race — color differences. A few included physiognomic differences as well, but essentially, a thorough analysis of the child's development of the concept of racial classification remains to be made.

Preference and Evaluative Statements about Dolls
and Pictured Situations

As indicated in section B-2-b above, a variety of measures has been used which purport to index blacks' and whites' attitudes toward black and white races. (I consider here the research emphasizing the over-all favorability of attitudes and in section B-3 the question of occurrence, recognition, and acceptance of "stereotypes," i.e., patterns of attributed traits.)

Using 253 black, southern, 4-5-year-olds, K. B. Clark and M. K. Clark (1947) introduced the technique of showing a black and a white doll and asking their respondents "Give me the doll that . . . " (you want to play with best; that is good; that is a nice color). Among the Clarks' subjects, the white doll was preferred for play (67%), considered good looking (59%), and thought to have a nice color (60%). (These children showed 93%/94% accuracy in selecting the doll which looked like a colored/white child.)

In 1961, 20 years after the Clarks' data had been collected, Greenwald and Oppenheim (1968) collected their data from 39 black and 36 white northern 4-5-year-olds, adding a third (mulatto) doll and phrasing the questions "Is there a doll that . . . ?" (you want to play with best, you don't want to play with best, that is good, that is bad, that is a nice color, that is not a nice color). Negative evaluations of the black and mulatto dolls characterized both races, the black subjects' response trends from Greenwald and Oppenheim's work appearing to be essentially similar to those obtained by the Clarks. No significance tests were given by Greenwald and Oppenheim for white versus black evaluative responses of black and mulatto dolls, but to 5 out of 6 questions, the percent of black respondents giving a poor evaluation to the black or mulatto doll was smaller than the percent of whites doing so.

Gregor and McPherson's (1966) 175 6-7-year-olds from segregated schools in a Deep South metropolitan area were shown two dolls about which they were asked: "Show me the doll that . . ." (you would like to play with; you like best; is a nice doll; has a nice color; looks bad). Testers were of the same race as the subjects. The authors state: "Over 79 per cent of the white responses on the four preference requests . . . favored the S's own group. Negro responses favored their own group on the same requests just short of or in excess of 50 per cent" (p. 100). Each of the 4 racial comparisons was significant.

On the fifth request ("Show me the doll that looks bad") . . . approximately 93 per cent of the white Ss chose the brown doll, only one white S refusing to identify either doll as looking "bad." In comparison, only eight Negro Ss chose to identify either doll as "bad," and all the choices were hostile to the ingroup. . . . Eighty-four Negro Ss refused to identify either doll as "bad." [P. 100]

As part of her study mentioned earlier, Simon (1974) asked 42 white and 120 black children adopted by white families and 121 white children born to these families the following: Point to the doll [among 3] that you like to play with the best, is a nice doll, looks bad, is a nice color. Among these children, aged 3–8, she found no racial differences in the number of times the white doll was evaluated favorably.

Goodman (1946) and Radke and Trager (1950) also used a doll technique, although not that of the Clarks.

Goodman (1946) gave her 15 black and 12 white northern children (aged 2-9 to 4-4)

> four different opportunities to indicate their esthetic preference with respect [to color of doll—medium brown vs. white baby doll; dark brown vs. light brown vs. white baby doll; medium brown vs. white young child doll] . . . 70 to 90% of each responding group preferred the white doll. The fraction of Negroes who designated the white doll was as great as the fraction of whites who did so. [P. 627]

No significance tests were reported.

Radke and Trager (1950) asked the questions "Which man (for girls, woman) do you like best? Why?" Among their 5–8-year-old respondents, 57% of the 90 black children chose the black doll and 89% of the 152 white children chose the white doll.

> [The whites'] reasons for preference show feelings of identification with the race of the doll and feelings of prejudice against Negroes. . . . Few [Negro children who choose the black doll] give reasons except to say "He is a Negro" or "a colored man." Those Negro children who prefer the white doll often mention factors of appearance or circumstance which express an under-valuing of their own race. [P. 32]

These data come from the same children about whom Radke, Trager, and Davis wrote in their 1949 publication described in more detail below.

In a doll study too briefly reported to permit evaluation, Aptowitz (in Freyberg & Shapiro, 1966) found "the [80 5–8-year-old] Negro children showed a marked preference for the white doll and a marked degree of rejection of the Negro doll" (p. 107).

Thus, six doll studies, covering black and white boys and girls, aged two years nine months through eight years, from northern and southern locations and from both integrated and segregated schools, yielded trends for devaluation of blacks by both black and white children. In those studies in which two racial groups were used, the blacks' attitudes toward their own group did not appear to be as negative as that of the whites toward the blacks. The exceptional study (reporting no racial difference) involved a very unusual sample of black and white children, all the blacks and some of the whites having been adopted by white parents.

Using their picture-based color meaning and racial attitude scales described earlier in this section, J. E. Williams and Roberson (1967) tested 3 age groups of southern white boys and girls from "better than average" socioeconomic levels. Age ranges were 35-59 months; 60-68 months; 69-81 months. Medium or high consistency was defined as giving between 9 and 12 responses in the same direction (i.e., white is good, black is bad; Caucasian is good, Negro is bad). On the color test, percents of such consistent subjects at successive age levels were 51.3, 81.1, and 89.2, with the difference between 51.3 and 81.1 significant. On the racial attitude test, percents of consistent subjects at successive age groups were 70.2, 91.9, 94.6. The difference between 70.2 and 91.9 was significant. No comparative information from black children was presented in their study, but it appears that before age 7 a great majority of these southern white children showed consistently prowhite (antiblack) and pro-Caucasian (anti-Negro) attitudes. (Only 2 out of 111 children showed a "clear tendency" toward problack and no subject showed a "clear tendency" toward pro-Negro consistency.)

As part of her study mentioned earlier, Simon (1974) used the Williams and Roberson color-attitude test. The 112 black children adopted into white families did not differ on this test from the 189 white children born into or adopted into these same midwestern families. Obviously, Simon's samples were very unusual; so generalization to other samples is not warranted. Of considerable interest are the age trends in the black sample: "Only among the black children did age make a difference in their scores. The older black children were more likely to associate black pictures with positive adjectives and white pictures with negative adjectives than were the younger children" (p. 51). No significance test was given for this comparison.

A different technique was used by Radke, Trager, and Davis (1949) and by Stevenson and Stewart (1958), namely the presentation of picture cards showing social situations. Respondents were asked questions which, it was hoped, would reveal their racial attitudes and, by inference, their attitudes toward themselves as members of a racial group.

Subjects for the Radke, Trager, and Davis (1949) research were 250 children, aged 5–8, in Grades K through 2, from Philadelphia public schools representing various religious, ethnic, and racial groups. All 95 black children were Protestant, but the 155 whites included Jews, Catholics, and Protestants. Although subjects were "mainly of the lower-middle income levels . . . (with) some of them . . . in the low income groups" (p. 335), it was not specified whether black and white groups were comparable regarding socioeconomic level and cognitive abilities.

Pertinent to the racial aspects of their extensive inquiry, their Social Episodes Test included a Negro Barrier picture and a Negro Non-barrier picture, presented to each child in separate interviews about a month apart (presentation order not counterbalanced). The Negro barrier picture showed a drawing of a black child on the periphery of a playgroup comprised entirely of white children. After requesting the child to "Tell me about this picture," and "Tell me about this little boy," the tester went on to inquire "Why isn't he [the peripheral child] playing? Why don't they ask him to play? Is this little boy glad he is colored? Would he sometimes want to be a white boy? Why?" (p. 349). The Racial Nonbarrier picture showed three white children and one black child playing together. Respondents were asked, "Tell me about this picture. These children are all playing together. This little boy is colored. [point] These aren't colored. Is this little boy glad he is colored? Why? Would he sometimes want to be something else? What would he like to be?" (p. 355).

It is noteworthy that, in response to the initial noncommital request to "Tell me about this picture," only 8% and 7% of children spontaneously included race in their descriptions of the two pictures respectively. One has no basis to decide whether this low percentage of spontaneous racial allusions is due to the low salience of the children's racial feelings, their emotional inhibitions against recognizing or accepting the pictured social situation, or their unwillingness to express their feelings to the interviewer.

After the tester raised the questions specifically about race, expressions coded as rejecting and accepting occurred in the following percentages of all children in their responses to the Barrier picture (first-listed percentage) and Nonbarrier picture (second-listed percentage): rejection of black, 51%, 34%; rejection of white 9%, (no opportunity to express acceptance or rejection); acceptance of black, 4%, 8%; acceptance of white, 41%, (no opportunity to express acceptance or rejection). These percentages were not broken down separately by race of respondent. However, race and age breakdowns were provided for the Barrier picture only. "Taking all the associations, judgments, and expressions of attitude which appear in the reactions to the Barrier picture, each child was rated for attitude of acceptance or rejection [by a described procedure]" (p. 373). Successive percents of children listed below are from kindergarten, Grade 1, Grade 2:

Black respondents rejecting whites	26,	21,	20
Black respondents rejecting blacks	17,	30,	17
Black respondents accepting whites	4,	18,	20
Black respondents accepting blacks	35,	3,	5
White respondents rejecting whites	0,	0,	0
White respondents rejecting blacks	63,	72,	67
White respondents accepting whites	39,	72,	45
White respondents accepting blacks	0,	0,	0

Thus, an increase of black acceptance of whites and a decrease in black acceptance of blacks was inferred. No particular trends occurred for whites except an increase in white acceptance between kindergarten and first grade.

Although, as the authors contend, these figures show that, among both white and black children, "there is far more rejection than acceptance of [the] Negro," it seems to me to be noteworthy that black rejection of blacks never exceeded 30 percent, even under the influence of leading questions. Also, these data seem not appropriate to warrant the conclusion that for "a quarter of the Negro children [there is] involved some measure of 'self-hatred'" (p. 374).

In response to the question "Is the little boy glad he is colored?" the percentage of yes responses to Barrier and Nonbarrier pictures were as follows: black respondents—Barrier, 63%; Nonbarrier, 74%; white respondents—Barrier, 24%; Nonbarrier, 32%.

Of course these answers are ambiguous in at least two ways: what the little boy in the picture is said to feel is not necessarily what the black respondents feel about themselves, and reasons for saying the pictured boy isn't glad are not known—specifically, a respondent could be realistically acknowledging the seriously handicapping discrimination experienced by blacks without having a deprecatory attitude toward the black race or himself as a black person.

After the tester introduced the mention of race, the percents of children interpreting the Barrier picture in the following ways were: group excludes him (for racial or unspecified reason) — black respondents, 64%, white respondents, 62%; boy doesn't want to play — black respondents, 39%, white respondents, 23%; game requirements don't allow him to join — black respondents, 22%, white respondents, 17%; is going to play, black respondents, 14%, white respondents, 6%.

Space precludes summarizing here other data analyses and sample quotations from protocol data which give plausibility to the authors' conclusions:

> [Comparing white Jews, white Catholics, white Protestants, and Negro Protestants,] the group receiving the greatest amount of hostility and rejection is Negro. Responses toward Negro correspond to adult culture patterns: (a) segregation of white and Negro ("White and colored can't play together"); (b) racial hostility ("I don't like nigger kids"); and (c) stereotypes of Negro character ("tough," "dirty," "kills whites"). . . . The Negro children have learned the same culture patterns of rejection by the white group and hostility between the races. [P. 437]

However, nothing in their formal presentations and analyses of data can be cited as direct support for their plausible hypotheses "Group membership is one aspect of the self-concept of children" (p. 441); or "Negative self-feelings and personal conflict concerning group-belonging arise frequently in minority children" (p. 442). Detailed qualitative examination of their protocols is apparently their basis for making the transition from their data to their stated opinions about self-concepts. However, for reasons discussed in the general methodological statement at the beginning of this section, and also mentioned in connection with the above presentation of this particular study, the technique used does not yield a sufficient basis for unequivocal interpretations in terms of the respondents' *self-conceptions*.

Working in segregated schools, Stevenson and Stewart (1958) asked 125 whites and 100 blacks between the ages of 3 and 7 to select persons from picture cards in response to questions aimed at discerning the children's accuracy (identifying their own mothers) and their propensity to choose a person of their own race in evaluative situations, namely: Who was mean and pushed the boy down, who would help a boy that had been pushed down, who was the winner of a rope, who was a bad man, who would go home with the child in the story, who would attend a birthday party, who was the child the central figure feared, and which child the black child would choose to pull him in a play situation. No reliability or validity information was given for this idiosyncratic instrument, but proportions of own race choice were tabulated by age and race, with chi square values for overall race differences being compared for answers to each question. At chronological age (CA) 3, the proportions in both races were below chance in the control discrimination task of choosing their own mothers' pictures, and the proportions increased to 1.00 by ages 6 or 7. The tables of proportions of own race choices in the evaluative situations show that, with one exception, there was a significantly higher frequency among blacks of replies supposedly indicative of negative attitudes toward own race. The frequency of discrimination was "rather consistently greater by the white children" (p. 407), a fact the authors speculate may be due to (a) the differing socioeconomic levels (and associated cognitive experience and functioning levels) of the two racial groups; or (b) the lesser experience of whites with opposite-race persons and their pictures, which might sharpen the whites' perception of the object choices as being "different" from each other. Also, as emphasized in the general methodological discussion at the beginning of this section, the respondents' replies to these projective questions were not necessarily indicative of their conceptions of themselves as members of a particular racial group.

Studies Using Multiple Observational Techniques in Natural Settings

From all that has been said above, it is clear that none of the limited types of tests used thus far warrants complex inferences regarding the development of children's "racial awareness" or of their own racial identity, or of evaluations of their feelings about the racial aspects of their own self-conceptions. Thus it would appear plausible that multiple observations in a natural setting might be more scientifically fruitful in revealing valid information on these complex points. I summarize two studies here; one is more rigorous and limited, the other more extensive and varied in its approach, but of unknown scientific quality. The former was directed toward "racial awareness"; the latter to this question and to evaluative reactions to own racial status as well.

The youngest subjects were looked at by H. W. Stevenson and N. G. Stevenson (1960) who chose to study only 5 black and 5 white children by observing them very intensively and systematically throughout their first year in one interracial nursery school. Racial groups were comparable with respect to age (between 2-8 and 3-6 upon entering school); parental educational and occupational levels (said to be "above average"); the specific desire of the parents to have their children in an interracial school; the self-reported lack of parental race prejudice; and the scarcity of children's cross-racial contacts outside the nursery school. The IQ range of the whites slightly exceeded that of the blacks (92-125 vs. 83-113). The policy of the school and the researchers was to avoid all teaching about race. Fourteen individual observations were made on each child in the fall, 6 in the spring. In November and April, mothers were interviewed about a number of matters, including the children's racial awareness. Teachers' day-to-day observations were also considered. Specifically defined behavior units were shown to be highly reliable.

H. W. Stevenson and N. G. Stevenson (1960) say:

> It is of interest that even though the quantitative analysis revealed no differences in the behavior of Negro and white children or in the frequency and types of intraracial and interracial behavior, the observational records contained many examples showing awareness of the physical differences related to race.
>
> The general opinion of the observers and the teacher was that none of the children appeared to show racial awareness either verbally or behaviorally at the beginning of the nursery school year. There were no indications of racial awareness during the first three weeks of nursery school and none were found in the observations after the middle of the nursery school year. [P. 60]
>
> The majority of the Ss showed some indication of racial awareness. Two Negro and three white children verbalized the differences between the two races or categorized people by race, and two Negro and one white child identified some distinguishing features of his own or the other race without noting differences between the races. Only one Negro and one white child gave no indication of racial awareness. [P. 69]

H. W. Stevenson and N. G. Stevenson suggest that the lack of indications of racial awareness during the first several weeks in nursery school might have been due to gradual learning or to the relative unimportance of racial characteristics in comparison with other attributes of the new situation.

Racial awareness did not result in the children's showing negative behavior towards members of the other race. All combinations of awareness and behavior were found. . . . The children did show some concern about their own racial status, as indicated by the questions they asked their parents. In view of this, it seems likely that the discovery of physical differences between the races may disturb the process of self-identification in some children. . . . Perhaps in a less neutral environment for interracial interaction the children's anxiety would have been reflected in more negative interracial behavior. [P. 69]

Goodman (1964), a cultural anthropologist, intensively studied 103 black and white 4-year-olds in 3 interracial nursery-school groups in a northeastern United States city, using many widely varied techniques, including nonparticipant observation, participant observation, reports from teachers, examination of school records, home interviews with parents, and 4 idiosyncratic projective techniques which were supplemented by informal interviewing and individualized probing as judged necessary. The materials and rationale for the projectives are reported in some detail. The data accumulated from all the above sources were finally "ordered on a case basis," following a published outline, and from the total accumulation of case material, Goodman prepared her report.

Although this report is book length, it is informal, discursive, anecdotal, case-oriented, and "deliberately nontechnical," rather than providing the needed information to enable a scientific reader to appraise the adequacy of her methods of data collection and analysis. However, since this study is so often cited and because it represents the most extensive available attack on the problem of developing racial awareness and evaluation in this age group, I give some substantive information about it, despite my severe reservations.

Criteria were set up for low, medium, and high "awareness," using three main headings: perception (noticing), vocabulary (description and labeling), and concepts (ideas and modes of thought). For example, *low awareness* was the label applied when the following features were seen in the case history (as excerpted from table 1, pp. 76-77). *Perception:* erratic interest in and attention to personal color (primarily) or other racial attributes; sees isolated and unique items about individuals. *Vocabulary:* race terms used infrequently and often inaccurately; experimentation in use of [race terms]; some associational terms used (dark, dirty). *Concepts:* little generalization or abstraction; think in terms of the specific and concrete; some idea of color kinds—attempts at classifications in these terms; uncertainty; some differential valuing of race attributes and the people possessing them; [in blacks] some rejection of Negro attributes, focus on and favoring of lightness or whiteness; [in whites] impartial or somewhat favorably oriented toward whites and unfavorably oriented toward blacks—dirty, dark, old, don't like, scared.

According to Goodman's judgments, 15% of blacks and 15% of whites fell in the low awareness category; 45% of blacks and 61% of whites in the medium category; and 40% of blacks and 24% of whites in the high awareness category.

Goodman states (without systematic supporting data) that race differences occurred within each awareness level. For example, when the low-aware black did see a difference, this difference was allegedly important to him, whereas the white's occasional evidences of awareness were said to be "sporadic and off hand." Within the medium awareness level, blacks were seen to be more uneasy the more they knew, with whites' emotions being little involved, although they saw " 'Black people' as a type [as] strange, unlovely and unloved if not actively rejected" (p. 79). At the high awareness level, the keener the blacks' awareness, the greater insecurity they manifested regarding racial status, while the keener the whites' awareness, the greater the security in their own racial status. All these statements must be viewed with strong reservations since no way is afforded the reader to evaluate these data based on the interpretative contribution of the data providers and the author.

In an admittedly "highly inferential" appraisal, Goodman sums up the superiority-inferiority feelings of the children in this way:

> Our white children never indicate a sense of inferiority in relation to browns. . . . About half of our white children give us no reason to suppose that they feel anything more than a passive neutrality. The other half falls close to the superiority end of the scale. . . . Never in our experience do [our Negro children] assume a posture of superiority toward whites. . . . They express neutrality (some 40% of them), but over half of our Negro children convey a sense of inferiority to whites. [P. 86]

In view of this apparently common black acceptance of the inferiority of their group (which, as we have seen, is agreed to by many researchers), it is interesting to note Goodman's opinion, expressed immediately following the above quotation: "In *rare* instances [emphasis added] this kind of acceptance [of black inferiority] leads to a depreciation, not only of the We-group, but even of the self" (p. 86).

In view of the consistent finding that some awareness of racial differences occurs at ages 3, 4, and 5, it is interesting to note Rohrer and Edmonson's (1960) remark that

> none of our New Orleanians remembered being introduced to color at such early ages as Goodman's three-, four-, and five-year olds in Boston. On the other hand, the folkloristic repetition of stories about the segregation "screen" on New Orleans buses has an apocryphal ring that has led us to the seriously intended psychiatric pun that these are largely screen memories. We conclude that in New Orleans, as in Boston, Negro children experience color awareness much earlier than they will as adults be able to (or care to) recall. [P. 77]

The adults to whom the quotation refers were 47 of the persons originally studied by A. Davis and Dollard (1940) in 1937–38 and restudied in 1953–56 by Rohrer and Edmonson.

Miscellaneous Studies of Possible Oblique Relevance

Dennis (1968) reports a comparison between the figure drawings of 80 black introductory psychology students at Howard University in 1957 and 88 black introductory psychology students at the same university in 1967. According to independent confirmations by psychologists naïve as to the purpose of the study, none of the 1957 drawings but 18% of the 1967 drawings represented black persons.

As part of a regular science lesson, and without the pupils' awareness that a skin-color preference test was involved, 74 blacks and 45 whites in Grades 3, 4, 5 of a nonsegregated Detroit elementary school were asked to color two human figures. Seventy-two percent of the blacks colored both figures brown, whereas 75% of the whites colored both figures white (Ogletree, 1969). The author contrasts these findings with those he attributed to the Clarks, namely that 52% of black children refused to color figures either brown or black in a study done "20 or 30 years ago."

Both authors wish to infer an improvement in blacks' attitudes toward their own racial characteristics. The data are congruent with such an assumption, but various factors preclude a firm agreement with their inference.

Palmer and Masling (1969) thought that the black group's greater cultural preoccupation with skin color as a correlate of social superiority should show itself in larger skin-color vocabularies among black than among white children when describing a series of pictures of black and white baseball players. However, the blacks used smaller vocabularies to describe a series of blue paint samples as well as skin color, perhaps because IQ and verbal facility were not controlled between racial groups. In any event, Palmer and Masling tried to compensate for this by creating discrepancy scores for each subject. Unfortunately, this approach yields uninterpretable values, as explained in Wylie (1974, pp. 88-94). Also, the order of task presentation was not controlled since the skin-color judgments were always made first, as the authors pointed out. Owing to these methodological problems, no conclusions about their original proposition can be made from their data.

Over-all Summary of Research Results and Interpretations

Although the following are intertwined, it is clear that we must conceptually differentiate among development of: (a) the general concept of race as a category; (b) more sophisticated knowledge about such a category; (c) evaluative attitudes toward racial groups, one's own and others'; (d) a cognitive sense of one's own racial identity; (e) an evaluation of oneself, as this is dependent on one's sense of racial identity. Often, the studies I have described have not used methods which enable one to infer the aspect(s) which their authors purported to be indexing.

In general, some notion of racial differentiation (between black and white) seems to begin to appear before the third birthday, with classification of clear-cut exemplars and self-classification by doll identification or verbal self-labeling being virtually errorless by age seven. Recent evidence suggests no racial difference in this sort of conceptual development, especially if socioeconomic level and general cognitive developmental level are taken into account.

Both blacks and whites tend to express rejecting attitudes more toward the black group, but the percent of white respondents expressing rejection of the black group exceeds that of the blacks who express rejection of the black group (such rejection being evidenced by 25% or fewer black subjects in some studies). It is also important to note that expressions of rejection of one's own group, even though they may be supplemented by expressions of awareness of the derogatory stereotypes directed toward one's group by the outgroup, were not shown to be methodologically adequate bases for inferring self-rejection. The common misinterpretation of these data may have been one reason why so many authors have mistakenly taken for granted that blacks' self-esteem must be inferior to that of whites (see section B-4 below).

Studies Involving Groups Other than Black and White

The following authors have looked at some aspect of racial awareness or identity in groups other than American black and white subjects. Morland (1972), American whites and blacks, and Hong Kong Chinese; Simon (1974), American whites and blacks, and American Indians; Springer (1950), Chinese, Japanese, Korean, Caucasian-Oriental, Hawaiian-Oriental, Caucasian, Filipino, and Hawaiian-Caucasian, all from Hawaii.

3. Stereotypes about Specific Personality Characteristics of Racial/Ethnic Groups

a. THEORETICAL ASSOCIATIONS BETWEEN STEREOTYPES AND SELF-CONCEPTS

The question of over-all favorability of attitudes of the black and white groups toward each others' groups, the degree of cognitive recognition of these attitudes directed toward one's own group, the acceptance of their validity for one's own group, and over-all self-regard, as it is presumably related to these attitudes toward one's group, were considered in the immediately preceding section. Here I turn to a closely related set of questions emphasizing the occurrence of attribution of specific trait patterns to a specified group, the acceptance of the validity of such attributes, and the correspondence, if any, between such "stereotyped" patterns and the pattern of traits attributed to oneself, i.e., one's self-conception along these particular dimensions.

Brigham (1971) has shown that, almost 50 years after Lippman coined the word stereotype, there is no consensus about the conceptual meaning of the term. He proposed the following definition: *"An ethnic stereotype is a generalization made about an ethnic group, concerning a trait attribution, which is considered to be unjustified by an observer"* (p. 31). Presumably "an observer" is usually a qualified psychologist or sociologist. If one accepts Brigham's definition, there is no research which operationalizes it (especially its unjustifiability restriction), let alone relates self-concept indices to stereotypes in Brigham's sense. Nevertheless, I report here some studies which use a variety of less explicitly rationalized definitions of the concept "stereotype," mostly involving the generalization aspect of Brigham's definition. Most of these studies follow the so-called Katz-Braly paradigm in which respondents are provided with a list of words or statements and asked to choose a limited number which they believe to be especially characteristic of a designated group. Stereotyped traits are usually defined as those attributed to the group by some arbitrarily large proportion of respondents.

Our main interest is to see if this research throws any light on the following questions: Are stereotypes of any ethnic group held by nonmembers and/or members of this group? If so, are the members' and nonmembers' stereotypes similar? To the extent that stereotypes occur, a basis is provided for the group members' self-concepts to be affected by their acceptance of the validity of the stereotypes of the *group*. Thus we come to the second question—do the self-concepts of individual members of the group correspond to stereotypes about their group?

If there were a correspondence between a stereotype and group members' self-descriptions (called vereotypes by Abate & Berrien, 1967), such evidence would suggest that stereotyping may be a factor in influencing the development of self-concepts in one or both of two ways: Perhaps the group members accept the stereotypes and develop these characteristics as a result of believing the stereotypes, or perhaps they *believe* and report that they have individually developed these characteristics, whether or not an objective observer would agree that they had.

But of course one can make an alternate interpretation of stereotype-vereotype correspondence, namely that the coincidence occurs because each is factually descriptive of group members' characteristics which were developed independently of stereotype influence. This is a possible interpretation since the typical operational definition of stereotype does not restrict itself to "false" descriptions as Brigham's proposed definition would demand.

b. ACCEPTANCE OF GROUP APPLICABILITY OF TRAITS
ATTRIBUTED TO ONE'S GROUP

Research on stereotypes of blacks and whites has had a long history, and some indications of the occurrence of stereotypes have been reported. Summing up earlier work, Brigham (1971) states:

> Stereotypes of Negroes as assessed by the Katz and Braly paradigm have tended to be rather definite and quite negative. Such traits as superstitious, lazy, dirty, and ignorant usually have headed the list in frequency of attribution. Recent psychological research and public opinion polling results indicate that although the United States white's view of Negroes may be becoming somewhat less negative, it is still radically different from his view of white Americans. [P. 20]

But this does not give us direct evidence that blacks share the whites' stereotypes. Brigham cites an early study by Bayton in which black college students assigned some of the above traits to "the Negro," but assigned quite different, more favorable traits to the typical student at their black college. This suggests several possibilities: (a) at that time (1941), black college students shared some of the white college students' stereotypes about blacks "in general"; (b) blacks were discriminating among members of their group, perhaps along lines of education and/or friendship, so that it would be oversimplified to assume that blacks hold only one stereotype of the black group.

Pursuing the idea that more than one stereotype of a racial group may exist, Bayton, McAlister, and Hamer (1956) proposed (a) that both black and white respondents' stereotypes of both black and white target groups may be determined more by the target groups' socioeconomic level than by their race; and (b) most whites simply assume that instructions to identify characteristic traits of blacks means to describe lower-class blacks, because so many blacks are categorized in the lower socioeconomic levels. Their study was aimed not only at exploring this point; it is also one of the few researches which attempted to make direct comparisons between black and white stereotypes of black and white persons. Unfortunately, no exact information is published about the instructions given to the respondents, the definitions of upper class and lower class which they were supposed to use as a basis for responding, the list of 85 adjectives from which they could choose, or statistical significance tests (if any were made). Moreover, the order in which respondents characterized upper-class whites, upper-class blacks, lower-class whites, and lower-class blacks was not counterbalanced. Thus, inspection of the lists of most frequently chosen adjectives is only suggestive, and, of course, the list represented opinions of a relatively small group of college students, not a representative sample of black and white Americans. Nevertheless, it is interesting and suggestive that there appeared to be some agreement between black and white respondents regarding the characteristics of each of the four groups. For example, among blacks and whites, the following adjectives were among the 10 most frequently chosen to characterize upper-class blacks: intelligent, ambitious, progressive, industrious, neat. Similarly, there appears to be more coincidence between stereotypes of blacks and whites *within a class* than between attributions to upper and lower class whites or between attributions to upper and lower class blacks. For example, the following adjectives were among the 10 most frequently chosen by both whites and blacks to describe both white and black upper-class groups: intelligent, ambitious, industrious, neat, progressive. The following adjectives were among the most frequently chosen by both blacks and whites to describe both black and white lower-class groups: ignorant, lazy, loud, physically dirty.

Another interesting point in these data is that even the 10 adjectives chosen most frequently from the given list of 85 were relatively infrequently picked. The range of percents of respondents choosing any one of these top 10 adjectives ranged from 66 down to 13, and only 6 of the top 80 choices (10 top-chosen adjectives × 4 target groups × 2 racial-respondent groups) were chosen by ≥ 50% of the respondents. Thus one can scarcely say that a great deal of consensus of any kind was evidenced.

Bayton and his colleagues attempted to look into other variables which might affect blacks' perception of personality traits, namely how the sex of the black respondent and the sex of the assessed group affect trait attributions to blacks and whites (Bayton, Austin, & Burke, 1965) and how the sex and skin color of the respondents and skin-color of the assessed black groups would affect the choice of attributed traits (Bayton & Muldrow, 1968). In both of these studies, however, respondents were instructed to guess how the average target group member would describe himself/herself. Thus, the results cannot tell us what traits the respondents thought actually characterized the target groups they were describing.

A report by J. D. Campbell, L. J. Yarrow, and M. R. Yarrow (1958) and L. J. Yarrow, J. D. Campbell, and M. R. Yarrow (1958) is suggestive of another determinant of trait attribution, namely the segregation/integration of children's group activities. This study was made in a setting ideally adapted to examining an additional question I raised earlier—to what degree do "actual behavior" and attributed behavior correspond? These investigators applied various observational techniques to low socioeconomic-level black and white children occupying segregated or integrated camping cabins for a 2-week period. From about 1,100 8-12-year-old children, 8 cabins of 6-10 children each were chosen for intensive study in each of 5 2-week periods, i.e., apparently about 360 to 400 children were intensively studied. Each such child was interviewed on the first or second day and asked to choose and describe the camp peer he/she knew best and then to respond to a "guess who" technique involving behavior dimensions not fully specified in the published article. At the end of the camping period, "essentially the same interview" was given. At the beginning and end of each session, counselors rated children in their cabins, using behavior variables parallel to those of the "guess who" technique. Undescribed time-sampling observational techniques were applied by the 10 members of the research staff to some of the children.

Insufficient information is given about the exact content and format of the instruments and observational techniques used in this study, and nothing is reported about the psychometric properties of the resulting scores or ratings. Likewise, the published report is quite incomplete concerning the modes of analysis of the mass of data which must have been accumulated, and quantitative outcomes are also incompletely reported, with no significance tests given in the published article. Thus it is not possible to make an adequate independent assessment of their methods and the implications thereof for possible alternate interpretations of their results.

The authors present the following verbal summary which appears to be justified so far as one can determine from the limited amount of technical information provided.

> The behavior of Negro and white boys in segregation is impressively similar, as is the behavior of Negro and white girls. We can assume, therefore, that the Negro and white children in this sample came into the desegregated cabins with similar culture patterns of peer behavior. The matched social class background of the Negro and white children of this sample may contribute significantly to this similarity (p. 17). . . . The [free

descriptions of peers and responses made to "guess who" questions about peers] were analyzed with reference to the race of the perceiver and the perceived child. Few descriptions, as gestalts, are dominated by racial stereotypes. This is in contrast to the many findings from attitude studies based on questions about race in the abstract (such as, what are Negroes [whites] like?). It would appear that face-to-face contact and attention to the individual of the other race decrease the potency or permissibility of verbalized stereotypic generalizations. The descriptive categories for peers of own and other race are remarkably comparable in aspects of sociability, conformity, and affiliation. We know from the behavior that white and Negro children are providing highly similar behavioral stimuli. This similarity is not distorted in perceptions of one another. [P. 23]

Although the above quotation makes it appear that their data give no support to stereotyped descriptions of either racial group by either racial group of child observers, the authors feel that some of the results evidenced "indirect effects of racial stereotyping."

Thus, for white children, comments on aggressive characteristics rise from 15 per cent in segregated groups to 53 per cent in desegregated settings when the object of description is a Negro child. Their reports on aggression in other white children (17 per cent) do not increase in desegregation. . . . [Negro children's] reports on aggressive behaviors of Negro peers are 29 per cent in segregation, 48 per cent in desegregation. Alertness to the same dimensions in their white peers occurs in 33 per cent of the cases. . . . The screen of racial stereotypes or stereotyped expectations may account for these emphases, for the behavior of Negro children and white children is not sufficiently different to account for these differences in perceptions. [P. 25]

Although the above-cited study offers no firm support for overt racial stereotyping in 8–12-year-old children from low socioeconomic levels, Radke, Sutherland, and Rosenberg (1950) report evidence of stereotyping in essentially the same age group (7–13) in 475 black and 48 white children in the predominantly black Hill District of Pittsburgh, Pennsylvania. Twenty-four personality-descriptive statements published in the article were read to the children as they viewed specially prepared photographs of black and white children. Thirty-two photographs (8 black males, 8 black females, 8 white males, 8 white females) were assorted into 4 slides of 8 pictures each (these 8 being equally divided among 2 races and 2 sexes). The four different slides were presented in the order 1, 2, 3, 4, 1, 2, . . . etc., so that each slide was eventually used for 6 statements. From whatever slide was on the screen at the moment when a statement was read, the respondents indicated which pictured child they supposed the statement described. The frequency with which each of the statements was assigned to one race by more than 70% of the children of either race was determined. At least 55% of blacks and at least 74% of whites assigned the following characteristics to whites: always neat and clean; never swears or uses bad words; smartest in the school; always fair and waits his [sic] turn; returned a lost purse; does not tell lies; very nice and kind. At least 68% of blacks and 72% of whites assigned the following characteristics to blacks: started a fight; always comes to school dirty. (No information is given about the remaining statements.) It is descriptively clear that 7 favorable characteristics were attributed to whites by both races and 2 unfavorable ones to blacks by both races. However, for each of the 9 statements, the percent of blacks attributing the favorable pole to blacks exceeds the percent of whites attributing the favorable pole to blacks. No significance test results are given. (Parenthetically, I note that it is possible that this tendency of black choices to approach 50-50 could plausibly be attributed to the reliability artifact, if one assumes that the black children were behaving more randomly since they were less able to follow the directions about choosing and writing down. the letter belonging to the picture of their choice. But, from the information given, it is impossible to evaluate the merits of this proposed alternate interpretation.)

Over-all, the descriptive evidence suggests some interracial agreement on stereotyping of each racial group, and the attributions of both blacks and whites are more favorable to whites.

The reader will remember that L. J. Yarrow, J. D. Campbell, and M. R. Yarrow (1958) found no direct evidence of stereotyping when children were rating black and white fellow campers, and they contrasted this with the common finding that stereotyping occurs "in the abstract." It seems that the Radke et al. study exemplifies such stereotyping in the abstract among children of this age and socioeconomic level. Interestingly enough, on a sociometric test, 76% of Radke et al.'s younger white children's in-class friendship choices were black and 47% of the older white children's in-class friendship choices were black. The black children showed 89% to 95% black in-class friendship choices. Thus, unfavorability toward blacks manifested itself more in the abstract situation than in real-situation friendship choices.

The most recent study to compare black and white trait attributions to both black and white groups dealt with 501 white and 315 black students in Grades 4-12 in each of 2 predominantly segregated, private, university-affiliated schools in the Deep South (Brigham, 1974). On the basis of cited previous research, 50 traits were selected as especially relevant to stereotypes about blacks and whites. Anonymously, and under the direction of a same-race tester, each student rated each trait as more characteristic of the Negro (scored 3), no difference (2), more characteristic of the white (1), or don't know. Two tables reporting only data from Grades 4-5 and 11-12 show the 5 traits most commonly attributed by each group to each group, i.e., the 5 traits with means nearest 3.0 (Negro) or 1.0 (white). Considering only these traits, in Grades 4-5 there was no overlap between white and black attributions to whites, and one common trait between white and black attributions to blacks (athletic). In Grades 11-12, there was no overlap between white and black attributions to whites, and 2 out of 5 overlapping traits between white and black attributions to blacks (good dancer, sense of rhythm). Going beyond the top 5 attributions to each race, Brigham says:

> Both black and white children attributed 10 traits more to blacks than to whites for at least 7 of the 9 grade levels. These traits were: able to do hard work, athletic, easy to make angry, fond of music, loud, musical, quick-tempered, revengeful, sense of rhythm, and wears flashy clothes. Perhaps due to the particular sample of traits used, there was much less agreement on attributions to whites—selfish and cruel were the only traits attributed more to whites than to blacks by at least 7 of the 9 grade levels in both samples. [Pp. 151-152]

About 10 months later, likeability ratings for each trait were obtained from samples of the same groups, the rating instructions making no reference to the race of the hypothetical person characterized by the trait. Across 50 traits, the mean likeability ratings made by the two racial groups correlated strongly (median $r = .935$). Within each grade and race, mean likeability ratings were then correlated with "direction of attribution" to one's own race (using the original Ns). Here the mean r was .54 for blacks and .38 for whites, showing a significantly stronger tendency for blacks than for whites to attribute likeable traits to their own race. These rs were doubtless affected in part by the much greater tendency of whites to use the "no difference" response in the trait attribution task. Numerous additional analyses are presented, and the results need cross validation since many significance tests on overlapping data analyses are given.

Direct comparisons of the last two studies are, of course, impossible since they differed with respect to year of data collection, racial school context, southern as opposed to northern subculture, techniques of data collection and analysis, characteristics from which the student could choose to make attributions to members of the two groups, and presumably with respect to socioeconomic level, since the Brigham study was done in private schools. About all one can say is that, in both groups, blacks appeared to resist attributing unfavorable attributes to their own race, with the tendency toward own-group favorability being much stronger in the Brigham study.

From a completely different culture comes some suggestive evidence that stereotypes of a derogated group are not necessarily accepted by that group. With university students as subjects, Morsbach (1972) used a 20-trait semantic differential technique to obtain descriptions of the six major "white" and "non-white" groups in South Africa. On 10 to 14 different traits, the Indians evaluated their own group more favorably than their group was evaluated by Afrikaans, English, Jewish, Coloured, or Africans. Morsbach (1972) points out that

> in spite of the general wariness shown towards "the Indians" by the other groups tested, the Indian Ss do not seem to have developed a self-hatred, as is evidenced by their high self-evaluation. Quite to the contrary: they show a very positive autostereotype, not matched by any stereotype the other groups have of them. [P. 166]

c. Stereotypes and Self-Concepts

Although there is some evidence that groups may stereotype themselves as others stereotype them, no study I have mentioned thus far has tried to relate stereotypes to self-descriptions, an important point for a self-concept theorist. To my knowledge, the only attempt to do this has been made by Abate and Berrien (1967) who used an idiosyncratic set of 15 descriptions of Edwards Personal Preference Schedule variables. Subjects sorted these descriptions into piles, each pile to contain a restricted number of statements. Male and female students in Japan and the United States used this method to describe Americans in general and Japanese in general. Mean ratings of the 15 descriptions from the stereotyping assessment form were converted into ranks. For describing themselves, students used the Edwards Personal

Preference Schedule itself, and mean scores on the 15 variables were converted into ranks. Rank order correlations are presented between the stereotypes of each group by itself and by the other group. They are: for American males, .82; for American females, .81; for Japanese males, .56 (not significant); for Japanese females, .89. Thus, some agreement is manifested between Japanese and American stereotypes of Americans and between Japanese and American stereotypes of Japanese. However, one sees little agreement between mean ranks of self-descriptions (called vereotypes by Abate and Berrien) and stereotypes of one's group by one's own group members. The rank order correlations are: for American males, .64 ($p < .05$); for American females, .40 (n.s.); for Japanese males, -.01; and for Japanese females, .10.

Unfortunately, the lack of correspondence between vereotype and stereotype is somewhat ambiguous in that the vereotype came from the EPPS scores themselves whereas the stereotypes came from sorts of the 15 summaries of EPPS variables. Had the correlations been high, something definite could be said. However, one cannot confidently say that these data show that subjects do not see themselves as embodying the stereotypical attribute patterns.

Another interpretive problem is seen when one looks at these low vereotype-stereotype correlations from another angle. It is known that the EPPS yields a range of scores on each variable (i.e., discriminates among individuals) and that the forced choice procedure used in the test means that this range of scores among individuals depends on each subject's having, in effect, rank ordered the traits as they apply to himself/herself. This being the case, a rank order of mean rank orders should yield a set of data which quite probably is comprised of steps that do not differ very reliably from one another. If this argument is correct, low correlations between vereotype ranks and any other variable (in this case, stereotype ranks) would be expected.

In short, this study attacked an important problem and showed considerable intergroup agreement about stereotypes, but the method used does not enable us to get very far in answering the question whether individuals find group stereotypes descriptive of themselves as individuals.

d. Summary

The word *stereotype* has never been adequately defined, either conceptually or operationally, and research on racial/ethnic "stereotypes" has actually looked at specified amounts of agreement among specified groups of evaluators in their attributions of traits to "members of group X." The entire collection of above-cited studies gave no direct support to the "obvious" proposition that blacks' and whites' self-concepts are associated with different agreed-upon patterns of trait attributions which each group agrees to be respectively valid for its own group. First, these researches have failed to turn up impressive evidence that blacks and whites agree on a distinctive pattern of trait attributions respectively applicable to each group. Secondly, although blacks may have given some evidence, especially in earlier studies, of accepting certain unfavorable trait attributions as applicable to their group, the evidence favors their resistance to accepting the validity of these attributes for "blacks in general." In fact, recent evidence suggests a greater group-favorability bias in blacks' attributions to blacks in general than in whites' attributions to whites in general.

In any event, no one has yet adequately approached directly the key question for self-concept theorists — to what extent do self-concepts of individual group members correspond to what they (or others) agree to be "group characteristics"? To the extent that one might want to hazard an indirect approach by comparing the results of stereotype studies and the results of studies of specific aspects of self-concept (see section B-6), the characteristics which were reported in the present section as possibly stereotypic of blacks do not appear to correspond to traits which blacks are more apt to endorse as self-descriptive. This statement must be made with extreme caution and skepticism, however, since there are not adequate methodological grounds for trying to examine in this indirect way the possible correspondences between stereotypic and self-concept descriptions.

4. Over-all Self-Regard as a Function of Racial/Ethnic Status

As already shown in section A above, one can develop a priori arguments that the variations in social favorability accorded varying racial/ethnic groups are positively related, negatively related, or unrelated to the average self-regard of the racial/ethnic group members. I turn now to the research relevant to such arguments.

Because reliability, validity, and other psychometric characteristics of self-regard instruments are so important in interpreting reported results, I present the studies below in two categories: those using relatively well-known and psychometrically explored instruments and those using idiosyncratic instruments, the characteristics of which are relatively less well known and often are not given in a published source.

a. Self-Regard Indexed by Relatively Well-Known Instruments

Because the Rosenberg Self-Esteem Scale and the Coopersmith Self-Esteem Inventory are by far the most frequently used in the racial/ethnic studies I examined, results involving these instruments are presented first. Within each group of reports, studies are presented according to increasing ages of the subjects used.

As usual, many of the investigations are characterized by serious methodological limitations or flaws. Those judged to be so badly flawed as to be uninterpretable are simply listed in the appropriate section.

Coopersmith's Self-Esteem Inventory (SEI)

J. H. Williams's (1973) study of 133 Hispano and Anglo first-graders applied a multiple-regression technique which used among its predictors an idiosyncratic, orally administered form of the SEI for which some reliability information is given. Although Hispano subjects had lower mean IQ and Reading Readiness scores, zero-order rs between each of these variables and self-esteem scores were "essentially zero." It is not clear that socioeconomic level or school context were controlled when making ethnic comparisons. Many zero-order rs involving SEI scores were computed, and the correlation with ethnicity was "essentially zero."

In two different references (Zirkel & Moses, 1971; Moses, Zirkel, & Greene, 1973) identical analyses of SEI scores are reported for exactly the same subjects: 120 fifth- and sixth-graders from 3 schools in a large Connecticut city. Within each school, 20 children represented the majority group (black, white, or Puerto Rican in each school, respectively), whereas in each school, 10 children represented each of the other 2 (minority) groups at that school. All children were classified as 6 or 7 on Warner's socioeconomic level, and groups were matched with respect to IQ. SEI items were projected on a screen and coordinated with a tape-recorded oral presentation, with both English and Spanish versions being presented. An ethnically mixed group of examiners was used. In an ANOVA (3 ethnic groups × majority-minority status), ethnicity was found to be significant, but this must have been due to the lower Puerto Rican mean (24.52), the black and white means being almost identical (27.97 and 27.72, respectively). Majority-minority status yielded an insignificant F.

In some research reported in overlapping publications (Trowbridge, 1972a, 1974), 3,789 children from 133 third- to eighth-grade classrooms, mainly from central Iowa, were classified for an ANOVA according to *school* socioeconomic level (see chapter 3 of this book), race (681 blacks vs. 3,108 "others"), and population density (urban/suburban vs. rural/small town). Classroom teachers administered the SEI. Age and sex were omitted from the 3-way ANOVA because sex was not significantly related to SEI scores, and the author believes that there was a "low probability that age or sex differences account for the important SES effect" (p. 529). As reported elsewhere in this book, a *negative* relationship between socioeconomic level and SEI scores was obtained by Trowbridge. Relevant to the topic of this chapter, a significant *negative* relationship with race was also reported (black mean = 73.6; "other" mean = 70.0). No significant interactions were obtained. IQ differences between races were not reported or controlled in this ANOVA, but if one assumes that the blacks' IQ mean was lower than the "other" IQ mean, this lack of control should operate against rather than in the direction of the obtained main effect of race. Likewise, the reliability artifact (see Wylie, 1974, pp. 119-121) would operate in the direction opposite to the obtained main effect of race. Accordingly, the higher mean SEI of the black group in this study cannot plausibly be attributed to these possibly uncontrolled irrelevant determiners. We are not told whether blacks attended mainly low socioeconomic schools, in which case they might be subjected to fewer invidious comparisons than were the "others" to whom their SEI scores were compared. Trowbridge (1972a) cautions that "a shortage of middle SES blacks in the sample leaves the question as to race partially unanswered" (p. 535).

Baughman (1971) reports an otherwise unpublished study by Bridgette in which 252 eleventh graders in village and country areas of North Carolina, attending one high school which had been desegregated 3 months before testing were given the SEI by one black and one white examiner, randomly assigned to the integrated classrooms. Although whites were found to have slightly higher self-esteem (exact significance level not mentioned) when the effect of IQ was "removed" by an unspecified statistical procedure, the race difference on the SEI was no longer significant. Although influences of southern as opposed to northern subculture were held constant, no information is given about controls for socioeconomic level.

Finally, SEI studies by Getsinger, Kunce, Miller, and Weinberg (1972) and by W. F. White and Richmond (1970) seem so seriously flawed as not to warrant substantive summary. In any case, neither publication reports significant associations between racial status and SEI scores.

Altogether, the above substantively summarized studies involved three sets of black-white comparisons based on subjects ranging from first through eleventh grade. Two of them yield no significant black-white differences in SEI scores, whereas one (Trowbridge) shows the black SEI mean to be slightly higher than the mean for "others." Since, in Trowbridge's study, IQ, own socioeconomic level, and school socioeconomic level were not controlled when making race comparisons, and there was a shortage of middle-class blacks, interpretation of her data is moot. In any event, no support is given by these investigations to the hypothesis that racial/ethnic status per se is related to self-regard as measured by the self-esteem scores from Coopersmith's SEI.

Rosenberg's Self-Esteem Scale (RSE)

In D. W. Edwards's (1974) complex investigation, most comparisons were made between schools which varied with respect to racial composition and socioeconomic level. That is, individuals were not assigned to race groups according to their individual racial status; racial context and, to some extent, socioeconomic level were confounded with "race" differences. However, in one analysis, 297 Detroit eighth-grade boys in 2 junior-high schools which sent their pupils to a 70% black high school were divided into blacks ($N = 237$) and whites ($N = 60$) according to each individual's racial status. Bachman's (1970) version of the RSE was administered by a mixed-race examining team. The racial groups did not differ on socioeconomic level, on an idiosyncratic "social exploration scale," or on a matrices test of intelligence. Neither did they differ on mean RSE score.

Hulbary's (1975) small and admittedly nonrandom samples were chosen on an apparently informal basis in an attempt to "reduce the systematic bias which might result from factors unique to a particular location" and to obtain "roughly equal numbers of blacks and whites and males and females and so that students with widely differing levels of deprivation and racial isolation would be represented" (pp. 107–108). Subjects were 88 black and 98 white adolescents, aged 14–19. In a multiple-regression analysis, race, socioeconomic level, exposure to political/social information, age, racial isolation, and sex were related to RSE scores, with race added last so that the estimate of its variance contribution is conservative. Race accounted for 2.7% of the variance in self-esteem scores (almost half of the self-esteem variance explained by all the factors). Blacks had significantly higher self-esteem scores than did whites.

Although Bachman's (1970) study is by far the largest of those looking for race effects on RSE scores, only 256 of his 2,213 tenth-grade boys were black, and he stresses the fact that his nationwide sampling was not set up to study race differences adequately. (See chapter 3 of this book for a fuller description of his methods and his results regarding socioeconomic level.) Whites (N = 1912) were compared to blacks in three subgroups: in integrated schools with $\geq$ 40% whites (N = 73); in northern segregated schools with $\leq$ 10% whites (N = 72); in southern segregated schools with $\leq$ 10% whites (N = 111). Self-esteem was indexed by a score based on 6 RSE items plus 4 others "quite similar to the Rosenberg items" (see table 7–2, p. 124, for items and percentage frequencies).

In a multivariate analysis called multiple comparison analysis, he obtained "an estimate of the effect of each predictor as if it were uncorrelated with all the other predictors" (p. 64). Beta estimates the explanatory ability of a given predictor with other predictors held constant. Predictors included socioeconomic level, number of siblings, broken home, family relationships, religious preference, family political preference, community size, and race. "After adjustments for background and Quick Test [of intelligence] differences, blacks in integrated schools are 30 per cent of a standard deviation higher than whites, and those in segregated schools are 50 per cent of a standard deviation above the whites" (p. 128). Beta for race = .14 for an analysis which includes "other racial minorities" (N = 45) in addition to the above-listed subdivisions of blacks and whites (p. 130). Noting that these results fall opposite the common prediction of low self-esteem among blacks, Bachman speculates that the results may "reflect a need among young black men to portray themselves in favorable terms" (p. 131), by which he may be implying that the scores indicate self-presentation tactics rather than valid reports of self-concept. In the light of Rosenberg's (1973) and others' hypotheses (mentioned earlier in this chapter) about the cushioning effects on self-esteem of living among significant others of one's own race, it is interesting to note that the self-esteem levels of the blacks are higher in the integrated than the segregated schools. (No significance test for this difference is given, however.)

In Rosenberg's (1965) study for which he developed the RSE scale, 5,024 juniors and seniors from a random stratified sample of 10 high schools in New York State were categorized into various racial and ethnic groups. The rank order of these 14 groups according to the proportion of high self-esteem responses was shown not to be a function of socioeconomic level and not to be a function of the rank order of the prestige accorded them by society, as indexed by Bogardus's published values from his Social Distance scale. So far as racial comparisons are concerned, the distribution of high, medium, and low self-esteem percentages were almost identical for black Protestants, English-Welsh Protestants, and Irish Catholics—all three groups falling in the lower half of the list of 14 groups. However, this investigation was not planned especially to look at self-esteem as a function of racial/ethnic status; the above statements are based on only 80 blacks and 122 English-Welsh Protestants, and variables other than socioeconomic class and religion are not held constant in the black-white comparisons. Accordingly, definite conclusions regarding race per se and its possible interaction with other variables in influencing self-esteem cannot be reached on the basis of these data. (Rosenberg & Simmons's [1972] extensive study of black and white self-esteem, discussed below, did not use the RSE.)

Selecting male and female, black and white high-school students from 21 target programs of the Project Upward Bound (a precollege enrichment program for students from low-income families), D. E. Hunt and Hardt (1969) compared RSE scores between races at each of 6 times between June, 1966, and March, 1968, inclusive. (Ns = 213 blacks and 90 whites.) Although all students were disadvantaged, no exact information is given regarding the comparability of socioeconomic levels between the two racial groups. GPAs appear to be fairly comparable between groups, but of course the meaning of GPA is unclear when so many schools are involved. It would appear plausible that many of the blacks attended segregated schools. On each of the 6 testing occasions, the RSE scores of blacks fell above those of whites. Significance tests for these comparisons are not given, however.

In a study by Herman, Sadofsky, Bensman, Lilienfeld, and Manos (1967), 9 of the RSE items were included in interviews of the following groups of male respondents: 601 blacks, ages 16–21, seeking job counseling or placement at 2 centers located in the 2 largest New York City black ghettos; 196 freshmen and sophomores at predominantly black Howard University, in Washington, D.C.; 442 freshmen and sophomores at predominantly white, Catholic, Fordham University in New York City; 260 freshmen and sophomores at predominantly white, Catholic, Cardinal Hayes High School in New York City. The RSE responses of the five groups were pooled and divided approximately into tertiles to define the range of the grand-above-average, grand-average, and grand-below-average (more precisely 30.7%, 39.8%, and 29.5%, respectively). The 5 groups were then ranked according to their separate percentage distributions of below-grand-average, within the grand-average range, above-grand-average. Although marked between-group differences emerged, with the Brooklyn black-ghetto group being especially self-derogatory, no inferences about racial influences per se can be drawn, since the groups obviously differed among themselves in numerous ways of possible relevance to RSE scores.

The only researchers who studied racial associations with RSE scores among adults are Yancey, Rigsby, and McCarthy (1972), who interviewed heads of households (or, where necessary another adult in the household) in Nashville, Tennessee, and in Philadelphia, Pennsylvania. Results are based on 1,179 interviewees, 602 white and 577 black. Their multivariate statistic *beta* is "a measure of the relative importance of predictor variables in this sample" (p. 350) [as in Bachman's, 1970, study cited above]. The 6 predictors—marital status, work-force participation, sex, race, age, and education—explain .147 of the RSE variance in Nashville, .183 in Philadelphia. *Beta* for race = .143 in Nashville (p = .001) and .098 in Philadelphia (p = .05). Interpreting these results is not possible, however, for 2 reasons: (a) in Nashville, the black self-esteem mean exceeded that of whites, whereas the reverse was true in Philadelphia; (b) in table 3, p. 350 and on p. 351, the Philadelphia effect is said to be significant, but in another sentence on p. 351, it is said not to be significant.

Because of various limitations or flaws, these seven studies do not provide an adequate basis for conclusions about the relationship of racial status per se to RSE scores, or about the interactions of racial status with other variables in influencing these scores. The most obviously uncontrolled variables, including the possible operation of the reliability artifact, would appear to work toward whites' having higher RSE scores. The reported results from the better studies, however, are either null or favor blacks, albeit by very small amounts. Thus, one possibility is that the black RSE means would be more consistently and absolutely higher if there were better control of some of the irrelevant variables plausibly operating against high black scores in the reviewed studies. In any case, no support is given to the hypothesis that the socially rejected position of the black group has led to self-derogatory RSE mean scores for blacks. Although, as Bachman (1970) has suggested, higher black means may be attributable to self-presentation strategies rather than to higher self-esteem, this remains to be tested.

The only ethnic study involving RSE scores of over-all self-regard which did not compare blacks and whites was done by Husaini (1974). He administered the RSE scale to 108 American and 66 Indian students from India, all of whom attended a private college in Detroit. These volunteer groups were similar in grade-point average, academic standing (junior or senior), and age. The Americans obtained a significantly higher mean RSE score. However, Ns were small for this sort of comparison and there is no way to evaluate the degree to which each sample was representative of its respective subculture.

(See Wylie, 1974, pp. 180–189, for a detailed review and evaluation of the RSE scale.)

Self-Social Esteem (SSE)

A clear, interpretable trend does not emerge from the 3 studies I examined which were directed toward comparisons of self-esteem scores (SSE) from the Long, Henderson, and Ziller Self-Social Esteem scale. Long and Henderson (1970) report that blacks had significantly lower self-esteem. Their subjects were 192 children entering first grade in 13 rural southern counties. For carrying out ANOVAs, the subjects were divided into 8 equal-sized groups, according to race, sex, and class. One must note 3 factors which preclude firm interpretation of their significant race effect on self-esteem: (a) 12 ANOVAs were performed, one on each of 12 types of scores from their instrument, including the self-esteem scores. Out of 36 possible main effects, including racial self-esteem differences, 7 were significant at "about .05" or better, 5 clearly equalling or exceeding the .05 level. But one has no way to evaluate the probable replicability of the racial self-esteem effect obtained in the context of multiple significance testing without cross-validation and involving dependent variables which were based on overlapping operations and intercorrelated scores. (b) It is plausible that the reliability artifact could be operative here to depress blacks' scores. (c) As the authors note, the use of all white experimenters may have "inhibited or otherwise changed" the responses of the black children.

Richards and McCandless's (1972) data were based on 181 black and white 4-5-year-olds and 74 black and white children from 3 experimental prekindergartens in Atlanta, Georgia. Children were "mostly poor." The SSE score was among 43 variables subjected to a factor analysis within each of the 2 groups (of 181 and 74 subjects). In neither factor analysis did race load on the same factor as SSE.

A variety of uncontrolled variables and the presence of many significance tests without cross-validation or regard to the intercorrelation among SSE scores renders Harootunian's (1968) study uninterpretable so far as racial differences in SSE self-esteem scores are concerned.

(See Wylie, 1974, pp. 190-200, for detailed description and evaluation of Long, Henderson, and Ziller's SSE instrument from which SSE scores are taken.)

Tennessee Self-Concept Scale (TSCS)

Four of the five studies I examined which used the Total Positive score of the TSCS to make racial comparisons on self-regard were seriously flawed or limited and are therefore not summarized here. They are Healey and deBlassie (1974), T. M. Hughes (1968), Powell (1973), and R. L. Williams and Byars (1968)—all of whom found no significant racial differences on the TSCS total positive score, except that, in her southern group, Powell found blacks' scores to be significantly higher.

Wendland's study as described in Baughman (1971), although methodologically better than the others, must be regarded cautiously. Among her 685 black and white subjects, aged 13-17, all were from North Carolina and of lower or lower-middle socioeconomic class, but the groups differed simultaneously on race and school context (i.e., each racial group came from an essentially segregated school). Also, IQ and GPA were not controlled. However, the latter, as well as the reliability artifact, if operating, might be expected to work against Wendland's reported findings that the black mean Total Positive score was significantly higher than that of the whites (significance level not specified). A multivariate analysis of these data could be enlightening. Since the blacks exceeded the whites on Harrison and Kass's (1967) Estrangement and Cynicism scores from the MMPI, Wendland speculates that the blacks' self-esteem may have been raised by their interpreting dis-esteem from others as indicative of "pathology in the discriminator." However, no r is published between either the Estrangement or Cynicism score and the Total Positive score of the TSCS; so one cannot evaluate this speculation. Alternately or additionally, one should note that the segregation of the black children could theoretically have protected their self-esteem in the manner described in section A of this chapter. (See Wylie, 1974, pp. 230–236, for a detailed review and evaluation of the TSCS scale.)

Piers-Harris Self-Concept Scale for Children (PH)

The main point of Vance and Richmond's (1975) study of 240 children selected to contain approximately equal numbers of each sex and race was not to make comparisons in self-esteem scores. Therefore, although they report that black and white PH medians did not differ significantly, it is not entirely clear whether this happened as an incidental finding or whether it was attained purposely as a step toward forming groups needed to accomplish their main purpose. All subjects were defined as lower middle class by school officials, and they lived in a rural area of the southeast United States.

(See Wylie, 1974, pp. 174–180, for a detailed review and evaluation of the PH scale.)

Bernreuter Lack of Self-Confidence

In Roen's (1960) study of 50 pairs of black and white males, chosen from hundreds of files at a southwestern army post, age, education, occupation of parents, income of parents, geographical area of childhood, army rank, number of years in service, marital status, urban/rural background, and plans for reenlistment were all matched between pair members. Although the racial groups did not differ significantly on Bernreuter Total Adjustment scores, the blacks had significantly greater Lack of Self Confidence scores ($p <$ .005). However, an intelligence score which was also significantly lower in the black group, was highly correlated with Lack of Self Confidence scores ($-$.79 for blacks, $-$.50 for whites). This renders the differences in self-confidence between groups ambiguous despite the careful matching on the many other variables.

Other Well-Known Instruments

The studies of possible racial differences in over-all self-regard indexed by other well-known instruments seem to me to be too flawed and/or limited to warrant substantive summary. They are: Davids (1973), using an idiosyncratic score based partly on the Adjective Check List (ACL); Butts (1963), Engle (1945), and R. M. Roth (1961), using the Sense of Personal Worth scale from the California Test of Personality; and Dales and Keller (1972), using an unspecified scale from Bills's Index of Adjustment and Values. (For detailed reviews and evaluations of two of these instruments, see Wylie, 1974, pp. 200–213, for the ACL, and pp. 150–165, for the IAV.)

Summary of Studies Using Well-Known Instruments
of Over-all Self-Regard

Altogether, this section is based on an evaluation of 30 publications concerning relationships between racial/ethnic status and some relatively well-known alleged index of over-all self-regard. In each of 2 instances, 2 publications were devoted to analyzing the same set of data.

Both the methodological problems and the overview of outcomes imply that we are in no position to make firm generalizations from these studies about racial/ethnic differences in over-all self-regard. Null results, by far the most commonly reported finding, are always ambiguous. However, since there is a fair amount of information available about the reliability, construct validity, and psychometric properties of many of the relatively well-known instruments used in the above-mentioned publications, it seems rather implausible that null findings could be attributed simply to psychometric deficiencies of the alleged self-regard indices. In the case of black-white comparisons, null results could easily arise from counteracting influences which cannot be evaluated with the data at hand. For example, the depressing effects of the reliability artifact might counteract the "cushioning effects" which segregation has been hypothesized to have on blacks' self-esteem, or poor self-esteem among blacks might be counteracted by allegedly defensive self-presentation tactics among black subjects.

By a slight margin, the significant trends are for blacks to have higher self-esteem scores. But obviously, box-score counts are not sufficient to decide what the meaningful conclusions should be, especially when there is such a variation among studies in instruments, subjects, and methodological adequacy; also little consideration has been given to interactions. In my opinion, the studies reporting lower black self-esteem tend to be methodologically less adequate than those reporting them to have higher self-esteem.

In view of the relatively recent social emphasis on increasing blacks' self-regard, as indicated by the black power movement, the "black is beautiful" trend, and by numerous advisory articles and books written by educators, one might wonder whether a tendency appears for earlier studies to lean in the direction of lower black self-regard with the more recent ones tending toward null findings or higher black self-regard. So far as I can discern, no such trend appears among these publications or among those to be discussed in the next section (which is based on idiosyncratic instruments purporting to index self-regard).

In any case, the firmest thing one can say is that these 30 publications place the burden of proof on those who have contended that the derogated social position of the blacks must obviously have resulted in seriously damaged self-esteem in that group.

b. SELF-REGARD INDEXED BY IDIOSYNCRATIC INSTRUMENTS

Turning to studies which looked for racial differences in over-all self-regard as allegedly indexed by idiosyncratic instruments, it is important to note that these studies are usually more difficult to interpret than the ones just reviewed, since much less is known about the reliability, validity, and other psychometric properties of the idiosyncratic instruments. Also, although there may be several studies using the same well-known instrument, each index in the investigations covered in the section below was used in only one study, so far as I know. Obviously, this further hampers generalization.

Of the 29 publications (covering 28 studies) which I have examined for possible inclusion in the present section, 20 are so seriously flawed and/or so incompletely reported that they do not seem to me to provide a basis for substantive description and evaluation; they are, therefore, simply listed at the end of the section. The text of this section is based on the remaining 9 investigations. Of the 4 researches based on Ns exceeding 1,000, 3 span a considerable age range (Crain & Weisman, 1972; Rosenberg & Simmons, 1972; Greenberger, Campbell, Sorenson, & O'Connor, 1971). These 3 are presented first. Thereafter, the studies are discussed approximately in order of the age of subjects tested.

Substantively Described Studies

Rosenberg and Simmons (1972), whose main point was to look at black and white self-esteem, published by far the most information about their specially devised self-esteem index, other aspects of their method, and results. Theirs is the most extensive study directed toward self-esteem as a function of race.

Modeling after the cluster sampling method of the U.S. Census Bureau, the authors drew a sample of 2,625 third- through twelfth-grade pupils from the records of 26 schools in Baltimore City, Maryland. Of those drawn, 1,917 were available to be interviewed, of whom 63.5% were black. Details about school size, racial context of school, and median family income of school census tract are given. Because the RSE which Rosenberg (1965) had developed for use in his New York State study was deemed unsuitable for the wider age range of the Baltimore subjects, a new 6-item Guttman scale was developed to index self-esteem levels in the Baltimore research. Considerable information about the scale, its development and psychometric properties, is given on pages 11-20 of Rosenberg and Simmons (1972). For secondary-school subjects, the value of *gamma* for the new instrument versus the RSE was 0.6119. Virtually no results of significance tests for reported trends are given by Rosenberg and Simmons. Race of experimenter was shown not to be a factor in the obtained distributions of self-esteem scores.

Over-all, and within each of 3 age groups (8-11; 12-14; 15-19), the percent of blacks attaining high self-esteem scores exceeded the white percents by at least 12, and the percent of whites attaining low self-esteem scores exceeded the black percents by at least 14. Relatively little racial variation is seen in percents attaining medium self-esteem scores.

These figures take no account of such possibly relevant factors as socioeconomic levels of individuals or schools, racial context of school or neighborhood environment, variations in family structure, IQ, GPA, or skin color—many of which might be expected to have operated *against* the finding of higher self-esteem among blacks. Accordingly, the authors turn to an examination of such variables in an attempt to account for these results.

They raise the question whether insulation in segregated environments has preserved or inflated black self-esteem, since only 12% of black children attended predominantly white schools, only 3% lived in predominantly white neighborhoods, and 99% and 98% of black and white children respectively reported that the majority of their friends were of the same race as themselves.

In support of the insulation hypothesis, black self-esteem of secondary-school students seemed to be higher in predominantly black schools. (Too few elementary-school students attended predominantly white schools to permit analysis at the earlier age levels.) Also, black children in integrated schools and neighborhoods were somewhat more likely than those in segregated environments to be subjected to racial teasing. In turn, there appeared to be a small but consistent association between self-esteem and reports of being teased about race. This trend was found at all 3 age levels (8-11; 12-14; 15+).

One might imagine that the objectively lower socioeconomic levels of the black children might be a factor in depressing their self-esteem. However, Hollingshead socioeconomic levels, which did appear to be related to self-esteem scores among whites, were unrelated to self-esteem among blacks, in an age-controlled analysis. In evaluating this, a number of factors must be considered. The black children were much less likely than whites to be below the average socioeconomic level of their own schools. Moreover, blacks were much less likely than whites to say they knew richer children. Thus they were more protected than were the whites from local invidious economic comparisons. Within each of 4 socioeconomic categories (1-2, 3, 4, 5), the percent blacks exceeded the percent whites who said their parents had "done very well in life," and, in 4 out of 5 occupational levels below the professional-executive status, larger percentages of black than white children said that "most people rate father's job as 'best' or 'good.' " Thus, whatever the socioeconomic level, the blacks did not seem to perceive the prestige of their parents as lower.

The authors also bring evidence to support their assertion that the black children hold inflated ideas about their group's evaluation by society. Asked to rank which of four groups (Jews, white Catholics, Negroes, white Protestants) *most people* in America think is best, 43% of the blacks replied that blacks are considered best. (This inflation mechanism also tended to occur to some extent in each of the other groups, but 1% or less of white respondents thought *most people* in America ranked blacks as the best group.

Looking at family structure as a possible factor in determining the obtained differences in self-esteem, Rosenberg and Simmons noted that certain types of family structure might have been expected to lower self-esteem, and these types might be more frequent among blacks. The authors point out that

> black children are considerably more likely than whites to originate from homes characterized by illegitimacy, legal separation, or abandonment. . . . Since in our society in general the socially least desirable family structure would appear to be one characterized by illegitimacy or desertion, the self-esteem of the children from such families may certainly be expected to suffer as a consequence of the associated stigma. [Pp. 75–77]

Although they did find that white children from separated or never-married families had self-esteem levels considerably below those of other white children, no such difference was found among the blacks. Thus, even though the incidence of these supposedly stigmatized families was higher among blacks, it did not seem to counteract the over-all black trend toward higher self-esteem. In trying to explain this, they note:

> In the predominantly black schools [attended by 82% of the black subjects] we see that it apparently makes no difference to the child's self-esteem whether or not he comes from a separated or never-married family. In the mixed or predominantly white school, on the other hand, a substantial impact is observed; 42 percent of the black children from separated or never-married families have low self-esteem compared with only 19% of the other black children. [P. 81]

The reason this difference did not affect the over-all black-white results is that so few black children came from predominantly white schools.

"Black children from separated or never-married families are virtually no more likely than other black children to say they have often or sometimes been teased about their family; but white children from such families are considerably more likely than other white children to report this type of teasing" (p.81). Refining this analysis, the authors say, "In predominantly black schools, black children from separated or never-married families are no more likely than other black children to say they have ever been teased about their families, but in the integrated schools they are" (p. 83).

But since so few blacks attended predominantly white schools, this difference by school did not substantially affect the over-all black-white comparison of teasing about family status.

In short, this series of analyses suggested to the authors that the normative standards of the black and white groups differed sufficiently with respect to stigmatization of separated or never-married families so that this family influence operated much more to depress white self-esteem than to depress black self-esteem.

Finally, Rosenberg and Simmons note that the lower average school grades actually characteristic of the blacks did not seem to counteract the trend toward higher black self-esteem.

> School grades seem to make less difference for the self-esteem of black children. This is especially striking among the near-failing pupils; the self-esteem of such white pupils is vastly lower than that of other whites, whereas the self-esteem of such black children is only moderately lower than other blacks. This suggested that blacks, particularly those whose school achievement is low, may more successfully employ certain defense mechanisms. . . . We found that the black child who did poorly in school was less likely than the corresponding white to feel that his school marks represented an accurate appraisal of his intelligence, to believe that his parents considered him unintelligent, and to care strongly about the quality of intelligence. It was suggested that the black child's social environment was more hospitable to the use of these protective mechanisms. [P. 102]

(One should note that these researchers did not control for measured ability when looking at self-esteem and achievement, nor did they look at self-esteem and ability scores, with achievement held constant, as recommended in chapter 7 of this book.)

Rosenberg and Simmons's (1972) results verified the frequently reported earlier findings of an aesthetic preference for lighter skin color within the black community. Earlier authors had confidently inferred that this preference indicated poorer self-regard among blacks. Surprisingly, then, Rosenberg and Simmons found virtually no association between the child's self-esteem and the interviewer's judgment of the child's skin color. To explain these unexpected null findings, the authors suggested two points: (a) Black children plausibly evaluate their physical attractiveness with reference to their own group, whites with reference to theirs. This was suggested by the fact that 63% of blacks and 65% of whites said they were either "very good looking" or "pretty good looking," whereas blacks within each age group were far more likely to say they were "very happy" with their looks and whites were likely to say they were "pretty happy." (b) Although there was a relationship within each racial group between self-esteem and self-evaluation of looks, certain self-protective mechanisms were plausibly at work among the black children, including a devaluation of the importance of looks for one's personal worth (self-designated very dark children were more likely to say that physical attractiveness did not matter to them and that their parents considered good looks unimportant).

Two methodological comments are in order about this thoughtfully conceived and executed major piece of research. First, one must consider the implications of the fact that the sample was comprised only of children from the public schools of one large city in a border state, a city which has 64.1% black school population and a great proportion of de facto residential and educational segregation. While the results as given are of interest and importance, replications in settings having other geographical and demographic characteristics would, of course, increase the generalizability of the results. Second, while numerous very important cross-tabulations have been examined and plausibly interpreted in an effort to see what factors might be related to the main findings about race and self-esteem, it would also be very helpful to have some form of multivariate analysis to enable one to estimate simultaneously the independent contributions to self-esteem scores made by race, socioeconomic level, age, sex, racial context of school, racial context of neighborhood, family status, skin color, and school performance. Such a multivariate analysis could not, of course, substitute for the selective analyses directed at particular issues, e.g., the relationships between skin color and perceived good looks and between the latter and self-esteem, but they could provide a supplementary overview and an estimate of significance levels of each association.

In contrast to Rosenberg and Simmons's (1972) work, Greenberger,

Campbell, Sorensen, and O'Connor (1971) based their racial comparisons on an ad hoc analysis of data originally gathered by the Board of Education of Pennsylvania; the samples and procedures are very incompletely described. From "a random sample of 20,000 children at each of two grade levels—grades 5 and 11— . . . a randomly selected subsample of approximately 3,000 children at each grade level was obtained [by Greenberger et al., 1971] for use in the construction of a maturity scale" (p. 9). Since these samples contained only 5% blacks, they "obtained the total black sample, consisting of 1,194 youngsters in grade 11 and 1,276 in grade 5" (p. 23).

From an initial pool of 199 attitude items, 55 were drawn on the bases of their judged theoretical relevance to "psychological maturity" and their empirical discrimination between fifth- and eleventh-graders. An item factor analysis with orthogonal rotation to simple structure was performed on 2 successive subsamples ($N = 850$ per subsample) at each grade level. The replication was intended to validate the initial structure. Five factors (including only 54 items) resulted, one of which was called "self acceptance." All items and their factor loadings are given in Greenberger and Marini (1972). All 10 items defining the Self-Acceptance factor scale are verbatim or modified statements from Coopersmith's Self-Esteem Inventory. Considerable psychometric information about the Psychosocial Maturity Scale is given in Greenberger and Marini (1972) and Greenberger et al. (1971).

The factor structure was found to be virtually identical for black and white samples. Self-acceptance accounted for 25% and 23% of the total variance accounted for by the 5-factor solution for whites and the 4-factor solution for blacks, respectively. Items of the entire 54 item Psychosocial Maturity Scale were divided into blocks of about 10 each, according to the degree to which they discriminated between races. In Grade 5, 2 out of 10 least discriminating items were from the Self-Acceptance subscale and 0 out of 9 of the most discriminating items were from that subscale. In Grade 11, 3 out of 10 least discriminating items were from the Self-Acceptance subscale, and 0 out of 9 most discriminating items were from that subscale.

Accordingly, so far as it goes, this study gives no support to the hypothesis of racial differences in self-acceptance. However, no information is given about controls over other possibly relevant variables such as the possible operation of the reliability artifact, socioeconomic level, GPA, IQ, or school racial context.

Crain and Weisman's (1972) report is based on a block-quota sample of 1,651 black males and females aged 21–45 from 25 different northern metropolitan areas and 1,326 whites from "another NORC national survey." With so little information given, one has no way of knowing whether other variables were properly taken into account in the racial comparisons. The 10 items in their idiosyncratic self-esteem scale were published in their book, along with item intercorrelations and some factor-analytic results, but the psychometric information given is not sufficient. Instead of using scores based on their factors, they presented racial comparisons item by item and for a total score. No information about significance was offered for these comparisons. In any case, since the items involved in the numerous comparisons were intercorrelated, it would not be possible to evaluate the significance levels, even if they had been stated. Thus one cannot evaluate their conclusions that "blacks born in the South have generally lower self-esteem than whites, but blacks born in the North tend to have self-esteem as high or higher than whites" (p. 74).

St. John's (1971) study of 957 Boston sixth graders, which is described in chapter 3 of this book, used multiple regression analysis to predict "general self-concept," but race was not one of the predictor variables. Instead, separate regression analyses were made within each race group (N = 496 whites, 416 blacks). Although St. John verbally compared the outcomes of these separate computations by race, her statements are not supported by any data analyses which enable one to infer that race per se was an independent variable in those multiple-regression outcomes which differed between the races.

Knight's (1969) research is unique in the use of educable mentally retarded black and white subjects. Ns were small (40 black boys, 43 white boys), but groups were matched on IQ, MA, CA (unspecified range), and socioeconomic level. She tabulated replies to the idiosyncratic question "How well do you like yourself?" (a lot, a little, not very much, not at all), and a chi square test showed no significant racial differences in the percentage distributions in the table. No information is presented about control of such possibly relevant variables as school or neighborhood context or interviewer effects, or about the psychometric characteristics of the instrument used.

In the earliest study of this topic I examined, Hurlock (1927) used 30 trait pairs, grouped into 3 levels of undesirability according to the judgments of 5 graduate psychology students who were instructed to rate the undesirability from the probable viewpoint of the seventh- and eighth-grade subjects. Traits were taken from the Will Downey Temperament Test. The 219 white and 204 black children were comparable with respect to mean IQ (107), and all were enrolled in one public school in Manhattan, New York City. Desirable responses were not always at the same end of the printed pair of trait opposites, affording some control of acquiescence response set, and the experimenter explained the meanings of each pair of terms before the subjects made the self-rating with respect to that pair. The over-all percent of undesirable responses was extremely small, and no significant racial differences were observed (7.3% by whites and 4.6% by blacks). An examination of the particular undesirable self-descriptions made by each racial group showed a high degree of overlap between races (e.g., proud [as opposed to humble], bad tempered, stingy, cowardly, stupid).

In their well-known, extensive examination of 1,222 black and white children from segregated schools in a rural North Carolina community, Baughman and Dahlstrom (1968) included (for the eighth graders only) an interview question about self-regard: "Again, to sum up, are you pretty much satisfied with the sort of person you are?" (very, kind of, so-so, not too much, very dissatisfied). Interviewers were of the same race as respondents. Data from this question were based on small Ns (28 white boys, 30 white girls, 32 black boys, 46 black girls). No tendency for lower self-esteem among blacks appeared in the descriptive data, and the p value for chi square was not significant. Relevant to interpreting these null results, there is no way provided in Baughman and Dahlstrom's book to evaluate the role of the reliability or other psychometric properties of the one-question self-esteem index or to evaluate the possibly mutually counteracting contributions of such factors as segregated context (which is confounded with racial status), IQ, GPA, or socioeconomic-level variations in determining answers to the index question.

Like a number of other reports, Gordon's (1972) publication concerning racial comparisons is based on a reanalysis of data already gathered by others for somewhat different purposes. In this instance, a 5% systematic subsample of 1,684 ninth graders was drawn from the complete tapes of 337,000 metropolitan northeastern ninth graders used in the Coleman report (Coleman et al., 1966). Possibly serious sources of bias in the original Coleman sample were mentioned by C. Gordon (1972, p. 10).

Rather than use Coleman's two-item "self-concept" index, Gordon constructed another idiosyncratic "global self-esteem" measure by combining seven "self-determination" items, two "academic competence" items (Coleman's original "self-concept" index), one "basic self-acceptance" item, and two "general competence" items. Some details about subscale-total rs, distributions, and inter-subscale rs were published. Inspection of the items suggests that this so-called global self-esteem index is heavily loaded with achievement-oriented self-appraisal statements. A path analysis technique yielded a null relationship of race to global self-esteem scores when verbal ability scores, socioeconomic level, family structure (strongly male, matriarchal, weakly male, neither present), and parental aspirations were held constant by this type of multivariate analysis.

Hodgkins and Stakenas (1969) compared 142 black high school and college subjects to 150 white high school and college subjects who were alleged to be "fairly representative" of such populations in that region of the Deep South. Scores from an idiosyncratic semantic differential instrument were used to index "self adjustment" and "self assurance." The scales and needed psychometric information were not published. They report that, when parents' socioeconomic status according to Duncan's index was controlled by an unspecified method, there were no racial differences in "self assurance in school" or "self adjustment." Relevant to interpreting these null results, however, there was no way provided to evaluate the role of the reliability or other psychometric properties of their idiosyncratic index or to evaluate the possibly mutually counteracting contributions of such factors as segregated racial context (which was confounded with racial status), IQ, or GPA in determining the scores on the self-regard instrument.

Summary of Studies Relating Racial/Ethnic Status to Self-Regard Indexed by Idiosyncratic Instruments

Altogether, this section is based on an evaluation of 29 publications concerning relationships between racial/ethnic status and idiosyncratic indices of self-regard. Since two publications covered the same study, only 28 different investigations were involved.

As was the case with research on racial self-esteem using relatively well-known instruments, both the methodological problems and the overview of outcomes imply that we are in no position to make firm generalizations from these studies about racial/ethnic differences in over-all self-regard.

Among the 9 substantively summarized researches, 4 large scale ones were reviewed. The one I judge to be best methodologically (Rosenberg and Simmons, 1972) shows rather strong tendencies for self-esteem to be higher among black than among white children from one large city, and they offer supplementary data to support plausible interpretations of this unexpected finding. However, this publication gives no systematic reports of significance tests, nor were multivariate analyses performed. One (Crain and Weisman, 1972) asserts without supporting data that racial differences among residents of the metropolitan Northeast United States depend on the blacks' region of birth.

Six of the substantively considered studies yielded null findings which are moot for various reasons explained in the summary of section B-4-a, above.

As was the case with the 30 publications based on relatively well-known instruments, the results presented in the 29 publications place the burden of proof on those who have contended that the derogated, disadvantaged social position of the blacks in the United States must obviously have resulted in seriously damaged self-esteem in that group.

Studies Not Substantively Described

Of the 29 publications involving idiosyncratic self-regard indices, I judged 20 to be so severely flawed and/or to give so little essential technical information as to warrant their being listed below rather than being substantively considered. Of these 20, 6 were concerned with ethnic comparisons other than or in addition to black-white. Among the 15 involving blacks and whites, 5 report blacks to have significantly lower self-esteem, 1 reports them to have significantly higher self-esteem, and 9 report null findings.

Obviously, all the publications reporting significantly lower black self-regard have been evaluated as not meriting substantive consideration according to the criteria stated in sections A-2, A-3, and A-4 of this chapter. The reader who wonders whether there was a bias in my application of these criteria for dividing studies into those I substantively considered and those I simply listed may wish to examine these primary sources. Listed in alphabetical order they are: Carpenter and Busse (1969); Davids (1973); Denmark (1970); Deutsch (1960,

1963); Fein, O'Neill, C. Frank, and Velit (1975); Getsinger, Kunce, Miller, and Weinberg (1972); Henton and Johnson (1964); Hishiki (1969), concerning sixth-grade girls of Mexican-American descent; Keller (1963); Lefley (1974), regarding Miccosukee Indian children; McCormick and Balla (1973), regarding Lebanese who varied in attachment to their ethnic subculture; Muller and Leonetti (1974), concerning primary level Chicano and Anglo students; Petersen and Ramirez (1971), regarding Negro-American, Mexican-American, and Anglo-American students from Grades 5–8; Powers, Drane, Close, Noonan, Wines, and Marshall (1971); Reeves and Shearer (1973); R. M. Roth (1969); Samuels (1973); Schaar (1974), regarding Trimble's work on American Indian self-image; Shulman (1968).

The reader interested in black-white comparisons may wish to refer to reviews by Christmas (1973), Shuey (1966, pp. 508–512), and Zirkel (1971) for substantive allusions to unpublished sources and references from the *Dissertation Abstracts* which are not included in the above section. Hernandez's (1973) review includes some unpublished studies concerning self-concepts of Mexican-American children.

5. Over-all Self-Regard as a Function of Integration

The Supreme Court decision of 1954 was based in part on the argument made by educators and social scientists that black self-esteem as well as black achievement is impaired by segregation. On the other hand, some have argued that segregation should not be expected to lower self-esteem and that integration might actually impair it, at least under certain conditions. For example, Hodgkins and Stakenas (1969) say:

> Within the segregated community, where most if not all significant others are Negro and the majority of prior experience is with other Negroes, no difference would be expected in the incidence of positive or negative self-concepts in a specific situation in the Negro or white segments of that community. Because the Negro is segregated, race as a basis of self-evaluation is eliminated within situation boundaries. [P. 372]

Going even further, Rosenberg and Simmons (1972) have argued that the blacks in an integrated setting may have lower self-esteem than those in a segregated setting, for the following reasons: (a) Blacks who attended integrated schools were teased more about their race (p. 27). (b) Blacks made lower marks than whites in integrated schools (even though they tended to make better marks than blacks in segregated schools, i.e., a B average was more outstanding in a segregated black school than in a predominantly white school). (c) Entering an integrated school situation, blacks may experience the white group's devaluation of aspects of their group's values and behaviors which they had previously considered acceptable, right, or even admirable. For example, blacks from separated or never-married families were teased more often about their families if they were in a predominantly white school (p. 82). (d) Integration could increase the black children's realization of their families' relatively depressed socioeconomic status. (In evaluating the data-based assertions in this argument, the reader should examine the details of the Rosenberg and Simmons [1972] research, as summarized in section B-4-b above and should remember that no significance tests were presented.)

In view of the importance of this issue, it is surprising and disappointing that only a small amount of published research has been directed toward it and that most of the published items are open to serious methodological criticisms. So that the reader may be assured that no relatively adequate study has been excluded, I summarize below all the ones which came to my attention.

The most controlled one, Bachman's (1970), is considered in some detail in sections B-4-a and B-6-a of this chapter. Even this investigation was not set up primarily to look at racial comparisons, let alone segregation effects, as Bachman stresses. In this national sample of tenth-grade boys, Bachman found the following increasing order of self-esteem means: racial minorities other than blacks, whites, blacks in integrated schools, blacks in northern segregated schools, blacks in southern segregated schools. *Beta* (controlling for 8 background factors and scores on the Quick Test of Intelligence) was a significant .14.

Rosenberg and Simmons (1972) in their research report, described in detail in section B-4 of this chapter, present a table of percents of black children obtaining low, medium, and high self-esteem scores, with the respondents classified according to whether their school context was predominantly black or white and according to level of school (junior high or senior high). Inspection of the table shows that a larger percent of black children in predominantly white schools tended to have low self-esteem and a smaller percent tended to have high self-esteem than the black children in predominantly black schools. Differences in percents with medium self-esteem were very slight.

Certainly no evidence in this table suggests that segregation damages self-esteem, but since the table was not standardized on other variables such as socioeconomic level, ability scores, or school performance measures and no significance tests were given, this trend must be viewed with caution. In any event, it is noteworthy that the descriptively evident trend went in a direction opposite that which would be expected from the direct operation of the uncontrolled socioeconomic and ability/achievement levels on self-esteem scores.

In a later report involving some additional data from the same investigation, Rosenberg (1975) tabulated percents of black children in predominantly black and white schools who manifested "stability of self-concept." The latter construct was indexed by an idiosyncratic six-item Guttman scale directed toward the children's sense of certainty or confusion about their concepts and evaluations of themselves. The items, but no psychometric information, were published in the report. Standardizing for self-esteem (with which stability scores correlated) and dividing the groups into percents showing unstable, medium, and stable self-concept, Rosenberg (1975) found significantly higher percents of unstable self-concept among blacks in predominantly white schools as contrasted to blacks in predominantly black schools. The difference in percents with unstable self-concept was significant at $< .05$ level at each of three school levels (elementary, junior high, and senior high). Again, this analysis involved no control for socioeconomic, ability, or school performance levels; so the results must be viewed with reservations. However, like the self-esteem trends, the stability trends fell in a direction opposite to that which would be expected from the direct operation of these uncontrolled variables on stability of self-concept.

In Harootunian's (1968) study of ninth graders, 200 segregated blacks were compared with 65 desegregated blacks on 8 scores from Long, Henderson, and Ziller's Self-Social Symbols Task (1970). As Harootunian points out, segregation was confounded with lower socioeconomic and educational level of parents and lower performance of the segregated subjects on several cognitive tests. Also, Harootunian made multiple comparisons involving intercorrelated scores from the Self-Social Symbols Task. Accordingly, the results cannot be confidently interpreted. In any event, the uncontrolled variables might be expected to operate *against* the obtained results, namely that desegregated blacks, especially boys, obtained the lowest self-esteem scores, whereas segregated blacks showed the highest. (A third group comprised of whites is not relevant here.) (See Wylie, 1974, pp. 190–200, for a detailed description and evaluation of the Self-Social Symbols Task from which the SSE [social self-esteem score] was obtained.)

R. E. Hughes and Works (1974) compared 58 black twelfth graders in a 34% black school with 37 twelfth graders in a 97% black school. The small Ns; the lack of control of socioeconomic level, ability measures, and achievement measures; the use of an idiosyncratic semantic differential instrument about which no psychometric information is given; and the performance of multiple significance tests all preclude interpretation of their reported trends toward greater favorability of self-concepts and various social-self-concepts among segregated students, especially males.

For a number of reasons, Strauss's (1967) report comparing second and third graders in one relatively segregated and one relatively integrated school is not interpretable in terms of the effects of integration on black pupils: (a) An idiosyncratic, 50-item, self-concept instrument was used to measure three categories of an "individual's school self," viz., intellectual self, school and peers, and personality-self-worth; no information about the instrument is given. (b) The data from blacks and Puerto Rican children were combined. (c) Multiple significance tests were made on probably intercorrelated scores. The study reports significantly more favorable self-concept scores from minority children in integrated schools, a trend differing from most of the studies described in this section.

In some survey research more fully described in section B-4-b of this chapter, Crain and Weisman (1972) used an idiosyncratic self-esteem scale to study a block-quota sample of 1,651 black males and females, aged 21–45, from 25 northern metropolitan areas. One table involves the following cross-classifications of conditions *experienced by the subjects as children:* segregated versus integrated schools; number of whites in neighborhood (none, few, many); and played versus did not play with whites. The authors point out that the largest percent of subjects with high adult self-esteem came from the completely segregated childhood condition (i.e., segregated schools, no whites in the neighborhood, did not play with whites); the next highest percent of subjects with high adult self-esteem came from the completely integrated childhood condition (integrated school, many whites in the neighborhood, played with whites). Lowest percentages of high self-esteem adults were found among persons having had two integrated and one segregated childhood experience. However, there are several reasons to reserve judgment about the interpretation of this table. Besides the limited information given about psychometric properties of the self-esteem total score, one should note that $N \leq 10$ in 5 out of 12 of the cells of the table; there was no information offered as to whether socioeconomic level and ability and achievement levels were controlled in these comparisons, and there were no significance tests.

The very small Ns, the presentation of multiple comparisons involving intercorrelated scores, and the lack of control of socioeconomic level, ability scores, or achievement scores renders uninterpretable R. L. Williams and Byars's (1970) report that Total Positive scores from the Tennessee Self-Concept Scale (TSCS) were slightly higher among 22 newly desegregated than among 72 segregated eleventh-grade blacks, a trend also differing from most of those described in this section. No significance test for this comparison is given, nor could one have been interpreted, owing to the making of multiple comparisons.

Denmark (1970) attempted to study the effects of newly instituted integration on 87 black children, Grades 1-6. No interpretation of her study is warranted, however, for a number of reasons, including the following: (a) An idiosyncratic, semiprojective, self-concept test was used about which no definite descriptive details and no psychometric information were given. (b) No control group of blacks not undergoing integration was used.

Works's (1962) report on the self-esteem of adult blacks living in integrated or segregated public housing cannot be evaluated because (a) only 118 subjects were interviewed; (b) an unknown idiosyncratic self-concept measure was used, for which only 1 out of 20 items was published and for which no psychometric information was given; (c) the subjects' retrospective reports about their self-concepts before moving to the project would be of dubious reliability and validity, it seems; (d) psychometrically indefensible gain scores in self-concept were used to evaluate the effects of integration. (See Wylie, 1974, pp. 88-95, for a commentary on the pitfalls in the use of gain and discrepancy scores.)

In summary, no study that I examined has fulfilled the necessary criteria to enable one to draw conclusions about the effects of integrated education or living on over-all self-regard in black children or adults. Either the sampling was not specifically and adequately planned for that kind of analysis, or other relevant variables were not controlled, or both. The most one can say at this point is that the burden of proof is on the person who asserts that children in segregated schools as compared to those in integrated schools have depressed self-esteem. If anything, the opposite trend may possibly emerge in future research which is appropriately planned and analyzed so as to look at this question. The latter statement is suggested by the facts that (a) in the two largest and methodologically best studies cited above, higher self-esteem was found in the segregated group; (b) even in the studies in which the uncontrolled variables were of the sort which might be expected to create the opposite effect, i.e., lower self-esteem in the segregated group, the trends were toward higher self-esteem in that group.

It is important to note that newly instituted integration, legally forced integration, and integration of longstanding which has arisen from the geographical relationships of neighborhoods to schools may conceivably have quite different impacts on the self-regard of black children, but no data are at hand to sustain even preliminary speculative conclusions about such factors. The same can be said about variations in minority ratios in integrated schools.

The reader may wish to refer to Christmas's (1973) review of studies of blacks' self-concepts, to Roberts and Horton's (1973) review of the extent and effects of segregation, to Rosenberg and Simmons's (1972) book, and to Zirkel's (1971) review of self-concept and ethnic group mixture, all of which allude to some *Dissertation Abstracts* and unpublished studies not included in this section. So far as one can discern from the information given in these sources, the conclusions drawn from the published studies cited in this section would not be modified by inclusion of these additional items.

6. Specific Aspects of Self-Concept as a Function of Racial/Ethnic Status

a. SELF-CONCEPT OF ABILITY

Methodological Considerations

In looking for possible racial differences in self-concepts of intelligence or schoolwork ability, it is especially important to control for ability and/or achievement scores and for socioeconomic level. This is true because each of these variables differentiates the black and white population, and each is known or thought to be related to measures of self-concept of ability or self-estimated intelligence. (See chaps. 7 and 3 of this book.)

However, even when one attempts such controls, one cannot be sure of having done an adequate job. First, racial subgroups which are drawn from any specified restricted range on an objective socioeconomic-level indicator (e.g., 4-5 on the Hollingshead occupational scale) may actually have proportionately more black persons in the low end of the range and proportionately more whites in the upper end, i.e., the two groups are not strictly comparable with respect to objective socioeconomic level. To the extent that self-estimates of ability are a function of objective socioeconomic level, this could create an artifactual tendency for blacks to have lower self-estimated abilities than do whites.

On the other hand, even if objectively equal socioeconomic levels do characterize the black and white samples being compared, this does not necessarily mean that subjective socioeconomic level has been equalized. For example, the white-collar classification, being more unusual for a black than a white person, may carry more prestige among black subjects if they are using their own group as a reference group. If this argument is correct, objectively equated racial groups may contain more blacks who experience prestige as a result of their own (or their fathers') job classification. This might be expected to lead to higher self-estimates of ability among black subjects at any given socioeconomic level, except perhaps the very lowest. Third, if one tries to choose groups comparable on IQ, standardized achievement tests, or GPA, one may attain this in objective terms, yet have included in the black group persons who are actually more able, knowledgeable, or proficient than are those in the white group having comparable scores. This possibility occurs to the extent that IQ, school tests, and standardized achievement-test scores are unfair to black groups, as has been frequently asserted. If the blacks are more able, although objectively comparable to the whites, this should lead to their giving higher self-estimates of ability.

Related to the latter point is one connected with the racial context of the schools from which subjects are chosen. In segregated schools, blacks may make grades equal to or better than the whites with whom the researcher is comparing them, i.e., the reference group against which members of each racial group are judging their schoolwork ability are respectively different. This kind of uncontrolled factor would tend to lead to more favorable self-concepts of schoolwork ability among the blacks if all or most of them in a given study came from segregated schools.

Thus, comparing racial groups chosen so as to be comparable regarding IQ, GPA, standardized achievement-test scores, and objectively defined socioeconomic level might well lead to finding that the self-concept of schoolwork ability or intelligence of blacks is close to that of whites or even exceeds it significantly, despite any possible hypothetical general tendency for a disparaged minority group to have lower over-all self-regard.

Finally, blacks have more reason than do whites to assume that their school performance does not represent their ability. This is partly because they may well assume that the teachers are prejudiced and/or that society has deprived them of the opportunity to develop their potential. For example, in A. B. Wilson's (1969) study described below, "two-fifths of the Negroes and one-fifth of the remaining students thought that teachers preferred white students" (p. 48). Rosenberg and Simmons (1972), in their study extensively described in section B-4-a above, report that the correlation between children's grades in school and "how smart" they said they were was much stronger for whites than for blacks (*gammas* = 0.7134 and 0.3609 respectively). Thus, if the blacks do make the above-mentioned assumptions, this could be one more reason to expect their estimates of their schoolwork ability to equal or exceed the self-estimates made by whites, when socioeconomic level, ability, and achievement scores are controlled.

Substantively Described Studies

Immediately below, I substantively summarize 6 studies in which *N*s equalled or exceeded 1,000 and 1 with small *N*s. These researches varied greatly with respect to geographical representativeness of samples, the degree to which the above-discussed control problems were confronted, and the type of instrument used to index self-concept of schoolwork ability or self-estimates of intelligence.

Undoubtedly the most famous research on this topic is the so-called Coleman Report (Coleman, Campbell, Hobson, McPartland, Mood, Weinfeld, & York, 1966, 1972), which was based on a stratified two-stage probability sample of the public schools in the United States and the District of Columbia. Included in the report were 645,000 pupils in Grades 1, 3, 6, 9, and 12 from 4,000 schools.

What Coleman et al. called simply "self-concept" is more appropriately labeled "self-concept of schoolwork ability," as an examination of the questions reveals. No self-concept question was asked in Grade 1; a single question, unique to that group, was asked of third graders; three questions (two of which were unique to that group) were asked of sixth graders; and three questions were asked of both ninth and twelfth graders, only one of these being the same question as one used in the sixth grade. Why Coleman et al. used such different indexes in different grades is not explained or self-evident. The report gives no information about the reliability of the self-concept measures and gives no formal consideration to problems of their validity or psychometric properties, as these might affect interpretations of group differences in self-concept. One can locate in the appendices means, standard deviations, and correlations between self-concept scores and reading comprehension and math achievement. The latter run between .2 and .4 for all black and all white students.

Although a major point of the research was to make racial/ethnic comparisons, substantive statements about racial/ethnic differences in "self-concept" are made only about the ninth- and twelfth-grade findings:

> Three questions were used at the 12th- and 9th-grade levels to obtain an indication of the child's self-concept. These are:
> (1) How bright do you think you are in comparison with the other students in your grade? [5 steps] . . .
> (2) Agree or disagree: I sometimes feel that I just can't learn. . . .
> (3) Agree or disagree: I would do better in schoolwork if teachers didn't go so fast. . . .
> In general, the responses to these questions do not indicate differences between Negroes and whites, but do indicate differences between them and the other minority groups. Negroes and whites show similar levels of response to these items, though there are variations among regions. Each of the other groups shows lower self-concept on each of these questions than does either the Negro sample or the white sample. [Coleman et al., 1966, p. 281]

Although the appendices show that achievement tests correlated 0.2 to 0.4 with the self-concept measures and that parents' educational level correlated 0.1 and 0.2 with self-concept measures, there is no indication that data analyses relevant to racial/ethnic comparisons on self-concept indices controlled for ability and achievement or for socioeconomic level. Also, there is no indication that racial school context and the possible influence of the reliability artifact (see Wylie, 1974, pp. 119-121) were controlled in the racial/ethnic comparisons. Because of this, and for other reasons given above, the conclusions of Coleman et al. are moot.

(See section B-6-b below for a discussion of the "sense of environmental control" scores used in racial comparisons made in the Coleman report.)

Bachman's (1970) survey of 2,213 tenth-grade boys in 87 public high schools is described more fully in chapter 3 of this book. He emphasizes that there were only 256 black respondents and that his sampling was not set up to study race differences adequately. His idiosyncratic index of self-concept of schoolwork ability is based on 3 questions, with item intercorrelations ranging from .29 to .53, and with item-total rs ranging from .74 to .81. Racial/ethnic categories were: all whites, blacks in integrated schools, blacks in northern segregated schools, other racial minorities, blacks in southern segregated schools. In his multivariate analysis which held constant socioeconomic level, number of siblings, broken home, family relationships, religious preference, family political preference, community size, and Quick Test of Intelligence scores, *Beta* for the relationship of these categories to self-concept of schoolwork ability = .14. It is interesting that all three black groups exceeded the white self-concept mean.

In commenting on these results, Bachman (1970) points out:

> One of the things that makes interpretation difficult is the very nature of our measure of self-concept of school ability. Respondents were asked to rate themselves "compared with those in your grade in school" or "compared with other boys your age." In principle, the appropriate reference groups would be a very broad cross-section of young men; however, to the extent that respondents actually used friends and acquaintances as their reference group, their answers may contain some built-in controls for socioeconomic level and intellectual ability. For example, a black respondent in a southern segregated school may quite correctly see himself as above average in scholastic ability compared with his friends, yet be closer to the average when compared with our total sample. In this example, the respondent has already matched himself with others of roughly equal socioeconomic level and intellectual ability; the adjustments provided by Multiple Classification Analysis in such a case might actually overcompensate. [Pp. 101-102]

In A. B. Wilson's (1969) research, a population of 17,000 pupils in 11 public junior and senior high schools in industrial urban Western

Contra Costa County, California, were stratified by sex, race, school, and grade level; random samples were taken at each stratum; and "unequal sampling fractions were applied to various strata so that the sample would contain sufficient numbers of minority-group children to provide an adequate sample base for analysis" (p. 2). Of the 5,545 pupils drawn, three-fourths

> completed an extensive set of questionnaires. . . . Those who completed the questionnaire were somewhat better students than those who were chronically absent, dropped out, made numerous response errors or whose parents refused [so that they did not complete the questionnaire]. Corrective weights have been applied to the estimate based upon the 4,077 students who remained in the final sample to allow for differential attrition between strata as well as the initial disproportionate sampling. [Pp. 2–3]

Two-thirds of the area's residents were manual workers, about 12% were blacks, and there was considerable segregation by race and socioeconomic level.

A multivariate analysis was made of sources of variation in percentages of students who said they were capable of obtaining A and B grades. When looking at the contribution of black-white status to these estimates of schoolwork ability, the following sources of variation were independently estimated: eighth-grade verbal ability, lower-class junior high school, lower-class intermediate school, first-grade mental maturity, lack of supervision by mother, number of objects in home, number of siblings, family socioeconomic status, and sex. The partial regression coefficients for black and white were small but significant. In the secondary-school sample, 70% of whites and only 44% of blacks reported that they thought they were capable of making A and B grades. However, commenting on the results of the multivariate analysis, Wilson said, "In fact, although the difference is not large, allowing for differences in measured achievement and other related variables, Negroes report slightly higher perception of their academic ability than whites" (p. 48). (Wilson's work has also been published in a report of the United States Commission on Civil Rights [1967, Appendix C–3].)

For their analyses of race, Wylie (1963) and Wylie and Hutchins (1967) used idiosyncratic questions to index self-concept of schoolwork ability in 4 main groups of subjects totaling 3,429: 2 junior high school groups (taken from the same school in 1959 and 1965), and 2 different high school groups. All subjects were from schools in small industrial northern cities which had had integrated schools for many years. In the city from which 3 groups came, blacks comprised about 11% of the population; the fourth group came from a city including 23% blacks. In each of 3 of these schools, subjects were divided into ability subgroups according to 10-unit IQ levels (e.g., 60-69; 70-79), while subjects in 1 of the schools were trichotomized on the basis of the Differential Aptitude Test (deciles 7-8-9; 3-4-5-6; 0-1-2). Then, on the basis of Hollingshead's Occupational Scale, each IQ (or DAT) subgroup was divided into high [Classes 1-4] versus low [Classes 5-7]. Because there were few blacks in Classes 1-4, the analyses for race were based on only those subjects in Classes 5-7.

In each school, the students were told, "By ability we don't mean necessarily how well you *actually* do your schoolwork, but rather how well you *could* do schoolwork if you tried your best . . . decide whether you would probably belong in the top half of the students in your homeroom, or . . . somewhere below the top half." They were also asked [assuming parental approval, your desire to attend college, and enough money, do you] "feel right now that, so far as your ability to do the work is concerned, you will be able to go through college?" (Answers were dichotomized.)

To look for relationships between race and self-concepts of schoolwork ability with ability scores controlled, 11 pairs of comparison subgroups of black and white students were formed such that each pair of comparison subgroups was equated with respect to ability scores and was comprised of at least 10 cases per racial subgroup.

Out of 11 subgroup pair comparisons, 6 showed a larger percent of whites stating that their ability was in the top half of their homeroom (one of these differences being significant). However, in 8 out of 11 subgroup pairs, a larger percent of blacks reported they thought they had the ability to go to college. It is interesting that no consistent trend in college-ability estimates was observed at the junior high school level (3 out of 6 pairs yielded higher percents for blacks), whereas the trend was entirely consistent in the senior high school groups (5 out of 5 pairs yielded higher percents for blacks, 1 of these pair-comparisons being individually significant). In 2 of the schools, 1 junior high school and 1 senior high school, students who thought they had college ability were asked to list 1 or 2 colleges at which they believed they could succeed and get a worthwhile education. Inspection of the names of the listed colleges offered no basis for suggesting that the blacks' expressions of self-confidence depended on their imagining themselves succeeding at easier colleges.

Among the limitations of this study are 3 of special relevance to the present topic: (a) The indices of self-concept of schoolwork ability are idiosyncratic, and no psychometric information on them is available (except that percents of students estimating they had "top half" or college-level ability increased regularly as a function of IQ class interval). (b) Only subjects from Hollingshead occupational classifications 5–7 were used. (c) Because of restrictions set in forming subgroups of comparable IQ with N at least equal to 10, the total Ns used for racial comparisons were reduced to 252 blacks and 1,192 whites. (d) The method of data analysis did not provide for statistical analysis of interactions.

Within these limitations and with socioeconomic level and ability scores held constant, these data offer no support to the idea that blacks' self-concepts of schoolwork ability are seriously depressed; the burden of proof is on those who offer such an hypothesis.

In Rosenberg and Simmons's (1972) study, extensively described in section B–4–b of this chapter, subjects were asked "How smart do you think you are? (very smart, pretty smart, a little smart, not at all smart)." For 441 black and 346 white secondary-school pupils in Baltimore City, Maryland, schools, response percentages were published for each of 3 grade levels: B average, C average, D average. (Too few A averages were available to warrant comparisons.) Visual inspection of their table suggests great racial similarity in self-estimated smartness by subjects attaining B and C averages. However, more black than white students with D averages thought they were "pretty smart" (63% vs. 45%), and 0% of blacks as compared to 20% of whites with D averages thought they were "not at all smart." Since no significance tests were presented and neither socioeconomic level nor racial school context was controlled in this analysis, firm inferences cannot be drawn. However, one would expect both these uncontrolled variables to operate against the presented slight trend toward higher black self-estimates; so perhaps these figures underestimate this trend, if anything. In any event, no support is given by this study to the hypothesis that blacks' estimates of their schoolwork ability are depressed.

In a sampling procedure designed to represent the total noninstitutionalized population of the United States who were at least 21 years old, Brim, Neulinger, and Glass (1965) report answers of 1,273 whites and 187 blacks to the following question: How do you think you compare to other people in intelligence? (father, mother, brothers in general, sisters in general, wife [or husband], your children, average person in the United States today, people who do the same kind of work, people you went to high school with, most of your friends today). Respondents could choose: I am much higher, higher, the same as, lower, much lower, or does not apply.

The authors report that 75% of whites and 75.4% of blacks thought themselves higher than others on one or more comparisons, whereas 60.6% of whites and 61.5% of blacks thought themselves lower on one or more comparisons. However, since racial answers were compared without regard to ability or achievement scores, socioeconomic level, or actual ability differences in the respective reference groups, these results are uninterpretable. The lack of control of ability scores and socioeconomic level would be expected to operate against the possibility of blacks' self-estimates of intelligence equaling or exceeding those of whites, but the lack of control of reference groups would probably tend to increase the possibility that black self-estimates would equal or exceed those of whites.

The final large-scale study summarized in this section involves the frequency of occurrence of Student Role, Academic Concerns, Positive Intellectual Ability, and Negative Intellectual Ability responses in the self-descriptions of 2,150 ninth-grade students in 8 Pittsburgh, Pennsylvania, schools (Wellman, 1971). Included were 1,212 blacks and 938 whites, classified into 3 socioeconomic levels according to Duncan's Socioeconomic Index for All Occupations. Responses to the Who Am I? test were analyzed into 92 categories of self-conception by using a specially constructed 'dictionary' in conjunction with the General Inquirer content analysis system of B. McLaughlin (1966). (See Wylie, 1974, pp. 240-247, for a description and evaluation of this instrument and scoring system.)

Whether response totals were controlled between races is not clear, and this could affect the comparisons in unknown ways. In an analysis which did not control for socioeconomic level or ability scores, Wellman reported that whites more often used Student Role self-characteristics (73.0% to 64.8%) and significantly more often used Negative Intellectual Ability self-characterizations (12.4% to 7.7%). No race differences were observed regarding Positive Intellectual Ability or Academic Concerns responses. The significant findings about Negative Intellectual Ability are opposite to the direction which might plausibly be produced by the uncontrolled socioeconomic level and ability score variables. Unfortunately, although data regarding

Student Role were also tabulated by socioeconomic level, race, and racial school context, they were not analyzed for race effects with these other variables controlled.

In Baughman and Dahlstrom's (1968) well-known research involving 1,222 children, small groups of eighth graders (58 whites and 78 blacks) were intensively interviewed with a schedule which contained a question relevant to self-concept of schoolwork ability: "If you really did your very best, what do you think your average would be? A, A−, B+, B, B−, C+, C, C−, D+, D, D−, F." Interviewers were of the same race as respondents. The trend toward higher proportions of blacks reporting they could attain A− grades or better was not significant. Parenthetically it is relevant to note that there was a significant trend for more blacks to report that their actually attained grade average was B− or better. Therefore, the index of academic accomplishment relevant to estimates of self-concepts of schoolwork ability favored blacks and perhaps determined the blacks' optimism. Although both groups were from the rural south and of relatively low socioeconomic level, in both these comparisons, segregated school context was confounded with race, and the comparisons were but two among many significance tests made on dependent variables which must have been intercorrelated. Therefore, no conclusions can be reached on the basis of this study regarding racial differences in reports of self-concepts of schoolwork ability.

Summary of Substantively Described Studies

Three of the above-described researches neglected to take socioeconomic level and ability scores into account when looking for racial differences in self-conceptions of ability or intelligence. Their typically null findings are uninterpretable for a variety of reasons, but at least it is clear that their lack of control did not suffice to push the blacks' self-estimates significantly below those of the whites, the direction of difference predicted by many theorists, and also the direction in which these uncontrolled variables would be expected to operate.

In the four studies which tried in various ways to control for one or both of these variables, the blacks tended to make higher self-estimates of ability, but in three of these reports the trend was either not significant or its significance was not reported.

As explained in the beginning of this section, one has no way of knowing whether the attempts to hold ability and socioeconomic level constant by use of objective measures may actually have led to the blacks' having higher ability and more prestigious socioeconomic level (in terms of their own reference groups, at least), than did their objectively comparable white counterparts. How much of the trend toward higher black self-estimates might be due to this cannot be evaluated with the information available.

Finally, it should be remembered that none of these reports gave adequate information concerning the psychometric properties of the responses to the idiosyncratic questions used to index self-conceptions of ability; so the possible influence of unreliability, invalidity, or distribution characteristics of the index scores cannot be evaluated.

Studies Not Substantively Described

In addition to the researches described above, I examined the following studies concerned with racial/ethnic differences in self-estimates of ability. They appeared to me to be even more flawed and limited than those already described. J. G. Anderson and Johnson (1971) and Carter (1968), both based on Mexican-Anglo subjects; Gibby and Gabler (1967), Herman, Sadofsky, Bensman, Lilienfeld, and Manos (1967), Hunt and Hardt (1969), Paschal and Williams (1970), all based on black-white comparisons. (Some information about the reports by Herman et al. [1967], and Hunt & Hardt [1969] are given in section B-4-a of this chapter.)

A racial-comparison study by Kleinfeld (1972) was directed at correlations between teachers' and students' and between parents' and students' evaluations of students' academic abilities. This study lacks several important controls, and the comparisons are not interpretable in any event, in view of the lack of psychometric information about the correlated measures.

b. SELF-CONCEPTIONS OF OTHER SPECIFIC
PERSONALITY CHARACTERISTICS

Because self-conceptions can include many other relatively specific dimensions besides self-evaluations of schoolwork ability or intelligence, this section is devoted to examining studies which can be construed as being directed toward some of those other dimensions. The makers of many well-known self-report "personality tests" typically have considered their instruments to be potentially valid indices of the respondents' "actual" personality characteristics, rather than indices of their self-conceptions. However, other researchers have used these same instruments in their attempts to index specific aspects of self-concept, arguing or implying that, since these self-report personality tests are operationally indistinguishable from many other tests which have been explicitly called self-concept indices, these, too, may be construed as self-concept indices.

The first part of this section deals with racial comparisons on scores from several relatively well-known self-report tests about which some reliability and validity information has been published. Unfortunately, most of these researches are undefinitive regarding racial differences in self-conception since they fall far short of fulfilling many of the methodological criteria given in sections A, 2–4 above, and/or the published reports are characterized by vagueness and omission of essential information. Accordingly, they are simply listed rather than being substantively summarized.

Interpersonal Check List (ICL)

McDonald and Gynther (1965) and McDonald (1968) look at racial differences in Dom and Lov Self scores from the ICL. In the earlier study, urban southern high school seniors were subjects, whereas rural southern high school seniors served as subjects in the later research. Race was confounded with segregated school context in each study, and in neither study were IQ and GPA controlled by the ANOVAs which did not take socioeconomic level and sex into account. In each report, multiple significance tests were given, involving correlated dependent variables, which makes evaluation of the significance of any outcome impossible. In the 1965 report, blacks are said to have obtained significantly higher Dom and Lov Self scores than did whites, with the racial Dom difference being greater for males than for females (interaction significant at < .01 level). In the 1968 publication, blacks again were reported to have higher Dom scores, even though a reversal occurred for higher socioeconomic males (but with no significant interaction). The racial main effect for Lov was not significant in the second report, with significant interactions occurring for sex × race and for race × class. In view of the inherent methodological problems in each study and the failure to replicate, even within a southern high school population, it seems unwarranted to conclude that Dom and Lov differences attributable to racial status per se have been demonstrated. (For a description and evaluation of the Interpersonal Check List, see Wylie, 1974, pp. 213-223.)

Minnesota Multiphasic Personality Inventory (MMPI)

More racial-comparison studies have been done with MMPI scales than with any other self-report instrument. Ages of subjects have ranged from 14 through adulthood, and researchers have included racial comparisons within groups of southern pupils, southern and northern prison inmates, medical outpatients, VA tuberculosis patients, VA mental-hygiene applicants, and low-income pregnant women. Harrison and Kass (1967) tabulated the results of researches appearing before theirs, providing a useful overview of reported findings.

A quick inspection of Harrison and Kass's table in conjunction with their own reported results and those of Baughman and Dahlstrom (1968) leaves the impression that considerable agreement has occurred with respect to racial differences on the following scales: *Hs* (5 out of 11 studies show black males, black females, or blacks higher, while 1 shows whites higher). *Hy* (4 out of 10 show white females or whites higher; no reversals). *Ma* (7 out of 11 show black males or black females or blacks higher; no reversals). The results for remaining scales either show mixed results or no differences.

These trends are suggestive, but before interpreting them as indicative of *racial* differences in self-reporting, self-conception, or clinical characteristics, one must introduce grave reservations based on an examination of the primary sources. In every research, the racial groups differed on one or several important variables, e.g., racial context of school, socioeconomic level, IQ, or degree of literacy. Of particular interest is the fact that the black samples tended to score higher on *L* and *F* scales (5 out of 11 studies on *L*; 6 out of 11 on *F*). One way that this might be explained is in terms of the operation of the reliability artifact. (See Wylie, 1974, pp. 119-121, for a fuller discussion of the reliability artifact.) For example, if reading or comprehension was lower in the black samples and more random choosing was therefore occurring, the *L* or *F* scores would thereby be increased. If this interpretation is correct, the reliability artifact might also account for higher black scores on the clinical subscales. However, this line of thought does not account for the fact that some scales rather than others tend most consistently to yield higher black scores. An examination of the grammatical complexity and vocabulary of the items in these particular scales might throw some light on this question. Harrison and Kass (1967) report that 213 out of 550 *items* showed race differences significant at < .05 level. Factoring the most significant 150 of these, they obtained 20 factors, each of which discriminated between their racial samples at < .001 level. This work has not been cross-validated using racial samples adequately equated with respect to other variables. Accordingly, interpretations must be held in abeyance. (Harrison and Kass, 1968, also analyzed a subset of their original data, with cases chosen to represent northern whites, northern-born blacks, and southern-born blacks. Although they state that their results closely parallel those from the samples which included this subset, no significance information is given specifically for comparisons between northern whites and northern-born blacks. In any event, one is still not assured that the samples were adequately equated with respect to literacy level.)

For another viewpoint on racial differences in the MMPI, the reader may wish to look at Dreger (1973).

Studies Using Well-Known Instruments Not Substantively Summarized

Activity Vector Analysis (AVA)
   Hasler and Clarke (1967)

Allport-Vernon Study of Values
   S. Gray (1947)

Bernreuter's Four Scales
   Eagleson (1938)
   Patrick and Sims (1934)

Cattell's Sixteen Personality Factor Questionnaire (16 PF)
   McClain (1967)

Children's Manifest Anxiety Scale (CMAS)
   Palermo (1959)

California Psychological Inventory (CPI)
   Ageton and Elliott (1974)

California Test of Personality (CTP)
   Engle (1945)

Depression Scales (MMPI and others)
Marsella, Sanborne, Kameoka, Shizuru, and Brennan (1975), comparing Chinese-Americans, Japanese-Americans, and Caucasians at the University of Hawaii

Edwards Personal Preference Scales (EPPS)
Brazziel (1964)
Grossack (1957)

Body-Cathexis Scale (BC)
Arkoff and Weaver (1966), comparing Japanese-Americans and Caucasian-Americans from Hawaii

Taylor Manifest Anxiety Scale (TMAS)
Roen (1960)

Tennessee Self-Concept Scales (16 dimensions besides Total Positive score)
Williams and Byars (1968)

Studies Using Idiosyncratic Measures

Turning now to *racial comparisons of self-conception* which used idiosyncratic measures to index relatively specific aspects of self-concept, one finds that most of these results, too, are inconclusive because researches fall very short of fulfilling many of the methodological criteria given in sections A, 2–4 above, and/or the published reports are characterized by vagueness and omission of essential information. The seven least adequate studies which do not seem to warrant substantive summaries are listed at the end of this section. Six others, although also suffering from serious methodological limitations, seem to warrant some substantive attention and are dealt with below in order of increasing ages of subjects.

Perhaps one could consider "sense of environmental control" as used by the authors of the famous Coleman Report (Coleman, Campbell, Hobson, McPartland, Mood, Weinfeld, & York, 1966), to be a specific aspect of self-concept. For this variable, only one question was used for sixth graders, only three questions for ninth and twelfth graders, and apparently none for third graders. All the questions appear to be directed toward the subjects' sense of environmental control as related to attaining "success in life," and there is no discussion of reliability, validity, or psychometric properties of this index. (The appendices give means, standard deviations, and correlations of this variable with all other variables used in the study. Also, frequency distributions of percentages of subjects giving each answer's alternate are tabulated on pp. 289–290, for each separate question, although not for the total index score labeled "sense of environmental control.") Coleman et al. (1966) state:

> On all these items, Negroes and other minority children show much lower sense of control of their environment than do whites . . . there is an objective basis for this difference in feelings of control, since these minority children have less chance to control their environment than do the majority whites. What is not clear, however, is how much of this can be accounted for by school factors, how much by family difference, and how much by their general position in society. [P. 289]

One might also add that, in making these racial/ethnic comparisons, Coleman et al. did not control for achievement levels (mathematics and reading scores correlated between 0.2 and 0.4 with sense of environmental control scores among all Negroes and all whites) or for the possible influence of the reliability artifact (see Wylie, 1974, pp. 119–121).

As reported in section B-4-b above, Hurlock (1927) found a great amount of overlap in the specific undesirable characteristics used in self-descriptions made by seventh- and eighth-grade blacks and whites.

Hartnagel (1970) was interested in studying the effect of both father absence and racial status on self-perceived "potency," as indicated by an idiosyncratic set of four semantic-differential scales previously determined by an undescribed factor analysis to indicate "potency." The sum of self-ratings on these potency scales (brave-cowardly, strong-weak, powerful-powerless, big-small) were used to approximate the "masculine self-concept." No reliability or validity information was given. The question defining father availability is poor, as the author points out. Boys from one inner-city high school in Indiana comprised the sample of 74 whites and 201 blacks. IQs all exceeded 90, and presumably the use of the one inner city school implied some control over socioeconomic level and racial school context of racial comparison groups.

For "actual self" potency, race was significant (with blacks giving more potent self-descriptions), whereas father availability and the interaction were not significant. Similarly with respect to self-ideal discrepancies on the potency dimension, race was significant (with blacks having greater self-ideal congruence), and father availability was insignificant. However, in this analysis a significant interaction was obtained coming from smaller self-ideal discrepancies among blacks with fathers absent than among whites with fathers absent. (As might be inferred from the above, no significant effects were obtained with the ideal-self potency scores.)

Short and Strodtbeck's (1965) extensive research on gang and nongang boys in a large city is very difficult to evaluate because of serious problems in sampling, instrumentation, scoring techniques, and data analysis. Nevertheless, a detailed examination of the report suggests that racial differences seem to vary as a function of socioeconomic level and gang membership of the racial groups being compared, implying important cautions which one should bear in mind when evaluating outcomes in this research area.

Altogether, 703 blacks and 362 whites were studied, divided as follows: 12 lower-class black gangs (N = 504); 15 lower-class white gangs (N = 191); 165 black and 117 white lower-class, nongang boys recruited from youth-serving agencies in gang areas; 34 black and 54 white middle-class nongang boys from YMCA and Hi-Y groups. Eighteen pairs of opposite adjectives and 4 unpaired adjectives were used in the idiosyncratic measure of self-concept dimensions, about which virtually no reliability or validity information is given. Each subject had to describe himself separately with respect to each member of an adjective pair, e.g., to tell how friendly he was and also how unfriendly.

Because Short and Strodtbeck used a questionable form of discrepancy score, I present here some brief descriptive observations culled from their tables of mean self-rating values on the 18 adjective pairs (pp. 149 ff.). Only if the racial difference was consistent have I listed it below, e.g., only if more friendly and also less unfriendly mean self-ratings characterized one racial group as compared to the other, is the adjective pair listed as an instance of a racial difference.

Considering first the *lower-class gang members:* whites' self-descriptions were more friendly and less unfriendly, more smart and less dumb, more kind and less mean, more cool and less square, more manly and less womanly. Blacks' self-descriptions were more cheerful and less sad, more brave and less cowardly. The remaining 11 dimensions did not yield such consistent within-adjective-pair racial differences. Altogether, in 5 out of 18 comparisons, whites' mean self-descriptions were more favorable; in 2 out of 18 comparisons, blacks' mean self-descriptions were more favorable, and no consistent trends were noted for the other 11 scales.

A different picture emerges in black-white comparisons based on *lower-class nongang members*. Here whites' self-descriptions were both more studious and less lazy, but this is the only adjective pair on which the whites consistently exceeded the blacks. The black lower-class nongang self-descriptions were, as in the gang comparisons, more cheerful and less sad, and more brave and less cowardly. However, the lower-class nongang black self-descriptions were also more cool and less square, more friendly and less unfriendly, more good and less bad, more obedient and less disobedient, more lucky and less unlucky, more strong and less weak. Thus, the black-white comparisons yield different results, depending on whether one is talking about lower-class gang or lower-class nongang boys. (Altogether, 8 out of 18 comparisons favored the blacks, 1 favored the whites, and 9 showed no consistent trend.)

Turning to the *middle-class nongang members*, one finds that more studious and less lazy were, as with lower-class nongang members, more characteristics of the whites' self-descriptions, and this was the only dimension out of 18 on which whites' self-descriptions were consistently more favorable. Nine of 18 dimensions favor the blacks in the middle-class nongang comparisons: more friendly and less unfriendly, more clean and less dirty, more polite and less rude, more brave and less cowardly, more helpful and less troublesome, more exciting and less boring, more tough and less soft, more manly and less womanly, more strong and less weak. It is evident that there is considerable lack of overlap in the specific dimensions of self-report favoring the blacks in the three sets of racial comparisons.

In the absence of psychometric information and significance tests, all these descriptive contrasts between blacks' and whites' self-report means must be viewed with extreme caution. However, it is interesting to note the following two points: (a) The number of self-descriptive adjective pairs which yield racial differences varied, depending on whether one was making racial comparisons among gang or nongang members, or among lower-class and middle-class nongang members. Among lower-class nongang and middle-class nongang boys, 8 out of 18 and 9 out of 18 self-description means of blacks were more favorable, with only 1 out of 18 white self-description means being more favorable. Only when making racial comparisons among lower-class gang members do we find 5 out of 18 self-description means favoring whites, with only 2 out of 18 favoring blacks. (Over-all, these differences do not give consistent support to the hypothesis that black self-esteem is depressed.) (b) Although there is no way to know how replicable the results involving each specific scale might be, if there is any lesson to be learned from these means, it is that *we had better not assume that specific self-description differences found in racial comparisons at one socioeconomic level will characterize racial comparisons at another socioeconomic level.*

In Steinmann and Fox's (1970) study of "female values" among 100 black and 126 white female undergraduates, socioeconomic level was approximately controlled, but racial school context and southern (as opposed to northern) subculture varied between racial groups. Subjects responded to an idiosyncratic instrument, not published in the article, which purportedly indexed family orientation as opposed to self-achievement orientation among women respondents (the Maferr Inventory of Female Values). No significant difference in mean scores for self-descriptions were obtained. Obviously interpretation of these null findings is not possible.

As was the case with a number of national surveys described in this chapter, analysis by race was not the main purpose of the large scale study done by the National Council on the Aging (1975), described in chapter 2 of this book.

With respect to the responses of those at least 65 years old to the idiosyncratic 7-item self-image scale, the report states that larger percentages of whites than blacks considered themselves to be very friendly and warm (73% to 69%), very wise from experience (70% to 63%), very bright and alert (69% to 54%), very open-minded and adaptable (64% to 51%), very good at getting things done (56% to 45%), very physically active (50% to 31%). On self-reports of being very sexually active there was essentially no racial difference (10% to 11%).

With respect to the entire age range, but giving details on only three of the self-image questions, the report states,

> Some of these same differences exist between younger blacks and whites, but to a much lesser extent. Seventy-three percent of whites 18 to 64 see themselves as very bright and alert, compared with a lower 65% of blacks 18 to 64. In some areas, however, younger blacks match younger whites in self-esteem: 60% of whites 18 to 64 see themselves as very good at getting things done, compared with a comparable 61% of blacks. [P. 150]

The table on p. 150 also shows that 66% of the younger whites and 59% of the younger blacks report that they are very physically active.

Although these descriptive percentages are based on a large random probability sample of the American public ≥ 18 years old, supplemented by additional samples of (a) respondents aged 55-64, (b) respondents aged ≥ 65, and (c) black respondents aged ≥ 65, one cannot draw firm inferences about racial differences. This is the case because (a) the instrument used is idiosyncratic, and its psychometric properties are not reported; (b) no significance tests are given; (c) when making racial comparisons, no controls are described for such variables as educational level and performance, socioeconomic level, possible operation of the reliability artifact, or interviewer effects.

Also dealing with older persons, Messer (1968) asked 118 black and 125 white respondents ≥ 62 years of age "How do you think of yourself as far as age goes?" Answers were coded into two categories of self-conception of age (elderly; middle-aged or young) by an incompletely described procedure. All respondents had occupied public housing at least 2 years and were presumably roughly comparable with respect to socioeconomic level. Controls for ability levels, state of health (of plausible relevance to the feelings of being old), or effects of interviewer's race were not mentioned. In each of 3 chronological age brackets, more blacks reported that they conceived of themselves as elderly. The author speculated that blacks may more readily see themselves as elderly because having suffered more deprivations in their lifetimes, they "may well think of themselves as having lived through the worst of it" and "old age may be perceived as a kind of reward in itself" (p. 248). One may also wonder whether health differences could be a factor in this racial difference in self-conception of age, and whether, since fewer blacks live to be old, the surviving elders may have a more unusual, honorific status. But before concluding anything, we need replication of these findings, with more controls incorporated in the procedure.

Overview of Studies of Specific Aspects of Self-Concept

Obviously the six researches reviewed in this section are extremely heterogeneous with respect to self-concept dimensions examined, instruments which purportedly indexed these dimensions, other aspects of method, and reported results. No interpretative generalizations can be drawn.

This group of studies does not enable us to see whether self-descriptions correspond in any way to racial/ethnic stereotypes, as discussed in section B-3. Accordingly, both the question as to racial/ethnic differences in specific aspects of self-conception and the question whether there are correspondences between racial/ethnic self-conceptions and stereotypes are unanswerable at this point.

Studies Using Idiosyncratic Instruments, Not Substantively Summarized

Arkoff and Weaver (1966), Japanese- and Caucasian-Americans at University of Hawaii; Attenborough and Zdep (1973); Back and Paramesh (1969), whites, blacks, and Madras Indians; Carter (1968), Mexican-Americans and Anglos; Gaier and Wambach (1960); Knight (1969).

7. Values and Ideals for Self as a Function of Racial/Ethnic Status

As is true in all areas of self-concept research, relatively few investigators who looked at racial/ethnic variables have been concerned with comparing individuals' conceptions of their ideal selves as opposed to their conceptions of their actual selves or their levels of self-regard.

Although the term "ideal self" has not typically been defined so as to include educational and occupational aspirations, I include these constructs under that rubric because it seems to me the type of person one ideally wishes one could become must include his or her educational/occupational identity. Accordingly, I include this kind of variable in the first section below. A few publications which dealt with explicit statements about ideal self or with miscellaneous "self values" (which I also construe as self-ideals) are in the second section below.

a. EDUCATIONAL AND OCCUPATIONAL ASPIRATIONS

Methodological Considerations

There is no agreement among researchers about the operations used to measure educational or occupational aspirations, and in the studies I examined very little or no information is given about the reliability, validity, or psychometric properties of the purported indices of educational or occupational aspirations. It seems obvious that one should not expect to get equivalent answers to interview or written questions which explicitly refer to wanting, wishing, or aspiring, as opposed to planning or expecting. Particularly when comparing groups which have unequal access to educational institutions and occupations, answers concerning planning and expecting could reasonably be quite different from those concerning wanting, even when socioeconomic level and ability and achievement scores are controlled. In particular, if family size at the same socioeconomic level varies between groups being compared, realistic financial constraints might make the groups' plans and expectations differ even if their aspirations were similar.

Some investigators have compared wanting, expecting, and planning statements and have found them to be about the same (Gist and Bennett, 1963) or have found them to yield practically identical relationships with other variables (St. John, 1966). Others have found that plans or expectations were more modest (C. S. Johnson, 1967; Stephenson, 1957), or that they were by no means identical (A. J. Lott & B. E. Lott, 1963). The burden of proof is on the person who asserts that these varieties of questions yield essentially the same distribution of answers or the same relationships of answers with other variables.

Although precise comparability of socioeconomic level between racial/ethnic groups is probably impossible to attain for reasons discussed in chapter 3 and in section A-2 of this chapter, studies which attempt some such control are better than those which do not, since there appears to be a trend for both educational and occupational aspirations to be a positive function of the family socioeconomic level of young persons, even when ability scores are held constant (see chapter 3 of this book).

Because IQ and educational achievement tend to vary as a function of racial/ethnic status, even with socioeconomic level constant, and since educational and occupational aspirations tend to be related to ability and achievement levels, the latter as well as socioeconomic level should be held constant when making racial/ethnic comparisons regarding educational or occupational aspirations. And because grading standards vary so widely between schools, either standardized achievement tests or standardized IQ tests or both are preferable to the use of the GPA. However, as I have noted earlier, the racial/ethnic groups that are matched on IQ may actually be unequal regarding ability if the tests are more unfair to one group than the other.

Altogether, I have examined 23 studies purporting to look for racial/ethnic differences in educational and/or vocational aspirations.

Of these, 8 seem so seriously flawed and/or incompletely reported as to be uninterpretable. They are listed at the end of this section.

Substantively Considered Researches

The publications which are given some substantive consideration immediately below vary greatly in methodological adequacy, as is noted. They are presented approximately according to the grade levels of the subjects studied: eighth (Baughman & Dahlstrom, 1968); ninth (Gordon, 1972; Sprey, 1962; Stephenson, 1957); tenth (Antonovsky, 1967; Bachman, 1970; H. P. Smith & Abramson, 1962); third-twelfth (Rosenberg & Simmons, 1972); seventh-twelfth (Reiss & Rhodes, 1959; A. B. Wilson, 1969; Wylie, 1963; Wylie & Hutchins, 1967); ninth and twelfth (Gist & Bennett, 1963); ages 16-20 (Antonovsky & Lerner, 1959); twelfth (Coleman et al., 1966; A. J. Lott & B. E. Lott, 1963); college seniors (J. H. Davis, 1964).

The reader may wish to refer to Dreger and Miller's (1968) review of racial comparison studies appearing between 1959 and 1965 and to Kirkpatrick's (1973) more recent review of racial differences in occupational and educational aspirations for some unpublished studies and some published reports I have not been able to examine, and therefore did not include in this section.

As one part of Baughman and Dahlstrom's (1968) well-known research discussed more fully in section B-4-b, extensive interviews with 58 whites (28 boys, 30 girls) and 78 blacks (32 boys, 46 girls), all *eighth graders,* contained some questions relevant to educational and occupational aspirations. Significant chi square values were reported for the following racial differences: fewer blacks said they would drop out of school now if free to do so; more blacks said they wanted to go to college. No race difference was found regarding stated expectations of realizing educational ambitions. (The phrasing of the occupational questions does not permit analyses in terms of socioeconomic level of the occupational aspirations.)

Some important variables were held approximately constant in these racial comparisons, but others were not. For example, all subjects were from the rural South and a relatively low socioeconomic class, but race was confounded with school context since all children attended segregated schools, and the achievement measure by which subjects might reasonably judge themselves and their aspirations was not comparable between groups (according to self-reports, significantly more blacks than whites obtained B- averages or better).

Altogether, then, some of the uncontrolled variables in Baughman and Dahlstrom's racial comparisons of educational aspirations might be expected to increase black aspirations, others to decrease it; so the net reported results cannot be evaluated as coming from racial status per se. Moreover, *N*s for these comparisons were small and multiple significance tests were made with intercorrelated dependent variables. These are additional reasons why these results should not be regarded as interpretable.

Stephenson (1957) asked his *ninth-grade* subjects for both their plans and wishes. After asking whether the respondent planned to quit high school, complete high school, or go to college, he inquired "After you (quit high school, complete high school, graduate from college) what kind of work do you *intend* to do? If you could do what you *really wanted to do,* what would you do?" [emphasis added]. The stated occupations were coded according to A. Edwards's socioeconomic levels. Of 1,000 ninth graders in 4 semiindustrialized medium-sized communities in New Jersey to whom the questionnaire was submitted, occupational plans and aspirations were reported by Stephenson for about 850, cross-tabulated according to race and A. Edwards's level of fathers' occupations. Only the 3 lowest socioeconomic groups could be used for racial comparisons, owing to the scarcity of black subjects whose fathers' occupations fell in the 3 highest groups. Without giving significance-test results, Stephenson (1957) says, "The Negro students tended to plan lower than the whites at each of their fathers' occupational groups, but their aspirations were uniformly high" (pp. 209–210). No control for ability scores or achievement was taken; so these verbally described trends must remain uninterpretable. In any event, the aspirational results do not fall in the direction one would predict from the lack of control of ability and/or school achievement to date. Nothing was said about the control of racial context when comparing between racial groups.

To look at "adolescent orientation to achievement," Gordon (1972) chose a 5% systematic subsample of 1,684 *ninth graders* drawn from the complete tapes of 337,000 metropolitan northeastern ninth graders used in the Coleman Report (Coleman, Campbell, Hobson, Mc-Partland, Mood, Weinfeld, & York, 1966). (Possibly serious sources of bias in the original Coleman sample were mentioned by Gordon [1972,

p. 10], as was the lack of information about just how a single verbal
ability score was obtained by Coleman et al. [1966] from the 60 items
from the Educational Testing Service's Schools and College Ability
Tests.) Since Coleman et al. presented aspiration data only for twelfth
graders, and they did not use multivariate analysis to predict
aspiration levels, Gordon's report does not overlap that of Coleman et
al. (which is briefly considered below).

Relevant to the topic of this section, Gordon (1972) chose the
following Coleman question to define "desire for education": How far
do you want to go in school? I want to finish high school only, to go to
technical, nursing, or business school after high school, some college
training but less than four years, to graduate from a four-year college,
to do professional or graduate work after I finish college.

To predict desire for education as a function of race with certain
other variables controlled, Gordon used a path analysis method within
each racial group. He then presented a low estimate of the direct path
from race to desire for education holding constant the following:
verbal ability scores, social class, family role structure (strongly male,
matriarchal, weakly male, neither present), self-esteem (measured by
an idiosyncratic instrument described in section B-4-a above), and
parental aspiration. The path coefficient (identical with a standardized *beta* weight) between race and desire for education was
− .109, indicating that blacks have a stronger desire for education than
do whites. Gordon considered this to be a low estimate of the direct
relationship of race to desire for education because the oversampling
of blacks had increased the race variance in the sample, leading to
smaller coefficients of every variable with race than would have been
the case had race been represented proportionately in the sample.

In still another study of *ninth graders*, Sprey (1962) compared
responses of 971 white and 183 black public high school students in
New Haven, Connecticut, and 1,092 white and 350 black public high
school students in Harrisburg, Pennsylvania. The actual questions
used to index aspirations and expectations were not published, and
aspirations were reported only in terms of discrepancies between
father's occupation and the student's desired occupation, a procedure
which does not enable one to look at the actual socioeconomic level of
the desired or expected occupations and which involves the inevitable
interpretative ambiguities in discrepancy or gain scores. (See Wylie,
1974, pp. 88-95, for a discussion of the pitfalls in such scores.) Some
but not all of the ambiguity in such scores is removed by the fact that

comparisons could be made only for children with parents in the skilled manual or lower manual group, since the sample did not contain enough blacks in the higher groups to warrant computation of percentages. Unfortunately, available scholastic aptitude test data "appeared to be too unreliable to be used"; so this factor was not controlled between races. No information about racial school context was published. Respondents were classified according to the Hollingshead classification of the parent's (usually the father's) occupation. In both cities, percents of black boys whose aspirations were above the parents' actual occupational levels were smaller than those of white boys (chi square significant at $\leq$ .05 level), but the black-white differences among girls did not appear to be large and consistent. Regarding expected differences between parents' and own occupational levels, the differences appear more consistent for both sexes, with such differences being smaller among the blacks. The many methodological shortcomings in this study, especially the lack of control for ability or achievement scores, make these findings uninterpretable, however.

Three researches involving only *tenth-grade* students came to my attention, one of which (Antonovsky, 1967) is simply listed below. Although Bachman's (1970) is by far the best in terms of representativeness of sampling and sophistication of multivariate analysis, he stresses that it was not planned to be an adequate basis for racial comparisons. It is also noteworthy that his questions were framed in terms of plans and/or expectations rather than aspirations or wishes. Thus, the differences cited may be conservative estimates of aspirational differences. The sample of 2,213 tenth-grade boys in 87 public high schools in the United States included 256 black respondents. Replies to the question "What sort of work do you think you might do for a living?" were coded according to Duncan's socioeconomic status index. With parents' socioeconomic level, number of siblings, broken home, family relations, religious preference, family political preference, community size, and students' scores on the Quick Test of Intelligence controlled in a Multiple Comparison Analysis, the mean occupational "aspirations" fell in the following order: all whites, racial minorities other than black, blacks in integrated schools, blacks in northern segregated schools, blacks in southern segregated schools. *Beta* = .12. Respondents naming a definite occupation in response to the above question were asked "How do you *plan* [emphasis added] to get this sort of work?" Those not stating an occupational expectation were asked what they *expected* [emphasis added] to do after high school. Bachman states:

> According to the Multiple Classification Analysis, if other family background factors were equal, 10 percent *fewer* whites than southern segregated blacks would plan to enter college. And controlling for Quick Test scores in addition to family background increases this difference to about 22 percent. Blacks in integrated schools show college aspirations slightly higher than whites, without any adjustments for other factors. Of these black students, 66 percent plan to go to college, in contrast to the 59 percent of whites. The difference of 7 percent is increases [*sic*] to 12 percent when family background differences are controlled, and to 15 percent when Quick Test scores are also controlled. [P. 186]

Although *N*s in H. P. Smith and Abramson's (1962) study were small (33 blacks, 33 whites), the racial groups of *tenth graders* in one high school in Albany, New York, were comparable in the following respects: racial school context, age, sex, intelligence (test unspecified), socioeconomic level (according to an index modified from Hollingshead). A 67-item interview contained the questions: "Have you ever thought about the kind of job or career you'd like to have when you finish school?" and "About your plans, what you actually intend to do, do you think you might go to college?" Subjects were classified as having high or low occupational "aspirations" according to some published criteria. Applying a chi square test to each set of dichotomized data, the authors reported that the black students had significantly higher educational and occupational "aspirations."

In five of the researches substantively summarized in this section, a range of grade-levels or ages was included. The widest range (*third through twelfth grades*) was covered by Rosenberg and Simmons (1972) whose work is more fully described in section B-4-b of this chapter. Eleven of their interview questions, printed verbatim in their monograph, referred to such "aspirations" as desire for wealth, importance of wealth, desire for fame, desire for a professional or executive job, aspiration to an occupation or wealth level higher than parents', level of excellence desired on one's job, level of excellence one expects to attain on one's job, desire for college, chances of going to college. Examination of a table where black and white percents were presented for each question, with age controlled, shows larger percents of blacks having high aspirations/expectations, except for a reversal regarding desire for a professional/executive job, and 0 or 1 percentage points difference regarding desire to be better than most or at the very top on the job, and regarding statements of the probability of going to college. Although Rosenberg and Simmons (1972) used a representative sample of pupils in Baltimore City, Maryland, schools and had large groups of both blacks and whites, the above-mentioned differences cannot be evaluated because ability and achievement scores, racial school context, and parental socioeconomic levels were not taken into account in making these comparisons; nor were significance tests presented. It is plausible that the differences favoring black respondents would be larger rather than smaller if these factors had been controlled. The same criticisms and speculative statements are applicable to their table giving aspiration/expectation percentages broken down according to three school levels (elementary, junior high school, senior high school).

A. B. Wilson (1969), whose sampling techniques were described in section B-6-a of this chapter, did not publish verbatim his questions about "educational aspirations for college" or "aspirations for manual occupations," which were asked of his *junior and senior high subjects.* Using covariance analysis to control for such variables as eighth-grade verbal ability, lower-class junior high school, lower-class intermediate school, first-grade mental maturity, lack of supervision by mother, number of objects in home, number of siblings, family occupational status, and sex, he concludes, "allowing for differences in achievement and school and home environments, twenty-five percent more Negroes than whites have college desires" (p. 52). On the basis of further analyses of sources of variation in college aspirations among white students and among black students, Wilson comments:

> The relatively high proportion of Negro students who are low achievers yet aspire to go to college . . . [is shown by the fact that] thirty percent of the white students whose measured verbal ability is below the thirtieth percentile say they would like to go to college; forty-three percent of the Negro students in this lowest achievement bracket have college aspirations.
>
> Differences in self-conception of ability do not account for the disproportionate number of poor-achieving Negroes who report college aspirations. Forty-one percent of the Negroes who do not think they are able to get better than C, D, or F grades nevertheless say they want to go to college . . . as we can see from the regression coefficients . . . academic performance and confidence in ability to achieve good grades are more relevant to the aspirations of white students than Negroes.
>
> It is particularly among the poor-achieving, lower-class students in predominantly lower-class schools that the reversal in educational aspirations is pronounced. [Pp. 53-55]

In a parallel multivariate analysis of sources of variations in aspirations to manual occupations, Wilson comments:

> We see analogous reversal.
>
> While a slightly higher proportion of Negroes than whites say they would like manual occupations, when allowing for differences in achievement, the relationship is reversed. Negro students whose achievement is poor eschew manual labor.
>
> The consequences of poor academic achievement are quite different for Negro and white students. White students perceive manual jobs as a viable alternative in the event of school failure. If the Negro student drops out he has good reason to expect to be unemployed. [Pp. 56-57]

(Wilson's work has also been published by the United States Commission on Civil Rights, 1967, Appendix C-3.)

Another publication based on *seventh–twelfth graders* is that of Reiss and Rhodes (1959), who administered an undescribed questionnaire to 21,270 students in the city and county of Nashville, Tennessee. The report, which is incomplete and vague on a number of important points, states in regard to their partial r technique: "Each of the four factors, race, sex, IQ [three levels on an unspecified test], socioeconomic status [blue collar vs. white collar on an unspecified index], (and in some cases a fifth, age), is successively introduced as a test factor so that we have first, second, third and fourth order partials for all relationships" (p. 256). Multiple significance tests using one-tailed probabilities preclude interpretation. To the statement, " 'Schooling is the most important thing in life for me,' . . . Negroes agreed . . . by roughly 30 percent more than did whites" (p. 257). Only in the county schools did they "inquire about subject's educational aspirations"; where, they report, "there is only a small racial difference in subject's educational aspirations such that Negroes are somewhat more likely to aspire toward a college education" (pp. 261-262). They also assert, "There is only a very small race difference in the per cent who want to quit school because they feel the coercive pressure of the norm [compulsory attendance law]; whites are somewhat more likely to want to quit" (p. 264). Additionally, "there is almost no race difference in the desire to quit school and go to work" (p. 266). The incompleteness and vagueness of this report greatly diminish its usefulness, but, at any rate, some attempt was made to control socioeconomic level and IQ, and such observed trends as were verbally reported are not in the direction one could plausibly attribute to the apparently limited precision of control of these factors.

How to interpret these trends is not self-evident. That they are related to blacks' search for self-esteem seems plausible, especially in the light of Glenn's (1963) survey of 16 Negro stratification studies published between 1899 and 1960, which showed formal education to have been the most important prestige criterion among blacks. Although no comparable survey of studies among whites was presented, Glenn noted that North and Hatt (in National Opinion Research Center, 1953) had demonstrated that correlations for a national sample between prestige ratings of occupations and (a) their median income, and (b) their median years of schooling was exactly the same (+ .83). Glenn suggests, then, that for blacks, education has a stronger relationship to prestige than does income, whereas for whites this is not the case.

Although some would say that blacks' high aspirations are compensatory for their depressed self-esteem (the latter stemming from their derogated minority status), a large number of recent studies give no support to the premise that blacks do experience lower over-all self-esteem. (See section B-4-a and B-4-b of this chapter.)

A plausible suggestion is based on the facts that job opportunities for uneducated blacks are fewer, and their access to skilled trades has been barred, with the consequence that education remains more necessary to them in getting available employment of any kind, especially of a prestigious and financially rewarding variety.

In 3 (or in some instances, 4) of the junior and senior high schools studied by Wylie (1963) and Wylie and Hutchins (1967), several questions relevant to educational and occupational aspirations were asked. As explained in detail in earlier sections of this chapter, racial comparisons involved only subjects from families with Hollingshead occupational ratings of 5-7, because too few blacks were available from the categories 1-4. Within each school, pairs of comparison subgroups were formed having the same IQ or DAT score ranges and $Ns \geq 10$. School racial context was controlled in the sense that all comparison groups were made up within each integrated school.

In response to the question (Assuming parental approval, enough money, and enough ability, do you) "feel right now that you would be interested in going to college after graduating from high school?", 9 out of 11 pairs of comparison subgroups showed more blacks reporting they wanted to go to college. Of the 9 pair comparisons, 3 were separately significant. The 2 exceptional pair comparisons (which yielded almost zero difference) were comprised of junior high school students.

Subjects' responses to the question "Please describe . . . the career you are thinking about for yourself" were coded and dichotomized into Hollingshead occupational levels 1-2 and 3-7. This question was asked in only 3 schools; so only 9 racial comparison groups were available. Of the 9, 7 showed more blacks aspiring to careers at levels 1 and 2. Again, the only 2 exceptions were found at the junior high school level.

In view of the strong trend toward higher long-range aspirations among blacks, it is interesting to note racial comparisons of the responses to the short-range aspiration question "What grades do you honestly aim to make when doing your schoolwork?" Out of six available racial-comparison pairs, five showed more whites saying "very high grades" or "good grades." Two of these five comparisons favoring whites were separately significant. Moreover, in five out of six racial comparison groups, a larger percent of whites reported "top half" to the question "If you think your grade average for the year is probably in the top half of your home room, put an X. . . ."

Thus, in groups roughly comparable with respect to IQ and parents' socioeconomic level, more blacks report high long-range educational and occupational aspirations, but more of them report that their present aims and accomplishments are not high.

In evaluating the reported trends, one should note that the race comparison data came from only two small, industrial, long-integrated northern cities and that socioeconomic level was equated only in the sense that all subjects were in the range 5-7 on Hollingshead scales. This obviously limits the generalizability of the results. However, if blacks more often fell in the 6 or 7 occupational categories, this lack of control should have operated against the reported findings, not enhanced them artifactually.

Gist and Bennett (1963) questioned all the *ninth- and twelfth-grade* students in four urban Kansas City high schools: 412 blacks and 461 whites. The schools were in neither the richest nor the poorest districts, but nothing was said about racial school context. The exact wording of the questions was not published, but occupational aspirations and plans were defined in terms of the subjects' statements concerning the occupations they "would like to have" and "actually will have" at age 30. No racial differences were found in 5 comparisons involving 5 IQ levels, or in 3 comparisons involving socioeconomic levels of fathers according to a trichotomized version of the North-Hatt Scale. (A multivariate analysis was not made.) Without telling how college aspirations were defined, the authors report, "Proportionately as many white students as Negroes aspired to college and University education. These findings held for both sexes and for all social classes" (p. 44). Evidently IQ was not controlled in this comparison; if it had been, one would expect higher proportions of blacks to aspire to college. Their "occupational mobility" score is uninterpretable, because it was computed as a discrepancy between father's occupation and student's aspired occupation, and it seems probable that the blacks and whites were not sufficiently comparable with respect to fathers' occupation in the comparisons of mobility scores.

In an early investigation covering approximately the age range of the three just discussed, Antonovsky and Lerner (1959) interviewed 61 blacks and 64 whites aged *16–20 years* from a highly industrialized upstate New York city. "No over-all differences between Negroes and whites on IQ scores" were observed (p. 134), and all subjects had lived in "the poorest neighborhoods" (p. 133). The greater unavailability of whites (because they had moved away and could not be traced) could have been due either to their families' being drifters, as the authors hypothesize, or to their moving because they were more ambitious. From a larger interview, 6 questions about aspirations were given verbatim in this publication, including desired work when in the first year of high school, desired work at the time of the interview, money the subject (or her husband) would be expecting to make 10 years hence, intention to apply for college entrance, and "Suppose your wildest dreams could be realized, and absolutely nothing would stand in your way, what would you be doing ten years from now? . . . Thinking realistically, what do you think you will probably be doing ten years from now?" (p. 134). Giving quantitative racial comparisons of the responses, the authors state, "Wherever trends and significant differences appear, the Negroes have a higher level of aspiration than the whites with a comparatively low socio-economic background" (p. 133). Antonovsky and Lerner (1959) speculated that these "surprising" higher black aspirations might be attributed to such factors as: (a) the family's serving as a negative role model; (b) "the traditional stress within the Negro community, particularly of late, on great black men" (p. 135); (c) the fact that "it is quite unrealistic for Negro youth in particular to seek success through the skilled trades, small business outside the Negro community, or corporate hierarchies" (p. 135); (d) a compensatory search for enhanced self-esteem stemming from the "acute problem of lack of self-esteem which besets the members of a minority group which has psychologically accepted its inferior status" (p. 135).

Since the Ns were small and the reasons for greater white attrition unspecifiable, about all one can say is that these reported trends go opposite the direction to be expected if ability and socioeconomic level had been uncontrolled (which they were not). The trends are in the direction obtained by other investigators who had larger, more representative samples and more precisely specified control of IQ, socioeconomic level, and other relevant variables. The authors' fourth explanatory factor is called into question by more recent research which does not support its basic assumption that blacks have lower self-esteem (see sections B-4-a and B-4-b of this chapter). (The authors state that their findings were reported in greater detail in Antonovsky and Lorwin, 1959, pp. 103-146, a source I have not examined.)

The following two publications are based on *twelfth-grade* respondents only. They are discussed substantively here because they are well-known studies, but the results regarding educational/occupational aspirations are inconclusive for the reasons stated below.

A. J. Lott and B. E. Lott's (1963) samples from two county and two city schools in Kentucky were found to differ with respect to many background factors; so two matched groups of *twelfth graders* were selected (17 whites and 23 blacks), who were comparable in the following respects: enrollment in city schools, "middle-status" occupation of the major breadwinner, IQs between 85-104, number of working mothers, number of homes with both natural parents at home, mother's and father's education. These matched groups differed in the following respects: significantly more persons lived in the black homes; more blacks saw their parents as belonging to the working class, and the racial school context was black for black subjects, white for white subjects.

So far as their responses were concerned, the matched groups did not differ significantly regarding socioeconomic level of occupations desired or occupations expected in 10 years. On an idiosyncratic instrument purporting to index the goal preference for academic recognition, social recognition, and love and affection, nonsignificant differences are reported for the latter two goal preferences, but the blacks were significantly higher on academic recognition scores. Although this study commendably tried to hold constant a number of relevant variables while making racial comparisons of aspiration and expectation, its conclusiveness is impaired by the following factors: (a) after matching, Ns were necessarily extremely small; (b) school racial context was confounded with race; (c) IQ was apparently only roughly controlled; (d) subjective socioeconomic level was uncontrolled; (e) multiple significance tests were made, so that the significance of those tests with reported $p \leq .05$ level could not be evaluated; (f) null findings are always ambiguous.

In the Coleman Report (Coleman, Campbell, Hobson, McPartland, Mood, Weinfeld, & York, 1966), discussed and evaluated throughout this chapter, information is published concerning only the *twelfth graders'* responses to certain questions about educational and occupational aspirations and plans. Blacks and whites are reported to be similar in saying they "would do almost anything to stay in school" (p. 278). "When asked whether they wanted to be good students, . . . in every region, a considerably higher proportion of Negroes than of whites gave [the] response" that they "wanted to be one of the best in the class" (p. 278).

> Turning to college plans and aspirations . . . a smaller proportion of Negroes than of whites report wanting to go no further than high school, in each region, though a slightly smaller proportion report wanting to finish college or go beyond. . . . More Negroes report wanting to go to technical, nursing, or business school after college. [P. 279]
>
> . . . fewer Negroes have definite plans for college, but fewer have definite plans not to attend. . . . This indicates the lesser concreteness in Negroes' aspirations, the greater hopes, but lesser plans. [P. 279]

As I have repeatedly emphasized in this chapter, IQ, achievement level, socioeconomic level, and racial school context were not held constant when making racial comparisons in the Coleman Report. The lower percentages of Negroes reporting that they wanted to finish college or go beyond are in the direction which might have been expected from the influence of these uncontrolled variables.

The reader will remember that in Gordon's (1972) multivariate analysis of a 5% sample of Coleman et al.'s ninth-grade data, blacks expressed a stronger desire for education than did whites, with verbal ability scores, social class, family role structure, self-esteem, and parental aspirations controlled in path analyses. This, of course, does not say that Coleman et al. would have found the same trend among twelfth graders had they instituted similar statistical controls, but it is suggestive of possible limitations on the interpretability of the trends stated by Coleman et al.

In the report of the United States Commission on Civil Rights (1967), Appendices C-1 and C-2 include detailed cross-classifications of twelfth graders' responses regarding educational plans and aspirations, the bases for cross-classifications including some combination of the following in various tables: individual parents' education, school average parents' education, teacher average earned degree, proportion white classmates, parents' educational desires, students' verbal ability scores, and geographical region. Unfortunately, no systematic multivariate analyses were presented. Thus, the table which classifies respondents into two levels of verbal ability, four degrees of school segregation, four regions, and two sexes does not control for socioeconomic level. Also, the median split on verbal ability scores in these tables does not, I believe, provide sufficiently precise control over this variable. Consequently, I conclude that these re-analyses, too, are inconclusive regarding the relationship of racial status to reported plans and aspirations of twelfth-grade respondents in the Coleman et al. study.

J. H. Davis (1964) authored the only publication I examined which presents race comparisons regarding educational plans and interests of subjects *older than twelfth graders.* The National Opinion Research Council gathered information by a self-administered questionnaire given to 33,982 June, 1961, college graduates from 135 colleges and universities. The questionnaire included inquiries as to whether the students planned to do graduate work the following year, and if not, which of several reasons they had for not going on next year. The black respondents, comprising only 3.6% of the sample, were not subdivided according to other variables such as socioeconomic level, but for purposes of looking at racial correlates of plans and motivations for further education, blacks were compared sometimes with all whites, sometimes with smaller-city, lower-class, Protestant whites (since the blacks tended to be Protestants with lower-status, smaller-city backgrounds).

To attempt to control for academic ability and achievement, an Academic Performance Index was developed, based on self-reported GPAs, adjusted according to rankings of the difficulty levels of the colleges, as estimated from knowledge of entering scores on the National Merit Examination (or substitute, correlated data) for each school.

One table compares plans between races with sex and Academic Performance Index controlled; a more refined cross-tabulation compares plans and reasons for not going on next year, with background characteristics, career field, sex, and Academic Performance Index controlled. From these tables, Davis drew the following statements:

a. When compared with whites in general, Negroes were a little less likely to anticipate immediate study, but when matched with comparable whites, more *Negroes* were going on next year (29 per cent vs. 23 per cent).

b. Negroes were considerably *less* likely to report low motivation (31 per cent) when compared with either group of whites, in both of which about one-half reported low motivation.

c. Negroes were considerably *more* likely to report external financial obstacles (34 per cent) when compared both with whites in general (12 per cent) and with Protestant low SES, smaller-city whites (20 per cent).

d. There was no difference by race in the per cent reporting non-financial external obstacles.

[In the more refined table] no tabulation is given for some groups in the arts and science careers since there were too few Negro women or high API Negro men, nor were there enough Negro cases to tabulate law and medicine. In the remaining groups, the trends noted above remained when sex, API, and career field were controlled. [Pp. 102-104]

Summary of Substantively Considered Researches

Obviously the above 16 investigations vary greatly with respect to the sizes and demographic characteristics of the samples, the methods used to index educational or occupational aspirations, and the adequacy with which relevant variables were controlled when making race comparisons. Nevertheless, most of the published trends were in agreement that blacks' educational and/or occupational aspirations exceed those of whites. This was even true in a number of studies which completely failed to control for ability or achievement levels or for socioeconomic level (a lack of control which would tend to counteract rather than artifactually produce or enhance the general finding that blacks' aspiration levels were higher). More convincingly, this consistent trend occurred in several large-scale studies where serious attempts were made to control a number of important factors including socioeconomic level, ability, and achievement levels.

There were four exceptional findings, two null and two favoring whites. These studies either failed to control ability and achievement levels, or did not simultaneously control for these variables plus socioeconomic level, or used very small *N*s.

It should be remembered that none of these reports gives adequate information concerning the psychometric properties of the responses to the idiosyncratic questions used to index educational and occupational aspirations; so the possible influence of unreliability, invalidity, or distribution characteristics of the index scores cannot be evaluated. In particular, the differentiation between wished for and expected attainments has not been systematically operationalized.

Although many of the substantively summarized studies are extremely limited and/or flawed, and/or incompletely reported, the following appear to me to be even more so. Consequently, I only list them. J. G. Anderson and Johnson (1971) (re Mexican-Americans and Anglos), achievement and socioeconomic levels not controlled, small Ns; Antonovsky (1967); G. F. Boyd (1952); Deutsch (1960); Hunt and Hardt (1969); Lorenz (1972); Powell (1973); Rumaldo and Kuvlesky (1968); Singer and Stefflre (1956).

b. IDEAL CONCEPTIONS OF MISCELLANEOUS PERSONALITY TRAITS

Regarding ideal-self conceptions other than those concerning desired educational or occupational levels, the literature is sparse, extremely heterogeneous, and methodologically weak. Of 11 publications I considered to be relevant to this topic, 6 are simply listed at the end, owing to their extremely serious methodological deficiencies and/or very incomplete reporting. The remaining 5, also characterized by some important methodological limitations or inadequacies, cannot be synthesized. Accordingly, each is briefly considered immediately below.

Probably the best known researches in this category are those of McDonald (1968) and McDonald and Gynther (1965), using the Interpersonal Check List Dom and Lov scales. These studies were also described in section B-6-b of this chapter. In both, southern subculture was common to the racial groups compared, but race was confounded with school racial context. Socioeconomic level was used in the ANOVAs. In each study, the ANOVAs made with Dom and Lov ideal-self scores were among several ANOVAs performed with Dom and Lov scores; so interpretation of the significance levels of the ideal-score difference is moot. In any event, nonsignificant differences in ideal-self Dom or ideal-self Lov were reported by McDonald (1968), with rural subjects, whereas whites' ideal-self Dom and ideal-self Lov were both significantly higher among McDonald and Gynther's (1965) urban subjects, although the ideal-self means for Lov appear to be extremely close. Because of the methodological limitations cited and the failure to get the same trends, the pair of studies does not form an adequate basis for conclusions about racial differences in ideal-self Dom or ideal-self Lov.

Hartnagel's (1970) study, described more fully in section B-6-b of this chapter, yielded no significant racial differences among high school boys on ideal-self "potency" scores taken from an idiosyncratic semantic differential instrument. Null findings, always ambiguous, are especially uninterpretable when no reliability information is given for the instrument used.

In Steinmann and Fox's (1970) study of "female values" among 100 black and 126 white female undergraduates, socioeconomic level was approximately controlled, but racial school context and southern (as opposed to northern) subculture varied between racial groups. Subjects responded to an idiosyncratic instrument, not published in the article, which purportedly indexed family orientation as opposed to self-achievement orientation among women respondents (the Maferr Inventory of Female Values). No significant difference in mean scores for "own ideal woman" were obtained. Obviously, interpretation of these null findings is not possible.

Studies Not Substantively Summarized

Arkoff and Weaver (1966), re Japanese-Caucasian ideals for sizes of body parts; Back and Paramesh (1969), comparing United States whites and blacks and Madras Indians on WAI values; G. F. Boyd (1952); Hishiki (1969), comparing Mexican-Americans and Caucasians; J. H. Hughes and Thompson (1954); Powers, Drane, Close, Noonan, Wines, and Marshall (1971), using A. Soares and L. Soares's instrument.

8. Integration/Segregation and Specific Aspects of Self-Concept, Including Ideal Self

In section B-5 of this chapter, it is pointed out that no studies of *over-all* self-regard as a function of degree of residential or school segregation have provided adequate tests of such possible relationships. There are even fewer publications concerned with *specific* aspects of self-concept as a function of degree of integration, and only two of these were chiefly directed at a study of degree of integration as an independent variable. In section B-5, one of those which dealt with both over-all self-regard and specific aspects of self-conception (Williams & Byars, 1970) is said to form an inadequate basis for conclusions. The other, St. John (1966), is considered first in this section.

St. John (1966) looked at educational preferences of 227 black and 1,038 white high school juniors in one middle-sized New England city as a function of average percent of black pupils in the elementary schools the students had attended, i.e., as a function of "ASPN." The students' elementary schools were divided into those having the following ASPN values: 0-39; 40-69; 70-100. The group studied included almost all students ever enrolled in the high school class of 1962 in that city. Since plans for education were identical to stated preferences in the case of 95% of whites and 93% of blacks, results were published in terms of plans, under the following categories: graduate school, 4-year college, technical or business school, high school graduation only, intention to drop out, already dropped out. (The study is described in this section on the assumption that educational goals or preferences are specific aspects of the ideal-self concept.)

St. John hypothesized that "regardless of whether schooling had been in the South or the North, the greater the average (pre-high school) percent Negro (ASPN), the lower the educational aspirations of Negro high school students" (p. 287). Failing to support this hypothesis, she found no significant differences in educational plans of black students by degree of segregation in their early schooling. The hypothesis was still not supported when data analysis was restricted to those blacks who had been educated entirely in the North. Considering only nondropouts, she classified each racial group according to three levels of ASPN and two categories of socioeconomic level (1-4 vs. 5) according to Hollingshead's two-factor index. Among blacks within each of the two categories, the greater the segregation of the students' early education, the *higher* the percent who planned post-high school education. No significance test was given for this comparison. Among whites within each of the two Hollingshead categories, no trend occurred for plans to be a function of ASPN.

In his extensive investigation described in chapter 3 and in section B-4-a and B-6-a of this chapter, Bachman (1970) found that mean scores on an idiosyncratic measure of "schoolwork ability self-concept" fell in the following *in*creasing order: all whites, blacks in integrated schools, blacks in northern segregated schools, other racial minorities, blacks in southern segregated schools. As reported in section B–6–a, the *Beta* for relationship between "schoolwork ability self-concept" and these racial/ethnic categories was a significant .14 when 8 background factors and Quick Test Intelligence scores were controlled in a Multiple Classification Analysis. Bachman presented some evidence supporting the construct validity of the 3-item measure of schoolwork ability self-concept. However, he emphasized that all his results involving racial/ethnic breakdowns should be viewed with caution inasmuch as his sampling was not specifically set up to furnish an adequate analysis of relationships involving this class of variable.

Certainly the Coleman Report (Coleman, Campbell, Hobson, McPartland, Mood, Weinfeld, & York, 1966) is the largest and best known piece of research which provided information about possible associations between degree of school integration and specific aspects of self-concept. Details of their method are given in section B–6–a of this chapter, where it is pointed out that (a) their idiosyncratic "self-concept" measures were different from grade to grade; (b) the content of the self-concept questions was directed toward self-concept of schoolwork ability rather than to over-all self-regard; (c) no reliability or validity information was published about these measures.

Another variable allegedly indexed by Coleman et al. was the subjects' "sense of control of the environment," a construct which also might be considered to be a specific aspect of self-concept. For this variable, only one question was used for sixth graders, and only three questions for ninth and twelfth graders and apparently none for third graders. All these questions appear to be directed toward control of the environment in terms of attaining "success in life," and no reliability, validity, or other psychometric information was provided.

In regard to the association of degree of school segregation with the "self-concept" and "sense of control of environment" scores, Coleman et al. say without providing tabulated data:

> This study provides little evidence concerning the effect of school factors on these attitudes. If family background characteristics are controlled, almost none of the remaining variance in self-concept and control of environment is accounted for by the school factors measured in this survey. One variable, however, is consistently related to control of environment and self-concept. For each group, as the proportion white in the school increases, the child's sense of control of environment increases, and his self-concept decreases. This suggests the possibility that school integration has conflicting effects on

attitudes of minority group children: it increases their sense of control of the environment or their sense of opportunity, but decreases their self-concept. This relationship may well be an artifact, since the achievement level of the student body increases with percent white, and may be the proximate cause of these opposite relationships. If so, these effects are merely effects or [sic] achievements and motivations of fellow students, rather than direct effects of integration. Whatever the time structure of causation, the relations, though consistent, are in all cases small. [Pp. 323-324]

Going beyond the cautions already quoted above, I conclude that nothing can be safely inferred from the Coleman Report regarding associations between segregation and these two self-concept variables. My reasons for such skepticism are: (a) The instruments used varied widely among grade levels; they were obviously extremely limited in content and length, and nothing was published about their reliability or validity. (b) No information is given about the statistical significance of the descriptive trends. (c) Not enough information is published to enable one to evaluate whether other variables besides school achievement were uncontrolled when trying to establish the association of school integration with the self-concept scores.

In some survey research more fully described in section B-4-b of this chapter, Crain and Weisman (1972) used an idiosyncratic internal-control scale to study a block-quota sample of 1,651 black males and females, aged 21-45, from 25 northern metropolitan areas. One table involves the following cross-classifications of conditions *experienced by the subjects as children:* segregated versus integrated schools, number of whites in neighborhood (none, few, many); and played versus did not play with whites. The authors point out that the largest percents of adults with a high sense of control came from either the completely segregated or completely integrated childhood conditions. Lowest percentages of high internal-control adults were found among persons having had two integrated and one segregated childhood experience. This observed trend does not seem to agree with the one just quoted from Coleman et al. where the sense of control of the environment was said to increase directly as a function of degree of integration. This discrepancy between the studies occurs even though 3 out of 5 of the internal-external control questions used by Crain and Weisman (1972) are the ones used in the Coleman Report. However, just as we found the Coleman trends uninterpretable, there are several reasons to consider the Crain and Weisman table also uninterpretable.

Besides the limited information given about the psychometric properties of the control scores, one should note that $N \leq 10$ in 5 out of 12 of the cells in the table; there was no information offered as to whether socioeconomic level and ability and achievement levels were controlled in these comparisons, and there were no significance tests offered.

The main point of Rosenberg and Simmons's (1972) investigation was to study variables relevant to black and white self-esteem, but one of the later analyses of their data may be classified as relevant to the topic of special aspects of self-conception, because it concerned the subjects' sense of racial identification (Rosenberg, 1975). (The Rosenberg and Simmons study is extensively summarized in section B-4-a of this chapter, and their reported associations between segregation and over-all self-regard are discussed in section B-5 of this chapter.)

A "racial identification score" was obtained by combining answers to six interview items on the basis of their seeming content validity for indicating degree of satisfaction and pride in being black and degree to which the subject reported vicarious shame upon hearing something bad said about another black person. No reliability, validity, or other psychometric information is given about this score, which was used to divide subjects into strong, medium, and weak racial identification levels. The tabulated data show some tendency for larger percents of blacks in predominantly black schools to show a strong sense of racial identity. But since the properties of the instrument are unknown, and other relevant variables were not held constant when looking at degree of segregation as a predictor, one cannot draw conclusions from these data.

Wellman's (1971) analysis of several kinds of Who Am I? (WAI) responses as a function of race and socioeconomic level are described and criticized in section B-6-a of this chapter. Relevant to this section are percentages of respondents identifying themselves in terms of Student Role, these data being broken down according to three socioeconomic levels and four levels of school racial composition (highly white, predominantly white, predominantly black, virtually all black). Among black respondents at the high and middle socioeconomic levels, significant U-shaped functions appeared, with the highest percentages of Student Role responses being given by students in highly white and virtually all black schools. No trend as a function of school racial composition was apparent among lower-class blacks. Wellman suggested, "In schools at either racial composition extreme, evidently, there is relatively less emphasis on race as a social differentiator; here blacks may be freer to adopt other identities, including the one most directly identified with attending school, Student Role" (p. 431).

While this could be one interpretation, lack of published information about the properties of the WAI scores renders the findings moot.

He published no information about his other self-identity scores from the WAI (Academic Concerns, Positive Intellectual Ability, Negative Intellectual Ability), broken down according to school racial composition and socioeconomic level; so I assume he found no trends in such analyses of these specific aspects of self-concept as a function of integration.

(See Wylie, 1974, pp. 240-247, for a description of the WAI test and a criticism of its scoring and interpretability.)

In the light of the variety among these six studies and their methodological limitations, no over-all statement can be made about associations between segregation and any one specific aspect of self-concept. St. John's (1966) work, clearly the most adequate, suggests that segregation does not impair blacks' educational aspirations, even though it seemed plausible to assume that it might.

5
Sex of Subject and Self-Concept Variables

A. Introduction

1. General Theoretical Considerations

The question of a relationship between sex and self-concept variables appears again and again in psychoanalytic and personality theories, in sociological and anthropological writings, and in the recent outpouring of work on female psychology. Some theorists focus on self-concept. Most treat it as peripheral to other larger issues such as psychosexual development or social stratification. Some dwell equally on male and female self-regard. Most are preoccupied with women either as deviants from an implied male norm or as an underprivileged group deserving of special attention. Some are explicit about the nature of the association between sex and self-concept. Most deal in implication. Some theories have inspired research intended to test specific predictions. Most have not. Nevertheless, theoretical rationales provide an orienting framework from which to embark on the major task of this chapter: to review and evaluate empirical research on the relationship between sex and selected self-concept variables.

I emphasize *selected* because theoretical speculation has ranged across a profusion of self-concept variables. Such global concepts as overall self-regard and feelings of inferiority/superiority have figured in numerous theories that speak to the issue of sex and self-concept. This question also has been raised with respect to specific dimensions of self-conception, including anxiety, competence, affiliation, adjustment, aggression, dominance, nurturance, ambition, and practically any other conceivable facet of personality. Accorded a key role in Kohlberg's (1966) cognitive-developmental theory is gender identity, the categorization of oneself as either male or female. (See chap. 2.) Kagan (1964) emphasizes sex-role identity, the degree to which a person regards himself or herself as "masculine" or "feminine," as culturally defined. Taking a social learning perspective, Mischel (1966) raises the possibility that the sexes set different standards for dispensing self-rewards and self-punishments.

To treat fully the question of how males and females conceive of the self would require a consideration of these and other self-concept variables — a task which far exceeds the scope of a single chapter. From this abundance I have selected three topics for review: over-all self-

Peggy Miller is the author of this chapter.

THE SELF-CONCEPT

regard, self-conceptions in relation to sex-role ideology, and self-reported affiliation. These topics are considered in sections B, C, and D, respectively. In each case theoretical rationales are presented first in order to provide a context from which to view the empirical research that follows. For the most part, I consider only studies that were published since the 1961 edition of this book.

Before turning to methodological considerations it is necessary to raise a conceptual issue that has methodological implications: I question the prevailing assumption, mostly implied, that the self-concept is a fixed entity, a stable quality "possessed" by each individual. One consequence of this assumption is the relative neglect of situational variation in self-conceptions. Is an individual's self-concept a function of the type of situation (e.g., work, school, home, etc.)? If so, what are the implications of this variation for the relationship between sex and self-concept variables? Perhaps the self-concepts of one sex are more consistent across diverse situations. Perhaps women feel more self-confident in certain kinds of situations, men in others. Perhaps specific dimensions of self-concept, such as self-reported affiliation or competence interact with situational factors in different ways for males and females. These and other related possibilities have received little theoretical elaboration or empirical exploration.

Traditional conceptions of self-regard have also failed to take into account the frame of reference which is used in assigning the self a value along some dimension. Self-appraisal requires a basis for comparison, a person or group which serves as a reference point. When men are asked to express their level of self-esteem, do they compare the self to people in general, to men, or to women? Which of these groups do women use in making analogous self-appraisals? Perhaps such broad and remote groups are not really to the point. Mischel (1970) suggests that social comparisons may be based on "highly select special reference groups" (p. 46). What kinds of special reference groups do men and women spontaneously use in evaluating the self? How do women's (and men's) self-conceptions differ across different special reference groups? Both theory and research remain mute on these and related questions.

These objections to traditional conceptions of self-concept variables are in line with Kagan's (1967) critique of the absolutistic orientation toward psychological constructs. He calls for a conceptual reform, involving relativistic definitions of certain constructs, including the self-concept: "'Relativistic' refers to a definition in which context and the state of the individual are part of the defining statement. Relativism does not preclude the development of operational definitions, but makes that task more difficult" (p. 131). It is likely that the development of such definitions will lead to a much more complex and subtle understanding of the relationship between sex and self-concept variables. But, at present, such understanding is beyond reach, as the research considered below continues to reflect an absolutistic orientation.

2. General Methodological Considerations

I present here the major guidelines that I used in evaluating research on sex and self-concept variables. These guidelines are similar to those applied in other chapters of this book. See Wylie (1974) for a more detailed discussion of methodological problems involved in measuring self-concept variables.

1. Are procedures described clearly and in adequate detail? In many studies the reporting of procedures is so vague, incomplete, or garbled as to preclude any interpretation of findings.

2. Does the study use an appropriate sample size? In order to answer this question I weighed several factors: (a) What is an adequate sample size, given the purpose of the study? (b) Is the sample large enough to sustain main effects of sex in sex groups which are heterogeneous with respect to other variables—such as social class, race or ethnic status, family relationships—which might affect self-concept? (c) Is the sample large enough to allow for analysis of interaction between sex and one or more of these other variables? (d) Is the sample large enough to sustain significant sex effects where empirical trends have been small thus far? (e) How homogeneous are the sex groups with respect to other variables which may be related to self-concept? (f) Is the sample so large that sex differences however small in absolute terms and lacking in psychological significance attain statistical significance?

3. Is any information given about whether the sex groups are comparable with respect to other variables that are possibly empirically related to self-concept, variables such as social class, racial or ethnic status, and grade-point average (GPA)? The samples are often so sketchily described as to preclude any assessment of whether the male and female groups were comparable on other pertinent variables. As has been urged in previous chapters, multivariate studies are needed so that the separate effects of sex, race, and social class and their interactions can be examined.

4. Do researchers report whether the data collection methods and conditions were comparable for males and females? A special case of this question is the following: do researchers account for or even consider the possibility of experimenter-related effects in interpreting the self-concept reports of male and female subjects? In a review of research on experimenter-subject interactions, R. Rosenthal (1969) states:

> Sex differences are well established for many kinds of behavior. But a question must now be raised as to whether sex differences which emerge from psychological experiments are due to the subject's genes, morphology, enculturation, or simply to the fact that the experimenter treated his male and female subjects differently so that, in a sense, they were not really in the same experiment at all. [P. 186]

Rosenthal mentions other potential sources of artifact, including (a) interaction between sex of experimenter and sex of subject; (b) interaction of expectancy effects (i.e., the influence of the experimenter's hypothesis) with sex of experimenter and sex of subject. The possible implications of these effects for research on sex and self-concept variables remain largely unrecognized and unexplored. Only rarely do investigators even report the sex of the experimenter. Once again multivariate studies are called for.

5. Does the study use one of the better developed instruments, the psychometric properties of which are known from previous publications? Or does it use an idiosyncratic instrument for assessing self-concept variables? If an idiosyncratic instrument is involved, do the authors provide information concerning the content, scoring, validity, and reliability of the instrument? In the absence of such information it is impossible to choose among alternate interpretations of the reported findings. The majority of studies considered for this review relied upon idiosyncratic instruments, which have received little or no psychometric exploration.

6. Are uninterpretable discrepancy scores used? For example, one type of discrepancy score is used to determine the degree to which women's self-conceptions are intrafamily versus extrafamily oriented. This score is determined by taking the difference between her scores on two sets of test items, representing an intrafamily orientation and an extrafamily orientation, respectively. (See Wylie, 1974, pp. 88–95, for a detailed criticism of discrepancy scores.)

7. Could purported direct associations between sex and self-concept scores stem from the reliability artifact? At least in the early grades,

boys, compared with girls, may be poorer readers[1] and less motivated in schoollike tasks. These factors may lead to more unreliable responding on the part of boys — which translates into low self-regard scores on some self-concept measures. (See Wylie, 1974, pp. 119-121, for a more detailed explanation of this kind of contamination between low self-regard and unreliability.)

8. Were statistical tests appropriately applied and interpreted? Most of the studies cited in this chapter at least presented statistical tests. Some investigators computed statistical tests which were not independent of one another, thereby rendering the results uninterpretable. Others made numerous comparisons between groups without regard for the fact that some comparisons will be statistically significant by chance alone. Rarely were the results of such multiple comparisons cross-validated with new samples.

The above questions served as general guidelines for evaluating research on sex and selected self-concept variables. (Other methodological issues will be raised below in connection with specific topics.) I encountered very few studies which met most of the desirable methodological criteria. Nevertheless, it was possible to distinguish more adequate from less adequate studies. In general, I describe in detail the better studies, while merely listing studies which are plagued by serious methodological shortcomings. However, I also take into account several other factors: (a) Is the value of the study augmented because it is part of a larger, systematic research effort? (b) Does the study contain useful detailed descriptive information about the subjects' responses even though other results are uninterpretable? (c) Have the results of the study been widely disseminated with widespread misinterpretation? I tend to give critical attention to such studies even when they fall far short of methodological adequacy.

The prevalence of methodological problems in even the better studies and the use of diverse methods and instruments seriously impede attempts to interpret and synthesize the evidence. In light of these difficulties I adopt Anastasi's (1937) policy, "the only available criterion for the acceptance of a conclusion is the *consistency of results of different investigators*" (p. 415). Accordingly, I draw conclusions only when the better studies consistently yield similar results. If the less

---

1. In her review of the literature Maccoby (1966) concludes that girls learn to read earlier than boys and that more boys than girls need remedial training in reading. But by about age ten, according to Maccoby, boys catch up in their reading skills. Maccoby and Jacklin (1974) and Sherman (1971) note that reading problems are more common among boys than girls.

adequate studies consistently support or oppose these conclusions, I note this as well. On many issues only a few methodologically adequate studies are available, but trends are sometimes discernible, nonetheless. I call such trends "hypotheses" in order to emphasize their tentativeness, and to alert researchers to possibly fruitful lines of study.

Even when consistent results emerge across many studies, it is difficult to arrive at definitive interpretations. On some self-concept variables considered below, the sexes do not differ, indicating areas of possibly genuine similarity between the self-concepts of males and females. However, null findings do not prove that no sex differences exist on these variables: future research involving better measurement procedures or different item content may yield different results. The finding of no difference between the sexes is ambiguous in another way, possibly reflecting sex similarities in social desirability response sets. (See Wylie, 1974, pp. 52–62, for a discussion of social desirability response sets in relation to self-concept measurement.)

This sort of interpretational ambiguity also arises with respect to sex differences on self-concept variables. Take, for example, the finding of a slight trend favoring females in studies of self-reported affiliation (see section D–2). Does this mean that women regard themselves as more affiliative or that they are just more likely than men to *say* that they are affiliative? Mischel (1970) suggests that "the sexes may give different self-reports in part because the *admission* of particular attributes or behaviors may have different value and may lead to different consequences as a function of the individual's sex" (p. 13). Perhaps a high level of self-reported affiliation is socially desirable for women, while for men a lower level is socially desirable. That is, sex differences on self-concept variables may reflect sex differences in social desirability response sets rather than differences in actual self-conceptions. There are ways of minimizing this kind of interpretational ambiguity. For example, testing conditions can be arranged so as to promote rapport between subject and experimenter and to encourage honest reporting. However, many studies have not used such procedures.

B. Over-all Self-Regard as a Function of Sex of Subject

1. Theoretical Rationales

The question of a relationship between sex and self-concept variables has most often been phrased in terms of over-all self-regard. Do men have higher self-esteem than women? Are the self-concepts of women more positive than the self-concepts of men? How do the sexes compare with respect to feelings of inferiority/superiority? The purpose here is not to document the pervasiveness of such questions, for this hardly needs documenting, nor to present an exhaustive list of theoretical statements on the matter. However, I give much more attention to theory about over-all self-regard than to theory about other self-concept variables included in this chapter. This emphasis reflects, in part, the greater volume of theorizing on over-all self-regard. It also reflects an attempt to alert the reader to the kinds of factors that might enter into a relationship between sex and self-concept variables. My aim, then, is twofold: (a) to offer a sampling of the numerous theoretical rationales that have been proposed to account for the assumed relationship between sex and over-all self-regard; (b) to illustrate how complex and richly varied are the possible factors that underly a relationship between sex and conceptions of the self.

Theoretical rationales concerning the relationship between sex and over-all self-regard may be divided into two main categories: those that accord at least a minor role to biological factors and those that define the relationship entirely in terms of social or cultural influences. I first consider rationales that are based partly on biological variables.

a. RATIONALES INVOLVING BIOLOGICAL FACTORS

Discernible in Freud's (1927, 1932, 1933) writings on psychosexual development are two themes that bear on the issue of biological sources of self-regard in males and females. The first and most important of these leaves little doubt as to the impact of gender on self-regard: it rests upon the presence or absence of the penis. The little boy's feeling of superiority originates in his discovery that he possesses something that the little girl lacks, while her sense of inferiority springs from the corresponding realization that she has been shortchanged. She "develops, like a scar, a sense of inferiority" (1927, p. 138). This insult to her pride sets the girl upon a prolonged and tortuous developmental course along which her penis envy is overcome only with great effort, if at all. Only in maternity do women find a measure of satisfaction and, by implication, a source of self-worth. If the child is male, the mother's satisfaction is the greater. In this account is the suggestion of a strong relationship between sex and feelings of inferiority/superiority, a relationship which is rooted in the assumption of the relative superiority of the male genitals.

However, Freud does not specify the degree to which feelings of inferiority/superiority operate consciously, as opposed to unconsciously. Is the woman who manages to achieve "normal" femininity plagued throughout life by a conscious sense of her inadequacy? Does her biological deficiency continue to trouble her—consciously or unconsciously—even during motherhood? And what of those women who fail in varying degrees to attain "normal" femininity? The woman who develops a masculinity complex denies that she lacks a penis and adopts masculine behaviors, according to Freud. Does she, then, experience conscious feelings of superiority appropriate to a "masculine" facade, concealing unconscious feelings of deficiency? Or is she aware all the while of her inferiority? Freud does not provide clear answers to these questions. Nor is he more explicit about neurosis, the other form of abortive femininity. And, with regard to male feelings of superiority, he is equally vague, never indicating to what degree such feelings are consciously or unconsciously held. Taking these considerations into account, one is left with the possibility that feelings of inferiority/superiority are not entirely conscious. It is impossible to say how this qualification affects the implied relationship between sex and feelings of inferiority/superiority.

Also found throughout Freud's work on psychosexual development is the theme of bisexuality. Just as each sex possesses a mixture of the sexual characteristics of its own and the other sex, so does each exhibit the psychological traits of both men and women. According to Freud (1927), "all human individuals, as a result of their bisexual disposition and of cross-inheritance, combine in themselves both masculine and feminine characteristics, so that pure masculinity and femininity remain theoretical constructions of uncertain content" (p. 142). As indicated above, Freud associates feelings of superiority and inferiority with masculinity and femininity, respectively. Assuming that the bisexual rule applies here, one would predict that women do not hold a monopoly on feelings of inferiority nor men on feelings of superiority, but that inferiority is more commonly felt by women and superiority by men.

Horney (1967) agrees with Freud that the little girl sees herself as comparatively disadvantaged in that she lacks a penis. Her envy is an expression of the mutual attraction of the sexes and is based upon the realistic assessment that she has fewer possibilities for gratification than does the little boy. But by this account, it is not this "primary" penis envy but the later Oedipal complex which is a critical source of the girl's lasting feelings of inferiority. She experiences guilt and anxiety as a result of her libidinal desires for the father. This conflict causes her to regress to her earlier penis envy. That is, in order to protect herself from the anxious feelings occasioned by her love for her father, she flees from a feminine identification into a masculine one. In the process her self-worth is damaged: "This attempt to deviate from her own line to that of the male inevitably brings about a sense of inferiority, for the girl begins to measure herself by pretensions and values that are foreign to her specific biological nature and confronted with which she cannot but feel herself inadequate" (p. 67). Horney goes on to show how this retreat into masculinity and the consequent injury to feminine self-regard are promoted by the social reality of women's subordination. From a very early age the girl is reminded of her inferiority, and when she reaches adulthood, her opportunities for achieving a fulfilling sublimation are limited by a society which discourages women from undertaking meaningful work outside the home.

Despite the suggestion throughout that women's prospects for self-worth are bleak compared with men's, Horney alludes to other factors which presumably temper any predictions about the relationship between sex and self-regard. To Horney, the female's biological capacity for creating life and the actual experiences of pregnancy and motherhood are rich sources of satisfaction. The implication here is that these may provide a basis for positive self-regard in women. Approaching the issue from the male point of view, Horney recognizes the dread of not being able to sexually satisfy the female as a potential threat to masculine self-respect. There is also the matter of man's envy of women's life-giving power. Both of these factors may pose problems for males with respect to how they view themselves. However, Horney does not dwell on these implied problems for masculine self-regard. Instead, she places the accent upon the role that dread and envy of women play in forming the unconscious foundation for the tendency of men to devalue women.

Fromm (1949) also considers the effects of biological sex differences on the formation of male and female personality, assigning to biology an insignificant part, compared with the impact of culture on personality. Cultural influences may augment, eliminate, or reverse biologically rooted sex differences in personality. Within this framework, he examines a single biological sex difference, namely the respective roles of men and women in sexual intercourse.

For men the sex act is a matter of performance, according to Fromm.

In order to satisfy his partner, the man must show that he can achieve and maintain an erection. His peculiar vulnerability arises from the necessity of proving his potency: he risks failure. That is not the case for the woman, in Fromm's estimation. She need not "prove" anything in order to satisfy her partner. Her lack of responsiveness can be concealed in a way that the male's cannot. Nevertheless, she is dependent for her sexual satisfaction upon the man's desire for her and upon his potency. She risks abandonment and frustration.

Men and women, then, suffer with different fears as a result of their distinctive roles in sexual intercourse. So do they develop different character traits, according to Fromm. In order to guard against fear of failure, men strive for prestige. One expression of this drive is a particular form of vanity which requires continual demonstrations of prowess in sexual and other domains. Feminine vanity is of another sort. It serves to protect the woman from frustration and dependency. She needs to attract, to prove to herself that she is desirable. Fromm is saying not that one sex is more vain than the other but that men and women are susceptible to distinctive kinds of self-admiration. These masculine and feminine brands of vanity are rooted in the sex act but are supported primarily by social roles.

Fromm, like Horney, also discusses women's capacity to bear children as it relates to character differences in the sexes. This natural gift inspires feelings of superiority in women but moves men to envy, feelings of inferiority, and compensatory efforts. In modern industrialized society these feelings are held unconsciously, according to Fromm, and so, presumably, are not necessarily expressed as differences in self-regard between males and females.

In summary, these theorists have seized upon a variety of biological factors as sources of self-regard in males and females — the possession or lack of a penis, the capacity or incapacity to bear children, the bisexuality of each sex, and the respective roles of men and women in sexual intercourse. The rationales that have been constructed around these factors may be called upon in support of the following predictions: the self-images of males are more positive than the self-images of females (Freud, Horney), the self-images of females are more positive (Horney), the sexes do not differ (Fromm). These theories accord an important role to unconscious aspects of personality but are vague as to how the unconscious influences the self-concept of males and females. In the theories of Horney and Fromm biological variables interact with societal or cultural influences to produce male and female personality.

b. Rationales Involving Social or Cultural Factors

The assertion that one or another biological difference provides a basis for positive (or negative) self-regard is a matter of the value imputed to that difference. Freud argues on behalf of the penis, Horney on behalf of maternity. But these biological facts have no significance in and of themselves. De Beauvoir (1949), author of *The Second Sex*, states: "It is not merely as a body, but rather as a body subject to taboos, to laws, that the subject is conscious of himself . . . —it is with reference to certain values that he evaluates himself" (p. 32).

This emphasis on society's interpretation of biology is shared by C. Thompson, a psychoanalyst who sees in women's position of underprivilege ample grounds for feelings of inadequacy. C. Thompson (1950) analyzes the derogatory attitude towards female sexuality prevalent among both sexes in western culture and relates it to woman's negative appraisal of herself. This attitude consists of three components: the belief that the female sexual drive is not urgent or important, the depreciation of women's sexual organs, and the association of the female genitals with uncleanness. In the derogation of their sexuality, women encounter a formidable obstacle, for "the acceptance of one's body and all its functions is a basic need in the establishment of self-respect and self-esteem" (p. 353). Since men do not labor under a similar disadvantage, the implication here is that they have higher self-regard than women.

C. Thompson (1942, 1943) alludes to three other conditions which presumably sustain such a relationship: the training of girls in insincerity about sexual matters; the devaluation in industrialized societies of woman's unique biological contribution—the bearing of children; and women's social and economic dependency.

Highlighted in Thompson's papers is the relative devaluation of female sexual and procreative powers as these attitudes bear on the self-regard of women. That is, she focuses on one portion of the cultural ideology that accompanies those (western) social arrangements in which men occupy the higher position. Adler (1973) also begins with the assumption of male domination over females, but illuminates another facet of western sex-role ideology, namely the complementary beliefs in the inferiority of women and superiority of men. These are far-reaching beliefs, he maintains, touching upon all manner of concepts so that the "good" become aligned with masculinity, the "bad" with femininity. Boys are bolstered in their self-love by this ideology and by their position of relative privilege. But the difficulties of subordination and prejudice combine to convince girls that the feminine role is unsatisfactory and that they themselves are inferior. It is clear from this account that Adler expects the self-evaluations of girls to compare unfavorably with boys'.

One qualification is necessary, however, with respect to the strength of this relationship. Adler describes a variety of ways in which women adapt to their situation. Some resort to exaggerated displays of obedience, humility, and weakness, whereas others accept the stigma of inferiority and embrace the system that produces it. Apparently, such women give voice to their low opinions of themselves. But Adler identifies a third group of women who reject a feminine ideal for a masculine one. It is unclear whether women of this type express the feelings of relative superiority associated with masculinity or feelings of inferiority stemming from their inevitable failure to achieve a masculine ideal.

Hacker (1951) also draws upon social structural and ideological factors, incorporating them into a more sophisticated sociological analysis of how women regard themselves collectively and individually. As the starting point for her argument, she adopts Wirth's definition of a minority group: "A minority group is any group of people who because of their physical or cultural chracteristics, are singled out from the others in the society in which they live for differential and unequal treatment, and who therefore regard themselves as objects of collective discrimination" (p. 60). Hacker shows that, by this definition, women cannot be considered a minority group in the full sense, for they do not meet the subjective criteria. For instance, a woman may believe her group identity to be different from what others hold it to be. Consequently, she may be unaware that her sex group affiliation influences the way she is treated. Or she may see herself as belonging to a group but not realize that the group is devalued. Still another possibility is that she knows that she is a member of a category but fails to recognize the group significance of the category. In all of these cases, women do not realize that they are being discriminated against as a group. But even if women are aware that they are treated unequally on the basis of their sex group affiliation, they may deem this an appropriate response to their distinctive characteristics.

Despite their possible lack of minority group consciousness, women, like other minority groups, often interiorize the prevailing attitudes of the dominant group, thereby developing *group* self-hatred. This may be expressed in denigration of other members of their sex group and in acceptance of the dominant group's stereotype of women. On the level of *individual* self-regard, women may exempt themselves from this group evaluation by imagining themselves to be different from the average woman. Or they may come to apply their negative evaluation of women to themselves as individuals. Hacker states: "Since a person's conception of himself is based on the defining gestures of others, it is unlikely that members of a minority group can wholly escape personality distortion. Constant reiteration of one's inferiority must often lead to its acceptance as a fact" (p. 61). This argument leads one to expect that women, as occupants of minority group status, do not necessarily develop negative self-images but are much more susceptible than men to such self-appraisals.

Also adversely affecting women's conceptions of themselves is the condition of marginality. Hacker explains that this type of role conflict occurs when women are socialized to fill opposing roles. The marginal woman receives contradictory messages: she ought to excel scholastically and she ought to defer to men in intellectual matters. Self-hatred is among the psychological concomitants of this conflict, according to Hacker.

Bardwick (1971) also conceives of female self-regard in terms of sex roles but in her rendition the real and ideal selves figure prominently in the dynamics of self-appraisal. The ideal self is composed of a number of roles and their associated motives and values. To the extent that a person realizes the full range of roles within her ideal self, her self-esteem will be high. In other words, the size of discrepancy between the ideal self and the real self is the crucial determinant of self-regard. This way of approaching the problem allows for alternative routes to self-worth. Some women fashion their ideal selves entirely out of feminine roles. To the degree that they perform well in these roles, they enjoy high self-esteem. For other women the ideal self is not wholly feminine: it encompasses traditionally masculine roles which carry with them the motive for worldly achievement. If such a person successfully enacts both the masculine and feminine roles of her ideal self, she too will regard herself positively.

But fulfillment of both kinds of roles is often difficult. The female adolescent may be encouraged to develop her talents as a musician, scholar, or athlete and simultaneously advised to cultivate a femininity which precludes achievement in these fields. The individual who incorporates these contradictory roles into her ideal self but performs only feminine behaviors is likely to suffer from feelings of low self-esteem.

That is, in failing to gratify her motives for masculine achievement, she feels that she is not utilizing her full potential. Since role conflicts of this type are "more likely to exist in women, in particular situations and in general women have lower self-esteem than men" (p. 155).

This, then, is the drift of Bardwick's general account of self-regard. She also speaks to the issue of the specific bases for self-regard, and here the achievement and affiliation motives take on special significance. The achievement motive refers to the desire to act alone according to personal standards of excellence. The affiliation motive is directed toward securing and dispensing love. Beginning in adolescence, males and females diverge in their paths toward self-esteem. For boys, achievement is the paramount source of self-esteem in childhood and remains so in adolescence. Girls follow a more discontinuous course: when they reach adolescence, heterosexual affiliation surpasses achievement as the dominant source of self-esteem. Thus, in adulthood the self-regard of males is rooted primarily in achievement and secondarily in affiliation, whereas the situation is reversed for females. This line of reasoning leads Bardwick to the following conclusion:

> I think that if a woman has a feminine and normal core identity, failure in the feminine roles will preclude feelings of self-esteem. Normally, women will not participate in roles which threaten their affiliative needs, because these needs are critical in their basic concept of themselves. [P. 158][2]

Sharing many features with Bardwick's account is Carlson's (1965) developmental perspective on self-regard. In her view, the self-image includes two independent dimensions, one of which she calls social/personal orientation. A social orientation is one in which interpersonal experiences and social appraisals figure importantly in a person's self-conception, whereas a personally oriented self-image is relatively immune from such influences. As preadolescents, both boys and girls are preoccupied with mastery and autonomy, tasks which are personally oriented. In adolescence, however, adult sex-role expectations begin to assume significance for both sexes. According to Carlson, the stereotypes of the feminine and masculine roles imply social and personal orientations, repectively. She hypothesizes that during adolescence sex differentiation occurs with respect to this dimension:

---

2. There is at least the suggestion in Bardwick's account that the affiliative motive has a physiological basis in women and that the achievement motive has a physiological basis in men.

the self-concepts of girls become more socially oriented, while the self-concepts of boys become more personally oriented.

Carlson envisions a different developmental path for self-esteem, the second dimension of the self-image. This construct is defined as the degree of correspondence between an individual's self-concept and his or her ideal self. In contrast to the social/personal dimension, self-esteem is held to be independent of sex role and relatively stable from preadolescence through adolescence. Carlson expects the degree of congruence between the self-concept and the ideal self to be equivalent for males and females despite differences across sex in the content of each component of self-esteem.

So far in this section I have reviewed several claims for a relationship between sex and over-all self-regard, claims which are based entirely on social or cultural factors. Thompson, Adler, and Hacker make much of women's subordinate position in the social hierarchy and of cultural ideology that favors men over women, weaving these factors into rationales for a relationship in which women compare adversely to men with respect to self-regard. Also supporting such a relationship is the greater likelihood of role conflict among women than men, a rationale offered by both Hacker and Bardwick. Carlson proposes a different relationship and a different rationale, expecting no sex differences in self-esteem on the grounds that males and females do not differ in the degree to which their self-concepts correspond with their ideal selves. The two rationales presented next also consider female self-regard against the background of women's relative position in the social structure. But here the emphasis shifts to the mother-daughter relationship as a mediator between the social structure and personality.

Central to Chesler's (1972) account of the plight of women in patriarchal society is the identification of various aspects of the plight of mothers. Because mothers have no power—economic, military, or political—they have no legacy of female pride or individual selfhood for their daughters. Instead "their legacy is one of capitulation via frivolity or drudgery" (p. 18). Knowing what lies in store for their female children, mothers are severe in training them to accept the subservient role necessary for survival. They do not nurture daughters as much as they nurture sons, prompting daughters to turn to their fathers for affection. Nor are mothers equipped to help their daughters accept their sexuality: they have learned to dislike the female body, to fear lesbianism, and to envy their daughter's youth.

In this version of female psychology self-hatred looms large, one of many crippling traits which purportedly arise out of the interaction among female reproductive biology, patriarchal culture, and the mother-daughter bond. The clear import is that women are at a great disadvantage compared with men in regard to their chances for developing positive self-images.

Chodorow (1974) also fixes her attention on the mother-daughter relationship as the crucial mechanism through which women internalize the social structure. In the course of presenting her theory of feminine personality, she describes several cross-cultural variations of the mother-daughter bond and the consequences of each for female self-regard.

The possibilities for positive self-regard are illustrated by three matrifocal societies in which mothers and daughters have close ties throughout childhood and adulthood. In these societies women have multiple sources of esteem independent of their relationships with their children: they contribute to the economic support of the family, engage in mutually supportive relationships with other women, and acquire prestige with age. As a result, mothers have nothing to gain by keeping their daughters bound to them in dependency. Daughters are further blessed in that they are offered an attractive gender identity, strong, self-accepting women with whom to identify, and the security of continued mutually rewarding and culturally sanctioned contacts with their mothers. Under these opportune circumstances daughters achieve a firm sense of self and of their own worth.

Matrifocal societies are not the only kinds in which women may find sources of self-worth. Chodorow maintains that even in patrilineal, patrilocal societies, women do not necessarily translate their low status and cultural devaluation into low self-esteem. Segregation may enable women to exert real control over an exclusively female domain. The existence of close ties with other women means that women are not dependent on the mother-child relationship as their only source of self-worth. Under such conditions daughters may become "allies against oppression" (p. 65).

The situation is quite different for the western middle-class housewife who has meager resources for building self-esteem in herself or her daughters, according to Chodorow. She does not contribute to the economic support of the family, is relatively isolated from other adult women, and cannot look forward to increased prestige as she ages. Instead, her energies are concentrated almost exclusively on childrearing. Lacking other sources of esteem, she is dependent on her children for a precarious sense of self-worth. Such mothers tend not to encourage separation or foster independence in their female children who, in turn, have difficulty developing a strong sense of self. Since daughters are offered a devalued gender identity and identify with individual mothers who themselves have low self-esteem, they are not likely to develop a sense of their own value.

These examples indicate that "women . . . although always of secondary social and cultural status, may in favorable circumstances gain psychological security and a firm sense of worth and importance in spite of this" (p. 66). Chodorow shows that circumstances are favorable to the extent that women are not confined to childrearing but have access to other valued roles such as economic provider or member of a mutually supportive network of women.

c. SUMMARY OF THEORETICAL RATIONALES

Most of the theorists cited above suggest that females compare unfavorably with males on over-all self-regard. Most locate the reasons for this relationship in manifestations and concomitants of women's substandard place in the social order. These include social and economic dependence, minority group status, segregation, and relative powerlessness; cultural ideology that calls women inferior, accords them less prestige with age, and derogates their bodies, sexuality, and capacity to bear children; a greater prevalence of role conflict; and certain problematic aspects of the mother-daughter relationship.

However, women do not necessarily translate these adverse social conditions into low self-regard. Hacker raises the possibility that individual women may exempt themselves from the cultural devaluation of women. Perhaps, as Freud implies, evaluations of the self are at least partly unconscious, having untold consequences for women's (conscious) self-regard. Several theorists allude to possible sources of *positive* self-regard available to some women in spite of their subordination. These include the capacity for creating life, the experiences of pregnancy and motherhood, the acquisition in certain societies of prestige with age, the availability of important economic roles and of mutually supportive relationships among women, including strong, positive ties between mothers and daughters. These represent one set of factors which may partially offset if not actually eliminate or reverse the predicted imbalance between male and female self-regard.

Other factors which operate similarly may be gleaned from the above theories. One set includes proposed sources of *negative* self-regard in men: envy of female procreative powers and fear of being unable to perform sexually. Also incorporated into some theoretical rationales is the suggestion that men and women possess equivalent "amounts" of *distinctive* types of self-regard. Fromm, for example, describes a characteristically masculine form of vanity which is qualitatively different from the feminine form. Similarly, Carlson suggests that the contents of the real self and the ideal self differ for men and women, but the discrepancy between these components is equivalent for the sexes.

Thus, while there are many good a priori reasons to predict that women compare unfavorably with men on over-all self-regard, there are also some good reasons to remain skeptical. Many other theories, not included here, add still other reasons to both sides of this controversy. Unfortunately, the research findings presented below are of little help in resolving this question.

But before appraising the empirical evidence, it is necessary to consider another matter related to theory—namely, the effect of the theories themselves upon the relationship between sex and self-regard. To the extent that Freudian theory has been absorbed into the general cultural ideology, it may promote the belief that substandard female anatomy leads to feelings of inferiority and standard male anatomy to feelings of superiority—thereby perpetuating the very self-evaluations that Freud hypothesized. I use Freud as an example because his ideas have had an indisputable impact upon western culture. But theories that hold social and cultural factors responsible for women's predicted disadvantage in over-all self-regard have also been widely disseminated. These too may influence male and female self-regard in the theorized direction. Or, in emphasizing factors that are less immutable than anatomy, they may lead to positive changes in women's self-regard. The same possibility applies to such recent theories as Chodorow's which, acknowledging the subordination of women, nevertheless, credit women with various sources of positive self-regard. It is likely that as such theories gain currency, they will affect women's self-regard in positive ways.

Of course, changes in scientific theory constitute only one type of historical influence upon the self-images of males and females. In 1909 Cooley remarked, "The fact that law and opinion now permit women to revolt against the abuse of marital power operates widely and subtly to increase their self-respect and the respect of others for them" (Cooley, 1956, p. 371). Since then changes have occurred in the social, economic, sexual, and political roles of women. In the conclusion to *The Feminine Character: History of an Ideology*, published first in 1946, V. Klein (1971) observed:

> through the acceptance of a great variety of new functions, through socially valuable and remunerative work woman's status has been improved; many of her inferiority feelings tend to disappear; as a consequence she is more inclined to regard herself as an equal partner. [P. 177]

In recent years, the feminist movement has reemerged, promoting the goals of sex equality, female pride, and solidarity among women. These historical developments raise the possibility of positive changes in the self-regard of women, while possibly posing new problems of self-conception for men.

2. Research Concerning Over-all Self-Regard as a Function of Sex of Subject

I have grouped studies into (a) those using relatively well-known instruments which have received relatively more psychometric exploration; (b) those using idiosyncratic instruments about which there is little or no published information regarding reliability, validity, and other psychometric characteristics. Obviously, studies in the first category yield results which are more easily interpretable.

Occasionally I include factor analytic or correlational evidence where it sheds some light upon the interpretation of results on sex and over-all self-regard. But it is beyond the scope of this section to assay the evidence concerning (a) the correlations between over-all self-regard scores and other variables for males and females; (b) the factor structure of over-all self-regard in males and females. To my knowledge, there are few factor analyses, separately by sex, of over-all self-regard.

a. Self-Regard Indexed by Relatively Well-Known Instruments

Most of the studies I have examined involve children and adolescents; relatively few deal with college students and adults. Consequently, I first consider instruments used to index self-regard in children and adolescents.

Revisions or modifications of relatively well-known instruments will be considered in the immediately following section along with other investigations involving idiosyncratic instruments.

Coopersmith's Self-Esteem Inventory (SEI)

J. Williams (1973) orally administered the SEI to 133 Hispanic and Anglo first graders. Approximately half the sample was male and half female. Some information on test-retest reliability is presented. The sexes did not differ significantly on IQ, reading readiness, or reading achievement. The author computed many correlations and found that the r between sex and SEI was near zero. (Correlations between SEI scores and ethnicity, IQ, and reading readiness were also near zero.)

W. E. Simon and M. G. Simon (1975) investigated the relationship between self-esteem and academic achievement among 42 female and 45 male fifth graders. Mean achievement and IQ scores computed separately for girls and boys indicate only slight sex differences which are not evaluated statistically. Boys and girls did not differ significantly with respect to mean SEI scores. The authors report (a) significant moderate level correlations between SEI scores and achievement scores for both sexes; (b) moderate level correlations between SEI and verbal IQ, significant for males but not for females; (c) nonsignificant correlations between SEI and nonverbal IQ for both sexes.

Coopersmith's (1967) book, *The Antecedents of Self-Esteem*, is based on an exclusively male sample of preadolescents. However, in describing the development of the SEI, Coopersmith alludes to two analyses of sex differences. The test was first administered to two fifth- and sixth-grade classes consisting of 43 girls and 44 boys. The mean SEI scores of the boys and girls did not differ significantly. The test was later administered to 1,748 children attending public schools in central Connecticut. The author notes that these subjects varied more in ability, interests, and social background than the first sample. Once again the sexes did not differ significantly.

In W. E. Simon and Bernstein's (1971) study 61 male and 68 female sixth graders served as subjects. (W. E. Simon, 1972, is a report of the identical study.) The authors report a nonsignificant sex difference in mean SEI scores. L. H. Primavera, Simon, and A. M. Primavera (1974) used the SEI to measure the self-esteem of 94 female and 70 male sixth graders attending a Catholic school in a middle-class neighborhood. A nonsignificant sex difference emerged. Correlations between SEI scores and each of 7 achievement subtest scores were consistently significant for females but not for males.

Reschley and Mittman (1973) administered the SEI to 90 seventh graders from mostly lower-class homes. (The number of subjects per sex group is not reported.) Once again males and females did not differ significantly on the SEI. Trowbridge (1972a), who was concerned primarily with self-esteem as a function of socioeconomic status, drew a large sample of children from 133 classrooms (Grades 3 through 8) in central Iowa schools. There were 1,947 boys and 1,842 girls. The sample varied with respect to socioeconomic status, race, and urban/rural status. A t-test revealed that girls and boys did not differ significantly in mean SEI scores.

These seven studies (plus one duplicate) report null results in samples of first, fifth, sixth, and seventh graders. However, it is impossible to assess the degree to which various sources of artifact contributed to these findings. Such variables as GPA and SES were not controlled, perhaps reflecting the fact that most authors did not set out to test specific hypotheses concerning sex and level of self-esteem. None of these studies reported or controlled for sex of experimenter effects. It is also possible that the reliability artifact contributed to these findings by depressing the mean of the boys' SEI scores. That is, although boys may actually exceed girls in level of self-esteem, this difference may be offset by a greater tendency for boys to respond unreliably—where unreliable responding reflects relatively poor reading ability or lack of motivation on school-related tasks. (See Wylie, 1974, pp. 119-121, for a discussion of the reliability artifact.)

Five other studies which contain serious methodological problems (see section A-2) either report null results or slight sex differences which are not evaluated statistically. These are Bridgette, cited in Baughman (1971); Flammer and Matas (1972); Friedman, Rogers, and Gettys (1975); Getsinger, Kunce, Miller, and Weinberg (1972); and J. S. Greenberg (1972).

A study by Bagley and Evan-Wong (1975) is relevant to the question of how to interpret the pattern of null findings involving the SEI. They conducted separate factor analyses of the SEI scores obtained by male and female high school students from southern England. The sample consisted of 143 male and 131 female subjects, 14- to 15-years old. Two-factor principal components analyses "produced similar components in boys and girls" (p. 253). The first of these loaded highly on items indicating self-disparagement, unhappiness at home, and general unhappiness. The second had high loadings on items measuring social confidence and extraversion. Unfortunately, the authors do not report factor scores for each sex. It is possible that girls obtain more positive scores on one factor, boys on the other. In a comparison of the total SEI scores of boys and girls, these differences may cancel out one another, resulting in a finding of no significant sex difference.

Altogether, the evidence from the SEI, though suspect in various ways, consistently fails to support a relationship between sex and self-esteem. It is impossible to say whether this trend toward null results reflects genuine similarity between girls and boys, or whether it may be better explained in terms of other factors.

(See Wylie, 1974, pp. 171-174, for a detailed review and evaluation of the SEI.)

Piers-Harris Self-Concept Scale for Children (PH)

In the test manual Piers (1969) cites three unpublished studies which failed to find significant sex differences in PH mean scores or standard deviations. Millen's sample consisted of 275 fourth graders, 265 sixth graders, 231 eighth graders, 221 tenth graders, and 191 twelfth graders—all from public schools in small towns. Farls's results were based on 221 students from the fourth grade, 211 from the fifth grade, and 207 from the sixth grade. In the third unpublished study, Piers used 54 male and 57 female fourth graders and 58 male and 55 female sixth graders enrolled in public school. She also conducted a factor analysis of PH scores and found that boys' self-ratings were significantly lower than girls' on the behavior and anxiety factors.

Piers and Harris (1964) found no consistent sex differences in samples of third graders (56 girls, 63 boys), sixth graders (56 girls, 71 boys), and tenth graders (53 girls, 64 boys). The structure of the PH scale was explored by factor analyzing the scores of the sixth-grade sample and an additional sample of sixth graders from another school system (total N = 457). Sex was included as a variable in the item intercorrelation matrix. Six interpretable factors emerged: Behavior, General and Academic Status, Physical Appearance and Attributes, Anxiety, Popularity, and Happiness and Satisfaction. The sex variable appeared only in the Anxiety factor, with boys tending more than girls to deny feeling nervous or worried.

Bradley and Newhouse (1975) investigated the relationship between sociometric choice and self-conceptions among a sample of 158 sixth graders from a single community in central Kansas. The data were collected in the children's classrooms by two male experimenters who orally read and repeated each PH item. This procedure possibly reduced the likelihood of a reliability artifact, as the subjects' responses were less dependent upon their own reading ability. A nonsignificant sex difference was found.

Vance and Richmond (1975) report a nonsignificant difference between the median PH scores of boys and girls in a sample of 240 elementary-school children, containing approximately equal numbers of each race and sex. The subjects ranged in age from 8 to 12 years, attended rural elementary schools in the Southeast, and were classified by school officials as lower middle class.

The value of these findings is reduced by several factors: (a) these studies were not designed primarily to test for sex differences in self-concept; (b) it is impossible to tell whether the sex groups are comparable on other variables such as GPA or SES; (c) the reliability artifact may have contributed to some of these results by lowering the scores of the less able readers (who may be overrepresented among the boys); (d) apparently sex of the experimenter was not controlled in any of these studies. An additional point applies to the scoring of the PH—which is based on three judges' opinions as to whether an item reflects adequate (high) or inadequate (low) self-concept. Judgments about whether an item indicates high or low self-concept may not be equally applicable to both sexes, thereby making it more difficult to interpret sex comparisons of PH scores.

In sum, research involving the PH consistently fails to disclose evidence of sex differences among elementary-school children. As null results are ambiguous in various ways, the question of a relationship between sex and PH scores must remain unanswered at this point. (See Wylie, 1974, pp. 174–180, for a detailed review and evaluation of the PH scale.)

Long, Henderson, and Ziller's Self-Social Esteem Scale (SSE)

In the best of the available studies, Long and Henderson (1970) obtained a sample of 192 children who were entering first grade in 13 southern rural schools. The sample was divided into 8 equal groups on the basis of sex, race, and social class. The sex groups did not differ significantly in IQ, amount of preschool education, number of older and younger siblings, and presence or absence of the father. Six white female experimenters administered the test. An ANOVA (sex × race × class) revealed a nonsignificant main effect of sex and nonsignificant interaction effects.

Three other studies report nonsignificant relationships between sex and SSE scores. Henderson and Long (1971) administered the SSE to 47 male and 48 female Negro children attending first-grade classes in southern rural counties. Half of the children were classified as lower class and half as higher class. The authors report that the self-concept scores were independent of IQ. The sample used by Long, Henderson, Gantcheff, and Kastersztein (1972) consisted of 50 girls and 50 boys, 11- to 13-years old, in each of 4 groups: English, French, English-Canadian, French-Canadian. There were no significant sex × culture or sex × locale effects on SSE scores. Long, Henderson, and Platt (1973) studied 46 male and 53 female Israeli children, aged 11 to 13 years. The samples involved in these studies are too diverse to permit any meaningful integration of results. Moreover, since these studies lack adequate controls, it is impossible to evaluate the degree to which their null results reflect (a) noncomparability of sex groups on other possibly related variables; (b) effect of sex of experimenter. The reliability artifact may also contribute to these results.

Null results are also reported in two of three other studies (Flammer & Matas, 1972; Getsinger, Kunce, Miller & Weinberg, 1972; Hollender, 1972). These studies are not described here as they contain serious methodological problems. (See section A-2.)

Carlson (1970) contends that the SSE, in requiring spatial representations of self-esteem, may contain unintended masculine bias.

In sum, the available evidence seems too limited to warrant any conclusion about the relationship between sex and SSE scores.

(See Wylie, 1974, pp. 190-200, for a detailed review and evaluation of Long, Henderson, and Ziller's Self-Social Symbols Tasks, from which the SSE score is derived.)

Tennessee Self-Concept Scale (TSCS)

In the TSCS manual Fitts (1965) does not present norms separately by sex, noting that the effects of sex on TSCS scores are "quite negligible." Supporting evidence is not provided.

Healey and de Blassie (1974) studied the self-concepts of 314 female and 293 male ninth graders. The sample varied with respect to eth-

SEX OF SUBJECT 267

nicity (Anglo, Spanish-American, Negro) and socioeconomic status. Despite such large *N*s, no significant sex difference emerged on the Total Positive Score of the TSCS. Interactions among ethnicity, sex, and SES also failed to attain significance. One of the major purposes of W. B. Walsh and Osipow's (1973) study was to identify sex differences in self-concept variables. They report no main effect of sex on the Total Positive Score in a sample of 81 male and 81 female undergraduates. Neither of these studies provides adequate information concerning the comparability of sex groups or reports the sex of the experimenter. Both involve multiple ANOVAs. The reliability artifact cannot be ruled out in interpreting the Healey and de Blassie results but is probably less of a problem in the Walsh and Osipow study which involved college students.

The following three studies are not described because they are seriously flawed: Tapp and Spanier (1973); Wendland, cited in Baughman (1971); and K. White and Howard (1973). (See section A-2.) Two of these studies report nonsignificant sex differences.

Once again the evidence is inadequate to sustain even tentative conclusions concerning the relationship between sex and over-all self-regard scores.

(See Wylie, 1974, pp. 230–236, for a detailed review and evaluation of the TSCS.)

Rosenberg's Self-Esteem Scale (RSE)

Although Hulbary (1975) was concerned mainly with the effects of race and socioeconomic deprivation on self-concept, he included sex among his independent variables. The sample consisted of 88 black and 98 white adolescents aged 14–19 years and representing a diversity of socioeconomic levels. There were roughly equal numbers of males and females. A multiple regression analysis was applied to assess the effects of race, socioeconomic status, exposure to political/social information, racial isolation, age, and sex on self-esteem, as measured by the Rosenberg scale. The influence of the sex variable was found to be small and statistically insignificant.

J. S. Greenberg and Archambault (1973) present mean RSE scores separately by sex, but, owing to various methodological problems (see section A-2), this study is not described here.

(See Wylie, 1974, pp. 180–189, for a detailed review and critique of the RSE.)

Bills's Index of Adjustment and Values (IAV)

Bills's IAV is designed to permit three different responses to each item: Self (How often are you this sort of person?); Self-Acceptance (How do you feel about being this way?); and Ideal Self (How much of the time would you like this trait to be characteristic of you?). Of relevance to over-all self-regard are the total Self score, total Self-Acceptance score, and total [Self — Ideal] discrepancy score, from which self-satisfaction is inferred.

Meissner, Thoreson, and Butler (1967) used a sample of high school juniors from three Wisconsin high schools. Among those students who admitted to having a physical problem or handicap (173 females, 157 males), nonsignificant main effects of sex were found on the Self and Self-Acceptance scores.

B. W. McCarthy and Rafferty (1971) obtained IAV Self-Acceptance scores from 282 male and 282 female college-student volunteers. A significant main effect of sex emerged, with males exceeding females. The authors note, "Although a significant difference was found on the sex variable, the magnitude of the difference was not great" (p. 579).

The purpose of Rule and Hewitt's (1970) study was to explore, separately by sex, the factor structure of anti-Semitism, cognitive structure variables, and self-concept, as measured by the IAV. The sample consisted of 113 female and 91 male college students enrolled in introductory psychology classes. In line with the results of McCarthy and Rafferty (1971), men obtained a higher mean Self-Acceptance score than women (170.90 and 164.91, respectively). Women scored higher than men on the mean [Self — Ideal] variable, whereas the sexes obtained similar mean Self scores. Unfortunately, none of these mean differences was subjected to statistical test. The results of the factor analysis revealed different factor structures for men and women. For example, from women's responses a single self-concept factor emerged which the authors interpreted as descriptive of a positive, satisfied person. For men, two self-concept factors were obtained, indicating projected self-assurance and neurotic, dissatisfied self-concept.

M. C. Shaw and Alves (1963) compared the IAV scores of achieving and underachieving high school students for each sex separately. Although they present the mean Self, Self-Acceptance, and [Ideal — Self] scores for males and females, they do not compute statistical tests of sex differences in these scores.

In sum, only four studies present IAV data separately by sex. The authors of these studies did not demonstrate the comparability of the sex groups on other possibly relevant variables, nor did they report or control for sex of experimenter. The diversity of samples involved and the scant amount of evidence on any one IAV score preclude any conclusions at this point.

(See Wylie, 1974, pp. 150-165, for a detailed review and evaluation of the IAV.)

Shostrom's Personal Orientation Inventory (POI)

In the POI manual Shostrom (1966) presents scores separately by sex for a sample of college freshmen (792 females, 1,254 males). A slight but significant sex difference favoring females occurred on the Self-Acceptance scale, but the sexes did not differ significantly on the Self-Regard scale. Analogous comparisons among 196 male and 216 female high school students yielded nonsignificant sex differences on both scales.

Two researchers undertook investigations with the express purpose of testing for sex differences in the twelve POI scale scores. Schroeder (1973) administered the test to a large stratified sample of freshmen living in residence halls at Oregon State University. There were 278 men and 290 women in the sample. Separate t-tests computed on each of the scales revealed that females scored significantly higher than males on 11 of the 12 scales, including the Self-Acceptance scale. However, in terms of absolute magnitude, females exceeded males by only a slight margin on the Self-Acceptance scale. The sexes did not differ significantly on the Self-Regard scale. In a study conducted by Wise and Davis (1975) 86 female and 86 male college students, predominantly juniors and seniors, took the POI twice, at a two-week interval. Significant sex differences emerged on 4 of the scales. But the Self-Acceptance and Self-Regard scales yielded nonsignificant main effects of sex and nonsignificant sex × trials interaction effects.

Doyle (1975), Ginn (1974), and Tapp and Spanier (1973) also present some information concerning the sex variable in relation to POI scores, but, owing to various methodological problems (see section A-2), these studies are not described here.

In sum, four samples yielded null results on the POI Self-Regard scale, while the equally sparse evidence from the Self-Acceptance scale is not consistent. Conclusions concerning the relationship between sex and POI Self-Acceptance and Self-Regard are premature at this point. (See chapter 11, pp. 631-632 of this volume for a critique of the POI.)

Gough and Heilbrun's Adjective Check List (ACL)

The ACL Self-Favorability and Self-Unfavorability scale scores are analogous to over-all self-regard scores derived from other instruments. In the ACL manual, Gough and Heilbrun (1965) explain that the adjectives comprising the Self-Favorability scale were identified on the basis of college students' choices of the 75 most favorable adjectives among the 300 adjectives in the test. The Self-Unfavorability scale items were identified in a similar way. This type of scoring is subject to the same criticism that I raised earlier with respect to the PH: it is possible that favorability/unfavorability judgments are not equally applicable to both sexes. The authors present standard scores separately for males and females, implying that there are sex differences in Self-Favorability and Self-Unfavorability raw scores.

In a small sample of adults (22 males, 19 females), Weinstein and Hanson (1975) found nonsignificant sex differences on ACL standard scores, including Self-Favorability and Self-Unfavorability. Costantini and Craik (1972) and Ramos (1974) present ACL standard scores separately by sex. But, as Costantini and Craik note, direct statistical comparisons of the sexes are not appropriate in light of the fact that Gough and Heilbrun (1965) established standard scores separately by sex. Silverman, Shulman, and Wiesenthal (1970) apparently did not convert college students' raw ACL scores into standard scores. In a rare exception to usual practice, these authors attempted to control for sex of experimenter. They computed many statistical tests and found no main effect of sex on Self-Favorability or Self-Unfavorability.

Clearly, the evidence from research involving the ACL does not help to resolve the question of whether sex and over-all self-regard are empirically related.

(See Wylie, 1974, pp. 200-212, for a detailed review and critique of the ACL.)

Interpersonal Check List (ICL)

The ICL counterpart of over-all self-regard scores is the total [Self—Ideal] discrepancy score. I have found only 2 studies that analyzed for sex differences in such scores. Eberlein, Park, and Matheson (1971) report that "only small and nonsignificant (sex) differences were observed" (p. 98) within 3 different samples—counsellor trainees, teachers-in-training, high school students. Lockwood and Guerney (1962) found that high school girls, compared with boys, obtained higher [Self—Ideal] discrepancy scores, called "Self-Dissatisfaction." However, this finding was not evaluated statistically, and sex groups were extremely small (13 boys, 15 girls).

(See Wylie, 1974, pp. 213-223, for a detailed review and critique of the ICL.)

Worchel's Self-Activity Inventory (SAI)

In a study designed to test an hypothesis not related to sex differences in self-concept, G. Becker and Dileo (1967) found a significant main effect of sex on SAI [Self—Ideal] discrepancy scores. Female college students obtained larger discrepancies than male college students. This is the only investigation I have found which presents data relevant to the question of a possible relationship between sex and SAI [Self—Ideal] discrepancy scores.

(See Wylie, 1974, pp. 165-169, for a detailed review and critique of the SAI.)

Summary of Studies Using Well-Known Instruments of Over-all Self-Regard

A clear trend emerges from these 47 investigations of the relationship between sex and self-regard: null results prevail. This is consistent with Maccoby and Jacklin's (1974) assessment of the evidence concerning generalized self-esteem. The pattern is the same whether one considers the many studies of children and adolescents or the relatively few studies of college students and adults.

As null findings are inherently ambiguous, one can only speculate about the meaning of these results. It seems unlikely that instrument deficiencies are primarily responsible for null results which obtain across several instruments, many of which have received a good deal of psychometric exploration. Questions concerning reliability and construct validity, then, seem less important here than certain other methodological problems which appear again and again in these studies. Investigators often failed to establish that their sex groups were comparable on other variables (e.g., GPA or SES) which may be related to over-all self-regard. Sex of experimenter was controlled in only one case. These failings are perhaps symptomatic of the tendency for studies to deal only incidentally with the variable of sex. Another problem, particularly applicable to studies involving children, is the possible confounding of low self-regard scores and unreliable responding. The reliability artifact may depress the self-regard scores of boys who, perhaps, are more likely than girls to read poorly or lack motivation in school-related tasks. (See footnote 1, p. 247.) With the evidence at hand, it is impossible to determine the degree to which these and other methodological problems contributed to null results.

Another possible explanation for null findings is related to the practice of summing across items in order to obtain a global self-regard score. Most of the instruments involved in this section rely upon such summation scores. Any given score of this type could result from any one of many item combinations. Perhaps males and females obtain equivalent total scores by endorsing different sets of items. Item analyses separately by sex are needed in order to explore this possibility. Factor analytic studies would also be useful here. Perhaps the factor structures of over-all self-regard are similar for the two sexes, but females obtain higher scores on some factors, males on others.

(A related issue concerns whether a given item is of equal importance to males and females. Rosenberg [1965] presents some data indicating that while male and female adolescents share many of the same self-values, they also differ substantially in the qualities that they say are personally important to them. One has no way of knowing how the sexes would compare in over-all self-regard if items were weighted according to their perceived importance to the individual.)

Of course, it is also possible that the recurrent failure to find significant sex differences indicates genuine similarity between the sexes in level of over-all self-regard. This would be inconsistent with the many theories that predict lower self-regard in females than males. But it would not be totally implausible. (See section B-1.) Despite their subordination, women may draw upon various resources that enable them to develop positive self-concepts. Despite their position of relative privilege, men may encounter various obstacles to such development.

Still another possibility is suggested by the fact that most of the studies under review were published in the late 1960s and early 1970s. Perhaps null results obtained with college student and adult samples reflect, in part, the influence of the recent feminist movement. Unfortunately, earlier evidence is too meager to permit detection of historical trends. (See Wylie, 1961, pp. 144-145.)

In sum, the evidence from studies involving well-known instruments fails to support a relationship between sex and over-all self-regard. Although various speculative interpretations may be offered to explain the repeated finding of null results, no firm conclusions can yet be drawn. The question of a relationship between sex and over-all self-regard remains unresolved.

b. SELF-REGARD INDEXED BY IDIOSYNCRATIC INSTRUMENTS

Also relevant to the issue of over-all self-regard as a function of sex are studies which use idiosyncratic measures of self-regard. Here the problems of evaluation and interpretation are compounded by the practice of using in a single study an instrument about which little or nothing is known concerning its reliability, validity, and other psychometric properties. Of the 43 studies (plus 2 duplicate reports) which I examined, most were so deficient methodologically (see section A-2) or lacking in information that I merely list them at the end of the section. The 10 studies which I chose for substantive review, although flawed in various ways, seemed less flawed than the others. These 10 studies are presented in order of increasing age of subjects.

Substantively Described Studies

Children of welfare mothers were subjects in Carpenter and Busse's (1969) developmental study of self concept. The sample consisted of 40 first graders and 40 fifth graders, equally divided by race and sex, all from father-absent families. The Where Are You Game was individually administered. This instrument requires no reading, thereby minimizing the effects of the reliability artifact. Reliability and validity information is not included in this article. Because the data were extremely skewed, the authors used Mann-Whitney U-tests rather than ANOVAs. For the total sample (race and grade groups combined) girls obtained significantly more negative self concepts than boys. When sex comparisons were made within racial groups, this relationship held for blacks but not for whites. However, since multiple statistical tests were involved, these findings cannot be clearly interpreted.

On the basis of Bardwick's theory (see section B-1), Fein, O'Neill, C. Frank, and Velit (1975) predicted that boys' self-esteem would be higher than girls' among children who were on the verge of adolescence, but not among younger children. The sample included 279 urban children, 52% female, 48% male, from Grades 2 through 6. A variety of ethnic groups was represented (white, black, Spanish-speaking, other). Items were drawn from the SEI and the PH to form a 26-item questionnaire in which acquiescence response set was controlled. The authors pretested the questionnaire with second and fourth graders in order to verify its comprehensibility. Kuder-Richardson reliability, based on the 279 subjects, was .76. Although the main effect of sex was not significant, a significant grade × sex interaction effect emerged. Boys, but not girls, showed an upward trend in self-esteem. Consistent with the authors' prediction, a significant sex difference favoring the boys occurred only at the sixth-grade level. However, this comparison was based on only about 28 subjects per sex group. Correlations between reading and self-esteem scores were moderate and significant at each grade level for boys but consistently near zero for girls. This finding, coupled with the rise in boys' self-esteem scores, suggests that the reliability artifact may have contributed to the self-esteem scores of boys. In an item analysis, the authors found significant sex differences on only 2 items, with more boys than girls scoring in the positive direction on each.

In a study by J. W. Greenberg, Gerver, Chall, and Davidson (1965) the main purpose was to explore various attitudes presumed to be important to academic achievement among disadvantaged children. Serving as subjects were 56 male and 59 female fourth graders, all of whom attended public school in a "severely depressed urban area" (p. 57). Inspection of the Metropolitan Primary Reading Test scores presented in the article indicates that the sexes were roughly comparable in reading achievement. An idiosyncratic semantic differential involving 6 evaluative scales and 2 potency scales was used to measure 13 concepts including Myself. No reliability or validity information is provided. In order to avoid penalizing the poor readers, the experimenter orally read the test directions. Nonsignificant main effects of sex and nonsignificant sex × achievement effects were obtained on the summed evaluative score and the summed potency score.

Large numbers of sixth-grade pupils from 36 Boston classrooms were involved in St. John's (1971) study. The sample consisted of 496 white, 416 black, and 45 Chinese, Puerto Rican, and other ethnic group members and varied with respect to SES and percentage of black students attending the school. General Self-Concept was measured by means of an idiosyncratic semantic differential consisting of 10 bipolar adjectives. Data concerning the reliability and validity of this instrument are not presented. The sex variable correlated −.03 with General Self-Concept for black students and −.08 for whites. Sex was also entered into a multiple regression analysis along with five other independent variables: IQ, GPA, class SES, own SES minus class SES, and class percent white. For blacks a nonsignificant regression coefficient of $-.10$ was obtained between sex and General Self-Concept. The analogous figure for whites ($-.15$) was significant at the .05 level, indicating higher self-concept scores for boys than girls. Of the six independent variables, GPA was most strongly related to General Self-Concept for both blacks and whites.

P. Katz and Zigler (1967) conducted a developmental study of self-image disparity among children from Grades 5, 8, and 11. The sample was randomly drawn from a single school system in a homogeneously middle-class community. Subjects were classed as either high or low IQ on the basis of scores on the Otis Quick-Scoring Mental Ability Test. A three-way factorial design was used involving an equal number (10) of male and female subjects within each age by IQ classification. Two idiosyncratic instruments were employed, a 20-item questionnaire, including some items from the SEI, and a 20-item ACL. In each case a balance between positive and negative items was achieved, but no reliability or validity data are reported. Subjects responded to each instrument under instructions to describe the real self, the ideal self, and the social self. Repeated measures ANOVAs (measure × age × IQ × sex) apparently revealed no main effect of sex on either the real self questionnaire score or the real self ACL score. Interaction effects involving sex also failed to reach significance.

Gill and D'Oyley (1970) describe their attempt to develop a new self-concept instrument. They drew a large sample of ninth-grade students (782 males, 642 females) from 5 academic high schools in Toronto. The test consisted of 2 sets of 65 items used to measure perceived self and ideal self, respectively. Apparently, acquiescence response set was only partially controlled. Eight week test-retest reliability estimated from the perceived-self scores of 67 students was .60 for girls and .69 for boys. Internal consistency reliability coefficients ranged from .89 to .92. Girls obtained a higher over-all mean score (187.1) than boys (183.9), but this difference was not evaluated statistically. A principal components analysis of the perceived-self scores yielded 15 factors for both boys and girls. Eight of these were psychologically interpretable: Achievement-Related Characteristics, Acceptance by Peers and Teachers, Self-Confidence, Originality, Feeling of Adequacy, Reaction to School Program, Concentrating Ability, Self-Satisfaction. Inspection of the factor scores computed separately by sex provides some clues as to the type of item content that does or does not differentiate the sexes. Girls scored slightly higher than boys on Achievement-Related Charac- teristics, Acceptance by Peers and Teachers, and Feeling of Adequacy. Boys scored slightly higher than girls on Concentrating Ability, while the sex groups obtained roughly equal scores on the other factors. Un- fortunately, these factor score comparisons were not subjected to statistical test.

Monge (1973) set out to examine age and sex differences in the structure of self-concept among adolescents. Included in the sample were children from Grades 6 through 12 of 4 small public school districts in central New York. There were 1,027 girls and 1,035 boys, with each sex × grade subgroup containing more than 100 subjects. An idiosyncratic semantic differential involving 21 bipolar adjective pairs was used to assess the concept, My Characteristic Self. No information concerning reliability or validity is reported. After preliminary factor analyses indicated a high degree of structural similarity across grade and sex groups, the author conducted a principal components anal- ysis of the scores for the total sample. The 4 factors which emerged were called Achievement/Leadership, Congeniality/Sociability, Ad- justment, and Masculinity-Femininity. These factors were highly similar to factors obtained when the same items were administered to different samples in 3 other studies. Factor scores were computed and were subjected to sex × grade ANOVAs. Compared with girls, boys obtained significantly higher scores on Achievement/Leadership and Adjustment, whereas girls scored significantly higher on the Con- geniality/Sociability factor. The sexes did not differ significantly in the sex appropriateness of self-concept, as measured by the Masculinity- Femininity factor score. Complex and significant interactions between grade and sex occurred on the Achievement/Leadership and Mascu- linity-Femininity factors.

Age and sex differences were also the focus of A. R. Kohn and Fiedler's (1961) investigation of person perception. They administered an idiosyncratic semantic differential to three groups of subjects: high school freshmen, second-semester college freshmen, and college seniors. There were 20 female and 20 male subjects per group. All subjects were from the upper middle-class as determined by father's occupation. The instrument consisted of 20 bipolar items used to describe 7 concepts, including the self. Corrected odd-even reliability coefficients for the 7 concepts ranged from .64 to .85, with a median of .77. The authors computed ANOVAs for each of the concepts and found a significant main effect of sex for self. Females described themselves more favorably than males. The sex × age interaction effect was not significant.

In L. R. Good and K. C. Good's (1975) study undergraduate students responded to the 32 items of a new measure of self-esteem. There were 83 female and 75 male subjects. Following an item analysis, 27 items were retained for which the Kuder-Richardson reliability estimate was .81. Acquiescence response set was partially controlled. The application of a t-test disclosed a significant difference favoring males.

For their large-scale survey of northern blacks, Crain and Weisman (1972) developed a self-esteem scale designed to measure the degree to which a person is willing to say that he or she is better than other people. They drew a block-quota sample of 1,651 black men and women, aged 21 to 45, from 25 different northern metropolitan areas. A sample of 1,326 whites served as a comparison group. The 10 items comprising the scale are presented in the book and refer to evaluation of one's character, ability, and merit as a family member. Kuder-Richardson reliability was found to be .74 for the black sample and .70 for the white sample. Item intercorrelations and some factor analytic information are presented. The authors conclude:

> The average white male rated himself above average on 3.3 items; white females, on 2.5; black males, on 2.6; and black females, on 2.2. Relative to men, black women do not rate themselves as low as do white women; black women have higher esteem relative to black men than white women do relative to white men. [P. 74]

However, no statistical evaluation is provided in support of these generalizations.

Summary of Studies Relating Sex to Self-Regard Indexed by Idiosyncratic Instruments

Described above are 10 studies concerning the relationship between sex and over-all self-regard as indexed by idiosyncratic instruments. Of these studies, 7 involved children and adolescents, whereas 3 used college student or adult samples. Among the commonly appearing methodological problems were (a) the failure to demonstrate that the sex groups were comparable on other possibly relevant variables; (b) the omission of reliability or validity information; (c) the use of multiple statistical tests or the failure to provide any statistical evaluation. In no case was the sex of experimenter controlled or even reported. The evidence from these studies is inconsistent: null results appear as frequently as results favoring males. In two studies females exceeded males on over-all self-regard.

Below I list studies which I judged to be even more deficient methodologically or lacking in necessary information. Most of these investigations dealt with children and adolescents. The majority report null results, while no trend in favor of either sex is discernible among the rest.

In sum, this evaluation of studies involving idiosyncratic instruments serves only to reinforce what has already been said concerning research based on well-known instruments. While the present evidence does not support a relationship between sex and over-all self-regard, resolution of this question awaits further, better research.

Studies Not Substantively Described

The following 33 studies (plus 2 duplicate reports) contain serious methodological problems (see section A-2) or too little information: Antley, Antley, and Hartlage (1973); Bledsoe (1964, 1973); Bledsoe and Wiggins (1973); Carlson (1963); Eagly and Whitehead (1972); Epps (1969); Gecas (1971); Getsinger, Kunce, Miller, and Weinberg (1972); Gold and Coghlan (1973); C. A. Grant (1973); Henton and Johnson (1964); Herbert, Gelfand, and Hartmann (1969); D. Hill (1970); Hughes and Works (1974); Kirchner and Vondracek (1975); Larkin (1972); Lawrence and Winschel (1973); Lekarczyk and Hill (1969); Lepper (1973); Lundgren and Schwab (1974); Lyell (1973); Miskimins and R. B. Baker (1973); Pannes (1963); Parker and Kleiner (1966); Preston (1967); Sarason and Koenig (1965); Sarason and Winkel (1966); M. S. Smart and R. C. Smart (1970); L. Soares and A. Soares (1970) and duplicate report, A. Soares and L. Soares (1970b); Ward (1971); W. F. White, H. E. Anderson, and Cryder (1966) and duplicate report, W. F. White, H. E. Anderson, and Cryder (1967); D. S. Wright (1962).

C. Sex-Role Ideology and Self-Concept

1. Theoretical Rationales

By drawing attention to the ideas of C. Thompson, Adler, and Hacker in section B-1, I anticipated the question of a possible relationship between sex-role ideology and self-concept. In this section I consider this question with respect to one portion of sex-role ideology[3] — namely, beliefs and attitudes concerning the personality characteristics of males and females. What kinds of qualities do people feel are typical in a man and in a woman? Are some of these qualities more highly valued than others? Do people impute prescriptive powers to certain attributes, calling some more appropriate to women, others more appropriate to men? And, if asked to envision their ideals, how do men and women respond? Which virtues do they bestow upon the ideal woman and the ideal man?

These questions have been explored empirically through the use of self-reports. Most research has dealt with sex-role stereotypes (beliefs about the typical chracteristics of males and females). Relatively less attention has been devoted to sex-role standards (beliefs about the appropriate characteristics of the sexes) and sex-role ideals (beliefs about the ideal characteristics of males and females). In the following section I examine research on each of these categories of beliefs and consider, where possible, studies that attempt to relate these beliefs to the self-concepts of males and females.

Most of these studies share the assumption, either implied or expressed, that the prevailing beliefs about the sexes shape the self-concepts of males and females. Just how this happens is unclear. Authors talk vaguely in terms of social pressures to conform to sex-role standards, of the incorporation of sex-role stereotypes into self-conceptions, of cultural conditioning, rewards, and punishments.

Although it seems highly plausible that sex-role ideology exerts an influence on self-concepts, this issue is far more complicated than is commonly recognized. Cooley's (1902) notion of the looking-glass self suggests one means by which beliefs about the sexes may affect the self-concepts of males and females and illustrates the complexity of this issue. The looking-glass self involves three elements: the individual's perception of how he or she appears to the other person; the individual's perception of the other's evaluation of that appearance; the individual's resulting feelings, such as pride or mortification. If a girl's self-appraisal is dependent upon other people's views of her (which views reflect their beliefs about females), she may eventually come to conceive of herself in

---

3. Sex-role ideology refers to that portion of a society's ideological heritage which includes beliefs, notions, attitudes, and feelings about males and females, their behaviors, personality chracteristics, motivations, and aspirations, interests, activities, and occupations.

terms of those beliefs. This may happen even though she does not realize that other people's perceptions of her are colored by their beliefs about females. This is one simple application of the looking-glass self to the issue at hand.

However, there is room within this concept for many more possibilities. First, questions may be raised with respect to each of the elements of the looking-glass self. Does the individual accurately perceive how he or she appears to others? Does he or she accurately perceive the others' evaluation? How does he or she feel about the other person's perception and evaluation? The answers to these questions obviously have a bearing on whether beliefs about the sexes influence the self-concepts of males and females. Second, according to Cooley, the nature of a person's feelings about the reflected self depends in part, on the other person in whom the self is reflected. This suggests, for example, that a boy may value especially highly the views of certain persons. Perhaps these special persons do not subscribe to the prevailing beliefs about the sexes. And even if they do, their perceptions of him may be based more on his individuality than on his membership in the male sex group.

Hacker's (1951) paper on women as a minority group raises other questions related to the issue of sex-role ideology and self-conceptions (see section B-1). Do women have a sense of group identification, a minority group consciousness—which includes awareness of sex-role ideology concerning women? (In a recent revision of her 1951 paper, Hacker [1975] implies that one outgrowth of the contemporary feminist movement is a new sense of group identification among women.) Do men have an analogous sense of group identification, a majority group consciousness? Do men and women accept the prevailing sex-role ideology as applicable to their respective *sex groups*? Do they accept it as applicable to the *self*?

Rosaldo's (1974) theory specifies some of the conditions under which women do and do not accept the devaluative aspect of sex-role ideology as applicable to women as a group. Drawing upon anthropological evidence, she documents the universal asymmetry in cultural evaluations of the sexes. She shows that it does not matter whether the society is relatively equalitarian or highly stratified as to sex: in every case it is men, their roles and activities, that are accorded the greater value and importance. Despite this, women are able to achieve a sense of female worth under certain social structural arrangements, according to Rosaldo. One such arrangement is relatively equalitarian:

women participate with men in the public sphere, while both sexes share domestic responsibilities. In more hierarchial societies, women may also acquire a sense of their own value:

> The very symbolic and social conceptions that appear to set women apart and to circumscribe their activities may be used by women as a basis for female solidarity and worth. When men live apart from women, they in fact cannot control them, and unwittingly they may provide them with the symbols and social resources on which to build a society of their own. [P. 39]

According to this view, then, conditions auspicious to the development of female pride—even in nonequalitarian societies—are those which enable women to transcend the domestic sphere. This may be achieved by participating in public activities or by elaborating a separate female domain. The opposing set of conditions in which women spend their lives in domestic isolation, engaging in neither public pursuits nor in interaction with other women may lead women to accept the cultural devaluation of their own sex group.

Aside from the social structural variation which Rosaldo describes there are undoubtedly many other factors which affect the degree to which males and females accept the prevailing sex-role ideology as applicable to men and women, respectively. The list of possible factors includes age, social class, racial/ethnic status, religious background, educational level, political orientation, geographic location, family structure, childrearing practices, and individual temperament.

When males and females do subscribe to sex-role ideology concerning their respective groups, a basis is provided for them to develop self-concepts that are in line with that ideology. But if an individual believes that certain personality characteristics are typical of women, does she necessarily conceive of herself as possessing any or all of those attributes? Does her conception of the ideal woman and of man's ideal woman necessarily influence her self-concept? Does a man who believes that certain characteristics are expected of men necessarily take these as standards in evaluating himself? Available theory has not dealt with the question of which conditions lead males and females to accept (or reject) the prevailing sex-role ideology as self-applicable.

This brief look at theory reveals a host of questions related to the issue of the influence of sex-role ideology on self-conceptions. As will soon become apparent, research provides answers to only a few of these questions.

The following survey of research is confined, for the most part, to studies conducted since the publishing of the 1961 edition of this book. A notable exception is the frequently cited, systematic work of Sherriffs and colleagues. The reader who is interested in earlier research on sex-role ideology is referred to reviews by I. K Broverman, Vogel, D. M. Broverman, Clarkson, and Rosenkrantz (1972), Kagan (1964), and Sherman (1971).

2. Sex-Role Stereotypes

As noted in chapter 4, section B-3, most investigators have defined the term ethnic stereotype rather vaguely as a commonly held generalization about an ethnic group, concerning a trait attribution. Sex-role stereotypes have been similarly defined as widespread beliefs about the attributes that differentiate the sexes. Paralleling the study of ethnic stereotypes, sex-role stereotypes have been explored empirically by asking subjects to describe the typical male and female (or males and females in general), usually with reference to a list of words, statements, or bipolar items.

In the 1961 edition of this book, Wylie cites four studies (Lynn, 1959; McKee & Sherriffs, 1957, 1959; Sherriffs & McKee, 1957) relevant to the issue of sex-role stereotypes, concluding that college student subjects hold stereotypes of males and females. Additional evidence from various samples supports the claim that adults agree as to which traits differentiate males and females. These samples include college students (Rosenkrantz, Vogel, Bee, I. Broverman, & D. Broverman, 1968; Ross & Walters, 1973; Sherriffs & Jarrett, 1953; Spence, Helmreich, & Stapp, 1974, 1975); Catholic mothers of male college students (Clarkson, Vogel, I. K. Broverman, D. M. Broverman, & Rosenkrantz 1970); several samples of adults, varying as to age, religion, marital status, and level of education (Broverman et al., 1972); female homosexuals and heterosexuals (Hassell & Smith, 1975); and clinicians (I. K. Broverman, D. M. Broverman, Clarkson, Rosenkrantz, & Vogel, 1970).

Researchers also report that college men and women subscribe to the same stereotypes about the sexes. For example, Reece (1964) notes that males and females agreed in their concepts of typical masculinity and typical femininity. Rosenkrantz et al. (1968) found that the average rating of the typical female made by women correlated .950 with the average rating of the typical female made by men. The corresponding correlation for the typical male ratings was .960. Sherriffs and Jarrett

(1953) and Lunneborg (1970) present further data indicating that college women and men share the same sex stereotypes. In a review of their own research Broverman et al. (1972) note that in samples of adults—varying as to age, religion, educational level, and marital status—men and women agree as to the characteristics of men and women.

In sum, studies involving various samples of adults consistently show that certain traits are differentially ascribed to the typical female and the typical male. Moreover, it appears that sex stereotypes held by female college students strongly resemble those held by male college students. But what is it that people agree upon? Which specific personality characteristics are ascribed to females, which to males? Are the characteristics associated with one sex more highly valued than those associated with the other? I consider, in turn, these questions of the content and value of sex stereotypic traits.

First, however, it is necessary to raise two conceptual and methodological issues which apply to both questions. The first of these was anticipated in section A-1 and concerns the frame of reference within which judgments are made about the typical male and female. There is a variety of distinctions that can be made here. A person may harbor some notion of "society's" definition of the typical male and female, an expectation about how "people in general" describe the average woman and man. It is likely that he or she also has some understanding of how specific groups—family, friends, feminists—characterize men and women. Then there is his or her own personal view on the matter, a view that may be similar to that of any of the above groups, but need not be.

These distinctions have generally not been recognized in the literature on sex stereotpyes. In most of the studies discussed below, instructions to subjects do not clearly specify a reference group, or the reporting of procedures is too vague to determine whether a reference group was specified.

Another issue concerns the type of design used in research on sex-role stereotypes. Most studies employ a within-subjects design in which the same subjects make separate ratings of each sex. The investigator subsequently compares these characterizations, inferring differences in the traits ascribed to the sexes and in the value conferred upon those traits. Two other designs are represented far less frequently in research on sex-role stereotypes: (a) a between-subjects design in which different groups of subjects chosen from the same population describe *either*

THE SELF-CONCEPT

males or females, e.g., Broverman et al. (1970); (b) a within-subjects design in which subjects make direct comparisons of males and females, e.g., Spence, Helmreich, and Stapp (1975). It is unclear whether and in what ways choice of design influences the findings on sex-role stereotypes. At least in principle, the within-subjects design involving direct comparisons yields information of a different type. A subject's own comparison of males and females is wholly phenomenal, whereas the other types of comparisons are not. This distinction between phenomenal (direct) comparisons and inferred comparisons has not been recognized in research on sex-role stereotypes.

a. CONTENT OF SEX-ROLE STEREOTYPES

In order to determine the content of sex stereotypes it is necessary to examine directly the items that subjects assign to males and females. Unfortunately, many of the studies on sex stereotypes do not report the data in such a way that the content of stereotypes can be ascertained. Those that do yield consistent findings.

Sherriffs and McKee (1957) explored this question using data collected in McKee and Sherriffs (1957). Fifty male and 50 female college students described first one sex and then the other, using the 200 adjectives of Sarbin's Adjective Check List (ACL). Half of the subjects began with women, half with men. The authors report the results in terms of favorable and unfavorable adjectives; another group of college students had previously rated the desirability or undesirability of each item as it applied to men and women, respectively.

Thirty favorable adjectives were ascribed significantly more often to men than women by both males and females. The authors intuitively interpreted those adjectives as falling into three clusters: straightforward, uninhibited social style (e.g., informal, frank, easygoing); rational competence and ability (e.g., industrious, realistic, logical); and action, vigor, and effectiveness (e.g., self-confident, aggressive, dominant). The eight unfavorable adjectives applied more often to men than women by both sexes generally referred to exaggerations of the positive characteristics attributed to males. These included, for example, boastful, outspoken, hardheaded, stern, and reckless.

Twenty-one favorable adjectives were ascribed significantly more often to women than men by both male and female subjects. These were grouped as follows: social skills and grace (e.g., poised, well-mannered, sociable); warmth and emotional support (e.g., gentle, affectionate, kind); and concern with the spiritual aspects of experience (e.g., sensitive, religious, artistic). Again, the 17 unfavorable adjectives seemed to be exaggerated forms of these positive qualities, including, for example, snobbish, vain, fearful, emotional, and frivolous.

Another sample of college students used an open-ended technique to characterize the typical male and female, yielding results similar to those described above.

An earlier study (Sherriffs & Jarrett, 1953) provides additional clues as to the stereotypic profiles of men and women. The authors used an idiosyncratic instrument consisting of 58 items which they and several colleagues had judged to represent the female stereotype (17 items), the male stereotype (17 items), and neither stereotype (24 items). A balance between positive and negative items was achieved within both stereotype and nonstereotype items. Using a forced-choice format, 212 female and 179 male college students indicated whether each item was more applicable to men or women. (The subjects also indicated which items more appropriately characterized one of two age groups and one of three religious groups. This attempt to conceal the authors' intention of studying attitudes toward the sexes was successful, according to Jarrett and Sherriffs [1953].) The following evidence of sex stereotyping was obtained: 19 items were assigned to women and 27 to men by significantly more than 50% of both male and female subjects. However, these differences between the items attributed to men and women are probably inflated to some degree as a consequence of the forced-choice format.

Inspection of the content of these stereotypic items reveals a strong resemblance to the results obtained by Sherriffs and McKee (1957). The male stereotype included such attributes as objective, intelligent, courageous, and careless. The female stereotype included warm, sensitive, imaginative, and vain. Other stereotypic qualities do not fit as easily into the Sheriffs and McKee clusters: for instance, women were chracterized as relatively faithful in marriage, men as relativley loyal to friends and causes.

Further evidence supporting this general picture of the content of sex-role stereotypes emerges from Rosenkrantz et al. (1968), a study conducted more than a decade after the research by Sherriffs and colleagues. The Stereotype Questionnaire developed for this study consists of 122 bipolar adjectives obtained by asking 2 classes of undergraduates to list characteristics which they considered to differentiate men and women. Eighty females and 74 males from several New England colleges indicated on a scale from 1 to 7 the degree to which they expected each adjective to characterize the average adult male. They took the questionnaire a second time under instructions to describe the average adult female. The order was counterbalanced. An item was identified as stereotypic if 75% or more subjects rated it as more typically masculine than feminine or vice versa. Forty-one items met this criterion for both sex groups. The difference between the mean typical masculinity and femininity responses of each of these stereotypic items differed beyond the .001 level of probability in both sex groups. The remaining items were classed as either differentiating or non-differentiating, depending on whether or not the mean typical masculinity and femininity responses differed at the .05 level of probability for both males and females. All items were further classified as female-valued or male-valued, according to whether the masculine or the feminine pole was rated more socially desirable for the population at large. (A more detailed description of these desirability ratings is presented in the following section.)

The authors present only the stereotypic items for examination as to content. Many of these are similar to the adjectives comprising sex stereotypes in the studies by Sherriffs and colleagues. For example, the 29 male-valued items include direct, logical, objective, dominant, active, and self-confident. The 12 female-valued items include tactful, gentle, aware of the feelings of others, expresses tender feelings, religious, and appreciates art and literature. Other stereotypic items which do not accord as well with the earlier findings include for men worldly, feelings not easily hurt, and hides emotions; and for women interested in own appearance, strong need for security, and quiet.

Spence, Helmreich, and Stapp (1974, 1975) offer evidence which is largely consistent with the results of previous studies. They administered the Personal Attributes Questionnaire, a revision of the Rosenkrantz et al. (1968) Stereotype Questionnaire to 282 female and 248 male college students. This instrument includes 55 items on which significant differences in the ratings of the typical adult man and woman and the typical male and female college student were consistently found in previous samples of college students. Subjects made direct comparisons of the typical male and typical female on each attribute. When the ratings of the typical male and typical female were examined, all 55 items yielded significant departures from the scale midpoint for both male and female subjects, confirming the authors' previous findings.

The female stereotype included such items as tactful, kind, gentle, warm to others, creative, enjoys art and music, religious, emotional, neat, strong conscience, likes children. The male stereotype comprised, for example, independent, self-confident, feels superior, dominant, ambitious, intellectual, aggressive, makes decisions easily, outgoing, not easily influenced, knows ways of world.

Lunneborg's (1970) findings also lend some support to the patterns of sex stereotypic content presented thus far. She administered the Edwards Personality Inventory, Booklet IA to two groups of college students, under instructions to predict either the answer that most women or most men would give in describing themselves. The female instruction group consisted of 87 males and 107 females; the male instruction group, of 75 males and 129 females. Significant differences between the stereotypic male and stereotypic female responses emerged on 13 of the 14 scales. Females as a group were assigned higher scores on 6 scales—plans and organizes things, has cultural interests, conforms, kind to others, worries about good impression, interest in others' behavior. Males were assigned higher scores on 7 scales—intellectually oriented, persistent, self-confident, enjoys being center of attention, carefree, is a leader, and likes to be alone. The remaining scale, seeks new experiences, did not differentiate the two stereotypes. Male and female subjects were in almost complete agreement as to which characteristics applied to women and which to men.

Broverman et al. (1972) performed separate factor analyses on the typical female responses and the typical male responses made by male and female subjects to the Rosenkrantz et al. (1968) Stereotype Questionnaire. The results indicated that the male-valued items represented a competency cluster, while the female-valued items represented a warmth and expressiveness cluster. Since the authors do not fully describe their methods, it is impossible to evaluate these findings.

Reece (1964) conducted the only other factor analysis of sex-role stereotype ratings. The Concept Meaning Measure, a 45-scale semantic differential, was administered to 40 female and 40 male college students, with instructions to rate each of several concepts, including typical femininity and typical masculinity. The scales were presented in a 7-point, bipolar format, with one pole representing an apparently masculine quality and the other an apparently feminine quality. In a notable exception to the usual practice, subjects were provided with a specific frame of reference for their ratings: "the concepts of typical masculinity and femininity referred to the stereotypes held by most people as perceived by S" (pp. 124, 125).

The results of the factor analysis yielded two major factors, potency and social behavior, in both typical masculinity and typical femininity. Inspection of the scales that loaded highly on these factors and comparison of the factor scores for typical femininity and typical masculinity revealed a resemblance to the content of sex-role stereotypes obtained in the above studies. I present only this brief description of the results because it is questionable whether a factor analysis based on such small samples, and in the absence of cross-validation, yields interpretable information.

Bayton, Austin, and Burke (1965) present findings that depart somewhat from the trends delineated so far. They administered the Guilford-Zimmerman Temperament Survey (GZTS) to 120 Negro college students of each sex, who were randomly assigned to each of 4 groups. Instructions were as follows: " 'How do you think the Average Negro Male [Average Negro Female, Average White Male, Average White Female] would answer these items?' " (p. 251). Three-way ANOVAs (sex of subject × sex stereotype × race stereotype) were computed for the 10 scales. None of the scales yielded significant main effects of sex of subject. Significant main effects of sex stereotype occurred on 3 scales: the average female was given higher scores on Sociability, the average male on Emotional Stability and Masculinity. Descriptions of the average male and average female did not differ significantly on General Activity, Restraint, Ascendance, Objectivity, Friendliness, Thoughtfulness, and Personal Relations. An examination of the definitions of traits allegedly measured by the GZTS (Anastasi, 1968) indicates that (a) the findings with respect to Sociability, Emotional Stability, and Masculinity are consistent with the results of studies already cited; (b) the failure to attribute higher Ascendance and Objectivity scores to the average male is *not* consistent with other studies. The authors also report 3 significant interaction effects to which the sex stereotype variable contributed. On the Restraint scale, the average white male was seen as more restrained than the average Negro male, but the descriptions of white and Negro females did not differ. On the Friendliness scale, male subjects attributed higher scores to males than females, while female subjects attributed greater friendliness to females than males. A triple interaction for Friendliness indicated that "male Negro subjects made their basic differentiation on this trait in terms of

racial stereotyping. . . In contrast, the female Negro subjects made
their basic differentiation on the basis of sex stereotyping" (p. 251).
The remaining studies that deal with sex stereotypes either do not
report content in sufficient detail or are methodologically inadequate
according to the general criteria presented in section A-2: Clarkson et
al. (1970); Cowan, Weiner, and Weiner (1974); Ellis and Bentler
(1973); Elman, Press, and Rosenkrantz (1970); Ross and Walters
(1973); Seward and Larson (1968); and Steinmann (1963).

In summary, the evidence on the content of sex stereotypes is not
extensive, despite the substantial number of studies that have inquired
into the ascribed characteristics of males and females. Most of the
studies cited in this section relied upon idiosyncratic instruments about
which little or no psychometric information is available. Most computed
multiple statistical tests without recognizing that some tests will be
significant by chance alone. With the exception of Spence, Helmreich,
and Stapp (1975), the necessary cross-validations involving the *same*
items were not made. Nevertheless, the evidence across different instruments is largely consistent, revealing a common core of stereotypic
characteristics. Females are described as warm and sensitive, socially
skilled, inclined toward interpersonal and artistic interests; males as
competent and logical, possessing self-confidence, direct in manner,
dominant. These then are the distinguishing characteristics of the sexes,
as perceived by both male and female college students. This picture
holds whether the data were collected in the 1950s or the late 1960s. It
holds whether the subject generates his or her own response, chooses
from among a list of adjectives unselected as to their relevance to sex-
role dimensions, or rates men and women on traits specifically chosen to
differentiate males and females.

In addition to these core characteristics that appear most often as
stereotypic, other attributes — including some negative attributes —
emerge as stereotypic in one or another study, reflecting, in part, the
diversity of content represented in the different instruments.

But what about those characteristics which are not differentially
ascribed to males and females? Unfortunately, one has very little information to work with here, as most authors do not report these
"neutral" characteristics. This omission may be traced to the preoccupation with differences that is a natural consequence of defining
stereotypes in terms of attributes which differentiate the sexes.

Also neglected in research on sex-role stereotypes are subject
populations other than white college students. In the only study in-

volving black college students (Bayton, Austin, & Burke, 1965) some, but not all, of the core characteristics emerged as stereotypic. This raises the question of whether the conclusions reached here are generalizable beyond white college student samples. Obviously, work is needed in this area.

b. EVALUATIVE DIMENSION OF SEX-ROLE STEREOTYPES

Some early evidence relevant to this issue may be gleaned from Sherriffs and Jarrett (1953). As described above, large groups of male and female college students indicated whether each of 58 test items was more applicable to men or women. This procedure yielded evidence of stereotyping: 19 items were assigned to women and 27 to men by significantly more than 50% of both male and female subjects.

On another occasion these same subjects responded to the test under instructions to rate along a 7-point scale the value of each item "in your own scale of values" (p. 162). Comparison of the mean ratings made by men and women on each item revealed a striking pattern of agreement between the sexes as to the value of the attributes. However, women were significantly more extreme in their ratings than men. Sherriffs and Jarrett state: "Thus the women seem to place more extreme values on most of our behaviors and attributes, even though they agree very closely with the men as to the value which any given behavior deserves" (pp. 165–166). Although the authors do not compare the values assigned to the previously identified male stereotypic and female stereotypic items, my examination of the published data indicates that (a) qualities that were negatively valued by both men and women were about equally distributed between the female stereotype and the male stereotype; (b) only 7 of the female stereotypic items were positively valued, compared with 16 of the male stereotypic items. This is highly tentative evidence, then, that the female stereotype includes substantially fewer positive attributes than the male stereotype.

These findings raised the issue of the differential evaluation of the sexes, prompting McKee and Sherriffs (1957) to undertake a more thorough investigation of this issue. The study consisted of three phases, each of which involved a different measuring technique and a different sample of college students ($N \geq$ 50 for each sex subgroup). In the first phase, subjects rated directly the " 'relative over-all general worth, merit or value of men and women' " (p. 359). Subjects were specifically instructed to give " 'your view' " on the matter (p. 359). Half of the subjects received a 6-point rating scale and half received a 7-point scale which included a neutral point. A second group of subjects responded to the 200 items of Sarbin's ACL under instructions to characterize men and women, and under forced choice and unforced choice conditions. Their responses were scored as favorable/unfavorable on the basis of ratings of the desirablity or undesirability of each item for men and for women separately, as judged by another group of college students. In the final phase of the study still another group of students used an open-ended procedure to characterize males and females. These lists were later rated as favorable, neutral, or unfavorable by students and by expert judges.

The results indicated that male and female college students are favorable to both sexes, but they regard males significantly more positively than females. This generalization held across all measuring techniques. The greater favorability toward males can be more specifically chracterized on the basis of data from the ACL and open-ended procedures: both men and women ascribed a significantly greater number of favorable qualities to males than to females. In other respects, the results varied somewhat, depending upon the type of technique used. For example, when given the option of choosing a neutral rating (7-point scale), most subjects endorsed the equality of men and women. Results obtained under the forced choice ad-ministration of the ACL were exaggerated relative to the findings obtained with the unforced choice procedure. The authors also report greater partiality to males on the part of females than males, but since this finding emerged only under the ACL procedure, it must be viewed as highly tentative.

Further evidence supporting the generalization that the charac-teristics ascribed to the typical woman are less highly valued than those ascribed to the typical man was obtained by Rosenkrantz et al. (1968). As described above, the original form of the Stereotype Questionnaire was administered to 80 female and 74 male college students. The authors report that 41 of the 122 bipolar test items were rated as more typically masculine than feminine (or vice versa) by more than 75% of both males and females. They call these items stereotypic. Those items that fell short of the 75% criterion were classified as either dif-ferentiating or nondifferentiating, depending on whether or not the mean typical masculinity and typical femininity responses differed significantly for both sex groups. Forty-eight items were identified as differentiating, 24 as nondifferentiating by this procedure. (The remaining 9 items were not analyzed.)

Another sample of 48 female and 73 male college students indicated which pole of each item of the questionnaire was more socially desirable for the population at large. The mean social desirability ratings of the 2 sex groups correlated .964 over the 113 items. In addition, the mean social desirability ratings made by males and females were virtually identical, permitting the authors to combine the sex groups for further analysis. (The social desirability judgments of another sample of 35 college men obtained under different procedures correlated .85 with the ratings of the original sample of males.) Correlations were computed between the social desirability ratings and judgments of typical masculinity and typical femininity in each of the 3 item sets—stereotypic, differentiating, nondifferentiating. These correlations, all positive and significant, ranged from .691 to .884, indicating a generally favorable view of both sexes.

But, as in the McKee and Sherriffs (1957) study, the evidence points to a more positive view of males than females. In order to explore the relative value attached to the items comprising the 3 item sets, the authors analyzed the data in several ways. They found, first, that the mean proportion agreeing that the masculine pole was more desirable on the 41 stereotypic items was .650, a figure which differed significantly from the proportion expected by chance. The corresponding figures for the differentiating and nondifferentiating items were not significant. Second, of the 41 stereotypic items, 29 (about 70%) were found to be male-valued. (This finding was verified in additional, undescribed samples of men and women; Broverman et al. [1972].) That is, subjects more often viewed the masculine pole as more desirable than the feminine pole. In contrast, only 12 items (30%) were female-valued. A chi-square analysis yielded a significant difference in these figures: more of the stereotypic items were male-valued than female-valued. Corresponding analyses of the differentiating and nondifferentiating item sets produced no significant results. Third, the absolute levels of social desirability of the male- and female-valued items were compared. No significant difference was obtained between the mean social desirability ratings of the male- and female-valued stereotypic items. The differentiating and nondifferentiating items also failed to produce significant differences. These findings lead the authors to conclude, with regard to the stereotypic characteristics, that "the greater valuation placed upon masculinity, then, is a function of more male than female traits being positively valued rather than a greater value per se of individual masculine traits" (p. 291).

Broverman et al. (1970) used a modified form of the Stereotype Questionnaire to investigate the concept of mental health as applied to women and men. Since the notion of mental health is evaluative by implication, the results of this study are relevant to the issue of the relative value attached to the sexes. Three groups of clinicians received the Stereotype Questionnaire, along with instructions to describe *either* a "mature, healthy, socially competent adult man" (adult woman, or adult person) (p. 2). The groups were small, each including approximately 26 clinicians. Only the stereotypic items were analyzed, i.e., those items on which 75% or more of the Rosenkrantz et al. (1968) college sample had agreed as to which pole characterizes men or women.

The authors computed an adult agreement score for each item. This was the percent of clinicians who agreed as to which pole of an item was healthier for an adult person. Analogous feminine and masculine agreement scores were also computed for each item. The adult agreement scores were summed across 38 stereotypic items and averaged to yield a mean adult agreement score for the item set; masculinity agreement scores were summed across the 38 items and averaged to yield a mean masculinity agreement score for the item set; and analogous operations yielded a mean femininity agreement score for the item set. Each of the three mean agreement scores significantly exceeded a mean of 50% agreement per item. That is, for each category of persons (adult, woman, man) there was substantial agreement among the clinicians as to which pole represents a healthier characteristic. Male and female clinicians did not differ significantly on any of the three agreement scores, a finding which is hardly surprising in light of the small sample sizes.

The adult agreement score on each of the 38 stereotypic items was compared with the social desirability values of the same items as judged by college students in the Rosenkrantz et al. (1968) study. A significant relationship was found between clinicians' judgments of the healthy pole of each item and the students' ratings of the socially desirable pole of the corresponding items.

The authors also computed a femininity health score for each item — the proportion of clinicians who, under instructions to describe a healthy woman, checked that pole of an item which another group of clinicians judged to be healthier for an adult person, sex unspecified. An analogous masculinity health score was also computed for each item. Thus, the femininity health score and the masculinity health score are measures of the degree to which descriptions of the mentally healthy woman and man, respectively, coincide with descriptions of the mentally healthy adult person (adult agreement score).

The authors then compared the masculinity and femininity health scores on (a) the male-valued stereotypic items and (b) the female-valued stereotypic items. (These were items on which college students in Rosenkrantz et al. [1968] had rated either the masculine pole or the feminine pole as more socially desirable.) On 25 of the 27 male-valued stereotypic items, the masculinity health scores exceeded the femininity health scores. On 7 of the 11 female-valued stereotypic items, the femininity health scores exceeded the masculinity health scores, while on 4 items, the masculinity health scores exceeded the femininity health scores. These findings, significant by a chi square analysis, support the authors' hypothesis that clinicians' judgments of mental health with respect to sex stereotypic traits parallel college students' judgments of social desirability on the same traits. Moreover, they interpret the finding that clinicians ascribe male-valued stereotypic traits more often to healthy men than to women as indicating "a powerful, negative assessment of women" (p. 4).

Further analysis of the femininity and masculinity health scores involved the computation of mean scores. The femininity health scores were summed across items and averaged to yield a mean femininity health score. A mean masculinity health score was obtained in the same way. Comparisons were made among the mean femininity health score, the mean masculinity health score, and the mean adult agreement score, using t-tests. No significant difference was found between the masculinity health score and the adult agreement score. However, both the masculinity health score and the adult agreement score were significantly higher than the femininity health score. The authors interpret these findings as supporting the hypothesis of a double standard of health, whereby men but not women are seen as mentally healthy by the adult standard.

However, this is a dubious interpretation in light of the following considerations. The masculinity health score is based, in part, on the adult agreement score: it represents a discrepancy between the mean masculinity agreement score and the mean adult agreement score.

Similarly, the femininity health score represents a discrepancy between the mean femininity agreement score and the mean adult agreement score. That is, the masculinity health score, femininity health score, and adult agreement score — all contain an overlapping component, namely, the adult agreement score. Consequently, the t-tests used to make comparisons between these three scores are not independent, and the resulting findings are not clearly interpretable.

Three other studies present results relevant to the question of the relative favorability or social desirability of sex stereotypic traits (Broverman et al., 1972; Clarkson et al., 1970; Ross and Walters, 1973). As these studies contain methodological problems (see section A-2), I do not describe the findings except to note that they indicate a greater favorability toward men than women.

In summary, these studies explored the evaluative dimension of sex-role stereotypes by means of various idiosyncratic instruments which have received little or no psychometric exploration. The evidence, although small in amount, consistently shows that (a) male and female college students endow both sexes with favorable qualities; (b) they regard males more favorably than females. This partiality to males, on the part of both sexes, may be further characterized as follows: a larger number of male-stereotypic traits is positively valued, compared with female-stereotypic traits. These generalizations hold despite method-ological differences across studies with respect to such matters as type of instrument and choice of frame of reference for judgments of favorability (e.g., own personal view vs. view of population at large). One may also hypothesize, on the basis of tentative evidence, that female college students, male college students, and clinicians agree as to the value of various stereotypic traits, whether value is expressed as social desirability ratings or judgments of mental health.

An important qualifier must be added to these remarks, one which is related to the issue of phenomenal (direct) comparisons raised earlier. In most of the studies described above, one group of subjects described males and/or females with respect to various characteristics, while another group (or the same group on another occasion) rated the value of these characteristics. The investigators then made inferences about the value of various stereotypic traits. The data from these studies are not relevant to the question of how individuals evaluate the charac-teristics comprising their own stereotypes of males and females. That is, subjects were not asked to express their evaluations of the qualities that they themselves believed to be typical of males and females. Nor were they asked to evaluate the characteristics that they believe to comprise the sex stereotypes of other specified groups, such as "most college students." These kinds of direct comparisons remain to be explored empirically.

c. Sex-Role Stereotypes and Self-Concepts

Survey of Findings

The evidence reviewed thus far indicates that male and female college students subscribe to stereotypes about the sexes, consistently ascribing one set of characteristics to men and another to women and regarding men more favorably than women.

Given these findings, one may suggest alternate hypotheses about the relationship between sex-role stereotypes and self-concepts. It is possible that the self-concepts of individuals are influenced by their acceptance of the same sex stereotype, so that eventually the self-concepts of women come to resemble the female stereotype and the self-concepts of men come to resemble the male stereotype. However, it is also possible, as Hacker points out (see section B-1) that an individual may exempt herself from her evaluation of women as a group. Presumably, individual men may similarly exempt themselves from their evaluation of men as a group. This line of reasoning leads to the hypothesis that the self-concepts of men and women show little resemblance to the appropriate sex stereotype. In order to choose between these alternate hypotheses, it is first necessary to ask whether the self-concepts of males and females correspond to the stereotypes of men and women, respectively.

The paradigm that has been used consistently to explore this question is one in which college students describe the self with reference to the same instrument on which they or similar groups of individuals had described the typical male and female. The investigators then compare these self-descriptions with the same and/or opposite sex stereotypes. Many of the relevant studies have already been cited above. The evidence is sufficient to resolve some questions of content. But relatively few data are available on the evaluative dimension of the self-concept in relation to sex-role stereotypes.

Beginning with the Sherriffs and McKee (1957) study, it is possible to anticipate the conclusions of this section. One hundred male and 100 female college students took Sarbin's ACL under instructions to check those adjectives which applied to themselves. Of the 200 adjectives in the test, 40 were ascribed to the self significantly more often by women than men, while 13 were attributed to the self significantly more often by men than women. This suggests a rather substantial difference in the self-ratings of males and females. However, the disproportionate number of adjectives endorsed significantly more often by women than men may be a function of women's tendency to check a larger number of adjectives. Apparently, the authors did not control for the possibly different response totals of men and women.

Several comparisons were made between subjects' self-descriptions and the sex stereotypes generated by another group of college students, using the same instrument. The number of items endorsed significantly more often by one sex or the other as self-descriptive was markedly reduced, relative to the number which differentiated males in general and females in general. That is, many of the adjectives which comprised the male and female stereotypes failed to produce sex differences in self-ratings. Notable in this regard were two clusters of the male stereotype — straightforward, uninhibited social style, and rational competence and ability. Discrepancies in the opposite direction also occurred in which significant sex differences emerged on self-ratings but not on stereotypic responses. Examples of such discrepancies were pleasure-seeking and quarrelsome for men; generous, resourceful, serious, cold, meek, and mischievous for women. Nevertheless, there was considerable overlap, with many of the stereotypic items also yielding significant sex differences in self-descriptions. Inspection of the data reveals that for women these overlapping items were distributed across all three favorable content clusters of the female stereotype — social skills and grace, warmth and emotional support, and concern with the spiritual aspects of experience. The unfavorable dimension of the female stereotype was also represented among the overlapping items by such items as high-strung, temperamental, shy, and moralistic. But for men, the overlapping items were concentrated mainly in a single cluster of the male stereotype, namely — action, vigor, and effectiveness.

The authors also present a more detailed analysis of the relative favorability of self and stereotype descriptions. (The items had been rated as to relative favorability, as applied to men or women separately by another sample of college students from the same population, McKee and Sherriffs, 1957.) Of the 40 adjectives which were ascribed to the self significantly more often by women than men, 21 were favorable and 19 were unfavorable. Of the 13 items which were checked as self-applicable by significantly more men than women, 10 were favorable and 3 were unfavorable. Both men and women assigned more favorable adjectives to the self than to males or females in general. The 20 favorable adjectives (omitting "feminine") that both men and women had assigned to the female stereotype were endorsed, on the average, by 68% of women and 50% of men, as self-descriptive. This difference was significant. A significant difference also emerged with respect to the 17 unfavorable female stereotypic items: these were checked, on the average, by 29% of women and 18% of men as true of the self. The corresponding comparisons for the male stereotype (omitting "masculine") revealed that significantly more men (53%) than women (45%) endorsed the 29 favorable male adjectives as applying to the self, but the sex difference for the 8 unfavorable adjectives was not significant. For both favorable and unfavorable adjectives women selected adjectives from the same sex stereotype to a significantly greater degree than did men.

McKee and Sherriffs (1959) report results that are largely consistent with their previous findings on the relative favorability of self-ratings on stereotypic items. In this study another sample of 100 male and 100 female college students described the self and several other concepts, using Sarbin's ACL. The results were analyzed only for stereotypic male and stereotypic female adjectives — those adjectives which had been identified by both males and females in a previous sample of the same population as characterizing the male and female stereotypes, respectively. (By this previous determination, there were 29 favorable and 8 unfavorable male stereotypic words, and 20 favorable and 17 unfavorable female stereotypic words.) Compared with men, women endorsed significantly more favorable words and significantly more unfavorable words in describing the self. These two main effects of sex of respondent were actually determined only by women's greater choice of favorable *female*-stereotyped words and unfavorable *female*-stereotyped words, respectively. Moreover, significant interaction effects were obtained for both favorable and unfavorable words, because the men, unlike the women, did not select significantly more same sex-stereotypic adjectives as descriptive of the self. That is, women were more likely than men to endorse as applicable to themselves items previously identified as stereotypic of their sex.

Lunneborg (1970) used the 14 scales of Edwards Personality Inventory, Booklet IA to explore the relationship between self-descriptions and stereotypic descriptions of men and women. Edwards's normative sample, including 203 male and 329 female college students, provided the data on self-descriptions. Lunneborg's sample consisted of another group of college students who were informed as to the author's intention of studying the sex stereotypy of items. Subjects received *either* female stereotypic instructions (87 males, 107 females) or male stereotypic instructions (75 males, 129 females). That is, they were told to predict the answers which most men or most women would give in describing themselves.

In the Edwards study significant sex differences in self-descriptions emerged on 8 of the 14 scales: males scored higher than females on intellectually oriented, self-confident, enjoys being center of attention, is a leader; females exceeded males on conforms, has cultural interests, kind to others, and interest in others' behavior. In all cases the differences, though significant, were small in magnitude. A *phi* coefficient was also computed, correlating sex status with item response (true/false). Of the 295 items, 42 discriminated the sexes at the .05 level. More than half of these sex-discriminating items represented 3 scales: intellectually oriented, has cultural interests, is a leader.

This pattern of sex differences in self-ratings contrasts with the more sharply differentiated pattern obtained under Lunneborg's stereotype instructions: the stereotypic descriptions of women differed significantly from the stereotypic descriptions of men on 13 of the 14 scales. In other words, of the 13 scales which differentiated the male and female stereotypes, 5 did *not* discriminate between the self-descriptions of men and women in the Edwards sample. These scales are plans and organizes things, worries about making a good impression on others (on which the female stereotype exceeded the male stereotype), persistent, carefree, and likes to be alone (on which the male stereotype exceeded the female stereotype). This finding of more dramatic discrepancies between the stereotypic descriptions of males and females compared with the difference between the self-ratings of men and women on the same scales is revealed also by the stereotype *phi* coefficients for item comparisons. Instructional set (male/female) was correlated with item response (true/false), yielding 48 items which differentiated the stereotypic male from the stereotypic female but did not differentiate the self-descriptions of males and females.

But once again there was substantial overlap between self-conceptions and sex stereotypes, with the eight scales that had differentiated the self-ratings of men and women also differentiating between the male and female stereotypes. Three of the four overlapping male scales—self-confident, enjoys being center of attention, is a leader—appear to be similar to the action, vigor, and effectiveness cluster represented by the overlapping male items in the Sherriffs and McKee (1957) study. The corresponding data for women yield similar evidence of consistency across the two studies. Three of the overlapping female scales—kind to others, interest in others' behavior, has cultural interests—are reminiscent of two clusters from the Sherriffs and McKee study. These are warmth and emotional support and concern with the spiritual aspects of experience.

Rosenkrantz et al. (1968) also report findings of interest here. As described above, college students responded to the Stereotype Questionnaire under instructions to characterize the average adult male and female. They then took the test a third time, under instructions to describe the self. Recognizing that self-ratings vary, depending upon the frame of reference, the authors adopted this constant-order procedure in which all subjects made their self-ratings after they had described the typical male and female. This was done in order to encourage subjects to judge themselves from within the framework of sex-role stereotypes. It is possible that this method promotes overlap of stereotype descriptions and self-descriptions: having made a previous commitment as to what is characteristic of his or her own sex, the subject may be unwilling to admit to deviations from "normality-for-my-sex." Or, for subjects who accept the newer, androgynous version of sex-roles this method may promote an opposing response set. That is, subjects may be eager to admit to deviations from "normality-for-my-sex," where normality is conceived of as rigid adherence to traditionally defined sex roles.

Comparison of the mean self-ratings of males and females on the stereotypic items yielded a significant difference. That is, on those items on which at least 75% of the subjects had agreed as to the sex-typing of the items, male and female subjects also differed in their self-ratings. A significant sex difference in self-ratings was also obtained on the differentiating items (those items on which the mean stereotypic masculinity and femininity responses differed significantly), but not on the nondifferentiating items. These findings suggest that sex differences in self-ratings parallel differences in subjects' conceptions of the average female and male.

For each set of items, comparisons were also made between each sex group's mean self-rating and their mean rating of the average member of their own sex. On the stereotypic items, females' self-descriptions differed significantly from their depiction of the average adult female, while males' self-ratings differed significantly from their descriptions of the average adult male. In other words, the self-conceptions of females were not as stereotypically feminine as their conception of the average female, and the self-conceptions of males were not as stereotypically masculine as their conception of the average male. In contrast to these findings, neither the differentiating nor the nondifferentiating items yielded significant differences between (a) females' mean self-ratings and their mean descriptions of the typical female; (b) males' mean self-ratings and their mean descriptions of the typical male.

These findings show that subjects' self-conceptions are less extreme than their same-sex stereotypes on those (stereotypic) items which maximally differentiate the average male and female. But on those items which discriminate between the average male and female to a moderate degree (differentiating) or not at all (nondifferentiating), subjects' self-descriptions do not differ from their descriptions of the average member of their own sex.

The authors also computed correlation coefficients between subjects' self-ratings and ratings of the social desirability (for the population at large) of the items made by another group of college students. These correlations were computed separately by sex within each set of items — stereotypic, differentiating, nondifferentiating. All correlations were positive and significant, ranging from .674 to .879. Thus, the mean self-descriptions of both men and women correlated to a substantial degree with the rated social desirability of the items, indicating that the self-descriptions of both sexes are generally favorable.

Another analysis of the same data is not presented here as it involves psychometrically ambiguous discrepancy scores (see Wylie, 1974, pp. 88–95).

Another source of evidence relevant to the question under consideration is Spence, Helmreich, and Stapp (1974, 1975). As I mentioned earlier, 282 female and 248 male college students responded to the Personal Attributes Questionnaire. Subjects first rated the self on each of the items. They then made direct comparisons of the typical male and typical female. On 35 of the 55 items, significant differences were found in the self-ratings of the two sexes in the direction of the stereotype. Comparisons of the ratings of the typical male and typical female revealed that all 55 items yielded significant departures from the scale midpoint for both male and female subjects. Thus, the subjects' conceptions of the typical male and typical female are more sharply differentiated than are the self-conceptions of males and females. The authors note, however, that "the self-ratings more often than not confirm the stereotype data" (p. 33).

Results are also reported separately for the subscales of the Personal Attributes Questionnaire. The test items had been previously grouped into 3 subscales—*female-valued* (18 items on which the mean ratings of both the ideal male and female made by another group of college students were toward the stereotypically feminine end of the bipolar item); *male-valued*[4] (23 items on which the mean ratings of both the ideal male and female were toward the stereotypically masculine pole); *sex-specific* (13 items on which the mean ideal female differed from the midpoint in the direction of the stereotypically feminine pole, and the mean rating of the ideal male differed in the direction of the stereotypically masculine pole). Comparison of the mean self-ratings of men and women on each of the subscales revealed that men, compared with women, obtained significantly higher stereotypically masculine scores on the male-valued and sex-specific subscales and less stereotypically-feminine scores on the female-valued subscales. Once more, the self-descriptions of men and women correspond to some degree with the male and female stereotypes, respectively.

Using a shortened form of the Rosenkrantz et al. (1968) Stereotype Questionnaire, Elman, Press, and Rosenkrantz (1970) found that male and female college student subjects' self-ratings were less divergent than their same sex stereotypes. These and other findings are not presented in detail here, owing to lack of sufficient information about certain procedures and apparent methodological shortcomings.

Three other studies (Hassell & Smith, 1975; Seward & Larson, 1968; Steinmann, 1963) report findings of possibly oblique relevance here. Since they employ methods of questionable value (see section A-2), I do not elaborate on these findings.

In summary, in several studies male and female college students described themselves with reference to the same instrument on which they or similar groups of individuals had described the typical male and

---

4. Note that the terms *female-valued* and *male-valued* are defined here in terms of androgynous *ideals*. The female-valued subscale consists of stereotypically feminine items attributed to both the ideal male and female, the male-valued subscale consists of stereotypically masculine items ascribed to both the ideal male and female. Above I describe the Rosenkrantz et al. (1968) study in which the terms *female-valued* and *male-valued* are used in a different sense — to refer to stereotypic items on which either the feminine pole or the masculine pole, respectively, was judged more *socially desirable*.

female.[5] These studies failed to demonstrate that the sex groups were comparable on other possibly relevant variables and used idiosyncratic measures about which little or no psychometric information is known. Sex of experimenter was not reported or controlled. In many cases, authors computed multiple tests of the significance of sex differences in self-ratings. Although the necessary cross-validations involving the same items or scales were not made, the evidence across different instruments consistently reveals: (a) sex differences in college students' self-descriptions on instruments used to measure sex stereotyping; (b) considerable overlap between the self-concepts of each sex and the same sex stereotype, with sex differences in self-ratings frequently emerging on the same items or scales that differentiated the male and female stereotypes.

This overlap can be further characterized for each sex on the basis of still tentative evidence. The self-descriptions of men correspond with the male stereotype on such qualities as self-confidence, leadership, independence, ambition, aggression, and ruggedness. For women an analogous correspondence between self-descriptions and the female stereotype is suggested with respect to such attributes as kindness, interest in others, sympathy, sensitivity, and cultural interests.

But this correspondence between self-conceptions and same sex stereotypes is not complete: the evidence also consistently shows that the self-descriptions of male and female college students are less divergent than their sex-role stereotypes (or those of similar groups of students). This evidence is of two sorts: (a) sex differences with respect to fewer characteristics emerge on self-ratings, compared with the number of significant differences between male and female stereotyped attributes; (b) on stereotypic items, female subjects' mean self-rating is significantly less stereotypically feminine than the mean rating of the typical female, and male subjects' mean self-rating is significantly less stereotypically masculine than the mean rating of the typical male. These results imply the possibility that the smaller discrepancy between male and female self-descriptions reflects greater variation among subjects' self-descriptions than among their descriptions of the stereotypic male or female.

---

5. This summary is based exclusively on studies that compare self-descriptions and sex-role stereotypes. Many other studies report sex differences on self-reported personality characteristics, without relating these findings to sex-role stereotypes. In section D I consider one such characteristic, namely affiliation.

Only a few studies furnish evidence relevant to the question of whether the relative favorability of subjects' self-conceptions corresponds to the relative favorability of sex-role stereotypes. The results of these studies point to two hypotheses which await further testing: (a) both college men and college women are favorable in their self-descriptions on sex stereotypic attributes; (b) college women, compared with college men, endorse as self-applicable both more favorable attributes and more unfavorable attributes from the same sex stereotype.

Interpretation of Findings on Sex-Role Stereotypes and Self-Concepts

An answer cannot yet be given to the question of whether a person's relative favorability toward himself or herself corresponds to the relative favorability of the same sex stereotype. But with respect to content, the evidence supports a substantial degree of correspondence between the self-conceptions of each sex group and the same sex stereotype. The possible interpretations given to this correspondence parallel those offered in chapter 4, regarding ethnic stereotypes and self-concepts.

First, this correspondence may be construed as evidence that sex stereotypes influence people's conceptions of themselves. Such influence may occur as follows: as a result of accepting the stereotype as applicable to his or her sex group, an individual may form a self-concept which incorporates characteristics from the same sex stereotype. For instance, a woman who believes the female stereotype to be true of women as a group, and who regards herself as a member of that group, may eventually believe that the qualities comprising the female stereotype apply to her.

Second, it is possible that the influence of stereotypes upon self-concepts takes a more circuitous route. A parent who believes the male stereotype may consciously or unconsciously inculcate independence in a son, with the result that the son comes to conceive of himself as independent. This possibility allows that the son may believe that he developed independence through an idiosyncratic process even though, in actuality, he acquired the characteristic through the indirect influence of the stereotype.

Thus, the correspondence between sex-role stereotypes and self-concepts may mean that stereotypes influence self-concepts either directly or through one or more intervening variables. However, it is also possible that both self-conceptions and sex-role stereotypes are factually descriptive of people's characteristics and that these characteristics developed independently of stereotype influence. On the basis of the available evidence, it is impossible to decide whether sex stereotypes do or do not influence self-conceptions.

It is also important within the context of the present question to raise again the issue of frame of reference for judgments of the typical male and female. As I mentioned earlier, investigators tend not to specify a reference group for such judgments. One may ask whether there is a correspondence between a person's self-concept and each of the following: (a) his or her conception of "society's" definition of the typical man and woman; (b) his or her conception of the way in which his family or his classmates or his coworkers or any other significant group views men and women; (c) his or her own personal beliefs about the typical characteristics of males and females. Different answers may result, depending upon which of these frames of reference is assumed to be operating. Moreover, the degree of congruence among the subject's descriptions of the typical male and female made from these different viewpoints is an interesting question in its own right.

A related issue concerns the frame of reference within which self-ratings are made. A woman may judge her standing on a particular dimension by comparing herself to adults in her society, to most men or most women, to her coworkers, or to any number of other groups. A man may rate himself with reference to a similar variety of groups. In most of the articles under review subjects were not explicitly instructed as to which reference group to use. Of course, when a reference group is provided, other measurement problems may arise. As I mentioned earlier in connection with the Rosenkrantz et al. (1968) study, certain kinds of response sets may be promoted when the subject is asked to rate the self relative to most women or most men. In any case, one is left with the empirical question of whether different frames of reference for self-ratings affect the relationship between sex-role stereotypes and self-conceptions. Also deserving of study is the question of which reference groups male and female subjects spontaneously choose when asked to describe the self.

So far my comments have been directed toward stereotype descriptions and self-descriptions, where each is made separately. This is the design used by all the studies on sex-role stereotypes and self-concepts. That is, subjects make (a) ratings of the typical male and female and (b) ratings of the self. The investigator subsequently compares these two sets of ratings. Once again one must distinguish such inferred comparisons from wholly phenomenal comparisons in which the subject directly compares himself or herself with perceived sex-role stereotypes. In no case were such direct comparisons made. We have no way of knowing, then, on which characteristics and to what extent subjects see themselves as similar to the same (or opposite) sex stereotypes.

3. Sex-Role Standards

There seems to be some confusion, from a conceptual standpoint, about the terms sex-role stereotype and sex-role standard, with some authors using the terms interchangeably, while others (e.g., Ellis & Bentler, 1973) assert that the terms refer to different but related concepts. I distinguish the two concepts as follows: sex-role stereotypes refer to beliefs about the typical characteristics of males and females, sex-role standards to beliefs about the appropriate (and inappropriate) characteristics of the sexes. Whether these concepts are empirically distinct but related is another matter.

The evidence is of little help in resolving this question. Spence, Helmreich, and Stapp (1975) found significant negative correlations, small to moderate in size, between the degree of college students' sex-role stereotyping on the Personal Attributes Questionnaire and their scores on the Attitudes toward Women Scale, a test of beliefs about appropriate roles for women. This result points to a relationship between the perception of larger intersex differences and the expression of more traditional beliefs about appropriate female roles. Consistent with this finding, Rothbart and Maccoby (1966) report significant, moderate-level correlations between parents' beliefs about the differences that actually exist between girls and boys and their beliefs about the differences that should exist. This finding must be viewed with caution as it is based on psychometrically ambiguous difference scores concerning what should exist. Ellis and Bentler (1973) provide correlational evidence that for female subjects, the greater the difference between stereotypic ratings of men and women, the greater the belief in the appropriateness of traditional sex-role standards. The corresponding correlation for males was not significant. Once again, however, the interpretation of these findings is unclear because difference scores were used. Thus, until further evidence becomes available, the question of whether sex-role stereotypes and standards are distinguishable and related must remain unanswered.

Citing several studies, Kagan (1964) summarizes as follows the personality attributes that comprise sex-role standards in our culture:

> Females are supposed to inhibit aggression and open display of sexual urges, to be passive with men, to be nurturant to others, to cultivate attractiveness, and to maintain an affective, socially poised, and friendly posture with others. Males are urged to be aggressive in face of attack, independent in problem situations, sexually aggressive, in control of regressive urges, and suppressive of strong emotion, especially anxiety. [P. 143]

However, it is unclear whether the studies to which he alludes defined sex-role standards in terms of appropriate characteristics. Using this definition as my criterion, I found 6 other studies of sex-role standards. Four of these investigations involved college students or adult samples (Ellis & Bentler, 1973; Gump, 1972; J. Joesting & R. Joesting, 1972; Rothbart & Maccoby, 1966) and two used high school students (J. Joesting & R. Joesting, 1975; Ponzo & Strowig, 1973). Ellis and Bentler (1973) and Ponzo and Strowig (1973) explicitly defined sex-role standards in terms of behaviors which are appropriate for one sex but inappropriate or less appropriate for the other. (Ellis and Bentler [1973] computed alpha coefficients for their scale of traditional sex-role standards: females .91; males .88.) Rothbart and Maccoby (1966) inquired into parents' beliefs about what differences *should* exist between boys and girls. J. Joesting and R. Joesting (1972, 1975) used a measure of equalitarianism which may be construed as tapping sex-role standards, as defined above. Subjects in the Gump (1972) study responded to an inventory of sex-role concepts containing many items that appear to measure sex-role standards. Unfortunately, these studies contain methodological problems (see section A-2) which preclude any generalizations about sex-role standards.

4. Sex-Role Ideals

So far this review has dealt with the self-report data relevant to two sets of beliefs about ·the sexes, sex-role stereotypes and sex-role standards. There remains still another set of beliefs about men and women, namely sex-role ideals. A few attempts have been made to explore the relationship between sex-role ideals and stereotypes, and these will be discussed below. How sex-role ideals relate to sex-role standards is not at all clear. These two sets of beliefs are at least conceptually distinguishable. Authors seem to use the term sex-role standard to refer to beliefs about the appropriate characteristics of the sexes, to what males and females ought to be and do. The implication is that sex-role standards represent the dictates of "society." Sex-role ideals refer not to the socially prescribed but to the ideally desirable in men and women. With sex-role ideals the connotation shifts to what men and women aspire to be and do, to what they admire in their own and the opposite sex. That is, in contrast to sex-role standards, sex-role ideals imply a *personal* (not a societal) point of view. Of course, there may be considerable overlap between an individual's sex-role ideals and society's sex-role standards. Or the two sets of beliefs may be very different.

Sex-role ideals have been approached from a variety of perspectives. How do women envision the ideal woman? The ideal man? What do women believe men view as ideal in a woman? Is there a discrepancy between what women view as ideal in a woman and what they believe men see as ideal in a woman? What do men consider to be ideal in a man? In a woman? What are their beliefs about women's ideal man? Is there a discrepancy between men's ideal man and their beliefs about how women perceive the ideal man? How closely do men's beliefs about women's ideal man coincide with women's own descriptions of the ideal man? Do women's beliefs about men's ideal woman accurately represent the ideal woman as portrayed by men? And, finally, how do people's sex-role ideals relate to their self-conceptions? These are the kinds of questions that have been raised about sex-role ideals. Unfortunately, answers may be offered for only a few of these questions and then only tentatively.

In some of the following studies reference groups are not clearly specified, but in most an explicitly personal frame of reference is provided: subjects are asked to describe the ideal female or male as they themselves conceive of these ideals. This is in keeping with the definition of sex-role ideals suggested above.

Two studies concerning college students' ideal male and female are considered here in some detail. The first of these is the McKee and Sherriffs (1959) study which already has been described in part. Each of 100 female and 100 male college students used Sarbin's ACL to describe 4 different concepts, including the ideal member of the opposite sex. A personal reference group was specified: subjects were told to describe " 'your ideal woman' " or " 'your ideal man' " (p. 357). Only the responses to female and male adjectives were analyzed, that is, those adjectives on which male and female subjects in the Sherriffs and McKee (1957) study had agreed as to whether the characteristics were stereotypically masculine or feminine. These adjectives were further classified as favorable or unfavorable on the basis of judgments made by still another sample of college students (McKee and Sherriffs, 1957). These categorizations yielded 29 favorable male-stereotypic adjectives and 20 favorable female-stereotypic items.

Women chose, on the average, 80% of the favorable female adjectives in characterizing their ideal man, a figure which nearly equalled the average percentage (82) of favorable male adjectives which they ascribed to the ideal man. That is, female subjects endowed their ideal man with stereotypically feminine and masculine qualities in roughly equal amounts.

In describing their ideal woman, men selected, on the average, 78% of the favorable female adjectives and 63% of the favorable male adjectives. They chose 10 of the 29 favorable adjectives in the male stereotype significantly less often than other favorable male adjectives. These were aggressive, courageous, daring, deliberate, dominant, dynamic, forceful, independent, rugged, and sharp-witted.

Further evidence that accords well with these results emerges from Spence, Helmreich, and Stapp (1974, 1975) which is partially described above. In the course of developing the Personal Attributes Questionnaire, they administered a series of bipolar items (from the Rosenkrantz et al., 1968 Stereotype Questionnaire) to groups of college students, under instructions to rate either the typical adult man and woman, the typical male and female college student, or the ideal man and woman. On 55 items significant differences between the ratings of the typical adult man and woman and the typical male and female college student were found for both male and female subjects. These items were selected for inclusion in the Personal Attributes Questionnaire.

The ratings of the ideal male and female provided the basis for grouping these items into three subscales. On 18 items the mean ratings of both the ideal male and ideal female were toward the feminine pole of the item, as determined by the stereotype ratings. This set of items (female-valued subscale) included expressive characteristics such as emotional, considerate, devotes self to others, strong conscience, kind, creative, warm to others, enjoys art and music, understanding, likes children. On 23 items the mean ratings of both the ideal male and female were toward the stereotypical masculine pole. These items (male-valued subscale) referred to predominantly instrumental characteristics such as independent, active, competitive, knows ways of world, outspoken, interested in sex, acts as a leader, intellectual, self confident, feels superior. Thus, the majority of male and female stereotypic items were assigned to both the ideal woman and the ideal man. But on 13 items (sex-specific subscale) the mean ratings of the ideal female differed from the midpoint in the direction of the stereotypically feminine pole, and the mean rating of the ideal male differed in the direction of the stereotypically masculine pole. These items included aggressive, dominant, loud, and sees self running show, as exclusively characteristic of the ideal man; and needs approval, feelings hurt, cries easily, religious, as exclusively characteristic of the ideal woman.

These findings, along with those of McKee and Sherriffs (1959), show that college students endow their ideal woman with many stereotypically masculine characteristics as well as stereotypically feminine characteristics. Similarly, they equip their ideal man with attributes from both the feminine stereotype and the masculine stereotype. To put it another way, college students in these two studies envision an ideal man and woman who share a large number of stereotypically feminine and masculine attributes, rather than being limited to attributes from the appropriate sex stereotype. However, the evidence also suggests that there remains a relatively small number of characteristics which are assigned exclusively to either the ideal male or the ideal female.

Elman, Press, and Rosenkrantz (1970) and Reece (1964) report results consistent with the finding that college students' sex-role ideals possess many characteristics stereotypic of both the same and the opposite sex. These results, based on college students' ratings of the typical man and woman and the ideal man and woman, are not presented in detail, owing to methodological difficulties in both studies. (See section A-2.)

In summary, the evidence points to two hypotheses concerning sex-role ideals: (a) college students depict an androgynous ideal man and woman, endowing each with many characteristics from both the feminine and masculine stereotypes; (b) they assign a relatively small number of characteristics exclusively to the ideal man and ideal woman, respectively.

The remaining studies which inquire into sex-role ideals do not present evidence relevant to this hypothesis. However, a related question is broached in the majority of these studies — namely, the degree of intrafamily versus extrafamily orientation characteristic of women's ideal woman (A. F. Rappaport, Payne, & Steinmann, 1970; Steinmann, 1963; Steinmann, Doherty, & Fox, 1970; Steinmann & Fox, 1966, 1970; Steinmann, Levi, & Fox, 1964; Voss & Skinner, 1975). These studies use a variety of samples of women, including black and white college students, nuns, mothers of female college students, businesswomen, and professionals. The evidence, to the extent to which it can be evaluated, consistently shows that women portray an ideal woman whose satisfactions derive about equally from service to home and family and from personal achievement. A much smaller amount of evidence from these studies indicates that men's ideal woman possesses a similar balance between intrafamilial and extrafamilial orientations. However, these findings are of limited value, as they are based on uninterpretable discrepancy scores (see Wylie, 1974, pp. 88-95). M. S. Richardson (1975) also investigates women's ideal woman, but owing to various methodological problems, the results are not discussed here.

A very small amount of evidence is also available concerning women's beliefs about men's ideal woman and men's beliefs about women's ideal man. In the McKee and Sherriffs (1959) study, each subject used Sarbin's ACL to express his or her view as to how the opposite sex conceives of the ideal for the subject's own sex and age group. Men chose, on the average, 78% of the favorable male adjectives and 76% of the favorable female adjectives when indicating their belief about women's ideal man. Women ascribed to men's ideal woman 58% of the favorable male words and 86% of the favorable female words. A significant subjects effect was obtained: men selected a larger number of favorable adjectives in expressing their belief about women's ideal man than women chose in describing men's ideal woman. The words × subjects interaction was also significant, indicating that women ascribe significantly fewer opposite sex characteristics to men's ideal woman than men ascribe to women's ideal man.

When these results are viewed in the light of the previously described findings reported in the same study, several interesting comparisons emerge. These results must be interpreted with caution since none of the comparisons was subjected to statistical test. Men's beliefs about women's ideal man accorded well with what women themselves ascribed to the ideal man, namely a large and equal number of male and female characteristics. Likewise, women's belief that men's ideal woman possesses a substantial number of characteristics of both sexes but relatively fewer stereotypically masculine than feminine characteristics was largely consistent with how men themselves envisioned the ideal woman. However, women attributed to men a more stereotypically feminine ideal woman than men themselves depicted.

Steinmann and Fox (1966) report some data that help to clarify this comparison between men's description of their ideal woman and women's perception of how men portray the ideal woman. The study involved a variety of samples of adult women and men who took the Inventory of Female Values. This instrument has been widely used in the study of the ideal woman. Split-half reliability has been estimated to be .81 (Fand, cited in Steinmann, 1963). The test is scored by taking the difference between the subject's subscores on two sets of items — those describing a family-oriented woman and those describing a woman who seeks her own fulfillment and achievement. Since these difference scores are subject to all the criticisms raised in Wylie (1974, pp. 88-95), the findings based on these scores will not be discussed.

The evidence of interest consists instead of an item-by-item breakdown of the responses that men gave in describing their ideal woman, compared with the responses that women gave in delineating their belief about men's ideal woman. On 19 of the 34 items, the modal response of the women differed from that of the men. Women sketched a more family-oriented woman as men's ideal, whereas men themselves described an ideal woman whose interests included personal achievement as well as devotion to husband and family. Men tended to take a less "traditional" position when responding to such abstract or global items as "likes to create something" and "capable woman has duty to be active" (p. 271). But on the more specific items, men sided with tradition, equipping their ideal woman with such concerns as "main goal of life is well-adjusted children" (p. 272) and "ambition should be subordinated to family" (p. 271).

In summary, on the issue of women's beliefs about men's ideal woman, the results of these two studies point to the following hypothesis: women believe that men envision an ideal woman who exhibits a preponderance of stereotypic or "traditional" female qualities. The strength of this generalization is enhanced somewhat by the fact that six of seven[6] other studies — all of which use uninterpretable discrepancy scores — obtained similar results: women attributed to men's ideal woman a relatively strong orientation to home and family

---

6. Interestingly, the one exception, Steinmann and Fox (1970), was the only study from this list to use black subjects. These black college women believed that men's ideal woman possesses a balance between intrafamilial and extrafamilial orientations.

(Rappaport, Payne, & Steinmann, 1970; Steinmann, 1963; Steinmann, Doherty, & Fox, 1970; Steinmann & Fox, 1969, 1970; Steinmann, Levi, & Fox, 1964; Voss & Skinner, 1975).

Two studies compared women's beliefs about men's ideal woman with men's expressed ideal. In both cases a discrepancy emerged in which women attributed to men a more stereotypically or traditionally feminine ideal woman than men themselves depicted. The remaining evidence from studies that are less methodologically defensible supports this generalization in one instance (Steinmann, 1963) but fails to support it in a study involving black college students (Steinmann & Fox, 1970). Once again, because the thread of evidence is so slender, this generalization must stand as hypothesis rather than conclusion.

Parallel evidence concerning men's beliefs about women's ideal man is too sparse to sustain even tentative generalizations.

Several studies that utilize the Inventory of Female Values offer findings that bear on the questions of whether women's self-conceptions are related to (a) their concepts of the ideal woman; (b) their beliefs about men's ideal woman (Rappaport, Payne, & Steinmann, 1970; Steinmann, 1963; Steinmann, Doherty, & Fox, 1970; Steinmann & Fox, 1966, 1969, 1970; Steinmann, Levi, & Fox, 1964; Voss & Skinner, 1975). Involved in these studies were a variety of samples of women — black and white college students, nuns, business and professional women from the United States, and middle-class, adult women from Peru and Argentina. The subjects responded to the test under instructions to describe the self, their ideal woman, and their conception of men's ideal woman.

For each construct a difference score was obtained, reflecting the discrepancy between the subject's orientation toward home and family and her orientation toward self-achievement. Since a difference score of any particular size can be obtained by any one of a large number of combinations of component scores, these scores are open to serious interpretational ambiguity (see Wylie, 1974, pp. 88-95). This reduces the value of the finding that, in all the United States samples, women's self-conceptions were less family oriented relative to their beliefs about men's ideal woman. (In the two South American samples women described both the self and men's ideal woman as family oriented. Data concerning women's ideal woman were not collected from these samples.) Moreover, certain results of this research are inconsistent even if taken at face value: inspection of the mean difference scores for self and ideal woman indicates that in some studies women saw the self as being more oriented to the home than their ideal woman would be, while in other studies, they imagined an ideal woman who was equally or less inclined toward home and family.

The remaining empirical information concerning the self in relation to sex-role ideals is too limited to allow even tentative generalizations (Elman, Press, & Rosenkrantz, 1970; McKee & Sherriffs, 1959; Richardson, 1975).

5. Other Studies of Sex-Role Ideology

In the preceding sections I reviewed studies dealing with three categories of sex-role ideology—stereotypes, standards, and ideals. These categories were chosen with an eye to the quantity of available research. Other studies falling within the domain of sex-role ideology do not fit easily into these categories. For example, Unger and Siiter, excerpted in Unger (1975), inquired into the relative importance that college students assign to certain values as "guiding principles" for oneself, members of one's own sex, and members of the opposite sex. J. N. Block (1973) conducted cross-cultural research on the ideal self which she views as an index of what a culture values in a person of each sex, respectively. I mention these studies here as a reminder that other aspects of sex-role ideology may have a bearing on the self-concepts of men and women.

D. Self-Reported Affiliation as a Function of Sex of Subject

1. Theoretical Rationales

From the several studies surveyed in section C–2, we learned something of the image of females embodied in college students' stereotypes. Among the qualities assigned to the typical woman were sensitivity, social skill, and interest in others. These attributes also distinguished females' self-descriptions from males' in studies of the correspondence between sex-role stereotypes and self-concepts. In this section I return to the social dimension of self-conception with the aim of bringing further evidence to bear on the question of whether self-reported affiliation varies as a function of sex.

Any number of theorists have lent a social cast to female personality. Women are thought to want or need or seek contact with others, to possess an abiding interest in people, a human responsiveness, a talent for the social. Women are portrayed again and again as *engaged with others* in a way that men are not. Having pursued the concept of feminine character across various disciplines and historical periods, Klein (1971) arrives at a surprisingly small number of feminine traits on which theorists have agreed. One of these is "greater intensity of personal relationships" (p. 164). Cooley (1902) notices a sex difference in the development of the social self:

> Girls have, as a rule, a more impressible social sensibility; they care more obviously for the social image, study it, reflect upon it more. . . . Boys are more taken up with muscular activity for its own sake and with construction, their imaginations are occupied somewhat less with persons and more with things. [P. 171]

Lynn (1962) hypothesizes a greater need for affiliation in females than males on the grounds that a girl's identification with her mother occurs within the context of a close, rewarding, personal relationship. This kind of relationship is not central to the boy's experience. He identifies not so much with his father as with an abstract masculine role. Taking a slightly different perspective on sex-role learning, M. M. Johnson (1963) elaborates Talcott Parsons's equation of femininity with expressive roles, masculinity with instrumental roles. To enact an expressive role, as the mother does, is to understand, to please, to cultivate "a direct sensitivity and responsiveness to the attitudes of others" (p. 321). The father, being the instrumental leader of the family, is primarily oriented toward goals that preclude this kind of close personal and emotional involvement. Chodorow (1974) proposes that "in any given society, feminine personality comes to define itself in relation and connection to other people more than masculine personality does" (p. 44). This sex difference arises from the fact that women everywhere are primarily responsible for the care of young children and the later socialization of girls.

Reviews of the literature on psychological sex differences have added empirical weight to the claim of women's greater social orientation. In their survey of studies from 1920 through 1952, Terman and Tyler (1954) conclude: "It is a common belief that one of the characteristically feminine traits is an absorbing interest in persons and personal relationships. That in fact a sex difference exists in this respect is indicated by data from subjects over a wide range of ages" (p. 1095). These data are of various sorts: dreams, wishes, question topics; play, reading, and occupational preferences; social IQ scores; and behavioral ratings of sociality. Anastasi (1958) reaches a similar conclusion concerning interests, preferences, attitudes, and values. Garai and Scheinfeld's (1968) appraisal of the evidence leads them to say that males have a greater interest in objects and a stronger need for acheivement, females a greater interest in people and a stronger need for affiliation. The tabled summaries of studies prepared by Oetzel (1966) show that girls and women exceed boys and men on diverse measures of need for affiliation and interest in and positive feeling for others. Sherman (1971) offers still another concurring opinion. The only dissenting voice is that of Maccoby and Jacklin (1974) whose survey of research on attachment, affiliation, and positive interaction revealed "surprisingly little sex differentiation" (p. 225). Their review of studies on social self-concept disclosed almost as many null results as results favoring females.

Both theory and research, then, agree that the social dimension of personality, broadly defined, is more salient in females than males. One might imagine from this that females, compared with males, are more likely to conceive of themselves in social terms. But in narrowing down the field to the social dimension of self-conception, one finds few theories concerning the variable of sex.

One of these is Bardwick's (1971) account of female psychology, already presented in section B-1. In her view, gratification of the affiliative motive, the need to love and be loved, is the critical requirement for positive self-esteem among women, but not among men. For young children of both sexes, self-esteem derives largely from the mastery of skills, the fulfillment of achievement motives. In adolescence and adulthood, males continue to be rewarded primarily for achievement, which remains their basic source of self-esteem. As girls approach adolescence, they are pressured by parents, peers, and society to make heterosexual affiliation their major concern. As a result, the primary locus of female self-esteem shifts to the affiliative motive. This account suggests that adolescent and adult females would be more likely than adolescent and adult males to define themselves in social terms, to report that they are affiliative. However, it is important to point out that Bardwick uses the term affiliative rather loosely to apply not only to the motive to receive and give love, but to femininity and the marital relationship. The implication throughout is that women's affiliative motive is directed specifically toward men and children; it is expressed through the traditional roles of wife and mother. Whether the importance of affiliation to women's self-concepts extends beyond the heterosexual and domestic realms is less clear from this account. That is, are women more likely than men to say "I am friendly; I enjoy the company of others; I initiate and cherish friendships"?

Carlson's (1965) notion of the social-personal dimension of self-conception is also relevant to the issue at hand. She conceives of this as a qualitative distinction between a self-concept defined in social terms and one defined in personal terms. Central to the socially oriented person's self-image are social experiences and personal relationships, while the personally oriented individual creates a self-image based on nonsocial criteria. As described in section B-1, Carlson proposes that during adolescence the self-concepts of girls become more socially oriented, the self-concepts of boys, more personally oriented. Further mention of Carlson's theory is made below in the context of her empirical work.

In sum, the theories and reviews considered here lead one to expect higher self-reported affiliation among females than males, at least from adolescence onwards. Below I evaluate the evidence from studies that used self-report measures of affiliation. Often the definition of this construct varies across studies. Whereas the reviews cited above included all manner of affiliation measures (e.g., play and occupational preferences, behavior ratings, self-reports), this survey is confined to self-reports of affiliative aspects of personality. With the exception of one test manual, I present studies that were published since 1961.

2. Research Concerning Self-Reported Affiliation as a Function of Sex of Subject

The studies in this section are grouped by instrument. I begin with the better-known instruments, although in no case is the evidence sufficient to justify drawing conclusions with respect to a single measure of affiliation. Four studies which used idiosyncratic measures of affiliation are presented next. Finally, I simply list investigations which used idiosyncratic instruments and contained numerous methodological flaws (see section A-2).

The majority of studies concerning self-reported affiliation as a function of sex of subject used adolescent and adult samples. I have found comparatively few investigations involving children younger than 13 years of age.

a. Carlson's Measures of Social-Personal Orientation

In a series of studies Carlson explored empirically the relationship between sex and the social-personal dimension of self-conception. Because in several cases her inquiry is theoretically directed, contrasting with most research in this area, I describe her studies despite their serious methodological limitations.

In the initial study Carlson (1963) describes the development of a questionnaire designed to measure "the child's reliance upon current social experiences in defining his self-image" (p. 569). The questionnaire consisted of 27 sentences judged by 9 psychologists to imply a social orientation and 28 judged to imply a personal orientation. At least 7 of 9 judges agreed on 76% of the judgments. Items were arranged in a forced-choice format in which response alternatives were equated on judged social desirability. No reliability information is presented. The social orientation questionnaire was scored as follows: for each subject a social score was obtained by summing the social items chosen as *most* characteristic of the self plus the personal items chosen as *least* characteristic. A personal score for each subject was obtained by an analogous operation. *The subject was then classified as socially oriented if the social score equalled or exceeded the personal score.* This kind of dichotomous scoring results in a crude index of social orientation: if a woman describes herself as possessing a balance between personally oriented and socially oriented characteristics, she is classified with the person who portrays himself or herself as exclusively socially oriented. Conversely, if her social score is just slightly lower than her personal score, she is called "personally oriented" even though her self-description is very similar to the "socially oriented" individual who obtains equivalent social and personal scores. Although the author had not made any predictions concerning the relationship between sex and social orientation in this initial study, she, nonetheless, made comparisons across sex groups. A nonsignificant difference emerged among a very small sample of middle-class sixth graders (25 girls, 18 boys).

Carlson (1965) elaborates her earlier definition of social-personal dimension: "Social orientation refers to the salience of interpersonal experiences in the individual's conceptions of himself and implies a degree of vulnerability to social appraisals, while personal orientation refers to conceptions of self which are independent of concern with social experiences" (p. 660). She sees a connection between social-personal orientation and sex-role differentiation during adolescence, hypothesizing that from Grade 6 to Grade 12, girls will increase in social orientation, boys in personal orientation. That is, each sex will move in the direction of its respective sex-role stereotype, where the feminine stereotype implies a social orientation, the masculine stereotype a personal orientation. Unfortunately, the longitudinal evidence which she offers in support of this hypothesis cannot be accepted for several reasons: (a) information concerning the comparability of the sex groups is not given; (b) the initial (sixth-grade) testing involved the social orientation questionnaire described above, but for the second (twelfth-grade) testing, a different form of the questionnaire was used (reliability and validity data are not provided for either the preadolescent or adolescent versions); (c) only 16 boys and 33 girls participated in the second testing; (d) the two testing conditions were not comparable: the test was group administered to the sixth graders; questionnaires were mailed to the twelfth graders; (e) dichotomous scoring, as described above, was used.

Smart and Smart (1970) administered Carlson's social orientation questionnaires (preadolescent and adolescent forms) to Indian students attending private schools in Delhi. Fifty male and 50 female subjects at each of 2 age levels (11–12 years and 18 years) served as subjects. All groups were equated on socioeconomic status. Subjects were tested in large groups and instructions were given both verbally and in writing. Carlson's method of dichotomous scoring was followed. Among the younger age group, a significantly higher percentage of girls than boys were socially oriented, but the adolescent males and females did not differ significantly.

Carlson and Levy (1968) describe the development of a different measure of social-personal orientation, called the Carlson Adjective Checklist. Two kinds of evidence were brought to bear on the construct validity of the instrument. On the basis of past theoretical and empirical work, the authors first predicted that males would describe personally oriented self-concepts, while females would portray themselves as socially oriented. Second, they conceived of social-personal orientation as representing "qualitative differences in the organization and functioning of the self-concept" (p. 912). Accordingly, they expected that social-personal orientation would be more directly related to modes of processing information than to the "objects" of processing.

That is, they hypothesized a closer relationship between social-personal orientation and the Jungian functions of sensation, intuition, thinking, and feeling than between social-personal orientation and extroversion-introversion. They also made the related prediction that socially oriented subjects would be more inclined toward sensing and feeling, whereas personally oriented subjects would be more inclined toward thinking and intuition.

Comprising the sample were 58 males and 75 females who were either college students or employees of an aerospace firm. The subjects responded to the Carlson Adjective Checklist during class periods or working hours. The Myers-Briggs Type Indicator, a measure of introversion-extroversion, and of Jungian types (sensation, intuition, thinking, feeling) was given as a take-out assignment.

The Carlson Adjective Checklist consists of 30 socially desirable adjectives equally divided between those which implicitly require a social object and those which do not. The social items include, for example, attractive, compassionate, considerate, cooperative; the personal items include, for example, ambitious, confident, creative, and efficient. Subjects first were told to check the 10 adjectives which "best describe yourself" and then to circle 5 of those as most descriptive of the self. Each checked item received a score of one; each circled item, a score of two. Once again, subjects were classified as *either* socially oriented (weighted sum of social items exceeds weighted sum of personal items) *or* personally oriented. One month test-retest reliability coefficients, based on small samples of college students, were .79 ($N = 25$) and .72 ($N = 44$). Internal consistency was estimated to be .82 for another sample of 79 college students who received instructions which differed from the standard instructions.

The authors' predictions, evaluated by means of chi square tests, were supported in every case: (a) more males were personally oriented, more females were socially oriented; (b) social-personal orientation was significantly related to the Jungian functions but not to introversion-extroversion scores; (c) socially oriented subjects were more likely to be sensing and feeling types; personally oriented subjects were more likely to be intuitive and thinking types.

Although Carlson and Levy (1970) did not formulate any hypotheses involving the sex variable, they did test for sex differences in social-personal orientation as measured by the Carlson Adjective Checklist. In two samples of Negro college students from the same university ($N = 52$ males, 150 females; $N = 20$ males, 20 females), nonsignificant sex differences emerged when subjects were dichotomously classified as socially oriented or personally oriented. Information concerning the comparability of the sex groups on such variables as SES is not presented.

The Carlson Adjective Checklist was also used to measure social-personal orientation in Carlson's (1971) investigation of sex differences in ego functioning. Of relevance to the present issue is her prediction that males would conceive of the self in individualistic (personal) terms, whereas females would define themselves in interpersonal (social) terms. The subjects were college students and community adults who varied with respect to age, education, socioeconomic status, and marital status. The 39 females and 37 males were apparently not equated on other possibly related variables. When their dichotomously scored responses were compared by means of a chi square test, significantly more females than males emerged as socially oriented, thereby supporting the author's hypothesis.

In sum, Carlson's notion of social-personal orientation in self-conception has generated research and led to the construction of instruments designed to measure this theoretically delineated construct. Unfortunately, the value of this research is diminished by (a) the largely unexplored psychometric nature of these instruments; (b) the prevalence of other methodological problems. While the prediction of sex differences in social-personal orientation has not received consistent support, it is still too early to draw firm conclusions.

b. EDWARDS PERSONAL PREFERENCE SCHEDULE (EPPS)

The EPPS purports to measure 15 manifest needs proposed by Murray (1938). One of these is Affiliation. In the revised EPPS manual, A. L. Edwards (1959) defines this variable as follows:

> To be loyal to friends, to participate in friendly groups, to do things for friends, to form new friendships, to make as many friends as possible, to share things with friends, to do things with friends rather than alone, to form strong attachments, to write letters to friends. [P. 11]

Data on the internal consistency, test-retest reliability, and convergent validity of the EPPS scales are presented. Sex comparisons among the normative college sample (760 males, 749 females) yielded significant differences on 12 scales, including Affiliation. Although females obtained significantly higher Affiliation raw scores than males, the difference was small in absolute terms. The normative adult group, consisting of a very large nationwide sample of household heads (4,031 males, 4,932 females), also produced a small but significant sex difference favoring females on the Affiliation scale. It is possible that these sex differences are inflated to some degree by the forced-choice format of the EPPS.

Although Sampson and Hancock (1967) were concerned primarily with birth order effects on personality, they included the sex of subject variable in their analyses. Included among the dependent variables was affiliation, as measured by a slightly modified form of the EPPS Affiliation scale. High school students (100 males, 128 females) from Grades 10, 11, and 12 completed the scale at home. Comparisons across the 10 subgroups formed by the various combinations of birth order, sex of subject, and sex of sibling revealed some variation in terms of father's occupation and education but only slight differences in age, grade in school, and sibling spacing. The application of an ANOVA to the Affiliation scores produced a nonsignificant main effect of sex and nonsignificant interaction effects among sex, ordinal position, and sex of sibling.

Spangler and Thomas (1962) administered the EPPS to 80 disabled adult patients at a county hospital and 80 nondisabled adults. The groups were comparable in IQ and educational level and contained equal numbers of males and females. Within each group there were 20 subjects from each of 4 age ranges: 40-49, 50-59, 60-69, 70-79. Of the 15 EPPS scales, 5, including Affiliation, yielded significant main effects of sex. Females obtained higher Affiliation scores than males. However, this result is ambiguous, as many statistical tests were computed without cross-validation. Interactions among sex, age, and physical status were not significant for the Affiliation scale.

In order to explore the need structure of Negro college students, Brazziel (1964) administered the EPPS to a lower South sample (60 males, 80 females) and an upper South sample (60 males, 62 females). Whether the sex groups were comparable on other variables such as socioeconomic status is impossible to tell. Sex comparisons on each of the 15 EPPS scales were made by means of t-tests, revealing nonsignificant sex differences on the Affiliation scale in both the lower South and the upper South samples.

A study by Schaie and Strother (1968) is not presented here because it contains various methodological problems. (See section A-2.)

In sum, the evidence from these 5 reports is too sparse and inconsistent to sustain conclusions concerning sex and self-reported affiliation, as measured by the EPPS.

c. INTERPERSONAL CHECK LIST (ICL)

McDonald and Gynther (1965) examined the effects of sex, race, and class on ICL scores. Participating in this study were high school seniors (151 Negro females, 110 Negro males, 114 white females, 97 white males) from segregated schools in a southern city. The sex groups did not differ significantly in age, but other potential sources of noncomparability between males and females were not considered. Subjects made self and ideal self ratings on the ICL, from which 4 scores were derived, including "Self-love." This score allegedly measures "friendly, warm, cooperative characteristics" (p. 85). A main effect of sex was obtained on Self-love, with females scoring higher than males. Sex did not enter into any significant interaction effects with race or class on this variable.

In a replication of McDonald and Gynther (1965), McDonald (1968) administered the ICL to two consecutive graduating classes from the only Negro high school and the only white high school in a southern rural area. There were 131 females and 87 males from the segregated black school and 168 females and 142 males from the segregated white school. No attempt was made to demonstrate the comparability of the sex groups on such variables as social class or GPA. Subjects rated self, ideal self, mother, and father on the ICL. Altogether 8 scores were derived, each of which was subjected to a sex × race × class ANOVA. Of primary interest here are the findings of (a) a main effect of sex on self-love, favoring females; (b) a significant sex by race interaction in which Negro males obtained higher self-love scores than white males but Negro and white females did not differ; (c) a significant sex by class interaction in which females scored higher than males only among the 2 higher classes. However, since multiple statistical tests were involved, these results are not clearly interpretable.

Although Mahoney and Hartnett (1973) did not make any predictions concerning the variable of sex, they did test for sex differences on ICL Lov scores. A regression analysis revealed a nonsignificant sex difference among a sample of 28 male and 47 female college student volunteers of comparable ages.

In sum, it is impossible to say whether ICL Lov scores vary as a function of sex of subject.

(See Wylie, 1974, pp. 213–223, for a detailed description and critique of the ICL, and, in particular, the Lov score.)

d. Cattell's High School Personality Questionnaire (HSPQ)

Baltes and Nesselroade's (1972) study of adolescent personality was directed toward examining ontogenetic and generational change during the period from 1970 to 1971. At the initial testing a large number of students from 32 junior and senior high schools in West Virginia responded to Cattell's High School Personality Questionnaire, Form A. The sample—stratified by sex, grade, and homeroom—included 5 successive cohorts, aged 12-1/2, 13-1/2, 14-1/2, 15-1/2, and 16-1/2 years, respectively. A year later 75.9% of the subjects ($N = 1,249$) were retested. The authors report no selective dropout effects on the dimension of interest here, Factor A (sizothymia/affectothymia). One-year test-retest stability coefficients for Factor A were .55 for females and .50 for males. Each of the 14 HSPQ dimensions was subjected to a cohort × time of measurement × sex ANOVA, yielding 12 significant main effects of sex. On Factor A (sizothymia/affectothymia), females scored significantly higher, i.e., toward the warmhearted, outgoing pole. However, the value of this finding is reduced by the number of statistical tests involved. The sex variable did not enter into any interaction effects, nor did the cohort or time variables exert significant main effects on Factor A scores.

e. Jackson's Personality Research Form (PRF)

In developing the PRF D. N. Jackson (1967) based his definition of personality traits largely on Murray's (1938) work. In the test manual he provides a list of adjectives which define Affiliation: "neighborly, loyal, warm, amicable, good-natured, friendly, companionable, genial, affable, cooperative, gregarious, hospitable, sociable, affiliative, good-willed" (p. 6). The high scorer "enjoys being with friends and people in general; accepts people readily; makes efforts to win friendships and maintain associations with people" (p. 6). An impressive amount of data is presented in support of the internal consistency, test-retest reliability, convergent validity, and discriminant validity of the PRF scales, including Affiliation. The large normative sample, drawn from more than 30 colleges and universities of varying size and geographic location, included 1,002 females and 1,029 males. Females obtained a higher mean Affiliation score than males (16.15 and 14.98, respectively), but no statistical test is presented. In data furnished to us by Jackson (personal communication, 1975), sex differences favoring females occurred on 18 of the 20 items in the Affiliation scale.

f. GOUGH AND HEILBRUN'S ADJECTIVE CHECK LIST (ACL)

Among the dependent measures employed in Silverman, Shulman, and Wiesenthal's (1970) study of deception and debriefing effects was the Affiliation subscale of Gough and Heilbrun's ACL. Subjects were 42 female and 56 male introductory psychology students. In a rare departure from the usual practice, the authors attempted to control for sex of experimenter effects. The sexes did not differ significantly in raw scores on the ACL Affiliation scale.

The ACL Affiliation scale was also used by Ramos (1974), but owing to various methodological problems (see section A-2), this study is not described here.

(See Wylie, 1974, pp. 200-212, for a detailed description and critique of the ACL.)

g. IDIOSYNCRATIC MEASURES OF SELF-REPORTED AFFILIATION

For his study of temperament traits Walker (1967) devised a questionnaire which includes a 16-item social scale. Inspection of the item content of this scale indicates (a) a focus on friendliness and enjoyment of group activities; (b) a failure to control for acquiescence response set. One year test-retest reliability coefficients based on a total sample of 368 children from Grades 3 through 6 ranged from .35 (third- and fourth-grade boys) to .59 (third- and fourth-grade girls). Moderate-level split-half reliability coefficients are also presented. The data of primary interest here were provided by 199 boys and 207 girls from Grades 3 through 6 in 2 urban elementary schools. Each item was read aloud to the subjects who responded by circling "yes" or "no." A t-test revealed a nonsignificant sex difference on the social scale.

As described in section B-2, Monge (1973) conducted a series of factor analyses on adolescents' self-concept scores. The subjects — 1,027 girls and 1,035 boys from Grades 6 through 12 — described My Characteristic Self using an idiosyncratic semantic differential. A principal components analysis of the scores for the total sample yielded 4 factors including Congeniality/Sociability. (This factor had also emerged for both boys and girls when scores from the same sample were factor analyzed separately by sex.) The Congeniality/Sociability factor loaded highly on such items as kind, friendly, nice, good, and happy, suggesting "an image of self as open to and pleased by social stimulation" (p. 387). Compared with boys, girls obtained significantly higher Congeniality/Sociability scores.

In an effort to explore the values and goals of Negro and white youth, A. J. Lott and B. E. Lott (1963) drew subjects from 4 senior classes in Kentucky. Two of the schools were located in the country, two in the city, and within each geographic locale one school was entirely or predominately Negro, one white. The Negro sample included 52 girls and 64 boys; the white sample included 109 girls, 76 boys. Since the authors were primarily concerned with racial comparisons, they provide no information concerning the comparability of the sex groups. Among the instruments used in this investigation were modified forms of the Goal Preference Inventory (GPI) and the Study of Values. For each a limited amount of psychometric information is provided. The GPI score of interest here is called Love and Affection, purporting to measure "'need for acceptance and indications of liking by other individuals in a social atmosphere . . . to feel the sheer joy of being with others regardless of any advantage to yourself . . . to feel part of a social group, that is, to be valued as a friend in social activities'" (p. 13). The Study of Values also provides a measure of apparent relevance to affiliation, namely the Social value orientation, "characterized by *love of people,* altruism or philanthropy, kindness, sympathy, and unselfishness" (p. 15). The computation of numerous sex × race ANOVAs yielded (a) a significant main effect of sex favoring females on the GPI Love and Affection score; (b) a significant sex × race interaction effect on the same score, indicating that the sex difference applies to whites but not to blacks; (c) a significant main effort of sex on Social value in the direction of higher scores for females and a nonsignificant interaction effect.

Fifty male and 50 female graduate students from India participated in Mukherjee and Sinha's (1970) study of achievement values and self-ideal discrepancies. Within each sex group subjects were equally divided by area of study (arts or sciences). Although the sex groups were not equated intentionally on other variables, the authors note that males and females were comparable in mean age, education, income and family size, and birth order. The Self Insight Test (Form A) provided a measure of self-ideal discrepancies on each of six dimensions including Sociability. The test was administered first under real self instructions and a week later under ideal self instructions. Subjects were encouraged to respond honestly and were promised confidentiality. Estimates of two week test-retest reliability, based on the current

sample, ranged from .66 to .80 for the 6 scales. The ANOVA performed on the Sociability scores revealed a nonsignificant main effect of
sex and nonsignificant interaction effects among sex, level of achievement values, and area of study.

h. STUDIES NOT SUBSTANTIVELY DESCRIBED

The following studies, all of which employed idiosyncratic measures
of self-reported affiliation, were judged to be methodologically deficient
according to the criteria presented in section A-2: Boyd (1975); Henton
and Johnson (1964); Kagan and Moss (1962); Kosa, Rachiele, and
Schommer (1962); Lansky, Crandall, Kagan, and Baker (1961); M. E.
Shaw (1974).

i. SUMMARY OF STUDIES CONCERNING SELF-REPORTED
AFFILIATION AS A FUNCTION OF SEX

These 28 studies of the relationship between sex and self-reported
affiliation are about equally divided between those reporting higher
scores for females and those reporting null results. In no case did males
significantly exceed females on self-reported affiliation. The outcome of
this review is thus consistent with Maccoby and Jacklin's (1974) survey of
studies on social self-concept.

Comparisons across age groups reveal that the pattern of results is the
same for adolescents and for college students and adults. Whether this
pattern applies to studies involving younger subjects is impossible to tell
on the basis of so few investigations.

Certain methodological problems have turned up with monotonous
regularity throughout this chapter, and this section is no exception. The
familiar list includes (a) the failure to establish that the sex groups are
comparable on other possibly relevant variables; (b) the use of instruments which have received little or no psychometric exploration; (c)
the failure to report or control for sex of experiementer; (d) the computation of multiple statistical tests without cross-validation. A related,
and equally tenacious problem, is the tendency to conduct empirical
inquiry, unguided by theoretical formulations.

Aside from whatever contribution these problems made to the
pattern of results, there is the fact of variability across studies in the
definition of affiliation. Most of these definitions are heavily saturated
with friendliness, friendship, and participation in social groups. Still
there are important differences in nuance: the suggestion of' intense

personal involvement or simple gregariousness, of loyalty, or warmth, or a need for acceptance. Translated into item content, these differences may account, in part, for apparent inconsistencies in results.

In sum, the expected relationship between sex and self-reported affiliation has received only limited support. Even when females scored significantly higher than males, the absolute difference between the means was small, indicating substantial overlap between the two distributions. On the other hand, there were no instances of sex differences in the reversed direction. That the relationship is not stronger is somewhat surprising in light of the trend that emerged from studies of the correspondence between self-concepts and sex-role stereotypes (see section C-2): compared with males, females were more likely to describe themselves in social terms. This discrepancy between the two sets of studies may reflect the fact that (a) different instruments were used; (b) there were comparatively few studies of self-concepts in relation to sex-role stereotypes, and all used college student samples.

E. Concluding Remarks

Of the many topics worthy of treatment in a chapter such as this, I chose only three: over-all self-regard, self-concept in relation to sex-role ideology, and self-reported affiliation. In giving my attention to these, I passed over self-reported anxiety, aggression, and dominance, the ideal self, sex-role identity, and confidence in task performance—to name a few of the self-referent variables which have been studied as a function of sex of subject. Even within the chosen topics certain territory was not covered. I was concerned primarily with sex comparisons in *level* of self-regard. I did not take up the equally important question of how males and females compare with respect to the patterning of relationships between self-regard and other variables.

Still, the task of evaluating and integrating the evidence was a formidable one, impeded by the prevalence among researchers of a kind of conceptual carelessness toward the variable of sex. Although a popular variable, it was rarely a variable of theoretical significance. Most studies provided no theoretical rationale for their analyses of sex in relation to self-concept variables.

This review has raised many questions and answered few. Perhaps future research, grounded in theory and methodologically improved, will offer deeper insights into the self-concepts of males and females.

6

Family Variables and Self-Concept Variables

A. Scope and Limitations of the Chapter

An overview of psychological, social, and educational writings shows that a wide variety of family variables are supposedly relevant to children's self-concepts. Most frequently mentioned are the following: (a) parent variables such as parents' characteristics, values, self-acceptance, and child-rearing practices; interparental relationships; absence of one parent through death or divorce; never-married status of the parents; working status of the mother; (b) family role structure and role specialization; (c) family size; and (d) birth order of children.

Theories about most of these variables are undeveloped and ambiguous, and there are few researches on most of them. Therefore, this chapter focuses selectively on some of the available publications.

Elsewhere in this book we consider a number of possible influences on self-conception which plausibly operate partly by way of experiences within the family. For example, hypothesized self-concept differences between persons of different race, sex, or socioeconomic status are presumed to be mediated partly through family variables such as differing degrees of parental self-acceptance in different racial or socioeconomic groups; differing kinds of child-rearing patterns in differing racial or socioeconomic groups; and different sex-role models provided in different kinds of family structure. Likewise, hypothesized associations between acceptance of self and acceptance of others presumably come about partly through intrafamily experiences. Accordingly, respectively relevant family variables are considered in chapter 3 on socioeconomic level, chapter 4 on race, chapter 5 on sex differences, and chapter 8 on self-concept variables as related to interpersonal attraction and regard. The reader is referred to those chapters for ideas about family variables which are not included in the present chapter.

References on parent-child interaction summarized in the earlier edition of this book (Wylie, 1961) are not substantively considered here, but are simply listed, inasmuch as their many methodological limitations were analyzed in detail in the earlier edition.

B. General Theoretical and Methodological Considerations

1. Theorizing about Parental Influences

It is a generally accepted premise in the psychological literature that the family plays a significant role in the development of a child's self-

---

Alice Wilson had the primary responsibility for preparing this chapter.

concept. We tend to assume that parents, serving as models and as sources of reinforcement, mold and shape the child's ideas and feelings about the kind of person he is and would like to be.

Both the theory and the research in this area lean heavily on the concepts of identification and learning in trying to explore and to explain the developmental aspects of the self-concept. Starting with the basic fact of the child's dependence on his parents and his affection for them, many psychologists believe that parents have a unique opportunity to reinforce selectively a child's learning, and in so doing, to influence his general perceptions of himself, the development of standards of conduct to which he should aspire, and his self-acceptance (including his negative feelings and limitations).

Both direct parental reinforcement and the reward value of imitating the parental model presumably play important parts in shaping the children's "actual" characteristics and behaviors. Partly as a function of these actual characteristics (especially as they are reflected to the child by others' reactions) children develop self-conceptions. However, self-conceptions about "actual" characteristics which meet with disapproval from significant others may be excluded or distorted (Rogers, 1951; Sullivan, 1953). Hence, accuracy of self-conception may depend in part on unconditional regard from significant others, especially parents.

Presumably, children's learning of values (development of the "ideal self") also depends on both direct parental reinforcement and the reward value of imitating the values of the parental model.

So far as children's over-all "self-acceptance" is concerned, this is presumably affected greatly by parental self-acceptance, since a self-rejecting parent would be unable to give adequate love and unable to provide an adequate model of self-acceptance. Rogers (1951) would stress the value of the parents' *unconditional* positive regard for self and child.

But what might appear at first glance to be a straightforward and obvious relationship between identification, learning, and the ensuing self-concept of the child, on further examination turns out to be a relationship involving specific theoretical questions which have never been explicitly drawn out and organized, let alone tested. Those questions which have been posed have proven to be by no means easy to study empirically. Part of the problem is due to the fact that over the years identification has come to have several meanings in the psychological literature (even in Freud's own writings there are semantic changes), and theoretical propositions about it are extremely unclear;

part is due to the difficulty in defining terms operationally, and another part of the problem is due to the difficulties inherent in designing research which can explore identification with parents and learning from them as independent variables.

Consider these problems briefly. The concept of identification originated in psychoanalytic theory, but as Bronfenbrenner (1960) points out in his essay on Freudian theories of identification, not only does Freud

> often use the same terms to refer to what are basically different concepts . . . but the above confusion becomes confounded in the later developments and modifications of Freud's theories by contemporary writers. . . . Most often, as in his discussion of the Oedipus Complex, Freud treats identification as a *process* — the sequential interplay of forces, internal and external, which impel the child to take on the characteristics of the parent. . . . But, on occasion, Freud also uses the term identification to describe the *product* or outcome of the process — the resultant similarity in the characteristics of the child and the model. Moreover, there is the further question of what aspects of the model are being emulated. At times . . . it is the overt behavior of the model which is being adopted. . . . In other instances . . . identification would appear to include internalization of the *motives* as well as the behavior of another. Finally, . . . in his later writings it is not the parent's ego with which the child identifies but his superego, his idealized standards for feeling and action. [Pp. 15,22]

Over the years many psychologists have proposed modifications of Freud's ideas about identification, and some have even suggested that we abandon the concept entirely. Kagan (1958), for example, defines identification as an acquired cognitive response which a child has. Sears (1957) proposes the idea of an "apparent absorption" of parental characteristics by the child, a process which appears to occur "without specific training, either by direct guidance or by reward and punishment" (p. 152). Mowrer (1950) suggests that the child goes through a series of identifications, a kind of progressive sequential differentiation of social objects, first with respect to age, then to sex. T. Parsons (1953) feels that the concept of identification should include not only the influence of the nuclear family, but of the broader context of society, as well. And N. Sanford (1955), in concentrating on the overt behavior aspect of identification, suggests that this could better be explained using the familiar model of learning through reinforcement by punishment and reward.

More recently, Bandura (1969) notes that "although wide differences of opinion exist among personality theorists in what they consider to be the most suitable reference events for identification, it is generally agreed that identification refers to a process in which a person patterns his thoughts, feelings, or actions after another person who serves as a model" (p. 214). However, for Bandura, identification occurs only "under conditions where the model's behavior has served as the determinative cue for the matching responses" (p. 217).

Kohlberg's (1969) "cognitive developmental account distinguishes identification (generalized enduring modeling and perception of a portion of the self as shared with parents) from imitation" (p. 426). Moreover, "enduring tendencies to model are only one component of a larger constellation of attitudes termed 'identification' " (p. 426). This constellation includes such relationships to parents as emotional dependency and attachment, tendency to conform to parents' expectations, perceived similarity to parents, idealization of parents, vicarious self-esteem derived from parents' competence or status, and ability to derive self-esteem from parental approval. On page 427 Kohlberg says, "We have referred to satellizing or developmental identification as a constellation of attitudes of attachment, imitation, and conformity to the expectations of the model. This is because definite causal priorities are not definitely implied by a cognitive-developmental identification theory. Insofar as these three attitudes are linked in other theories, such causal sequences are assumed."

With so much diversity of interpretation, it is not much wonder that, in moving from theory to research, it has proved difficult to develop an adequate operational definition of the term identification.

The third major difficulty mentioned above, the problem of exploring identification and learning from parents as independent variables in the development of a child's self-concept, has also proved to be troublesome in empirical research. As Bronfenbrenner (1960) has said, "theories have grown all out of proportion to the facts. They offer elaborate and intricate explanations for phenomena presumed to be universal; yet the evidence for the prevalence, or even the sheer existence of these phenomena is extremely sparse" (p. 38).

2. Characteristic Topics and Designs of Extant Studies

In sum, I have noted that theoretical ambiguities not only severely limit the possibility of deriving clearly implied, testable hypotheses, but also make instrumentation extremely difficult. There is, nevertheless, the possibility that atheoretical or common-sense hypotheses about parental and family influences on children's self-conceptions might be developed and tested. However, in 1961, Wylie pointed out that neither theoretical nor atheoretical research to that date had been able to establish any clear-cut cause-and-effect relationships between parental influence and the development of the child's self-concept (stimulus-response [S-R] research) but only to explore some of the many conceivable response-response (R-R) relationships between these two variables. This limitation in research design is no less true today. No study has attempted to obtain longitudinal information on objectively indexed parental characteristics, behaviors, or values in relationship to development of children's conceptions and evaluations of self.

In general, the kinds of relationships which empirical studies have tried to explore over the years have been those involving (a) the perceptions of children and parents of themselves and each other, and (b) the factors postulated as influencing these perceptions. In the first area, the area of perceptions, studies have been devised which attempt to assess the relationship between (a) the child's perception of self and of parent, and (b) the parent's perception of self and of child. And in the second area, the area of family variables postulated as influencing these perceptions, studies have considered such factors as (a) emotional support by the parent, (b) parental acceptance/rejection, (c) parental control/permissiveness, (d) intrafamily tension, (e) birth order, and (f) broken homes.

3. Methodological Evaluations of Extant Studies

The conclusiveness of these researches is seriously impaired or vitiated by many methodological limitations in addition to the already-mentioned reliance on R-R and cross-sectional designs. In evaluating whether studies warranted substantive summary, I noted the following:

1. Many publications were based on a very small number of subjects.

2. The parental or other family variables were most frequently assessed by instruments of unknown reliability and validity. Often children's retrospective reports were used. Or parental interviews, which are notoriously subject to bias and distortion, were often depended upon to index family variables. Even the use of a relatively well-known instrument such as the Parent Attitude Research Instrument is

questionable in the light of W. Becker and Krug's (1965) review of this instrument. No studies used independent observations of parental behaviors and characteristics.

3. Self-conceptions were measured most frequently by idiosyncratic instruments of unknown reliability and validity.

4. Similarity measures often involved indefensible types of scoring. (See chapter 8, section D-1-b of this book for a detailed discussion of the problems in similarity scores; and Wylie, 1974, pp. 88-95, for a consideration of difficulties with dyadic indices generally.)

5. Although self-concept variables are generally agreed to be multiply determined, practically no studies involving family variables used multivariate designs. Thus, generalizability and the possibility of looking for interactions were precluded.

6. In many investigations, multiple significance tests, often based on overlapping or correlated scores, impaired the interpretability of individual significance levels.

7. Possible contaminations between family variables and self-concept variables sometimes occurred. For example, if similarity between parent and child (as reported by the child) is taken as a measure of "identification," and this score is related to, say, scores on the Children's Manifest Anxiety Scale, the relationship between "identification" and "anxiety" could be attributable to the correlation between two self-reports, with the mother component of the identification score being irrelevant to the correlation.

C. REVIEW OF EXTANT RESEARCH

With these limitations in mind, let us consider briefly several illustrative studies in the literature designed to explore some of the relationships mentioned above, studies employing various self-concept measures with different kinds of subjects.

1. Studies of Children's and Parents' Perceptions of Themselves and Each Other

First, several studies relating to the matter of perceptions. If there is similarity between the child's perception of his own qualities (self-concept) and his perception of his parent's qualities, theories of identification would suggest that the child admires the parent and is striving to be like him/her in terms of the way the child perceives the situation. However, to interpret such similarities as relevant to *parental* influence, one needs a way to evaluate their discriminant validity. For example, does the child perceive more similarity between self and parent than between self and a hypothetical "average other" person? The question of discriminant validity was raised by Wylie in 1961, but no recent study has satisfactorily addressed itself to the issue. Sopchak's (1952) early attempt to obtain such evidence of discriminant validity yielded null results.

Indirect light might be thrown on the issue by predicting which of two classes of children would be expected to perceive greater similarity between self and parent. For example, Deitz (1969) postulated that delinquent children (as compared to nondelinquents) should be expected to show less perceived similarity between self and parent.

To test this hypothesis, Deitz (1969) compared the self-concept, self-acceptance, and parental identification of 40 delinquent males and 42 nondelinquent males ranging in age from 14 to 18 years. Nine scales of bipolar adjectives from Osgood's Semantic Differential (Osgood, Suci, & Tannenbaum, 1957) were administered to all subjects on a voluntary basis. (For a critical discussion of this measuring instrument in self-concept research see Wylie, 1974, pp. 224–230.) Subjects were asked to respond using the following concepts: (a) Me as I Really Am, (b) Me as I Would Like to Be, (c) Father as He Really Is, (d) Mother as She Really Is, (e) Me as My Father Sees Me, and (f) Me as My Mother Sees Me. The first of Deitz's hypotheses was not confirmed, namely that the delinquents would have a significantly lower self-concept than the nondelinquents (Me as I Really Am) when the level of self-concept was evaluated against judges' opinions. He found, as predicted, that the delinquent group had a greater discrepancy between the Self-Concept score and the Self-Ideal score than did the nondelinquents (Me as I Really Am and Me as I Would Like to Be), implying that "delinquents are less self-accepting than non-delinquents" (p. 289). Delinquents had higher self-expectations (Me as I Would Like to Be) than non-delinquents, but identified less closely with their parents (particularly father) than was the case for nondelinquents (Me as I Really Am compared to Father/Mother as He/She Really Is). Delinquents also believed themselves to be less accurately perceived (less understood) by their parents than did nondelinquents (Me as I Really Am compared to Me as Seen by Both Parents). Since the delinquents and nondelinquents had similar self-concepts, the delinquents' lesser assumed similarities to father (parents) presumably came from the father (parent) component of the assumed similarity score.

In the light of some reservations about the use of the Osgood Semantic Differential as a self-concept measuring instrument (Wylie, 1974, p. 228), the results of this study should be viewed with considered skepticism. Perhaps a modification of the scale in the direction of developing "bipolar scales especially selected for self-concept relevance" (p. 228) might make more meaningful research possible. In addition, there is only perceived similarity measured in this study inasmuch as the subjects described both themselves and their parents, and this kind of information may tell one more about the perceiver than about the one perceived. On the other hand, phenomenological theory holds that assumed similarities are important intervening variables apart from their correspondence with actual similarities.

Two different questions are raised in a study by Medinnus (1965): (a) Will children's self-acceptance be directly related to their perceptions of how well their parents accept them? and (b) Will children's self-acceptance be directly related to the amount of similarity children assume to exist between themselves and their parents?

Medinnus (1965) attempted to explore these questions by administering two measures of self-acceptance and a parent-child questionnaire to a group of 44 students in an introductory psychology course: 26 females and 18 males whose mean age was 18 years. The Bills Index of Adjustment and Values (Bills, n.d.) was used to measure self-acceptance. (See Wylie, 1974, pp. 150–165, for a critical discussion of the reliability and validity of this measuring instrument.) A semantic differential scale of 9 bipolar adjectives (Osgood et al., 1957) representing the 3 factors of evaluation, potency, and activity was also used. On the semantic differential the difference between the subjects' ratings of Me as I Am and Me as I Would Like to Be was defined operationally as the degree of self-acceptance, and the difference between Me as I Really Am and Mother/Father as She/He Really Is was the operational definition of the extent of identification with parents. The Parent-Child Relations questionnaire (PCR) (Roe & Siegelman, 1963) was also administered at another meeting of the class. This questionnaire provides scores on 10 subtests: Loving, Protecting, Demanding, Rejecting, Neglecting, Casual, Symbolic-Love Reward, Direct-Object Reward, Symbolic-Love Punishment, and Direct-Object Punishment. Both mother and father forms were used.

One way in which Medinnus tried to answer the first question was to compute Pearson rs between each of the two measures of "self-acceptance" and each of the 10 subtests of the PCR for mother and for father. Of the 40 rs, 14 were significant at the $\leq$ .05 level. Adolescents high in self-acceptance and adjustment were likely to perceive their parents as loving and not neglectful or rejecting, which was not true for subjects low in self-acceptance. Seven of the correlation coefficients with the mother PCR form were significant, and 7 of the coefficients also reached this level for the father form. In general, the size of the coefficients appears to be somewhat larger for the mother than for the father. This suggests, according to Medinnus, that mothers exert a greater influence than fathers on the child's personality development. (Medinnus's second purported method of indexing perceived parental acceptance involved the uninterpretable use of two kinds of discrepancy scores, a procedure characteristic of this research area and is not commented on further here.)

The second question which Medinnus raised, the question of whether children's self-acceptance is directly related to the amount of similarity children assume to exist between themselves and their parents, also exemplifies the uninterpretable use of discrepancy scores. That is, "self-acceptance" from the semantic differential was based on a [Self—Ideal] discrepancy, and identification with mother on a [Self—Mother] discrepancy. Thus, he does not have independent estimates of "self-acceptance" and "perceived similarity to mother."

In conclusion, then, this study cannot tell us whether response sets are operating in these three measures of perception (all done by the same subjects), and/or whether the subjects who perceived their parents as loving and not rejecting were more self-accepting on that account. Studies in which so many correlations are used with the same subjects are at best highly questionable, inasmuch as each significance test cannot then be assumed to be independent of every other one. Cross-validation studies might be used to see if the same variables keep yielding significant results.

Concerning Medinnus's question of whether there is a relationship between children's self-acceptance and their perceptions of parental attitudes toward them, it appears that information from Bachman's (1970) survey may be pertinent. Bachman (1970) devised a measure of interpersonal relations with parents, the development, contents, and psychometric characteristics of which are described. Ten items pertain to parental punitiveness and 11 deal with closeness to parents and the feeling that parents are reasonable. In his sample of 2,213 tenth-grade boys, associations were not strong between scores from this scale and the other background variables used as predictors of self-esteem. There was some tendency for sons from smaller families and families high in socioeconomic level to report better parent-son relations; family-relations scores were lower in homes broken by separation. In any event, Bachman states, "By far the largest relationship between self-esteem and the dimensions of family background involves family relations" (p. 126). *Eta* was .35 after adjustment for 7 other family background factors plus intelligence test scores. Bachman repeatedly stresses the fact that his index of family relations is subjective and that its associations with self-esteem scores must be viewed in the light of that fact. (More details about this survey are given in chapters 3, 4, and 7.)

Up to this point I have considered several studies which related children's conceptions of self and parent. I turn now to a different kind of question about child and parent conceptions, namely the possible relationship between children's self-concepts and parents' assumptions about their children's self-concepts.

For a number of years clinical psychologists and psychiatrists have assumed that good communication between parent and child is important as a basis for keeping problem behavior to a minimum. And good communication involves, in part, an awareness by the parent of the child's self-concept. In a study entitled "Parent Prediction of Children's Self-Concepts," Piers (1972) was interested in measuring whether parents of normal children were more aware of their child's thoughts and feelings concerning themselves than were parents of disturbed children. There were, in the first group, 188 normal children 8 to 14 years of age from 2 separate schools, who had never attended a clinic. Responses from only 140 of the mothers and 132 of the fathers were obtained. The second group of 97 clinic children were outpatients from 3 separate clinic facilities. Of this group, responses were available from 51 mothers and 28 fathers; so not only was the original number of clinic families smaller, but the attrition rate for them was also higher. The measuring instrument used was the Piers-Harris Children's Self-Concept Scale (Piers, 1969; Piers & Harris, 1964). (For a critical discussion of the Piers-Harris scale see Wylie, 1974, pp. 174–180.) The same scale was used with the parents with instructions to "answer the way your child would answer." Clinic children and their parents completed the scale during the usual clinic procedure, the parents working independently. The younger normal children, working in groups, filled out the scales at school, and the two parent scales were sent home with a covering letter. Parents of the older normal children were contacted at a PTA meeting and invited to take home an envelope containing all 3 scales and a covering letter.

To assess the degree of parental awareness of their children's self-concepts, the percent of agreement between each parent and child was calculated over individual items. For each parent-child pair, two kinds of agreement scores were computed: one based on positive responses, one on negative responses. This analysis showed that, on the positive responses, the parents of normal children agreed with their children and with each other significantly better than did the clinic parents, and that the opposite was true for the negative responses (although the latter was significant for only clinic mothers). Then, for each parent-child pair, percent of agreement scores were computed for each of 6 groups of items respectively, based on factors determined from a previous factor analysis: Behavior, Intellectual, Physical, Anxiety, Popularity, and Happiness. One of the percent agreement scores for each factor was based on positive responses, the other on negative responses. Each of these separate analyses yielded the same trends as obtained for the whole scale. That is, mothers of normal children agreed better with their children than did clinic mothers with their children on positive items, with the reverse being the case on the negative items. The trends for mothers were separately significant on 11 out of 12 comparisons. The analogous trends for fathers were significant on 7 out of 12 comparisons.

Although such results as these do not give us any indication of a causal relationship, the fact that parents of normal children tend to overestimate their children's self-concept whereas the reverse is true for parents of clinic children does raise some interesting questions which Piers (1972) points out. For example, "To what extent is a child mentally healthy because his parents think he is? Future studies should investigate the degree to which such factors as social desirability or defensiveness might be operating selectively on the part of the children, and projection, justification, and wish-fulfillment on the part of the parent" (p. 432).

The problem of multiple significance testing based on overlapping scores is a troublesome one in this study since the total scores were studied first in terms of a dichotomous grouping of high and low self-concept items, and then in terms of the six factors mentioned above.

Other studies of children's and parents' perceptions are listed in section 3 below. All in all, such studies have not offered interpretable results let alone any methodologically adequate support for any version of identification theory.

2. Studies of Self-Conceptions as a Function of Objective Family Variables

Turning now to the second of the two areas of studies indicated above, that of objective family variables influencing the child's self-concept, I consider first the factor of *broken homes*. No systematic line of reasoning has been developed to link broken homes with children's self-conceptions, but it seems to be commonly assumed that intact homes are most favorable for children's psychological development, including the development of self-regard and sex-role identity. There seems to be some agreement (e.g., see Bachman, 1970; Rosenberg, 1965) that breaks due to divorce or separation might be more damaging to the child's self-regard than breaks resulting from parental death. A few investigators have looked for possible relationships between this class of family variables and self-regard. For example, Thomes (1968) compared two groups of children whose families were similar in socioeconomic level and in structure except for the distinguishing variable of the presence of the father in the home or his absence because of divorce or separation. Subjects from homes in which the father was absent were selected from files of families receiving aid to dependent children and met the following criteria: (a) at least one child between 9–11 years of age, (b) the father had been absent from the home a minimum of two years, (c) the child was legitimate, and (d) all family members were Caucasian, had been born in the United States, and were of low socioeconomic status. Subjects from homes in which both mother and father were present were obtained through referral by the mothers in the father-absent homes, each mother being asked to suggest three families known to her which had a child between 9 and 11 years of age with both parents in the home. There were 47 children in the father-absent group and 36 in the father-present sample.

All children were interviewed individually in their homes without a parent present, and the variables explored were: (a) the child's self-concept, (b) the child's concepts of parental roles, (c) their attitudes and feelings concerning family members, and (d) peer relationships. The child's self-concept was measured by 3 instruments quite distinct from one another in approach. The first measure, developed specifically for this study, was a check list of 32 personal qualities (17 of them labeled desirable qualities and 15 of them undesirable qualities). No examples of what is meant by desirable or undesirable are given. Each child was given the set of words 4 times and asked to check the words which (a) describe himself as he is, (b) describe what he would like to be, (c) describe most fathers, and (d) describe most mothers. Scores were computed by subtracting the number of undesirable qualities checked from the number of desirable qualities checked.

The second assessment of self-concept used 2 scales from the California Test of Personality (L. P. Thorpe, Clark, & Tiegs, 1953), the scales labeled *belonging* and *self-reliance*. The questions in these scales ask the child to describe some of his own habits and feelings in relation to his peers, to his family members, and to certain tasks.

The third instrument used was a portion of the Bene-Anthony Family Relations Test (1957) dealing with statements ascribed to the self. In this test the child assigned statements of affectionate or hostile feelings to various family members including himself.

Thomes states that "for all three instruments there were no significant differences between children from father-absent homes and children from father-mother homes, and this similarity suggests that there were not gross differences between the groups of children in the conscious perceptions of certain aspects of self" (p. 95). In considering what may account for the similarity of the two groups on all 3 measures the author considers the following: (a) the years 9-11 are relatively quiescent ones in personality development, and (b) since all fathers had been absent for at least 2 years, the immediate period of adjustment to the father's absence was past.

The use of an idiosyncratic instrument to measure self-concept in this study (the check list of 32 personal qualities) raises questions concerning validity and reliability. And the almost complete lack of reporting numerical scores and statistical analysis of them makes it impossible to study critically the results and conclusions which the author presents.

These null findings are in agreement with those obtained in Bachman's (1970) multivariate analysis based on a sample of 2,213 tenth-grade United States boys. He predicted scores on an idiosyncratic measure of self-esteem, using as predictors intelligence test scores and 8 background factors. (This research, already mentioned earlier in this chapter, is described in greater detail in chapters 3 and 4.)

Several researchers have thought that *birth order* or *family size* might be among the objective family variables related to children's self-conceptions.

In 1969 Kohn and Schooler analyzed data from the National Occupation Study to determine whether there was a relationship between birth order within the family and various aspects of the person's self-concept. The data used as a basis for this analysis were but one part of a large study which they conducted on the social-psychological consequences of occupation experience. Interviews were conducted by the National Opinion Research Center with 3,101 men representative of all men throughout the United States employed in civilian occupations. Birth-order differences were examined by dividing subjects into the following 5 groups: (a) first-born, (b) first half and not first-born, (c) middle child in odd-sized families, (d) last half and not last-born, and (e) last-born. In all analyses effects of family size were controlled through covariance, and only children were excluded. The dependent variables used were self-concept variables, based on factor analyses of the subject responses in the interview which, on the average, lasted 2-1/2 hours. Aspects of the self-concept which were among the 21 dependent variables listed in the study were: (a) self-confidence, (b) self-deprecation, (c) sense of control over fate, (d) anxiety, (e) believes ideas conform to those of groups to which one belongs, and (f) compulsiveness (Schooler, 1972). No statistics are given in this study so it is not possible to determine exactly how scores were computed or groups were compared with each other. In commenting on this study Schooler says that no significant birth-order effects were found for these dependent variables, and

> this lack of findings is, in fact, a record of sorts, since, given the large number of cases and the relative discriminatory power of the dependent variables, nearly all other analyses with this body of data have produced some pattern of significant results regardless of whether the independent variables represented occupational conditions, background factors, or even aspects of family structure such as family size, intactness of family, and having a mother who worked. [P. 170]

In other words, birth order was not an independent variable for these self-concept dependent variables. And, in a related issue, Schooler (1972) comments that "analysis of the responses of 1,516 men in the sample who had children between 3 and 15 years of age also failed to reveal any differences related to birth rank of the child in child-rearing values or in the reported display of affection or anger" (p. 171).

These null findings agree with those reported by Bachman (1970), whose large multivariate study of 2,213 tenth-grade boys is mentioned above, and with Rosenberg's (1965) survey of 5,024 New York State high school students, using the Rosenberg Self-Esteem Scale (RSE).

In discussing his own results and the results of many other studies concerning the influence of birth order, Schooler (1972) raises the question as to why birth-order analysis has had such a fascination for researchers "given the pitifully few replicable findings that have emerged from this relatively large body of research" over the past 30 years. He suggests that this may have been because birth order has been considered to be a seemingly simple independent variable, when, in fact, it is not. He concludes by suggesting that "in order to be fruitful the study of birth-order necessitates dealing with the complexities of such variables as the sex of siblings and family density, or of collecting data on hard-to-define control groups" (p. 174).

Bachman (1970) included family size in his study of tenth-grade boys mentioned above, which Schooler did not. Bachman reports "We did find, as did Rosenberg (1965), a tendency for *only* children to be slightly higher than others in self-esteem. Once we adjust for [socioeconomic level] through [Multiple Classification Analysis] this is the only difference in self-esteem that relates to family size, and it amounts to only one-tenth of a standard deviation" (p. 126). And Rosenberg (1965) comments as follows:

> If we simply look at the child's birth order in the family, we find little association with self-esteem. What does make a difference is whether the subject has *any* brothers or sisters. Only children, we find, tend to have higher self-esteem than others. . . . It is interesting to note, however, that it is the male only children, rather than the female only children who are especially likely to have high self-esteem . . . and it is the Jewish only boys who have conspicuously high self-esteem. [Pp. 107–109]

The effect of other family variables in addition to broken homes, birth order, and family size have been studied—less objective variables such as parental interest, warmth, concern, and control, to name a few. In his 1967 report, *The Antecedents of Self-Esteem,* Coopersmith devotes five chapters to discussing his research concerning the relationship between a number of parent characteristics and the self-esteem of a group of boys aged 10-12. These boys, all from middle-class, urban, intact families and free from personality disturbances were subjects in an extensive study of self-esteem which involved gathering data from a number of sources. Based on a belief in the importance of emphasizing the positive, constructive aspects of personality, this study attempted to identify those variables within the child's family which were associated with feelings of high and low self-esteem. Assessment measures were used with both the boys and their mothers. An interview of approximately 2 hours was conducted with each of the 82 mothers who participated in this part of the study. The questions covered 6 areas of information concerning the family: (a) social background and history, (b) pregnancy and infancy, (c) developmental history of the child, (d) current parent-child relationships, (e) parent's appraisal of the child, and (f) interviewer's appraisal of the mother. In all there were 182 questions, 116 asking for straightforward information and 66 open-ended questions (Coopersmith, 1967, Appendix D, "Mother's Interview," pp. 274-279). In addition, the mothers completed a questionnaire of 80 items taken from the Parent Attitude Research Instrument (PARI) (E. S. Schaefer and Bell, 1958) (Coopersmith, 1967, Appendix C, "Mother's Questionnaire," pp. 269-273). This scale consists of 14 subscales grouped under 3 headings: (a) Democracy-Domination, (b) Acceptance-Rejection, and (c) Indulgence-Autonomy. Each item is in the form of a statement with which the mother indicates she agrees or disagrees, e.g., "Children should be allowed to disagree with their parents if they feel their own ideas are better."

Information from the child came from his responses to the Rosenberg Self-Image Questionnaire (Rosenberg, 1965) and from the Thematic Apperception Test (TAT). Thus, information on parent-child interactions was obtained from both the mother and the child, and this included information concerning the father's attitudes and behaviors also since the father was not contacted directly.

To measure the child's self-esteem from the perspective of the subject, a specially constructed 50-item self-esteem inventory, the Coopersmith Self-Esteem Inventory (SEI) was used (Coopersmith, 1967, Appendix A, "Self-Esteem Inventory," pp. 265-266). For each item the child was asked to check whether it was "Like Me" or "Unlike Me." Sample items are: "I'm proud of my schoolwork," and "Most people are better liked than I am." (For a critical discussion of this inventory see Wylie, 1974, pp. 171-174.)

For another measure of the child's self-esteem, teachers were asked to rate each child on a 13-item 5-point scale of behaviors, the Behavior Rating Form (BRF), e.g., "To what extent does this child show a sense of self-esteem, self-respect, and appreciation of his own worthiness?" (Coopersmith, 1967, Appendix B, "Behavior Rating Form" [BRF], pp. 267–268).

On the basis of data from the SEI, the boys were put into three groups (high, medium, and low self-esteem) and relationships were explored statistically between the degree of the boy's self-esteem and a number of parent-child attitudinal and behavioral variables. (The relationship between the child's self-esteem and many other variables such as physical attractiveness and family income were also explored but they will not be discussed here.)

Statistical results dealing with the relationship between self-esteem and some 58 family variables are presented in tables, expressed as percentages of responses characteristic of parents of high, medium, and low self-esteem boys, and are expressed in terms of whether the differences among the 3 groups of parents were or were not statistically significant. Few of these family variables can be termed objective in the sense that father-absence and birth order were objective in the previously discussed studies. Examples of objective variables in Coopersmith's study are such things as mother working outside the home (p. 92, not significant) and the number of nonparents in the home (p. 102, significant). But the majority of the significance tests are based on statements made by the mother concerning, for example, her acceptance of the mother role (p. 107, not significant) or her ideas concerning the child's right to privacy (p. 228, significant). These are obviously subjective reports, and this makes the Coopersmith study more a study of perceptions by and of the parent for self and child than a study of more objective factors influencing the child's self-esteem.

Of the 58 family variables in this study, 38 are significant at the $\leq$ .05 level, 13 are not significant, and significance or nonsignificance is not reported for the remaining 7 variables. In summing up his results, Coopersmith says, "The most general statement about the antecedents of self-esteem can be given in terms of three conditions: total or nearly total *acceptance* of the children by their parents, clearly defined and enforced *limits,* and the *respect* and latitude for individual action that exist within the defined limits" (p. 236).

But generalizations tell only part of the story, as Coopersmith points out in his summary. Looking at the details of the statistical data, a somewhat more complicated picture of the situation emerges. Consider, for example, the fact that about 12% of the mothers of the high self-esteem group did not enforce limits consistently and with care and that, on the other hand, 60% of the mothers of the low self-esteem group *did* enforce limits (table 10.3, p. 186, significant). These figures and others would suggest, says Coopersmith, that self-esteem is the result of no one single parent variable, but a combination of positive conditions together with a "minimum of devaluating conditions" — the whole forming a pattern (p. 240).

In spite of the fact that the Coopersmith study is so extensive in time and effort, there are some outstanding problems with it. For example, the sample is very small for such an extended statistical analysis and description of its characteristics is limited. Then there is the matter of measuring instruments. Regarding the use of the SEI, Wylie (1974) states that "the state of development of this inventory and the amount of available information about it do not make it an instrument of choice for self-concept research on child subjects" (p. 174). And W. Becker and Krug (1965) in their review of research in which the Parent Attitude Research Instrument has been used comment that "the bulk of the evidence suggests that the PARI does not predict much very well" (p. 229).

One glaring omission in this study is any information gathered from the fathers of these boys, and another is the absence of any observation of parent-child interaction. All information about the father's attitudes and behaviors comes indirectly from statements made by either the mother or the son — a decided limitation.

Another complicating factor is the matter of the grouping of the boys. Originally there were 5 groups with 17 boys in each, set up using the combined scores from the SEI and the BRF as follows: High-High, Medium-Medium, Low-Low, High-Low, and Low-High (p. 12). (The rationale for combining scaled scores from a subjective measure of self-esteem with scaled scores from a behavioral measure of self-esteem appears dubious to the writer.) But, in reporting results in the 58 tables involving family variables, the 5-fold classification is used in only 4 of the tables, whereas in the other 54 tables, percent of responses is given for 3 groups only, and the general heading of the groups is "Subjective Self-Esteem." No reason for this shift from 5 groups to 3 groups is given (High-Medium-Low), nor is a restatement made concerning the number of boys in each of the 3 groups.

Another problem for the reader is the matter of trying to evaluate such a large number of significance tests based on data gathered from several different sources. In fact, the total number of significance tests made is never specified in the text at all. In the 58 tables, data are used from the subject interview, the subject questionnaire, the mother interview, the mother questionnaire, the interviewer report, and the TAT.

Then there is the problem of generalizations in the text which do not always agree with figures in the tables. Consider, for example, the statement in which Coopersmith describes the parents of low-esteem children by saying that "they rely upon harsh treatment to exercise control over their children" (p. 215). But, when we consult table 10.5 (p. 192) titled "Type of Control Generally Employed by Mother When Rules Are Violated," we find that the difference among the parents of the three groups of boys is not statistically significant.

All in all, the Coopersmith study is a difficult one to follow systematically or to analyze critically. It is such a potpourri of subjective variables and behavioral variables, full of such confusing and conflicting statements, that the reader will find it practically impossible to assess. To my knowledge no attempt has been made to repeat the Coopersmith study in recent years.

In this section we have taken a look at some studies which have attempted to investigate the influence on self-conceptions of such objective family variables as father-absence in the home, birth order, and family size, as well as such subjective family variables as parental interest, rapport, and permissiveness. We have looked critically at some of the measuring instruments used and have considered some serious flaws in the experimental design of these studies.

3. List of Additional Studies Not Substantively Summarized

Readers who wish to examine additional studies in this general area of family variables and self-conceptions are referred to the following. Many of these studies also suffer from the same methodological limitations which were discussed in section B-3 above. (Studies critically discussed in the 1961 edition of this book are also included in the lists below.) Concerning the relation between self-concept and the perceptions of parents and children of self and each other: Bieri and Ratzeburg (1953); Bieri and Lobeck (1961); Bieri, Lobeck, and Galinsky (1959); Carlson (1963); Davids and Lawton (1961); Donnenwerth, Teichman, and Foa (1973); Gecas, Calonico, and Thomas (1974); Havighurst, Robinson, and Dorr (1946); Helper (1955, 1958);

350 THE SELF-CONCEPT

Hollander and Marcia (1970); Hollender (1973); Jourard (1957); Jourard and Remy (1955); Kagan (1956); Kagan, Hosken, and Watson (1961); Kagan and Lemkin (1960); Kreiger and Worchel (1960); Lazowick (1955); Levitt (1959); Long and Henderson (1968); Manis (1958); Medinnus and Curtis (1963); D. E. Payne and Mussen (1956); Porter and Stacey (1956); Rosenberg (1963, 1965); Sears (1970); Serot and Teevan (1961); Tarwater (1955).

Concerning the relation between self-concept and objective family variables: Baruch (1973); Biller and Bahm (1971); Eisenman (1970); Farley (1968); Gecas (1971, 1972); Hetherington (1972); J. M. Kelly (1970); Rosenberg (1963, 1965); Rosenberg and Simmons (1972).

An additional group of studies in these two general areas which appear to the writer to be even more flawed than those mentioned above are listed as follows: Bigner (1971); Block (1958); Brooks and Hillman (1965); Cass (1952a, 1952b); Chang and Block (1960); Couch (1962); David (1968); Davids (1973); Dien (1964); Diener (1972); Felker (1968); Felker and Kay (1971); Gartner and Goldstein (1973); S. W. Gray (1959); Gunderson and Johnson (1965); Henry (1956); Kaplan (1970, 1975b, 1976); Kaplan and Pokorny (1971); Kauffman (1971); Koenig (1969); Langford and Alm (1954); Maskin and Flescher (1975); T. W. Miller (1971); Pedersen and Stanford (1969); Teichman (1971, 1972); Voss and Skinner (1975); Ward (1971); Ward and Day (1969); Washburn (1961, 1962); Wechsler and Funkenstein (1960); Wilkinson and Worchel (1959); D. S. Wright (1962); B. Wright and Tuska (1966).

D. SUMMARY AND CONCLUSIONS

Our discussion began with the commonly accepted premise in the psychological literature that family variables play an important role in the development of a child's self-concept. It has been assumed that children develop their ideas and feelings about themselves, in part, as a result of identifying with their parents and learning from them through rewards and punishments.

We have considered the confusion that exists in the literature concerning the definition of the term identification and the difficulty, therefore, in translating the idea into an operational definition which can be explored empirically.

A number of limitations in self-concept research in this area were pointed out — problems with experimental design and with measuring instruments. A survey of the literature has shown that, at present, it appears difficult if not impossible to design empirical studies which can establish clearly an antecedent-consequent relationship between family variables and the child's self-concept. And so, contemporary research is still involved in exploring a relatively limited number of R-R relationships, and, on occasion inferring (perhaps erroneously) cause-and-effect relationships from them.

We have considered several studies which were directed toward assessing the similarity between the child's perception of himself and of his parents as compared to his parent's perception of him, and several studies of objective family variables postulated as being influential in the development of the child's self-concept.

There is some limited evidence from these studies that a child's level of self-regard may be associated with the parent's reported level of regard for him and that parental interest and rapport are associated with the child's level of self-regard. The evidence is stronger for an association between the child's perception of himself and his perception of the parent's attitudes toward him. There is some evidence that parents of normal children tend to perceive their children more positively than do parents of emotionally disturbed children and that delinquents believe themselves to be less accurately perceived by their parents and less similar to them than do nondelinquents. There is no evidence here that birth order, per se, is an important determiner of a child's self-concept, or that father-absence in the home lowers a child's self-esteem. There is more evidence of a relationship between family size and a child's self-esteem and of the likelihood that the self-esteem of the male only child will be especially high.

When we consider how much lip service has been paid in the literature over many years to the idea that family variables are important determiners of a child's self-concept, it is remarkable how few extant studies there are, and what a host of questions remains to be answered, or even raised.

One apparent lack in self-concept research in this area is any attempt to conceptualize broadly a model of relationships of the variables involved as has been done in some areas of child-rearing, e.g., E. S. Schaefer's (1959) circumplex model of parental behaviors or Baumrind's (1971) model of seven axes of parental authority. Such a proposed model would make it possible, perhaps, to formulate more clearly the rationale concerning the psychologically relevant variables in identification and self-concept development and could serve as a focal point from which empirical research might be designed.

The present state of research in the area of relationships between family variables and the development of the child's self-concept suggests a need for this sort of conceptualization as a basis for experimental design, as well as a need for a careful reexamination and/or modification of extant measuring devices and a more considered treatment of data gathered as a result of their use.

7

Achievement, Ability and Creativity Indices as Related to Self-Concept Variables

A. Achievement and Ability Scores and Self-Concept Variables

1. General Theoretical and Methodological Considerations

Basically this section deals with four classes of variables: measures of abilities or aptitudes; measures of achievement or accomplishment; measures of over-all self-regard; and measures of self-evaluation along specific dimensions, especially those which are possibly relevant to ability and/or achievement.

a. Relationships of Achievement and Ability Indices to Self-Concept Variables

Many persons, especially educators, have unhesitatingly assumed that achievement and/or ability indices will be strongly related to self-conceptions of achievement and ability and to over-all self-regard as well.

It does seem intuitively plausible that variations in success in scholastic activities could lead to variations in approval or disapproval from significant others, thereby yielding variations in over-all self-regard; that academic success could increase the sense of self-potency, which should promote self-regard, while failure could have the opposite effect; and that the degree of success could lead the subject to envisage attainment of more or less prestigious vocational goals, with correlated effects on over-all self-regard.

Conversely, over-all self-regard might influence achievement in several kinds of ways, leading to positive associations between achievement scores and self-regard scores. According to McCandless (1967), "It can be predicted that poor self-concepts, implying as they so often do a lack of confidence in facing and mastering the environment, will accompany deficiency in one of the most vital of the child's areas of accomplishment—his performance in school" (p. 270). Moreover, since we know that low over-all self-regard is associated with anxiety and depression, perhaps the latter emotions might impair concentration, or lower the willingness to put in the effort needed for achievement. Alternately, according to consistency theories such as Rogers's, low self-evaluation should lead a person to act in such a way as to maintain

---

Susan S. Cowles drafted evaluative summaries of a substantial number of the studies considered in this chapter.

congruence between self-concept and environmental feedback, even if this entails failing as a way to maintain congruence between objective behavior and a poor level of self-evaluation.

So far as IQ is concerned, it may seem obvious that subjects having differing ability levels will differentially experience success in school, on the job, and in similar activities; they will have differential potential for learning to behave in ways which lead to the approval of significant others whose evaluations affect their self-regard; and they will vary concerning the sense of self-potency which should affect self-regard.

However, the situation is much more complex, both theoretically and methodologically than is typically assumed. In developing an understanding of some of the possible complexities, it is helpful to envisage a hypothetical chain of events connecting ability and achievement indices to self-concept indices.

First, if achievement and/or ability indices and self-concept scores are to be highly related empirically, it seems plausible that individuals must become aware of their achievement and ability levels as manifested in these indices. Self-conceived achievement and ability levels may then play some part in determining over-all self-regard levels.

But at the first step, both awareness and evaluation of achievement and ability levels may be distorted, naïvely and/or defensively. Although the achievement and ability scores or performance indices in a given piece of research usually come from a heterogeneous group, an individual may see and evaluate his own grades, comments, and test scores mainly in terms of more limited reference groups, e.g., the special class, the subculture, or the gang. The reference groups may simply be those which happen to be available, or they may be chosen by the individual. Insofar as the reference group is relatively homogeneously low on achievement and ability indices, the person whose standing in a heterogeneous group is low may consider his abilities and achievements to be near or above the average as compared to this more limited reference group. Insofar as the reference group is relatively homogeneously high on ability and achievement indices (e.g., upper track classes, elite college groups, friendship groups among children of professional persons), the individual whose standing in a heterogeneous group is high may see his abilities and achievement as not especially good in comparison to this more homogeneously high reference group. Thus, self-estimates of ability and achievement may correlate quite imperfectly with IQs and GPAs drawn from a heterogeneous group, the range of which may be unrecognized or considered irrelevant by the respondents when stating their own self-estimates of achievement or ability.

It seems plausible that self-estimates of ability are even harder to ground in firm evidence than is the case with self-conceptions of achievement. There is comparatively little opportunity for most persons to become acquainted with their ability scores per se, or with other relatively direct indicators of their ability (their "potential"). Consequently, their estimates of their *ability* levels in relationship to others must, to a large extent, come indirectly from such *achievement* indices as grades, teachers' comments on work, acceptance into various levels of schooling, and, perhaps, from occasional feedback from standardized achievement tests. This necessary reliance on indirect evidence of one's ability could play a part in lowering the accuracy of one's self-conceptions of ability; this inaccuracy could, in turn, influence the level of correlation between ability indices and self-conceptions of ability, with achievement held constant.

Not only is it difficult to ground ability estimates in firm evidence, but it seems plausible that over-all self-regard may depend more heavily upon self-conceptions of ability than upon self-conceptions of achievement. This would increase the tendency to distort what indirect evidence there is, if such evidence seems unfavorable. Thus, if achievement indicators are disappointing, they can be reinterpreted as representing insufficient effort or interest, thereby protecting the low achiever's self-conception of ability, and, in turn, protecting his or her self-regard. Alternately, members of culturally disadvantaged groups have the socially sanctioned possibility of explaining poor achievement and/or ability scores as due to their educational deprivation or perhaps to the prejudices of their teachers and testers, as opposed to being indicative of their own ability limitations. The above arguments imply an attenuation of the relationship between ability scores and ability estimates, especially when achievement scores are held constant.

Chapter 12 of this book presents evidence that upward distortion of self-evaluations, especially self-evaluations of ability, are common. If this is true, the range of self-estimates of ability may be considerably truncated at the lower end. This would operate statistically to lower correlations between achievement or ability scores and self-conceptions of ability.

Finally, one must consider possible links between achievement and ability estimates on the one hand and indices of over-all self-regard on the other. As argued above, there are several reasons why self-conceptions of achievement and ability may not correspond well with achievement and ability indices. These are also some of the routes by which the connections between achievement and ability indices and over-all self-regard are necessarily attenuated. Moreover, self-conceptions of achievement and ability are at least potentially determined by a more limited set of relevant input information than is the case with over-all self-regard. From this standpoint alone, one would expect lower *r*s between over-all self-regard and achievement or ability scores than between self-conceptions of achievement and ability and scores from achievement and ability measures.

Additionally, it seems safe to assume that persons work hard to preserve and enhance over-all self-regard and that they will emphasize or minimize the salience of various aspects of self-concept as needed to accomplish this. Thus, to the person who is able and achieving and so conceives of himself, these factors may be salient to over-all self-regard, especially if significant others indicate their importance. But the person whose achievements and abilities are manifestly limited may minimize the importance of "grades and brains," especially if these factors are not particularly salient to significant others.

Moreover, parents and educators may specifically encourage limited individuals not to evaluate their over-all personal worth in terms of ability and achievement. Ways of attaining love and approval without being an intellectual star or even ordinarily competent are often compassionately provided. At the other end of the range, very capable persons might set higher goals, experience greater expectations and pressures from teachers and parents, and experience as much or greater failure in relation to the goals they feel that they should be attaining as do persons of lesser abilities who are allowed to strive for lesser attainments.

All these factors imply a very low correlation between IQ scores and indices of over-all self-regard, especially with achievement indices held constant.

In summary, the above arguments suggest the following very tentative predictions which are obviously different from the oversimplified assumptions often stated.

1. Correlations between self-concept indices on the one hand and achievement and ability indices on the other should be ordered in magnitude, as specified below, with even the largest being rather modest in absolute size.

2. When achievement indices are correlated with various self-concept measures (holding ability scores constant), the partial rs with self-conceptions of achievement should be highest, those with self-conceptions of ability next, and those with over-all self-regard lowest (perhaps insignificantly different from zero).

3. When ability indices are correlated with various self-concept measures (holding achievement indices constant), correlations with self-estimated achievement, self-estimated ability, and over-all self-regard should all be quite low, with the latter probably the lowest (quite possibly insignificantly different from zero).

b. Need for Simultaneous (Controlled) Examination of Achievement and Ability Measures in Relationship to Self-Concept Measures

There are several reasons for casting one's predictions in terms of partial rs or alternate statistical analyses which control for one predictor while looking at the contributions made by the other. First, achievement measures are typically correlated with so-called ability scores such as IQs. Hence, if one wishes at the purely empirical level to infer anything about the unique predictive value of one, the other must obviously be controlled. (Sharma [1971] has made this point in his review of some of the studies relating self-acceptance to achievement scores.)

Then there are the conceptual reasons already implied in the arguments preceding the predictions. That is, a correlation between an ability score and a self-concept score could come about by way of some direct information the person is given about his ability scores or others' comments about his ability. Alternately, this correlation might come about indirectly by way of the subjects' knowledge of grades or achievement-test scores which are on the one hand correlated with IQ and on the other interpreted by the subject as to some degree indicative of ability.

In a parallel fashion, a correlation between an achievement index and a self-concept score could come about by way of direct information the person is given about his achievement indices, or by way of others' comments about his achievement. Alternately, such a correlation might come about indirectly through the subject's being told about his ability scores which, on the one hand, are correlated with achievement scores, and on the other hand may be interpreted by the subject as to some degree indicative of achievement.

c. METHODOLOGICAL CRITERIA

In evaluating the methodological adequacy of all the studies, I used a number of criteria in addition to those already mentioned. Of greatest relevance to this chapter are the following:

1. What were the characteristics of the achievement measures? Did the researchers use standard achievement tests for which needed psychometric information is available? If GPAs were used, were there serious limitations (e.g., lack of comparability across classes and/or across schools) adequately taken into account (see Thorndike, 1963)? Was an idiosyncratic achievement test used? Was enough psychometric information provided about the range, reliability, and content of GPAs or idiosyncratic achievement tests to serve as a basis for interpreting outcomes involving them?

2. What were the characteristics of the ability measure? Was sufficient psychometric information provided or available to serve as a basis for interpreting outcomes?

3. Was a standard or idiosyncratic self-concept measure used? If the latter, is sufficient information given about its content and psychometric characteristics to serve as a basis for interpreting reported outcomes?

4. Were multiple significance tests made without regard to the number of significant relationships to be expected by chance? Were reported associations cross-validated?

5. Could response unreliability artifactually account for the reported associations between ability, achievement, and self-concept measures? One should note that poor reading skills, poor attentiveness to directions, and unwillingness to cooperate will affect achievement and ability measures and will also artifactually produce "low self-regard" scores on tests having certain formats, as fully explained elsewhere (Wylie, 1974, pp. 119-121). To the extent that these extraneous variables are influencing each set of correlated scores, the size of the correlation coefficient between self-regard scores and achievement or ability measures will be artifactually inflated, and the rs should not be psychologically interpreted.

6. Was a sufficient range covered and a sufficient number of points on this range represented to allow one to look for curvilinearity in the

relationships between IQ and self-concept variables, or between achievement measures and self-concept variables? If so, were such relationships looked for by use of *etas* or other appropriate techniques? Sharma (1971) has pointed out the need for this methodological precaution in this area of research, since some studies suggest the possibility of curvilinear relationships.

2. Studies of Achievement Measures and Self-Concept Measures (Ability Scores Not Controlled)

a. ACHIEVEMENT MEASURES AND OVER-ALL SELF-REGARD

A number of studies have correlated achievement or accomplishment measures without controlling for IQ or ability-test measures. I have divided these studies according to whether they used grade-point averages or standardized achievement tests as a measure of achievement.

Among the more widely used tests of self-regard, I have found no information relating either of these types of achievement measures to over-all self-regard scores for the California Psychological Inventory (CPI), the California Test of Personality (CTP), Lipsitt's Self-Concept Scale for Children, or the Rosenberg Self-Esteem Scale (RSE).

Grade-Point Averages and Over-all Self-Regard

The correlations between grade-point averages and the tests of over-all self-regard for which information was found are mostly around .30, although about half the examined correlations between idiosyncratic measures of over-all self-regard and GPA examined were insignificant.

Concerning Bills's Index of Adjustment and Values (IAV), Boshier and Hamid (1968) correlated IAV Self, Self-Acceptance, Ideal Self, and [Self — Ideal] discrepancy scores with grades in the final exam of a psychology course. Of these 4, the only correlation which was significant (at the .05 level) was that of Self-Acceptance and grades ($r = -.31$).

Boshier (1972) examined the same IAV scores in a test-retest situation in which experimental subjects were given false information concerning a test grade. In a group of 66 second-year university students, half the subjects were given no feedback concerning an examination grade, whereas the other half were given a low examination grade designed to induce a sense of failure. No test-retest self-esteem differences were found on Self, Self-Acceptance, or Ideal Self within either of the 2 groups except that the failure group showed an unpredicted significant drop in their Self/Ideal-Self discrepancy scores on the retest. Multiple significance testing precludes interpretation.

In Ullman's (1957) study of 162 males and 154 females in the ninth grade, "self" scores on the California Test of Personality were significantly higher for those students who were on the eleventh-grade honor roll than for those not on the eleventh-grade honor roll, and significantly higher for those graduating versus those withdrawing from high school prior to graduation.

Coopersmith's Self-Esteem Inventory (SEI) was found to be related to several different measures of achievement. Coopersmith (1967) reports an $r = .30$, significant at the .05 level, between his SEI score and grade-point average in children aged 10 to 12. T. L. Morrison, Thomas, and Weaver (1973) report an $r = .34$ ($p = .01$) between SEI score and grades on an objective test on material about learning theory. T. L. Morrison and Thomas (1975) report an $r = .26$ ($p = .05$) between SEI score and proportion of thoughts contributed to a class discussion. Correlations ranging from .35 to .45 were found by Trowbridge (1972a) between SEI scores and reading level scores for children within different socioeconomic levels. In a study by J. H. Rosenthal (1973), the mean SEI score of dyslexics, 61.8, differed significantly from that of controls, 75.5. In Kunce, Getsinger, and Miller's (1972) research, scores on a modified 15-item version of the SEI were correlated with GPAs of 247 ninth graders for the first, second, and third academic quarters. The 15 items were chosen on the basis of an item analysis designed to determine which questions differentiate students on measures of social class and welfare status. The correlations between self-concept scores and GPA in the first, second, and third quarters were .20, .15, and .15 respectively. All correlations were significant. (Although zero-order rs are also reported between self-esteem and IQ, no partial rs are given.) However, in a study by C. W. Perkins and Shannon (1965) with 78 sixth-grade boys, no significant correlation was obtained between self-concept as measured by a modified version of the SEI and average grades in the third quarter of the current school year. This lack of agreement with the results from the other studies relating SEI scores to grades of various types may be a function of the modification of the total number of items and the response categories for the SEI in this particular study.

Felker and Stanwyck's (1971) investigation involving *PH* scores and a 10-word spelling test seems too limited to be relevant.

The relationships between the Self-Social Esteem Scale (SSE) and achievement were examined in the studies reported above by Morrison, Thomas, and Weaver (1973) and Morrison and Thomas (1975). Neither the grades on an objective test on material about learning theory nor the proportion of thoughts contributed to class discussion were found to be significantly related to SSE scores.

Achord and McCary (1975) examined the relationship between the Total Positive score from the TSCS and achievement, defined in terms of staying versus withdrawing from a nursing program during the freshman year. Although the statistical procedure used is not given, they report a difference significant at the .05 level. C. R. Smith (1972) found that the difference between the means of blind students who either dropped out of school during their freshman year in college or persisted in their school work was significant for 13 out of 29 TSCS scales. However, the Total Positive score did not differentiate significantly between the groups. In any case, the results from this study are uninterpretable due to the multiple significance tests with overlapping scales and the lack of cross-validation. Hughes's (1968) study involving the TSCS gives too little information to sustain interpretation.

(Of the well-known tests mentioned above, the IAV, SEI, and SSE are reviewed and evaluated in Wylie [1974].)

Among 10 studies involving various idiosyncratic measures of self-regard, 3 (Fiedler, Dodge, Jones, & Hutchins, 1958; Jervis, 1959; and A. Soares & L. Soares, 1971) found no significant relationship between their over-all self-regard measures and grades. Among their 1,917 black and white subjects in Grades 3 through 12 in the Baltimore, Maryland, public schools, Rosenberg and Simmons (1972) found a strong association between marks in school and scores on their idiosyncratic self-esteem scale about which some psychometric information is presented. The authors state that "while grades make a difference for the self-esteem of children of both races, it seems to make less difference in the case of blacks" (p. 92). In a study involving an idiosyncratic measure of self-regard known as the "Class Play," Cotler and Palmer (1970) found significant correlations between the percentage of negative self-selections by girls in Grades 4–6 and their teachers' ratings of their achievement in reading and arithmetic. The correlations obtained for teachers' rating of achievement in reading and percentage of negative self-selections was −.38, while that for teachers' ratings of achievement in arithmetic and percentage of negative self-selections was −.35.

Although both of these correlations were significant at the .01 level for the girls, no significant correlations were obtained for the boys in the same grades. In a representative national sample of 2,213 tenth-grade boys attending United States public high schools in 1966, Bachman (1970) found a significant correlation of .23 between an idiosyncratic self-esteem score based on Rosenberg's Self-Esteem Scale and self-reported grades for the ninth grade. In a 1974 follow-up of 1,608 of these subjects, the previously self-reported ninth-grade marks correlated .10 with 1974 self-esteem scores (Bachman and O'Malley, 1977).

Boshier (1973), in his study of 2,436 participants in an adult education program in New Zealand, used an idiosyncratic scale to examine the 4 concepts Myself, Myself-As-I-Would-Like-To-Be, Other Adult Education Students, and My Adult Education Lecturer. He then compared discrepancies between Myself and each of the other 3 concepts to persisting versus dropping out of the program and found that large self/other discrepancy scores are correlated with dropping out. Multiple significance testing involving discrepancy scores, each based on the self component, preclude interpretability, however. In Gill and D'Oyley's (1970) investigation involving 1,424 ninth-grade students in 5 Toronto high schools, correlations of .42 for boys and .35 for girls were obtained between scores on an idiosyncratic perceived-self scale and final average marks, but correlations of only .25 for boys and .19 for girls were obtained between the ideal-self scale of the same test and final average marks. The two sets of zero-order rs cannot, of course, be independently interpreted owing to probable correlations between perceived self and ideal-self scores.

In a study by R. Rubin, reported by Curtis (1963-67), black and Puerto Rican elementary-school students were classified as high achievers if their reading level was near or above grade level and they were in the highest ranking fourth-grade class; they were classified as low achievers if their reading level was one and a half years or more below grade level. She found that high and low achievers did not differ in their self-concepts as measured by an apparently idiosyncratic scale. However, low achievers had significantly higher total ideal-self scores as measured by the same scale.

Standardized Achievement Measures and Over-all Self-Regard

There is not much information available on the relationship between well-known tests of self-regard and standardized tests of achievement, with ability levels uncontrolled. The only tests for which I found any such information are the 24 scales of the Adjective Check List (ACL), Coopersmith's Self-Esteem Inventory (SEI), the Piers-Harris Children's Self-Concept Scale, and the Tennessee Self-Concept Scale (TSCS). The correlations between standardized achievement tests and these tests of over-all self-regard as well as some idiosyncratic tests of over-all self-regard tend to range from approximately .10 to .50.

In an examination of the relationship between the 24 ACL scales and speed and comprehension on a Reading Versatility Test, Brunkan and Shen (1966) found 9 of the 24 ACL scales to be significantly related to the reading test scores in an analysis of variance. However, the self-acceptance scales (Fav, Unfav) were not among these 9. These results are not really interpretable at any rate due to multiple significance tests and lack of cross-validation.

The manual for the Piers-Harris test (Piers, 1969) includes correlations between an 80-item version of the test and an unspecified achievement test for boys and girls in Grades 4 and 6. All of the correlations were significant, ranging from .32 to .43, except the correlation for Grade 6 girls, which was only .06. A study by Piers and Harris (1964) also obtained significant correlations of .19 and .32 between a 95-item version of the Piers-Harris and an unspecified achievement test for children in Grades 3 and 6 respectively.

Concerning the SEI, Coopersmith (1959) reported a correlation of .36 between SEI scores and the Iowa Achievement Test and a correlation of .30 between SEI scores and Iowa Achievement Tests with sociometric choice partialled out. Both correlations are significant at the .01 level. Simon and Simon (1975) obtained a significant correlation of .33 between SEI scores and scores on the Science Research Associates (SRA) Achievement Series for boys and girls in the fifth grade. Significant correlations of .30 and .42 were also reported by J. Lewis and Adank (1975) between the SEI and a composite of raw scores from the Stanford Achievement Test in fourth, fifth, and sixth graders who were enrolled in classrooms with an individualized instructor's program and a self-contained program respectively. A study done by Trowbridge (1972a) obtained correlations between the SEI and the Iowa Tests of Basic Skills ranging from .35 to .45 for children within different socioeconomic levels. Trowbridge (1972b) correlated SEI scores and the most current reading test scores of children in target area and nontarget area classrooms. The target area classrooms were composed of disadvantaged, low socioeconomic level children. She found a significant correlation within the target area classrooms of .33 and a significant correlation within the nontarget area classrooms of .38. However, when the data from both types of classrooms were combined, a nonsignificant correlation of .08 was obtained. Therefore SEI self-concept and reading test scores were correlated only within each socioeconomic level in this study.

However, in the study of Perkins and Shannon (1965), discussed earlier, no significant correlation was obtained between self-concept, as measured by a modified version of the SEI, and median achievement scores on the Metropolitan Achievement Test for a group of 78 sixth-grade boys from middle-class socioeconomic backgrounds. This lack of agreement with results from other studies relating SEI scores to scores on standardized achievement measures may be a function, however, of the modification of the total number of items as well as the response categories for the SEI in this particular study.

Total Positive scores on the Tennessee Self-Concept Scale (TSCS) were correlated with scores on the reading and arithmetic sections of the California Achievement Test battery, in a study by R. L. Williams and Cole (1968). In a sample of 80 sixth graders, significant correlations (.31 and .33) were obtained.

Some information on the relationship between scores on the TSCS and standardized tests of achievement is also given in the study by Hughes (1968), mentioned above. However, as indicated there, too few details are reported to permit interpretation.

(The ACL, PH, SEI, and TSCS are reviewed and evaluated in Wylie [1974].)

The majority of the studies examining the relationship between over-all self-regard and standardized tests of achievement used idiosyncratic measures of self-regard. The researches which fall into this category include Bennett, Sorensen, and Forshay (1971); Bledsoe (1964); Caplin (1968, 1969); Chotin as reported by Curtis (1963-67); Cotler and Palmer (1970); Deo and Sharma (1970); Fein, O'Neill, C. Frank, and Velit (1975); Greenberg, Gerver, Chall, and Davidson (1965); Greenberger, Campbell, Sorensen, and O'Connor (1971); Greene and Zirkel (1971); Guggenheim (1969); Henton and Johnson (1964); Hishiki (1969); Lekarczyk and Hill (1969); Perkins (1958b); Rosenblatt reported in Curtis (1963-67); Sears (1970); Wapnick reported by Curtis (1963-67); Wattenberg and Clifford (1964); and Yellott, Liem, and Cowen (1969). The standardized tests used in these studies included the California Achievement Test, the Inter-American Test of General

Abilities, the Iowa Tests of Basic Skills, the Level of Previous Learning Test, the Metropolitan Reading Achievement Test, the N.Y.S. Pupil Evaluation Program, the Punjab University Higher Secondary Exam, the SRA Achievement Series, and the Stanford Achievement Test. Although many of the correlations between these achievement measures and the idiosyncratic self-regard measures are significant, insufficient information about these idiosyncratic self-regard measures used and other methodological flaws preclude interpretation of these data.

b. ACHIEVEMENT MEASURES AND SPECIFIC ASPECTS OF SELF-CONCEPT

Grade-Point Averages (GPA)

A number of studies looked at the relationship between specific aspects of self-concept and achievement as measured by grade-point average (GPA). As might be expected, self-concept of ability correlates more highly with grade-point average than does over-all self-regard.

Concepts of Schoolwork Ability. In his 1965 investigation of New York State high school students (fully discussed at other points in this book), Rosenberg found that good grades were closely related to the students' reports of being "a good student in school," but only slightly related to self-descriptions of being "clear-thinking and clever" or "imaginative and original." Brookover, LePere, Hamachek, Thomas, and Erickson (1965) found correlations between GPA and self-concept of ability ranging from .56 to .65 in a study of seventh to tenth graders. In a longitudinal study of boys and girls in the seventh through the tenth grade in which general self-concept of ability and self-concept of ability in mathematics, English, social studies, and science were compared to grades in each subject area respectively, correlations between self-concepts of abilities and grades ranged from .30 to .60. In research by J. G. Anderson and Johnson (1971) involving 114 Mexican-American and 49 Anglo junior and senior high school students, self-concept of ability scores were used to predict students' most recent semester grades in English and mathematics. In a stepwise multiple linear regression analysis with self-concept of ability and 7 home background factors, as the independent variables, the *beta* coefficients for self-concept of ability were .3097 for English and .3059 for mathematics. Self-concept of ability was found to be the most significant of the 8 predictors. Joiner, Erickson, Crittenden, and Stevenson (1969) obtained correlations in 3 different schools between general self-concept of ability and GPAs. The correlations obtained were .51 in an Indiana school for the deaf, .32 in a Michigan school for the deaf, and .53 in a public school group. From their survey mentioned in the immediately preceding section, Rosenberg and Simmons (1972) conclude, "Whether he be black or white, the child's grades in school turn out to be closely related to 'how smart' he thinks he is . . . but the relationship among blacks, while strong (*gamma* = 0.3609), is still weaker than among whites (*gamma* = 0.7134)" (p. 93).

In the study by Richmond and Dalton (1973) ANOVAs for educable mentally retarded students rated by their teachers as high or low in academic proficiency are given for the 4 subdivisions of the SEI. ANOVAs for school self-concept, as well as for general and home self-concept were significant. The ANOVA for social self-concept was not significant. However, since the significance tests involved some scores based on overlapping items, they must be regarded with caution. Morrison and Thomas (1975) obtained a significant correlation of .40 between the school self-esteem subset of the Coopersmith SEI items and the proportion of thoughts contributed by college students in class discussion. Morrison, Thomas, and Weaver (1973) obtained a significant correlation of .38 between the same school self-esteem subset and grades on an objective test about learning theory.

In Bachman's (1970) study of 2,213 tenth-grade boys reported above, a significant correlation of .48 was obtained between self-concept of schoolwork ability and self-reported grades.

A. Soares and L. Soares (1971) compared students' self-concepts of what grades in English and science they thought they would get at the end of the semester with the actual grades they received and found a significant correlation of .48 between self-concept of grade in English and actual grade in English, but no significant correlation between self-concept of grade in science and actual grade in science. In the study by R. Rubin (in Curtis, 1963–67) discussed previously, no significant difference was found between high and low achievers in reading on the school-related self-concept from the scale "How I Feel About Myself."

Finally, an examination by Start (1963) of the relationship between self-estimates and group-estimates of success on first-year university examinations is uninterpretable because of the artifact introduced by using discrepancy scores; whereas Roth's (1959) work, involving an idiosyncratic measure of "self as a student" and Frease's (1972) report, based on an idiosyncratic measure of academic self-concept, are uninterpretable, owing to many flaws and gaps in the published information.

Specific Aspects of Self-Concept Other Than Self-Concepts of Schoolwork Ability. Davidson and Lang (1960) found a significant positive relationship between academic achievement and children's perceptions of their teachers' feelings toward them in 203 fourth, fifth, and sixth graders. Children who were rated by their teachers as having high academic achievement had a favorable perception of their teachers' feelings toward them.

In the study by Achord and McCary (1975) reported above, a significant difference on the Self-Satisfaction scale of the TSCS was found between nursing students who withdrew from the program and those who continued. However, there was no significant difference between the two groups of nursing students on the Identity Self-Concept scale of the TSCS. The interpretation of these results is limited, however, by the overlapping of these specific TSCS scales with each other as well as with the Total Positive TSCS scale.

In the study reported above by C. R. Smith (1972), blind students who dropped out of school during their freshman year in college were compared to those who persisted in their schoolwork on an idiosyncratic semantic differential scale with concepts of special significance to the blind. The bipolar adjectives used to describe the concepts were taken from Osgood, Suci, and Tannenbaum (1957). The differences between the means of persisting and nonpersisting students was significant for the potency dimension, but not for the activity or evaluative dimensions. Smith also found a significant difference between the two groups on the self-criticism score of the TSCS, although this finding is really uninterpretable because of the multiple significance tests performed on overlapping scales.

A. S. Waterman and C. K. Waterman (1972) found a significant difference between the grade-point averages of students withdrawing from college who upon entering college were in different stages of identity status, according to Marcia's ego-identity status questionnaire. Students who had entered college in the achiever status and later withdrew had significantly higher grades than those who entered in the foreclosure or diffusion status and then withdrew. The grades of those who persisted in college and who were in different stages of identity upon entering did not differ significantly.

No significant difference was found by Gustav (1962) between

370   THE SELF-CONCEPT

superior, average, and failing college students in the total number of responses, the number of "academic" responses, the rank of the first "academic" response, or the content of "academic" responses on the Twenty Sentences Test (TST). (See Wylie, 1974, pp. 240–247, for a criticism of this test.)

Among seventh graders, Paschal (1968) examined the relationship between grade-point average based on grades in English, geography, mathematics, and science for the first 6 weeks of a grading period and responses on the Spivack Response Form, a test measuring self-acceptance and self-rejection. Significant chi square values were obtained for relationships between over-all GPA and scores on the Spivack test, and between GPA in English, geography, and science and Spivack responses. The relationship between GPA in mathematics and the Spivack test was not significant. However, the use of multiple significance tests involving the same variable and the lack of cross-validation render the results of this study uninterpretable.

In a group of 114 high school seniors in a small rural town, Sims (1952) obtained a correlation of .25 between marks in the senior year and scores on a Social Class Identification scale. The author attributes this low correlation to the unreliability of marks themselves.

In Mehta's (1968) study of the self-concepts of bright high school males in India, all subjects had a score above the 75th percentile on Jolata's Group Test of Mental Ability. Of these subjects, 100 were classified as underachievers, and 192 as achievers on the basis of marks in the previous annual school examination in compulsory subjects. The idiosyncratic self-concept inventory administered to the subjects was designed to measure five dimensions. The underachievers differed significantly from the achievers on all 5 dimensions, being more characterized by inadequacy, instability, and withdrawal, and less by positive attitude toward achievement and self-confidence.

Standardized Achievement Measures

Only a few studies were concerned with the relationship between specific aspects of self-concept and achievement as measured by standardized tests. In Caplin's (1969) study reported above, the correlation between the Iowa Tests of Basic Skills and a personal/social quality score from his idiosyncratic self-concept scale was .45, and the correlation between the Iowa test and a school-related items score from the self-concept scale was .58. Both of these correlations are significant.

In the study by Brunkan and Shen (1966) reported above, the Self-Confidence scale of the ACL was found to be significantly related to both speed and comprehension on the Reading Versatility Test at the .05 level. However, multiple significance tests and lack of cross-validation preclude interpretation of their results.

Sears (1970) correlated unspecified reading and arithmetic achievement tests with various measures of specific self-concept. These included the self-satisfaction and comparative rating scales of the Sears Self-Concept Inventory (SCI), a self-criticism scale, a self-aggression scale, and a scale oriented toward hypersensitivity to other people's reactions to the self. Out of 20 correlations reported, only 6 are significant. The use of multiple significance tests without cross-validation precludes interpretation.

Ringness (1961) used an idiosyncratic self-concept scale to assess the self-concept of low, average, and high IQ children of their success in learning in the areas of arithmetic; English, spelling, and writing; and reading. Several other areas of social self-concept were also assessed. Ringness compared these self-estimates of achievement with scores on the California Achievement Test and found that children in all three IQ groups overrated their achievement. However, since discrepancies between self-ratings and external criteria were used as determiners of overrating, the results of this study are uninterpretable.

In Chotin's work (Curtis, 1963-67) cited earlier, scores of socially disadvantaged black fifth graders on the Metropolitan Achievement Test were not significantly related to scores on the Academic and Interpersonal-Social subsections of the Davidson-Greenberg Self-Concept Check List, but the scores of the high achievers were higher on the Personal-Emotional subsection of the self-concept test.

Coleman, Campbell, Hobson, McPartland, Mood, Weinfeld, and York (1966) studied approximately 900,000 pupils in Grades 1, 3, 6, 9, and 12 in United States public schools with roughly half of the subjects being white and half nonwhite. Their achievement test is an unspecified vocabulary test measuring verbal skills, and their idiosyncratic self-concept of ability measure differed from grade to grade. Coleman et al. list the unique contribution for self-concept of ability to the accounted-for variance of verbal skills in regression equations with 8 background variables for Grades 6, 9, and 12 as being .98%, 1.16%, and 2.91% for Negroes and 3.95%, 3.49%, and 5.82% for whites.

The results from a study by Yellott, Liem, and Cowen (1969) in which scores on the Anxiety and Lie scales of the Children's Manifest Anxiety

Scale were correlated with various standardized achievement test scores
and results reported by Joseph and McDonald (1964) in which EPPS
scores and Diagnostic Reading Achievement test scores were correlated
are also uninterpretable because of the poor reporting by the researcher
and numerous serious methodological flaws.

c. Conclusions

A wide variety of achievement measures and self-concept measures
have been correlated in the 78 publications cited in this section. Even
though many of the studies reported significant correlations between
grade-point averages or standardized achievement tests and either over-
all self-regard or specific aspects of self-concept, none of these
correlations is interpretable as indicating either a null or a significant
relationship between achievement and self-concept variables with
measured IQ or other relevant ability held constant. Probably other
variables such as socioeconomic level should also have been controlled
in some of these studies when looking at self-concept of achievement as a
function of achievement tests.

Accounting for variations in obtained rs among studies is not usually
possible since range and type of achievement scores and self-concept
measures varies so much from study to study. The correlations tend to
run higher when self-concept of achievement is involved as contrasted to
correlations between over-all self-regard and achievement measures.
However, the incomparability of the studies requires that this statement
be made very tentatively. Unwillingness or lack of ability to concentrate
may impair achievement test scores or GPAs and also artifactually yield
"low self-regard" scores on certain self-regard measures, as already
mentioned, leading to an unknown amount of spuriousness in some
achievement-test–self-regard correlations.

*3. Studies of Ability Measures and Self-Concept Measures
(Achievement Scores Not Controlled)*

Most of the available correlations involving IQ or other ability scores
come from manuals for self-concept tests or self-report personality tests.
Each manual presents these correlations primarily to give information
relevant to the construct validity, especially the discriminant validity, of
the self-report instrument being described and evaluated in the manual.
Accordingly, the data from manuals cannot be faulted for failing to

present the data necessary to evaluate theoretically interesting relationships between ability and self-concept measures, with achievement controlled. Nevertheless, such correlations do not lend themselves to testing these theoretical points, and this must be kept in mind when examining the rs given below.

a. ABILITY MEASURES AND OVER-ALL SELF-REGARD IN NORMAL
   OR HETEROGENEOUS GROUPS

Correlations obtained with a variety of self-regard measures and a variety of IQ tests or similar kinds of ability tests tend to be rather low, often insignificant.

Among the more widely used tests of self-regard I have found no information relating ability measures to over-all self-regard scores for Bills's Index of Adjustment and Values (IAV) or Rosenberg's Self-Esteem scale (RSE).

Gough and Heilbrun (1965) report 4 correlations involving the Fav and Unfav scales of the Adjective Check List (ACL), the Terman Concept Mastery Test, and Wesman's Personnel Classification Test. The largest and only significant r of the 4 = .20 for the Terman Concept Mastery Test versus the Fav scale. Mason, Adams, and Blood (1968) report nonsignificant rs between a "Verbal Composite Test" and Fav or Unfav scores.

Gough (1957) reports nonsignificant rs = .11 and .12 between Self-Acceptance scores on the California Psychological Inventory and scores from the Terman Concept Mastery Test and the Wesman Personnel Classification Test. Purkey (1966) reported a gifted group to have a significantly higher Self-Acceptance score than an average group, but the Terman Concept Mastery Test was used to define "gifted" while the School and College Ability Tests (SCAT) was used to define "average."

C. L. Mayer (1966), comparing normal and educable mentally retarded groups, reported an insignificant difference in self-esteem as measured by Lipsitt's Self-Concept Scale for Children.

Richards and McCandless (1972) correlated verbal facility with SSE scores from Long, Henderson, and Ziller's (1970) Children's Self-Social Construct Test in a sample of four- and five-year-olds including 220 black and white kindergarten children and 120 black and white prekindergarten children, all of whom were disadvantaged in terms of family income. In a factor analysis of 43 variables, a factor "verbal facility" emerged; high self-esteem loaded .29 on this factor.

Concerning the Piers-Harris Self-Concept Scale for Children (PH), Piers (1969) and Piers and Harris (1964) give 11 correlations involving either the Otis, WISC, California Test of Mental Maturity (CTMM), or unspecified IQ tests. Of these 11 correlations, 4 are significant ≤ .05 level. The range of the 4 significant rs is from .25 for the unspecified IQ test to .48 for CTMM for Grades 6-9.

More correlations are available for the Coopersmith Self-Esteem Inventory (SEI) than for any other self-regard test. In large scale studies in which correlations were computed for numerous subgroups (Trowbridge, 1970, 1972b), rs ranged from .10 to .15, with an over-all r = .136 reported in the first study (1970) and an over-all r = .146 in the other (1972b). All these rs involved the Lorge-Thorndike Intelligence Test. Trowbridge (1974) presented SEI means according to IQ deciles and found that subjects in both the top 2 and bottom 2 deciles had significantly lower self-esteem scores than the average for the entire group. This tendency toward curvilinearity may explain why the Pearson rs for this test tend to run low. In two different groups, J. Lewis and Adank (1975) obtained significant rs = .24 and .34 between SRA Tests of General Ability and SEI self-esteem scores. Simon and Simon (1975) found significant rs = .30 and .23 between SEI scores and Lorge-Thorndike verbal and nonverbal IQs. Coopersmith (1967) reports a significant r = .28 between WISC IQs and SEI scores. Richmond and Dalton (1973) report an F value significant at the .01 level in a one-way analysis of variance for educable mentally retarded subjects given the SEI and rated by their teachers as either high or low on academic ability. However, the ability measure they used actually implied proficiency or achievement in academics more than academic ability.

Contrary to most of the findings above, Perkins and Shannon (1965) obtained no significant correlation between scores on a modified version of the SEI and IQ for a group of 78 sixth-grade boys in the study discussed earlier. However, this lack of agreement may be a result of the modification of the total number of items and the response categories for the SEI in this study as well as the use of school records containing the results of apparently different group-administered IQ tests given over a 2-1/2-year period prior to the research.

No information is given in the manual (Fitts, 1965) for the Tennessee Self-Concept Scale (TSCS) regarding relationships between Total Positive scores and ability scores. Collins, Burger, and Doherty (1970) report no significant differences between Total Positive mean scores of retarded and nonretarded adolescents. Hughes (1968) reports a correlation of only .10 between TSCS scores and an unspecified IQ test given to sixth graders. Also using sixth graders (N = 80), Williams and Cole (1968) obtained a significant correlation of .31 between the TSCS Total Positive scores and ability scores from the California Short-Form Test of Mental Maturity.

Mason, Adams, and Blood (1966) compared bright groups of students to normative groups on the Adjective Check List (ACL), California Psychological Inventory (CPI), and the Who Are You? (WAY) test, but the results of their study are uninterpretable due to insufficient published information and serious methodological flaws.

(The ACL, IAV, RSE, SSE, and TSCS are reviewed and evaluated in Wylie [1974].)

A number of studies involve idiosyncratic measures of self-regard and a variety of ability tests. When the studies are looked at as a group, the incidence of significant associations and the magnitude of them seems about the same as those given above for the better known and more developed tests. The immediately preceding statement is based upon the following publications: Bachman (1970); Bachman and O'Malley (1977); Badgett, Hope, and Kerley (1971); V. D. C. Bennett (1964); L. A. Bennett, Sorensen, and Forshay (1971); Bledsoe (1964); Cotler and Palmer (1970); Gellert (1975); Gill and D'Oyley (1970); Greene and Zirkel (1971); J. E. Hall, Morris, and Barker (1973); Harrison and Budoff (1972a); Henton and Johnson (1964); Hishiki (1969); Kunce, Getsinger, and Miller (1972); S. C. Larsen, Parker, and Jorjorian (1973); Lekarczyk and Hill (1969); Meyfrowitz (1962); Perkins (1958b); Sanders, Mefferd, and Bown (1960); Sears (1970); Wattenberg and Clifford (1964); Yellott, Liem, and Cowen (1969); and Zigler, Balla, and Watson (1972). It should be noted that many of the above studies are characterized by so many serious flaws that they are virtually uninterpretable.

b. Self Evaluation in Mentally Retarded Persons

Within the area of relationships between ability and self-concept variables, some special questions arise when one is dealing with mentally retarded persons. Concerning method, Knight (1970) cites and agrees with the opinion of several previous writers that retarded children do not possess the skills to perceive clearly and report truthfully their own inner feelings. As shown below, however, research results cast doubt on this assertion, at least so far as educable mentally retarded (EMR) persons are concerned.

Theoretically, the most interesting questions center around whether mentally retarded persons perceive themselves as belonging in a stereotyped group, whether they have an accurate idea of the stereotype (if one exists), whether they accept the stereotype as being accurately self-descriptive, and whether their over-all self-regard or some aspects of self-evaluation are poor, as might be predicted if the retardates recognize their severe limitations and the relatively low regard others have for them.

Research is meager concerning the existence, content, and strength of stereotypes about the mentally retarded. J. J. Greenbaum and Wang (1965) used a 21-scale semantic differential to measure conceptions of the mentally retarded by parents of retarded children, professionals who are likely to deal with the retarded, paraprofessionals who supervise institutionalized retardates, and business executives who are in a position to hire vocationally rehabilitated mentally retarded patients. Their results indicate that, even though parents and paraprofessionals who work daily with the retarded have more favorable views of the retarded than do professionals and business men, even the attitude of the parents is ambivalent. None of the respondents had positive views concerning the retardate's social-stimulus value, psychological attributes, or physical health. From several small researches which he briefly describes, Guskin (1963) concludes, "The content of the associations, the degree of consensus about them, how favorable they are . . . must be independently investigated and cannot be summarized in a single statement regarding the strength of the stereotype" (p. 339).

So far as I know, there are no investigations available concerning mental retardates' specific ideas of stereotypes of their group or their ideas as to whether particular stereotyped traits characterize them as individuals. Of indirect relevance is a small pilot study reported in R. L. Jones (1972) which indicates the stigma perceived by a group of 23 high school boys enrolled in a special class for the educable mentally retarded. Seventeen of these boys lied when asked about their school work, indicating they were enrolled in regular classes. None of the students felt that the special class was his preferred placement in school. Jones (1972) reports similar results in a follow-up study of 116 EMR junior and senior high school students in self-contained classrooms. He also reports that in a study of 269 former special class students, 65% of these adults had told no one or only a few persons about their former special class placement. Although these reports provide some evidence that EMR students feel a certain stigma attached to their special class placement, they are so vague that the results are not really conclusive.

Despite Knight's (1970) and others' skepticism, several investigators have found extant self-concept tests appropriate for use with EMR subjects, and several persons have devised new self-concept tests especially for them. At least two of these investigators have also called into question the a priori assumption that EMR persons have a generally unfavorable self-concept.

Richmond and Dalton (1973) used an oral presentation of Coopersmith's SEI with 100 EMR children aged 9-15 whose IQs were between 50 and 75. The article does not say whether the obtained means and standard deviations on the SEI correspond to those of the normative samples. In any event, it is implied in the report that the authors found the test usable with these subjects. (Within the group, they obtained F values significant at the .01 level in ANOVAs comparing teachers' ratings of the pupils' academic proficiency and the pupils' general self-esteem, school self-esteem, and home self-esteem scores from the pupils' SEI. Unfortunately, multiple significance tests were made and no cross-validation is reported.) Morena and Litrownik (1974) found the SEI mean of 24 EMR children aged 11.5 years to be 1 SD below Coopersmith's norms (1967, p. 10).

Mayer's (1966) subjects were 98 pupils aged 12-17 who had Binet or WISC IQs of 50-75. These children, who had no observable physical, sensory, or emotional disabilities, showed no significant difference from the standardization samples used for the Lippsitt Self-Concept Scale for Children and the Piers-Harris Children's Self-Concept Scale (PH). (A psychologist administered the test orally to the children who worked in small groups where their questions could be handled and their understanding monitored.) As mentioned earlier, Collins, Burger, and Doherty (1970) report no significant differences between TSCS Total Positive mean scores of retarded and nonretarded adolescents.

Piers and Harris (1964) obtained trends different from Mayer's when they compared PH scores of normal third, sixth, and ninth graders to PH scores from 88 institutionalized retarded females (mean age = 16.8 years; mean IQ = 69.6; reading level at or above third grade). While the mean PH scores of the normals ranged from 64.5 to 69.4, the mean of the retardates was 57, a significant difference. One cannot rule out the possibility of accounting for this difference in terms of the reliability artifact.

(The Lipsitt, PH, and SEI scales are reviewed and evaluated in Wylie [1974].)

Agreeing with Piers and Harris in not supporting Mayer's (1966) null findings, Meyfrowitz (1962) reported that significantly more self-derogatory statements were endorsed by educable mentally retarded (EMR) first graders than by normal controls who were matched with the retarded subjects on father's income, occupation, and residential area. The means are 3.2 and 2.6 self-derogations out of a possible 22 on the Illinois Index of Self-Derogation, suggesting that the absolute differences in self-derogation between groups are very small, despite the statistical significance of the mean difference. Moreover, only 3 out of 22 items significantly discriminated EMR first graders from normal controls. Opposite to Mayer's hypothesis, the mental retardates who remained in first grade endorsed fewer self-derogatory statements than did the retardates assigned to special classes (the means being 3.0 and 3.4, respectively). W. J. Goldman and May's (1972) comparison of 100 EMR children and 100 normal children is too flawed to warrant a substantive summary.

Supporting Mayer's hypothesis, but opposite to Meyfrowitz's findings, Schurr, Towne, and Joiner (1972) found that taking students out of regular classrooms and placing them in special classes tended to increase their self-concept of ability. They administered Brookover et al.'s Self-Concept of Schoolwork Ability scale to EMR students twice while they were attending regular classes and four times a year during the first and second years of their special class placement. SCA scores showed a significant ascending linear trend during the first and second years of special class placement. The means of an EMR control group tested only twice during the second year of special class placement in order to examine possible effects of repeated testing were not significantly different from the group tested four times that year. This rules out repeated testing as an explanation for the ascending trends, according to the authors. Also, the SCA scores of a small group of students reassigned to regular classes after spending one year in the special class decreased after one year of attending regular classes again (significance level not given).

Three attempts have been made to create scales especially for mentally retarded subjects, although none of them has been used to make comparisons between retarded and normal persons.

McAfee and Cleland (1965) modified Bills's IAV and reported nonsignificant associations between IQ and Self or Ideal Self within an

EMR group. [Self—Ideal] discrepancies correlated significantly with IQ, however, indicating supposedly that higher IQ tended to be associated with poorer self-regard within this group. Unfortunately, psychometric information is not given for this new test.

Another more extensive effort to create a special self-concept test for mentally retarded persons was made by workers at Laurelton State School in Pennsylvania (Guthrie, Butler, & Gorlow, 1961, 1963; Kniss, Butler, Gorlow, & Guthrie, 1962). Using 50 retarded women as their subjects, the researchers carried out an inverse factor analysis of 150 items in an attempt to identify groups who were homogeneous with respect to patterns of self-attitudes. Then a replication of the inverse factor analysis was done, using 50 more retarded women. Three generally favorable and 4 generally unfavorable factors were identified. A 50-item scale was developed from the original Laurelton scale, using items which had met stated standards of reliability ($\geq$ .40), response variability (item split between .10 and .90), and judged "appropriateness of the item content for a wide range of retardates and school children of normal intelligence" (pp. 245–246). With this abbreviated scale, ideal-self patterns of female retardates were studied (Kniss, Butler, Gorlow, & Guthrie, 1962). More recently, Harrison and Budoff (1972b) factor analyzed 137 items of the Laurelton Self-Concept Scale and the 23 items from the Bialer Locus of Control Scale for children, using 172 special class and institutionalized EMR children.

In section A-4 below, I consider two studies which correlated the Laurelton scale or an abbreviated form of it with standardized achievement test scores, with IQ purportedly controlled (Gorlow, Butler, & Guthrie, 1963; Snyder, 1966). Both studies involved only retarded subjects.

In a third attempt to develop a self-concept scale especially for mentally retarded persons, D. A. Burke and Sellin (1972) modified the General Self-Concept of Ability Scale of Brookover and his associates for use with EMR adolescents. Putting special emphasis on the vocational aspects of the education received by the subjects, all of whom attended a special school offering an unusually comprehensive training program, the authors created a standardized interview schedule which included 8 items pertaining to self-concept of ability as a worker, and 4 pertaining to job and school aspirations. Thirty-day test-retest reliability of the self-concept-of-ability-as-a-worker scale was .81, and each of the 8 items significantly correlated with the total subscale (*phi* values ranging from .48 to .59). No validity data are offered.

It seems clear from all the information given above that, despite the opinion of a number of writers, various aspects of the self-concepts of mentally retarded persons can be reliably measured by extant tests or by one of the newly devised tests for the retarded. Within the retarded group, correlations between self-regard and ability or achievement have been obtained. (See section A-4 below for a study by Snyder, Jefferson, and Strauss [1965] in which reading achievement of EMR subjects was varied while holding IQ constant, and a study by McCoy [1963] in which standardized achievement test scores of EMR subjects were varied while holding IQ constant.)

It would be interesting to see the outcomes of using the specially devised tests to compare self-concepts of educable mentally retarded and normal subjects.

To my knowledge, the only self-concept study involving severely retarded subjects is one by Pechacek, Bell, Cleland, Baum, and Boyle (1973) who unsuccessfully attempted to develop their subjects' capacities to recognize themselves in a mirror. As the authors point out, their null findings leave open the question whether limitations of method and/or subjects determined their lack of success.

c. ABILITY MEASURES AND SPECIFIC ASPECTS OF SELF-CONCEPT

Concepts of Schoolwork Ability

One would expect self-concepts of ability to correlate with IQ scores more highly than over-all self-regard indices correlate with IQ scores. That this is the case is shown in several publications. Brookover, LePere, Hamachek, Thomas, and Erickson (1965) report that rs between Self-Concept of Schoolwork-Ability—General (SCA) and IQs from the California Test of Mental Maturity (CTMM) run between .44 and .54 for 8 samples (males and females, Grades 7, 8, 9, 10). Brookover, Erickson, and Joiner (1967) report $rs = .51$ and .59 between SCA and CTMM IQs. Joiner, Erickson, Crittenden, and Stevenson (1969) report rs between .41 and .49 for 3 samples: 2 deaf samples given a version of WISC adapted for the hearing impaired, and a normal sample tested with CTMM.

The correlations between the Intellectual and School Status Factor from the Piers-Harris Self-Concept Scale for Children (PH) and the WISC Full Scale and Verbal Scale IQs $= .43$ and .50 according to Eastman (in Piers, 1969).

Paradoxically, Trowbridge (1974) reported that high-IQ children scored significantly *lower* than average-IQ children on the 8 school-academic items of Coopersmith's Self-Esteem Inventory (SEI).

In a one-way analysis of variance for educable mentally retarded children rated by their teachers as either high or low on academic ability, Richmond and Dalton (1973) obtained significant F values for the general, school, and home self-esteem subtests of Coopersmith's Self-Esteem Inventory (SEI), but not for the social self-esteem subtest of the SEI. However, their measure of academic ability actually implies academic proficiency or achievement rather than ability.

Ringness (1961) used an idiosyncratic self-concept scale to measure self-estimates of achievement in 8 different areas, including academic as well as social areas, in 3 groups of fourth graders: educable mentally retarded children with IQs of 50-80, normal children with IQs of 90-110, and bright children with IQs greater than 120. In an analysis of variance, he found that IQ was a significant factor in the self-concept ratings of the students, with bright students having the highest self-concept ratings, retarded students the second highest ratings, and normal students having the lowest self-concepts.

In the representative national sample of 2,213 tenth-grade boys attending United States public high schools reported on above, Bachman (1970) found *eta* = .46 between an idiosyncratic 3-item purported measure of self-concept of schoolwork ability and the Ammons Quick Test of intelligence. The former yielded r = .48 with self-reported grades, but the value of *eta* between the self-concept and the intelligence test measure has not been given with the factor of grades held constant, nor has the correlation between the self-concept measure and achievement been reported with intelligence test scores held constant.

In Wylie's (1963) and Wylie and Hutchins's (1967) work based on a total of 4,245 subjects in Grades 9-12 in 3 different communities, the point was not to look at self-conceptions of ability as a function of IQ, but rather to hold IQ constant while looking at sex, race, and socioeconomic level. Nevertheless, the data were analyzed in such a way as to show incidentally a strong relationship between ability scores and measures of self-conceptions of ability. For example, within high socioeconomic and within low socioeconomic groups, subgroups ≥ 10 were formed according to rather narrow class intervals of ability scores (e.g., 10 IQ points). Within each of 4 school cohorts, curves were plotted for pairs of high socioeconomic level and low socioeconomic level groups with comparable IQs: these curves showed the proportion of each IQ subgroup who said they were in the top half of their homerooms in ability to do schoolwork ("By ability we don't mean necessarily how well you *actually* do your schoolwork, but rather how well you *could* do schoolwork if you tried your best"). Each of the 8 curves showed a clear upward trend as a function of IQ. The same thing appeared when the proportions plotted referred to students at each IQ level who felt that "so far as your ability to do the work is concerned, you will be able to go through college." Since achievement indices were not controlled in preparing these curves, nothing can be concluded about the association between ability scores and self-conceptions of ability with achievement held constant. (See chapters 3 and 4 for more information on procedures and data analyses in these studies.)

Anastasiow's (1967) sample of 510 boys and girls from Grades 4-6 consisted of those scoring in the top and bottom 26% on the SCAT 4-A ability test. In comparing these 2 groups on the subscales of the Sears Self-Concept Inventory, he found that, among girls, those low in ability scored significantly lower on all 3 subscales concerning aspects of schoolwork ability—mental ability, work habits, and school subjects. According to Anastasiow, among boys, those low in ability scored significantly lower on the school subjects and mental ability subscales (but the mean for the low ability boys is actually reported to be higher in the data table given).

Specific Aspects of Self-Concept Other Than
Self-Concepts of Schoolwork Ability

The California Psychological Inventory manual (Gough, 1957) reports correlations of each of the 18 scales with various intellectual measures including the Terman Concept Mastery Test and Wesman's Personnel Classification Test. The lack of correlation of the latter two measures with the CPI Self-Acceptance scale has already been reported, but the question remains whether the other, more specific, self-evaluative scales are associated with ability. Since there were 17 scales (excluding Self-Acceptance) and 2 intellectual measures, 34 rs were generated. The Terman Concept Mastery Test correlates significantly with 12 of the 17 scales, and the Wesman Test with 7 of them. However, aside from the problem that achievement has not been partialled out of these rs, their statistical and psychological significance cannot be evaluated because (a) so many *r*s were generated; (b) the CPI scales intercorrelate; (c) the ability measures intercorrelate; (d) no cross-validational information is available.

As was true of the CPI, the Adjective Check List (ACL) over-all self-regard scales (Fav and Unfav) did not correlate significantly with scores from the Terman Concept Mastery Test or the Wesman Personnel Classification Test (Gough & Heilbrun, 1965), which we have already noted above. But what about the other 21 ACL scales which purport to measure more specific dimensions of self-evaluation? With 21 scales and 2 intellectual measures, 42 *r*s were generated (I am excluding the Number Checked scale). Gough and Heilbrun (1965) report that 8 out of 21 scales showed significant *r*s with the Terman Concept Mastery Test (ranging from .20 to .29, including one $r = -.26$), whereas 4 out of 21 of the scales showed significant *r*s with Wesman's test (ranging from .21 to $-.27$). However, aside from the problem that achievement has not been partialled out of these *r*s, their statistical and psychological significance cannot be evaluated because (a) so many *r*s were generated; (b) the ACL scales intercorrelate; (c) the ability measures intercorrelate; (d) no cross-validational information is available.

In research concerning Edwards Personal Preference Schedule scores and IQs in 1,521 high school students, Klett (1957) found that scores on the California Test of Mental Maturity correlated with several EPPS variables. (Apparently about 10 out of 15 *r*s are large enough to differ significantly from 0.) However, the large *N*s make small *r*s significant, and multiple significance testing without cross-validation precludes interpretation. In the Sanders, Mefferd, and Bown (1960) research reported in the previous section, only 3 out of 15 EPPS scales yielded significant differences among three groups of male university freshmen differing in their verbal-quantitative abilities. The 3 groups, consisting of (a) those with both high verbal and quantitative ability, (b) those with high verbal and low quantitative ability, and (c) those with low verbal and high quantitative ability, differed significantly on the Autonomy, Dominance, and Endurance scales. Correlations involving these 3 variables were apparently significant in the Klett (1957) study as well, albeit with *r*s between .08 and .15.

Sears (1970) examined the relationship between many different specific self-concept measures and an unspecified IQ test in boys and girls in the sixth grade. The specific self-concept measures administered were a self-criticism scale, an ideas of reference scale (measuring hypersensitivity to other people's actions or presumed feelings toward the self), a self-aggression scale, and the self-satisfaction and comparative rating scales of Sears's Self-Concept Inventory. When each of these measures was correlated with IQ in boys and in girls, the only significant correlation out of 10 coefficients computed was an $r = .24$ between the comparative rating scale and IQ in boys.

In the study of fourth- to sixth-grade boys and girls reported in the previous section, Anastasiow (1967) also compared those scoring high or low in ability on the SCAT on subscales of the Sears Self-Concept Scale which are unrelated to schoolwork ability: self-concepts of physical ability, social relations with boys, social relations with girls, social relations with teachers, physical appearance, social virtues, and happy qualities. High ability girls scored significantly higher than low ability girls on self-concept scores of school subjects, mental abilities, physical appearance, work habits, social relations with teachers, social virtues, and happy qualities, while the significant differences in the self-concept scores of high and low ability boys were in mental ability and school subjects. However, multiple significance testing without cross-validation precludes interpretation of these significance levels.

Sims (1952) administered the Social Class Identification scale to 900 college freshmen, 114 high school seniors, and 95 vocational high school seniors. He found no significant correlations between Social Class Identification scores and scores on the Bennett Mechanical Comprehension Test or the Minnesota Clerical Aptitude Test for the vocational students. For the high school senior sample, the correlation between Social Class Identification scores and scores on the American Council on Education Psychological Examination (ACE) ranged from .18 for the quantitative score to .38 for the linguistic and total scores. The correlation between Social Class Identification scores and Otis Beta IQ was .31 in this sample. Lastly, the data for the college students showed correlations between Social Class Identification scores and the quantitative, linguistic, and total scores of the ACE test of .085 (n. s.), .186, and .185, respectively. Correlations between the scores on the subtests of the Cooperative English Test and Social Class Identification scores ranged from .163 to .252 for the college students.

R. C. Bailey and Shaw (1971) compared scores on an idiosyncratic 15-item self-confidence scale of students who were overraters, realistic raters, or underraters of their college ability (as determined by a comparison of a self-rating scale of college ability and an objective measure of college ability) and found no significant difference in the three groups of students. However, the use of discrepancy scores prevents one from inferring anything about ability self-ratings per se and self-confidence reports.

A study by Yellott, Liem, and Cowen (1969) included Otis IQ scores and scores on the Anxiety and Lie scales of the Children's Manifest Anxiety Scale (CMAS) for third graders, but unfortunately did not report any correlations between the two measures.

d. CONCLUSIONS

A wide variety of ability measures and self-concept measures has been correlated, according to the published reports examined, and significant positive, although low, rs have been the most typical findings. However, none of these rs is interpretable as indicating either a null or significant relationship between an ability dimension and a self-concept dimension, because measured achievement was not held constant, even in those studies which used both ability and achievement measures. Probably other variables such as socioeconomic level should also have been controlled in some of these studies when looking at self-concept of schoolwork ability as a function of scores on ability tests (e.g., see Trowbridge, 1974).

Accounting for variations in obtained rs *among studies* is not possible since the range and type of ability scores and self-concept measures varies so much from study to study.

The correlations do appear to run higher when they involve the more specific aspect of self-concept, self-concept of schoolwork ability, as contrasted to correlations involving measures of *over-all* self-regard and ability measures. However, the incomparability of the methods among these researches requires that this comparative statement be made very tentatively.

There is no methodologically adequate evidence regarding associations between other specific aspects of self-concept and ability measures.

Unwillingness or lack of ability to concentrate may impair IQ or other ability scores and also artifactually yield "low self-regard" scores on scales of certain format, as already mentioned. This could lead to an unknown amount of artifactual inflation of some of the correlations reported between ability measures and self-concept measures.

4. Simultaneous (Controlled) Examination of Ability and Achievement Measures and Self-Concept Measures

a. TECHNIQUES USED

I consider it methodologically most defensible to offer interpretations based only on those studies which used both IQ and achievement measures and which attempted in some way to relate one of them to one or more self-concept variables while holding the other constant. The available approaches took one of several forms:

Some studies used *partial* rs between achievement and self-concept measures with IQ held constant, or partial rs between IQ and self-concept measures, with achievement held constant.

Other studies used *multiple regression* techniques, to see whether both IQ/ability and self-concept variables yielded significant increments to the value of the multiple R with achievement measures.

Still other studies compared so-called *overachievers* and *underachievers*. Overachievement and underachievement were said to have occurred when a student's achievement score differed positively or negatively by a specified minimum amount from the most likely achievement score predicted by the regression of achievement scores on ability scores. This method is full of potential pitfalls, as well described by Thorndike (1963), and one needs to keep them in mind when evaluating the interpretability of such studies.

In some studies, *groups are matched* with respect to IQ, and varied with respect to self-concept scores, while differences in achievement scores between groups are looked for.

b. STUDIES OF OVER-ALL SELF-REGARD AND ACHIEVEMENT WITH ABILITY CONTROLLED

I have examined 29 studies which looked at relationships between over-all self-regard and achievement while purportedly controlling for ability by one or more of the methods just listed. None of these researches met all the methodological criteria listed in section A-1 above. For example, when GPAs were used, psychometric information about them was routinely omitted, and no report based on an idiosyncratic measure of self-regard provided enough psychometric information about it. Nevertheless, completeness of reporting and adequacy of method seem more adequate for some studies than for others, and these are given substantive consideration here, while the most incomplete and/or severely flawed reports are simply listed at the end.

Studies Using Well-Known Tests of Over-all Self-Regard

Two studies used the Butler-Haigh Q sort, one with high school and one with college students.

The z values of self-ideal correlations obtained from the Butler-Haigh Q sort (BHQ) were reported by Quimby (1967) to be significantly higher on a one-tail test for a group of "achieving" than for a group of "underachieving" eleventh- and twelfth-grade students. However, even though IQs from the California Test of Mental Maturity were all $\geq$ 110, it is not reported that achieving (higher GPA) and underachieving (lower GPA) subjects were strictly comparable with respect to IQ, leaving the interpretation of this already weak trend equivocal.

From 175 college students who had responded to the Butler-Haigh Q sort, Turner and Vanderlippe (1958) chose the 25 persons with the highest and the 25 persons with the lowest self-ideal congruence scores. ACE scores were shown to be nonsignificantly different between these two groups, whereas mean cumulative GPA was shown to be significantly higher in the high self-regard group. One should note that they used a one-tailed t-test and that this comparison was one of a number made with the same subjects without cross-validation on another sample.

One study used Bills's Index of Adjustment and Values as a source of self-regard measures: Shaw and Alves (1963) looked for differences in Self, Self-Acceptance, and Ideal Self scores between a group of achievers and a group of underachievers, equated with respect to IQ on the California Test of Mental Maturity. All subjects were eleventh or twelfth graders, and all IQs $\geq$ 110. It is not clear that IQs were precisely comparable between achievement groups. Male achievers (those attaining a GPA $\geq$ 3.0 = B) exceeded male underachievers (those attaining a GPA $\leq$ 2.5) with respect to Self, Self-Acceptance, and Ideal Self scores, with the first 2 differences being significant. Similar, but not significant trends for the 3 score differences were attained for the female subjects.

Two studies employed a version of the Laurelton scale, especially developed for use with retarded subjects. Among 164 institutionalized retardates, Gorlow, Butler, and Guthrie (1963) found significant but low partial rs between total positive self-regard scores from their Laurelton Self-Attitude Scale and California Achievement Test scores in reading and arithmetic when Wechsler IQs were held constant. Their matrix is large and needs cross-validation. Included in it are several types of self-regard scores, among them SS + (number of positive self-descriptions accepted) and SS − (number of negative self-descriptions rejected). Of these two, the SS − scores correlated more strongly with achievement tests.

Snyder (1966) also reported on retarded subjects who were said to be comparable with respect to socioeconomic level and IQ (different IQ tests being used for different subjects, however) and to be "significantly dichotomous" with respect to "academic attainment" (different standard tests being used for different subjects, however). The self-regard of the higher achievers was significantly higher than that of the lower achievers, when self-regard was measured by an abbreviated form of the Laurelton Self-Attitude Scale. The fact that the author read each Laurelton item twice, and only a *yes* or *no* answer was required diminishes, but does not eliminate, the possibility that the obtained r may be artifactually created by the common influence of unreliability of responding.

In yet another study involving educable mentally retarded persons, 26 pairs of black subjects were chosen so as to equate groups with respect to Otis or California Test of Mental Maturity IQs and vary scores on the Verbal Comprehension subtest of the California Achievement Test (Snyder, Jefferson, & Strauss, 1965). The subjects responded to an oral administration of the California Test of Personality, Elementary Form, from which an idiosyncratic "self-concept score" was obtained by combining 3 subscales of the personality test: Self-reliance, Sense of Personal Worth, and Feelings of Belonging. The high-achievement group significantly exceeded the low-achievement group on this self-concept score, as well as on the Total, Personal Adjustment, and Social Adjustment subscales of the California Test of Personality.

F. W. Black (1974) administered the Piers-Harris Self-Concept Scale for Children (PH) and the Wide Range Achievement Test (WRAT) to normal and retarded readers all of whom were diagnosed as learning-disabled and who were matched on the basis of WISC full-scale IQ scores. He obtained significant rs between self-concept and WRAT reading, spelling, and arithmetic scores ranging from − .46 to − .57 for these children, with little difference in the size of the correlation for the retarded and normal readers.

In another investigation using the Piers-Harris test (PH), R. N. Morse and Piers (n.d.) compared 10 Stanford Achievement Test scores of 15 high-self-esteem and 15 low-self-esteem black, sixth-grade boys. The 2 groups were said to be comparable with respect to Lorge-Thorndike IQs. The direction of 2 significant and 8 nonsignificant differences on the Stanford Achievement subtests favored the hypothesis that achievement and self-regard would be positively associated. Without cross-validation, however, there is no way to evaluate their multiple significance tests. Moreover, in consideration of the characteristics of the subjects used, the question must be raised whether unreliability of responding could artifactually account for the obtained relationships between achievement test and self-regard scores.

Two studies used Coopersmith's Self-Esteem Inventory (SEI) or a modified version of SEI. In an incomplete published description of a dissertation, P. B. Campbell (1967) reported using "multiple regression techniques" to examine the contribution of IQ scores and Coopersmith's SEI scores to the prediction of Iowa Composite Achievement Test scores. He did not consider the use of the SEI scores "worth while . . . because the contribution of self-concept to prediction is too small" (p. 512).

J. H. Williams (1973) used stepwise multiple regression to try to predict first- and second-grade reading achievement on the California Achievement Test from five variables: Kuhlmann-Anderson IQs, Metropolitan Reading Readiness Test scores, self-esteem scores from a modification of Coopersmith's Self-Esteem Inventory, ethnic background, and sex. She found all the correlations between self-esteem scores and the other predictor variables to be essentially zero, and the self-esteem scores failed to add to the prediction of either first- or second-grade reading achievement beyond the prediction made from intelligence and reading readiness scores.

(The BHQ, IAV, PH, and SEI are reviewed and evaluated in Wylie [1974].)

Studies Using Idiosyncratic Measures of Over-all Self-Regard

Finally, each of the nine studies I have chosen for substantive summary involved a different idiosyncratic index of over-all self-regard.

Borislow (1962) formed 2 groups of college freshman students: underachievers whose GPAs fell $\geq$ 0.5 standard errors below the mean predicted for their Scholastic Aptitude Test (SAT) and achievers (all those not defined as underachievers). It is not completely clear whether achiever and underachiever groups were equal with respect to their aptitude test scores. Each achievement group was further divided into those students who were high and low with respect to "scholastic achievement motivation." To evaluate self-regard, Borislow used an idiosyncratic modification of Fiedler's 24-item semantic differential scale. (See Wylie, 1974, pp. 224–230, for an evaluation of the semantic differential technique as a tool for measuring self-regard.) Altogether, he made 4 comparisons of self-regard means between underachieving and achieving groups, a presemester and a postsemester comparison for each of his 2 pairs of groups. None of the 4 differences was significant, thus yielding no support to the idea that over-all self-regard is significantly associated with achievement.

In a study reported in more detail below, Kubiniec (1970) used an idiosyncratic set of semantic differential scales to measure, among other things, Real Self on an evaluative factor. This score, which I assume is similar to other scores purporting to index over-all self-regard, showed no tendency to differentiate groups of high achievers, moderate achievers, low achievers, or dropouts, within either the male sample or the female sample.

Irvin (1967), using an idiosyncratic self-regard instrument and dealing with three groups of college students matched for sex, age, and SCAT mean percentile, found significantly greater self-favorability among the "good-standing" group as opposed to either the "probation" or "failed" group. In another study described as a "partial replication" of the above, LaPlante and Irvin (1970) actually varied rather than replicating Irvin's method in that extreme groups on the American College Test Service aptitude test were chosen, and aptitude scores were not held constant when correlating GPA with scores from their self-regard test. LaPlante and Irvin (1970) found no relationship between GPA and self-regard in this study and thought that ad hoc explanations of the discrepant results between the two studies were not possible.

In their large-scale multiple regression study, Nichols and Holland (1963) looked at the relationships of 141 predictor variables to 13 predicted variables, including self-reported GPAs for the college-freshman year. Their subjects were National Merit finalists polled by mail. Perhaps one might take as a measure of self-esteem their variable called "number of self-ratings above average," based on an idiosyncratic 20-adjective set of self-rating scales. This measure did not correlate with

GPAs or with other academic achievement variables such as achievement in science, drama, writing, music, or graphic art. (In a similar study with another sample of National Merit finalists [Holland & Nichols, 1964], different self-rating scales were used, but one cannot infer from the published information whether any idiosyncratic "self-esteem" score of the same general type as Nichols and Holland used was among the predictor variables.)

St. John (1971) performed a multiple-regression analysis in which scores on an idiosyncratic, undescribed self-regard instrument were predicted from six variables (sex, Kuhlmann-Anderson IQ, own socioeconomic level, GPA, class socioeconomic level, and percent of class white). GPA T-scores, but not IQs, yielded significant standardized regression coefficients on "general self-concept." This finding was obtained within each of two racial groups of sixth graders, black and white.

Rather than using regression-line techniques to define over-achievement and underachievement, Wyer (1965) took Scholastic Aptitude Test Verbal and Mathematics scores to define aptitude and formed "academic effectiveness" groups as follows: All subjects were placed in the high academic effectiveness group if the standard score value of their first-term college freshman GPA exceeded the standard score value of their aptitude test score by $\geq$ 1 *sigma*, and in the low academic effectiveness group if the standard score value of their GPAs fell $\geq$ 1 *sigma* below the standard score value of their aptitude scores. Subjects were placed in the normal academic effectiveness group if the standard score value of their GPA fell within $\pm$ 1 *sigma* from the standard score value of their aptitude-test scores. Employing a 5-point scale for self-rating on each of 24 specially chosen adjectives from the Adjective Check List (published in Wyer's article), he obtained idiosyncratic self-acceptance scores. For males but not for females, these self-acceptance scores were directly and significantly related to "academic effectiveness." It is not clear, however, that this technique sufficed to hold aptitude scores constant.

Bennett (1964) studied the relationship between the self-concepts of sixth-grade students and their achievement, as measured by Iowa Tests of Basic Skills. The idiosyncratic measure of self-concept was based on the Butler and Haigh Q sort and the Hilden Q sort (1954). The statements were modified for use with elementary age children and some psychometric information is given. The zero-order correlation between self-concept scores and achievement scores was .34 ($p < .01$). When IQ scores on the California Test of Mental Maturity or the Lorge-Thorndike Intelligence Test were held constant, a partial correlation of .24 ($p < .02$) was obtained.

Stenner and Katzenmeyer (1976) used an idiosyncratic scale to measure the self-concepts of 225 sixth graders in West Virginia. Achievement and ability measures were from the Scholastic Testing Service Educational Development Series. However, they feel that verbal IQ "is so achievement saturated as to be better considered an achievement test than an ability test" (p. 272); so their results are presented in terms of the percent of variance accounted for and the incremental predictive value of the self-concept scale and the ability measure (nonverbal IQ only) in predicting the achievement variables. Given the nonverbal IQ, the incremental values of the self-concept score, in predicting the 7 achievement measures, ranged from 8 to 13; while the incremental value of the nonverbal IQ score, given the self-concept score, ranged from 6 to 21 for the achievement measures.

The following studies were not included in the above substantive summaries, either because they gave insufficient information to permit evaluation or they appeared to be unusually seriously flawed methodologically, or both: Durr and Schmatz (1964); Fink (1962); Mitchell (1959); Norfleet (1968); Norman and Daley (1959); Passow and Goldberg (1962); Rabinowitz (1966); M. C. Shaw, Edson, and Bell (1960); Stewart (1968); A. M. Walsh (1956). The latter study is evaluated in Wylie (1961), p. 257.

Summary and Conclusions

Thirteen of the 19 discussed studies showed at least one significant positive association between over-all self-regard and achievement, with ability supposedly controlled, whereas 6 showed no significant trends of this sort. In studies in which male and female data were separately analyzed, 2 yielded significant associations for males but not for females. The reverse situation never occurred. None of the studies yielded any significant negative associations between achievement and over-all self-regard.

It is obvious that the 19 reports discussed above involved a wide range of types of subjects, self-regard measures, achievement measures, ability measures, and means of trying to control for ability while looking at the relationship between over-all self-regard and achievement. In one way, this variety is a weakness, since direct replications are not at hand, and systematic comparisons between or among studies are not possible. In another way, however, such variety may strengthen one's confidence in the more usual, albeit very small trends for higher over-all self-regard to be associated with higher achievement levels.

It cannot be said that the use of GPAs as opposed to standardized achievement tests differentiates the studies which report null findings as opposed to positive findings, or vice versa.

It might be thought that the type of self-regard measure could be a factor in whether positive trends were obtained. Of 9 studies using unmodified versions of better known and developed instruments, 8 reported at least one significant positive trend. The 1 of these 9 which yielded insignificant results was the only one using Coopersmith's SEI. Ten of the 19 discussed researches employed idiosyncratic indices of self-regard, and, of these, 5 show at least one positive trend, whereas 5 show no trends; the latter 5 include 1 failure to replicate 1 of the original significant positive trends. In the absence of psychometric information about the idiosyncratic self-regard instruments, it is impossible to speculate further about this possible reason why significant positive associations are or are not obtained.

Perhaps the weakness of the positive trends and/or the null findings in some studies may be due to the inappropriate use of methods of data analysis based on the assumption of linear relationships. But in the absence of testing for curvilinearity, this point remains moot.

Certainly these results give little support to the widely accepted lore that there is a psychologically important relationship between achievement and over-all self-regard. On the other hand, there are enough significant positive trends, weak though they are, to encourage further explorations which incorporate needed methodological improvements.

As Sharma (1971) has pointed out, one methodological omission which is rather striking is the general lack of search for interactions. For example, it seems plausible that achievement and self-regard might plausibly be more closely associated among children from higher as opposed to lower socioeconomic levels.

c. Studies of Over-all Self-Regard and Ability with Achievement Controlled

In section A-3 above, it is reported that correlations between over-all self-regard and IQ or ability tests tended with only one exception to run no higher than .20s and .30s, with many of them being lower than that.

The question remained, then, whether such zero-order rs represent relationships that would yield significant rs between IQ and over-all self-regard when tested levels of achievement are held constant.

Examining the 29 studies which are used as a basis for section A-4 immediately above, one sees that researchers have shown little interest in this question, having concerned themselves almost exclusively with the relationships between achievement levels and self-regard, with ability levels controlled. Only 2 items of possible evidence from section A-4 can be brought to bear on the question whether ability and self-regard may be associated with achievement controlled.

Turner and Vanderlippe (1958), it will be remembered, found no significant difference in ACE scores between their self-regard groups, even when these groups did differ with respect to achievement. Although in the multiple-regression study reported above, St. John (1971) found that GPA-T scores yielded a significant standardized regression coefficient on "general self concept"; she did not find IQ to yield such a significant standardized regression coefficient on "general self concept."

These two null findings cannot, of course, suffice to test the hypothesis that IQ and over-all self-regard are significantly related with achievement held constant. More research specifically directed to this point remains to be done.

d. STUDIES OF PARTICULAR ASPECTS OF SELF-CONCEPT AND ACHIEVEMENT WITH ABILITY CONTROLLED

Although all the researches which belong in this section included both ability and achievement measures, all but *two* were directed only to predicting achievement from self-concept measures with ability statistically controlled, not with seeing if self-concept variables would be significantly related to ability measures with achievement levels controlled.

As would be expected among studies which attempt to relate specific aspects of self-concept to achievement measures, the researches were most often concerned with the subjects' self-evaluations of their abilities and/or motivations for the type of achievement to be predicted. As indicated below, a few studies employ specific self-evaluations not obviously related to academic achievement, e.g., Dom and Lov scores from the Leary Interpersonal Check List.

The broadest of the more restricted achievement-relevant self-reports include several alleged measures of self-concept of academic ability or motivation without regard to particular areas of ability and achievement. These include the relatively well-known instrument, Self-Concept of Ability Scale — General, devised by Brookover and associates and used in studies by Brookover, Thomas, and Paterson (1964); Brookover, Paterson, and Thomas (1962); Brookover, Erickson, and Joiner (1967); Binder, Jones, and Strowig (1970); and J. G. Jones and Strowig (1968); the Word Rating List of "academic self-concept" on which D. A. Payne (1962) and D. A. Payne and Farquhar (1962) have done considerable developmental work; and 7 different idiosyncratic instruments used respectively by R. C. Bailey (1971); Borislow (1962); Brim (1954); Coombs and Davies (1966); Furst (1966); Passow and Goldberg (1962); and St. John (1971).

By contrast, some investigators have obtained self-evaluations of abilities and/or motivations in more specific educational fields such as art, writing, English, science, history, or mathematics (Baird, 1969; Brookover, Paterson, & Thomas, 1962; Brookover, Thomas, & Paterson, 1964; Holland & Nichols, 1964; Nichols & Holland, 1963; O'Hara, 1966). These workers have looked for relationships between these more specific self-evaluations and respectively appropriate achievement measures in various fields.

Finally, as I mentioned above, some researchers have looked for relationships between achievement and relatively specific aspects of self-concept which are not manifestly self-evaluations of academic ability or motivation, e.g., Dom and Lov scores from Leary's Interpersonal Check List (Guerney & Burton, 1967), factors from an idiosyncratic semantic differential scale (Kubiniec, 1970), CPI scales and ACL adjectives (Norfleet, 1968), California Test of Personality scales (Norman and Daley, 1959), and 8 scores from the Minnesota Counseling Inventory (Zoolalian, 1965).

Several of the studies which belong in this section were unusually seriously flawed in a number of respects, and they therefore are simply listed at the end of the section. The other reports are considered immediately below in the following order: (a) those which used purported measures of more general self-concept of academic ability; (b) those which used purported indices of more restricted self-concepts of ability; (c) those which used other specific kinds of self-evaluations than those of ability and/or motivation for achievement.

Self-Concept of Schoolwork Ability—General

Brookover, Paterson, and Thomas (1962) and Brookover, Thomas, and Paterson (1964) both published correlational data from the same group of white seventh-grade students as follows: After partialling out IQ scores from the California Test of Mental Maturity, they obtained partial *r*s between the Self-Concept of Schoolwork Ability Scale— General and GPAs = .42 and .39 for the 513 males and 537 females, respectively. Also using partial *r* technique to relate self-concept of schoolwork ability to achievement with IQ controlled, Brookover, Erickson, and Joiner (1967) obtained partial *r*s of .39 and .63 for 100 delinquent and 100 nondelinquent subjects.

Binder, Jones, and Strowig (1970) and J. G. Jones and Strowig (1968) report high school GPA predictions which were cross-validated in two replications of a procedure using as predictors Brookover's Self-Concept of Ability Scale—General, the Hemnon-Nelson Test of Mental Ability, and a specially developed Expectations Inventory (which purportedly represents "behavioral correlates of the role 'student' "). All the variables significantly added to the multiple *R*; and the *beta* weights for each predictor variable differed nonsignificantly from one replication to the other.

(Jones and Strowig's [1968] report on Jones's study, the second of the two replications mentioned above, describes the development of an Identity Rating Scale coded from students' answers to the Who Am I test. [See Wylie, 1974, pp. 240–247, for an evaluation of the Who Am I Test.] Based on Eriksonian theory, the 5-point scale purports to be a continuum extending from a "diffused concept of identity to a cohesive, well-defined concept of identity" [p. 79]. Although this identity rating scale correlates significantly with both the Brookover scale scores and the GPAs, the *beta* weight in a multiple regression analysis was significant only for the females.)

Word Rating List (Academic Self-Concept)

D. A. Payne and Farquhar (1962) describe the content and development of a 48-item Word Rating List (WRL) intended to measure "academic self-concept." A multiple scalogram analysis indicated that the WRL is a multifactor instrument, but total WRL scores were used in the analysis reported by Payne (1962). According to Payne (1962), 4 "random normal samples" were chosen from approximately 4,200 eleventh-grade students: 254 males and 261 females for a first data analysis; and 117 males and 120 females for a cross-validational analysis. Multiple correlations for predicting cumulative ninth- and tenth-grade GPAs from Differential Aptitude Test — Verbal Reasoning and the Word Rating List are presented. In all but the second male sample, the multiple r with the achievement measure was significantly increased by the inclusion of WRL scores to the aptitude test scores.

Payne (1962) also presents data for groups of underachievers, overachievers, achievers, and a general sample, all groups having comparable mean scores on the Differential Aptitude Test — Verbal Reasoning. Overachievers and underachievers fell at least ± 1 S.E.$_{est.}$ relative to the regression of the aptitude test scores on the achievement measures. *Within* each of these groups, there were significant zero-order rs of WRL versus GPA, only one out of 16 rs failing to reach the .05 level.

Idiosyncratic Measures of Self-Concept of Ability

Brim (1954) correlated the GPAs and self-estimated ranks of general intelligence of 103 college students, with ACE scores held constant, obtaining a nonsignificant partial $r = .20$.

In a study described in section A–2 above, Borislow (1962) used Fiedler's semantic differential scales not only to get an index of over-all self-regard, as already reported above, but also to obtain the subjects' more specific evaluations of themselves as students. Although "achievers" and "underachievers" did not differ in general self-evaluation, some positive findings were obtained with the more restricted, idiosyncratic measure of "self-evaluation as a student." In two groups reporting high scholastic achievement motivation, achievers significantly exceeded underachievers in regard to "self-evaluation as a student," both at presemester and at postsemester testings. In two groups reporting low scholastic achievement motivation, achievers exceeded underachievers in "self-evaluation as a student" at the postsemester test, with no significant difference appearing at the presemester test.

Furst (1966) reports some, but not enough, information on a new 9-item Achievement Motivation Scale about which he says, "The scale essentially samples aspects of the self-concept, reflecting both the person as he sees himself and as he thinks his peers and teachers see him" (p.

933). The item content is clearly concerned with academic functioning. In 5 groups, the zero-order rs of this scale with ninth-graders' GPAs = .30, .44, .50, .52, and .76, all but the first being significant at $\leq$ .01 level. The study offers multiple rs involving 9 predictors of GPAs, but unfortunately, the predictive value of the Achievement Motivation Scale is not separately evaluated in the published data presented.

In still another study based on an idiosyncratic self-concept index, Bailey's (1971) subjects were asked to indicate "how they felt they compared to an average student of their class rank in their ability to do college work" (Self scale), and "how they would ideally like to be in their ability to do college work as compared to an average student of their own class rank" (Ideal Self scale) (p. 188). No psychometric information is given except that 2-week test-retest rs are reported to equal .84 and .87 for Self and Ideal respectively. Achieving and underachieving groups who were equal with respect to mean Hemnon-Nelson IQ but significantly different with respect to GPA (1.45 vs. 2.25), differed significantly in their Self and Ideal Self reports. The achievement group mean was higher for each of these scores. This work has not been cross-validated.

Coombs and Davies (1966) studied the relationship of college-grade achievement to idiosyncratic measures of self-conception of scholastic ability and expectation of obtaining superior college grades. The former involved a 5-point scale ranging from "must study somewhat hard to pass" to "get A's and B's without working very hard," whereas the latter involved asking students to estimate their chances of getting a B average during their first year in college. Ability was measured by the ACE aptitude test, and self-conceptions were related to mean college GPA within the group above median ACE and within the group below median ACE. With ACE held "constant" to this extent, students tended to get significantly higher GPAs if they had favorable self-concepts and expectations of achieving. The only exception to this finding was that the expectation of obtaining superior grades did not differentiate significantly on college grade achievement for the low aptitude students.

In a report cited in section A-4 above, St. John (1971) briefly mentioned an idiosyncratic measure of "academic self-concept" in which she showed a 10-runged ladder with the instructions: "At the top are the best students in the 6th grade in this school; at the bottom are the worst students in the 6th grade. Write the word 'Me' on the step where you think you are" (p. 584). Insufficient psychometric information is given about this scale. Zero-order rs of this academic self-concept measure with Metropolitan Reading Achievement Test scores and with sixth-grade GPAs were significant for a white sample and also for a black sample. In a multiple-regression analysis in which academic self-concept was predicted from sex, IQ, own socioeconomic level minus class socioeconomic level, GPA-T-scores, class socioeconomic level, and class percent white, GPA-T-scores but not IQ yielded standardized regression coefficients significant at the .01 level. These regression weights are numerically larger than the corresponding ones with St. John's "general self-concept" measure, mentioned earlier, but there is no way to say from the information provided whether the relationship of GPA-T-scores with academic self-concept is significantly stronger than with general self-concept.

Self-Concepts of Specific Ability Dimensions

In a large-scale attempt to predict 13 measures of college achievement from a very large (unspecified) number of predictors, Baird (1969) included 31 idiosyncratic self-rating scales previously factor analyzed by Richards (1966). Several of these scales ask the subject to evaluate his/her specific abilities in areas such as mathematics, art, and writing. For males and females separately, multiple correlation equations to predict each achievement measure were computed so as to get the respectively "best predictors" for each of the 13 kinds of college achievement, using specified, published standards for defining "best predictors." A cross-validation was then done. A thorough evaluation of this study is not possible because not all the needed information is given. However, it is interesting to note that, among the 9 college achievement areas for which corresponding self-rating scales are available, 4 show the corresponding self-ratings to be among the best predictors. Baird points out, "It is possible that similar ratings would have appeared among the best predictors of achievement in other areas if the lists of ratings and goals had included items which were directly relevant to those areas" (p. 252).

Brookover and his colleagues have developed not only the Self-Concept of Schoolwork Ability—General scale, referred to above, but they have also made scales which purport to measure students' self-concepts of their abilities in mathematics, English, social studies, and science. In samples of 513 white males and 537 white females in the seventh grade, the following partial correlations were obtained between the self-concept and corresponding achievement measures, for males and for females: mathematics = .46, .44; English = .31, .34; social studies = .46, .44; science = .49, .38. These appear to be about the same size as the partial rs between the Self-Concept of Schoolwork Ability—General scores and total GPAs (Brookover, Thomas, & Paterson, 1964).

These correlations involving the very specific aspects of schoolwork ability are interesting. However, it is theoretically appropriate to wonder whether each respective self-concept scale is a discriminating predictor of achievement in the respectively corresponding subject-matter area. No partial rs to answer this sort of question are available. But examination of the zero-order rs given in Brookover, Paterson, and Thomas (1962, p. 109) shows that there is a tendency for correlations involving the same subject-matter area (e.g., self-concept of arithmetic ability vs. arithmetic achievement scores) to exceed the corresponding cross-correlations (e.g., self-concept of arithmetic ability vs. English achievement scores). This support for discriminant validity is not strong since only about three-quarters of the convergent coefficients exceed the respectively corresponding discriminant coefficients, and the absolute sizes of the differences between rs are small. The latter facts are not surprising in view of the relatively high correlations among the special self-concept-of-ability scales and among the achievement measures.

O'Hara (1966) tailored each of his 9-point self-rating scales to correspond to the achievement measures he wished to predict: (a) yearly GPA, and grades in English, Latin, foreign language, mathematics, and science for twelfth graders; and (b) yearly GPA and grades for English, Latin, history, and mathematics for ninth graders. Altogether, including self-ratings, he used 72 predictor variables and examined separately the results for 308 ninth-grade males and 152 twelfth-grade males.

For each of 6 twelfth-grade achievement criteria and each of 5 ninth-grade achievement criteria, he computed 72 rs, making 432 rs in the twelfth grade and 360 rs in ninth grade.

Out of 432 rs from the twelfth-grade group, 24 $rs \geq$ .31. For each of the 6 achievement criteria, between 2 and 6 such $rs \geq$ .31 were found, and we may call these predictor variables "best predictors." Of these 24 "best predictors," 11 were self-ratings. In a parallel analysis of ninth-grade data, out of 360 correlations, 13 $rs \geq$ .33 were obtained between predictors and achievement criteria. Three of these 13 "best predictors" were self-ratings. This is an intuitively impressive "batting average" for self-ratings, but of course there is no way of evaluating this set of data for over-all statistical significance.

An examination of the "best predicting" self-ratings shows that they are "sensible," e.g., self-rated literary and creative abilities were among the best predictors of English grades. The one exception is that self-rated numerical ability was a "best predictor" of Latin achievement in the twelfth-grade data.

O'Hara then used a multiple correlation technique on the data for each criterion for each grade, first finding the multiple correlation between the criterion and test scores (including five subtests of the Differential Aptitude Test); then finding the multiple correlation when test scores and "selected self-rating variables" were correlated with the criterion. For the ninth-grade data, each of the five analyses (one for each achievement criterion) showed that self-ratings significantly increased multiple R; while for twelfth-grade data, three out of six multiple Rs were significantly increased by the addition of self-ratings.

Since somewhat different achievement criteria were used in the ninth- and twelfth-grade analyses and somewhat different findings were obtained, the two analyses cannot be considered to be replications yielding point-by-point mutual confirmation. Accordingly the study should be replicated.

Holly, Purl, Dawson, and Michael (1973) gave a 10-item Mathematics Self-Concept Scale (MSCS) to 183 seventh graders in southern California. They made several multiple-regression analyses predicting posttest scores on the Comprehensive Test of Basic Skills — Mathematics as the dependent variable measure of achievement. In one multiple regression analysis which included biographical and demographic predictors, but excluded cognitive predictors (e.g., verbal and nonverbal IQ, mathematics skill pretest), the MSCS was the first chosen and most heavily weighted predictor variable. But in another multiple regression analysis which included cognitive variables, the MSCS made no statistically significant contribution to the prediction. Thus one cannot assert that mathematics self-concept was correlated with achievement when abilities were held constant.

Specific Aspects of Self-Concept Other Than
Self-Concepts of Specific Abilities

Goldman, Hudson, and Daharsh (1973) obtained a single self-estimate measure of task persistence, based on the sum of self-estimated persistence (as compared to college peers) on 20 different, clearly specified cognitive tasks. The use of a single self-estimated persistence score was justified by the results of a factor analysis and an odd-even reliability of .91 for the 20 responses comprising the single self-estimate score. For 52 undergraduate experimental psychology students, a markedly curvilinear relationship was obtained between self-estimated persistence and GPA, the highest GPAs being associated with an intermediate amount of persistence. When ability scores on 5 tests from the Kit of Reference Tests for Cognitive Factors were removed as covariates, the curvilinear relationship between self-estimated persistence and GPA was undiminished, perhaps magnified.

In the study by Baird (1966), evaluated earlier in this section, quite a few of the 31 self-ratings among his very large number of predictors of 13 college achievements involved personality characteristics which appear not to be specifically related to academic ability or to academic interests and academic achievement motivation. For example, these nonacademic self-ratings included popularity, understanding of others, sociability, self-control, conservatism, and cheerfulness. It will be remembered from the previous discussion that self-ratings of specific abilities appeared with some consistency among Baird's "best predictors" of 13 kinds of college accomplishment. By contrast, none of the self-ratings involving nonacademic personality characteristics was among the best predictors for any of the 13 college accomplishments.

In a similar large-scale study by Holland and Nichols (1964), also described earlier in this section, 51 self-rating scales were among the 130 predictors used to predict 7 criteria of college achievement. Although the self-rating scales are not published, it is probably safe to assume that nonacademic self-evaluative traits were included among them. However, no nonacademic self-ratings appeared among the "best predictors" of GPAs or of specific college accomplishments in science, art, dramatic art, writing, or music.

In another large-scale study also referred to above (Nichols & Holland, 1963), 141 variables were used to predict 13 college-achievement criteria. Among the predictors were 20 self-ratings on characteristics which included such nonacademic traits as emotional stability, popularity, dependability, sociability, self-control, cheerfulness, conservatism, and self-understanding. These authors also used several scales from the California Psychological Inventory (Femininity, Socialization, Social Presence), and the Dom scale from Cattell's 16 PF

Test. For the following reasons it is impossible to evaluate the presented results: the matrix of correlations between predictors and criteria of achievement is very large; results are incompletely published; correlations among predictors and among achievement criteria undoubtedly occur, and they have not been taken into account in evaluating significance levels of predictor-criterion *r*s, and there was no cross-validation. However, it seems safe to surmise from the published report that personality inventory scale scores and self-ratings on the nonacademic traits did *not* show significant associations with general or specific college achievement criterion scores more often than would be expected by chance. If anything, such "significant" correlations occurred less frequently than would be expected by chance, it appears.

In Guerney and Burton's (1967) study of 51 high-achieving and 42 low-achieving college females who were matched with respect to verbal and mathematics scores on the College Entrance Examination Board (CEEB), the mean Dom Self score from Leary's Interpersonal Check List did not differ between achievement groups, whereas the mean Lov Self score was significantly higher in the high-achievement group. Neither Ideal Dom nor Ideal Lov scores differentiated achievement groups. These findings have not been cross-validated. (For an evaluation of the Interpersonal Check List, see Wylie, 1974, pp. 213–223.)

Kubiniec (1970) chose 5 semantic differential scales to represent each of Osgood's 3 "meaning dimensions": evaluative, potency, and activity. On the basis of her own factor analysis of her subjects' ratings of 8 concepts on each of the 15 scales, Kubiniec divided her semantic differential variables into *Self Evaluations* (i.e., Past Self, Future Self, Real Self, Ideal Self on good-bad, strong-weak, active-passive, important-unimportant, interesting-boring, enjoyable-unenjoyable) and *Self-Descriptions* (on the specific scales active-passive, energetic-lethargic, serious-humorous, masculine-feminine, complex-simple, excitable-calm, and rugged-delicate). She uses the term *Phenomenal Self* to refer to these 2 sets of self-report variables combined. "Relative academic achievement" was defined according to methods suggested by Thorndike (1963) for controlling for ability while differentiating the following groups with respect to GPAs: High Achievers (HA), Moderate Achievers (MA), Low Achievers (LA), and Dropouts (DO).

She predicted that the Self-Evaluation variables would discriminate more effectively between achievement groups than would the Self-

Descriptive variables. In the case of each set of Phenomenal Self Variables however, the order of the groups was predicted to be HA > MA > LA > DO.

Of the four Self-Evaluation variables (Past Self, Future Self, Real Self, Ideal Self on the scales indicated above), only Past Self significantly discriminated among the male achievement groups, but this significant effect came from the MA group's having the highest rather than (as predicted) the second highest score. None of the four Self-Evaluation Variables (Past Self, Future Self, Real Self, and Ideal Self on the scales indicated above) discriminated among the women's achievement groups.

All F tests for comparisons of men's achievement groups on each of the six Self Descriptive variables were insignificant, as was apparently also the case for the women's groups, although the individual F tests for women's groups are not published in this report.

In a discriminant function analysis, the entire set of Phenomenal Self Variables (i.e., a combination of Self-Evaluation and Self-Description) significantly discriminated among male achievement groups. However, the means for male groups were ranked in the order MA > HA > LA > DO. That is, the MA and HA groups were interchanged from their hypothesized order. In a corresponding discriminant function analysis of the entire set of Phenomenal Self variables (combined Self-Evaluation and Self-Description) for the female achievement groups, the Phenomenal Self variables failed to discriminate significantly.

This overview of Kubiniec's results gives no support to the idea that either over-all self-regard or self-evaluations regarding specific personality characteristics are significantly associated with achievement, when ability levels are controlled.

One other study involving the relationship between achievement and a specific aspect of self-concept was conducted by McCoy (1963) with 2 groups of 31 educable mentally retarded subjects who were matched with respect to sex, racial group membership, socioeconomic level, Stanford Binet IQ ($\bar{X}$s = 74.2 and 72.1), MA ($\bar{X}$s = 114.1 and 110.1 mos.) and CA ($\bar{X}$s = 158.0 and 156.0 mos.). On the California Achievement Test, each member of the first ("academically unsuccessful") group had a grade placement ≥ one grade level below that expected for his/her MA; each member of the second had a grade placement equal to or higher than the level expected for his/her MA. Results from an idiosyncratic test of "self-confidence" showed no significant difference between these academically successful and unsuccessful EMR students. Although his failure to find a significant relationship between a nonacademic specific aspect of self-concept and an achievement measure among the mentally retarded supports the results of studies reported above which were concerned with similar variables among normal subjects, the use of an idiosyncratic measure which may not even be appropriate for the educable mentally retarded and the omission of many details about the procedure limit the interpretability of these findings.

Seven other studies looked at relationships between achievement and specific aspects of self-concept other than self-concept of abilities, but since these researches are more seriously flawed than those considered above and will not sustain interpretation, they are simply listed here: Durr and Schmatz (1964); McDonald (1963); Norfleet (1968); Norman and Daley (1959); Passow and Goldberg (1962); Stewart (1968); Zoolalian (1965).

Summary and Conclusions Regarding Particular Aspects of Self-Concept and Achievement with Ability Controlled

The seven studies which are substantively discussed in this section include three very large-scale attempts to find predictors of academic achievement. So far as self-evaluations of *nonacademic* personality characteristics are concerned, there is no firm evidence that associations occur between self-reports on such characteristics and the achievement measures used in the five studies. This situation is in marked contrast to the rather consistently obtained trends toward positive associations between achievement measures and self-evaluations of personality characteristics which are intuitively specifically relevant to achievement, e.g., self-ratings of ability in English, self-ratings of "schoolwork ability."

5. Overview of Studies Relating Achievement and Ability to Self-Concept Measures

In summarizing this section, I first return to the predictions stated at the outset, to see how many have been tested and with what results.

Concerning relationships between achievement levels and self-concept measures with ability indices constant, arguments were developed that relationships with self-conceptions of achievement would be strongest, relationships with self-conceptions of ability would be next, and relationships with over-all self-regard weakest (perhaps insignificantly different from zero). The great methodological disparities among the discussed investigations render extremely hazardous any attempts to "test" this predicted rank order by an overview of the results of these studies. Only one researcher attempted to look at self-conceptions of achievement in relationship to achievement levels — an insufficient basis for evaluating that sort of relationship. It does appear that the relationship between achievement level and self-concepts of ability may be stronger and more replicable than the relationship of over-all self-regard to achievement level. This seems reasonable in the light of the arguments developed in the introduction in support of the prediction.

It is interesting that significant associations between achievement level and over-all self-regard indices have come more often from studies using well-known and relatively well-developed self-regard instruments, as opposed to idiosyncratic ones with unknown psychometric characteristics. As it happens, fewer of the studies of self-conceptions of ability have involved well-known and developed indices of that construct, probably because fewer such instruments were available in the literature. The fact that, despite this instrument deficiency, the trends involving self-conceptions of ability may be somewhat stronger and more reliable than the trends involving over-all self-regard goes against what one might expect on the basis of instrument limitations per se. In any event, the correlations of achievement indices and over-all self-regard indices tend to be small in absolute terms, offering no support to the commonly accepted lore that achievement and self-regard are strongly associated. (Even the correlations between achievement and self-regard indices with ability scores uncontrolled tend to run only around .30.)

It was also predicted that, with achievement level constant, ability scores should correlate only weakly with self-conceptions of achievement level, self-conceptions of ability level, and over-all self-regard (the latter quite possibly yielding correlations not significantly different from zero). To my knowledge, no studies have looked at the first two types of relationships mentioned, and only two researches looked at the third. Here, as predicted, null findings were obtained. While the two null outcomes are congruent with the prediction, they are obviously inconclusive. (Among the investigations in which achievement level was not controlled, slightly more than half yielded one or more significant associations between ability-level indices and over-all self-regard indices. However, such zero-order rs cannot, of course, be interpreted as indicating an association between ability level per se and over-all self-regard.)

Turning now to the situation with the mentally retarded, one finds a somewhat surprising and curious situation. Obviously, comparisons of retardates and normal persons involve both ability and achievement differences between groups. Even with both factors operating to produce lower self-regard in the retarded, two authors report finding no difference, one reports a very small (albeit significant) difference favoring the normals, and one a relatively large difference favoring normals. Certainly, evidence of a severe impact of retardation on over-all self-regard is not at hand. However, three studies do show that, within retardate groups (as within normal groups), associations occur between achievement level and over-all self-regard, with ability indices controlled. Both of the above sets of findings involving retarded persons are congruent with the idea that persons will tend to evaluate themselves against a restricted reference group which seems relevant to them.

The remaining studies in this section are too disparate to furnish a basis for a synthetic or comparative overview. They provide some suggestive leads concerning possible relationships between achievement and ability levels on the one hand and various specific aspects of self-concept other than self-conceptions of ability on the other.

B. Creativity Indices and Self-Concept Variables

1. Theory and Definitions

Insofar as theoretical interest has formed a basis for planning any of the published research involving relationships between purported creativity measures and self-concept scores, one cannot say that self-concept theories were explicitly involved. Indeed, the available publications regarding creativity measures and self-concept measures have usually reported such relationships among a much larger set of associations between creativity measures and personality measures of all kinds. When self-report personality measures were used, they were apparently construed by many researchers as only one of several ways of measuring traits, rather than as being self-concept indicators. In any case, a fairly atheoretical, inductive approach seems to be most typical, although discussion sections of research reports may refer to one or more personality theories in an ad hoc and speculative manner.

This situation may surprise any reader who realizes that some version of the concept "creativity" has appeared in the theoretical writings of personality theorists ranging from Freud and Rank to Rogers and Maslow. Nevertheless, since such a state of affairs exists, I believe the most comprehensible way to try to organize the research literature on creativity and self-concept variables is according to categories which emerge from the different measurement practices used in such studies.

To present a thorough survey and analysis of conceptual referents for the term creativity is impossible here. Few research psychologists have made formal attempts at literary definitions of this term, but instead have proceeded without such preliminary definitions to use one or more classes of operational definition which I mention later on. Among the few who offer a conceptual definition are Mednick and Mednick (1964). Working from an association-theory approach, they propose that *"creative thinking consists of forming new combinations of associative elements, which combinations either meet specified requirements, or are in some way useful. The more mutually remote the elements of the new combination, the more creative is the process or solution"* (p. 55). Drawing attention to the difficulties in using the word *new* in definitions of "originality," R. C. Wilson, Guilford, and Christensen (1953) state "rather than define original as 'new' or 'did not exist before' we have investigated three alternative definitions. We have regarded originality in turn as meaning 'uncommon,' 'remote,' and 'clever.' It was felt that these three definitions include significant aspects of the term original" (p. 363). Considering creativity in the sciences, Ghiselin proposes that "the measure of a creative product should be 'the extent to which it restructures our universe of understanding,' " while Lacklen, in an almost equivalent suggestion says one should judge the "creativity of a contribution in terms of the area of science which it underlies" (Lacklen & Harmon, 1957, p. 243).

Obviously, even those courageous enough to try to give a conceptual definition of creativity have left many terms within the definition incompletely explained. In short, the situation described in 1963 by Golann seems still to obtain:

A striking feature of the literature on creativity is the diversity of interests, motives, and approaches characteristic of the many investigators. Creativity has been viewed as a normally distributed trait, an aptitude trait, an intrapsychic process, and as a style of life. It has been described as that which is seen in all children, but few adults. It has been described as that which leads to innovation in science, performance in fine arts, or new thoughts. Creativity has been described as related to, or equatable with intelligence, productivity, positive mental health, and originality. It has been described as being caused by self-actualization and by sublimation and restitution of destructive impulses. Clearly there is a need for organization and integration within the psychological study of creativity. [P. 548]

Since a search of current psychological literature for agreed-upon conceptual definitions of creativity is fruitless, I attempt here only a brief classification and evaluation of the measures actually used in the studies reported in this section. It seems safe to say that most of the authors of these studies would at least agree that (a) creativity within any given kind of activity (e.g., painting, fiction-writing, mathematics) is probably not a unifactor dimension and, (b) considerable lack of transsituational generality is to be expected (i.e., perhaps a different set of creativity factors will be found within each of several areas such as fiction-writing, mathematics, or painting).

2. Methodological Considerations

a. CREATIVITY INDICES

The studies relating self-report data to creativity measures have used one of three classes of indices which purport to differentiate individuals and/or groups with respect to creativity: (a) nominations by teachers or professional peers; (b) scores on alleged tests of creativity such as Guilford's, Torrance's, the Barron-Welsh or Revised Art Scales, the Rorschach O +, or less well-known tests; (c) self-reports of activities or products such as time spent in painting, published research articles, patents obtained from inventions, prizes received for poetry.

Applicable to all these purported indices of creativity are some methodological questions about *construct validity*. In order to compare and synthesize studies we need to know to what extent measures from the three classes intercorrelate, i.e., show convergent validity. Some correlations of this sort are scattered throughout the literature I examined (e.g., F. Barron, 1955, 1957; McDermid, 1965), but not enough information is available to provide a systematic, adequate basis for a comparative substantive review of available publications using differing creativity indices. The correlations between creativity-test scores and creativity nominations or ratings appear typically to run low enough to suggest that different constructs are being tapped by these two types of procedures. It is partly for this reason that I divide the studies for discussion according to the creativity indices they involved.

Then, of course, there are problems of *discriminant validity:* How can we discriminate individual differences in creativity (by any one of these classes of measurement) from differences in tested intelligence and from differences in tested achievement? That these variables are correlated has been frequently recognized (e.g., by Torrance, 1967; Barron, 1957; C. E. Schaefer, 1969; Rivlin, 1959), but the correlations have not always been taken into account in the procedures used for selecting subjects and analyzing data. For example, it seems obvious, in view of the halo effect and the probable overlap between intelligence and creativity, that raters or nominators must be given very explicit instructions in order to maximize the discriminant validity of their creative nominations or ratings; yet one is often not given enough information in the published articles to evaluate how well this was done. Likewise, known correlation values of creativity-test scores with IQ values and/or achievement-test scores must be allowed for when evaluating correlations between creativity test scores and self-concept reports; yet many researches fall short on this point.

Psychometric information about the creativity scores is necessary in order to evaluate, for example, the influence of range of scores or the reliability of the scores and the relevance of such facts to interpreting the many null or weak trends characteristic of this area. Unfortunately for the interpretability of research in this area, such information is not routinely given in publications relating creativity and self-report variables.

The best known creativity tests have received considerable standardization and validation work, e.g., Guilford's tests (Guilford, 1957; Guilford & Merrifield, 1960; R. C. Wilson, Guilford, & Christensen, 1953); the Barron-Welsh Art Scale and the highly overlapping and highly correlated Revised Art Scale, consisting of items from the Welsh Figure Preference Test (Welsh, 1959); Torrance's tests (Torrance, 1966a, 1966b, 1974). Guilford's tests are derived primarily from a factor analytic approach to measures of performance based on his a priori conception that originality involves remoteness, unusualness, and cleverness. Although he feels that creative thinking cannot be allocated exclusively to any particular subdivisions of his factorial structure-of-intellect model (Guilford & Merrifield, 1960, p. 11), those of his tests which are most frequently used in creativity studies are among the ones which represent his "divergent production" factors of semantic spontaneous flexibility (brick uses, alternate uses) and originality (cleverness of plot titles, consequences of certain changes). The Barron-Welsh Art Scale was constructed by comparing the expressed preferences of known groups (artist vs. nonartist) for figures differing in complexity/asymmetry—simplicity/symmetry. Torrance (1974) has devised or developed both verbal and nonverbal tests which he judged to be representative of a stated set of criteria of creativity. Two of the verbal tests are modifications of Guilford's unusual uses and consequences tests, whereas two of the figural tests are adaptations of a drawing-completion test developed by Franck. The 1974 manual gives an overview of research which is relevant to the reliability and construct validity of the Torrance scores.

b. Types of Self-Concept Variables Examined

With what sorts of relationships between self-reports and creativity measures have researchers been concerned? The most common approach is to examine various specific self-reported personality characteristics, using for example, the California Psychological Inventory (Gough, 1969) and Gough's Adjective Check List (Gough and Heilbrun, 1965), as related to differences in creativity. Additionally or alternately, purported measures of over-all self-regard have been looked at in relation to creativity. Unique to the field of creativity is the attempt to have creative subjects describe their views of their own creative activities, as in the Gough and Woodworth (1960) Q sort for scientists. Obviously, all studies involving relationships of creativity to self-report must be evaluated methodologically partly in terms of the adequacy and appropriateness of the self-report measures used.

c. Methodological Criteria

In addition to considering the methodological adequacy of creativity measures and self-report measures used in each study, one must also appraise other methodological characteristics such as the comparability of test-administration conditions across subjects, the control of tested IQ and achievement, the means of keeping the evaluators of self-reports unaware of the creativity status of each subject, the use of multiple significance tests (especially when the variables involved are themselves correlated), the cross-validation of findings (especially when multiple significance tests have been involved in the initial study).

It is unfortunately the case, as is shown later on, that few of the available researches fulfill these rudimentary criteria of methodological adequacy.

3. Studies Classified According to Types of Creativity Indices

The studies to be cited and evaluated are presented below essentially according to the sorts of creativity measures involved, i.e., nominations/ratings, tests, and self-reported activities and accomplishments.

a. CREATIVITY INFERRED FROM NOMINATIONS

The most impressive series of researches using the nomination technique for designating creative persons was carried out at the Institute for Personality Assessment and Research (IPAR) at Berkeley. Unusually creative subjects and competent (but not unusually creative) comparison subjects were obtained from the professions of architecture (F. Barron, 1969; MacKinnon, 1963, 1964, 1965; W. B. Hall & MacKinnon, 1969); mathematics (F. Barron, 1969; Helson, 1967b, 1971; Helson & Crutchfield, 1970a, 1970b); writing (F. Barron, 1955, 1968, 1969); and from the seniors at a women's college (Helson, 1967a; F. Barron, 1969). An unusually innovative group of Irish business managers was also studied by F. Barron (1969), but without comparison to a comparable control group of competent, less innovative managers.

The general approach in this program of research was to assess the subjects intensively, obtaining many personality scores for each person (e.g., 200 or more scores per subject), and then to compare more and less creative groups and/or individuals with respect to each of the numerous personality scores.

Evaluation of these researches poses many difficulties. Although the data were mostly collected in the 1950s and numerous overlapping partial reports have appeared, it is exceedingly difficult or impossible to piece together all the information one needs to know in order to evaluate thoroughly their methodology and the interpretability of their results. Barron pointed out in 1969 that

> a comprehensive review of the results [of this series of studies] must await publication of full reports on each study separately, and some of these are not yet available. Even a thorough first-level correlational analysis based on test measures in relationship to the [creativity] criterion ratings has not yet appeared in print for the entire program of research. [P. 67]

The study in this series for which the most complete procedural and cross-validational information is available is the one by Helson (1967a) concerning creative college women. The strongest points of this series of researches are the great care with which the nominating techniques were applied, the use of very unusual groups of subjects (which could potentially facilitate generalizations concerning high levels of creativity in various fields), and the extensiveness of the exploratory work done in different studies using many of the same instruments, which should facilitate comparisons among studies.

On the other hand, it is not clear that all experimenters held tested intelligence constant between creative and comparison groups. The creative and comparison college women studied by Helson (1967a) were matched for Scholastic Aptitude Test scores. However, no information is given by Barron (1955, 1968) about the intelligence of the writers of varying levels of rated creativity which he studied. Architects who varied in rated creativity (MacKinnon, 1963, 1964, 1965; Hall & MacKinnon, 1969) were tested under differing conditions, with only the most creative ones being called to Berkeley for live-in assessment, while the others worked at home, using mailed materials. Consequently, no intelligence test scores are available, a drawback of this study, as MacKinnon (1964) recognizes. Although Terman Concept Mastery Test scores correlated .31 with rated creativity among women mathematicians (Helson, 1971), the more creative group was higher on this test at only the .10 level. I found no relevant information about the tested intelligence of the creative and competent male mathematicians. The Terman Concept Mastery Test was also correlated with creativity in the Irish manager group (Barron, 1969) and air force captain group (Barron, 1957, 1968), and some of the findings are reported with Terman Concept Mastery scores partialled out.

So far as the self-report measures most commonly used in these studies are concerned, the California Psychological Inventory (CPI) and the Adjective Check List (ACL) are both subject to a number of important criticisms. (See Buros, 1970, regarding the California Psychological Inventory; and Wylie, 1974, pp. 200–213, regarding the Adjective Check List.)

The most serious criticisms of the IPAR nomination studies stem from the fact that hundreds of measures of association between self-report measures and creativity measures were generated in each study of the research program. Thus, the particular self-report scores which yielded "significant" findings should not be psychologically interpreted before cross-validation has been carried out. Although Barron (1969) feels that "it is possible to pull together a wealth of findings that are of scientific interest, even though they have not yet been cross-validated" (p. 67), I contend that the suggestive scientific interest of the results is not the same as their scientific *value,* which can be demonstrated only by cross-validation. Except for parts of Mackinnon's (1962, 1963, 1964, 1965) and Hall and MacKinnon's (1969) study of architects, the number of self-report scores significantly associated with creativity was near or less than what might be expected by chance. However, in their extensive interpretive discussions of each set of their findings, the members of the research group seem to imply that the significant findings involving the Adjective Check List, may be particularly suggestive before cross-validation, insofar as there is an apparent overlap in meaning among the small number of *adjectives* which differentiate creative and comparison groups within certain respective professions. MacKinnon (1962, 1963, 1964, 1965) also argues for the internal consistency among the Adjective Check List *scales* which differentiate more and less creative architects and for the internal consistency of the 13 CPI scales which were associated significantly with creativity in his architect groups. When this sort of clustering of meaning occurs, it is indeed suggestive that cross-validation might be worth pursuing, but it does not substitute for cross-validation.

In 1969, Hall and MacKinnon reported a kind of cross-validational reanalysis of the data for all 124 architects' scores on 132 scales from 7 self-report inventories. As a basis for this cross-validation, the group of architects was divided into halves, comparable with respect to rated creativity. The program for multiple-stepwise correlational analysis of their data from the first half of their subjects provided for choosing and weighting 3 scale scores from each of 7 inventories in such a manner as to maximize the possibilities of obtaining variables which would hold up under cross-validation with the second half of the subjects. The weighted triad obtained from the CPI was based on scores from the Social Presence and Femininity scales (both positively associated with rated creativity) and the Achievement via Conformance scale (negatively associated with creativity). Weighted scores from this triad correlated significantly with creativity in the cross-validational group as well as in the original group. The weighted triad obtained from the ACL *scales,* which was also significantly correlated with rated creativity in the cross-validational group, was based on the Self-Confidence scale (negatively associated with creativity), and the Autonomy and Change scales (both positively associated with creativity). This type of analysis still leaves open, of course, the replicability of null or other findings from other CPI scales, other ACL scales, and the ACL adjectives, as previously reported by MacKinnon to be associated with rated creativity for this group of architects.

While MacKinnon reported 13 CPI scales to be significantly associated with rated creativity among his architects, the situation is quite different in the other IPAR nomination studies. Either there were no CPI scales significantly associated with creativity (the study of writers reported by Barron, 1955, 1968); or the one scale which discriminated at original testing did not do so at follow-up (Psychological-Mindedness among college women, reported by Helson, 1967a); or only a few scales discriminated significantly, with little overlap among those which did. For instance, in the study of Irish managers reported by Barron (1969) only the Femininity and Socialization scales were associated with creativity; in the study of women mathematicians reported by Helson (1971), only Communality, Achievement via Conformance, and Flexibility were associated with creativity, whereas Helson and Crutchfield (1970b) report CPI Self-Control and Flexibility to be significantly associated with creativity among male mathematicians. In the case of an IPAR study using tests rather than nominations as indices of creativity, 2 scales *not* among MacKinnon's discriminating 13 were the only discriminating ones (Social Dominance and Impulsivity in the study of United States Air Force captains, reported by Barron, 1957, 1968). This clearly shows the dangers in assuming that apparent internal consistency augurs well for generalizability across studies of "creativity." (Later on, I tentatively compare the ACL adjectives and scales found to be discriminating in a cross-validational study by J. M. Smith and Schaefer [1969] with those found to be discriminating in the above-discussed IPAR studies and 2 other studies to be discussed.)

Parloff, Datta, and Handlon (1968) factored CPI scale intercorrelations from two matrices, one based on responses of some of the mathematicians, research scientists, writers, and architects previously studied in the above-mentioned IPAR research, the other based on male adolescent Science Talent Search winners who scored above the eightieth percentile on a scientific aptitude test and whose projects had been rated as more or less creative by pairs of judges who were experts in the respective areas of the projects. Coefficients of congruence indicated a good match between each of the first four factors obtained from the matrices from the adult and adolescent groups, and factor scores were used to compare more and less creative subjects within the adult group and within the adolescent group. On Factor I (Disciplined Effectiveness), the more creative adolescents unexpectedly scored significantly higher than did their less creative counterparts, while the significant difference found in the adult group went in exactly the opposite direction. Adult and adolescent results were similar for each of the three remaining factors, as follows: On Factor II (Creative Self-Assurance) mean scores were significantly higher for creative adolescents and nonsignificantly higher for creative adults. On Factor III (Adaptive Autonomy) scores, both creative adolescents and creative adults significantly exceeded their less creative peers, whereas Factor IV (Humanitarian Conscience) scores failed to differentiate creativity levels within either the adolescent or adult group. Since the individual CPI scales have not repeatedly discriminated between creative and less creative groups, as we have just seen above, these findings are suggestive that the factor scores may be more reliable and potentially more indicative of some psychologically meaningful characteristics than are the individual scale scores. Replication of these findings, especially the unexpectedly opposite trend found in adolescent and adult Factor I scores, is needed before a firm interpretation can be offered.

So far as *over-all self-regard* is concerned, there is little in the IPAR studies to support the idea that creative persons differ from comparison persons. Helson (1967b, 1971) reported that for neither male nor female mathematicians was the mean Self-Acceptance score from the CPI significantly higher among the more creative subjects. Barron (1969) gives mean CPI Self-Acceptance values for the groups of architects and writers, but gives no significance tests. However, MacKinnon (1964) reports a significant $r = .18$ between CPI Self-Acceptance scale scores and rated creativity across all 124 architects studied. On the other hand, MacKinnon (1963) reported no significant differences between architect groups on either the Fav or Unfav scales of the ACL. Helson (1967a) reported no significant difference in Self-Acceptance means for creative college women as contrasted to a matched comparison group, or as contrasted to the rest of the college class from which the research subjects were drawn. Although the creative writers had significantly higher Self-Acceptance mean than "the general population," no difference between more creative and less creative writers was reported by

Barron (1968). Also, no significant associations between creativity and any of the CPI and ACL scales of over-all self-acceptance, self-favorability, or self-unfavorability were reported in Barron's (1969) publication about Irish managers. *From all the information available from the IPAR studies, then, no firm support is at hand for the conclusion that differences in rated creativity are associated with differences in over-all self-regard.*

Finally, I note an attempt by researchers to develop a measure of self-description of characteristic styles of activity, modes of research activity, and values among research scientists. This Q-sort device, originated by Gough and Woodworth (1960) and given to 45 professional research scientists in industrial laboratories, was subjected to a factor analysis "among scientists." The 8 "factor types" seemed to the authors operationally to represent stylistic types of self-described research methodologies. Unfortunately, no cross-validational research on this instrument was performed; so no substantive generalizations are warranted. (The reader should also note the evaluation of Q-sort methodology in Wylie, 1974, pp. 128–150.)

Helson (1967b) used some of Gough and Woodworth's (1960) items to form a 56-item mathematician's Q sort, descriptive of "professional style" in mathematics. Helson (1971) reports that 13 of these items discriminated significantly between more and less creative women mathematicians, but no cross-validational information is at hand.

Using the self-descriptive Q sorts made by all 109 creative and competent male and female mathematicians used in the IPAR study, Helson (1967b) performed a Tryon-type cluster analysis which yielded 4 clusters. She also computed another cluster analysis of the Q sorts made by the 34 creative male mathematicians among the 109 subjects. This yielded 6 clusters which are published both in Helson (1967b) and in Helson and Crutchfield (1970a). Although the 2 sets of clusters on the 34 and the 109 cases are based on overlapping subjects, they are quite dissimilar, and neither has been cross-validated. In a further analysis of the same data, Helson and Crutchfield (1970a) chose 4 of the creative males who "best represented" each of the five 5 "types" (clusters), and they attempted to describe the 5 types and relate numerous personality variables to the respective type scores. The Ns were extremely small, and cross-validation of these associations was not carried out; so substantive conclusions about self-concepts of various self-described types seem not to be warranted.

I have examined three other studies which relied mainly or exclusively on nominations to define creativity. (Studies using *both* nominations and tests are reported in the following section.)

Rivlin (1959) compared honors class high school students who were nominated by their teachers, using 14 stated criteria of creativity. Although the teachers attended conferences where the criteria were discussed, no information is available on the reliability of the nominations (there was only one nominator per subject), and no explanation is given as to how the teachers were supposed to carry out their instructions to pick high and low creative groups of subjects who were "equally able." (Results showed that, in the boys' group, high and low creative subjects did differ significantly in Pintner IQ.) Using Bills's Index of Adjustment and Values (Bills, undated), Rivlin reports no association between creativity and Self scores, Ideal Self scores, or [Self — Ideal] discrepancies. A finding the author considered contrary to common-sense expectation and which has not been cross-validated was a significantly higher Sociability mean score for the creative subjects on the Bell Adjustment Inventory.

In their study of petroleum engineers, R. F. Morrison, Owens, Glennon, and Albright (1962) used supervisor ratings of creativity and performance and number of patent disclosures during a 5-year period to define creativity. Although their principal means of predicting creativity measures was a 75-item life-history questionnaire on which some previous validational work had been done, this questionnaire contained a number of self-descriptive and self-evaluative items. The largest factor resulting from a factor analysis of the 75 questions and the creativity scores was called by them Favorable Self-Perception. The items loading most highly on this factor concern descriptions of oneself as a successful, fast worker who likes to work entirely autonomously, take responsibilities and risks, and handle many things simultaneously. Also loading on this factor is the self-description as friendly, easygoing, having many friends. Rated creativity and performance (but not patent disclosures) loaded $\geq$ .30 on this Favorable Self-Perception factor. However, one should note that the factor accounted for only 6.8% of the total variance.

In another nomination study, McDermid (1965) defined creativity differences among his engineering and technical personnel at an organ company by means of supervisor and peer ratings, the contents of which are described more fully in previous publications. For unknown reasons, the two types of creativity ratings agreed poorly (r = .30), and a combination of the two is the creativity score alluded to here. (Incidentally, neither patent disclosures nor Welsh's Revised Art Scale correlated with the combined rating criterion of creativity.) The Terman Concept Mastery Test did not correlate with creativity or performance ratings; so tested intellectual ability cannot account for relationships of creativity ratings to other variables. Anonymity was guaranteed but administrative conditions by mail provide questionable control over certain variables which could affect self-reports and ratings. No CPI scale and 5 out of 21 ACL scales correlated significantly with the combined creativity ratings. Although there is no way of knowing which, if any, of these 5 are significant by chance, the particular scale findings do tend to agree with some of those from other creativity studies using ACL scales, as I summarize below. As is typically reported, creativity measures were not associated with any over-all self-favorability or self-regard scores from the CPI or the ACL.

b. Creativity Inferred from Tests

Several studies have looked for possible associations between self-concept scores and creativity, when creativity is inferred from tests. The most frequently used tests which purport to measure creativity include those by Torrance (1966a, 1966b), Guilford (Guilford, 1957; R. C. Wilson, Guilford, & Christensen, 1953), and Welsh and Barron (Welsh, 1959).

The Torrance tests have had considerable use, and Torrance (1967) summarized briefly the results of surveying about 300 published references concerning the reliability and validity of these tests. Relevant to the question of discriminant validity, he tallied 178 rs between intelligence test scores and creativity scores from his tests, citing values ranging from $\geq$ .60 to $\geq$ $-$.30 for total scores, (median $r = .20$); from $\geq$ .60 to $\geq$ $-$.30 for verbal scores (median $r = .21$); and from $\leq$ .49 to $\leq$ $-$.40 for figural scores (median $r = .06$). Total Torrance scores correlated $\geq$ .70 to $\leq$ $-$.29 with various achievement tests (median $r = .29$); $\leq$ .69 to $\leq$ $-$.39 with teachers' grades (median $r = .21$); and $\leq$ .69 to $\leq$ $-$.19 with teachers' estimates of creative potentials (median $r = .20$). These rs cannot be clearly evaluated since Torrance reports no information about Ns, types of intelligence or achievement tests, ages of the subjects, or ranges of abilities included in the samples. Nevertheless, they at least indicate the need for trying to control IQ and achievement test scores when looking for relationships between self-concept variables and creativity or originality as measured by the Torrance tests. Unfortunately, only one of the following studies took this requirement into account.

R. J. Wright, Fox, and Noppe (1975) found no relationship between Total Positive scores on the Tennessee Self Concept Scale and any of the eight Torrance subtests. (See Wylie, 1974, pp. 230–236, for an evaluation of the TSCS.) They also attempted to look at "self-concept of creativity" by way of an idiosyncratic set of Likert scales for which no psychometric information is given. The total scores from these Likert self-concept scales correlated significantly with only three out of eight Torrance subscales. The numerous methodological limitations of this study preclude interpreting the reported results, however.

V. K. Phillips (1973) examined the correlation between Verbal Form B of Torrance Tests of Creative Thinking and two idiosyncratic self-concept instruments for which no psychometric information is provided. Procedures are vaguely described, evidently no attempt was made to control for intelligence or achievement differences, and multiple significance tests were made without cross-validation. Accordingly, the reported results are uninterpretable.

Dauw (1966) formed two extreme groups of high school seniors on the basis of Torrance's Test of Creative Thinking and looked for differences in "creative self-concept" between these groups in terms of scores on a personality check list developed by Torrance to include adjectives judged most characteristically descriptive of the "creative personality." Nothing is said about controlling for IQ or achievement scores. This, together with the paucity of information given about procedure and instruments, make it impossible to interpret the stated result that highly creative students had a significantly higher "creative self-concept" than did less creative students.

Using Torrance's Parallel Lines Test as a nonverbal measure of "originality," Long, Henderson, and Ziller (1967b) looked for associations between this kind of originality and (a) various scores on their nonverbal Self Social-Esteem (SSE) test, and (b) self-descriptive adjectives. IQ and Iowa Basic Skills test means were held constant between high- and low-originality groups. They found that "self-esteem" on their nonverbal test was significantly lower in the high-original group. However, they made multiple significance tests in this study, involving not only overlapping SSE scores but also an unpublished, idiosyncratic "self complexity" index of 110 adjectives. Thus their significant findings involving SSE scores and individual adjectives are uninterpretable without cross-validation. (See Wylie, 1974, pp. 190–200, for an evaluation of the SSE test.)

The CPI manual (Gough, 1969) and the ACL manual (Gough & Heilbrun, 1965) give correlations between the "Guilford Creativity Battery" and all scale scores from the CPI and ACL respectively. Unfortunately, several facts render these reported *r*s uninterpretable: (a) no information is given about the "100 males" on whom the correlations are based; (b) the exact composition of the Guilford Creativity Battery is not indicated; (c) multiple significance tests using correlated variables are made without cross-validation; (d) despite the need to control for IQ and achievement when examining relationships between creativity and self-concept variables, no account is taken of the 8 out of 24 significant correlations shown in the ACL manual between the Terman Concept Mastery Test and ACL scales, or the 12 out of 18 significant *r*s shown in the CPI manual between the Terman Concept Mastery Test and CPI scales. Thus, although the Guilford Creativity Battery is reported to correlate significantly with 7 out of 24 ACL scales and with 7 out of 18 CPI scales, one does not know what to make of this information.

Garwood (1964) examined selected scores on the CPI and the ICL for two groups of male science majors designated as high- or low-creative persons on the basis of a specially devised composite test score. Five tests of creativity, including 4 by Guilford and his associates, were administered to 105 male science majors, including graduate and undergraduate students and postdoctoral research fellows, all from southern California. From the original group of 105, personality test data were obtained from 18 of the top 20% and 18 of the bottom 20%. Among other personality measures, 10 CPI scales and 2 ICL scales were used. Garwood found that the high-creative group had significantly higher scores on CPI scales of Originality, Cognitive Flexibility, Dominance, Sociability, Social Presence, Self-Acceptance, Sense of Destiny. The high-creative group was significantly lower on CPI Socialization, Self-Control, Good Impression and on ICL Love. Garwood also compared the 2 groups on two measures involving the integration of the nonconscious and the conscious self. However, since the unconscious self was involved, these results are not reported here. (See Wylie, 1974, chap. 5, for an evaluation of measures of unconscious self-concept.) The small sample size, the multiple-significance testing based on intercorrelated dependent-variable measures, and the lack of cross-validation limit the interpretability of the results from this study.

THE SELF-CONCEPT

Guilford, Christensen, Frick, and Merrifield (1957) studied the relationship between (a) various questionnaire scores purporting to indicate traits of temperament and motivation, and (b) various purported measures of creative-thinking aptitudes. Eleven of the 40 questionnaire variables were said by the authors to be indices of various respective aspects of "self concept." These include ascendance, individual moral conformity, personal decisiveness, dejection, adaptive divergent thinking, emotional immaturity, excitability, general activity, impulsiveness, self-confidence, and nervousness. These "self-concept" variables were measured by items from the following tests: Guilford-Zimmerman Temperament Survey, G-IPAR Rigidity scale, Guilford Martin Inventory of Factors (GAMIN), and STDCR. To measure "creative thinking aptitudes," a number of different tests were used pertaining to various forms of fluency, originality, and flexibility. The 3 samples included 212 coast guard cadets, 221 naval air cadets, and 164 air force cadets.

The results of this study are very difficult to interpret for a number of reasons. The correlations between each of the 40 questionnaire variables and each of the measures of creative-thinking aptitudes are given for each of the 3 samples individually, but no significance values are given for these correlations. The 40 questionnaire variables were collapsed for the purpose of data analysis into 24 personality-trait scores. Of these, apparently 9 were comprised partly, but not necessarily entirely, of original questionnaire scores the authors had labeled "self-concept" measures. Also, each of the 3 samples was not given exactly the same creativity-aptitude tests, although there is some overlap among the 3 groups. The correlations between the 24 collapsed questionnaire scores and the creativity scores are reported separately for each sample. Also reported are average correlations between each of the 24 questionnaire scores and each creativity measure which was common to 2 or more samples. Of the 36 average correlations between the 4 creativity measures common to 2 or more of the samples and the 9 questionnaire variables based at least partly on alleged "self-concept" indices, only 6 are significant, the largest of these being only .22.

Although there was no actual control for IQ or achievement in this study, subjects' scores on tests of verbal comprehension and general reasoning were also correlated with the personality scores. The 5 self-concept questionnaire scores found to be significantly correlated with 1 or more of the 4 creativity measures were not found to be significantly correlated with either verbal comprehension or general reasoning (1 out of 10 rs was significant). Obviously, multiple significance testing throughout this study precludes interpretation of the results.

Barron (1957, 1968) reports on a study in which 100 United States Air Force captains were intensively evaluated at the Institute for Personality Assessment and Research (IPAR), using an idiosyncratic "Originality Composite" test score to define creativity and, as self-descriptive instruments, the California Psychological Inventory (CPI) and Adjective Check List (ACL) which (as noted above) were used throughout the IPAR studies. The Originality Composite score was the sum of standard scores from each of 8 parts: 3 Guilford tests, Rorschach O + , originality ratings on TAT stories, an idiosyncratic Barron Movement-Threshold Inkblot Test, an idiosyncratic anagrams test, and an idiosyncratic originality rating of a story written under specific task requirements. Except for the 3 Guilford tests, the parts of the Originality Composite score tended to intercorrelate poorly with each other. The Originality Composite score yielded an $r = .55$ with originality as rated by assessment staff members after the 3-day live-in period. Since the correlation between the Terman Concept Mastery Test and the Originality Composite was .33, partial rs were computed between each CPI scale and the Originality Composite, with the Terman scores controlled statistically. Out of 20 CPI scales, only Social Dominance and Impulsivity yielded significant partial rs. In an attempt to control for intelligence while examining the ACL adjectives which differentiated creativity groups, two extreme groups were formed as follows: (a) originality high–intelligence low; (b) intelligence high–originality low. Adjectives from the ACL which significantly differentiated these groups are listed and discussed, but one cannot interpret them because there are 4 possible explanations of these differences: (a) they could have occurred by chance (since only 18 out of 279 adjectives differed significantly between groups); (b) the groups differed in intelligence; (c) the groups differed in creativity; (d) the groups differed with respect to the direction of discrepancy between intelligence and creativity. Although Barron seems to feel that the discrepancy-group technique is acceptable, he himself remarks on the need for cross-validation to see how many of the multiple significance tests would be replicable. Incidentally, although the ACL provides for Fav and Unfav scale scores, nothing is said about these or the other ACL scales. Thus we do not know whether the preliminary observations made in this study would or would not suggest differences in over-all self-regard as purportedly indicated by the ACL.

As yet another way of purportedly measuring creativity by means of a test, Barron (1968), Welsh (1959), Cashdan and Welsh (1966), and Gough and Heilbrun (1965) used the Barron-Welsh Art Scale or the Revised Art Scale (RA), figure-preference tests which had been shown to differentiate artists from nonartists (Welsh, 1959). In all 4 studies, the Adjective Check List was used to obtain the subjects' self-descriptions, but, unfortunately for the comparability of the results, Barron (1968) and Welsh (1959) present their findings in terms of individual *adjectives* while Cashdan and Welsh (1966) present theirs in terms of ACL *scale* scores.

The Barron (1968) and Cashdan and Welsh (1966) publications report results of many significance tests involving some intercorrelated variables, thus precluding interpretive generalizations based on their results. Welsh (1959) does not state any significance levels for his 39 discriminating adjectives. Cashdan and Welsh (1966) attempted to set "stringent criteria [relevance to earlier theoretical formulations or empirical findings; F value closer to the .05 than the .10 level; only trends associated with over-all main effects considered] . . . in order to minimize consideration of results which, in a study of this size may well be speciously significant due to chance" (p. 448). But even these criteria do not appear to me to rule out the necessity for cross-validation before interpreting the results. Moreover, none of these reports mentioned any attempts to control for intelligence or achievement between groups or individuals differing in art-scale scores.

In the research edition of his manual, Welsh (1959) briefly alludes to comparisons between "the ten highest and ten lowest students on RA in a class of 74" (p. 15), listing adjectives "consistently more often checked about themselves" by the high and low groups. In Barron's (1968) study, 2 groups of 18 male graduate students with nonoverlapping distributions of Barron-Welsh Art scores were differentiated at the .05 level with respect to their frequency of endorsement of 16 adjectives. Since there were 279 adjectives used, this number was very close to what would be expected by chance. Again we have an instance of a point discussed earlier, that the content of the "discriminating" adjectives in the Barron (1968) study appears somewhat homogeneous. Despite this suggestive observation, psychological interpretations are unjustified without cross-validation. Moreover, inspection reveals that only one of the 16 adjectives which discriminated at the .05 level in the Barron (1968) study is among the 39 reported to be discriminative in the Welsh (1959) study. There is no way from the information given to account for this lack of correspondence, but it makes the necessity for formal cross-validation all the more obvious.

Nothing is said in either the Welsh (1959) or Barron (1968) reports about the scale scores, so not even preliminary information is available as to whether high and low Barron-Welsh Art groups differed in over-all self-regard (Fav scores and Unfav scores).

Khatena (1971a, 1971b, 1972, 1975a, 1975b) has developed a self-report check list (Something About Myself), involving both biographical and self-descriptive items. The total score on this instrument correlates with such variables as vividness and autonomy of imagery (Khatena, 1975a, 1975b), or verbal originality, using either sound or onomatopoeic word stimuli or a test of visual imagery control (Khatena, 1971a, 1971b); and with Torrance's Tests of Creative Thinking (Kaltsounis, 1975b). Something About Myself purportedly represents "three categories of creative functioning, namely, personality traits, use of creative thinking strategies, and creative productions" (Khatena, 1971a, p. 262). Thus, its author evidently regards it in part as an index of aspects of self-concept concerning creativity and/or relevant to creativity. The items of the scale were factor analyzed by Bledsoe and Khatena (1973), but published details are scanty, and cross-validation should be done before one can feel relatively confident of the factors and whether their content corresponds respectively to biographical and "creative self-concept" aspects of the test. Acquiescent response set is uncontrolled.

Another test purportedly indexing "self-perception of creativity" (What Kind of a Person Are You?) was developed in forced-choice format by Torrance and Khatena (1970a and b) and factor analyzed by Bledsoe and Khatena (1974). (See Wylie, 1974, pp. 76–80, for a criticism of the forced-choice technique.) Scores from this test were correlated with an idiosyncratic self-concept instrument by Khatena (1971b) and by Kaltsounis (1975a). However, published information is insufficient to serve as a basis for evaluating the idiosyncratic self-report test of attitude patterns and, hence, for concluding anything about the self-concept characteristics of those scoring high or low on "creative self-perception." Apparently, scores from What Kind of a Person Are You? and Something About Myself have never been correlated, although they both purport, at least in part, to reveal aspects of self-concept associated with creativity and should therefore be expected to correlate significantly.

Cashdan and Welsh (1966) studied adolescents from a special

summer school for the talented. They divided their subjects into those
$\geq \pm 1$ SD from the mean RA score for the talented group. Six out of 24
ACL scales differentiated the groups, but the Fav and Unfav scales are
not among those which differentiated creatives (high RA) from non-
creatives (low RA). Using only subjects with RA scores ≥ 40, Cashdan
and Welsh (1966) looked for ACL scale differences between science and
art students, but they found none. (See below for results from a study by
Schaefer and colleagues which replicate some of Cashdan and Welsh's
findings under better controlled conditions.)

Two other reports which used tests as purported indicators of
creativity (Coopersmith, 1967; Eisenman & Grove, 1972) will not be
discussed substantively either, because these researchers used
idiosyncratic creativity tests about which needed information is not
given; they apparently made no attempt to control for IQ and/or
achievement when looking at creativity, and one study (Eisenman &
Grove, 1972) used an idiosyncratic self-concept instrument about which
needed information is not given.

c. CREATIVITY INFERRED FROM NOMINATIONS PLUS TESTS

The study with the best method is one reported by C. E. Schaefer and
Anastasi (1968), C. E. Schaefer (1969), and J. M. Smith and Schaefer
(1969), involving 8 groups of 100 high school students each who attended schools which provided opportunities for creative productions in
art, writing, science, and mathematics. Subjects were classed as creative
if they met a double criterion: nominations by their teachers as having
produced one or more creative products *and* scoring above a cutoff
point on the Guilford Alternate Uses and Consequences tests. Subjects
were assigned to control groups if they were nominated by teachers as
having shown no concrete evidence of creativity *and* they scored below a
cutoff point on the Guilford tests. Creative and control subjects were
equated within each of 4 specialty fields for (a) school attended, (b) class
enrolled, (c) grade level, and (d) grade-point average. Nothing is said
about controlling for aptitude or IQ test scores. Eight groups of 100
each were formed: Creative Art-Boys; Control Art-Boys; Creative
Science-Boys; Control Science-Boys; Creative Art-Girls; Control Art-
Girls; Creative Writing-Girls; Control Writing-Girls. Identification
numbers were used to preserve the subjects' anonymity and encourage
truthful self-reports.

As part of the data analysis, Schaefer (1969) examined all 24 Adjective Check List (ACL) scales, having hypothesized directions of

difference for 14 of them, based on his "review of the literature." Of the 56 comparisons (14 scales in each of 4 pairs of groups), only 2 went nonsignificantly opposite the predictions, and 34 were significantly in the predicted direction. Schaefer (1969) recognized, however, that factor analytic studies of the ACL scales call into question the separate interpretability of all these significant findings. It is of interest that two of the six scales which significantly differentiated creative and control subjects in Cashdan and Welsh's (1966) study tended similarly to differentiate all pairs of creative and control groups in this study. In both studies, creatives were significantly higher on Lability and Change. MacKinnon (1963) had also found that scores on Lability, Change, and Deference correlated significantly with rated creativity in his study of architects. Not consistent with previous studies is Schaefer's (1969) unpredicted finding that creatives obtained a higher ACL Unfav score.

Following an item analysis procedure given in Schaefer and Anastasi (1968), Schaefer found that the following ACL adjectives discriminated with a "compound probability level" of .10 or better in one or more of the 4 specialty fields: Adjectives checked more often by creative subjects were imaginative, artistic, ingenious, original, independent, unconventional, individualistic, spontaneous, impulsive, assertive, outspoken, rebellious, complicated, reflective, cynical, idealistic, and aloof. Control subjects more frequently chose dependable, cooperative, contented, conventional, quiet, and silent.

Smith and Schaefer (1969) reanalyzed these data in a cross-validational design in an attempt to develop a creativity scale for the ACL which would discriminate better than any existing scale. For this purpose, each of the 8 criterion groups of 100 (Creative Art-Boys; Control Art-Boys; Creative Science-Boys; Control Science-Boys; Creative Art-Girls; Control Art-Girls; Creative Writing-Girls; Control Writing-Girls) was divided into a subsample of 50 subjects. Thus, 4 pairs of initial comparisons, using 50 subjects per group, could be made between creative and control groups, one comparison involving art creativity among boys, one involving science creativity among boys, one involving art creativity among girls, and one involving writing creativity among girls. On these initial comparisons, they found 27 adjectives which discriminated between creative and corresponding control subjects with $p \leq .20$ in 3 out of the 4 possible group comparisons, and for which the fourth comparison at least fell in the same direction (even if not reaching $p \leq .20$). The cross-validation subsamples of 50 were then compared on a total *scale* score based on these 27 items and also on 8 ACL *scale* scores which had proved to be the most valid scales in differentiating the original creative and control groups of 100 each (see Schaefer, 1969). This new 27-item scale discriminated significantly within *each* of the 4 pairs of creative-control cross-validational groups. By contrast, none of the 8 ACL scales previously found to discriminate the original 100-person creative and control groups did so for all 4 cross-validational comparison groups of Smith and Schaefer (1969). The adjectives comprising the 27-item "Creativity Scale" are as follows, with italics added to indicate adjectives which are the same as those reported to discriminate as described above for the entire group in the first data analysis: *artistic, assertive,* clever, *complicated, cynical,* foolish, *idealistic, imaginative, impulsive, ingenious,* insightful, intelligent, inventive, *original,* peculiar, progressive, quick, *reflective,* resourceful, sharp-witted, *spontaneous,* stolid, strong, talkative, *unconventional,* versatile, cooperative (the latter being endorsed more often by control than creative subjects). Unfortunately, no information is given as to individual significance levels for each adjective in the cross-validation groups.

Five of the IPAR publications discussed earlier in this section report particular ACL *adjectives* which discriminated more and less creative subjects, although not all the publications give significance levels at which their listed adjectives were associated with creativity. The 5 IPAR studies differed widely in respect to indices of creativity, size and type of subject groups, and control of key procedural and subject variables. Nevertheless, it is of some interest to see which 13 of the 27 adjectives used by Smith and Schaefer (1969) in their cross-validation study to form a Creativity Scale were also on any IPAR list. (Again, the italicized adjectives are those reported by Smith and Schaefer [1969] as discriminating for their entire group in their first data analysis.)

Smith and Schaefer Adjectives	Types of IPAR Subjects among Which Adjectives Discriminated (Maximum Possible Number = 5)
artistic	female mathematicians; Welsh manual students; architects
assertive	Irish managers
complicated	Welsh manual students; female mathematicians
cynical	Welsh manual students; Irish managers
imaginative	female mathematicians
impulsive	Welsh manual students
inventive	architects
original	female mathematicians
progressive	architects
sharp-witted	Welsh manual students
strong	United States Air Force captains; Irish managers
unconventional	Welsh manual students
cooperative	female mathematicians (less creative)

It is obvious that the coincidence is much less than the maximum possible number of five studies in addition to the Schaefer and Smith (1969) study.

Five years after the original study by C. E. Schaefer and his coworkers, Schaefer (1972, 1973) was able to get ACL results from 390 of the original subjects. With respect to age, educational level, high school grade-point average, and scores on the two creativity screening tests, the respondent and nonrespondent groups were comparable within each of the 8 criterion groups. Regarding ACL *scales,* the number of Unfavorable adjectives checked was significantly different in only 1 (instead of 2) of the 4 group comparisons, whereas the 8 most discriminating scales in the original study yielded significant group differences as follows (the first number in parentheses gives the number of significant comparisons out of 4 possible in the original study, while the second number gives the number of significant comparisons out of 4 possible in the follow-up study: Lability (3, 2); Exhibition (3, 1); Autonomy (3, 3); Aggression (3, 2); Change (4, 2); Self-Control (3, 3); Nurturance (3, 2); Deference (3, 2). Five of the scales showed one nonsignificant reversal in direction of difference between comparison groups in the follow-up study, whereas no such reversals occurred in the original study. Particularly noteworthy is the fact that the mathematics-science boys showed no significant differences on any of these scales at follow-up, even though, according to their biographical reports, the creative mathematics-science boys were continuing to do more creative things during the 5-year follow-up period. The specially developed and cross-validated Creativity Scale for the ACL (J. M. Smith & Schaefer, 1969) held up very well, discriminating each of the 4 pairs of groups of follow-up subjects. Three of the comparisons were significant at the $p \leq .001$ level, one at the $p \leq .05$ level.

d. Creativity Inferred from Self-Reported Accomplishments

I found several studies in which creativity was defined in terms of subjects' self-reports regarding their own activities, publications, prizes, inventions, patents, and the like. Unfortunately, most of these are so severely flawed methodologically as to preclude substantive summary (Bergum, 1973, 1974, 1975; Rees & Goldman, 1961).

Possibly a study by Lacey and Erickson (1974) also belongs in this category inasmuch as they used a "biographical creativity form" which had been cross-validated and found in previously published cited work to be "predictive of creativity ratings in several samples of engineers and scientists." Exactly what was in the "biographical creativity form" is not specified by Lacey and Erickson (1974) or in the primary sources cited by them. Apparently some self-descriptive items were included, as indicated in Morrison, Owens, Glennon, and Albright (1962).

In this study, anonymity of the 117 scientists and engineers who served as subjects was preserved, and the most and least creative thirds of their subjects were compared on all 24 Adjective Check List scales and on Smith and Schaefer's (1969) Creativity Scale for the ACL mentioned above. Lacey and Erickson (1974) were especially interested in the 8 ACL scales Smith and Schaefer (1969) had considered most discriminative before beginning to develop their ACL Creativity Scale. Of these, they found Exhibition, Autonomy, Aggression, Change, Deference to differentiate significantly between their creative and control groups, but they failed to find that Lability, Self-Control, or Nurturance significantly differentiated their groups. Although they repeated the finding that Smith and Schaefer's (1969) Creativity Scale discriminated between groups, it was not as highly discriminative as several of the other scales, especially the Deference scale. Unfortunately, nothing is said by Lacey and Erickson (1974) about equating the high and low "creativity" groups with respect to tested intelligence or achievement scores. And, of course, creativity differences were inferred from a quite different kind of observation than used in the nomination study by Schaefer and colleagues.

4. Summary and Conclusions

The studies in this section used several quite diverse alleged indices of creativity: nominations/ratings, tests, combinations of the latter two indices, and self-reported activities and accomplishments.

The scales of the California Psychological Inventory (CPI) and the individual adjectives and scale scores of the Gough Adjective Check List (ACL) were the self-report variables most often employed. This repeated use of one or two instruments has the potential advantage of permitting comparability among studies, providing the researches are properly done. However, wider generalizability could possibly be obtained if we had several groups of well-done studies, each group using a different self-report instrument.

Unfortunately there are many severe methodological flaws within individual studies, especially failure to cross-validate and failure to control for tested intelligence and achievement levels. Moreover, there are incomparable method variations across studies. Therefore, the conclusiveness of this body of reported results is severely limited, even within the kind of self-concept scores used, i.e., CPI and ACL.

Probably the safest generalization that can be made is that there is no trend toward association between over-all self-regard scores and creativity.

Regarding self-concept reports concerning various more specific personality characteristics, there seem to be no *CPI scales* which are consistently associated with creativity. Only the Flexibility scale discriminated in as many as four comparisons. Most studies report no more CPI scales to be significantly associated with creativity than would be expected by chance, and there is essentially no generality across studies in the one or two CPI scales which are reported to be significantly associated with creativity. Of course this could be due, at least in part, to the wide differences in areas of creativity examined in these researches.

In most studies, the number of *ACL adjectives* which are said to discriminate significantly between or among creativity groups is at or below chance expectations, and the overlap among studies in adjectives reportedly associated with creativity criteria is extremely low.

Only one adjective (artistic) was cited in as many as 4 studies, while 9 others were cited in 2 or 3 reports. Again, the paucity of findings may be partly due to the wide differences in areas of creativity examined, if one assumes that creativity factors vary greatly among types of activity such as artistic, scientific, mathematical, architectural, literary, or managerial.

Regarding the ACL *scales* given in the manual, the 8 for which we have the most published data were tested 10 times in relationship to creativity criteria, 4 of the tests being made within 1 cross-validational study. (I have not included the 5-year follow-up data from the subjects used in the cross-validational study.) Out of 10 opportunities to obtain significant associations with creativity, these 8 scales yielded significant associations with creativity as follows: Lability (5), Exhibition (4), Autonomy (6), Aggression (6), Change (5), Self-control (2), Nurturance (4), and Deference (7). Lability, Exhibition, Autonomy, Aggression, and Change were positively associated with creativity indices, whereas Self-control, Nurturance, and Deference were negatively associated with these indices. Order is the only other ACL scale which appeared to yield some consistent trends across a number of studies. Out of 8 published comparisons, 4 yielded significant differences. The studies from which all the preceding figures came involved adult male engineers, scientists, and architects; male and female mathematicians; and high school students in art, writing, and science. It must be remembered that a number of these studies did not attempt to control for IQ and/or achievement-test scores when looking at relationships between creativity indices and ACL scales.

Five opportunities occurred (four within one cross-validational study) for Smith and Schaefer's (1969) new Creativity Scale for the ACL to be found significantly associated with creativity indices. In all five, a significant association was obtained. When Schaefer (1972) followed up his entire group five years after initial testing, the Creativity Scale was still significantly associated with creativity within each of four pairs of comparison groups.

That there is some tendency for similar *ACL scale* findings to occur in studies involving different types of creative activities suggests that the above-mentioned lack of replication of findings regarding *ACL adjectives* cannot be explained entirely in terms of variations among studies in respect to types of creative activity involved.

An overview of all the research mentioned in this section suggests that some specific self-concept variables (though *not* over-all self-regard) are probably associated with some creativity indices. But we need further research which uses more adequate methods and includes a wider variety of measures of both self-concept and creativity constructs, each measure having met at least minimal criteria for reliability and construct validity.

8
Interpersonal Attraction or Regard and Self-Concept Variables

433

A. Associations between Self-Regard and Regard for Others

1. Theory

Research in the area of self-regard as related to regard for others was started by Rogers, his students, and colleagues. However, theoretical discussions of this general topic go back much further (e.g., to Freud and Adler) and also include other more contemporary theoretical statements besides Rogerian ones (e.g., Horney and Fromm).

a. Terminology and Definitions

As is common in personality theory, ambiguities in definitions of terms and vagueness of theoretical statements makes it difficult or impossible to be sure what each theorist is trying to say, whether apparent differences of opinion are only semantic, and what the research implications of respective theoretical positions might be. However, in order to offer plausible and useful research hypotheses and interpretations of results, one must look briefly at extant theory in order to see what is needed by way of more refined theoretical subpropositions.

Consistent with my earlier suggestion regarding terminology (Wylie, 1974), I use self-regard as a generic term. Theorists' statements involve many aspects of this very general, abstract concept, for example, love, narcissism, self-esteem, self-acceptance, self-hatred. Each of these undefined or only vaguely defined terms in theorists' writings may refer to the same or different concepts and potential measurements thereof. Within any one of these self-regard concepts there remains the question whether over-all self-attitudes are theoretically plausible or empirically definable. (See Wylie, 1974, pp. 101–102.) Virtually all extant research has been based on the assumed existence of such measurable, generalized predispositions. In trying to operationalize these varieties of global self-regard, researchers appear gratuitously and tacitly to assume that any assortment of items referring to evaluative self characteristics will suffice to index individual differences with respect to this construct. However, it seems likely that individuals differ concerning which of their characteristics are most salient in determining their self-regard. Both theorists and researchers have paid too little attention to this point and its research implications. (See Wylie, 1974, p. 48.)

In the research area now being discussed, a particular problem which

435

has been virtually overlooked by theorists and researchers is that of defining "other(s)." Typically, an unspecified generalized other is seemingly implied, or sometimes a generalized other is made explicit, as in Fromm's "love of mankind." One must be skeptical whether such a construct as level of regard toward "others in general" is theoretically plausible and whether interindividual differences in it are measurable. Surely any person makes important distinctions in level of regard and in salience of level of regard toward specified individual others and toward varying reference groups. It seems commonsensible to think that correlations between self-regard and regard for others would be a function of the particular target individuals or groups the subject has in mind when participating in research on self- and other-acceptance. For example, the ethnocentric person by definition values in-groups highly, out-groups lowly. The authoritarian person, although rejecting some others (e.g., intellectuals, nonconformists, homosexuals), accepts certain others (e.g., parents, patriots). Similarly, the younger child's evaluative reactions to unspecified others must be heavily weighted by his reactions to parents and teachers, whereas the college student's reactions to unspecified others might be quite different according to whether he decided to emphasize parents, teachers, or peers in choosing his answers to questions about "others." (The idea that level of regard varies with the target person is empirically supported by Pedersen's (1969) findings that semantic differential evaluative ratings of "generalized others" correlated imperfectly with ratings given regarding mother [.51 for male respondents, .21 for female respondents] and regarding father [.51 for male respondents, .28 for female respondents].)

b. FREUDIAN VIEWS

Obviously, Freud's economy model of libido functioning, the earliest theory relevant to this substantive research area, did not recognize the complex distinctions outlined above. In his view, one's love for self must be diminished if one directs large quantities of libido outward, since one has a limited quantity of libido. If the assumption is made that a subject's reports of self-regard are at least rough indicators of inward-directed libido, whereas his reports about his level of regard for others are at least rough indicators of amount of outward-directed libido, then one might expect to obtain *inverse* correlations across persons between such reports of self-regard and regard for others.

c. Adlerian and Neo-Freudian Views

Horney and Fromm make clear that their theoretical views about self-love and love for others are different from Freud's. They regard love not as a fixed quantity but as a capacity developed to a greater or lesser degree by interaction with others, especially parents. Fromm says, "Love of others and love of ourselves are not alternatives. On the contrary, an attitude of love toward themselves will be found in all those who are capable of loving others" (Fromm, 1947, *Man for Himself*, p. 129). In *New Ways in Psychoanalysis*, Horney (1939) makes the point that children who are not loved by their parents do not develop a capacity to love either themselves or others.

Adler proposed that the neurotic person characteristically uses depreciation of others as a means for raising his own self-esteem by comparing himself with the devalued others (Ansbacher & Ansbacher, 1956, pp. 267–269). Goldfried (1963), in reformulating Adlerian views, suggests that

> whether or not the individual is successful in alleviating these experienced feelings of inferiority might depend on the strength of these feelings, as well as his skill in depreciating others. Perhaps another important variable is the *effect* this depreciation has on others. Thus, if those other people who have been depreciated react negatively to the depreciator, this might only serve to further reinforce the individual's negative conception of himself. [P. 39]

There is also the possibility suggested by Goldfried (1963) that "depreciation of others . . . makes it easier for him to tolerate his inferior projected self-concept. This would be a 'misery-loves-company' interpretation of the effect of depreciation" (p. 45).

None of these theorists has considered the possible need to define self-regard rigorously or to separate it into subconstructs. For this reason, among others, one cannot know whether any of them would accept any of the extant self-regard and other-regard reports as indicators of what they had in mind as "love" or "depreciation." Moreover, they, like Freud have provided insufficient referents for the term "others." Thus, one cannot know whether available instruments purporting to indicate subjects' regard for others would be acceptable to them as measuring the constructs they have in mind. If they would find presently used measures of self-regard and regard for others plausibly valid, it appears that their general theoretical positions would be supported by the usually obtained positive correlations across persons between self-regard statements and statements of regard for others.

d. ROGERIAN VIEWS

Research predictions regarding concomitance of degree of regard for self and others were first stated by Rogerians (e.g., Raimy, Scheerer), and it is important to note that at first they appeared to be referring to a particular kind of self-regard which they called self-acceptance (as opposed, for example to self-esteem in the sense of a close congruence between perceived self and ideals for self, or a high self-rating on a scale with favorable and unfavorable ends determined by the experimenter).

As personally communicated to Shepard and Glass (1972), Raimy's idea of "self-acceptance in its traditional usage in psychotherapy referred to the acceptance of both one's faults and one's virtues as they were perceived by the person as aspects of his self-concept. The most important connotation of the concept, as used clinically, was that the self which was to be accepted or rejected was the individual's subjective concept of himself and not an objective or external assessment of his traits" (p. 2).

At a somewhat later date than the earliest Rogerian research on self- and other-acceptance, Rogers (1951) stated "When the individual perceives and accepts into one consistent and integrated system all his sensory and visceral experiences, then he is necessarily more un- derstanding of others and is more accepting of others as separate in- dividuals" (p. 520).

The rationale for this is that the person who denies some experiences must, as part of his defense against symbolizing them, misinterpret and attack reactions of others because these actions represent or resemble feared experiences. The other person cannot be experienced "for what he really is, a separate individual, operating in terms of his own meanings, based on his own perceptual field" (p. 521). And, in con- nection with the Chicago group's research on therapy, Rogers theorized that "the client will change his perception of self, will become more understanding of self and others, more accepting of self and others" (Rogers & Dymond, 1954, p. 4).

Jacobs, Berscheid and Walster (1971) propose one specific way in which perceptual distortion could occur and lead to correlations be- tween self-esteem and regard for others:

> In real life situations . . . unambiguous expressions of esteem or rejection are probably rather infrequent. In the course of social interaction, we rarely know for certain whether or not someone likes or dislikes us. . . . Expressions

of approval seem to be suspect in social interaction, since social courtesy, as well as a variety of ulterior motives on the part of others make such expressions more frequent than expressions of disapproval (cf. Jones, 1964). Given such ambiguity, it can be argued that low-self-esteem individuals appear to like others less (whether objectively accepting or rejecting) than do high-esteem individuals simply because low-self-esteem individuals generally perceive others as more rejecting than do those with high self-esteem. [P. 85]

(Evidence supportive of a reciprocity process is given in section C of this chapter.)

It was Raimy's and Rogers's general idea about self-acceptance and other-acceptance which Scheerer (1949) first tried to operationalize in terms of a scheme for coding therapy protocols and which formed the basis for development of scales by E. M. Berger (1952) and E. L. Phillips (1951).

Although the original predictions and research (Scheerer, 1949) involved self-acceptance as roughly described above, we have seen that this is only one kind of expressed self-regard; for example, there is supposedly over-all self-ideal congruence, or over-all self-assessment on rating scales to which the experimenter has assigned evaluative points summed across items, or over-all expressed positive or negative affect toward self. Analogously, there are various "kinds" of regard for others, for example, the perception a subject has of the congruence between another's self and that other's ideal self, or the subject's perception of the characteristics of the other(s) on rating scales, or over-all expressed positive or negative affect toward others.

It seems reasonable on theoretical grounds that, not only should self-acceptance and other-acceptance correlate, but there might also be correlations across persons between the just-mentioned global self-regard and global other-regard measures. And, at a more molecular level, one might predict across-persons rs between subjects' reports of their own standing on a particular attribute and the standing of particular or general others on that attribute.

But we must be wary in interpreting such positive rs, when and if they are obtained, because positive rs of any kind between evaluative reports about self and other(s) might also be a manifestation of naïve projection and/or individual differences in a construct-irrelevant response bias toward restricting ratings to one part of a scale. Most of the studies I have looked at provide no basis for evaluating these alternate interpretations.

2. Methodological Considerations

a. CONVERGENT AND DISCRIMINANT VALIDITY OF SELF-REGARD SCORES

Even though similar predictions might be made about (a) relationships between self-acceptance and acceptance of others, and (b) relationships between self-esteem and esteem for others, it is nevertheless important to see whether there is evidence for at least two constructs having different literary definitions (self-acceptance and self-esteem), and whether operationally distinct measures of each do relate to indices of acceptance of or esteem for others in the predicted manner. The attempt to make a distinction is important because the original Rogerian predictions pertained to self-acceptance as described above, yet, in the literature, one finds discussion and investigations involving different self-regard labels, presumably referring to respectively different varieties of self-regard. (In fact, in one of the earliest Rogerian researches, Stock [1949] used a scale of positive-neutral-negative *affect* to evaluate the subjects' feelings about self and others as expressed in counseling protocols.)

Some authors, working after Scheerer (1949) have explicitly labeled their instruments as measures of self-acceptance and have apparently, in some cases, tried to operationalize the type of literary definition given by Raimy (in Shepard & Glass, 1972). Unfortunately for both conceptual and operational clarity, others have used the term self-acceptance to cover instrument scores obtained by adding the subject's [Self—Ideal] discrepancies or evaluating the subjects' self-ratings against a favorable-unfavorable standard decided upon by the experimenter. Have those who tried to operationalize "self-acceptance" succeeded in producing instruments which correlate with each other (showing convergent construct validity), but which do not correlate as highly with instruments purporting to measure [Self—Ideal] discrepancies or socially evaluated self-ratings (showing discriminant construct validity)?

A great many publications pertinent to this question have appeared, and many of the relevant correlations are given in Wylie (1974, p. 96; pp. 155–159; pp. 208–209). These correlations involve scores explicitly labeled self-acceptance by their authors, namely, Berger's Acceptance of Self score, Bills's Acceptance of Self score. Crowne's Self-Acceptance score, Gough's Adjective Check List Self-Acceptance Scale, Medinnus and Curtis's (1963) Semantic Differential Self-Acceptance score, and

E. L. Phillips's (1951) Acceptance of Self score. In varying combinations, these self-acceptance scores have been correlated with each other, and also various self-acceptance scores have been correlated with [Self — Ideal] discrepancy scores, self-ideal r scores, and self-rating scores. Because the correlations come from many different studies which vary in numerous ways, straightforward synthesis is impossible. Nevertheless, the over-all picture clearly gives no comfort to the person who wishes to argue that "self-acceptance" is a construct which is alternately measurable by a variety of so-called self-acceptance instruments which yield high convergent validity values and low correlations with other types of self-regard measures (e.g., with Q-sort rs, [Self — Ideal] discrepancy scores from semantic differential scales, or other kinds of rating scales assigned evaluative numerical values according to the experimenter's preconceived notions of their favorability or unfavorability).

Recently, Shepard and Glass (1972) have reported an extensive attempt to use the multitrait-multimethod matrix of D. T. Campbell and Fiske (1959) to determine whether it is reasonable to infer a measurable construct called self-acceptance which can be indexed by alternate measures which are discriminable from "self assessment" (i.e., self-regard) measures such as Q sorts. (See Wylie, 1974, pp. 107–116, for a discussion of this method as it is applicable in self-concept research.)

Using the Berger (1952) Self-Acceptance and Other Acceptance Scales and a variety of specially devised or modified measures purporting to indicate respectively (a) self-acceptance, (b) self-assessment, and (c) acceptance of others, they obtained an average convergent validity value of .55 among so-called self-acceptance measures and .41 among so-called self-assessment measures. Obviously there was only weak evidence of discriminant validity between self-acceptance measures as a group and self-assessment measures as a group, inasmuch as the average convergent validity value of the self-acceptance measures (.55) only slightly exceeded the average correlation between self-acceptance and self-assessment measures (.41).

What is the implication of all this correlational information for the substantive questions at hand, namely, whether self-acceptance correlates with acceptance of others, and whether there is any sequential relationship between the two variables? At the least it seems clear that there are no grounds for organizing the presentation of research studies in this area according to whether self-acceptance or some other self-regard construct was ostensibly measured. Even if lack of discriminant validity among measures purporting to index differing aspects of self-regard proves to be found when measurement techniques are more adequately developed, it would not pose serious problems in deciding whether obtained correlations between self-regard and regard for others support theoretical predictions. This is so because the theorists who are interested in this general area presently seem to hypothesize associations between self-regard as an inclusive construct and regard for others as an inclusive construct. (Of course, if different aspects of self-regard prove to be discriminable by better developed instruments, theorists must refine and further clarify their expectations about possible associations between [a] different aspects of self-regard and [b] different aspects of regard for others.)

Not only do we find problems of convergent and discriminant validity among alleged measures of self-acceptance, but we find that most of those measures used in studies of self- and other-acceptance have fallen far short of adequate standards for building an instrument and checking on its reliability and construct validity. (See Wylie, 1974, pp. 38–123, for detailed specification of these standards.) Many have been used only once or twice. Their interchangeability, as indicated above, is unknown or doubtful. Self-regard scales which have been used most often in research in this area are those constructed by Bills (Index of Adjustment and Values), E. M. Berger, Fey, and E. L. Phillips. The characteristics of the IAV have been examined in considerable detail in Wylie (1974, pp. 155–159), while the Berger (1952), E. L. Phillips (1951), and Fey (1954, 1955, 1957) scales have been discussed in Wylie (1961, pp. 66–67), and some of their characteristics are also evaluated later in this section. Also evaluated in Wylie (1974) are Gough's Adjective Check List (ACL), Rosenberg's Self-Esteem Scale (RSE), and semantic differential techniques which are used in one or more of the studies mentioned below.

b. Coding of Interview Materials

Somewhat different methodological questions must be raised regarding the coding of interview materials for self-regard and regard for others. This has been done by Scheerer (1949) and Stock (1949), and Bills (1954), for example. Even when separate judges are used to code the protocols for self-regard and regard for others, there is a possibility of an artifactual inflation of the correlation, either within an interview across persons or across interviews and persons. For example, the judge who is evaluating the interviewee's self-regard is automatically exposed to the interviewee's statements pertinent to his regard for others. Hence the judge's evaluation of the interviewee's self-regard might be contaminated by his knowledge of what the interviewee has said about others. The judge who is supposed to be evaluating the interviewee's regard for others could be subject to a complementary effect.

c. Problems in Making Sequential Inferences

Rogerians were interested in seeing whether therapy would produce concomitant increases in self-acceptance and acceptance of others. They thought such research would perhaps reveal whether the increases in self-acceptance preceded the increases in acceptance of others. If and when such predicted concomitant or sequential increases are found, one must always allow for the possibility that they are a function of the subject's wanting to please the therapist by telling him what he wishes to hear regarding both attitudes.

d. Discriminant Validity of Regard-for-Others Scores

I have mentioned above that obtained correlations between self-acceptance and acceptance of others might be interpretable as artifacts of the measurement process or the subject's wishes to conform to the researcher's expectations. There remains one other methodological issue to consider: Are obtained correlations between self-acceptance reports and acceptance-of-others reports indicative of relationships between these two particular variables, or is acceptance of others simply one facet of the subject's acceptance or rejection of many aspects of life, for example, his home town, his college, his school environment? Associations have been found between self-regard scores and expressed satisfaction with home town (Levy, 1956), government (Kornreich, Straka, & Kane, 1968), school (Williams & Cole, 1968), and college (Graham & Barr, 1967). We should note, however, that the correlation obtained by Williams and Cole (1968) might be explained as due to the common influence of poor reading skills on (a) satisfaction with school, and (b) the reliability (and hence the evaluative level) of the self-regard scores, as explained in Wylie (1974, pp. 119–121). The Graham and Barr (1967) study was based on extremely small Ns. Moreover, Pervin (1967) found no association between self-scores and expressed satisfaction with the college environment, whereas Pervin and Smith

(1968) found environmental satisfaction "relatively independent" of self-ratings. (In both the latter studies, instruments with unknown validity were used.) R. E. Lee (1972) found patients' Rosenberg Self-Esteem scores to be positively associated with their expressions of satisfaction about the hospital (but information about the latter scale is not provided). All things considered, even the positive findings are small, they come from methodologically flawed or limited studies, and they do not provide comparisons needed to evaluate whether self-other associations are larger than associations between self-regard and evaluative attitudes toward "things in general."

If the above-mentioned positive findings, such as they are, are not artifactual, they may raise questions about the validity of the available research for supporting the particular Rogerian hypotheses regarding associations between self-acceptance and acceptance of others. But another view might be that phenomenological and psychodynamic theory imply that negative affect will generalize widely across self and environment, including other persons in the environment. The only way to separate these alternative interpretations is to develop instruments with respectively discriminant validity for measuring acceptance of or attitude toward varying aspects of the environment and compare their correlations with self-regard to the correlations between self-regard scores and scores specifically valid for indicating regard for other persons.

3. Findings Regarding Associations between Self-Regard and Regard for Generalized Others

Turning now to an overview of the research which is possibly relevant to hypotheses about correlations between self-acceptance and acceptance of others, one finds that the studies may conveniently be grouped as follows, in which order they are considered below:

1. Associations between self-regard measures and measures of regard for "generalized others."

2. Associations between self-regard measures and measures of regard for particular others or particular groups of others.

a. SCHEERER'S STUDY

As a basis for her pioneering attempt to test Rogers's ideas, Scheerer (1949) devised a detailed literary definition of self-acceptance and other-acceptance and translated these statements into rating scales by which judges rated experimenter-sampled "units" of therapy interviews from 10 cases. By interview, self-acceptance and other-acceptance ratings yielded an $r = .51$.

b. Berger's and Phillip's Scales

Following Scheerer's literary definition, both Berger (1952) and E. L. Phillips (1951) devised scales of self- and other-acceptance. Within the Berger and Phillips inventories, self-referent and other-referent items were intermingled, maximizing the possible influence of response sets upon the correlations between the self and other subscales. Acquiescence response set is also uncontrolled. Several investigators have found significant positive correlations between scores from the self-acceptance items and from the other-acceptance items, using these inventories.

E. M. Berger (1952) found rs ranging from .36 to .69 with various groups; Streitfeld's (1959) correlation, involving psychology graduate students, is .53, and Omwake (1954) obtained an r of .37 with female introductory psychology students. Omwake's correlation is lower than the Berger-Phillips self-acceptance r of .73, or the Berger-Phillips other-acceptance r of .60, suggesting that the Berger Self-Acceptance–Other-Acceptance correlation is not simply due to response sets elicited by the format of the Berger Inventory.

Shepard and Glass (1972) used the Berger scales as one method of measuring self-acceptance and acceptance of others in a multitrait-multimethod matrix involving 6 alleged measures of self-acceptance, 6 alleged measures of "self-assessment," and 4 alleged measures of acceptance of others. The Berger Self-Acceptance Scale correlated with the Acceptance of Others scales as follows: Berger Acceptance of Others, $r = .52$; newly devised Self-Acceptance Product Sum Q sort (based on the Butler-Haigh Q-sort items), $r = .37$; specially devised Semantic Differential Acceptance of Others, $r = .07$; specially devised Incomplete Sentences Acceptance of Others score, $r = .32$.

Coons, McEachern, and Annis (1973) report concomitant increases in Berger's acceptance of self and others in mental patients positively reinforced for endorsing self-accepting items.

Using his own scale, E. L. Phillips (1951) obtained self-acceptance versus other-acceptance rs ranging from .51 to .74, with 4 groups of subjects consisting of younger and older high school students, college

students, and older students. McIntyre (1952) reports a correlation of
.46, based on male college students, while Suinn and Hill (1964) found r
= .35, using introductory psychology students. In a small group of
introductory psychology students, the Self-Acceptance versus Other-
Acceptance correlation was .57 in a "stress" condition of an experiment
and .58 in a "neutral" condition (Suinn & Geiger, 1965). Omwake
(1954) reports r = .41.

Altogether, the range of Self-Acceptance versus Other-Acceptance rs
reported for the Phillips scale is about the same as for the Berger scale.
As with the Berger scale, Omwake (1954) found that the Phillips Self-
Acceptance versus Other-Acceptance r is below the r of .73 between
Berger Self-Acceptance and Phillips Self-Acceptance, and the r of .60
between the Berger Other-Acceptance scores and the Phillips Other-
Acceptance scores. This suggests that the Phillips Self-Acceptance
versus Other-Acceptance correlation is not simply due to response sets
elicited by the format of the Phillips inventory.

That common method factors may play a part in increasing Self-
Acceptance versus Other-Acceptance rs within each instrument,
however, is suggested by Omwake's (1954) findings that the r between
Berger Self-Acceptance and Phillips Other-Acceptance is only .25,
while the r between Phillips Self-Acceptance and Berger Other-
Acceptance is .34.

Of course, the above information is insufficient to evaluate
adequately the relative contributions of method and construct variance
to the within-Berger correlations and to the within-Phillips correlations
and to the correlations between the Berger and Phillips scales.

c. Fey's Scales

Fey (1954, 1955, 1957) constructed and used several slightly differing
forms of an Acceptance-of-Self and Acceptance-of-Others Inventory.
The definitions of the constructs and the means of establishing the
relevance of the items to the definitions are not given. As with the
Berger and Phillips inventories, self-referent and other-referent items
are intermingled, and acquiescence response set is uncontrolled.
Correlation values ranging from .40 to .50 are reported by Fey for
various student groups. J. E. Williams's (1962) study, intended as a
replication of Fey's work, yielded an r of .64 between Fey's Self-
Acceptance and Other-Acceptance scores.

d. OTHER SCALES

Other researchers have used a variety of purported measures of self- and other-regard, as described below.

Stock (1949) developed a rating scale of negative-to-positive "affect" toward self and others by which judges rated experimenter-designated interview units from 10 counseling cases, 7 of them the same as used by Scheerer (1949). For the 34 interviews where the number of units was $\geq$ 10, r was .66 across interviews between judged positivity of affect toward self and toward others. Although she was interested in a possibly sequential relationship between changes in self-regard and regard for others, her method and results permit no sequential inferences.

In his large-scale New York State study of adolescents, Rosenberg (1965) obtained a significant positive linear relationship between scores on his self-esteem scale (RSE) and an idiosyncratic Guttman scale (Reproducibility = 90.1%) which he labeled "faith in people" or "misanthropy." (The RSE scale is discussed in Wylie, 1974.)

The Index of Adjustment and Values scales of Self-Acceptance, Self, [Self—Ideal], and other scales have been examined by several investigators. This instrument is extensively described and evaluated in Wylie (1974). Of particular relevance here are the following points: First, there is no evidence that the alternate self-regard scores (Self, [Self—Ideal], or Self-Acceptance) have discriminant validity as measures of different self-regard constructs. Second, unknowable variations are caused by ambiguities and variations in the instructions for describing Others. One part of the instructions tells the subject to give an accurate description of "other people as you see them"; another directs the subject to think about "other people like you." At this point in the instructions, the examiner is told to help the subjects to determine their appropriate peer group, which, it is implied, will differ from administration to administration of the test. But finally, the subject is told to answer the questions "as you think the average member of this group would answer it for himself." Thus, the interpretation of the Other scale is completely unclear.

IAV Self-Acceptance scores correlate .49 and .55 with Self-Acceptance scores from Berger and Phillips, respectively, according to Omwake (1954), but only .24 with Phillips Self-Acceptance scores, according to Bills's undated manual. As might be expected from differences in the directions, the Other scale of the IAV correlates only .23

and .13 with the Other-Acceptance scales of the Berger and Phillips, respectively (Omwake, 1954).

In his undated manual, Bills reports the following rs relevant to hypotheses regarding the association of self-acceptance and other-acceptance: Self versus Other = .78; Self-Acceptance versus Other-Acceptance = .56; [Self — Ideal] for self and [Self — Ideal] for Other = .43 (N = 300). In Renzaglia's study (reported in Bills's undated manual), ratings assigned to Self correlate .50 with ratings given to Others. Bills's confusing directions regarding the rating of Others were evidently used. Omwake (1954) gives rs of .39 between IAV Self-Acceptance and IAV Acceptance of Others scores, but only .18 between IAV Self-Acceptance and Phillips Other-Acceptance scores, and .23 between IAV Self-Acceptance and Berger Other-Acceptance scores.

As detailed below, all but one of the remaining studies which used a variety of instruments found a tendency for self-regard and regard for others to be significantly associated, and only one of the significant relationships was curvilinear.

Lehner (1956) reported that the self-favorability of men's (but not women's) Adjustment scores on the California Test of Personality was positively associated with favorability of their answers concerning "average others," and, in a later study (Lehner, 1960), he reported such a positive association with sexes combined. Zuckerman, Baer, and Monashkin (1956), inferring self-acceptance and other-acceptance from scores on Buss's 16 subscales covering "clinically relevant dimensions," found self-acceptance significantly associated with expressed acceptance of mother, father, and "people." Pedersen (1969) used a specially devised semantic differential for inferring self-concept and concepts of father, mother, and generalized other and used Gough's Adjective Check List Self-Acceptance Scale to infer the respondent's self-acceptance. The semantic differential scales were presented with good and bad adjectives randomly assigned to right and left ends of the scales. He found that semantic differential self-concept scores correlated with "generalized-other" scores for both males and females (.36 and .42) and that ACL Self-Acceptance scores correlated with semantic differential evaluations of generalized others for both males and females (.37 and .35). With 35 variables altogether in the correlation matrix, it is impossible to evaluate which rs might have been significant by chance, however. (The semantic differential technique and the ACL are extensively discussed and evaluated in Wylie, 1974.)

In their final multitrait-multimethod matrix, Shepard and Glass (1972) included the Berger scales along with 5 other newly devised purported self-acceptance measures, 6 newly devised self-assessment measures, and 4 newly devised purported acceptance-of-others measures. Their rs involving the Berger scales have already been given above. Overall, they concluded that although the degree of overlap between self-acceptance and self-assessment measures was greater than expected from the use of the terms, the average correlation (.21) between self-regard measures and other-acceptance measures was small enough to warrant calling other-acceptance a construct which is separate from self-regard yet related to self-regard constructs to a degree congruent with theory.

B. N. Phillips, Hindsman, and Jennings (1960), using a variety of measures of self-satisfaction and other-satisfaction taken from the Texas Cooperative Youth Studies and the Brown-Holtzmann Survey of Study Habits, obtained rs between self- and other-dissatisfaction ranging from .13 to .74. It is not possible to tell from the information given just what correlation values were obtained involving more generalized others (in this study, criticism of youth, negative orientation to society), as opposed to values involving particular others, such as teachers.

Foulds, Girona, and Guinan (1970) found concomitant increases in favorability toward self and others in subjects participating in a marathon group, as compared to a nonparticipating group. The small number of subjects and the use of an idiosyncratic instrument about which little information is given severely limit the interpretability of this study.

The only curvilinear relationship is reported in Reese (1961) where fourth, sixth, and eighth graders whose Lipsitt scale scores indicated a medium self-esteem level were maximally accepting of others, as indicated by mean evaluative ratings they assigned to their peers.

Zelen (1954a, 1954b) obtained the only completely negative results in this area. Self-acceptance was indexed by the California Test of Personality and the Who-Are-You Test. Although the two measures of self-acceptance intercorrelated highly (.73), neither of these measures correlated with acceptance of others (indexed by the Bonney Sociometric Technique). Obviously response sets due to instrument format have been ruled out in this study. The interpretation of the negative findings is unclear, however, since this study differs from the others in several ways (different instruments were used, and the subjects were children rather than college students or young adults), and in-sufficient information is given regarding the Bonney Sociometric Technique.

e. SUMMARY

The studies reviewed above suggest the following. Significant positive correlations tend to occur between scores purportedly indicating self-regard and regard for "generalized others."

To some extent, the sizes of these rs are probably inflated by acquiescent response sets and/or response sets induced by common instrument format. On the other hand, there is some suggestion that the rs cannot be entirely accounted for in this artifactual way. Rather, it appears plausible, although not demonstrated, that self-regard may be positively associated with regard for others, when each is measured with some degree of respective discriminant validity.

The question then arises whether regard for "generalized others" might be simply one manifestation of a generally optimistic attitude toward all aspects of the environment, e.g., home town, college, school, hospital. No adequate direct tests of this kind of discriminant validity are at hand, so one must reserve judgment on this point. However, the few studies which looked for relationships between such general en-vironmental acceptance and self-acceptance do not offer much indirect support to the idea that regard-for-others scores represent merely a generally optimistic attitude toward the environment.

4. Findings Regarding Associations between Self-Regard and Regard for Specific Others

A second group of studies was concerned with associations between self-regard and regard for *particular* others, as differentiated from "generalized others." Although some of these investigations dealt with both "manipulated" and "chronic" self-regard, I allude here only to the results involving chronic self-regard indices.

The trends are mostly, but not unanimously, toward positive associations. But we must realize that there are great methodological disparities among these researches, no two of them using the same instrument for indexing self-regard or regard for others. This, coupled with serious flaws within a large number of these studies, indicates the impossibility of synthesizing, comparing, or generalizing.

The category "particular others" includes standard photographs (Bossom & Maslow, 1957); teammates from experimentally formed teams (Deutsch & Solomon, 1959; Skolnick, 1971); a novel person, briefly observed (V. J. Crandall & Bellugi, 1954); five unspecified persons of the subject's own choosing (Levanway, 1955); the student whom the teacher respondent considers most desirable to teach (Mc-Callon, 1966); an anonymous fellow student (Arrowood & Short, 1973); father and mother (Pedersen, 1969); teachers (B. N. Phillips, Hindsman, & Jennings, 1960); a hypothetical professor (C. R. Berger, 1973); the experimenter (Rosenbaum & Stanners, 1961); parents, Jews (Sarnoff, 1951); a graduate-student interviewer (Shrauger & Lund, 1975); fathers, teachers (Suinn, 1961); disabled persons, and a verbally described simple schizophrenic boy (Yamamoto & Wiersma, 1967); the experimenter, a teacher (Walster, 1965); specified members of the respondents' military living group (Wylie, 1957); one "harmonious" and one annoying peer (Zimmer, 1956).

As I indicated at the outset of this section, we need more examination of variations in regard for particular others and particular groups and how these varieties of other-regard relate to self-regard, since there is so much that is conceptually and operationally unsatisfactory about the referent(s) for "others in general." However, the above-listed researches do not enable us to examine these conceptual and methodological questions.

5. Grounds for Exclusion of Studies

As I have repeatedly said, many of the studies included in the above summary of reported results relevant to self- and other-acceptance are seriously limited or flawed methodologically. In addition to the research reports already specifically mentioned, I have examined the publications listed immediately below and judged them worthy of exclusion from substantive summaries relevant to this topic because they exhibited one or more of the following serious methodological faults: use of too small a number of subjects for the type of analyses made; describing procedures so vaguely as to preclude evaluation of the results; use of idiosyncratic instruments to measure one or more of the crucial variables, coupled with no or extremely limited information about the psychometric properties of the instrument(s); uninterpretable uses of discrepancy scores; failure to control for response totals when correlating two measures; making multiple significance tests or computing many rs involving scales which themselves intercorrelate and/or involve overlapping items, so that one cannot discern whether the "significant" findings exceed those to be expected by chance.

6. List of Excluded Studies

Excluded studies are: Alfert (1958); Davids (1973); Eisenman (1970); Garretson (1962); Jervis (1959); D. E. Lee and Ehrlich (1971); Maliver (1965); O'Leary and Hood (1969); Richmond, Mason, and Padgett (1972); Rosengren and Davids (1961); I. M. Rubin (1967a, 1967b); Rudikoff (1954); Trent (1959); Vavrik and Jurich (1971); Wilcox and Fretz (1971); Zuckerman and Oltean (1959).

B. SELF-REGARD AS A FUNCTION OF ACTUAL OR PERCEIVED ACCEPTABILITY TO OTHERS IN REAL-LIFE SITUATIONS

1. Theory

At first thought it appears obvious that the theories of Cooley, Mead, Rogers, and many others imply that a person's over-all self-regard and self-conceptions regarding particular characteristics are determined to an important degree by reflected appraisals from others. According to this view, if others in real-life situations seek a person's friendship, leadership, team participation, etc., the over-all self-regard of that person should be enhanced. Also, depending on the particular kinds of reflected appraisal, his or her self-conceptions concerning particular abilities and personality characteristics should be affected. Failure to be chosen should mean lack of an important factor needed for high self-regard. Being actively rejected by others should depress the self-regard level, since it implies the presence of bad characteristics in the rejected person. (Of course this argument also implicitly assumes that the accepting, indifferent, or rejecting feelings of others have been communicated to the potential nominees in the course of the group's interactions. This assumption in itself is questionable. If it turns out to be untenable, a negligible correlation between self-regard and sociometric choice scores would occur no matter how valid the theoretical point about one's self-evaluation being based on one's ideas of others' opinions.)

Most of the studies considered in this section are based explicitly or implicitly on the simple, supposedly self-evident propositions stated above. Accordingly, the researchers who did these studies predicted a linear positive association between subjects' scores allegedly indexing general (or specific) evaluations by others and scores purporting to index the subjects' over-all self-regard (or their self-conceptions regarding particular personality characteristics which correspond to those covered in the others' evaluations).

But, as with other research areas covered in this book, reflected-appraisal theories do not necessarily imply only this straightforward, strongly effective sequence. For one thing, even if one assumes that the necessary interpersonal communication has taken place in the group, other moderating factors must be considered. First, not all others are equally "significant" sources of appraisal (Rosenberg, 1973). If the influence of parents is especially important, the elementary-school child's popularity level with his peers may have relatively less impact, thus attenuating correlations between sociometric status and self-regard. That some peers may be relatively insignificant others may be true for adult subjects, for example those assigned to arbitrary groups in dormitories and military barracks. Thus the opinions of those others whom the researcher assumes to be "significant" may be of little importance to a person whose level of self-esteem is grounded in earlier family and school experiences and in many social contacts outside the arbitrary group. In fact, if we give credence to Horney's (1945) ideas, the adult person who indiscriminately emphasizes "moving toward others" (i.e., takes just about everyone as a "significant other") may actually be someone who is compensating for the esteem-damaging effects of previous appraisals from others. Recognition of such complexities leads one to predict that, in the usual research situation, the correlation between others' evaluations and self-evaluations may be considerably attenuated, perhaps especially so among adults in arbitrarily formed groups.

Another way in which the first-stated hypothetical sequence is simplistic is its implied emphasis on *numbers* of significant others, as opposed to their respectively individual importance in determining the chosen person's self-esteem level. That is, even if the group is not an arbitrarily formed one, many persons may feel that a few important mutual friendships within the group suffice to support their self-regard and provide the needed reflected appraisals of their specific personal attributes. Thus, although the person who is widely popular within a group *may* indeed have self-regard increased by this popularity, the self-regard of a person with a few good friends may be equally elevated if these friends are the ones whose opinions and company he or she particularly values. In short, the "head count" approach implied in a simple version of reflected-appraisal theory and in extant sociometric tasks and scoring schemes takes no account of the salience of the chooser for the self-regard of the chosen.

We should allow for still another factor which could theoretically attenuate the positive association between the sociometric scores and self-regard scores. An extremely able and attractive person may actually be chosen sociometrically by fewer others than would a typical person, because many potential choosers are overawed, envious, or anxious to avert invidious comparisons which would come with close associations with such a superior person. Therefore, such a superior individual may well have a realistically favorable self-conception, but a moderate sociometric score.

A variant of the immediately preceding point is implied by Byrne's (1971) theory that interpersonal attraction is a direct function of the amount of interpersonal similarity of beliefs, attitudes, and personal characteristics. On this view, a person with very unusual characteristics should have fewer persons sociometrically choosing him or her, since, by definition, few would be sufficiently similar. But, depending on the particular kind of characteristics which make the person unusual, he or she could have a realistically favorable self-concept or a realistically unfavorable one. Thus, the person with truly unusual desirable characteristics who is selectively chosen by only a few others and the more ordinary person who is chosen by many others could both have high self-regard, but for different reasons.

The simple reflected-appraisal view assumes that being actively rejected by others would be associated with the poorest level of self-regard. This seems plausible, but a number of cautions are in order. First, if rejections are assumed to represent the opposite pole of an accepting-rejecting dimension of the group's attitudes toward its members, it is important to check this by asking for rejection nominations as well as favorable nominations. Most researchers have assumed that those receiving few or no positive nominations include that extreme subset of persons, the actively rejected ones; however, they have not isolated them for study. If investigators did call for both accepting and rejecting sociometric nominations, they might find among the rejected ones some who are never chosen as most desirable choices, but also some who are occasionally chosen as most desired while also frequently being mentioned as rejected. The latter may be those who are *favorably* regarded within a salient subgroup, e.g., their religious or racial minority group, or their "delinquent" clique, precisely because they are rejected or relatively unchosen by the larger group whose members disavow the values of the subgroup. The persons who are (a) ignored "nonentities," (b) rejected by some while being ignored by others, and (c) rejected by some and chosen by a few are plausibly in quite different situations so far as the effects of group appraisal on the self-concept are concerned. Not to differentiate among them is to increase the likelihood of obtaining uninterpretable or null results.

Thus far I have dealt only with various possible ways in which being chosen as acceptable or unacceptable might affect the nominees' self-conceptions, if the nominators' feelings have been communicated to the nominees during group interactions preceding the sociometric study. But one must also consider the possibility that subjects with varying self-regard levels may, because of their differing characteristics, affect their potential nominators in a variety of ways. According to one common-sense view, others take one pretty much at one's own evaluation. Moreover, the self-derogating person would possibly be too withdrawn or socially unskilled to interact successfully. Either or both of these factors could mean that positive correlations between self-conceptions and nominators' statements represent, at least in part, the causal influence of the nominee's characteristics (which he describes in his self-concept report) on the nominator's behavior, rather than the other way around. In fact, a reciprocal or circular sequence appears to be quite plausible. This could, of course, contribute to a linear positive association between self-concept reports and sociometric scores.

But finally, looking at the situation from yet another vantage point, one might predict not just a strong linear relationship, or even a severely attenuated linear relationship, but perhaps a nonlinear one. For example, some have assumed that an extremely favorable self-regard report may represent a kind of defensive denial. Such a person could be unable to interact in an open and undefensive fashion with others, creating a poor impression. Thus, one might perhaps expect the person with a moderately favorable self-concept to be more able to function effectively in a social situation, garnering more sociometric nominations from his or her group than does the highly defended high-self-regard subject. Although all this is very speculative, there is enough room for a variety of a priori arguments to make it necessary on theoretical grounds to look for nonlinear relationships between sociometric scores and self-evaluative reports. Unfortunately, with one exception, all the many extant studies have failed to do this.

2. Methodological Considerations

Before trying to interpret the output in any research area, one needs to clarify the methodological criteria by which the researches should be judged, especially those standards of particular relevance to the topic under consideration. Here it is convenient to divide these criteria into those pertaining to the sociometric and related techniques; those pertaining to the self-concept measures; and those relevant to methods for examining relationships between these two classes of variables under suitably controlled conditions. (A discussion of measurement criteria relevant to purported indices of perceived acceptability to others is included later on, in the section which presents the results of studies involving that group of variables.)

a. SOCIOMETRIC TECHNIQUES AND SCORES

In so-called sociometric techniques, each person in a specified group is asked, privately or by interview, to name a limited or unlimited number of other persons in the group who belong in one or more designated categories, e.g., wanted by the respondent as friend, leader, teammate for a specified job, guest at a birthday party, confidant, roommate. It is also possible to ask for nominations for a limited (or unlimited) number of persons *not* wanted or *least* wanted for the designated categories. It seems plausible that furnishing privacy or anonymity to the respondents will promote honesty and thereby increase construct validity, but this has not been studied methodologically, nor even mentioned by most of the authors whose studies I review below.

Method Variations

There is no standard method of obtaining a popularity score or any other kind of score from this approach. (See Mouton, Blake, and Fruchter [1955a or 1960a] and Busk, Ford, and Schulman [1973] for an overview of types of questions asked, and Lindzey and Byrne [1968] and Busk et al. [1973] for an overview of scoring techniques and associated variations in reliability.) Also, there are no grounds for saying that sociometric techniques are basically different from the many idiosyncratic varieties of rating scales which have been introduced to measure intensity of interpersonal attraction (Lindzey & Byrne, 1968).

Lindzey and Byrne (1968) pointed out some time ago that correlations are usually

substantial . . . among the responses to [sociometric] questions if they deal with relatively similar activities or interactions [but it has been empirically demonstrated] that personal choice patterns vary to some extent with the activities in terms of which the choice is made [and since] there has been little investigation of the equivalence of the different approaches to sociometric measurement (that is friendship choices, ratings, rankings, etc.) . . . the relevance of findings based on one type of instrument for generalizations concerning other types of instruments remains a matter for conjecture. [P. 479]

The reports covered in the present section take no account of this situation; hence insufficient information is at hand to enable one to synthesize, compare, or even separately interpret the 34 studies below, almost all of which apparently used different sociometric techniques. (I say "apparently" because some of these reports are so vague one cannot know exactly what methods of inquiry and scoring formed the basis for the sociometric scores.)

Construct Validity

Obviously I am not arguing here that sociometrically measured attraction or rejection is a unified construct and that one should therefore search for and use the "true" or "best" measure. Rather, I contend that this construct domain is undoubtedly complex, so that casual proliferation of idiosyncratic instruments doubtlessly leads to an unwarranted assignment of a common interpretation or label to sociometric scores which represent a variety of constructs, and interstudy "disagreements" may well be a function of this overlooked complexity in the sociometric domain.

The following validity question is especially relevant to the use of sociometric techniques for testing hypotheses about the effects of reflected appraisals on the self-concept. Are differences in verbal nomination behavior associated with differences in actual behaviors of the nominators toward the nominee? If they are not, it seems unlikely that the nominee had a basis for becoming aware of the nominators' attitudes, and so there is no basis to believe that sociometric scores should be associated with the subjects' self-concept variations. Therefore, instruments should be chosen for which some evidence of this kind of validity has been demonstrated. In their overview of validity of sociometric measures, Mouton, Blake, and Fruchter (1955b or 1960b) cite a number of studies which suggest that some kinds of sociometric nominations are associated with relevant actual interaction patterns. However, for the many different idiosyncratic sociometric measures used in the studies considered in this section, no such validity information is given, nor do the authors indicate an awareness that such information would be desirable, let alone necessary as a basis for interpreting the outcomes of their work.

As mentioned above, a sociometric instrument should allow one to order subjects along a continuum of number of favorable choices received from their group members, but it should also permit separate examination of those who are simply ignored, those who are usually ignored but sometimes rejected, and those who are both rejected and accepted.

In order to identify those who are really ignored, it is necessary to allow nominators to make unlimited choices. Certainly the ignored status under limited and unlimited choice cannot be assumed to be psychologically comparable.

Harper (1968) has shown that the distributions of acceptance and rejection nominations are quite different and that there is more intergroup agreement about those who are undesirable than about those who are desirable as best or close friends. He hypothesizes that "the attributes of an individual that lead to social rejection are more clearly defined than those that lead to acceptance" (p. 226). If this is true, it emphasizes the need for separate analysis of self-conceptions in relationship to rejection status and acceptance status, respectively.

In any case, it is obviously a very dubious procedure to subtract rejections from acceptance and assume that the resulting score value (call it X) represents a person who has the same psychological position in the group as one who attains a score of X by receiving X favorable nominations and no rejections.

Consistency over Time

Virtually none of the reports considered in this section offers any information relevant to the test-retest reliability of the sociometric scores used, or any information about their distribution. Only if nominees' relative sociometric standings remain reasonably stable over a period of time would it be reasonable to assume a stable enough effect on the nominees' self-concept to lead to a significant association between sociometric status and self-concept. As far back as 1955, an overview of reliability indices and outcomes based on 53 studies was published by Mouton, Blake, and Fruchter (1955a or 1960a); in 1968, Lindzey and Byrne gave a comprehensive analysis of types of reliability indices and some of the factors on which the numerical values of such coefficients apparently depend; most recently, Busk, Ford, and Schulman (1973) published an examination of the reliability obtained with the use of a variety of methods and scoring procedures. One can perhaps assume from these sources and from Northway's (1971) analysis of 11 years of accumulated data that the null or low associations from the presently considered studies which used sociometric techniques are probably not due to the unreliability of the sociometric measure, since so many variants of sociometric measure were found to yield test-retest reliabilities between .50 and .90 for intervals up to one year. (However, for unknown reasons, Horrocks and Benimoff [1966] found low one-year retest reliability with 549 children aged 12–17.)

Finally, since so many assumptions can be made about the psychological meanings or effects of sociometric scores which fall along various points on the range, one should cover a sufficiently wide range and subdivide the groups into a minimum of three reliably different subranges in order to look for nonlinear relationships and to provide a basis for choosing a mode of statistical analysis appropriate to the form of the distribution, which is typically quite skewed (see, e.g., Northway, 1971; Horrocks & Benimoff, 1966).

b. SELF-CONCEPT SCORES

Since I have extensively discussed elsewhere (Wylie, 1974), the many methodological complexities in self-concept measurement, I shall not attempt to summarize that analysis. Four points, however, are especially relevant to evaluating the work reviewed in this section.

Although even the most developed instruments purporting to measure self-regard or other aspects of self-concept have not been sufficiently refined and validated, at least much more is known about them than is the case with idiosyncratic indexes invented for a particular piece of research. This becomes a major issue in evaluating studies of sociometric scores and self-regard, since so many of these researches relied on idiosyncratic instruments about which little or no reliability, validity, or psychometric information is given.

Discrepancy or dyadic scores (e.g., self-ideal discrepancies) or mother-child similarities in self-descriptions are almost always uninterpretable, especially (in the present case) when no separate analysis is given of the relative contribution of their components to the correlation between the supposedly self-relevant score and the sociometric score.

A self-concept score should provide enough discriminably different steps to enable one to divide subjects into several groups, not just two, for the purposes of looking for nonlinear relationships and interactions.

As with the sociometric nominations, honesty (hence validity) should be promoted by providing anonymity. This is seldom considered in the reports below.

c. PROBLEMS IN RELATING SOCIOMETRIC AND
   SELF-CONCEPT SCORES IN AN INTERPRETABLE WAY

*Need for Control of IQ, Achievement,
and Socioeconomic Level*

Lindzey and Byrne (1968) report that sociometric status has sometimes been found to be positively correlated with IQ, reading achievement, educational status (among adults), age, and socioeconomic level and that nominations tend to be associated with sexual similarity, i.e., boys choose boys, girls choose girls. Evidence reviewed elsewhere in this book (see chap. 2) suggests that over-all self-regard is not a function of age, at least between ages 6 and 50. Hence, if sociometric status correlates with over-all self-regard, one need not worry about a possible artifactual explanation in terms of associations of age with sociometric status. Moreover, even if an equal number of nominees of both sexes are not available, this lack of control should not be relevant in studies of over-all self-regard because there appears to be no sex difference in that respect, as shown in chapter 5 of this book.

However, IQ and/or achievement levels may be associated with self-regard (see chap. 7 of this book), and they may also be artifactually associated with self-regard scores under certain conditions which promote the operation of the so-called reliability artifact (see Wylie, 1974, pp. 119–121 for an explanation of how this may occur). Also, IQ and achievement scores are associated with self-evaluations of ability and certain ability-related traits. Thus, some method of controlling for IQ should be introduced into studies associating sociometric status and self-concepts.

Findings concerning associations between socioeconomic level and over-all self-regard are mixed, most investigators reporting null results (see chap. 3 of this book). Pending clarification of this situation, socioeconomic level should be controlled as a precaution if one wishes to interpret positive associations between self-regard and sociometric scores in terms of possible influences of popularity on self-regard.

Need for Multivariate Designs

In general, multivariate designs are much needed, both to control for the above-mentioned variables and to look for interactions among them.

Timing of the Testing

Given the unknown and quite possibly limited consistency over time of both sociometric and self-concept scores, it seems important to try to apply both techniques at approximately the same time. Otherwise the correlations do not represent the concurrent associations between the variables, and null or low relationships in general are subject to one more source of ambiguity.

3. Results

a. RESULTS OF SOCIOMETRIC STUDIES

Using the above-discussed criteria, I examined 34 publications reporting a search for associations between sociometric status and self-concept scores and 7 publications reporting attempts to relate the subjects' self-concepts to their perceptions of others accep-tance/rejection of them. (Since the latter seem conceptually related to the topic of this section, they are included here rather than in a separate section. Two of them are included among the 34 sociometric studies as well.) Since some of the sociometric studies include peer nominations of leadership, it seems appropriate and convenient to include here 4 other investigations which looked at nominated leadership status, even though the nominations were not made by the peers of the nominees. Altogether, then, 38 sociometric publications are considered, including the anomalous 4 which used nonpeer nominations.

Of the 38 sociometric and nominating researches, one (Mussen & Porter, 1959) used an unvalidated TAT measure of self-concept and therefore seemed not comparable to those aiming to study the phenomenal self-concept. Three of the 37 sociometric reports are based on dyadic scores which render the results uninterpretable (Goslin, 1962; Helper, 1955; Mannheim, 1966). (Helper's study is extensively analyzed and criticized in Wylie, 1961, pp. 132 f.)

Of the remaining 34 sociometric and nominating publications, 23 reported one or more positive associations between sociometric or nominated status and self-regard. With one exception, these associations were small in absolute terms, and in some of the 23 reports, one finding was significant whereas another was not. (For example, Guardo's [1969] associations reached the .05 level for girls, but not for boys; while R. B. Smith, Tedeschi, Brown, and Lindskold [1973] reported a significant association for boys, but not for girls.) In the 11 publications reporting insignificant results, sometimes more than 1 group yielded such findings (e.g., Fiedler, Hutchins, and Dodge, 1959).

Two questions arise: First, why were the trends so small even in those studies where satisfactory significance levels were reached? Second, what differentiated the 23 methods yielding at least one significant result from the 11 yielding only null associations?

Comparing the two sets of researches yields no definitive answers to these questions, but some suggestive facts may be noted.

All but two of the 34 publications based on sociometric and nominating techniques were based on a different idiosyncratic sociometric measure. While this could not differentiate between the two groups of studies, it could have a bearing on the generally small associations obtained in both groups. Could it be that all these idiosyncratic sociometric measures are unreliable? Although most of the publications do not give enough information to answer this question, unreliability seems to be an unlikely explanation, in view of the information about the relatively high reliability of sociometric techniques, summarized above in the discussion of methodological criteria.

At least three other methodological explanations remain, then: (a) the sociometric or nomination scores in all the studies may be invalid or only weakly valid indicators of the nominators' attitudes toward the nominees; (b) the nominations, while validly expressing the nominators' feelings, have little or no relationship to how the nominators or peers actually treated the nominees and/or how the nominators or peers were perceived by the nominees to be treating them; (c) the methods of statistical analysis chosen, e.g., Pearson r or a t-test between extreme groups were inappropriate to the distribution of scores and/or for the purpose of revealing possible nonlinear relationships.

The publications afford no way of systematically checking these 3 speculations since so little is told and so many researchers used only Pearson rs or t-tests on dichotomized data. However, regarding point (b), it is suggestive that two of the publications reporting no significant association between self-regard and sociometric standing give significant correlations between subjects' self-regard scores and their stated estimates of their acceptability to others (Fey [1955], $r = .71$; J. E. Williams [1962], replicating Fey, $r = .62$). Regarding point (c), it is suggestive that only one of those investigators who obtained significant results tried to find and did report a nonlinear association involving 3 groups (Reese, 1961).

As one alternative to these ad hoc methodological explanations, one might propose that the weakness and insignificance of the reported results from the 33 studies occurred simply because any and all versions of the underlying theory mentioned at the outset are wrong, i.e., sociometric status has negligible association of any kind with self-regard.

But we must remember that 23 publications did report significant associations, even though small in absolute terms. What, then, might differentiate these studies from those yielding null results?

Two facts emerge from comparative inspection of methods. Out of the 23 yielding some significant findings, 20 measured self-regard with a relatively well-known instrument about which some reliability and validity information has been established, whereas only 2 out of 11 studies yielding insignificant associations used such instruments. The 10 different, relatively well-known instruments used in the studies yielding significant results were: Butler-Haigh Q sort*; California Test of Personality, Personal Worth Scale; Bills's Index of Adjustment and Values*; Brownfain's Self-Concept Inventory**; Lipsitt's Self-Concept Scale for Children*; Piers-Harris Self-Concept Scale*; Coopersmith's Self-Esteem Inventory*; Long, Henderson and Ziller's Self-Social Esteem test*; Tennessee Self-Concept Scale*; Rosenberg's Self-Esteem

Scale*; and the Twenty Sentences Test (the Who Are You? test)*. (Tests marked * are described and evaluated in Wylie, 1974; those marked ** are described and evaluated in Wylie, 1961.) Among the 11 studies yielding insignificant findings, one used Coopersmith's SEI, and one Phillips's Acceptance of Self Scale**. It seems plausible, then, that lesser reliability and/or validity may have characterized most or all of the idiosyncratic self-regard instruments, with the insignificant trends being partly assignable to this.

The second marked difference between these two sets of studies is the age of subjects used. While the studies yielding significant trends covered the age range from Grade 3 (one study) to old age (one study), 12 of the investigations used sixth graders, sometimes alone and sometimes with groups from nearby grades (e.g., 4, 5, 6 or 6, 7, 8). By contrast, among the 11 yielding essentially insignificant associations, only 2 involved normal children, whereas the remaining 8 publications were based on 2 samples of disturbed children and 8 college, military, or medical school groups.

One might ask whether the theoretical point raised earlier is of any relevance, namely were the nominators or peers very "significant others" for the adult student and the military nominees (or for that matter, were their disturbed peers' opinions of great importance to the disturbed children)?

About all that can be said in a positive vein is that future research, with more sophisticated theorizing and instrumentation, might yield more consistent and psychologically enlightening results, since at least some indication of significant association has been reported in 22 publications. From the theoretical and methodological discussions above, it is obvious that the reported studies represent a very primitive beginning. In addition to their limitations which have been cited already, only 2 of them made any attempt to control for variables such as IQ, achievement, and socioeconomic level which would tend, when uncontrolled, to inflate obtained correlation values. Therefore, whereas most of the improvements suggested might be expected to lead to the uncovering of some kind of consistent trends, if these variables were controlled in multivariate design we might find that even the significant trends obtained thus far are artifactual rather than indicative of the need of more refined psychological analysis.

The 23 studies which yielded at least one significant difference per study are as follows: Alexandra (1946); Bauer (1971); Bills (n.d.); Bonney (1943); Bordeau, Dales, and Connor (1963); Bradley and

Newhouse (1975); Coopersmith (1959), achievement partialed out; Cox (in Piers, 1969); R. W. Davis (1962); Gebel (1954); Guardo (1969), girls' difference significant, boys' not; F. D. Horowitz (1962), anxiety partialed out; Izard (1959); R. N. Morse and Piers (n.d.); Rosenberg (1965), Washington, D.C. high school study; Scandrette (1953); R. B. Smith, Tedeschi, Brown, and Lindskold (1973), boys' difference significant, girls' not; Turner and Vanderlippe (1958); R. L. Williams and Cole (1968); Yellott, Liem, and Cowen (1969); Zelen (1954a, 1954b, which report the same data); Ziller, Alexander, and Long (in Ziller, Hagey, Smith, and Long, 1969).

The 11 publications which report only null associations are as follows: Bass and Fiedler (1961); Coopersmith (1967); Fey (1955); Fiedler, Hutchins, and Dodge (1959); Fiedler, Warrington, and Blaisdell (1952); McIntyre (1952) (only mean rs given; values too low to reach the .05 level, given the mean N); O'Connor (1960) (only 1 out of 12 comparisons reached the .05 level despite intercorrelations among dependent variable measures); Perkins (1958b); Reidy and Colvin (1959); Rosengren and Davids (1961); J. E. Williams (1962).

b. Results of Studies of Perceived Acceptability to Others

Turning now to the publications giving correlations between subjects' self-regard levels and their estimates of their acceptability to others, we should keep two points in mind. On the one hand, such comparisons are, in principle, appropriate tests of self-concept theories since, according to these theories, it is one's perceptions of others' reactions which are presumed to be the immediate determinant of self-concept. Although one might correctly maintain that these perceptions which the person has of others' views of him are factually inaccurate, the theoretical point is that both the correct and distorted impressions are presumed to influence the self-concept; therefore, so long as our measure of expected or perceived acceptability is a reasonably valid index of the subject's view, it is indexing a theoretically relevant variable, whether or not it is a valid predictor of what others actually think of the subject.

On the other hand, one must always be wary on methodological grounds of correlations between two self-reports, since such correlations may be artifacts of the common format of the measuring instruments, e.g., an acquiescent response set or an extreme response set might artifactually account for positive associations between the two sets of scores. Also, one needs to inspect item content closely, as it may well be that the self-regard measure contains within it items of essentially the same content as does the purported measure of acceptability to others. For example, in Kaplan's (1976) report (discussed below), one of the four items comprising his scale of perceived-peer-derogation is "I am not very good at the kinds of things the kids at school think are important." This seems intuitively quite similar to two of the seven Rosenberg Self-Esteem items Kaplan used: "I feel I do not have much to be proud of," and "I'm inclined to feel I'm a failure." Unfortunately, most authors do not publish enough information to enable one to check systematically on this possible artifactual source of obtained associations between self-regard scores and perceived acceptability scores.

Eight publications concern studies which looked at associations between self-regard and self-rated or self-reported popularity or acceptability. Two of the eight reported insignificant associations between self-regard scores and perceived acceptability to others, whereas six report a significant association.

One of the two null findings was reported by Wiest (1965) who correlated scores from Coopersmith's Self-Esteem Inventory with a dyadic index of congruency between the child's sociometric status and his estimation thereof. As is the case when such unanalyzed dyadic scores are used, the results are uninterpretable and would be moot even if they had been significant. The second nonsignificant finding was reported by Berman and Brickman (1971) who correlated scores from an idiosyncratic self-regard instrument with subjects' judgments as to whether photographed persons liked them, i.e., no actual interpersonal interaction was involved in the experiment.

The earliest studies yielding significant positive findings are those of Fey (1955) and J. E. Williams (1962) (whose sociometric work is discussed in an earlier section). Both used Fey's Acceptance-of-Self scale (described and evaluated in Wylie, 1961) and a 5-item Expected Acceptability scale (split-half reliability = .89). They report significant correlations (r = .71 from Fey's work, r = .62 from Williams's report, both significant at ≤ .01 level).

Simon (1972) and Simon and Bernstein (1971) (who report the same study in these two articles) obtained a significant correlation between the number of persons each child thought would sociometrically choose him or her (here interpreted as a self-regard measure) and the number of persons who actually did choose him or her on a sociometric measure.

In his large scale study of New York State high school seniors,

Rosenberg (1965) obtained a significant linear association between self-esteem scores on his own (RSE) scale and subjects' tendency to endorse the statement that most people thought very well of them. Likewise, proportions of subjects who described themselves as well respected and looked up to by others, likeable, popular, and well liked by many different people varied significantly as a function of RSE scores. Since the latter self-report variables must be intercorrelated, it is not possible to evaluate the significance of these "significant" trends. A significant linear relationship is also reported between subjects' RSE scores and proportions who reported having held any elected position in a club or school organization.

In a publication based on the response of a large national sample of college students, Skager and Braskamp (1966) report a positive association between (a) changes in self-rated popularity and (b) score changes on an idiosyncratic Interpersonal Competency scale which appears to be at least partially an index of self-regard, especially with respect to social interaction. They attempted to control for the regression artifact by making separate analyses of groups from each of four initial levels of self-rated popularity. However, they made so many comparisons and significance tests in this study that the interpretability of any one significant finding is questionable.

Among 7,618 seventh graders in Houston, Texas, Kaplan (1975b, 1976) obtained a correlation of .42 between the self-derogation factor score from Rosenberg's Self-Esteem scale and a perceived-peer-derogation score based on 4 items. No discriminantly valid association can be inferred from this finding since (a) correlations were also found between RSE self-derogation scores and other perceived derogation scores, i.e., derogation by family and by school; (b) common item content may have inflated one or more of the correlations. Kaplan also tried to predict shifts in self-derogation as a function of perceived derogation by others at the first of 3 testing times. However, questions about the defensibility of the gain scores and the performance of multiple significance tests on overlapping and correlated measures render moot the interpretability of these reported outcomes.

In short, in the only two studies reporting null associations between self-regard and self-perceived acceptability to others, the results may well have been determined by methodological characteristics. However, the five studies reporting positive associations are open to other methodological criticisms. Thus, while results are suggestive and are congruent with theory, definitive support remains to be obtained for the proposition that perceived acceptability to others is correlated with self-regard when each is measured by an appropriate method having unique content and discriminant validity for its intended purpose.

C. Differential Attraction toward Particular Others as a Function of Manipulated Self-Regard

Altogether I have examined 57 studies which were intended at least in part, to look at subjects' evaluative reactions to others following an experience of being evaluated by others. Although not all the researchers called their operations "manipulation of self-esteem" or "manipulation of self-evaluation," all the studies except one used operations of the general class which is commonly so labeled. Accordingly they are considered in this section.

The theoretical section immediately below presents first a general analysis of the expected outcomes of this kind of experiment, given varying assumptions about the relative strengths of self-enhancement influences and cognitive consistency influences; then a listing of various a priori suggestions which have been made about possible moderating variables in this class of experiments.

The methodological section lists the most important method criteria relevant to evaluating this class of studies, and simultaneously indicates the extent to which the group of studies as a whole fulfilled these criteria.

Finally, an overview of the chief results from these researches is given.

1. General Theoretical and Methodological Considerations

a. Major Theories and Their Methodological Implications

Two main theoretical notions (self-enhancement and cognitive consistency) underlie this experimental work concerning subjects' attitudes toward others following evaluation. Both these ideas were included in the writings of self-theorists such as Rogers (1951) and Lecky (1945), and of consistency theorists such as Aronson (1969). However, so far as the idea of consistency is concerned, self-theorists especially emphasized that persons would seek congruence among aspects of the self-concept and between self-concept aspects and input from the environment, whereas cognitive-consistency theorists considered the congruencies or dissonances involving the self-concept as just a subset of a more inclusive set of cognitive consistencies or dissonances to which their theoretical propositions are addressed.

Both sets of theorists agree that persons seek both self-enhancement and consistency as means to maximize positive reinforcement or pleasurable affective states and to minimize aversive or painful states. While an infinite variety of behaviors is conceivable in the presence of positive or aversive states, the authors of the publications under consideration here focused on their subjects' expressed attraction toward or evaluation of others in the experimental situation. In most cases, these others are the alleged evaluators of the subject, but, in some cases, they are not. It is assumed that others having some association with positive reinforcement will be liked or well evaluated, those associated with aversive states disliked or devaluated.

TABLE 1

Subject's "Original" Self-Regard Level (Chronic or Manipulated)	Evaluation of Subject in Experiment	Hypothetical pleasurable state (+) or aversive state (−) created by	
		Evaluation of Subject	Consonance/ Dissonance
High	Positive	+	+
Low	Negative	−	+
Low	Positive	+	−
High	Negative	−	−

Reference to table 1 should help the reader to understand what might be predicted from a combination of self-enhancement and consistency influences, given certain assumptions.

In some situations, both self-enhancement and consistency influences are expected to operate in the same direction, e.g., toward maximizing positive reinforcement or pleasure; hence the subjects' behaviors could be interpreted as due to either or both influences. For example, as in row 1 of table 1, a person with high self-regard who is given a favorable evaluation in the experimental situation would be expected to accept the evaluation and show a favorable attitude toward the evaluator because the evaluative input (a) enhances the subjects' self-regard level, and (b) creates no cognitive dissonance because there is consistency between the subject's self-concept and the evaluative input. As in row 4 of table 1, unfavorable evaluation of a person with high self-regard would be expected to create an aversive state on either or both of two counts: (a) self-regard is threatened and (b) cognitive dissonance is introduced because the subject's original high self-regard level and the unfavorable evaluation input are inconsistent. (The latter expectation has been extended to say that, up to a point at least, the larger the negativity/discrepancy of the evaluations received by high self-regard persons, the greater their tendency to derogate the source [Harvey, 1962; Harvey, Kelley, & Shapiro, 1957; H. H. Johnson, 1966; H. H. Johnson & Steiner, 1968; Pepitone & Wilpizeski, 1960].)

Only in the case of the person whose self-regard level is *low* before receiving a specified experimental evaluative input can the conceptually separable influences of consistency and self-enhancement be pitted against one another. Thus if a positive evaluation is given to a person of low self-regard, this inconsistency should create cognitive dissonance leading to an aversive state, while simultaneously creating self-enhancement leading to a pleasurable or positively reinforcing state. (See row 3, table 1.) If a negative experimental evaluation is given to such a person it will be consistent with his negative self-conception, leading to a pleasurable or positively reinforcing state, while self-enhancement is simultaneously thwarted, leading to a negative or aversive state. (See row 2, table 1.) In short, if inconsistency (dissonance) between the experimental evaluation and the person's self-regard level has an influence separate from the self-enhancing aspects of the evaluative input, then the low self-regard person who is given positive evaluations of self should tend to experience either conflict or (if the influences cancel one another) a more nearly neutral state.

The table shows self-enhancing and consistency influences to be of equal strength. However, one could imagine that they are not, i.e., that self-consistency tendencies are slightly more influential than self-enhancement tendencies or vice versa. Which one of the three assumptions one makes about the relative strengths of these two influences will determine the predicted rank order of the middle two rows of the table, as follows: (a) If self-enhancement and consistency influences are equally strong, both the originally low self-regard groups should have the same affective level and equal attraction to the evaluator. There probably would be no main effect of evaluations given to the subject, but should be an interaction between original self-regard level and manipulated self-regard level in determining affective state and attraction to the evaluator. (b) If consistency influences outweigh self-enhancement influences, the original low self-regard groups should be in the order listed so far as affective state and attraction to the evaluator is concerned. There should be an interaction, but no main effect of positivity of manipulated self-regard. This is what Deutsch and Solomon (1959) predicted. If self-enhancement effects outweigh dissonance effects, the order of the two middle rows of originally low self-regard subjects should be reversed from that in the above table, so far as affective state and attraction to the evaluator are concerned. In that case, we should see both a main effect of positivity of manipulated self-regard and an interaction between original and manipulated self-regard.

On the other hand, one could add complications to the above theoretical picture. For one thing, the above table says nothing about the subjects' general levels of need for enhancement, implying that all four groups would be initially comparable with respect to need for self-enhancement, so that the potential rewarding or punishing value of positive or negative evaluations received during the experiment would be comparable for all groups. However, some have assumed that originally low self-regard subjects have a stronger need for self-enhancement than do originally high self-regard subjects. If so, positive evaluations would be especially rewarding for the former and negative evaluations especially aversive for them. If this idea is correct, the difference in affective states would be greater between differently evaluated subjects having originally low self-regard than between differently evaluated subjects having originally high self-regard. The situation might be envisaged as in table 2. (See Dittes, 1959; Skolnick, 1971; Stotland, 1959; and Walster, 1965, for example.) If the order of affective states is as tabulated in table 2, one would predict that, in comparison to originally high self-regard subjects, originally low self-regard subjects should be more attracted to a positive evaluator and should devaluate a negative evaluator more.

TABLE 2

Subject's "Original" Self-Regard Level (Chronic or Manipulated)	Evaluation of Subject in Experiment	Hypothetical pleasurable state (+) or aversive state (−) created by	
		Evaluation of Subject	Consonance/ Dissonance
Low	Positive	+ + + +	−
High	Positive	+	+
High	Negative	−	−
Low	Negative	− − − −	+

In practice, the subclass of studies which may be examined for possible relevance to the theoretical views about consistency versus self-enhancement are divided according to the alleged nature of the "original" self-regard level: Some experimenters assumed that some sort of chronic or predispositional self-evaluation should characterize the high and low groups, and they have usually formed their groups according to some purported measure of such a construct (e.g., Dittes, 1959; Shrauger & Lund, 1975). They have then looked for differing effects of manipulated or acute self-regard upon subjects having different levels of "original" chronic self-regard.

Others purported to manipulate self-regard once within the experiment in order to create "original" levels of manipulated self-regard, then have purported to manipulate self-regard again to see what effects the second self-regard manipulation would have on the subjects who were presumably temporarily put into one or more "original" self-evaluative levels by the first manipulation. (See, for example, Deutsch & Solomon, 1959; Skolnick, 1971.)

It appears that workers in this field implicitly assume that "original chronic self-regard" and "original manipulated self-regard" are comparable with respect to what they portend for subjects' reactions to (additional) manipulations of self-regard within these experimental situations.

Thus far I have left vague the possible referents for the terms "original self-regard" (chronic or manipulated) and "manipulated self-regard." One could read them as follows:

Original (chronic or manipulated)	*Manipulated*
Over-all (e.g., global self-esteem)	Over-all
Over-all (e.g., global self-esteem)	Restricted aspect
Restricted aspect (e.g., self-evaluation of friendliness or anagram-solving skill)	Over-all
Restricted aspect (e.g., self-evaluation of friendliness or anagram-solving skill)	Restricted aspect

In many cases, theorists and experimenters have not been clear about which of these combinations supposedly describe the intentions behind their experimental operations, and disparate results across studies as well as null findings within a study could plausibly be attributable to the variety and mutual appropriateness of the particular combination(s) of operations chosen.

In connection with this more refined question, Secord (1968) has suggested an additional complexity, as follows: Suppose one considers how a subject should be affected by evaluation on a particular attribute (e.g., his evaluation of his skill on a fairly specific kind of task or his evaluation of a particular self-referent trait). According to the principle of dissonance per se, if a relatively restricted cognitive input is dissonant or inconsistent with a relatively restricted aspect of the subject's cognitions (e.g., to cognitions about his or her ability or performance on this type of task or cognitions concerning a particular trait), it should not matter whether the dissonance is in the direction of positive evaluation given to a subject with poor evaluation of self or negative evaluation to a subject with good evaluation of self. However, Secord proposes that there is an asymmetry involved: restricted "negative evaluations have the property of spreading to other related aspects of self which have a positive valence" (p. 353), whereas a similar spreading will not be seen from positive evaluative input to other aspects of the self having a negative valence. This supposedly could explain why the negativity of a *self*-referent input to the subject could have greater impact than would be predicted on the basis of its dissonance only and greater than a positive evaluative input of presumably equal dissonance.

If Secord's idea is correct, the subject who devalues self in one restricted respect and is given an inconsistent favorable evaluation in that particular respect does not experience general self-enhancement; instead he or she experiences a given amount of dissonance on a restricted dimension and a little increment in self-evaluation. By contrast, the subject who evaluates self highly in that one respect and receives inconsistent unfavorable evaluation concerning that particular aspect of self would experience general devaluation in addition to experiencing the given amount of dissonance. In the above table, then the high self-evaluating subjects receiving negative evaluations would supposedly be even more discriminable from the low self-evaluating subjects receiving negative evaluations than would be the case if this kind of asymmetry of spread of particular negative or positive evaluations did not obtain. However, I know of no experiment that has tried to explore the relative spreading effects of favorable and un-favorable input, and the operations which would be required to make a properly controlled test of this idea seem to be exceedingly difficult to specify, let alone carry out.

Ideas about the role of dissonance have not only influenced

predictions about interactions between "original" and "manipulated" self-regard in affecting subjects' reactions to evaluators, but these theories have suggested some other experiments as well. For example, Glass (1964) assumed that, among subjects known to be against the use of shock in experiments, degree of choice in shocking a confederate would interact with manipulated self-regard to affect subjects' liking for the shocked confederate. Whereas all subjects presumably experienced dissonance between their attitudes toward shock and their shock-giving behavior, differences in dissonance would be especially high between those who had high and low self-esteem who chose to give shock, whereas no further dissonance arousal was expected for either high or low self-esteem persons given no choice. Several authors have proposed that dissonance effects would be shown up only under special moderating circumstances to be discussed later in connection with the overview of results. (See the substantive discussion of publications by Dutton & Arrowood, 1971; S. C. Jones & Ratner, 1967; Krauss & Critchfield, 1975; and D. T. Wilson, 1965, given in the section below which summarizes methods and outcomes.)

Although I have given a fairly elaborate consideration of the comparative predicted outcomes which follow certain assumptions about the relative roles of self-enhancement and consistency influences, many of the available studies of attraction as a function of manipulated self-regard were designed primarily on the basis of additional or alternate theoretical considerations. The latter, while always including the idea of maximizing positive reinforcement and minimizing aversive states, are not rooted in any other well-known theoretical viewpoint. Many of the hypothesized processes appear to be common-sense intuitions. Partly because of this, there is such a variety among the theoretical suggestions that it presents an almost unsurmountable challenge to organize them into coherent subclasses to facilitate an overview. Accordingly, my categorizations may inadvertently do violence to the theoretical intentions of the investigators.

b. IDEAS ABOUT MODERATING VARIABLES

Generally speaking, I believe, these alleged moderators may be seen as operating in the following ways: (a) to minimize or maximize the objective necessity for the subjects to accept as self-applicable the evaluations given to them; (b) to provide alternate ways of behaving than liking or disliking others in the experimental situation, in order to see whether these alternate ways affect the appearance of effects on subjects' evaluations of others.

Substantively, I have found it helpful to classify these alleged moderating influences as follows: (a) characteristics of the source of evaluations of the subject; (b) the subjects' predispositional (personality) characteristics; (c) the motivations, goals, and/or expectancies of the subject in the particular experimental situation; (d) situational variables relevant to manipulated evaluation salience and/or opportunities for alternate behavior patterns.

Evaluation from a credible, respect-worthy source is expected to carry more weight in affecting self-regard (or in creating dissonance, for that matter) and, hence, in affecting the subjects' attractions to the source or to certain others.

Construing this idea broadly, one can perhaps class together the following publications. Dickoff (in E. E. Jones, 1964) expected subjects to be affected less by an evaluator whose motive was supposedly ulterior (to get the subject to do a favor) than by an evaluator whose alleged motive was to be accurate. In comparing derogated with bystander subjects, E. E. Jones, Hester, Farina, and Davis (1959) expected derogated subjects to console themselves with the thought that a maladjusted derogator's views of others are distorted as compared to the judgments of a well-adjusted derogator. In contrast, a bystander subject, having no need to protect herself against attack, would find her dislike for a maladjusted person compounded with her dislike for derogators; this would lead to the bystander's greater devaluation of the maladjusted derogator as compared to the well-adjusted one. Aronson and Linder (1965) offered the source's "discernment" as one possible ad hoc explanation of their findings that negative, then positive evaluations led to greater attraction to the evaluator than did continuously positive. With this idea in mind, Landy and Aronson (1968) attempted specifically to vary evaluators' discernment. Harvey, Kelley and Shapiro (1957) expected the subjects' reactions to their evaluators to depend in part on whether the evaluators were supposedly strangers or acquaintances. R. C. Howard and Berkowitz (1958) hypothesized that a person who gives a subject a performance evaluation deviating considerably from the consensus of several other evaluators is less attractive to the subject than the group of evaluators who are in agreement, regardless of whether the deviate's ratings are highly favorable or unfavorable. (Although this prediction could stem from a source-credibility idea, it could also be interpreted in dissonance terms or in terms of the subject's wanting to work with an accurate person in order to maximize his team's—hence his own—success.) H. H. Johnson and Steiner (1968) predicted that subjects' favorability toward their evaluators would be affected in the case of evaluations received from own fraternity members, but not in the case of evaluations received from members of a little-known "antagonistic" fraternity.

Others have theorized that *certain personality traits of the subject will operate as moderating variables* in this type of experiment. For example, Page and Markowitz (1956) hypothesized that defensive subjects would be less likely to express dislike toward their derogators. In the same vein, Fishman (1965) predicted that, among derogated subjects, those with high Marlowe-Crowne Social Desirability (MCSD) scores would evaluate their derogators more favorably than would those with low MCSD scores. Taking an alternate view, Shrauger and Jones (1968) thought subjects who were high in need for approval would be more rewarded by positive evaluations and more frustrated by negative ones, so that high scorers in MCSD would react more unfavorably than would low scorers to a person who evaluated them poorly. Without making the underlying rationales explicit, Hamilton (1969, 1970) proposed that several different personality variables might moderate the influence of manipulated self-esteem on the subjects' evaluations of their evaluators' competence: dimensions measured by the Interpersonal Check List; Repression-Sensitization scores; and Dogmatism scores. Harvey (1962) expected "intolerance of ambiguity" on the California F scale and extrapunitiveness on the Rosenzweig P-F scale to be associated with subjects' unfavorability to their derogators. At least part of the basis for all the above predictions lies in assumptions about the type and strength of the subjects' defenses against having to accept low evaluations and/or against expressing negative feelings toward others in the experiment.

Relating to the preceding group of hypothesized mediating variables within subjects are *the motivations, goals, and/or expectancies relevant to the particular experimental situation, and the ways the subject finds available to fulfill them within this situation.* For example, Aronson and Linder (1965) thought their negative-to-positive evaluation condition might have stimulated subjects to improve their impression of their evaluator, resulting in an increasing sense of competence when evaluations shifted from negative to positive.

In comparing subjects with high and low levels of task aspiration (correlated with high and low expectations of success), R. C. Howard and Berkowitz (1958) expected that high-aspiring subjects should see a favorably deviant evaluator as being more accurate and an unfavorably deviant evaluator as being less accurate relative to three other evaluators who agreed on an intermediate evaluation level.

S. B. Kiesler and Baral (1970) felt that realistic prospects of attaining the goal of "catching" a romantic partner would underlie a tendency for high self-esteem subjects to behave more romantically toward a very attractive (as opposed to a moderately attractive) confederate, and for low self-esteem subjects to behave more romantically toward a moderately attractive (as opposed to a very attractive) confederate. Also adopting the premise that subjects will maximize their prospects of getting a romantic partner and will avoid invidious comparisons, Walster (1970) reasoned that one could predict from a person's self-esteem the desirability level of partner which would be preferred.

E. E. Jones et al. (1959) hypothesized that a subject who is merely a bystander in a devaluation situation should not be so affected as the derogated subject. Stotland (1959) thought that whether the subject sees his private task as relevant or irrelevant to the group's goals will affect whether success or failure on that task determines the subject's attraction to the group. Persons expecting to undertake a competitive task will prefer a less desirable partner who can be outperformed, whereas those expecting to undertake a cooperative task will prefer a desirable partner to maximize team (hence their own) success. A similar difference was not expected in high self-esteem subjects who supposedly would have more confidence in their own abilities.

On the assumption that subjects aim to give "correct" answers, Shrauger and Jones (1968) hypothesized that "the tendency to respond positively to the agreement of others and negatively to their disagreement will be stronger when [separate] objective means of opinion validation are absent than when [separate] objective means of validation are present" (p. 316).

Friedman (1976) expected need for equity to override need for self-enhancement among high self-esteem subjects, with the opposite occurring among low self-esteem subjects when they rated their attraction to a highly personable confederate from whom they had just received inequitably high rewards and with whom they expected to interact further.

Other situational variables have also been supposed to moderate outcomes in experiments in which subjects evaluate others or indicate the attractiveness of others after having been evaluated themselves.

Most of these situational variations provide some kind of opportunity for some of the negatively evaluated subjects either to minimize the salience of the experimental evaluation or use some means to lower or forestall their aversive state before evaluating others in the experimental situation. For example, C. R. Berger (1973) assumed that the opportunity to attribute success or failure to impersonal environmental sources as opposed to own ability would attenuate liking or disliking felt toward an imaginary professor who announced subjects' test scores. Taking an opposing viewpoint, Snoek (1962) predicted that subjects given an "invidious" (personal) reason why a group has rejected them will be *more* attracted to the group than will subjects given a "noninvidious" (impersonal) reason for the group's rejection. As a basis for this "paradoxical" prediction, Snoek assumed that subjects in the invidious condition would more strongly need social reassurance and would especially value reacceptance into the group as a means of obtaining that reassurance.

Green and Murray (1973) theorized that subjects will be more vulnerable to threats to self-esteem following high as opposed to low self-disclosure on the part of the subject. Rosenbaum and deCharms (1960, 1962) assumed that the opportunity to communicate hostility toward a derogator would lower "residual hostility" expressed toward him at the end of the experiment.

c. METHODOLOGICAL EVALUATION OF EXTANT STUDIES

Several methodological comments are applicable to this entire group of complex researches.

1. They involved an extremely wide variety of operations for manipulating the subjects' self-evaluations (e.g., alleged failure or success on a rather narrowly specialized task, alleged failure or success on purportedly important intelligence tests, bogus clinical evaluations of subjects' personality characteristics, bogus peers' evaluations of subjects' personality characteristics, bogus feedback regarding subjects' desirability as bridge club members, insults to subjects' task motivations, and unprovoked verbal attacks). There is virtually no overlap among the 57 studies regarding exactly how the over-all or more restricted self-evaluations of subjects were purportedly manipulated, severely curtailing synthesized generalizations or interstudy comparisons.

2. With few exceptions, only two levels of manipulated self-evaluation were included: some of the two-level studies used positive versus negative, others two degrees of negativity. Occasionally a no-manipulation control group was run. Naturally, therefore, the search for nonlinear relationships was precluded in most studies.

3. Fewer than half the investigators attempted to check on whether the subjects' self-evaluations were actually affected by the manipulation in a way relevant to the researcher's hypotheses and suggested data interpretations. Hence one cannot know (a) whether the intended "acute" level of self-evaluation was affected at all by the manipulations, (b) what *range* of differences was created across the groups whose self-evaluations were supposedly manipulated in different directions or to different degrees. The latter is especially important in that null findings might result from working within too narrow a range.

Some investigators who have used self-regard measures to check on their manipulations have not found effects on self-evaluative indices while finding effects on one or more attraction measures, or they have found different effects on self-evaluative measures than on attraction measures. This kind of situation creates a difficult interpretative situation in that one could argue at least two ways: (a) the effect on the attraction measures was not mediated by self-regard changes, perhaps because devaluating others enabled the subjects to preserve their self-regard level, i.e., changing of evaluations of self or others are to a certain extent alternate modes of coping with evaluations given the self; (b) the measures used by the experimenter are insensitive to actual changes in those aspects of self-regard produced by the manipulations which are relevant to the subjects' changes in evaluations of others.

4. Where a purported self-esteem measure was used, either as a check on the effectiveness of the supposed manipulation of self-regard, or as a separate independent variable (i.e., to index chronic self-regard levels), or, occasionally as a dependent variable measure, an idiosyncratic index was used in all but eight studies. Usually even descriptive information about these idiosyncratic measures is not published, and no publication provides information about reliability, validity, or other psychometric characteristics. In the eight studies which used a chronic self-esteem measure about which some information is published elsewhere, the Janis-Field Scales were employed five times; and the Tennessee Self-Concept Scale, Coopersmith's Self-Esteem Inventory, and the California Psychological Inventory (six selected scales) once

each. Obviously, interpretation of results from individual studies and syntheses across studies are greatly hindered by this situation.

5. Although the theory behind these studies assumes that the subjects' chronic and manipulated self-regard are conceptually equivalent as independent variables, there has been no demonstration that this is the case.

6. Regarding the dependent variable measures of the subjects' attractions to or evaluations of others, almost every publication is based on a different, idiosyncratic index for which descriptive information is usually incomplete and for which no reliability, validity, and other psychometric information is published. The "evaluations of others" ranged from indicating others' desirability as teammates for a particular, specialized task, through evaluating their competence as evaluators of the subject, through evaluating their over-all attractiveness or likeability as persons. Six studies used Byrne's Interpersonal Judgment Scale for which some information about reliability and construct validity has been published (Byrne, 1971, pp. 52 and 229-235; Byrne, Ervin, & Lamberth, 1970). C. A. Kiesler and Goldberg's (1968) exploratory factor analysis suggests that at least two different factors are involved in the above kinds of attraction indices: one "closely related to what one might ordinarily call 'liking'. . . . the other a task category of interpersonal attraction related to what one might ordinarily call 'respect' " (p. 700).

Ironically, although the experimenters have invented ingenious and elaborate experimental procedures in order to attain improved control over many of those variables left uncontrolled by previous investigators, the potential value of the more rigorous experimental approach is counteracted to an unknown extent by the use of dependent variable measures having unspecified characteristics.

7. Some investigators have used two-part change scores or other two-part scores as a measure of the dependent variable(s) without regard to the pitfalls therein which usually preclude interpretability. (See Wylie, 1974, pp. 88-95, 304, 307.)

8. The discriminant validity of the dependent variable measures is still open to question in many of these studies. That is, one wonders whether positive or negative evaluation from another discriminantly affects subjects' evaluations of that other who is the source of the manipulation or is in some way relevant to it, or whether the subjects' general attitudes have been affected by the manipulation. A partial check on this could be made if there were studies yielding positive main

effects for within-subject comparisons of subjects' evaluations of others who positively evaluated them and who negatively evaluated them. None of the studies in question used such a design, however. A more direct check on the question of discriminant validity could be made if the subjects' reactions to the other who manipulated their self-evaluations were compared to their reactions to others not connected with the manipulation. Two of the studies did show that subjects devalued by the experimenter's manipulations in turn devalued others not involved in the original self-evaluation manipulation (Glass, 1964; Stotland, 1959). However, in each of these studies, there is another reason to predict the direction of the subjects' evaluations of the noninvolved others; so these findings do not constitute an adequate test of the discriminant validity question at issue.

9. Suitable multivariate analyses were never made to ascertain whether associations between chronic or manipulated self-regard and dependent measures of evaluation of others might actually be due to some association of a common variable with both the self-regard scores and the dependent variable scores (e.g., an extremity response set might be operating, or perhaps the experimental conditions induced an adjustment in the subjects' ideas of the meanings of various points or ranges on the scales provided).

10. Another common methodological failure of these studies is that (with one exception) subjects are asked to indicate their attraction to or evaluation of others whom they never see or see only briefly. While this enables the investigator to introduce certain controls which are not afforded by more "real life" research situations, it also obviously limits the generalizability of the results.

11. Since these experiments attempt to control certain variables by more or less complex, artificial, deceptive scenarios, the question of the subjects' suspiciousness is especially pertinent. More than half the studies made no mention of checking subjects' suspicions, whereas about a third of them indicated, without giving enough details about inquiry methods, that data from suspicious subjects were eliminated from the analysis. But Golding and Lichtenstein's (1970) results, among others, suggest that (a) many suspicious subjects do not confess their suspicions, even under pointed, systematic probing; (b) suspicious subjects who do reveal their suspicions (and are thereby eliminated from the analysis) tend to have complied less with the demand characteristics of the experiment than do suspicious subjects who do not indicate their suspicions and whose data are therefore included. Thus, findings

supporting the experimenter's hypothesis may not be generalizable to truly naïve persons.

12. Besides its methodological implications for suspiciousness of subjects, the use of deception techniques raises serious ethical questions which I have discussed fully elsewhere (Wylie, 1974, pp. 32–37). Opinions vary as to when (if ever) scientific work is sufficiently important and methodologically meritorious to warrant the use of deception. However, it appears to me that the other methodological limitations and flaws characterizing this set of studies makes it unlikely that one could defend their use of deception in terms of their scientific merit, regardless of the social importance of the questions to which they were addressed.

2. Overview of Results

Faced with this dismaying methodological situation, a reviewer may either yield to the temptation to avoid substantive comment altogether or she can attempt to present a very tentative set of generalizations, should any trends or patterns seem to be discernible. I have chosen the latter course, after eliminating 3 of the 57 studies from further consideration, owing to their extreme inadequacy of method and/or reporting (Freeman, 1973; Hart, 1973; Levanway, 1955).

I consider first the main effect of favorability of evaluations given the subject; then studies which purport to evaluate the relative influences of consistency and self-enhancement tendencies, and finally four groups of researches which examine classes of variables thought to moderate the influences of manipulated self-regard on the evaluation which subjects make of others.

a. Main Effects of Favorability of Evaluations Given the Subjects

Although most of the 54 studies substantively considered in this section were not solely or primarily concerned with main effects of manipulated self-evaluations upon the subjects' attraction to and/or evaluation of others, most of the reports can be examined for possible evidence of such an effect.

Of the 54, 34 (63%) showed significant support for the general proposition that subjects' evaluations of others are a direct function of the subjects' manipulated self-evaluation levels. These are: Aronson and

Linder (1965); Aronson and Worchel (1966); Arrowood and Short (1973); C. R. Berger (1973); Byrne and Griffitt (1966); Byrne and Rhamey (1965); Deutsch and Solomon (1959); Dickoff (in E. E. Jones, 1964); Dittes (1959); Eiser and Smith (1972); Fishman (1965); Glass (1964); J. W. Goldstein and Rosenfeld (1969); J. Gormly, A. Gormly, and Johnson (1972); Green and Murray (1973); Griffitt, Byrne, and Bond (1971); Hamilton (1969); Harvey (1962); Harvey, Kelley, and Shapiro (1957); Hewitt (1972) [two experiments]; H. H. Johnson (1966); H. H. Johnson and Steiner (1968); S. C. Jones (1966); Keislar (1961); Landy and Aronson (1968); Lowe and Goldstein (1970); Ludwig (1970); Pepitone and Wilpizeski (1960); Shrauger and Jones (1968); Sigall and Aronson (1967); Skolnick (1971); Stotland (1959); Tognoli and Keisner (1972).

Fifteen publications (28%) showed either nonsignificant main trends or did not present an analysis of such a main effect due to the authors' concerns with specified predicted interactions, as explained in later sections. They are: Dutton and Arrowood (1971); Friedman (1976); Howard and Berkowitz (1958); Jacobs, Berscheid, and Walster (1971); S. C. Jones and Ratner (1967); Kiesler and Baral (1970); Koeck and Guthrie (1975); Krauss and Critchfield (1975); Mettee (1971a, 1971b); Page and Markowitz (1956); Shrauger and Lund (1975); Walster (1965, 1970); D. T. Wilson (1965).

Four studies could not have been analyzed for such a main effect. Therefore, *34 out of a possible 50 which could have been analyzed for this kind of main effect yielded at least one significant trend for subjects' attraction to others to be a positive function of manipulated self-regard.* This is a conservative estimate in that some of the authors who did not choose to check the significance of such a main positivity effect might have obtained one or more such outcomes.

Only one significant reversal is reported — by Snoek (1962), who gave subjects either invidious (personal) or noninvidious (impersonal) reasons why a bridge group was rejecting them. Only one of his five intercorrelated dependent variables yielded a significant difference, and it was a change score of doubtful interpretability. In any case, Snoek argued that invidiously rejected subjects showed more change toward a desire to stay in the group because their invidious rejection had created a greater need for being socially reassured by the group.

As already indicated, the 34 studies varied greatly in methodological characteristics. Perhaps one could suggest that positive findings from such disparate operations for manipulating subjects' self-evaluations and for evaluating their reactions to others strengthens the generalizability of the significant trends. Moreover, in those few studies which used more than two levels of manipulated self-evaluation, or supplemented a two-level manipulation with a "no message" control group, essentially monotonic main effects were obtained (Arrowood & Short, 1973; Dickoff [in E. E. Jones, 1964]; Green & Murray, 1973; H. H. Johnson, 1966; H. H. Johnson & Steiner, 1968).

However, before generalizing from these results, one should reserve judgment in the light of one additional methodological point besides those already mentioned: Although each of the 34 yielded at least one significant main effect, several of them used a number of dependent variable measures purportedly indicative of alternate aspects of the subjects' evaluations of and/or attraction to others, and not every such dependent variable within these experiments yielded significant results, even if the dependent variables were intercorrelated.

Considering the strong intuitive plausibility that self-enhancement will be at least one factor in determining the degree of attraction to one's evaluators, it is perhaps surprising that there are not more such significant main effects reported. On the other hand, since little or nothing is known of the reliability and validity of the dependent variable measures, failures to reach satisfactory significance levels with all of them may be due in part to their unknown psychometric characteristics. Or the explanation may lie to an unknown extent in the fact than the positivity effect is diminished by a considerable number of moderating variables.

b. EXPERIMENTS RELEVANT TO TESTING CONSISTENCY
   INFLUENCES VERSUS SELF-ENHANCEMENT INFLUENCES

As explained in the theoretical discussion, if both consistency and self-enhancement influences are operative, and all groups are assumed to have the same need for self-enhancement, then experimentally inducing positive or negative self-regard should create greater differences in the attraction reactions of originally high self-regard persons than in the reactions of the originally low self-regard persons. On the other hand, whether or not both factors are operating, if originally low self-regard subjects have greater needs for self-enhancement (hence finding positive self-regard manipulations more rewarding and negative ones more aversive), the differences created between originally high self-regard subjects should be smaller than those between originally low self-regard subjects.

One of the first and most widely cited experiments on this topic (Deutsch & Solomon, 1959) yielded some evidence for a consistency effect counteracting a self-enhancement effect. That is, persons with manipulated high self-regard (task success) liked a positive note writer who said she wanted the subject on her team better than a negative note writer who said she did not want the person on her team, but persons with manipulated low self-regard (task failure) did not show a preference between positive and negative note writers. However, the findings do not support the idea that consistency influences will either act alone or completely override self-enhancement influences because low self-regard subjects did not significantly prefer the negative note writers. Moreover, criticisms can be made of Deutsch and Solomon's method, data analyses, and report, and their results have not been replicated.

Skolnick (1971) did a very similar experiment in which he first attempted to manipulate self-regard by manipulating task success, after which he gave notes to half the subjects in each self-regard group saying the team wanted them while to half he gave notes saying the team did not want them. The low self-regard subjects (task failure group) showed a greater difference in evaluation of positive and negative note writers than did the high self-regard subjects (task success group), but the interaction did not reach the .05 level. This nonsignificant trend fails to replicate Deutsch and Solomon's results and supports the idea that the stronger self-enhancement needs of the low self-regard subjects led to self-enhancement influences overriding consistency influences rather than the reverse.

As in the preceding two studies, S. C. Jones (1966) used one self-regard manipulation followed by a second self-regard manipulation in order to test consistency theory predictions against self-enhancement predictions. The first manipulation consisted of experts' judgments of the subject's success or failure on a design judgment task; the second consisted of a co-worker peer's judgments of the subject's success or failure on an oral continuation of the same task. Subjects' evaluations of their peers' abilities on the task constituted the dependent variable. Those whose peer evaluations were favorable gave these peers significantly higher percentages of positive evaluations than were given by subjects whose peer evaluations were unfavorable. Considering only the subjects whose initial (expert) evaluation was unfavorable, those receiving favorable peer evaluations gave significantly more positive evaluations to their evaluators than did those receiving unfavorable peer evaluations. A similar trend among those whose initial evaluation was favorable was not significant. This pattern of results supports the idea that the stronger self-enhancement needs of low self-regard subjects led to self-enhancement influences overriding consistency influences rather than the reverse.

The procedure of Jacobs, Berscheid, and Walster (1971) may be viewed as similar to that reported in the preceding three publications, with the addition of a third ("ambiguous") level in the second self-regard manipulation. First, the self-regard levels of male college freshmen were manipulated by bogus favorable or unfavorable personality test feedback and psychiatrists' evaluations of their personalities. In the second self-regard manipulation, they were exposed to either a clearly accepting, ambiguously accepting, or clearly rejecting evaluation of themselves which had supposedly been made by a college female who had judged their social skills on the basis of listening to five taped telephone calls which the subjects had been induced to make. Both subjects with high and low initially manipulated self-regard evaluated this female more favorably if she supposedly clearly accepted them as opposed to clearly rejecting them. This difference was somewhat larger among subjects with initially lowered self-regard. Although the latter trends were not separately evaluated for significance, they are similar to results reported by Skolnick (1971), S. C. Jones (1966), and Dittes (1959). Thus, they are in the direction predicted by the assumption that low self-regard subjects have greater self-enhancement needs so that enhancement tendencies override consistency influences. Subjects with initially raised self-regard evaluated the ambiguously accepting female about as favorably as the clearly accepting one. Those with initially lowered self-regard evaluated her more favorably than the clearly rejecting female, considerably less favorably than the clearly accepting female, and significantly less favorably than did the high self-regard subjects. The authors suggest that the person with low self-regard feels less favorable toward the ambiguously accepting person because he is less able to interpret her behavior as accepting. In other words, it appears that the subjects with low self-regard found clearly accepting input the most desirable of the three even though it is the most dissonant from their allegedly low self-regard level. If, as the authors believe, the ambiguous accepting input is perceived as less favorable by the low self-regard subjects than by the high self-regard subjects, it makes such ambiguous input less rewarding to the former, even though more nearly congruent with their low self-regard. Accordingly, the trends obtained from the subjects' responses following ambiguously accepting input also tend to support the idea that the low self-regard subjects had stronger self-enhancement needs, and the enhancement influences overrode the consistency influences.

Walster's (1965) results seem to support the idea that inducing low self-regard should increase need for favorable evaluation. She manipulated the self-regard of her female subjects by giving them bogus personality ratings from a therapist. Then she measured by an un-specified method the subjects' liking for an accepting, affectionate, physically attractive male confederate. The low self-regard subjects showed significantly higher attraction ratings toward the confederate than did the high self-regard subjects. It appears that manipulation of self-regard may have been successful since both subject groups ap-parently tended to accept as self-applicable the evaluations given them.

Unlike the first four investigations, Dittes (1959) varied original self-regard levels not by experimentally manipulating it but by choosing groups who were high, medium, and low on an idiosyncratic measure of chronic self-regard. One-third of each self-regard group was told by note that their acceptance by the group was well above average, one-third that it was average, and one-third that it was below average. A post-manipulation check using an idiosyncratic self-evaluation index suggested that the manipulation had affected the subjects' self-regard. Congruent with the idea that low self-regard subjects have especially strong self-enhancement needs which will override consistency in-fluences, the originally low self-regard subjects showed a significantly greater attraction to the positive and average than to the negative note writers, while the originally average self-regard and high self-regard subjects showed successively smaller differences of this kind, both differences being insignificant.

Koeck and Guthrie (1975) used subjects who were high and low on Berger's (1952) Self-Acceptance Scale, and they gave each subject a bogus evaluation (favorable, neutral, unfavorable) which had sup-posedly been made by a confederate with whom the subject had per-formed some cognitive tasks. Subjects with low Berger self-acceptance scores gave their evaluators poor evaluative ratings regardless of the evaluative level of the bogus appraisal they had received. Among subjects with high self-acceptance scores, however, there was a direct relationship between evaluative level of the bogus rating and subjects' evaluations of their supposed evaluators. These results are not explicable in terms of self-enhancement processes or the supposed greater need for enhancement among low self-regard persons. Also, the fact that the low Berger scorers did not favorably evaluate those who unfavorably evaluated them is not explicable on the basis of consistency per se. In effect, a check on the manipulation of self-regard was made in which subjects of both Berger groups seemed to accept their bogus evaluations as being self-applicable.

Also using a measure of chronic self-regard, Shrauger and Lund (1975) divided their groups into those with high and low self-esteem. Then, following an interview of each subject by a supposed graduate student in clinical psychology, the experimenters gave one-third of each self-esteem group bogus feedback from the interviewer to the effect that they were "self aware" (supposedly a favorable evaluation), or not "self-aware" (supposedly an unfavorable evaluation). The remaining one-third received no feedback. Subjects then rated their perceptions of the favorability of the interviewer's attitudes toward them; the interviewer's objectivity, competence, and degree of emotional bias in making judgments; and their emotional reactions toward the interviewer. The subjects' rated emotional reactions toward the interviewer gave entirely null results. The ratings of interviewer objectivity, competence, and bias failed to support self-enhancement views in that it was the high self-regard subjects who tended to rate favorable interviewers as more objective, competent, and unbiased than unfavorable interviewers, whereas low self-regard subjects showed little difference in these ratings of favorable and unfavorable interviewers. However, as in Deutsch and Solomon's study, the subjects did not give significantly better ratings to unfavorable evaluators, even though the unfavorable evaluators' feedback would supposedly be more congruent with the subjects' unfavorable self-evaluations. Thus, the evidence is not clearly in the direction to be expected if consistency effects override self-enhancement effects.

In attempting to decide whether this experiment constitutes a real test of self-enhancement influences as opposed to consistency influences, one can question whether self-regard was effectively manipulated. An idiosyncratic 11-trait self-evaluation measure was used to check on the manipulation. Although subjects did differ in their self-awareness ratings as a function of self-awareness feedback, the "evaluative feedback had no significant effect on the favorability of subjects' over-all self-evaluations [on the 11-trait measure], and high and low self-esteem subjects' impressions of themselves were not affected differentially by the evaluative feedback they received" (p. 103). Moreover, among both high and low self-esteem subjects, the over-all perception of the favorability of the interviewer's attitudes toward them did not vary as a function of the evaluative feedback that was given.

Eiser and Smith's (1972) work is unique in two ways. (a) They attempted to vary both accuracy and positivity of evaluations given to each subject by determining for each one individually which particular listed adjectives he thought were accurate and inaccurate as self-descriptions and how likely it would be that he would like another person he described by each adjective. (b) Dependent variable measures were taken purely on the basis of the subjects' imagination, i.e., "preference scores" were determined for each of the subject's adjectives by his answers to the question "If *you* overheard someone describing you as . . . , how likely is it that *you* would like that person?" Preference score means for each type of adjective were: accurate-positive, 2.6; inaccurate-positive, 3.4; accurate-negative, 4.8; inaccurate-negative, 5.7. Main effects of both positivity and accuracy were significant, the interaction not significant. Since accuracy as defined here is essentially the same as consonance, and inaccuracy is dissonance, we see that dissonance did play an independent role in diminishing subjects' imaginary liking for imaginary evaluators. This is most evident in that consonant favorable evaluations were preferred to dissonant favorable ones, even though the dissonant favorable ones would presumably add to the over-all favorability of the subject's evaluative input. In this respect, the results support the idea that consistency influences may operate independently of self-enhancing ones. However, the interpretation of the data on dissonant negative evaluations is moot. The results could imply that dissonance played a role independent of negativity in determining the subjects' liking for their evaluators. Alternately, it could imply that the subject was imagining himself receiving even more numerous unfavorable evaluations than he felt he deserved. In other words, in one sense negativity of input was held constant when looking for dissonance effects, but in another sense, the total amount of negative evaluation was being varied by the addition of unwarranted (dissonant) unfavorable evaluations to warranted (consonant) unfavorable ones. No study involving real or supposedly real social interaction has attempted such a within-subject manipulation of both positivity and dissonance; so one cannot say whether the subjects' reactions to real evaluators would turn out the same way as in this purely imaginary situation.

Excluding Eiser and Smith's (1972) work which is methodologically incomparable to the other eight studies, the results reported in five out of eight publications fell in a direction supportive of the idea that low self-regard persons have greater needs for self-enhancement and that self-enhancing influences override consistency influences. However, trends were not always significant. The remaining three gave some support for the counteraction of self-enhancement by consistency influences in that low self-regard subjects showed little difference in their attraction to positive and negative evaluators. However, these three did not show that low self-regard subjects were *more* attracted to negative than to positive evaluators, as would be expected if consistency influences acted alone or overrode self-enhancing influences. In any case, more questions can be raised about the adequacy or relevancy of the methods of these two investigations as compared to the other five. Taken as a group, these eight publications offer no firm basis for saying that a self-enhancement explanation must be supplemented by a consistency one in order to account for differing attractions or evaluations expressed toward evaluators by subjects having high and low self-regard.

But perhaps under special circumstances consistency influences will be needed to account for some of the results, whereas self-enhancement influences will not. The following four researches are aimed at exploring some of these possible special circumstances.

Although the obtained trends from the investigations cited below may sometimes seem to support the idea that consistency influences are operating alone or overriding enhancement tendencies in the special situations described, it appears to me that any significant findings can also be explained in terms of self-enhancement influences. Thus, these results provide no clear-cut demonstration of situations which demand a consistency explanation.

For example, Dutton and Arrowood (1971) predicted and found that, when subjects were arguing *for* their own positions on an issue (where their goal ostensibly would be to convince the hearer), the rated likeability of the hearer depended primarily on position agreement from the hearer and only secondarily on the hearer's agreement with the subjects' evaluation of her demonstrated skill in arguing. When subjects were arguing *against* their own position (where their goal ostensibly would be to argue well rather than to convince the hearer), the hearer's likeability depended primarily on his agreement with the subject's own evaluation of her performance in arguing and only secondarily on the hearer's agreement with the position for which the subject argued. It may appear that the latter finding suggests that, under certain conditions, subjects prefer negative, accurate evaluations of their performance to positive, inaccurate ones. However, as S. C. Jones (1973) points out, the particular procedures used in this experiment raise doubts about the defensibility of a consistency interpretation as opposed to a self-enhancement interpretation of these results. That is, subjects read aloud to their hearers either adequate or inadequate arguments prepared for them by the experimenter, and they either were or were not given the promised time to examine the provided materials and think of additional ideas before beginning to argue. It seems difficult to believe, then, that subjects in the "poor performance" condition could seriously attribute their necessarily poor performance to their own abilities or knowledge. They could see that the hearer who said they performed poorly was accurate and whatever positive attitudes his accuracy might induce would not have to be counteracted by taking his criticisms personally.

D. T. Wilson (1965) proposed another kind of special circumstance under which persons with low self-regard might prefer to receive low evaluations from others, supporting the operation of consistency influences alone or as opposed to self-enhancement influences. He argued that subjects who made a personal decision not to go on to a possibly rewarding main test after experiencing an "ambiguous pretest failure" would prefer to have someone confirm the low self-evaluation implicit in their announced decision. By contrast, persons who were arbitrarily denied the chance to decide whether to go on to the main test after the ambiguous pretest failure would have only a need for self-enhancement and would prefer a self-enhancing evaluator. Bogus evaluations were sent to each subject from their partners, half the notes implying the subject was competent and could pass the main test, half that he was incompetent and probably could not pass it. Wilson predicted that the personal-decision subjects could like a negative evaluator better and a positive evaluator less than would the subjects who had had no chance to make a decision. "Since the person decided to abandon his chance for reward [from the main test] he should prefer someone who attested to his incompetence" (p. 487). One of the problems with Wilson's study is that he made numerous t-tests on dependent variable measures which must have been correlated. However, I consider here only the attraction ratings which are germane to the present discussion. The personal decision subjects liked the positive evaluator nonsignificantly less than the negative evaluator, whereas the subjects who had no chance to decide liked the positive evaluator significantly more than the negative evaluator. The same trends, both significant, occurred with respect to an expressed preference for another partner. While D. T. Wilson (1965) and others have considered these results to be supportive of a consistency interpretation, this outcome is interpretable in self-enhancement terms as follows. If the subject has to decide to forego a chance for a reward, he would like to think his decision and decision-making ability are sound. Thus the positive evaluation of his chances of succeeding on the main task implies that the evaluator doubts the wisdom of the subject's decision and perhaps his decision-making ability. If their ability to make sound decisions is more important to the decision-making subjects than is their ability on this particular kind of task, a "positive" task evaluation might actually appear to be derogatory and cause them to dislike the "positive" evaluator.

S. C. Jones and Ratner (1967) proposed yet another circumstance in which subjects might prefer unfavorable evaluations consistent with their low self-evaluations, namely when the subject publicly commits himself to an unfavorable self-evaluation before receiving further evaluative input. Their "commitment" variable is somewhat similar to Wilson's "personal decision" variable. They believe that if consistency influences are operative, subjects should show attraction reactions to their evaluators essentially similar to Wilson's personal decision subjects, i.e., they would like a negative evaluator better than a positive evaluator.

All experimental subjects were told they had failed on an initial written test of "personality inference ability," supposedly inducing low self-evaluation with respect to that ability. Then half were allowed to choose a case-analysis task which supposedly involved the same ability, this task to be done at the end of the experiment. These "committed" subjects supposedly indicated their public acceptance of their manipulated low ability levels by choosing predominantly easy versions of this case-analysis task (as compared to the difficulty levels of the task chosen by a praised control group). The other half of the experimental (initially failed) subjects were told they could choose their final case-analysis task later, thus avoiding public commitment to their manipulated low self-evaluation. Before proceeding to the final task, both initially failed groups then experienced either positive or negative feedback from peers who jointly participated with them in an oral version of the initial test of "personality inference ability." Two dependent variable measures were used: (a) proportion of times the subjects thought their positive and negative peer evaluators were themselves giving correct answers to the personality inference test; (b) ratings of positive and negative peer evaluators with regard to liking, respect, candidness, competence, and effectiveness as a rater of personality-inference ability. The authors thought that public commitment should make positive evaluations more dissonant from the subject's low self-evaluations, leading to a greater tendency among committed subjects to evaluate positive evaluators unfavorably and negative evaluators favorably, if consistency influences were paramount in determining the subjects' behavior. However, the results fell opposite to this prediction. On the first dependent variable measure, subjects who had committed themselves to a low self-evaluation "more positively evaluated the positive evaluator than the negative evaluator, and subjects in the no-commitment condition more positively evaluated the negative evaluator than the positive evaluator" (significant interaction) (p. 445). The second dependent variable measure showed similar but nonsignificant trends among committed subjects and mixed non-significant trends among noncommitted subjects. Building an argument in terms of self-enhancement influences, they reason that when a subject commits herself to being poor on a certain type of task that means (in this context) that she has excused herself from even trying. Thus failing will not matter, and she therefore can accept praise from the other because it will not imply any action on the subject's part such as trying to live up to the positive evaluation.

One can also question whether the dependent variable measure which showed significant results in this study was really an attraction measure, because it actually indicated whether the subjects thought their peers' opinions of their answers were accurate. If this reasoning is correct, this experiment might be considered of marginal relevance to the question of whether consistency influences counteract self-enhancement in determining low self-esteem subjects' attractions for their evaluators.

Finally, Krauss and Critchfield (1975) agreed with S. C. Jones (1973) in assuming that subjects actually receiving evaluations should behave toward a confederate according to self-enhancement influences, while subjects who are passive bystanders should behave toward a confederate in such a way as to maximize consistency. Accordingly, they compared the reactions of subjects who succeeded or failed on a written anagram task with the reactions of subjects who worked the same anagrams in their heads and received no success or failure feedback. Both groups of subjects rated a stooge (ostensibly a third cosubject also working the anagrams in her head) on four idiosyncratic dependent variables: like-dislike, evaluative factor score, potency factor score, activity factor score. None of these analyses showed any differences between the ratings given to the stooges by the subjects who succeeded or failed on the written anagrams test and those who were only mental problem solvers. These null findings must be viewed in the light of two methodological points: (a) It was the experimenter who told the active-solver subjects they had succeeded or failed; the stooge whose attractiveness the subjects evaluated had nothing to do with scoring the subjects' anagram performance—she only gave out monetary rewards appropriate or inappropriate to their success or failure; (b) the main effect of the success-failure manipulation was nonsignificantly opposite that obtained in most experiments, viz., for unknown reasons, both active and passive solvers rated the stooge somewhat more favorably when the active solvers' performance was negatively criticized by the experimenter.

One cannot predict, of course, what might be brought to light by future, more programmatic research in which needed methodological improvements are made. Meanwhile, in my view, the available studies offer no clear support for the idea that dissonance operates alone or against self-enhancing tendencies to affect attraction ratings given by low self-regard subjects to positive and negative evaluators.

c. Source Credibility as a Moderating Variable

As I mentioned in my presentation of theoretical ideas, it seems intuitively plausible that source credibility would moderate the relationship between the favorability of the evaluations received by subjects and their opinions of the accuracy, competence level, and/or personal attractiveness of their evaluators. However, only some of the possibly relevant studies support this idea, and for the many methodological reasons outlined above, one cannot really make an intelligent guess why this mixed state of affairs exists.

Harvey (1962) and Harvey, Kelley, and Shapiro (1957) reported significant main effects of varying degree of acquaintance between evaluator and subject. However, H. H. Johnson and Steiner (1968) reported no such effect when own fraternity and other fraternity members were supposedly the subjects' evaluators.

For every level of evaluators' favorability toward subjects, Dickoff (in E. E. Jones, 1964) found greater favorability of subject to evaluator among those subjects who supposed their evaluators were motivated for accuracy than among those supposing their evaluators to have an ulterior motive (to get the subjects to do them a favor). Only between groups receiving the most positive evaluations was this difference significant. In light of the idea that subjects might be able to minimize criticism from an inaccurate source, it is interesting to note that even poorly evaluated subjects preferred the accurate evaluator (non-significant trend). Contrasting, perhaps, with Dickoff's findings are those of Landy and Aronson (1968). In this study no evidence was obtained that a supposedly discerning praiser or that a supposedly discerning derogator was liked less than a supposedly nondiscerning derogator.

Finally, E. E. Jones et al. (1959) found no evidence that criticized subjects preferred a maladjusted to a well-adjusted derogator (even though they did prefer the maladjusted derogator more than a bystander did, supposedly because they could downgrade the credibility of a maladjusted critic).

d. PERSONALITY CHARACTERISTICS AS MODERATING VARIABLES

As discussed in the theory section, it seems plausible that predispositional personality characteristics other than self-regard or self-evaluation on specific characteristics might moderate subjects' reactions to positive and negative evaluations from others. These personality variables could operate by way of helping the subject to distort input, or by determining which modes of reacting he or she will use toward the input which has been absorbed (e.g., differences in attraction reactions to positive and negative evaluators; failure to recall the evaluation).

Possible moderating personality variables which have been studied thus far include dogmatism/authoritarianism, defensiveness, certain dimensions ostensibly revealed by the Interpersonal Check List, and direction of punitiveness as ostensibly revealed by Rosenzweig's *P-F* Test.

As I have extensively documented in chapter 10 of this book, both theory and research concerning self-concept variables and scores on Dogmatism or the California F scale are weak and ambiguous. In the present area, too, results are impossible to interpret because of the use of ambiguous discrepancy scores and/or null findings and/or lack of cross-validation of multivariate analyses (Harvey, 1962; Hamilton, 1969, 1970).

Four publications allude to the possibly mediating influence of a defensive need for social approval on subjects' reactions to others who positively or negatively evaluate them. Using an idiosyncratic Defensiveness scale, Page and Markowitz (1956) found that only low Defensive subjects showed a difference in reaction to favorable and unfavorable evaluators, respectively. In a possibly related study, Fishman (1965) found that only low scorers on the Marlowe-Crowne Social Desirability Scale showed a significant difference in their evaluations of others who criticized or praised them, respectively.

However, in an exploratory multivariate study using several personality scores related to various predominant modes of reacting to devaluation from others, Hamilton (1970) failed to find that the Marlowe-Crowne Social Desirability Scale discriminated those subjects who characteristically rejected their critics. Seemingly opposite to Page and Markowitz (1956) and Fishman (1965), Shrauger and Jones (1968) found that Marlowe-Crowne Social Desirability scores correlated positively with the tendency to be less favorable to a negative than to a positive evaluator.

For obvious reasons, it is impossible to reconcile all these findings about defensiveness which seem to run the gamut of possibilities. However, one should note that the use of questionable discrepancy scores as dependent-variable measures raises especially serious doubts about the interpretability of the results reported by Shrauger and Jones (1968) and by Hamilton (1970).

Likewise, the use of discrepancy scores renders moot Hamilton's positive findings involving several scales from the Interpersonal Check List, and Harvey's (1962) null findings involving intropunitive, extrapunitive, and impunitive scores from Rosenzweig's P-F Test.

Taking a somewhat different approach to the question of how stable personality characteristics might affect responses in the kinds of experiments under discussion here, J. Gormly, A. Gormly, and Johnson (1972) proposed that the tendency to devaluate others who disagree might be a transsituational personality predisposition. It is known that, in many subjects, attraction is diminished toward a person who disagrees and increased toward a person who agrees (Byrne, 1971). The question is whether the same subjects who tend to react in this manner to attitude disagreements or agreements might also be less attracted to a person who disagrees with their answers to IQ tests (a possible kind of manipulation of self-regard), or with personal descriptions of themselves (another possible kind of manipulation of self-regard). To test this, the same subjects were exposed to disagreements in all three areas and given a number of behavior measures purportedly indicative of (a) underrecall; (b) changing attitudes, test answers, or self-descriptions to agree with disagreeing input; or (c) devaluating others who disagree. This interesting study suggests the occurrence of transsituational generality of a number of possible alternate modes of reacting to various sorts of disagreement, even when particular measures of a given dependent variable (e.g., of attraction) are used. Unfortunately, the procedures are so briefly described one cannot be sure whether disagreements with self-descriptions were in the negative direction, positive direction, or both. In any case, this study gives some credence to the idea that the tendency to have positive attitudes toward agreeing others and negative attitudes toward disagreeing others may itself be a stable predisposition which partially determines the subject's choice of mode of responding to self-regard manipulations. It also suggests a link between the studies discussed in this section and those considered in section D below on interpersonal attraction as a function of similarity between persons.

e. Motivations, Goals, and Available Modes of Goal Attainment within the Experiment as Moderating Variables

When discussing theory, I listed various authors' ideas about the *possible mediating influences of motivations, expectancies, goals, and the available means of goal attainment within the experimental setup.* From that listing it was clear that I placed a very heterogeneous array of studies in this category. Only a brief listing of outcomes is attempted here, as these studies cannot be compared or synthesized.

As predicted, Aronson and Linder's (1965) subjects showed significantly greater attraction to others who shifted their evaluations from negative to positive than to others whose evaluations were positive throughout. The attraction to others who shifted from positive to negative evaluations were less than to others who were negative throughout (but the difference was not significant). It is noteworthy that these findings involve the subjects' rated degree of liking for their evaluators, although there was no evidence for the above effects using another dependent variable measure of subjects' attitudes toward their evaluators (14 trait-rating scales). In fact, the only 3 trait scales yielding significant differences between groups showed "reverse effects," i.e., subjects who had received always-positive evaluations rated their evaluators as nicer, warmer, and friendlier than subjects who had received negative, then positive evaluations. This illustrates well the methodological point I made earlier that alternate dependent variable measures of attraction to or favorability toward evaluators do not necessarily yield comparable results.

Moreover, several attempts to replicate Aronson and Linder's gain-loss effect have failed to support their findings, even when the dependent variable measure is some kind of rating or ranking of liking (Hewitt, 1972, two experiments; Mettee, 1971a, 1971b; Sigall & Aronson, 1967; Tognoli & Keisner, 1972). Each of these attempts used a unique combination of relatively idiosyncratic dependent-variable liking scales, idiosyncratic bases on which differing aspects of self-regard were purportedly manipulated, and differing variables hypothesized to interact with the evaluation-sequence (gain-loss) effect. Thus it is obviously impossible to evaluate the import of the studies as a group except to say that they seriously call into question the replicability and generalizability of the gain-loss effect, as opposed to the influence on subjects' liking for their evaluators produced by the proportion of positive and negative evaluations given to the subjects by those evaluators.

As predicted, Howard and Berkowitz (1958) found that high-aspiring subjects (as contrasted to low-aspiring ones) considered a favorably deviant evaluator to be more accurate and an unfavorably deviant evaluator to be less accurate relative to three other evaluators who agreed on an intermediate evaluation level. (Since level of aspiration and level of expectancy were correlated, the role of expectancy cannot be separately determined from their results.)

Stotland (1959) manipulated three variables: the group's stated expectancy that the subjects would either succeed or fail on a task they performed privately; the relevance or irrelevance of that task to the group's success; and the subjects' success or failure on that task. Manipulated success and failure affected the subjects' attraction to the group (even though it was the experimenter, not the group, who said the subjects had succeeded or failed). On the other hand, neither the level of the group's expectations for the subjects' task success nor the relevance of the task to the group's success affected the subjects' attraction to the group. Moreover, only one interaction was significant, viz., among low-expectancy subjects, the success-failure manipulation affected attraction to the group more under task relevant than under task irrelevant conditions. Especially in the light of the generally null findings, this interaction should probably be cross-validated before being interpreted. Moreover, it cannot be said that the null findings concerning expectancy cast doubt on the significant findings reported by R. C. Howard and Berkowitz (1958) because the latter experimenters obtained their subjects' own views of their aspirations and expectancies, whereas in the Stotland experiment, subjects were told what their groups supposedly expected of them.

S. B. Kiesler and Baral (1970) and Walster (1970) wondered whether subjects would have the goals of minimizing invidious comparison and maximizing their realistic prospects of catching a romantic partner. Congruent with this idea, Kiesler and Baral (1970) found that low self-esteem subjects behaved more romantically toward a moderately attractive confederate than to a very attractive confederate, whereas high self-esteem subjects behaved more romantically toward a very attractive confederate than to a moderately attractive confederate. Failing to support this finding, in two experiments, Walster (1970) reported that subjects of both high and low self-esteem preferred the most attractive partners.

Although there is no clear way of reconciling these apparently contrasting outcomes, one consideration may be relevant: S. B. Kiesler and Baral (1970) employed interactions with a real confederate while Walster employed pictures of persons previously rated according to physical attractiveness. Thus, in Kiesler and Baral's situation, real risk of rejection was involved, and differences in romantic behavior may not be indicative of the relative attractiveness of the two confederates to the subjects. On the other hand, it surprises me that Kiesler and Baral (1970) got effects on romantic behavior by supposedly manipulating subjects' opinions of how well they had done on an "important intelligence test," whereas Walster got null results after giving variably favorable psychiatric analyses of the subjects' personalities. One might suppose that the latter would be more relevant than the former to confidence in one's ability to catch a romantic partner. Both investigators claimed that their self-regard manipulations were successful, although Walster gives no data to support this assertion, and Kiesler and Baral (1970) checked their self-regard manipulation in terms of performance on an idiosyncratic "mood measure" (differences not significant) and a self-rating of test performance (difference significant).

Two studies which compared the reactions of evaluated subjects and bystander subjects have yielded uninterpretable or inconclusive results. One, by Krauss and Critchfield (1975) is discussed in the section in which research relevant to consistency theory is considered. In the second by E. E. Jones, Hester, Farina, and Davis (1959) it was predicted and found: (a) for criticized subjects, the preference for a non-derogating confederate was slightly greater when the derogator was said to be maladjusted as opposed to adjusted; (b) for bystander subjects, the preference for the nonderogating confederate was greater when the derogator was said to be maladjusted as opposed to adjusted. The difference between the differences was significant at $< .05$ on a *one*-tail test. This was thought to support the idea that criticized subjects could be skeptical about the validity of derogations from a maladjusted person (taking the sting out of these derogations and partially counteracting their assumed tendencies to be less attracted to maladjusted than to adjusted persons). However, the discrepancy scores and the kinds of statistical analyses used in this experiment render moot the interpretability of these results.

Shrauger and Jones (1968) assumed that people like to give "correct" answers to questions and that they will seek appropriate reference standards in order to validate their correctness. If they are answering questions which have objectively correct answers, they will supposedly find that peer opinions are less important in this validation process than would be the case when there are supposedly no right or wrong answers. To test this, the investigators attempted to manipulate the importance of peer judgments by telling some subjects that the correctness of their answers to a Personality Inference Inventory would be scored by an objective answer key, while telling others there were no right or wrong answers. All subjects received information that one of their experimental peers considered 14 out of 16 of the subject's answers to be correct (positive evaluation), while another peer considered only 6 out of 16 of them to be correct (negative evaluation). There was a significant difference in the subjects' attraction to the positively and negatively evaluating peer, and the manipulation of the importance of peer opinion versus answer key yielded no significant main effect. One interaction was significant, viz., when the subject was operating under a condition conducive to relying on peer evaluations, the effect of peer evaluation was greater than when the subject was operating under a condition conducive to relying on an objective answer key to validate answer correctness.

Deaux and Coppess (1971) also assumed that subjects wish to succeed at experimental tasks and that the available paths to success within an experimental situation may affect the relationship between self-regard and attraction to others. They supposedly manipulated self-regard by bogus feedback from a personality questionnaire, then asked subjects to describe on evaluative scales the types of partners with whom they would prefer to work in a competitive or cooperative task. There was a significant main effect of self-regard manipulation on desirability of preferred partner, but this occurred only because the low self-regard subjects wanted a much less desirable partner in the competitive as opposed to the cooperative situation. Supposedly both high and low self-regard subjects were attracted to desirable partners if success at the task was to be shared between them, while low self-esteem subjects wished to avoid invidious comparisons and/or loser status on the task which required competing with the partner in a situation where only one of the two could win.

Arguing from a combination of self-enhancement and equity theories, Friedman (1976) predicted subjects' expressed attraction to a highly attractive confederate who gave all subjects inequitably large rewards for a task performance. In Friedman's view, subjects with low self-esteem should be attracted to such a confederate, especially when expecting to interact with her further. That is, the low self-esteem person's need for self-enhancement from continuing interaction with such a superior, rewarding person was expected to override the potentially embarrassing inequity effects created by further dyadic interaction. By contrast, a person with high self-esteem will dislike the confederate when expecting to interact with her again. The aversive prospects of possibly becoming beholden to a giver of inequitable rewards was expected to override the minimal need of the subject with high self-esteem to have her self-regard maintained or enhanced by continuing a relationship with an attractive, superior person. Congruent with these expectations, a significant interaction was obtained:

"Self-esteem did not affect liking when no future interaction was expected" (p. 689), but "for those subjects who expected to continue working with the confederate, the predicted [significant] difference in liking as a function of self-esteem was obtained" (p. 688).

f. Other Situational Factors as Moderating Variables

A few investigators have dealt with situational variables which provided an opportunity for some of the negatively evaluated subjects either to minimize the salience of the experimental evaluation or to use some means to lower or forestall their aversive state before rating others' attractiveness. Due to their extreme variety, these studies cannot be synthesized or compared.

C. R. Berger (1973) asked his subjects to imagine how they would feel towards a professor who told them one of four things: (a) you did very well on a difficult test, success due to your ability; (b) you did very well on an easy test, success not due to your ability; (c) you failed an easy test, failure due to your lack of ability; (d) you failed because test was too difficult, not because of lack of ability. On rated attraction toward the imaginary professor, there was a main effect of success-failure but this was carried chiefly by the clear separation of the attraction ratings made by success-ability versus failure-ability subjects ("manipulated self-regard"?). Dividing his subjects into thirds on a chronic self-regard measure, Berger found no main effect of chronic self-regard on attraction ratings given to the professor. However, chronic self-regard and imagined success or failure interacted in the following way: failure-ability and success-ability subjects (i.e., subjects with differing levels of "manipulated self-regard") showed no relationship between chronic self-regard and attraction to the professor, whereas failure due to test difficulty and success due to test easiness showed U-shaped and inverted U-shaped relationships, respectively, between chronic self-esteem and attraction ratings. Thus the findings give no consistent support for Berger's idea that subjects with chronic moderate self-esteem levels are less defensive than are subjects with either high or low chronic self-esteem.

Green and Murray (1973) assumed that high as opposed to low self-disclosure should make a person more vulnerable to self-regard manipulations. To test this they first required three groups of subjects to write letters to their partners on either high-disclosure topics, low-disclosure topics, or the topic of how they had solved some easy puzzles. The investigators attempted to manipulate self-esteem by having the partners send (bogus) written replies to the subjects' letters, either criticizing their writing skills and reasoning (criticism condition), impugning their genuineness and personality (derogation condition), or avoiding evaluative comment. On an undescribed "verbal hostility" measure, the criticized and derogated subjects expressed significantly more aggression toward their partners than did the control subjects. There was no main effect of self-disclosure level on expressed hostility toward partners. The significant interaction between self-disclosure level and manipulated self-esteem level did not seem to result from any clear between-cells effects supportive of the hypothesis.

Rosenbaum and deCharms (1960, 1962) reasoned that objectively equal derogation should frustrate persons with low self-esteem more than persons with high self-esteem. Moreover, they argued that the opportunity to reply to a derogator should reduce the effects of the criticism on the subjects' later dislike of their derogators and that this effect should be stronger among low self-esteem persons. In two experiments based on these ideas, subjects high and low on the Janis-Field self-esteem scales were subjected to severe personal verbal attack from a member of a discussion group. In Experiment I, attacked subjects were either allowed to respond to the attack (communication condition), listen to another group member respond in their defense (vicarious communication), or not allowed to respond. In Experiment II, only the communication condition was run, using only the subject and one attacker. Attacked subjects wrote personality sketches of the attacker (and, in Experiment I, of the other group member). "Residual hostility" scores were obtained from these sketches. Although the order of residual hostility means in Experiment I was in the predicted direction for all groups combined (i.e., no communication, highest hostility; vicarious communication, intermediate hostility; communication, lowest hostility), F was insignificant. Actually, the only separate curve which showed this trend across communication conditions was that for low self-esteem subjects when evaluating their attackers. In Experiment I, as compared to chronic high self-esteem subjects, chronic low self-esteem subjects clearly differentiated more sharply between their evaluations of the attacker and the other group member. In both Experiments I and II, there was a nonsignificant difference in the communication condition between the amount of residual hostility to the attacker shown by high and low self-esteem subjects. Altogether, then, only in the no-communication condition was there evidence that objectively equal derogation might be more frustrating to a low than to a high self-esteem person.

3. Summary

Self-enhancement and cognitive consistency are the two main theoretical notions underlying the large number of studies which looked at attraction toward particular others as a function of manipulations of self-regard. Alternate versions of basic theory about the combined effects of these influences remain to be clarified. A number of researchers examined factors which they thought might moderate the effects of manipulated self-regard and/or consistency.

Severe methodological problems plague the studies in this area; so general statements must remain very tentative. The most frequently obtained finding is the main effect of self-regard manipulations on subjects' attractions toward the manipulator: at least two-thirds of the main effects are congruent with self-enhancement theories. In my view, the available researches offer no clear support for the idea that dissonance operates alone or against self-enhancing tendencies to affect the attraction ratings given to positive and negative evaluators by subjects having low self-regard. (Only in the case of the person whose self-regard is *low* before receiving experimental evaluative input can the conceptually separable influences of consistency and self-enhancement be pitted against one another, and their possibly separate influences examined.) The investigations of supposed moderating variables do not lend themselves to synthesis, given the miscellaneous nature of these variables which have been examined thus far.

D. Interpersonal Similarities and Interpersonal Attraction

1. General Theoretical and Methodological Considerations

There is a long history of research and theorizing about interpersonal attraction as a function of interpersonal similarities (e.g., Flemming, 1932; E. L. Kelly, 1940; H. M. Richardson, 1940; Pintner, Forlano, & Freedman, 1937). Empirical tests of the theories have been difficult for many reasons, not the least of which is the fact that the theoretical roots are numerous, tangled, overlapping, and often unclearly delineated.

Below I attempt to begin to disentangle some of the possible ways of dealing with this topic conceptually. It will become clear that the extant literature has not provided a systematic specification of reasonable conceptual alternatives, so that my proposed analysis pulls together a miscellaneous assortment of published theoretical fragments and a generous collection of other possibilities which seem intuitively plausible to me. It also becomes clear in the section on empirical results that the research literature has touched on but a few of these possibilities.

In one way or another, all of the extant theorizing and my own ideas assume that interpersonal attraction depends in part on attaining positive reinforcement and/or averting or decreasing noxious states, although there are varying unresolved views of the nature and mode of operation of reinforcement, and there is no satisfactory way of in-dependently defining a supposedly reinforcing state of affairs. (See Byrne, 1971; Byrne & Clore, 1970; Byrne & Griffitt, 1973; Byrne & Nelson, 1965; Festinger, 1957; Heider, 1958; A. J. Lott & B. E. Lott, 1968; Murstein, 1971b). Moreover, many theorists have considered interpersonal similarities involving self-referent cognitions and attitudes to be special instances of interpersonal similarities with respect to all kinds of attitudes or beliefs. Accordingly, they have assumed that the functional relationships between interpersonal attraction and in-terpersonal similarities with respect to self-referent cognitions and attitudes should be the same as those between interpersonal attraction and similarities with respect to a wide variety of attitudes. In other words, the present topic might be subsumed theoretically under a much more inclusive one. (See, for example, Backman & Secord, 1962; Byrne, 1971; Griffitt, 1966; Newcomb, 1956.) However, close exam-ination of what is at issue reveals that this plausible and potentially useful theoretical strategy cannot be applied to the present topic in as simple and clear-cut a fashion as one might at first suppose.

a. Basic Definitional Considerations and Postulated Relationships between Variables

Any theory on this topic should clarify the referent(s) for "in-terpersonal attraction" and "interpersonal similarity," as well as specifying a rationale for predicting stated functional relationships between them. An overview of the literature reveals that each of these terms is a vague umbrella label for what is almost certainly a heterogeneous collection of concepts.

Definitions of Interpersonal Attraction

Interpersonal attraction has been indexed in terms of (a) verbal statements of liking for hypothetical strangers or photographs of unknown persons, or persons encountered once in an artificial laboratory situation; (b) verbal choices of best friends, acquaintances, and most disliked persons; (c) positive and/or negative sociometric choices of same sex or opposite sex persons taken under a wide variety of instructions (e.g., to name best friend, or work partner in a task) and referring to widely varying pools of selectees (school classmates, camp group, office mates); (d) heterosexual choices of fiancés or spouses (as compared to randomly selected unacquainted opposite-sex pairs); (e) married couples' reports of their congeniality level.

On a common sense a priori basis, it seems unlikely that any one functional relationship between interpersonal attraction and similarity should obtain across all such variants of interpersonal attraction, since the degree and qualitative characteristics of interpersonal interaction must certainly vary widely in the above-listed situations.

Types of Interpersonal Similarities and Postulated Relationships to Attraction

There is even more variety and unclarity on the side of defining "interpersonal similarities" and rationalizing why any particular kind could plausibly be an antecedent, correlate, or consequent of interpersonal attraction.

Actual Similarities. One major subdivision of interpersonal similarities involves "actual" resemblances between persons as opposed to resemblances which persons may "perceive" or "assume" to exist between or among themselves. One common referent for the term *actual similarities* includes likenesses in such ostensibly objective respects as sex, socioeconomic class, chronological age, IQ scores, and behavioral attributes (reputation) as judged by persons other than the subjects whose interpersonal attractions are being studied. These kinds of "actual similarity" have been found by some but not all researchers to bear some relationship to degrees of interpersonal attraction. (For positive results see for example, Flemming, 1932; Bonney, 1942; Maisonneuve, 1954; N. Miller, Campbell, Twedt, & O'Connell, 1966. For null findings, see for example, Murstein & Lamb [in Murstein, 1971b]; and J. G. Thorpe, 1955 [although Thorpe's results appear to be based on an inappropriate mode of data analysis].) Logically, there are at least three ways of interpreting such associations without necessarily including in the proposed explanation any recognition on the part of the attracted persons that actual similarities have anything to do with their degree of attraction.

First, *actual similarities could operate to increase or decrease attraction by way of mutually gratifying or frustrating behavioral interactions traceable to the actual similarities.* For example, actually similar persons may be capable of playing a certain level of game, thus getting mutual reward from their shared enjoyment of playing it. As another example, Izard (1960a, 1960b) suggests, that interpersonal similarity may facilitate the expression of interpersonal positive affect.

[Similar persons] have similar ways of expressing and receiving affect, and this actual similarity of affective characteristics might reasonably be expected to facilitate mutually satisfying interactions and experiences. For one thing, the same individuals, groups, and interpersonal situations that evoke positive affect in one member of an affectively similar pair would tend to evoke positive affect in the other. Actual personality similarity should also increase the accuracy of interpersonal perception and communication, particularly the perception and communication of attitudes, values and other affective aspects of experience. [Izard, 1960b, p. 50]

Conversely, *certain types of actual similarity might depend upon antecedent interpersonal attraction.* For example, actual similarity in skill tests could be a function of one friend's teaching another the given skill.

As yet another alternative, some actual similarity relationships with interpersonal attraction might depend upon the common influence of a third factor. For example, children of the same CA and IQ tend to be placed together in school, increasing the probability that friendship bonds will be formed between actually similar children. Or, as a possible artifactual common influence, raters may judge friend pairs as more behaviorally similar than they are because the raters' judgments are distorted by their perceptions of valid actual interfriend similarities such as in IQ or socioeconomic level (N. Miller, Campbell, Twedt, & O'Connell, 1966).

Beyond these kinds of possibility, "actual similarity" of the kind I am discussing may also operate toward increasing interpersonal attraction by way of each person's recognizing the similarities and being somehow reinforced directly by this awareness. Such *perceived* similarities are not, of course, the same as the actual ones and must be conceptually and empirically separated, the latter operation requiring multivariate analyses. (Further theoretical consideration of such perceived similarities is given shortly.)

A second common referent for the term *actual similarity*, one with which we are concerned here, is *likenesses between or among self-report responses, e.g., between self-descriptions or between ideal-self reports*. By what conceivable routes might this kind of "actual similarity" be related to interpersonal attraction? If the self-descriptions or the ideal-self reports are indicative of the subjects' actual behaviors (as many researchers using self-reports as "personality tests" have assumed), these scores are analogous to IQ scores or chronological age. Accordingly, the alternative kinds of explanation already outlined above are applicable here, too. That is, it may be the actual behavior similarities which are either antecedents or consequents of interpersonal attraction, or a third factor may account for the relationship—all these being possible without the subjects' awareness of the factors explaining the obtained association between interpersonal attraction and actual similarity of self-report scores.

One can illustrate these points with reference to actual similarity between ideal-self reports. First, *actual behavior similarities implied by actual similarities in ideal-self reports could operate to increase or decrease attraction by way of mutually gratifying or frustrating behavioral interactions*. For example, persons whose actual ideal-self reports are similar with respect to, say, striving toward excellence, may choose to engage in the same task activities which they enjoy. The reinforcement from enjoying the activities tends to become associated with the other with whom one is acting; hence attraction to the other may develop (Byrne, 1971; A. J. Lott & B. E. Lott, 1968).

Conversely, *certain types of actual similarity in ideal-self report might depend on antecedent interpersonal attraction*, as when one friend encourages another to strive toward excellence, or when one friend's striving behavior sets a model which the other emulates.

As yet another alternative, *some actual similarity relationships in ideal-self reports might depend upon the common influence of a third factor*. For instance, persons with similar ideal-self reports about their striving for excellence might, because of their actual similarity in striving behavior, be placed by a teacher or coach in the same team or work group, thus increasing the probability that friendship bonds will be formed between persons with actually similar ideal-self reports. To repeat, all these possible directions of relationship between attraction and actual similarity in ideal-self report could occur without the subjects' awareness of the factors which explain the association between interpersonal attraction scores and ideal-self report scores.

On the other hand, one might take a step further and infer that these self-report responses index various aspects of self-concept, including over-all self-regard, over-all ideal self, specific aspects of self-concept and evaluations attached thereto, or specific aspects of ideal self. Such inferences must, of course, be highly tentative and closely scrutinized in light of the complex requirements for construct validity. But if one is willing to make such an assumption, then the relationships between interpersonal attraction and any kind of actual similarity between self-descriptions, ideal-self reports and the like should be theoretically considered in terms of the possible modes of operation of "perceived or assumed similarities," as discussed immediately below. Again, the need for multivariate analysis is obvious, in order to try to discern the relative contributions of actual self-report similarities and perceived or assumed similarities between self-concepts.

For some, the rubric *actual similarities* also includes correspondences between the *subject's self-report and others' reports about the subject.* Here again, both these reports may be somewhat indicative of the subjects' actual behaviors. If so, the other might treat the subject in a way appropriate to these actual behavior characteristics. These behaviors on the other's part might yield positive reinforcement for the subject if he or she can react to the other's behavior with self-congruent appropriate reactions. But conceivably, the other's treatment, while appropriate to the subject's actual characteristics, might sometimes create aversive effects. For example, the other could criticize the subject on a realistic basis. Either of these eventualities could occur without the subject's perceiving or assuming similarity between his own self-concept and the view of himself held by the other, or without such a perceived similarity being involved in the positive or aversive state created by the other's behavior.

Alternately, if subjects become more or less accurately aware of the degree of such actual correspondences between their self-descriptions (self-concepts) and another's descriptions (conceptions) of them, various sources of reinforcement might stem from this variety of perceived similarity, as discussed below under assumed or perceived similarities. Again, there is need for multivariate analyses to try to discern the relative contributions to attraction-prediction made by (a) actual self-other similarities regarding the subject's characteristics, and (b) the subject's assumed or perceived similarities between his or her own self-concept and the view of self attributed to others.

Perceived or Assumed Similarities. Most writers have been primarily concerned with "perceived" or "assumed" similarities in relationship to interpersonal attraction, and these are, of course, the ones which are particularly relevant to this book. Operationally, "perceived" or "assumed" similarity means that the subject believes the other to have (a) a certain degree of actual behavioral similarity to himself or herself; and/or (b) a self-concept or ideal-self concept of a certain degree of similarity to the subject's; and/or (c) a view of the subject which is similar to the subject's view of self. Researchers have not clearly separated these possibilities, although it seems reasonable that they should be, in the interests of conceptual clarity.

One can conceive of both the *degree and kind of perceived or assumed similarity as possibly reinforcing to the subject.* Parenthetically, one should note that such perceived or assumed similarities can arise from real-life interactions, either in or out of the laboratory, or they can be artificially induced by presenting the subject with information about the characteristics of self-conceptions of another hypothetical or real individual (e.g., Griffitt, 1966, 1969).

Are perceived or assumed similarities of this sort reinforcing, and if so, in what ways? In an analysis of this question, it is important to keep separate *assumed or perceived similarities with respect to:* (a) particular corresponding aspects of own and others' ideal self; (b) over-all level of own and others' ideal self; (c) particular corresponding characteristics of self and others, e.g., traits or needs (both the cognitively perceived similarities and the evaluations attached to the similar/dissimilar characteristics are of theoretical importance); (d) own ideal self and others' characteristics; (e) own and others' over-all self-regard level; (f) particular corresponding aspects of one's self-concept and the concept that others have of one; (g) over-all self-regard level and the over-all level of regard others have for one.

There has been an almost complete disregard of the need to make the above distinctions when theorizing about the perceived or assumed interpersonal similarities and interpersonal attraction. I turn now to a more detailed elaboration of conceivable relationships.

Consider first the possibilities inherent in *comparing specific aspects of one's ideal self with one's views of others'* ideals for themselves. Festinger (1957) among others, contends, we are motivated to be correct in our knowledge and opinions, and, as is the case with many attitudes or opinions, the lack of an objectively correct reference source increases reliance on the social comparison process to reassure ourselves of our accuracy. Since there is no objectively correct standard against which to validate various aspects of the ideal self, we would be expected to compare our ideal-self aspects with those of others and to find it reassuring when we find or believe that similar values are held by them. Such positive reinforcement should tend to make the similar other attractive. This is analogous to the reinforcing mechanism which may be presumed to operate in the many studies by Byrne and his colleagues who find that subjects' reported attractions to hypothetical strangers are a function of the proportion of attitude similarities between the subjects' protocols and those of the hypothetical others.

An alternate view of the positively reinforcing value of assumed similarity of particular ideals for self seems to come from balance theory (Heider, 1958, especially chap. 7; Newcomb, 1956). In this view, the subject is presumed to be attracted to an other if he believes that both hold the same attitude toward X, any concrete or abstract "object." The ideal self values would seem to qualify as Xs in this analysis.

Alternately, the same activities may be chosen, hence shared, by persons who perceive themselves as having common ideals for self. Those associated with such reinforcement (i.e., the rewards intrinsic to or contingent upon the activities) tend to become reinforcing, hence attractive (Byrne, 1971; A. J. Lott & B. E. Lott, 1968). Precker (1952) has suggested that "valuings operate in the selection of associates . . . since they allow for a *universe of discourse,* an operational 'language,' which facilitates intercommunication and, thereby, interaction" (p. 406) and that "the similarity of values may also be psychologically equated with the acceptance of others, . . . [which] in turn reinforces the social bond" (p. 413).

Yet another source of positive reinforcement from similarity in aspects of ideal self might stem from Freudian theory. That is, the operation of narcissistic tendencies implies being attracted to others who are like oneself, in this instance alike with respect to particular values.

Secondly, it is possible to conceive of interpersonal attraction as a function of the reinforcing value of *assumed or perceived interpersonal similarity of over-all ideal-self level.* That is, with respect to the extreme ends of trait or behavioral continua on a multiitem instrument, individuals differ with respect to their ideal-self total scores (e.g., Bills's undated manual; Wylie, 1974). Presumably, the above arguments might apply to the reinforcing value of interpersonal similarity in respect to such over-all self-regard levels.

A final point might be entertained about possible reinforcements associated with both specific and over-all ideal-self similarities, viz., someone whose ideal-self level is slightly lower than one's own might be positively reinforcing in that one could take pride in one's own higher standards by comparison (Adler, e.g., in Ansbacher and Ansbacher, 1956, pp. 244–245; Horney, e.g., 1945, pp. 97 ff.). On the other hand, it is flattering to be accepted by a person with unusually high standards; so this type of person might on these grounds be attractive.

All in all, then, one might predict some positive relationship between interpersonal attraction and interpersonal similarities of ideal self (either with respect to specific characteristics or with respect to over-all level), but these could be attenuated if the arguments in the preceding paragraph are valid. In any event, whatever functional relationship is found would not constitute discriminant support to any of the above theoretical views about the reinforcing mechanisms involved.

Interestingly enough, the research literature is virtually devoid of anything relevant to any or all of the above possibilities.

Thirdly, I turn to the possible ways in which reinforcement might conceivably be associated with *perceived or assumed interpersonal similarities in particular aspects of self-concept,* e.g., as inferred from self-descriptions of specific needs, traits, or habits. I consider both the person's cognitive views about the degree to which any given aspect characterizes him or her, and the evaluations attached to these perceived standings.

Here, conceivable possibilities proliferate, and predictions about similarity-attraction relationships become quite indeterminate. In some predictions, interpersonal attraction is the consequent, in some the antecedent of phenomenal interpersonal similarity.

For example, *apart from evaluations attached to the attributes* which one perceives as similar between self and other, the *cognitive similarity* would plausibly increase feelings of competence in that one understands the other and knows how to interact appropriately. Both from the feelings of competence and the appropriate interactions, positive reinforcement, hence attraction, might be expected to ensue.

Alternately, using ideas from Berlyne (1960) it may be suggested that perceiving another as extremely similar could lead to boredom (an aversive state), whereas a person perceived to be moderately dissimilar would produce optimal arousal (a positively reinforcing state), and extreme dissimilarity would again produce an aversive state. On this view, one would predict a nonmonotonic rather than a direct functional relationship between perceived interpersonal similarity and attraction. One can complicate this further by assuming that insecure or anxious persons, being in a chronic arousal state, might be more likely to prefer more interpersonal similarity, because even a modicum of dissimilarity would bring their total arousal level into the aversive range.

Introducing now the *subject's evaluations* of particular aspects of self-concept, one can see that assumed or perceived similarities between one's own self characteristics and the self characteristics of another might be especially positively reinforcing if the imputed interpersonal similarities in self description involve highly valued aspects, i.e., the other's self characteristics are, in effect, seen as corresponding with the subject's ideals as well as with the subject's self. Griffitt (1969) hypothesized that "a person who is similar in behavior or description to one's ideal-self provides consensual validation of and precise comparisons for one's positive attitudes towards a particular ideal behavior pattern" (p. 143). This amounts to the Festinger argument as applied above to explaining the positively reinforcing properties of perceived correspondences between ideal-self characteristics.

Two other ways in which interpersonal similarity regarding highly valued specific aspects of self might be positively reinforcing are (a) the other is seen as behaving in a way which creates positive affect in the interaction; (b) one may feel honored by attaining the friendship of such a fine person.

But, according to more complicated arguments, it might be aversive to a person if the positively valued characteristic in question is seen as similar between self and others if one would like to feel uniquely superior with respect to the characteristic. Moreover, it is also possible that perception of interpersonal similarity involving a *poorly* evaluated characteristic could be positively rather than negatively reinforcing if it is reassuring to find that others have a similar fault or weakness, and one need not feel uniquely inferior. (This argument was inspired by, although not the same as, one offered by Jellison and Zeisset, 1969.)

In Davitz's (1955) view, interpersonal attraction may be the antecedent and perceived interpersonal similarity the reinforcing consequent. Based on a reinforced-learning theory of developmental identification, including supposed rewards to the child for imitating loved others, Davitz infers the development of an underlying general need to be similar to valued others. This need may be satisfied in part by distorting one's perceptions of interpersonal similarity, i.e., by perceiving more interpersonal similarity than is "actually there," once attractions have been formed.

There are other possible ways that perceived *dis*similarity regarding certain traits would be associated with positive reinforcement, and hence with interpersonal attraction. For example, in his *complementary need theory* of mate selection, Winch suggests that greater compatibility (interpersonal attraction) should occur when certain needs are complementary, increasing the possibilities for interactions which are positively reinforcing to both parties in the relationship. He suggests two types of such complementarity: (a) When one person is high and the other low on the same need, e.g., dominance; (b) when one is high on one need and the other is high on another "opposite" need (as in the relationship between Hostility and Abasement, for example) (Winch, Ktsanes, & Ktsanes, 1955).

This theory seems plausible, but certain difficulties have been pointed out (see Levinger, 1964, for example). For one thing, no clear basis exists for a priori theoretical predictions of what pairs of characteristics should be considered complementary. Moreover, as Newcomb (1956) suggests, the positively reinforcing value in such instances might ultimately depend on a certain kind of interpersonal similarity, namely that each agrees that the complementary relationship between them is appropriate (i.e., the persons have a certain kind of "attitude similarity"). By this means, Newcomb (1956) would propose to bring apparently dissimilar needs (to him theoretically analogous to "attitudes") within the explanatory rubric of balance theory. In a similar vein, Secord and Backman (1964) suggest that when person A behaves nurturantly toward person B who is succorant, this apparent dissimilarity actually implies that the two agree that B has a certain characteristic; this cognitive agreement amounts to a reinforcing kind of interpersonal similarity. But, as Marlowe and Gergen (1968) point out, such suggestions beg the question as to just what sorts of interpersonal similarity may be predicted from theory to be positively reinforcing, hence to lead to attraction.

Another way in which phenomenal *dis*similarity in self-characteristics might be associated with greater attraction behavior occurs when the person with a modest self-evaluation seeks to enhance self-esteem by attaining a friend or mate who (being seen as a superior person) will represent a "good catch," one whose reciprocal choice will increase the self-regard of the chooser. This kind of *dis*similarity in descriptive/evaluative characteristics seems plausibly to imply a fourth *kind of similarity*, viz., *between the subject's ideal self and the assumed characteristics of the other*, a type of similarity which should be considered in its own right, as well as the special case of assumed *dis*similarity between descriptive characteristics. Beginning with the latter, Murstein (1970), Walster (1970), and S. B. Kiesler and Baral (1970) have all raised the question whether persons will seek as romantic partners those who match them in one or more descriptive/evaluative respects or will instead seek those who are seen as having maximally desirable personal characteristics. If the individual fears rebuff by the maximally desirable person, "matching behavior" might occur (i.e., a correlation between attraction and assumed similarity in descriptive/evaluative characteristics will be found). This is plausible because the goal of attaining a friend or mate might be more surely fulfilled thereby than if one set one's sights for a maximally desirable other (one most similar to one's self ideal?) who is seen to be *dis*similar to one's own descriptive/evaluative characteristics. Parenthetically, one can question whether the actual choice behavior with reference to the friend or romantic partner is indicative of the chooser's degree of attraction in the sense of liking or preferring to be with the person. That is, what one realistically aspires to attain and hence chooses (in Murstein's [1970] terms, "settles for") may not be what is most attractive or likeable. Therefore, if matching behavior occurs, such a finding could be irrelevant to testing any similarity-attraction hypothesis.

In the same vein, another possible explanation of why phenomenal *dis*similarity in self characteristics could be associated with greater attraction might involve the idealization of the friend or spouse (i.e., the perception of similarity between the other and the ideal self) *after* one attains a reciprocal choice from that person. It is plausible that a person with relatively moderate self-regard might find it self-enhancing in at least three ways to idealize a person *after* mutual choice: (a) having been chosen by a superior person reflects especially well on one's attractiveness; (b) one's choice of a superior person reflects well on one's taste; (c) attributing superiority to a friend or spouse might indicate one's own modesty, a socially valued trait.

Above I have considered the possible simultaneous operation of *dis*similarities in descriptive/evaluative characteristics coupled with *similarities* between the subjects' ideal self and the other's descriptive/evaluative characteristics. One must remember also a simpler common-sense notion, that persons will be more attracted to persons whom they see as *high* on evaluative characteristics. This common-sense view obviously says, in effect, that a person is probably attracted to others whose attributes are seen as similar to the person's own ideal self, regardless of interpersonal similarities in descriptive/evaluative characteristics. A. J. Lott, B. E. Lott, Reed, and Crow (1970) offer a learning theory explanation of this kind of similarity-attraction relationship.

Fifthly, how could *assumed or perceived interpersonal similarities in over-all self-regard level* (i.e., over-all self-acceptance or over-all self-ideal correlation or over-all self-ideal discrepancy score) be associated with interpersonal attraction?

A priori, one can think of a variety of sources of both positive and negative reinforcement associated with either similarity or dissimilarity; so predictions seem indeterminate.

First, consider two ways in which positive reinforcement, hence attraction, could be associated with similarity in over-all self-regard level. One possibility is for positive reinforcement to occur through increasing mutual understanding of one another's feelings, leading to an increased sense of competence and also, potentially, to rewarding interactions. That is, a person with relatively poor self-regard could empathize with another whom he or she perceives to be in the same situation, whereas a person with higher self-regard might be better able to empathize with another having high self-regard. Another possibility is that a person with modest self-regard might be envious of another who is perceived as having higher self-regard. This, of course, implies that an aversive state could be associated with perceived *dis*similarity, and, relatively speaking, a less aversive state would be associated with similarity.

Alternately, could *dis*similarity in over-all self-regard conceivably lead in any way(s) to positive reinforcement, hence to interpersonal attraction? One could imagine that persons with high self-regard could feel sympathy for persons perceived as having lower self-regard and/or could feel relatively superior to these people, even perhaps achieving a fulfillment of their competence needs through being helpful to them. Both of these things could lead to *dis*similarity's increasing attraction for this particular person, i.e., for similarity to be negatively related to acceptance. Moreover, being accepted by a person who is seen as having high self-regard (especially if his self-regard is seen as being warranted by his attributes), might be especially rewarding to one whose self-regard is low. This is so because having such a friend would reflect well on one, and, in addition to this, the high self-regard person might be psychologically "freer" to be helpful to the low self-regard person than would be the case with a low self-regard person. To the extent that this line of argument is valid, similarity should be negatively related to self-regard.

The reader can doubtless think of other possible reasons why predictions are indeterminate concerning interpersonal attraction as a function of assumed interpersonal similarities in over-all self-regard level.

A sixth type of *assumed similarity* involves *one's self-conceptions as compared to the views of oneself which one attributes to others.*

Backman and Secord (1962) have postulated that, as a means of achieving "satisfying consistency,"

> individuals shape the interaction process so as to maximize congruency among three components of an interpersonal matrix . . . an aspect of the self-concept of the subject (S), his interpretation of those elements of his behavior related to that aspect, and his perception of the related aspects of the other person in the dyad (O). [P. 321]

In their 1962 paper, they are especially concerned with the supposedly rewarding properties of one kind of cognitive consistency—"congruency by implication [which] exists if S perceives O as attributing to S a trait that S attributes to himself" (p. 321). Relevant to the present topic, Backman and Secord (1962) hypothesize "those persons whom S likes will be perceived as having more congruent perceptions of him than those O's toward whom S feels neutral or whom he dislikes" (p. 322), and "the more he likes an O, the more S will distort O's presumed perceptions of him in the direction of congruency" (p. 322). This argument follows from the consistency theories of Heider (1958), Festinger (1957), and Newcomb (1956), among others.

However, I believe we must also consider whether such cognitive perceived congruence (similarity) is always positively reinforcing to the subject, or whether some such perceived congruencies are positively reinforcing whereas others are aversive, according to whether the others' assumedly congruent views of the subject are respectively acceptable or not acceptable to the subject's ideal for self. In other words, given cognitive congruency between the subject's self view and the view he assumes another has of him, the positively reinforcing value of such cognitive congruency might be increased if it concerns a characteristic which the subject values in himself, or it might be counteracted by the aversive effects of having unfavorable characteristics attributed (albeit congruently) to himself. As M. B. Smith (1968) remarked in his discussion of self and cognitive consistency, "The tendency to think well of oneself may complicate predictions from consistency theories, since it appears to be independent of trends toward consistency" (p. 372). Moreover, to complicate matters still further one needs to consider whether it may be positively reinforcing for a *friend* to recognize a fault one acknowledges in oneself (since this implies that the other likes one despite the fault, or perhaps even finds the fault endearing), whereas it would be aversive for a nonfriend to recognize the same fault in one.

A second type of assumed similarity involves that between the *subject's over-all self-regard level and the level of regard he perceives or assumes that others have for him.* By "other's level of regard for him" I do not refer to the other's degree of liking for the subject or the other's expressed attraction toward him, although these are often conceptually and operationally confused.

Common-sense and self-esteem theories might suggest that evaluative influences would override the effects of similarity here, i.e., that a subject at any level of regard would be more attracted to another whom he perceives as having a generally favorable view of him. However, if this idea is accurate, it would constitute a contradiction to consistency theory which would predict that positive reinforcement (hence attraction) should be determined at least partly by cognitive similarity per se. To my knowledge, little consideration has been given to the relationship between interpersonal attraction and this kind of assumed interpersonal similarity.

By now it should be obvious that it is exceedingly difficult or impossible conceptually, let alone methodologically, to separate the influence of assumed similarity-dissimilarity per se from the influence of variations in evaluation attached to the particular dimensions along which similarity-dissimilarity is perceived to occur. As is the case when one tries to tease apart cognitive-dissonance influences and self-favorability influences in experiments involving manipulated self-regard, it is usually impossible to specify whether a given outcome in the present area rules out one or the other alternate possibilities. (See section C of this chapter.)

Attitude Similarity and Self-Esteem

Before leaving the topic of assumed or perceived interpersonal similarity effects, one should note two tangential but relevant ideas. Both concern the widely replicated effects of perceived similarity on "impersonal" attitude dimensions such as politics, art, or campus life. These effects have been demonstrated most often with Byrne's (1971) paradigm of attraction to a bogus stranger, as indicated by the verbal attraction measure called the Interpersonal Judgment Scale. One may first ask whether manipulating perceived attitude similarities along these "impersonal" dimensions somehow affects the subjects' self-regard level, and perhaps by this route affects the subjects' attraction to the other. J. Gormly, A. Gormly, and Johnson (1972), for example, wondered whether a threat to the subjects' sense of competence might be posed by the lack of consensual validation presented by a person holding different attitudes. If so, not only disliking of the dissimilar other but also lowering of one's own self-esteem might result. Another idea is that the subject's chronic self-regard level might somehow mediate the degree to which dissimilarity with respect to impersonal attitudes lowers the expressed attraction of the subject to the other (Archibald, 1970; Byrne, 1971; Hendrick & Page, 1970; Leonard, 1973). Perhaps one aspect or result of a generally high level of self-regard is confidence in one's own opinions, so that failing to get consensual validation would be less threatening.

The reader may well be convinced by the entire set of arguments presented in this section that "interpersonal similarity" in any of its above-listed generic or specific self-referent senses is not a particularly fruitful theoretical variable for self-concept theorists and researchers. This may be the case even if (as Festinger, 1957; Newcomb, 1956; and Byrne, 1971 have suggested) interpersonal similarity with respect to more "impersonal" attitudes may be a useful, unifying theoretical concept. However, since a sizeable empirical literature has accumulated on the subject of interpersonal similarities referring to self dimensions, it behooves the serious student of self-concept research to examine the empirical as well as the theoretical aspects of the topic.

b. METHODOLOGICAL CRITERIA

As in the analyses of available publications on any topic, I prepared and applied a list of methodological criteria by which to evaluate the interpretability of the kinds of studies under consideration here. These criteria are given below, together with an overview of the methodological quality of the extant work.

Attraction Measures

Of the 61 publications examined, 56 used idiosyncratic attraction indicants, mostly of the sociometric variety. The vast majority of them gave little or no descriptive or psychometric information about the measure. Two investigators used Byrne's (1971) Interpersonal Judgment Scale and 2 the Burgess-Cottrell Scale of Marital Compatibility. Since section B-2 of this chapter thoroughly covers methodological considerations relevant to sociometric methods and section C-1 considers other attraction measures, the reader should refer to those sections for ideas pertinent to the present one. At the very least, comparison and synthesis of studies on this topic is seriously hampered by the wide variety of approaches to measuring "attraction."

Interpersonal Similarity Measures

Variety of Measures. Regarding similarity measures, somewhat the same situation obtains, in that at least 36 different self-report bases for devising similarity measures were used. Of these, 23 were idiosyncratic; 10 studies used the Edwards Personal Preference Scale (EPPS) or an idiosyncratic variant thereof; 3 used the Self Activity Inventory; 2 each used the Guilford-Zimmerman Temperament Survey, the Allport-Vernon Study of Values, or MMPI items; and 1 each used the Maudsley Personality Inventory, Maslow S-I, the Butler-Haigh Q sort, and the Gough Adjective Check List. (For an evaluation of the latter 2, see Wylie [1974].) Over and above the validity questions one might raise about each of these separately, the extreme variety precludes clear syntheses of results from various studies.

Interpretability of Measures. In comparing interpersonal similarity to attraction, several strategies have been used. Consider first *"actual similarities" in self reports* regarding, e.g., self-descriptions or ideal-self descriptions. In one approach, a given correlation across subject pairs within an attracted group (e.g., friend pairs) is compared to the corresponding correlation across subject pairs in a nonattracted group (e.g., pairs who know one another but have not chosen each other as friends). Cautions are in order in using this approach and interpreting results obtained with it. It is quite probable that the self-reports of 2 persons may be affected by inter-subject differences in their general ways of using the rating scales or the answer options provided. This applies not only to idiosyncratic instruments but to many of the more standard instruments as well. Therefore, the agreement (e.g., r) between pairs of self-reports regarding a certain characteristic is attenuated to an unknown extent by these irrelevant inter-subject variations in response styles. Thus, if actual-similarity rs in self-reports between attracted pairs or between nonattracted pairs turn out to be low or insignificantly different from chance, one has no way of guessing the contribution of differing response sets to the weakness of the obtained relationship(s). Of course one can argue that inter-subject variability in response style should be about the same among members of attracted-pair groups as among members of nonattracted-pair groups. Thus, any significant difference in actual similarity between the 2 groups could not be accounted for in terms of intergroup differences in subjects' response-style variations.

The troublesome influence of intersubject variability in response styles could, for some studies, be circumvented by appropriate use of methods in which each subject ranks himself vis-à-vis the same group with respect to the self-report variable in question. Of course discriminant reliability of rank steps would have to be demonstrated.

In a second strategy, the investigator obtains an *actual similarity score for each subject* and relates this in some way to the attraction measure. For example, interpersonal similarity is indexed by obtaining a correlation *within each pair of subjects,* across self-report scores. The EPPS has been frequently used, apparently because of the interest of many theorists in need similarity and complementarity. Its ipsative scoring scheme forces a rank order of self-reported needs within an individual. Thus, within-pair *rhos* are computed, and mean or median *rhos* are compared between, say, groups of friend pairs and groups of random pairs. However, within-pair *rhos* across ranked needs (or across any set of ranked self-report items or scores, for that matter) will be attenuated by unreliability of ranks. Forced choice or forced ranking may result in unreliable or invalid between-rank discriminations by the individual. This problem has yet to be recognized in interpersonal similarity studies and has not been taken into account by assuring the reliability of interrank differences within the self-report scores of each individual. Parenthetically, it should be noted that correlation of a given self-report score across persons is questionable whenever a forced-choice instrument such as the EPPS is used because, in effect, the subject has been indirectly forced to rank order things to which he would have assigned equal ranks if given an opportunity to express himself in a valid fashion. Some of the similarity studies of the EPPS are difficult or impossible to interpret on these grounds.

In a third approach, *each pair of subjects is assigned a difference score*, by, e.g., subtracting the self-report score of one person from the self-report score of another, or subtracting the ideal-self report score of one person from the ideal-self report score of another. Then these difference scores for each individual are related to the attraction measure. This is not a defensible procedure. *No matter what self-report measure is used, subtracting raw scores is not psychometrically defensible* since resulting differences of equal size cannot be assumed to represent equal degrees of similarity when the components of the difference score come from varying points on an ordinal scale. (See Wylie, 1974, pp. 88–95, 289, 305; and Cronbach & Furby, 1970.) Cronbach and Furby (1970) assert that difference scores "are rarely useful no matter how they may be adjusted or refined" (p. 68). They argue that there is no justification for computing and using difference scores for individuals in order to operationalize individual differences in standing with respect to *any* construct dimension. However, they suggest that, if the experimenter is determined to use two-part subtractive scores, a number of methodological refinements may increase the construct validity of such scores. The entire area of interpersonal similarity research has taken no account of these arguments, and insofar as difference scores have been used to measure interpersonal similarity, the interpretability of the study is minimized or vitiated.

It is interesting to note that one kind of "actual similarity" score is operationally identical to one kind of "insight" score, as studied by certain other investigators. That is, both scores are comprised of a discrepancy between the subject's social-self-concept ("How I think others see me") and others' expressed views of the subject. Apparently neither the insight researchers nor the similarity researchers have recognized this operational identity, and each has developed a separate body of hypothetical explanations of obtained findings. In any event, both the points about difference scores discussed above and Wylie's (1974) discussion about such discrepancy scores of "insight" are relevant to evaluating the interpretative pitfalls in this particular kind of interpersonal similarity score.

Some investigators have indexed similarity in yet another way—in terms of the number of responses to adjective-choice or inventory tasks which coincide, say, between two subjects' self descriptions or between two subjects' ideal-self descriptions. Careful control of response totals is in order when this method is chosen, needless to say.

Rather than using "actual similarity" measures between reports made by two different persons, many researchers have employed *"assumed similarity" measures involving two reports taken from the same subject.* These assumed similarity measures are plagued with psychometric shortcomings, most of which are the same as those just shown to be applicable to actual similarity measures.

In interpreting within-pair *rhos* across reported characteristics (e.g., between the subject's self-description and his description of another), one must still consider the possibly attenuating influence of unreliability of both the rank orders for self characteristics and the rank orders which the subject assumes to be descriptive of the other person. Both sets of rank orders could be unreliable under certain forced-choice conditions. Or the unreliability of one's ranks for a nonfriend might be greater than for a friend simply because of one's having less knowledge about the nonfriend (necessitating guessing). Thus, if the *rho* between the subject's description of self and his description of the nonfriend is lower than the *rho* between self and friend, the attenuation of the former could be primarily a matter of unreliability as opposed to being an index of the subject's assumed or perceived dissimilarity between self and nonfriend.

The objections to the use of raw difference scores are as germane to assumed similarity scores as to actual similarity scores. Of course, when one compares a self-minus-friend score to a self-minus-nonfriend score, for example, one is at least holding constant the subject's idiosyncrasies in general use of the instrument. This is all to the good. However, one must not forget that the subject may have relatively little knowledge about the nonfriend. Therefore larger differences could result as much from the unreliability of the ratings of the nonfriend as from greater perceived or assumed dissimilarity of nonfriend to self.

Cognitive versus Evaluative Similarity. A different kind of validity question also needs to be raised inasmuch as a validly indexed degree of assumed similarity is necessarily cognitive and also probably evaluative, since most personal characteristics are demonstrably rateable for their evaluative level. For example, suppose that subjects are found to show greater assumed similarity between self and friends than between self and disliked persons on attributes A, B, C, . . . *n*. Is this merely a cognitive report about the subjects' views concerning the characteristics in question, or does it stem from subjects' general evaluative attitudes toward friends and nonfriends?

Since much of the interest in the topic of interpersonal similarity stems from assertions that attraction is related to cognitive similarities (apart from evaluative similarities or evaluative levels), this question of discriminant validity is especially pertinent to these theorists' views. However, other theorists too should be concerned with the problem, in order to interpret research findings as unambiguously as possible.

Most of the publications have not been concerned with this basic question of the role of cognitively recognized similarities (with evaluative similarities held constant) or with evaluative similarities (with cognitively recognized similarities held constant). Certainly, adequate methods for handling this interpretative problem remain to be developed.

Confounding of Similarity and Attraction Measures. Related to the above point is the question whether the assumed similarity and attraction measures may be confounded in some of the studies discussed below. To understand the argument, consider first a situation in which this type of confounding is improbable. That is, when attraction is measured by choice of friend and acquaintance, by a sociometric technique, by a marital choice, by a direct liking or attraction rating, or by a social distance scale, there is no operational overlap (hence no confounding) between the attraction measure and the assignment of the evaluative trait ratings or rankings on which the experimenter will base the index of assumed similarity. Thus, if the attraction and similarity measures correlate, the outcome cannot be explained in terms of simple confounding.

By contrast, in numerous studies of attraction in this and previous sections of this chapter, attraction to other(s) is indexed by the subjects' evaluations of the other(s) on trait-rating scales. In the studies we are considering in this section, trait evaluations of the other(s) are also taken as the basis for the assumed similarity measure. Now we should recall that distributions of self-ratings are typically skewed, i.e., most persons have relatively favorable self-ratings. If they give favorable ratings to others, they will necessarily have given them "similar" ratings, too. But if the other tends to be favorably evaluated on the attraction measure and also on the assumed similarity measure, why say that "assumed similarity" has been shown to be related to "attraction"? More parsimoniously, two sets of ratings of others have been shown to be correlated, i.e., the attraction measure and the similarity measure are confounded.

Other Problems in Relating Attraction and Similarity Measures

It would be enlightening to compare within the same study the relationships of interpersonal attraction measures to both actual similarity and assumed similarity. Unfortunately, very few investigators looked at both relationships using the same subjects. Accordingly, conclusions are severely restricted on this ground alone.

As mentioned in the theoretical discussion of possible similarity-attraction relationships, any connections between actual similarities and attraction may be interpreted in terms of perceived similarities which are aroused by or somehow associated with the actual ones. This suggests that multivariate analyses are needed to examine the relative roles of actual and assumed or perceived similarities in predicting attraction.

As is true in many areas of self-concept research, this one is plagued by the presentation of many significance tests, usually involving overlapping data comparisons or intercorrelated variables. Without replication or cross-validation, there is no way to evaluate the significance of the reported outcomes.

2. Results, According to Types of Interpersonal Similarities Related to Attraction

a. Actual or Assumed Similarities between Ideal-Self Reports

Publications on these topics are rare, perhaps because investigators have assumed that there is so much stereotypy in ideal-self responses that little room would be left for interpersonal attraction to vary as a function of either assumed or actual interpersonal similarity in ideal self. Perhaps this mistaken assumption of extreme stereotypy rests indirectly on the well-known stability of Social Desirability means for self-report items. This kind of stereotypy might at first seem to imply virtually perfect intersubject correspondence in personal ideal-self report. However, as I have documented in detail elsewhere (Wylie, 1974, pp. 54–55, 130–131), individual differences in ideals for self are by no means adequately represented by mean Social Desirability values for items. Alternately, researchers may have been deterred by the well-known fact that variance in personal ideal-self reports, while occurring, is considerably smaller than variance in self-descriptive responses (see Wylie, 1974, pp. 93, 153–154, 217). Investigators may have assumed accordingly that the ideal-self score would yield weak or null relationships with other variables, owing to its restricted variance.

In any event, I have found only four publications which look at interpersonal attraction as a function of *actual interpersonal similarity with respect to particular aspects of ideal-self reports.* Three of them obtained null results (Fiedler, Warrington, & Blaisdell, 1952; Murstein & Lamb [in Murstein, 1971b]; Murstein, 1971a).

Perhaps Precker's 1952 research relating to 39 criteria for educational evaluation is essentially a study of actual ideal-self correspondences, but the article gives insufficient information to be sure. Among other analyses, *rhos* across 39 evaluative items were computed for each pair of subjects in the following combinations: student versus mutual peer choice; student with peer not chosen. The mean *rhos* from these two sets of correlations were significantly different. Therefore, if these evaluative items are in effect ideals for self, Precker's report stands as the only one giving a positive association between interpersonal attraction and actual interpersonal similarity in ideal-self report.

In contrast to null findings involving actual interpersonal similarity in ideal-self reports, 2 investigators found significant correlations between *interpersonal attraction and subjects' assumed similarity of particular aspects of own and others' ideal-self concepts.* In W. R. Thompson and Nishimura's (1952) Q-sort correlations across items, *rs* from subject's own ideal versus ideal attributed to friend ranged from .31 to .77. Unfortunately, no *rs* are provided for subjects' ideals versus ideals attributed to nonfriend or to "people in general." Also using Q sorts, Fiedler, Warrington, and Blaisdell (1952) found that correlations indexing assumed similarity of ideal-self were higher when they were based on "self-versus-most-liked-other" than on "self-versus-least-liked other."

Multivariate analysis would be necessary to see whether, in predicting interpersonal attraction, assumed similarities in ideal-self contribute separately from assumed similarities in self-description.

So far as I know, no one has looked at *interpersonal attraction as a function of assumed or actual interpersonal similarity in over-all ideal self.*

b. ACTUAL OR ASSUMED SIMILARITIES BETWEEN SELF-DESCRIPTIONS (SELF-CONCEPT CHARACTERISTICS)

Actual Similarities

If the above-stated methodological criteria were to be rigorously applied to the studies bearing on this topic, one would have to say that almost none should be considered as a basis for interpretive generalization. However, I have tried to divide the 31 available publications on the basis of their relative methodological adequacy. Those that seem to me to be relatively more defensible offer only very weak and spotty support for the idea that attraction is a function of actual interpersonal similarity in self reports. Unless otherwise indicated, all results are based on college-aged persons.

The relatively more adequate publications which report at least some positive findings are: Izard (1960a, 1960b, 1963); Lindzey and Urdan (1954); Pintner, Forlano, and Freedman (1937), children in Grades 5–8; Reader and English (1947); Rosenfeld and Jackson (1965), commercial office workers; and Van Dyne (1940), subjects aged 11–27. Even in these studies, it is typically the case that: (a) only one of several (possibly intercorrelated) variables yielded significant associations between intersubject attraction and intersubject self-report similarity; or (b) the results were not replicable when subject groups (e.g., Izard, 1963) or length of acquaintance (e.g., Rosenfeld & Jackson, 1965) were somewhat changed.

The relatively more adequate publications which report null results on this topic are: Bonney (1946), elementary school through college; Corsini (1956), married college couples; Davitz (1955), children, mean age 9.8; Fiedler, Warrington, and Blaisdell (1952); Hoffman (1958); Hoffman and Maier (1966); I. Katz, Glucksberg, and Krauss (1960), married couples, mean age = 29.6; N. Miller, Campbell, Twedt, and O'Connell (1966); Murstein (1970, 1971a), same group of premarital couples; Murstein and Lamb (in Murstein, 1971b); Reilly, Commins, and Stefic (1960). (One cannot be sure from Davitz's [1955] published report whether the instrument for indexing interpersonal similarity was a self-concept index.)

The following publications seemed to me to be so methodologically flawed and/or incompletely reported as to warrant exclusion from a substantive overview: Banta and Hetherington (1963), subject ages not given; G. Becker (1964), dating or engaged couples; Bowerman and Day (1956), engaged college couples; Day (1961), friends of Bowerman and Day's couples; Fitzgerald (1965), data analysis relevant to this topic not made; J. E. Gordon (1957); Kelly (1940), engaged couples; Manis (1955); Mehlman (1962); Rychlak (1965), telephone company employees; Schooley (1936), married couples; Taylor (1967), adult married couples; W. R. Thompson and Nishimura (1952), it cannot be determined whether the mean Q sort for friend pairs exceeded chance. Had these excluded ones been included, the "box score" count of studies reporting positive associations between attraction and subjects' actual similarities of self-report would have favored the similarity hypothesis somewhat more strongly, although (as with the included reports) these excluded ones which were said to yield significant positive associations actually gave only weak positive findings, or mixed weak positive and null findings.

Accordingly, there seems to me to be no adequate research base at present to support the idea that expressed interpersonal attraction is a function of "actual similarities" between subjects' self-reports about aspects of their self-concepts. There is, of course, no way to be sure whether such null and weak results would continue to be obtained if improvements in measuring techniques and other aspects of method were to be made.

Those positive findings that have been reported seem to me to furnish no basis for choosing among the previously discussed explanations of any associations which might occur between interpersonal similarity in self-reports and interpersonal attraction.

In no study yielding significant relationships between interpersonal attraction and interpersonal self-report similarity was "positivity" (as opposed to similarity per se) controlled. Accordingly, there is no way to be sure whether the significant results are attributable to any extent to similarity per se.

Methodological problems have plagued the few studies attempting to look for complementarity as opposed to similarity in relationship to interpersonal attraction. Thus far, no clear support is at hand for the complementarity hypothesis.

Assumed Similarities

We have seen that the evidence is only slightly suggestive that interpersonal attraction is associated with actual interpersonal similarity in self-descriptive reports (self-concepts). Perhaps this is because subjects' attractions to others determine or are determined by their *perceptions or assumptions of interpersonal similarities in self-characteristics,* regardless of the similarity of the actual self-descriptions given separately by each of the interacting persons. As shown below, attraction has more often been found to be associated with the *subjects' perceptions or assumptions that similarities exist* between their own self-reported characteristics and the self-descriptions they impute to others.

This has been looked at in two ways, and the evidence from the first class of studies is less consistent than that from the second: (a) The subject's perceptions of the self-report of another unknown person is artificially determined by means of showing the subject a bogus self-report protocol purportedly filled out by another, but actually rigged to create a specified degree of similarity between the subject's self-report and the other's self-report. Expressions of the subjects' attraction to this unknown other are examined as a function of degree of similarity between each subject's self-report and that purportedly made by the unknown other. (b) Subjects are obtained who manifest differing degrees of interpersonal attraction in real life situations (e.g., friendship pairs as compared to nonfriend pairs; married couples as compared to acquaintance pairs; married couples expressing differing degrees of interpersonal compatibility). The similarity of subjects' self-reports to their perceptions of others' characteristics (or others' supposed self-descriptions) are examined in relationship to real-life variations in attraction.

I turn first to investigations which purportedly manipulated the subjects' perceptions of self-other similarity with respect to the personal characteristics of self and other. This method has the following advantages: (1) If positive results are obtained, the perceived interpersonal similarity may be an antecedent of interpersonal attraction, and it certainly cannot be interpreted as a consequent of it. (2) Certain other possible influences on interpersonal attraction may be controlled, e.g., length of interaction and physical appearance. However, since no interpersonal encounters take place in most such studies, and, in any event, only brief interactions occur, one cannot say that effects obtained in these experiments will also be found in "real life" social interaction.

Griffitt (1966) gave each subject a self-report protocol from an unknown other person in which the subject's ideal self and the other's ideal-self statements on Worchel's Self-Activity Inventory (SAI) were identical for each self-other pair. For half the subjects, the proportion of self-descriptions common to the subject's and the other's self-reports was .33, for the other half it was 1.00. Among those receiving the dissimilar self-descriptions, half the subjects received protocols in which all the other's dissimilarities in self-report were in the negative direction compared to the subject's self-reports, and half received protocols with all dissimilarities more positive than their own. Amount of dissimilarity but not its direction was found to be inversely related to the subject's expressed attraction to the stranger, the latter being indexed by Byrne's Interpersonal Judgment Scale.

In Griffitt's (1969) second experiment, all subjects received SAI protocols from unknown others in which 40% of the other's ideal-self descriptions agreed with their own. Half the subjects examined protocols in which 20% of the self-descriptive items were the same as their own; the other half examined protocols in which 80% of the other's self-descriptions were the same as their own. Again, attraction to the hypothetical stranger was a direct function of proportion of similarity between the self-reports made by the subject and the other. There is no information given in either publication as to whether subjects' suspicions were checked. (Worchel's Self-Activity Inventory is evaluated in Wylie, 1974, pp. 165–169.)

The remaining eight experiments of this type (described immediately below) do not give results as straightforward as the above two. That is, interpersonal attraction is not always found to be a direct function of manipulated perceived similarity in self characteristics, with other variables controlled.

Having established two groups of subjects whose self-reports yielded high extraversion or high introversion scores on the Maudsley Personality Inventory (MPI), Hendrick and Brown (1971) gave half of each group bogus self-reports supposedly made by unknown strangers whose self-descriptions on the MPI would classify them as either introverted or extraverted. With four out of six attraction measures, significant interactions were obtained as follows: Introverts preferred others whom they perceived to be *dis*similar to them (i.e., others who gave extraverted self-reports), whereas extraverts preferred others whom they perceived to be similar to themselves. The authors interpret this as an exception to Byrne, Clore, and Worchel's (1966) hypothesized generalization that "it seems quite possible that in any type of social comparison with other human beings (e.g., opinions, attitudes, beliefs, values, abilities, tastes, income, overt behavior, etc.) similarity is preferable to dissimilarity" (p. 223).

The question arises why perceived *dis*similarity between self-descriptions might be preferred by introverts but not extraverts. Hendrick and Brown (1971) propose that indirect light is thrown on this question by evidence from Brown and Hendrick (1971) and Star (1962) that the ideal self of both introverts and extraverts tends to be extraverted. If this is true, then perhaps both Hendrick and Brown's introverts and extraverts were basing their interpersonal attraction for the unknown strangers on another kind of assumed or perceived interpersonal similarity — the similarity between the self-described personality characteristics and the subjects' ideal-self characteristics. It should also be noted that two of Hendrick and Brown's (1971) attraction measures did not yield the significant interactions obtained with the four attraction measures discussed above. Instead, on two of these dependent variable measures, both extraverts and introverts preferred similar others. This provides another example of the previously mentioned fact that results in this area may differ according to the attraction measure used. Inspection of the six attraction indices suggests no obviously plausible reason why different effects were obtained with them.

Hendrick and Brown (1971) checked on the effectiveness of their manipulation of perceived self-other similarity, but they do not mention checking on subjects' possible suspicions about the contrived nature of the others' protocols they examined.

Using somewhat the same paradigm as Griffitt's, Palmer and Byrne (1970) found in two experiments that both dominant and submissive subjects on Leary's Interpersonal Check List were more attracted to strangers whose bogus self-reports classified them as dominant. For the dominant subjects this might be interpreted as the effects of self-descriptive similarity on attraction. But the submissive subjects also showed greater attraction to the dominant stranger, suggesting a complementarity-attraction or dissimilarity-attraction effect. However, the difference was smaller for the submissive subjects, and this significant interaction is interpreted by the authors as supporting the hypothesis that similarity in self-descriptions determines attraction. (Incidentally, this interaction was obtainable only when extreme groups of subjects were used.) As with Hendrick and Brown's results, Palmer and Byrne's may plausibly be alternately interpreted as indicating an effect of similarity between the subjects' ideal self and the bogus stranger's descriptive self. Evidence for this is developed in a later section. "The results for attraction as a function of similarity on love-hate also from the ICL revealed strong support for the similarity hypothesis in the first experiment, but this interaction did not appear at all in the second experiment" (p. 110, footnote). This report does not mention checks on the manipulation of assumed similarity or on subjects' possible suspicions. (Leary's Interpersonal Check List is evaluated in Wylie, 1974, pp. 213-223.)

B. McLaughlin (1970) presented each subject with self-descriptions allegedly made by three others, but actually contrived by the experimenter so that the similarity between the subject's self-description and that by each of the others was respectively high, medium, or low. Subjects' amount of attraction to the others was directly and significantly related to the degree of perceived similarity between their own and the others' self-descriptions. However, the adjectives used to prepare the bogus others' reports had been judged on a "likeability" scale (before the experiment under discussion here). McLaughlin pointed out that the more the bogus others' reports were dissimilar from the subjects' self-reports, the lower the mean previously rated "likeability" of the adjectives was. In other words, similarity and independently rated adjective likeability of the others' reports were confounded. Accordingly, McLaughlin used analysis of covariance to show that the similarity-attraction relationship was not significant when rated likeableness of adjectives was held constant. No information is given about checking the effectiveness of the manipulation of perceived similarity or the subjects' possible suspicions that the others' protocols were contrived.

In a second experiment by B. McLaughlin (1971), subjects were required to describe themselves using either 20 high-likeable or 20 low-likeable adjectives (likeability having been previously rated by persons outside the experiment). They were then presented with bogus self-descriptions of unknown others using either the high-likeable or low-likeable list of adjectives. The subjects' mean attraction to the others (as indexed by a set of 10 evaluative adjective scales) varied significantly with both (a) the others' perceived similarity to self and (b) the rated likeableness of the adjectives used by both self and other for their self ratings. The interaction was not significant. When attraction of the subject to the other was measured in terms of statements of willingness to interact with the other, however, neither the main effect of likeableness of the adjective set nor the main effect of self-other similarity in self-description or the interaction reached satisfactory significance levels. As in Hendrick and Brown's (1971) study, the results differ according to the "attraction" measure used. B. McLaughlin (1971) comments, "Thus, in Byrne's terms, both similarity and likeableness function as reinforcers, but the extent to which they influence appraisal of others depends on the particular judgments the subject is asked to make about the stimulus person" (p. 68).

In this study, checks were made on the manipulation of perceived interpersonal similarity and likeability-values of adjectives, but not on the subjects' suspicions of the contrived nature of the others' protocols.

In Rosenfeld's (1964) study, each subject was supposedly led to believe that his own task competence was average, while that of five other persons in his group ranged from far below to far above him. Subjects indicated their cosubjects' attractiveness in terms of rank order of preference as task partner and rated degree of how much they "would like to associate with each of them." These expressed degrees of attraction were directly related to the subjects' perceptions of the others' competence levels, *not* to others' perceived similarity to the subject. Rosenfeld claimed without explaining how he did it that subjects' suspiciousness was controlled. There was no check on the effectiveness of the self-evaluation manipulation.

It is not possible to tell whether Goldstein and Rosenfeld's (1969) results may properly be interpreted as resulting from manipulation of perceived similarity between the subject's self-concept and that supposedly reported by an unknown other. This ambiguity occurs partly because no information is given about their idiosyncratic 40-item self-report instrument except that it included "interests and traits." A similarity main effect was reported; however, favorability was not apparently controlled when varying dissimilarity. Although the effectiveness of the perceived similarity manipulation was checked, only vague mention of subjects' possible suspicions was made.

Basing their procedure on the general orientations of balance theories, Lerner and Becker (1962) presented subjects with a similar and dissimilar profile based respectively on two hypothetical others' self-reports on Nowlis's Mood Adjective Check List and an idiosyncratic instrument. Subjects then chose one of these others as a partner for a hypothetical game in which either (a) the anticipated interaction would yield mutual gain, or (b) the anticipated interaction would yield gain for one at the expense of loss for the other. As predicted, subjects chose similar others for Condition a, dissimilar others for Condition b. If one assumes that Condition a implies sharing a desirable outcome with an attractive other, whereas Condition b implies "aggressive or combative acts" presumably more appropriately directed to an unattractive other, these results might indicate a similarity-attraction relationship consonant with balance-theory predictions. Some attempt was made to control for evaluative level when varying similarity, but reported results from a brief post-experimental interview suggest that subjects did not recognize the similarity manipulation, and no information is given about suspicion checks.

In short, the above 10 experiments do not give methodologically adequate and consistent support to the hypothesis that interpersonal attraction depends on manipulated assumed or perceived interpersonal similarity of self-descriptive characteristics, when other variables are controlled. The studies are so methodologically diverse that it is impossible to speculate fruitfully about the various possible causes of failures to support the hypothesis. A number of the findings may imply that assumed similarity between one's ideal self and others' descriptive attributes is a more important determiner of attraction than between one's own and another's characteristics.

In contrast to experimental work, the "real life" studies of the attraction-similarity hypotheses have certain methodological disadvantages and advantages. Obviously, positive results from such studies can be only correlational, and no directional hypotheses can be specifically confirmed. Also, when a variable such as attraction is "manipulated" by choosing different individuals or groups of subjects, one can never be sure that the persons or groups are comparable in regard to characteristics other than the one which formed the researcher's basis for differentiating them. For example, not only interpersonal attraction but also interpersonal propinquity and amount of interpersonal interaction may vary between friend and nonfriend groups. Therefore, aside from intergroup differences in interpersonal attraction, those other intergroup differences could conceivably influence the obtained relationship of assumed interpersonal similarity to interpersonal attraction. Conversely, there are so many ways that attracted or nonattracted groups could be personally similar (or dissimilar) that one cannot be sure of the relative contributions to the similarity-attraction relationship made by (a) the investigated variable and (b) other assumed similarities not under investigation. (Sęe Byrne, Griffitt, & Stefaniak, 1967.)

However, in the experimental situation, the effects of a particular manipulated similarity, e.g., in attitude or in ideal self, may be "exaggerated" since this is the only cue the subject can use as a basis for an attraction reaction. That is, in ordinary everyday interaction, these particular similarities might not often become apparent and/or they might be overriden by other, more important or interacting determinants of attraction. Moreover, "real life" situations provide more opportunities for psychologically meaningful interpersonal attractions of various kinds to develop. On these grounds, some have argued that correlational findings might provide the better basis for descriptive statements about factors associated with interpersonal attraction in actual social situations.

The following publications report some trend(s) toward a *positive association between interpersonal attraction and the degree to which subjects attribute similar characteristics to self and other.* The kinds of "comparison others" on which results were based are briefly indicated after each listed publication. Unless otherwise noted, respondents were college students.

Beier, Rossi, and Garfield (1961). Others were persons whom subjects held in very low or very high esteem.

Davitz (1955). Others were sociometrically ranked fellow campers, mean age 9.8. (It is not possible to be sure from published information whether the assumed-similarity measure is a self-concept index.)

Fiedler (1954). Others were sociometrically differentiated members of high school basketball teams or surveyor groups. No actual data are given to support their verbal statement of the similarity-attraction association.

Fiedler, Warrington, and Blaisdell (1952). Here, similarities involved subjects' predictions of self-descriptions which would be made by most and least liked fraternity members.

Kipnis (1961). Others were best friend and least-liked roommate.

Lundy (1958). Others were opposite-sex persons (spouses excluded) with whom subjects would most and least like to spend time.

Lundy, Katkovsky, Cromwell, and Shoemaker (1955). Others were positive and negative sociometric choices.

Murstein and Lamb (in Murstein, 1971b). Others were ranked peers in a small dormitory.

Although all the above studies may be faulted on various methodological grounds, there are no clear bases for discriminating among them, and all seem to be in empirical agreement. Unfortunately, none provided a basis for estimating the relative contributions to similarity-attraction correlations made by (a) assumed similarity per se and (b) favorability of assumed characteristics. As with the above-cited experimental results, this lack of control in the correlational researches leaves open the possibility that the kind of assumed similarity which determines attraction may be between the subjects' ideals for self and the attributes of others, rather than between the subjects' and others' attributes.

Some additional publications give correlations between subjects' descriptions of self and friend, but no control-pair correlations are available. R. C. Bailey, Finney, and K. G. Bailey's (1974) study about assumed similarity in intelligence is uninterpretable on this and other methodological grounds.

Sappenfield and Balogh (1970) and Levine, Ranelli, and Valle (1974) both attempted to look at the relationship between attraction and assumed similarity of self characteristics by engaging their subjects in completely imaginary manipulations of the variables. The former had subjects Q-sort photographs first for "similarity to me," and two weeks later for "perceived attractiveness." The latter asked subjects to imagine one of their habits of which they were proud (or ashamed); then to imagine another person who had once had the same (or a different) habit and who remained the same, remained different, became more like the subject, or became less like the subject on the imaginary habit dimension. Attraction ratings were analyzed by ANOVAs. In both these instances, the methods seem to me to be too artificial to warrant generalization of the results to actual interactions. In the Levine et al. study, one did not even have any idea what "habit" each subject may have been thinking of.

Actual and Assumed Similarities Compared

Thus far we have seen that *actual interpersonal similarities in self-descriptions* are related weakly if at all to interpersonal attractions, whereas *interpersonal similarities which are assumed* by respondents to characterize themselves and others are consistently related to interpersonal attraction. Having separately listed the respective groups of relevant publications, I now point out that only 5 studies compare both kinds of similarity measure taken from the same subjects. These are:

Brim and Wood (1956), 50 courtship pairs; Davitz (1955); Fiedler, Warrington, and Blaisdell (1952); Murstein and Lamb (in Murstein, 1971b); and Murstein (1970, 1971a), which give correlations across 99 premarital pairs. In each instance, actual interpersonal similarity of self descriptions was *not* related to interpersonal attraction, whereas subjects' assumptions of similarity between own and others' characteristics were significantly related to interpersonal attraction.

c. ACTUAL OR ASSUMED SIMILARITIES BETWEEN SUBJECTS' IDEAL-SELF REPORTS AND CHARACTERISTICS OF OTHERS

As mentioned several times, there is a strong possibility that subjects' attractions may be greater for others who are perceived or assumed to have especially favorable characteristics. Also, we have just seen that the results of many studies which purported to look at descriptive interpersonal similarity and attraction may plausibly be explained in terms of the *relationship of attraction and assumed similarity between one's own ideal self and the characteristics one attributes to others.* Below is some additional evidence on this point.

The reader will recall that Hendrick and Brown (1971) proposed that an extraverted ideal self characterizes both self-described extraverts and self-described introverts. On this view, when both introverts and extraverts were more attracted to others whom they assumed to be extraverts, one might suggest that similarity between own ideal self and assumed characteristics of others is relevant to one's attraction to those others. (Obviously *dis*similarity in *descriptive* attributes was related to attraction among the introvert subjects.)

Similarly, in Palmer and Byrne's (1970) experiments described earlier, both dominant and submissive subjects expressed greater attraction for self-described dominant strangers. The authors show that the social-desirability mean ratings of the items in the dominant stranger's profile exceeded that of the submissive stranger's profile. If the personal ideals of the subjects in these experiments agree to some extent with these "cultural norms," then the results of their study may be another example of attraction's being a function of assumed similarity between ideal self and attributes of another person. (And, again, interpersonal *dis*similarity in descriptive attributes was associated with greater attraction for one group of subjects—here, submissive ones.)

As described in section C, Walster (1970), found that subjects of both high and low self-favorability behaved more romantically toward more attractive partners. Again, presumably, similarity to ideal self overrode *dis*similarity to self in determining the attraction behavior of some of the subjects. By contrast (as described in section C), S. B. Kiesler and Baral (1970) report a correlation between attraction behavior and interpersonal similarity. (As explained earlier, the "romantic behavior" dependent variable in these studies may not indicate which other is most *liked* by the subject.)

Griffitt (1969) gave each subject a contrived self-description allegedly made by an unknown other, in which 40% of the other's self-descriptions were the same as the subject's. He varied the degree of similarity between the stranger's self-description and the subject's ideal self by giving half the subjects protocols from others in which 20% of the other's self-description corresponded to the subject's ideal-self responses, and giving the other half of the subjects protocols showing 80% correspondence between the other's self descriptions and the subject's ideal-self responses. The positive effect of this kind of similarity on attraction (as measured by Byrne's Interpersonal Judgment Scale) was significant.

On the assumption that the wish to be competent constitutes part of the ideal self for most persons, I include here studies by Rosenfeld (1964), Aronson, Willerman, and Floyd (1966), and Helmreich, Aronson, and LeFan (1970)—all of whom, in effect, varied similarity between subjects' ideals for self and the descriptive characteristics of others whose attractiveness the subjects were to judge.

As noted earlier, all of Rosenfeld's (1964) subjects supposedly thought they were of medium competence level, but they preferred others who were most *dis*similar to them, i.e., most competent.

By audiotape and videotape respectively, subjects in the two experiments by Aronson and colleagues observed an interview with a person who was either highly competent or incompetent ("average" in the first study) and who either committed a blunder or not. The intuitive hypothesis for both studies was that the highly competent person would be more likeable if he committed a pratfall, since an extremely competent person might be perceived as "too good [and] non-human." Although in both investigations the competent person was liked significantly better, in other respects the results of the studies do *not* agree. Only in the second did the other's pratfall per se significantly decrease the subjects' rated liking for the other. Only in the first was there a significant interaction of the other's competence level and his pratfall, i.e., the competent person was rated as more attractive, the less competent person as less attractive after the pratfall. In the second study, not only were the other's competence level and his pratfall varied, but subjects' chronic self-esteem was varied according to scores on an idiosyncratic self-esteem measure. A predicted triple-order interaction is reported, viz., for high and low self-esteem subjects, the pratfall of a competent person decreased his attractiveness, whereas for medium self-esteem subjects it increased the other's attractiveness. Over-all, the discrepancies between the two studies and the fact that no attempt was made to replicate the triple-order interaction suggests that the most solid finding from the pair of experiments by Aronson and colleagues is the greater attractiveness of competent others. Thus these results as well as Rosenfeld's suggest that the other's similarity to ideal self is of importance in interpersonal attraction, overriding interpersonal dissimilarities in descriptive attributes.

Perhaps a study by S. C. Jones and Shrauger (1970) may also be classifiable in this section, although not so conceptualized by the investigators. In this experiment, half the subjects heard another person quite fully described in very favorable terms and half heard the other quite fully described in very unfavorable terms (high and low reputation). Then half of each of the above groups of subjects heard the other describe herself in very favorable, half in very unfavorable terms (high and low self-evaluation). From the viewpoint of the present section, then, perhaps we may say that the experimenters manipulated the similarity between the subjects' ideal-self and others' self characteristics. Attraction, as measured by subjects' ratings of their "general emotional reaction to the stimulus person" varied significantly as a function of the favorability of the other's reputation, but not significantly as a function of her self-evaluation. The authors' interest in doing the experiment was to see whether the other's attractiveness as a function of her self-evaluation would be mediated by the previously given reputational evaluations of the others. Pertinent to this, an interaction was found, namely, the high-reputation other was more attractive when she presented consistent (high) self-evaluations, and the low-reputation other was also more attractive when she presented consistent (low) self-evaluations. As the authors suggest in somewhat different words, this interaction is congruent with either of two explanations: (a) subjects prefer cognitively consistent input and are attracted to others who are associated with such input; (b) subjects are attracted by the candidness and/or self-awareness on the part of the others, inasmuch as candidness and self-awareness are similar to (consistent with) the subjects' own ideals.

Using a correlational rather than an experimental approach, a number of investigators have reported that liked others are assumed to have more favorable characteristics (so, at least by implication, to be more similar to the subject's ideal self) than are less liked others and even that liked others have more favorable characteristics than does oneself.

Using selected Gough adjectives to index favorability, Newcomb (1961) reports that, for each of his 17 intensively studied subjects, the attraction rankings and the favorability rankings assigned to the other 16 persons correlated highly (mean *rho* at Week 14 = .70). Similarly, when A. J. Lott, B. E. Lott, Reed, and Crow's (1970) subjects described a liked, neutral, and disliked other using Anderson's adjectives, the mean likeability (favorability) values (based on Anderson's previous calibration of the adjectives) varied significantly among the 3 groups of others.

In Luckey's (1960a, 1960b, 1961) publications about subjects reporting themselves to be more or less maritally compatible according to Locke's scale, discrepancies were obtained for each subject between his or her ideal self on four Interpersonal Check List dimensions and his or her concept of spouse on these dimensions. For the wives, high marital compatibility was associated with small discrepancies on each dimension, for the husbands, parallel trends were significant on three of four dimensions.

W. R. Thompson and Nishimura (1952) found a significantly higher *r* between subjects' self ideals and their descriptions of friends than between subjects' self ideals and descriptions of nonfriends.

In an early study, E. L. Kelly (1941) found a significant positive association between reported marital compatibility (here taken as an attraction index) and the tendency to describe the spouse's actual characteristics more favorably than one's own. If one assumes that the "good" ends of Kelly's idiosyncratic trait scales correspond approximately to the subjects' self ideals, this finding indirectly supports the idea that attraction may be a function of perceived similarity between others' characteristics and one's ideal self.

Northway and Detweiler (1955) reported that their seventh-grade female subjects tended to rate their sociometrically chosen friends more favorably than self and their sociometric "indifferents" as lower than self on 10 idiosyncratic evaluative scales.

Similar trends were reported by Fiedler, Warrington, and Blaisdell (1952); Lundy (1958); and Lundy, Katkovsky, Cromwell, and Shoemaker (1955); and Murstein and Lamb (in Murstein, 1971b), whose studies were cited in the immediately preceding section.

McKenna, Hofstaetter, and O'Connor (1956) asked each of their subjects to describe self, own ideal, friend #1, and friend #2, using a modification of the Butler-Haigh Q sort. Within each subject, each sort was correlated with each other, and the r values transformed to z values. For each friend, the following comparisons were made:

Subject's self-description vs. subject's view of friend's
characteristics (with subject's ideal self constant)
compared to
Subject's ideal self vs. subject's view of friend's characteristics
(with subject's self-description constant).

The second correlation was significantly greater than the first for friend 1 and for friend 2, implying that perhaps assumed similarity between own ideal self and other's characteristics is more important in friendship relationships than is assumed similarity between own self-description and other's characteristics. Unfortunately no similar comparisons are available for subjects and their assumptions about non-friends' characteristics.

Although they did not so conceptualize it, perhaps Neuringer and Wandke's (1966) work might be classifiable in the present section. They provided their subjects with 10 imaginary situations in each of which the subject had supposedly given a hypothetical person either a friendly or an unfriendly rating and then was told that the person had done a bad or good thing, i.e., something more or less similar to what we may presume to be the subjects' self-ideals. The conditions were not orthogonally varied, i.e., originally attractive others always did bad things, originally unattractive ones always did good things. Subjects were to imagine how they would rate their feelings of friendliness (attraction) after hearing about the others' behaviors. The authors' interest in balance theory underlay their design, but the artificial nature of the purely imaginary situation, plus unclear and probably undefensible use of discrepancy scores and a nonorthogonal design lead me to omit further comment.

To my knowledge, there are no studies involving *actual similarities* between the subject's ideal-self reports and descriptive characteristics of others.

d. Actual or Assumed Similarities in Over-All Self-Regard Level

To my knowledge, Murstein (1970) is the only author who has concerned himself with *interpersonal attraction as a function of actual interpersonal similarities in over-all self-regard*. He obtained "self-acceptance" scores for each person among 99 premarital couples by correlating self-reports and ideal-self reports across 15 EPPS needs within each person. He found that girl friends of men with the highest self-acceptance scores showed significantly higher self-acceptance scores than did girl friends of men with the lowest self-acceptance scores. Conversely, boy friends of girls with the highest self-acceptance scores obtained significantly higher self-acceptance scores than did boy friends of girls with the lowest self-acceptance scores. (Naturally, these 2 findings are not independent of each other.)

So far as I know, no one has looked at interpersonal attraction as a function of *assumed* interpersonal similarities in over-all self-regard level.

e. Actual or Assumed Similarities between Subjects' Self-Reports and Others' Reports about the Subjects

Backman and Secord (1962), Broxton (1963), and Luckey (1960c, 1961) were theoretically concerned with attraction as a function of actual coincidences ("actual similarities") in the adjectives used by a subject and another to describe the subject. As explained earlier, consistency theory implies that greater similarity per se should be associated with greater attraction, aside from the evaluative characteristics involved in the similarities or dissimilarities. However, as noted in my earlier methodological discussion, these "actual similarity" measures are operationally identical with scores which have been called "insight scores" by other investigators, and, in the hands of these other researchers, an entirely different line of research and theorizing has grown up around such measures!

Backman and Secord (1962) had each of 30 sorority-house residents rank each other on degree of liking and also choose 5 adjectives from a list of 16 to describe (a) herself, (b) each other person, (c) what each other person would say about her. For each person, the others were divided into those most and least liked. The number of adjectives *actually* chosen by both the subject and her most liked others to describe the subject was significantly greater than the number chosen by both the subject and her least liked others to describe her. Broxton (1963) reports a parallel finding from the responses of female dormitory residents and their more- and less-liked roommates, using 100 of Gough's adjectives.

Luckey (1960c, 1961) subtracted each husband's self-description score from the description his wife made of him on each of four dimensions of the ICL. She found that these congruence indices were smaller among husbands with high (as opposed to low) marital satisfaction on Locke's scale (three out of four differences were significant). Parallel trends were found for wives, but only one out of four was significant. The use of discrepancy scores precludes evaluating the relative contributions of self-descriptions and other descriptions of self to the obtained correlations, and no formal attempt was made to control for favorability when looking at congruence per se in relationship to marital satisfaction.

As compared to their actual similarity effect, Backman and Secord (1962) found an even stronger effect when comparing (a) subjects' *assumed* similarity between self-descriptions and those they expected from most-liked others, to (b) subjects' *assumed* similarity between self descriptions and those they expected to receive from least-liked others. They made a commendable attempt to separate the possible influence of the social desirability value of the adjectives from the effects of the cognitive congruity introduced by actual or assumed similarities. However, one must question whether their method served adequately to separate these influences of cognitive similarity-dissimilarity from the subjects' *personal* evaluations of the adjectives in determining the association between similarity and attraction in this study.

Broxton (1963) did not make a comparable assumed similarity analysis of her data, although she might have. Instead, she looked for coincidences between the subject's *perception* of what others would say about her and the other's actual description of her. Broxton calls this perceived (i.e., assumed) similarity; however, its operational referent is *not* the same as that for Backman and Secord's assumed similarity. Moreover, Broxton's perceived similarity is operationally identical to one of the types of measures which other researchers have labeled "insight." No attempt was made in any of Broxton's analyses to control for evaluative level when varying similarity.

In one of the most famous investigations of interpersonal attraction, Newcomb (1956, 1961) studied 2 successive groups of 17 previously unacquainted men who lived together in the same dormitory for one year. His "assumed similarity" score is operationally equivalent to Backman and Secord's (1962) "assumed similarity" score. In a preliminary report on the first year's findings, Newcomb states, without giving formal supporting data:

> Attraction turns out to be closely related to perceived agreement [between subjects' self-descriptions and how they thought other house members would describe them] (at considerably less than the .001 level). When the same data are analyzed individually, only two of 17 subjects fail to show the relationship in the predicted direction, and only one of these reverses it. This finding is more impressive than it would be if it resulted from attributing only favorable judgments of oneself to high-liked others. Actually, eight of ten subjects who accepted unfavorable adjectives as describing themselves, and who indicated that one or more others agreed with them, showed more agreement in these unfavorable self-descriptions with high-liked than with low-liked others. The relationship between attraction and perceived agreement on favorable items is, not surprisingly, a good deal closer. At any rate, the finding that attraction varies with perceived cognitive agreement about the self is not merely an artifactual result of the common-sense assumption that one is attracted toward those who are believed to think well of one. [P. 582]

Unfortunately, one cannot get enough information from the published sources to make an evaluation of the methodology relevant to this conclusion, or to find whether such an effect also occurred in the second group of 17 men.

Using a living situation and attraction indices quite similar to Newcomb's, Curry and Emerson (1970) found a weak association between attraction and *assumed* similarity between self-descriptions and others' descriptions of self. During the first week, *gammas* ranged from .14 to .33 in various subgroups. In the eighth week, the relationship was considerably attenuated, with *gammas* ranging from .09 to .17 in various subgroups. No significance tests were made. Curry and Emerson erroneously thought that the use of the EPPS would enable them to separate social-desirability influences from assumed cognitive-similarity influences in determining their similarity-attraction findings. Over-all, it is not clear whether their results call for any interpretation other than chance. If psychological interpretation is warranted, the relative roles of personal desirability and assumed cognitive similarity cannot be separated in such a suggested interpretation.

Like Backman and Secord (1962), Broxton (1963), and Luckey (1960a, 1960b, 1961), Thompson and Nishimura (1952) looked at *actual similarity* between their subjects' and others' reports concerning the subjects, but all their subject-other pairs were friends; so the correlation is not useful in evaluating a similarity-attraction hypothesis.

In summary, the very small number of available studies agree in yielding some support for the hypothesis that there is a positive association between interpersonal attraction and assumed or actual similarities between self-descriptions and others' descriptions of self. Information is not at hand to distinguish the relative roles of cognitive similarity and favorability level of the attributed similarities in determining this relationship.

f. Subject's Over-All Self-Regard Level and the Over-All Level of Regard Others Have for the Subject

As pointed out earlier in my discussion of theoretical possibilities, I know of no research in which this type of attraction-similarity relationship has been investigated.

g. General Attitude Similarities, Interpersonal Attraction, and Self-Regard

Effects of Disagreement on Self-Esteem and Attraction

It has been frequently found that interpersonal agreement on an assortment of attitudes is positively related to interpersonal attraction (Byrne, 1971). According to Byrne and Clore (1970), one explanation of this could be that one's sense of competence is increased by receiving consensual validation from others and is decreased by failing to get such consensual validation. If that is true, it follows that manipulating attitude dissimilarity might not only decrease one's expressed attraction for a disagreeing other, but might also lower one's self-esteem, at least temporarily. C. D. Johnson, J. Gormly, and A. Gormly (1973) tested this notion by varying the degrees of attitude agreement which subjects received from fictitious others. Scores on the Coopersmith Self-Esteem Inventory as well as idiosyncratic attraction-to-other scores were lower among subjects receiving disagreeing messages as compared to those receiving agreeing messages. Although these findings are congruent with the Byrne and Clore theory, the authors discuss several alternate explanations as well. Checks on subjects' suspicions were only vaguely mentioned.

Self-Esteem as a Mediator in the
Agreement-Attraction Relationship

To my knowledge, four investigations have been planned to look for possible mediating effects of self-esteem on the relationship between manipulated agreement and attraction. Each used an idiosyncratic method, and four different kinds of results were obtained.

In Worchel and McCormick's (1963) work, subjects were selected as being high, medium, or low in self-esteem as indexed by Worchel's Self Activity Inventory, and each subject was presented with either an agreeing or disagreeing opinion from a bogus peer. The authors report the typical significant main effect of agreement on their idiosyncratic attraction ("depreciation") score, but this was determined by the strong tendency of the high self-esteem subjects to derogate the disagreeing other more than the agreeing other (interaction significant). No mention is made of checking subjects' suspicions. (The Self-Activity Inventory is evaluated in Wylie, 1974, pp. 165–169.)

Although Hendrick and Page (1970) recognized that arguments could be made for expecting any one of a number of kinds of interaction, they followed McGuire's (1968) idea that self-esteem and attitude change might be nonmonotonically related. Thus they predicted that persons with high and low chronic self-esteem might show a relatively large effect of disagreement on attraction for the disagreeing person, whereas persons with moderate levels of chronic self-esteem might show the disagreement-attraction effect less strongly than the other two self-esteem groups. Such an interaction effect was found, but only under the maximum disagreement condition, and it held for only some of the alternate attraction measures used. Idiosyncratic attraction and self-esteem measures were employed; multiple ANOVAs were made on probably intercorrelated dependent variables, and it seems that no formal checks on the subjects' suspicions were made. Accordingly, the conclusiveness of this study is quite limited.

Working from balance theory, Archibald (1970) expected a significant interaction between the subjects' chronic self-esteem levels (as indicated by an idiosyncratic modification of Bills's Index of Adjustment and Values) and the degree of others' agreement with the subjects about the Vietnam War. However, even though Archibald got the frequently obtained positive association between attitudinal agreement and rated liking for others, he obtained no evidence that self-esteem mediated this effect, i.e., there was no interaction.

Leonard (1973) chose subjects above and below the median on Ghiselli's Self-Esteem Index and had them interview a stooge who was presented as either similar or dissimilar to them with respect to attitudes on "salient campus issues." An idiosyncratic attraction scale was used, and no mention is made of checking the subjects' suspicions.

Leonard reports a significant interaction in which subjects with high self-esteem preferred the stooge who had similar attitudes, whereas the subjects with low self-esteem preferred the stooge having dissimilar attitudes. This is consonant with a reinforcement idea according to which a similar person could be a conditioned positive reinforcer for persons with high self-regard, whereas a similar person would be a conditioned negative reinforcer for a person with low self-regard.

One puzzling feature of the results is that the very frequently reported main effect of attitude similarity was not found. Also, there is no obvious way of reconciling Archibald's lack of interaction with the seemingly different kinds of interaction obtained by Worchel and McCormick (1963), Hendrick and Page (1970), and by Leonard (1973), since their methods differed in numerous ways.

Altogether, no conclusions are warranted at this time about the mediating role(s) of chronic self-esteem in the effects of attitudinal similarity on attraction.

3. Summary

In the study of relationships between similarity and attraction, the widespread use of a single word *similarity* has had the unfortunate effect of glossing over many important distinctions that should have been made both conceptually and methodologically, viz.: the differentiation of "actual" and "assumed" similarities; and within each of these, the differentiations of many subvarieties, ranging from objectively measured characteristics, through attitudes and opinions on a wide range of topics, through self-relevant descriptions and ideals. It is confusing, misleading, and empirically unjustified to oversimplify one's thoughts on "similarity" and "attraction" in this way.

Although much of the impetus for looking for similarity-attraction relationships has come from various consistency (balance, cognitive dissonance) theories, neither predictions nor outcomes may be related unequivocally to such views. Moreover, sources of reinforcement other than those alleged to come from dissonance or consistency per se are easy to imagine in the various kinds of similarity situations discussed. These have not been controlled in the studies carried out thus far. Accordingly, consistency theory has neither subsumed nor been clearly advanced by this line of research.

I list briefly below the reported relationships between "attraction" (measured in a disconcertingly large variety of ways) and a number of kinds of similarities involving self-relevant variables.

1. *Actual and assumed similarities in ideal-self reports:* (a) null or uninterpretable findings so far as actual similarities in particular aspects of ideal self are concerned; (b) two positive findings involving assumed similarities in specific aspects of ideal self; (c) to my knowledge, no studies of actual or assumed similarities in over-all levels of ideal self.

2. *Actual and assumed similarities in particular aspects of self-descriptions:* (a) regarding actual similarities, somewhat more numerous null findings than significant positive ones, and all of the latter small; no significant negative relationships; (b) regarding assumed similarities, mixed findings from experiments which manipulated assumed similarity by presenting subjects with bogus others' self-reports; consistently positive findings (albeit often small in absolute terms) from correlational studies done in "real life" situations.

3. *Actual and assumed similarities between the subject's ideal-self characteristics and corresponding descriptive characteristics of others:* (a) mostly positive findings involving assumed similarities; (b) to my knowledge, no studies on actual similarities.

4. *Actual and assumed similarities between own and other's self-regard level:* (a) one significant positive finding regarding actual similarity; (b) to my knowledge, no studies on assumed similarity.

5. *Actual and assumed similarities between subject's reports and others' reports regarding the subject:* a small number of studies of each; positive trends, although not always significant.

6. *Assumed and actual similarities between the subject's over-all self-regard level and the over-all regard level others have for the subject:* to my knowledge, no studies.

No conclusions can be drawn concerning the possible role of chronic self-esteem in mediating the often-demonstrated relationship between attraction and interpersonal similarity with respect to "impersonal" attitudes, since the four relevant studies yielded four different patterns of results.

9

Influencability and
Self-Concept Variables

A. Conceptual, Theoretical, and Methodological Considerations

Relationships between influenceability and self-regard or between influenceability and specific self-concept dimensions obviously fall within the larger domain of relationships between influenceability and personality factors. The latter, more inclusive topic has been cogently considered from conceptual, theoretical, and methodological viewpoints by McGuire (1968), many of his points being made specifically through his discussions of influenceability and self-esteem. Accordingly, this section draws heavily on his way of organizing and analyzing the present section.

To plan, interpret, or criticize empirical research regarding influenceability and over-all self-regard or other more specific self-concept variables, one must consider: (a) conceptual and operational definitions of influence situations and measures of influence effects; (b) conceptual and operational definitions of over-all self-regard or specific aspects of self-concept; (c) theorizing which has influenced hypothesizing and/or ad hoc interpretations of results; (d) general problems of research design and procedure which are particularly pertinent to establishing and interpreting theoretically relevant relationships between (a) and (b)

1. Conceptual and Operational Definitions of Influence Situations and Measures of Influence Effects

McGuire has suggested the use of the generic term influenceability to cover any tendency of a person to change as a function of social pressure. He believes it is useful to distinguish three classes of social influence situations, each of which may be operationalized in a variety of ways. These classes are suggestion, conformity, and persuasibility, to be identified more fully below. Within each class, he feels that operational definitions should yield converging results and that the alternate operations within a class should yield relationships to other variables which show a distinctive pattern for that class, since he posits a possible group factor within each of the variations in kinds of social influence within a class. In addition, he thinks there may possibly be a weak general factor underlying all three types of influence procedures. In my opinion, research adequate to evaluate this plausible network of assertions is not at hand, but, in any event, his three classes do serve as convenient bases for grouping available studies.

Suggestion situations are not directly defined by McGuire (1968), but, from the context, one can infer he is using the term to refer to hypnotizability and related waking suggestion tests such as body sway. This class of situations will not be dealt with in this review because the rather extensive research attempting to relate various measures of suggestibility and hypnotizability to self-reports about personality has been critically reviewed by Barber (1964) and Hilgard (1965). They agree that current measures of hypnotizability or suggestibility do not show replicable associations with scores from such tests as the California Psychological Inventory, Edwards Personal Preference Scale, Guilford-Zimmerman Temperament Survey, and Leary's Interpersonal Check List.

Conformity situations involve procedures in which the subject is simply informed that a certain source holds a certain position, without the subject's being given any arguments or explicit indications that he or she is expected to concur.

In persuasion situations, a source gives a position on an issue and also presents arguments for its correctness. In some influence situations first used by McGuire and Millman (1965) subjects are not actually exposed to arguments, but are forewarned that they will be. I think these situations could plausibly be subsumed under the persuasion category, even though not explicitly so categorized in McGuire (1968), since there is a presumption of a source who wants to convince by argument. I also include here those studies which induce the subject to produce arguments against his or her own initial opinion, i.e., the "forced compliance" or "active participation" studies.

Obviously when one uses any one of these influence procedures and attendant measures of their alleged effects on the subjects' attitudes or opinions, evidence for the reliability and the convergent and discriminant construct validity of the influence measures should be given. Unfortunately, authors of the many studies I have examined generally show little or no recognition that such problems even exist, and they give little or no information for the reader to evaluate the psychometric properties of their instruments in relation to the interpretability of their findings using data from those instruments. These measurement issues are considered in more detail below.

2. Conceptual and Operational Definitions of Over-All Self-Regard or Specific Aspects of Self-Concept

Of course, the reliability, discriminant validity, and convergent validity of the self-concept measures are just as crucial for interpreting results as are the psychometric properties of the influence measures. These measurement issues are considered below and in more detail in Wylie (1974).

3. Theorizing Which Has Influenced Hypothesizing and/or Ad Hoc Interpretations of Results

When it comes to positing theoretical relationships between self-concept variables and influenceability, one finds the theorizing has been done mostly by social psychologists as opposed to personality theorists such as Rogers. It is not difficult to discern, however, how Rogerian theory fits generally into the discussions presented by the social psychologists.

a. TYPES OF THEORIES

McGuire (1968) mentions the following four classes of theory as the major categories providing a priori and/or ad hoc interpretations of studies of personality and influenceability: (a) functional theories; (b) consistency theories; (c) learning theories; (d) perceptual theories. These categories overlap to a considerable extent, with the consistency and learning views, especially, being elaborations of the functional view. The functional theories assert most generally that the subject's behavior in an influence situation depends upon the instrumentality of the influence response to the attainment of one or more of the subject's goals. In order to state testable research hypotheses, one must ask what goals could be involved and how could the specified influence responses be instrumental in achieving these goals?

Relative to these questions, D. T. Campbell (1961) points out that human beings learn in at least six ways: trial-and-error, perception, observing another's responses, linguistic instruction about the characteristics of objects, linguistic instruction about responses to be made, and perceptual observations of the outcomes of another's trial-and-error.

Conformity research is usually centered around instances of incompatible dispositional tendencies induced on the one hand by individual modes such as trial-and-error and vision; and on the other hand by social modes such as observation of another's response, verbal instruction about another's response, or the like. . . . Differences in the degree of conformity are differences in the degree to which the different modes (e.g., the personal, 1 and 2; or the social, 3, 4, 5, 6) are weighted in achieving a composite. . . . In many instances, certainly, so-called conformity behavior is an intelligent part of a rational search for valid knowledge about a fallibly and indirectly known world rather than merely an interest in being like other persons whether or not they are correct. [Campbell, 1961, pp. 107-108] . . . Our normative model is thus one in which all persons give *some* weight to *all* dispositional sources. Differences in relative weighting in achieving the composite thus become the research issue. [p. 113] . . . Giving heavy weight to the social source will be regarded as synonymous with conformity, suggestibility, persuasability, or yielding, as these terms have been used in the literature. [P. 114]

Campbell thinks that a number of factors would be expected to enter into whether an individual finds it potentially reinforcing (hence functional) to give heavy weight to the social source in an influence situation, and he has posited what some of these factors should be. Of greatest pertinence to self-concept theorists' views of conformity are the relevant self-perceived competencies of the person being subjected to influence manipulations. Campbell predicts that the greater a person's self-perceived own ability, the less his conformity; the more self-esteeming, self-assured, ascendant, nonsubmissive, the less conforming. Presumably this would be so because the person has learned in the past that his abilities to use modes (1) and (2) have enabled him to attain useful ways of perceiving and acting in his environment without much reliance on modes (3), (4), (5), and (6).

Self-concept theories themselves are functional theories, of course, which stress certain kinds of needs and goal attainments, and the assertions of self-concept theorists seem to be implicitly assumed by the social psychologists who do much of the functional theorizing concerning personality and influenceability. For example, social psychologists assume that persons have a need to maintain as favorable a level of self-regard as possible. Accordingly, if one could correctly surmise which influence response in an experimental situation would maintain a high level of self-regard, one could (given knowledge about the other factors Campbell listed) state a definite hypothesis relating self-regard and influence behavior in a particular experimental situation. But, unfortunately, the vagueness of the major proposition about self-regard makes definite hypotheses impossible. Will the person with favorable self-regard resist influence because, as McGuire and Millman (1965) proposed his self-regard depends on "knowing his own mind," being confident of his own knowledge or skills, regardless of what others may say or do? Or will he yield to influence procedures because an important part of his favorable self-regard involves his conception of himself as an open-minded, reasonable person? As with the behavior possibilities of the high self-regard subject, the possibilities for functional influence responses of low self-regard subjects are numerous, and the predictions are again equivocal. For example, will a person with low self-regard conform to the responses or opinions offered by supposedly superior sources because doing so will make him more accurate, enhancing his self-esteem about his achievement, or because doing so will enable him to identify with the more worthy influencer? (The latter idea was suggested in a personal communication from William McGuire, December, 1975.) Or will he resist influence in an attempt to improve his image of himself as an independent person? Or, as another alternate, will a person of low self-regard assume that he must be wrong or inferior in the experimental influence situation, just as he feels he is in many or most situations, and will he, for this reason, be swayed by the influence manipulation since he has found in the past that he can get effective guides to action by using others' evaluations of the environmental situation, as Campbell would say? Or the low self-regard person might yield for yet another reason: Rogerians would argue that yielding would help the subject to maintain *congruence* between his unfavorable self-concept and his current actions or feedback from his current actions. The idea of a need for congruence apart from a need for self-enhancement has long been a tenet of Rogerian theory. The reader will recognize that this idea of a need for congruence takes us into the consistency theories as well as functional and learning views. In the following two quotations about attitude changes following counterattitudinal behavior, Aronson (1969), the dissonance theorist, recognizes the Rogerian points about congruence:

> Although we were not fully aware of it at the time, in the clearest experiments performed to test dissonance theory, the dissonance involved was between a self-concept and cognitions about a behavior that violated this self-concept. . . . dissonance theory allows us to predict that for people with low self-concepts the "good feelings" aroused by the products of success will be tempered by the discomfort caused by dissonance—the dissonance between a low self-concept and cognitions about high performance. [P. 28]

In short, we should be able to look separately at the attitude-change effects attributable to (a) the subject's need to reduce cognitive dissonance per se and (b) the subject's need for self-enhancement. Schlenker (1973) has also made this point, contending that most studies of attitude change following counterattitudinal behavior can be better synthesized by explaining them in terms of self-enhancement needs as opposed to dissonance-reduction needs. (The procedure of Schlenker's relevant study is too briefly reported to allow for evaluation here.)

Thus far I have argued that (a) dissonance theory is really a functional theory and that both dissonance and functional theories obviously involve learning; (b) dissonance theory and self-concept theories converge and overlap in their general ideas about what self-concept-relevant needs may be satisfied by responding or not responding to influence manipulations; and (c) each gives an unacceptably vague basis for predictions without the inclusion of further, more specific assumptions and facts about the subject's conceptions of himself and his conceptions of what usefulness various influence responses may have in helping him to attain his goals.

I think it is clear that many other needs of the subject besides self-regard and self-concept congruency may plausibly affect his influence responses, for example, the desire to attain valid knowledge of the situation, as Campbell would say; the desire to get the experiment over with quickly; the desire to cooperate with the experimenter in order to feel one has made an important contribution to science; the desire to defeat the experimenter in what the subject regards as an asinine undertaking. This being the case, any researcher who takes functional theorizing seriously must design the study to control these other needs.

In stressing functional and dissonance theories, I do not mean to imply that learning and perception theories are irrelevant. An examination of Campbell's analysis makes clear the importance of both learning and perception. Aside from the general points already made about the importance of learning principles in understanding influence behaviors, reception of the message obviously involves learning, and in McGuire's (1968) analysis, both reception and yielding are involved in influence behaviors. Of particular relevance here is McGuire's (1968) idea that self-esteem is positively related to learning the message while being negatively related to yielding. Moreover, learning theory is obviously involved in accounting for how the person's self-concept came to be what it is as a predisposing factor in the influence situation, and in understanding how the subject may come to interpret the message or the reinforcing contingencies in the influence situation. Then, too, there may be such a thing for each person as an operant level of influence behavior for a certain type of situation, understandable in terms of learning theory. Additionally, learning theory might predict that such things as the primacy-recency phenomenon conceivably could influence reactions to influence procedures, since the subjects' reactions to influence necessarily involve their acquisition and retention of the information given to them. By and large, however, the studies evaluated in this section have not derived their inspiration primarily from such aspects of learning theory.

Perceptual theories, too, are pertinent to the area of self-regard and persuasibility, for example, in respect to the use of perceptual distortion measures as conformity indices, or in respect to adaptation level as a factor in the subject's self-evaluation, or the subject's evaluation of the extremity of the pressure in the influence manipulation. As with certain aspects of learning theory, however, perceptual theories have not explicitly formed the basis for the studies examined.

b. MODERATING VARIABLES IN THEORIES CONCERNING THE ASSOCIATION OF SELF-REGARD AND PERSUASIBILITY

I have already illustrated the fact that no simple predictions about self-regard and influence behaviors are clearly implied by any theory, including self-concept theory. Moreover, there has been a widely recognized failure to get strong and replicable empirical functional relationships between measures of self-concept and measures of influence behavior. In the light of the preceding facts, there has been a move toward theorizing that self-regard variables may be expected to interact with or be moderated by other variables to produce a variety of functional relationships between self-concept variables and influenceability measures. For example, depending on the moderating situational and personality variables chosen, self-regard may be postulated to have a linear negative, linear positive, inverted U, or U-shaped relationship to influence-indicative behaviors. Although it seems quite defensible to say that an adequate theory must account for such complexities and Campbell's analysis amounts to a detailed listing of many of these possible interacting factors, there has been much more ad hoc than a priori talk about such possibilities. Clear tests of any of them remain to be made.

McGuire (1968) conjectures that such interactions should be theoretically expected and empirically explored, and he has done more than anyone else to try to propose quantitative models of some of the possible interactions, making explicit the methodological implications. His approach, although conceptual, does not clearly fall within the boundaries of any one of his four classes of theory mentioned above.

Following the view that influence behaviors are mediated by a chain of events, he proposes to theorize about the relationships of personality variables (in the present case, self-concept variables) to each of the steps in the mediating chain in order to arrive at a sensible a priori development of more complex hypotheses about possible relationships between self-regard and influence behavior. After reviewing the proposed mediating chain of attention, comprehension, yielding, retention, and action, McGuire chooses to base his analysis on two steps: reception (attention and comprehension combined) and yielding. He believes that the relationships of a personality variable to reception may be quite different from its relationship to yielding and that this must be taken into account both in deriving theoretical hypotheses and evaluating experimental situations which have been or might be used to study self-esteem relationships with influence behaviors.

Consider, for example, variations in the influence situation. If the message is either very hard or very easy to comprehend, then theoretically the personality variable such as a self-concept variable should be expected to operate on the consequent influence behavior mostly by way of the yielding mediator. Alternately, situations vary regarding whether they are plausible, moderately plausible, or unconvincing. Only to the extent that the situation is moderately plausible and hence puts moderate demands on yielding, McGuire thinks, will a personality variable have much association with influence behavior by way of the yielding mediator. By developing some of the implications of these ideas, he shows that the function relating self-regard to influence behavior might be expected to be positive linear, negative linear, or nonmonotonic, depending on the hypothetical way the self-regard and situational influences are supposed to act with respect to one or more of the alleged mediators.

McGuire (1968) has also recommended specific theorizing and testing regarding the possible interaction between self-regard and such situational variables as the status of the influence source and the characteristics of the message.

Another theoretical idea with important methodological implications is the likelihood of a confounding between the particular personality variable under study and other personality variables. For example, if self-regard is varied by selecting subjects with differing scores on a purported self-regard measure, one is most probably also confounding individual differences in self-regard with individual differences in both anxiety and depression, since it is well known that scores indicative of both these personality variables covary with self-regard scores. Thus, if the subject conforms to erroneous peer judgments, is it because he feels too depressed to care about resisting or arguing, feels so anxious that he is very distractible and/or afraid to assert himself in this strange experimental situation, or feels so inferior that he thinks his own judgments must be wrong? The theoretical statements about how either anxiety or depression would be expected to affect each of the postulated mediators and hence to affect the influence behaviors are virtually nonexistent. It is not necessarily incumbent on a self-regard theorist to clarify in advance what would be expected with respect to each of these confounding variables in relation to influence behavior. However, if one wishes to design a study to test the self-concept hypothesis that a person who feels inferior loses belief in his own adequacy to judge in this particular experimental situation, then one must take steps to rule out such alternate interpretations as would plausibly arise if confounding personality variables are operative. Two general methodological strategies seem relevant: (a) develop and use instruments having discriminant validity for measuring the self-regard variable they purport to measure (or for measuring other allegedly different personality constructs as appropriate); (b) study a wider net of possibly confounded personality variables in their relationships with influence behavior, trying to hold constant confounding variables while looking at self-regard variable X and at interactions between self-regard variable X and the other personality variables (McGuire, 1968). As it is, all extant studies are subject to serious confoundings of this type. As McGuire (1968) has shown, one could get artifactual trends toward positive linear, zero, negative linear, or nonmonotonic relationships between a purported self-regard variable and behavior in an influence situation, depending on the type of confounding action. Thus, extant studies lose interpretability since they provide no means of ruling out alternate interpretations made plausible by the confounding.

A special case of confounding of personality variables and failure to study discriminant validity arises when one fails to distinguish two common ways of varying self-regard: (a) by measuring predispositional ("chronic") levels of self-regard by means of a self-report device; or (b) by manipulating ("acute") levels of self-regard in the experimental situation by means of bogus feedback about personality or ability tests or about success or failure on a task used in the experiment. Occasionally an author seems to recognize the theoretical point that the self-regard independent variable may be quite different depending upon whether one is using the chronic-predispositional or acute-manipulating approach, but explicit recognition of this possibility is rare in research publications and authors of studies typically use the term self-esteem in their discussion of results as if the class of operational definition was irrelevant, which has certainly not been demonstrated.

Several methodological considerations are implied by thinking about the above problem. First, it is obviously highly desirable to be able to manipulate an independent variable experimentally as opposed to varying it by choosing subjects according to their different predispositional levels. Underwood (1957) has clearly explained the serious lacks of control intrinsic to the latter procedure of attempting to study the effects of an independent variable. Thus, attempts to manipulate self-regard are methodologically commendable *if* they accomplish their purpose and can be ethically defended (the latter being a very serious question, indeed, no matter how successful one may be in the former). Second, we need more studies which vary chronic and manipulated self-regard orthogonally, looking for evidence of their convergent and/or discriminant validity. That is, it is not enough to show that each relates to an outside variable such as influence behavior in the same way. Some of the apparent inconsistencies among studies quite probably depend on the fact that equivalence has been unwarrantedly assumed among a wide variety of operations for establishing individual or group differences in chronic or manipulated self-regard.

Parenthetically, one should note that the chronic-manipulated distinction implies other important methodological points besides those involved in clarifying the conceptual separateness or relatedness of the two self-regard constructs. As McGuire points out, even if chronic and manipulated self-esteem are conceptually comparable, one needs to consider which technique can yield a wider range of individual or group differences, inasmuch as the possibility of finding a relationship between self-regard and influence behavior will be diminished if the range of variation on the self-regard variable is very narrow. Moreover, the number and range of reliably and validly discriminable steps on the self-regard measure is of paramount importance so long as there is the very strong possibility that nonmonotonic relationships rather than rectilinear ones obtain between self-regard and influence behavior, at least under certain moderating conditions. The typical experiment using manipulated self-esteem has used only two levels, thereby not permitting one to look at the entire function. Perhaps the experimenter has concluded that there was a very weak or null relationship when, in fact, the relationship between manipulated self-regard and influence behavior could be curvilinear for the situational conditions of the experiment. On these grounds, if chronic self-esteem measures are conceptually comparable to manipulated self-esteem, they may be preferable, inasmuch as one can know, if a properly developed instrument is used, that more than two or three steps are reliably discriminable among subjects or among groups. Thus, one can look at the function in a more fine-grained way, being less likely to miss nonmonotonic relationships if they are actually characteristic of the self-regard and influence behaviors under the moderating conditions of the experiment. On the other hand, if chronic and manipulated self-esteem are not conceptually comparable, it is possible and necessary to create several discriminable steps of manipulated self-regard.

c. RELEVANT AND IRRELEVANT SELF-CONCEPT VARIABLES

Not only do we need to think carefully about the predispositional-manipulated tactics for varying self-regard, but we should also consider what aspects of self-concept are theoretically relevant to the influence situation and behavior under study, and whether our self-concept manipulations or measures are theoretically appropriate to the particular hypothesis being tested. For example, there is no very plausible a priori theoretical reason to think that manipulating the subject's success or failure on a particular task should lead to important "acute" changes in *over-all* self-regard. In fact, what literature there is on this topic would fail to support such an idea (Wylie, 1961, and other sections of this book). Yet it is often true that experimenters will gratuitously assume that feedback regarding a particular task somehow creates an over-all lowering of self-regard. If the experimenter's theory and interpretation depend on this unsupported assumption, then the conclusion seems indefensible. It seems sensible to theorize that bogus success or failure on a particular task, or feedback regarding a particular aspect of the personality might be expected to affect the subject's behavior in an influence situation involving *that task* or *that aspect* of personality.

And what about the converse situation in which the experimenter devalues the subject in some very general way, such as telling him he has many poor personality qualities or is very stupid on an intelligence test and evidently expects that this will create felt inferiority and yielding behavior with respect to a particular task such as line judging? Even if the general feedback has had some sort of general effect, it still seems questionable to think that this kind of ego-involving self-concept effect would spread to very restricted behavior in domains quite different from those in which the subject has been devalued and plausibly quite peripheral to his over-all level of self-regard. In short, separate theorizing, separate measures, and separate influence tasks are needed for (a) specific versus general self-evaluation as related to (b) whether the influence task is plausibly related to general self-regard level and/or specific self-evaluation.

4. General Problems of Research Design and Procedure Which Are Particularly Pertinent to Establishing and Interpreting Theoretically Relevant Relationships between Self-Concept Variables and Influenceability

Thus far I have been stressing theoretical and conceptual ideas regarding self-concept variables and influenceability, referring briefly and parenthetically to some of the implications of these theoretical and conceptual ideas for inventing and evaluating relevant methodology. But in order systematically to evaluate the interpretability of the studies I examined, I had to establish a more detailed list of specific methodological criteria. As will become apparent, no study survived scrutiny in the light of these criteria, and the incidence of serious method flaws renders the groups of studies essentially uninterpretable.

a. SELF-REGARD MEASURES

One must question the self-regard measures used in these studies. If an idiosyncratic instrument is used to index self-regard, the burden of proof is on the researcher (a) to explain why such a measure should have been used in preference to one of the more commonly used and better developed instruments; and (b) to give sufficient information regarding the idiosyncratic instrument's psychometric properties (range of individual differences, reliability, convergent and discriminant construct validity) to enable the reader to be convinced that the self-regard construct intended by the experimenter was plausibly measured by the idiosyncratic instrument. Research on self-concept and influenceability is characterized more strongly than other areas of self-concept research that I have examined by the use of unjustified idiosyncratic instruments, with insufficient or no information being given the reader about the properties of the instrument.

On the other hand, if a self-regard instrument is used which has been developed previously and has been used in a variety of other studies, the question then arises as to the already known psychometric properties of that instrument. Although no widely used self-regard instrument fulfills all desiderata (see Wylie, 1974), some are less inadequate than others. Unfortunately, the personality-persuasibility area has been dominated by use of various versions or modifications of the Janis-Field Scales. Typically the use of these scales is either unjustified or rationalized by brief allusions to their widespread use by previous researchers. But no version of this scale has received proper psychometric evaluation and development. On the whole there is no basis for determining how much one version yields an estimate of self-regard essentially comparable to that yielded by the others. In most versions, acquiescent response set is grossly uncontrolled by the use of all or almost all items keyed in one direction (i.e., agreeing yields poor self-regard). This, of course, means that the agreeing behavior in an influence situation could correlate with Janis-Field scores simply by means of the acquiescent response set. Additionally, scores on these scales may be influenced by extremity response set, a method factor which it may share with a number of extant influenceability measures, with possible correlations between self-regard and influenceability scores being determined artificially by the extremity response set (Levonian, 1968).

The problem of discriminant validity of any of the idiosyncratic instruments *or* the Janis-Field Scales is completely untouched. Thus, the interpretability of results in terms of association of self-regard with persuasibility is confounded with an unknown variety of other personality factors, probably most prominently anxiety, as I have discussed above.

Another question of discriminant validity arises when one asks whether a low self-regard score may be indicative of genuinely poor ability on the influence task. For example, League and Jackson (1964), in a study involving no attempt to influence subjects, found that poor performance in one of the extant conformity tasks (counting metronome clicks) was associated with low self-esteem reports. Thus, the correlations between low self-esteem and a high degree of counting "conformity" (i.e., counting inaccuracy) might be related to the actually poor counting ability of the subject rather than being attributable to his general level of self-regard affecting his conformity behavior.

We have already mentioned that enough reliably discriminable levels of self-regard should be used in these studies in order to enable one to look for nonmonotonic relations. This desideratum has been overlooked in many researches. If such relations obtain between the inferred self-regard and influenceability variables, conflicting empirical results may arise because the two ranges of self-regard which are used may be different from study to study, resulting in weak positive relationships in one study, weak negative ones in another, zero relationships in yet a third. But there is no way to be sure from published information that this methodological variation accounts for discrepant results.

b. Timing of Self-Regard Measures or Manipulations

The timing of the self-regard measure or manipulation in relation to the influence procedure is potentially very important. First, the test-retest reliability of the self-regard measure is of special relevance, since, in many studies, some time elapses between collecting the self-regard data and exposing the subjects to the influence situation. If the test-retest reliability of the self-regard instrument is poor, the subjects' standings on chronic self-regard may not be the same on the occasion of the attempt at influence as it apparently was at the time the subject was assigned to the high, medium, or low self-regard group, later to be used as a basis for data analysis. In Wylie (1974) where I have given detailed information on test-retest reliabilities of some of the more widely used instruments, one can see that such values over 6- to 24-week periods range from .92 to .31. This shows that the degree of test-retest reliability may not be a problem for certain instruments and types of subjects, but that the burden of proof is on the investigator to assure that the test-retest reliability of his instrument is high enough to avoid the problem discussed in this paragraph.

Then, too, one must question whether the self-regard data were collected in a time relationship which would increase the probability of subjects' becoming suspicious of the experimenter's intention of relating self-regard to influenceability. Including self-regard measures among influence measures as some experimenters have done seems especially likely to introduce common irrelevant method factors as explanations of any associations obtained. Moreover, such concomitances may increase the probabilities of the subjects' becoming suspicious. Perhaps suspicions create antagonisms in some subjects, decreasing the reliability and validity of their self-regard responses or influence responses, while, in some subjects, increasing attempts to cooperate with the supposedly understood intent of the experimenter, having unpredictable effects, depending on what the subjects' construction of the experimenter's intent is. Since we have no way of knowing what effect suspiciousness might have, precautions must be taken to eliminate the possibility of its arising. More is said below about the question of suspiciousness as dependent on other factors in the procedure.

c. Problems with Self-Regard Manipulations

Turning specifically to the commonly used attempt to manipulate self-esteem by bogus feedback or contrived success or failure within the experiment, one must first ask whether any checks were made on this manipulation. Did the experimenter attempt to find out to what extent the subject found the bogus feedback or artificial success or failure cognitively convincing? If it was unconvincing, it is implausible that it affected his or her self-regard. And did the subject who was *un*convinced also become suspicious of the experimenter? If so, all the unknown possible effects of suspiciousness must be allowed for, making interpretation of results difficult or impossible. If the subjects were both cognitively convinced and nonsuspicious, did the manipulation affect their self-regard in any way relevant to the experimenter's hypothesis? Most studies have omitted these crucial checks, simply assuming that if influence behaviors are associated with the manipulation, it indicates that the manipulation created differences in self-regard. Obviously such assumptions are hazardous. (One study attempted a check on this manipulation, found no evidence of its effectiveness in terms of self-regard report, but accepted the association between the manipulated self-regard and influence scores as indicative that manipulated self-esteem was associated with influenceability!) In some studies which have attempted one or more of these important checks on the manipulation of self-esteem, the check was made either with idiosyncratic self-regard instruments having unknown psychometric properties, or with measures which seem patently inappropriate to the type of manipulation attempted (e.g., checking on the effects of a restricted manipulation

involving one aspect of the personality by using an instrument supposedly measuring over-all self-regard). Obviously these procedures
vitiate the interpretability of the experiment.

Continuing with the methodological questions which must be raised
in connection with allegedly manipulating self-regard, one must ask
questions of *discriminant* validity here, as already discussed in connection with alleged variations in chronic self-regard. Perhaps the
manipulation has not affected the subject's self-concept but rather his
or her anxiety level, or distractibility. No extant study provides us with a
way of evaluating this.

d. INFLUENCE MEASURES AND THEIR PSYCHOMETRIC PROPERTIES

Of course self-regard variables constitute only one part of what must
be measured in studies purporting to relate self-concept variables to
influenceability. Turning now to the other type of variables which must
be considered, i.e., the influence procedures and influenceability
measures, one must ask many of the same types of questions as we raised
about the self-regard variables. Were an idiosyncratic procedure and
measure used? If so, was sufficient information given regarding the
procedure and the psychometric properties of the instrument to enable
one to evaluate the possible contributions of method factors to the
outcome of the experiment and to compare the given experiment with
another?

Since many null or very weak trends are reported in the literature
on self-regard and influenceability, an extremely ambiguous situation is
created. Such confusing outcomes could be due to a variety of theory-
relevant factors (e.g., undetected curvilinear relationships between self-
regard scores and influence behavior scores, theoretically relevant but
undetected interactions with other variables), *or* they could be due to
the unreliability of one or another of the instruments entering into the
correlation. Generally speaking, published researches give little or no
information about the reliability of the influence measures. Concerning
popularly used change scores (before-after difference scores), one of the
reasons they are to be avoided is that they may well be unreliable. As
Stanley (1971) among others has shown, the attainment of highly
reliable change or difference scores depends upon having a high average
reliability of the two component scores and a low correlation between
the component scores. That these conditions obtain in the researches I

examined is either unknown or probably untrue. Therefore, the chances that these studies produced unreliable difference scores probably are great, and inferences of weak or no relationships may be made on the basis of correlation coefficients which are lowered by the unreliability of the influence measure.

Turning to considerations of *construct validity of influence measures,* note first that acquiescence response set and extremity response set may determine scores on some of the influence measures used. Since, as explained above, the self-regard scores used are also often susceptible to such response sets, the obtained correlations between self-regard measures and influenceability measures may well be artifacts of common response sets.

The most serious validity-related charge which can be leveled against most of the studies of influenceability and self-regard variables concerns the widespread use of difference or change scores to index influenceability. As Cronbach and Furby (1970) say about such scores, "Although the unsuitability of such scores has long been discussed, they are still employed, even by some otherwise sophisticated investigators" (p. 68). This statement certainly applies to research on influenceability. In the studies I examined, there appears to have been little or no recognition of the fact recently reiterated by Cronbach and Furby (1970) that " 'raw change' or 'raw gain' scores formed by subtracting pretest scores from posttest scores lead to fallacious conclusions, primarily because such scores are systematically related to any random error of measurement. . . . [Such] scores are rarely useful, no matter how they may be adjusted or refined. [p. 68] . . . there appears to be no need to use measures of change as dependent variables and no virtue in using them" (p. 78). Their article suggests appropriate ways to analyze posttest data in influence studies.

The reliability and validity problems associated with any kind of difference scores constitute only one reason why studies using a pretest-posttest design may lead to uninterpretable findings, as I explain below.

In addition to the problems of artifact associated with use of change scores as purported indexes of influence, it is extremely important to raise questions concerning the convergent and/or discriminant validity among the influence measures used in the various studies. Is the measure used in a given study unique to that study and not correlated with those used in other studies? If so, general statements about "influenceability" are unwarranted when based on one type of influence measure, and comparison and synthesis across studies is not justifiable. Or, if there are respectively different influenceability constructs, as McGuire (1968) argues, one needs evidence for the convergent validity of alternate measures of each respective kind and evidence for the discriminant validity of the alleged indices of each purportedly different kind. To my knowledge, researchers in this area have given little or no evidence of realizing that this problem exists. They have certainly not taken steps to establish convergent validity information of any sort.

An additional validity problem concerns the question whether the alleged influence-indicative response really stems from deliberate response control by the subject. That is, in many studies the subjects' behavior could be determined simply by their desire to save trouble or to give the experimenter the response they think the experimenter wants to hear, rather than indicating a theoretically relevant change of opinion or attitude. We have here exactly the same sort of problem which arose in the early "dirty-word" studies where the subjects simply reported something other than what they saw. Theoretical conclusions based on the obtained data of any kind of study in which this problem is not handled are, of course, discreditable. Obviously, we have the same problem on the side of the self-regard instruments, as has been very frequently noted. But at least the problem has been more frequently recognized as a possibility there, and control measures have been developed to some extent to encourage honesty of reporting and rule out this sort of theoretically irrelevant determinant of response.

To some extent, the subject's deliberate response manipulation of both the influence response and the self-regard response should be able to be minimized by providing anonymity to the subject, and this point was carefully noted in evaluating the methodological adequacy of any study.

e. OVER-ALL DESIGN AND PROCEDURE

The final category of methodological criteria I set up for evaluating studies in this area includes problems of over-all design and procedure.

Group Formation

One should first ask whether the groups were established randomly, perhaps supplemented by relevant matching techniques, but not primarily determined by matching techniques. It is well known that any method of matching may yield groups which, unbeknownst to the experimenter, are unequal in respects other than the matching criteria. The necessity for using random groups in experiments in social settings, as well as in other work, was stressed as early as 1957 by D. T. Campbell and repeated by D. T. Campbell and Stanley (1963). Despite the wide publicity given to these authors' cogent arguments, many influence studies have failed to fulfill their requirements.

Experimenter Effect

Experimenter effects are possible in any research, but this consideration seems especially important in experiments dealing with social influence. One looks to see whether the same experimenter ran both the experimental and control groups, and whether experimenters were counterbalanced across groups if more than one experimenter was used. According to Campbell and Stanley (1963), it is better to run individuals or small groups, counterbalancing experimenters and orders, to hold constant experimenter effects between or among conditions. A very large group of the studies I examined either did not give sufficient information to evaluate this aspect of their method, or clearly did not control for experimenter effects adequately.

Timing of Aspects of Procedure

In this sort of experiment it is especially germane to ask whether the timing of the experimental and control group treatments was exactly comparable. That is, were pretest times, posttest times, and elapsed times between tests the same for each group? Then, too, as Campbell and Stanley (1963) point out, if all experimental subjects are run as a group and all controls run as another group, even if time relationships are the same between pre- and posttest, factors other than the influence procedure might be affecting the behavior of the influence group, inasmuch as each group has a unique pre-post history as well as a different experimental treatment. To get around this problem one might run both groups simultaneously, if other aspects of procedure permit, or run individuals or small groups in the manner explained in the above paragraph.

I have found that most of the research reports either do not give enough information to tell whether the above criteria were met, or they fell short with respect to these criteria.

Pretest-Posttest Design Problems

An important point concerns limitations on the generalizability of the study stemming from possible effects of pretesting in the pretest-posttest design. D. T. Campbell (1957, p. 302) warned us long ago that taking the pretest might in some way sensitize the subject to the influence procedure, and this warning was repeated by D. T. Campbell and Stanley (1963, p. 188), with the additional possibility being mentioned that perhaps the pretest might dampen rather than enhance the effects of the influence procedure. After surveying a number of experiments which looked for pretest effects, Lana (1969) concluded "at least in attitude research, pretest measures, if they have any impact at all, depress the effect being measured" (p. 139). Regardless of the direction of the pretest's effects on the subjects' susceptibility to the influence procedure, it is extremely important to evaluate these pretest effects and take account of them in the results, or, if sufficient groups are not going to be run to evaluate pretest effects, one should avoid the pretest effects by using random groups and a posttest only design. (As I said earlier, pretests are not even desirable as bases for change scores, since change scores involve serious reliability and validity problems.)

Extant conformity studies are superior methodologically to extant persuasion studies in respect to the problems associated with pre-post comparisons. This is so because many of them ran only the equivalent of a posttest.

Need for No-Influence Control Groups

Typically the subjects have been divided into two or more levels of chronic or manipulated self-esteem, the influence manipulation performed, and the data then analyzed in one of two ways: correlations between self-esteem scores and influence (change) scores were computed, or mean influence (change) scores of different self-regard groups were computed and compared.

Levonian (1970a) has argued that we need no-influence control groups, on the grounds that opinion change and self-esteem might be correlated in the *absence* of any influence attempts, and such a possibility needs to be evaluated as a basis for interpreting findings obtained with an experimental (influence) group. He has pointed out that only one of the nine well-known studies he examined ran a no-message control group, and even this study failed to use it to make the above evaluations. The nine studies are Cox and Bauer (1964), Dabbs (1964), Gollob and Dittes (1965), Janis (1955), Janis and Field (1959), Leventhal and Perloe (1962), Nisbett and Gordon (1967), Silverman (1964), and Silverman, Ford, and Morganti (1966).

But why should the opinion change of no-message control subjects having a particular level of self-esteem be *in the direction of the position advocated to the influence group,* whereas the opinion change of no-message control subjects of another level of self-esteem show less such change or change in the direction away from the advocated position, simply as a function of time? One reason might lie in the possibility of artifact stemming from the measurement methods. That is, if the experiment is to indicate yielding, subjects must be chosen whose initial attitudes differ from those the experimenter intends to advocate, and, therefore, the expressed opinions would plausibly tend toward one end if a multistep attitude scale is used. This would be true of both the to-be-influenced group and the no-message control group if the latter were matched or comparable to the former, as they should be. One reason subjects might give a relatively extreme attitude answer initially is that their responses are affected by an extremity response set. Now, with the commonly used multistep Janis-Field Scale, "low self-esteem" could also be obtained partly through the influence of such an extreme response set. We would expect then, on the basis of our knowledge of statistical regression effects, that subjects with low self-esteem scores would tend to make somewhat less extreme opinion responses on retest even in the absence of a message, thus moving their opinion reports in the direction of the communicator's position. A negative r between self-esteem and opinion change could result even in the absence of a message. Alter-nately, if multistep self-esteem scales are worded so as to yield high self-esteem scores to subjects operating under an extremity response set, one would expect "high self-esteem" subjects to show more movement of opinion toward the experimenter's position. A positive r between self-esteem and opinion change would result. Of course this argument is speculative, and needs to be examined empirically. The only study which has attempted to do this is one by Levonian (1968) in which virtually identical correlations between self-esteem and change toward the advocated position occurred in the influence ($r = -.14$) and the no-influence ($r = -.12$) groups.

In reply to Levonian's (1970a) criticisms, Dittes (1970) argued that some of the studies had run controls in the sense that they presented differing kinds of communication, predicting and getting effects in different directions, according to the type of communication. But this still does not answer the question whether no experimental influence at all might result in relationships between self-esteem and influence scores similar to one, the other, or neither of the influence groups. Accordingly, the results of all studies using no no-influence control group are in this sense uninterpretable.

One problem with Levonian's study is his use of very complex change scores. Since, as I have discussed, change scores of any kind, including all those in the nine studies he criticized, are methodologically suspect, a better way to proceed would be to form self-regard groups, randomly assign one of each to various levels of influence procedure and to at least one appropriate no-influence control group.

(The reader who wishes to follow further the specific interchanges between Levonian and some of those authors he criticized is directed to Levonian [1970b, 1970c] and Silverman [1970].)

At first one might suppose that some of the Asch-type conformity studies would not need a no-influence control group, inasmuch as the perceptual judgments to be made are so obvious that any person would attain 100% accuracy if not subjected to conformity pressures. However, not all such tasks yield 100% accuracy, as Crutchfield (1955) showed with respect to a variety of tasks. Whenever subject accuracy varies in a conformity task done in the absence of conformity pressures, a control group is needed to evaluate the relationship between self-regard and task accuracy in that no-influence condition. This point is aptly illustrated by League and Jackson's (1964) study showing self-esteem and metronome-count accuracy to be correlated significantly in the absence of influence conditions. Since conformity in many Asch-type experiments is measured in terms of inaccurate responses, there being no way to unconfound the subject's yielding and his perceptual correctness in his accurate responses, the findings of League and Jackson (1964) indicate the need for a no-influence control in such Asch-type experiments.

Subjects' Suspiciousness

As I have already explained to some degree, another crucial factor in experiments purporting to examine relationships between social influence manipulations and self-regard is whether the subjects' suspicions have been aroused by any aspect of the procedure and, if so, what effects this might have in distorting the obtained relationship away from the "true" relationships between self-regard and influenceability. Few studies tried to check this point, which is especially worrisome when one considers the following: (a) occurrence of suspicion seems intuitively plausible even to a lay critic of this research; (b) Stricker, Messick, and Jackson (1967) showed that suspiciousness in this type of experiment was widespread, even among supposedly naïve high school students; (c) Stricker, Messick and Jackson's (1969) report suggests the possibility that influence manipulations possibly produce different relationships between self-reports and influence behaviors among suspicious as contrasted to nonsuspicious subjects (but some flaws in their study make this statement equivocal); (d) Z. Rubin and Moore (1971), using a different measure of suspiciousness from that of Stricker et al. (1969), found that suspicion and self-regard scores were directly correlated; (e) Ettinger, Marino, Endler, Geller, and Natziuk (1971) showed that suspicious subjects conformed in a Crutchfield-type of situation significantly less than those who were not and that suspicious subjects rated themselves higher than did nonsuspicious subjects on self-competence measures. The preceding points imply that suspiciousness must be controlled when looking for associations between self-regard variables and influence behaviors.

McGuire (1969) has examined at some length the various possible ways in which suspiciousness could affect behavior in an influence experiment, for example, by motivating a preparatory defense, by enhancing one's personal commitment to one's opinion, by distracting the subject so that the message perception could be affected. In the light of these a priori, empirical, and sophisticated analytical considerations, one cannot help but wonder how to interpret results from experiments in which this variable has not been taken into account, and therefore has not been controlled. In the experiments in which the researcher evidently gave some attention to this problem, the way in which suspiciousness was indexed is often described exceedingly vaguely, if at all, leaving the reader unable to evaluate the adequacy of its control.

B. OVERVIEW OF EXTANT STUDIES

1. Categories of Studies

Finally we come to the question of how to summarize the results of the studies as a group. As should already be apparent, it is extremely discouraging to consider this problem inasmuch as so many of the studies contain serious, even fatal, flaws.

It seemed possibly defensible methodologically and conceptually to divide the studies into subgroups according to the types of self-concept variables and the types of influenceability measures looked at in each study. Following McGuire's distinctions and elaborating on them a bit, one can conceive of several relevant possibilities on the self-regard side, namely: (a) chronic over-all self-regard (hereafter briefly called *chronic self-regard*); (b) manipulated over-all self-regard (hereafter briefly called *manipulated self-regard*); (c) chronic self-evaluation concerning a restricted aspect of one's personality, for example, one's ability at a certain task, or one's affiliativeness (hereafter briefly called *chronic specific self-evaluation*); (d) manipulated self-evaluation concerning a restricted aspect of one's personality, for example, experimentally contrived success or failure on a specific perceptual task (hereafter briefly called *manipulated specific self-evaluation*).

Again following McGuire's analysis, it seemed possibly defensible and useful to divide the studies into subgroups according to the type of influence procedure used. The available studies lent themselves to two categories: conformity, as earlier defined, and persuasibility (including persuasion by a source, forewarning experiments, and experimentally induced counterattitudinal behaviors of the subject).

Combining these categories, I have divided the studies into groups as follows. If a study belongs in more than one group, as is the case, for example, when both chronic and manipulated self-regard are varied, it is considered in each subgroup in which it could be classified.

Chronic Self-Regard and Conformity
Chronic Self-Regard and Persuasibility
Manipulated Self-Regard and Conformity
Manipulated Self-Regard and Persuasibility
Chronic Specific Self-Evaluation and Conformity
Chronic Specific Self-Evaluation and Persuasibility
Manipulated Specific Self-Evaluation and Conformity
Manipulated Specific Self-Evaluation and Persuasibility
Both Chronic and Manipulated Self-Regard and Conformity
Both Chronic and Manipulated Self-Regard and Persuasibility
Both Chronic Self-Regard and Manipulated Specific Self-Evaluation and Conformity

Both Chronic Self-Regard and Manipulated Specific Self-Evaluation and Persuasibility

a. CHRONIC SELF-REGARD AND CONFORMITY

Seventeen studies have come to my attention which appear to fall into this category, according to McGuire's definitions of chronic self-regard and conformity behavior cited at the beginning of this section. Not all these authors use the term conformity, but, in each instance, group pressure was instituted by way of informing the subject of another's opinion or achievement without giving arguments or explicit indication that the subject should concur (imitate, conform). As is so often true in influenceability research, one finds an emphasis on the Janis-Field Scales or modifications thereof, for example, the Rosenbaum and deCharms Scale. Of the 17 studies discussed in this section, 5 employed some version of the Janis-Field Scales. Superficially it might appear that the use of these scales would promote comparability among studies, but the fact is that no information is at hand which systematically evaluates the interchangeability (convergent validity) of these various forms. One researcher (Eagly, 1969) has used a modification designed to control for acquiescent response set. Otherwise the uncontrolled acquiescent response set in the Janis-Field Scales leaves open the troublesome possibility that any obtained associations between a Janis-Field Scale and conformity behavior may be an artifact of individual differences in the acquiescent response tendencies of the subjects, affecting scores on both instruments. In general, it appears that none of the Janis-Field versions has undergone sophisticated psychometric development about which there is sufficient published information to convince one that it has reasonably satisfactory construct validity for inferring chronic self-regard.

The other researchers used a wide variety of indexes of self-regard, most of them idiosyncratic except for Crutchfield (1955), Tuddenham (1959), and Appley and Moeller (1963), all of whom used the California Psychological Inventory; and Gelfand (1962) and Coopersmith (1967), who used the Coopersmith Self-Esteem Inventory (SEI). Unfortunately, however, Coopersmith's conformity data are presented only as a function of uninterpretable discrepancy scores between SEI scores and teacher reports of the subjects' supposed self-esteem. Thus we can infer nothing about the association of phenomenal self-regard and conformity. One of the idiosyncratic instruments (Singh & Prasad, 1973) appears to allow for the common operation of extremity response set on both the self-regard and conformity measure.

One respect in which the studies in this section are better than those in some other categories is that most of them used more than two levels of chronic self-regard, permitting one to look for curvilinear relationships. Usually three levels were used, but sometimes Pearson rs or biserial rs are computed. Unfortunately, when Pearson rs are used and weak or null results occur, as is typically the case, the possible occurrence of theoretically plausible curvilinear relations has not been checked.

With respect to conformity manipulations and conformity measures, there is great variation from study to study. The Asch-type situation is used in six studies, but with entirely different kinds and numbers of stimuli (e.g., lines in Coopersmith [1967], Tuddenham [1959], and Appley & Moeller [1963]; metronome clicks in Stricker, Messick, & Jackson [1967, 1968]; men's suits in Venkatesan [1968]). Other investigators manipulated the teacher's expressed picture preferences (G. S. Lesser & Abelson, 1959); peers' expressed picture preferences (Gelfand, 1962); shifts in judgments of color, creativity, and aesthetic qualities of photographs of art work after hearing the expressed opinions of an art major (Gergen & Bauer, 1967); shifts in judgments of amount of black in ambiguous stimuli following expressions of a bogus opinion (J. C. Moore & Krupat, 1971; Z. Rubin & Moore, 1971); matching guesses on the outcomes of a hypothetical horse race (Rosenbaum, Horne, & Chalmers, 1962); shifts in answers to a vaguely described questionnaire (Eagly, 1969); and answers to an undescribed "conformity" questionnaire (Singh & Prasad, 1973).

There is no available information about the possible convergent validity of the conformity scores from these alternate procedures; so one cannot assume they are even approximately equivalent indicators of the same construct.

Alternately, if task and source characteristics interact in some theoretically sensible way, as McGuire plausibly surmises they may, one would never be able to evaluate this from a comparative view of these studies. This is because there is no way to place the conformity tasks on any meaningful psychological dimension in order to compare the associations between self-regard scores and conformity scores across studies which vary systematically in task characteristics. (Of course, as I said before, the studies used varied measures of self-regard as well; this means that, even if conformity tasks could be dimensionalized across studies, the variations in self-regard from study to study would preclude systematic evaluation of possible interactions of source and task characteristics with self-regard as they affect conformity behaviors.)

When the Crutchfield (1955) or Asch-type procedures are used, the researcher has the advantage of not having to deal with change scores which are unacceptable on grounds of questionable reliability, construct validity, and pretest sensitization influences, as fully described above. There is no reason why the other conformity procedures could not also avoid this pitfall, and some of them do (e.g., Lesser & Abelson, 1959; Rosenbaum, Horne, & Chalmers, 1962). However, a number of the studies unnecessarily use pre-post difference scores of conformity, thereby vitiating the interpretability of their results involving association between conformity scores and self-regard scores (e.g., Eagly, 1969; Gergen & Bauer, 1967; J. C. Moore & Krupat, 1971; Stricker, Messick, & Jackson, 1968).

In Asch-type and Crutchfield conformity manipulations in which one object is clearly longer, brighter, or otherwise perceptually different, it is often assumed that the subject would make perfectly accurate judgments if not subjected to majority pressure from the experimental stooges present in the room or quoted by the experimenter. Thus, researchers apparently assume that no control group is needed and that conformity may be evaluated with reference to the degree of departure of the subject's responses from a baseline of 100% accuracy. Or, if the objects to be judged are identical, but said by the experimenter's confederates or a quoted source to differ, one might at first assume that chance alone (for example, 50–50 in the case of two stimuli) would be a proper baseline from which to evaluate the percent of times in which the subject's stimulus choice agrees with that of the majority stooges or reported norms. However, it is not safe to assume that this is the case in the absence of control observations. Whenever there is room for ambiguity or judgment of any kind in the subject's uninfluenced reactions to the stimuli, the only way to know how choices might vary as a function of self-regard in the absence of any conformity manipulation is to run a no-influence group. Only one of the studies examined in this category did use this proper base (Venkatesan, 1968).

As I have said above, it seems plausibly important to know whether subjects in conformity experiments are suspicious of such aspects of the study as its purpose and the "phoneyness" of the stooges' or bogus judgments. Relevant to this methodological point is the study of suspicion by Stricker, Messick, and Jackson (1967, 1968). Their research is particularly germane here since it is classifiable in the presently discussed area of conformity behavior as a function of self-regard. They found a high incidence of suspicion even though their subjects were relatively naïve high school students, and they report an apparently somewhat different pattern of correlation of self-report scores with conformity scores among suspicious as compared to nonsuspicious subjects. This report alerts us to possible sources of uninterpretability in all the other studies which either did not control for suspicion or did not publish their control procedures. It must be noted, however, that Stricker, Messick, and Jackson's study cannot be taken as definitive regarding the ways, if any, in which suspicion might moderate self-regard associations with conformity. This lack of definitiveness depends upon the following facts: (a) they used change scores of conformity which, as explained above, are not psychometrically defensible; (b) they produced a large array of correlations; and, in the absence of cross-validation, one has no basis for evaluating the replicability of either the null or significant ones. However, since their study does show that suspicion is widespread and that there is a possibility that the association of self-regard variables with conformity behavior may be different for suspicious and unsuspicious subjects, one must be skeptical in interpreting any study which has not dealt with this control problem. This is the case in most of the studies reported below.

Of the 17 studies 8 were characterized by so many serious flaws that they do not seem to me to warrant attempts at substantive summary and speculative psychological interpretations. These 8 are: Coopersmith (1967); Eagly (1969); Gergen and Bauer (1967); J. C. Moore and Krupat (1971); Z. Rubin and Moore (1971); Singh and Prasad (1973); Stricker, Messick, and Jackson (1967); and Stricker, Messick, and Jackson (1968). On pages 590–592 I give specific criticisms of studies by Crutchfield (1955), Tuddenham (1959), and Appley and Moeller (1963)—all of whom report no significant association between Self-Acceptance scores on the California Psychological Inventory and Asch-type yielding behavior. The remaining 6 either do not give adequate information on some points or fail to measure up to some of the methodological criteria specified, but in some parts, at least they are relatively more adequate than the others and will be briefly mentioned substantively.

G. S. Lesser and Abelson (1959), used an idiosyncratic measure of self-esteem in young children (a measure about which inadequate psychometric information is given) and an influence procedure in which children told which of successive pairs of pictures of familiar objects they liked best. In one study, in which the teacher expressed her judgments first, conformity was measured in terms of number of agreements of the child's response with the teacher's response. There was no evidence of significant *r*s between these conformity scores and the self-regard scores. However, no evaluation of nonlinearity is given to help one to interpret the meaning of the consistently insignificant *r*s. In a second study, a first step was run in which the teacher elicited the children's preferences first and then either agreed or disagreed with them. In the next step of this second study, she expressed her preference within each of 14 pairs of pictures before the child expressed his preference. It was only after the teacher agreed with the child's preference in the first step that subjects having low self-regard exhibited significantly more conformity in the second step, as compared to the amount of conformity exhibited in the second step by the high self-esteem subjects. This finding was obtained in two replications. The authors speculated that the low self-esteem child reacts sensitively to the approval he seeks from others and is predisposed to be conforming only if the communicator indicates to him the likely possibility they will agree with each other.

Gelfand (1962) looked at children's picture preferences as affected by a peer confederate who chose the picture in each of several pairs previously shown to be the pair member which was less preferred by a pretest sample. She found no association of chronic self-regard, as measured by Sears's test, and conformity in terms of picture-preference scores.

Costanzo (1970) used a specially devised self-blame scale about which he gives only the statement that it had "content validity." Split-half reliabilities for each of his 4 age groups (7 years to 21 years) were $-.77$, $-.82$, $-.86$, $-.84$ [*sic*]. His use of 3 subgroups on the self-blame scale permits one to evaluate whether there might be curvilinear relationships between self-blame and conformity if one assumes the 3 points covered a sufficiently wide range. The influence procedure was a modification of Crutchfield's technique, using line judging. So far as one can tell, complete accuracy should have been expected in the absence of influence procedures, since he reports using "the simple straight line stimuli described by Asch." The conformity score was the "number of times a subject's choice corresponded with the erroneous judgments of the simulated peer majority" (p. 369). Nothing is said about checking on the suspiciousness of the subjects. An analysis of variance found a significant main effect of self-blame. In each of 4 age groups there was a linear negative relationship (not a curvilinear relationship) between self-blame and percent [sic] conformity.

Although Rosenbaum, Horne, and Chalmers (1962) labeled their dependent variable "imitation" or "matching," their influence procedure appears to fulfill the McGuire definition of conformity procedures. Self-regard was varied by establishing high and low groups on the Rosenbaum and deCharms scale, based on the Janis-Field Scales. The use of only two steps precluded looking for possible curvilinear relationships. Also, positive associations between Janis-Field scores and matching behavior could be a function of acquiescent response set influencing both self-regard and conformity scores rather than being a relation between self-regard and conformity.

The conformity procedure consisted of getting the subject A to guess the winning horse in a series of simulated horse races. Subject A first heard the alleged opinion of another subject, B, before making his own guess. In each of three reinforcement conditions, respectively, the subject A was rewarded (told his guess was correct) .80 or .50 or .20 of the times he chose the same horse as subject B had ostensibly chosen.

Only in the .80 reinforcement condition did low self-regard subjects show a significantly stronger matching tendency than did the high self-regard subjects to subject B's choice. Nothing is said in the report regarding the subjects' suspiciousness or control of suspiciousness.

DeCharms and Rosenbaum (1960) used the Rosenbaum and deCharms Scale (based on the Janis-Field Scales) to divide naval aviation cadets into only two levels of chronic self-regard, precluding the search for curvilinear relationships. The Asch-type influence task involved 24 trials of identifying which of 3 aircraft silhouettes matched a standard. Low self-regard subjects showed significantly higher conformity scores. However, the use of a self-regard scale susceptible to the acquiescent response set means that the obtained association may be an artifact of common acquiescent tendencies in the self-regard and conforming situations. (See the section on chronic specific self-evaluation and conformity, and the section on chronic self-regard and manipulated specific self-evaluation and conformity for results regarding these experimenters' manipulations of specific self-evaluations.)

Venkatesan (1968) used 23 Janis-Field items to measure self-regard and an Asch-type situation as his influence procedure. The objects to be judged by the naïve subjects were 3 identical men's suits, labeled A, B, C. In each group of 4 persons, the naïve subject made his choice of "best" suit after hearing 3 physically present experimental confederates choose B as the best suit. Post-experimental interviews revealed 7 suspicious subjects whose data were then eliminated from the published data analyses. When the subjects were divided into high and low self-regard on the basis of the Janis-Field scores, there was only a non-significant trend for greater conformity behavior (choice of the B suit) among low self-regard subjects. When 3 self-regard groups were formed (high, low, very low), there was a slight trend toward curvilinearity, with low self-regard subjects conforming more than high or very low, but this trend, too, was not significant. A no-influence control group was used as the basis from which to evaluate whether the percent of B choices was greater under the experimental as opposed to the control conditions, but the control group was not used to evaluate the proportion of B choices by high and low self-regard subjects under experimental and control conditions. Since the 3 suits were identical, it seems plausible that such analysis of the control group data is unnecessary for this study.

Insofar as these studies can form a basis for any psychological speculations, the trend seems to be for weak, often nonsignificant, associations to occur between low self-regard scores and high conformity scores. None of the studies found significant evidence of curvilinearity of the relationship between self-regard scores and conformity scores. Four of them did not permit looking for possible curvilinearity. The study with the most clear-cut results (Costanzo, 1970) yielded a linear relationship.

Definitive or strongly defensible comparative analysis of the studies is obviously impossible. In a strictly speculative vein, one might suggest that the lack of comparability among the results could be partly related to whether each of the respectively used self-regard measures could sensibly be expected to index a self-attitude having anything to do with the conformity behavior studied. Lesser and Abelson's (1959) idiosyncratic measure of self-regard involved children's feelings of being accepted by their peers, whereas their measure of conformity was degree of concurring with a teacher's preferences. Venkatesan (1968) used a supposedly over-all self-regard measure (Janis-Field items) coupled with a very specific conformity procedure (judgments of quality in men's suits). It seems plausible that one's over-all feelings about self might have little to do with one's confidence or ego-involvement in such a specific area of judgment, especially when the judgments are obviously so "subtle," the suits being identical. Costanzo (1970), who found the strongest associations between self-regard and conformity, used a self-regard measure which seems most plausibly aimed at a self-attitude relevant to conformity, namely, self-blame attitude. In short, one possibility is that self-evaluations which are not relevant to the conformity task should not be expected to determine one's behavior on the conformity task.

I return to this point later when presenting results regarding specific self-evaluations and conformity behaviors.

So far as the experiments by Costanzo (1970), Venkatesan (1968), deCharms and Rosenbaum (1960), and Rosenbaum et al. (1962) are concerned, another possible difference among them is possibly worthy of consideration: The conformity tasks in the Costanzo experiment and the experiments by Rosenbaum and associates involved multiple responses. The Costanzo and the deCharms and Rosenbaum experiments showed clear-cut associations between self-regard scores and conformity scores, and the Rosenbaum et al. experiment showed clear-cut association of self-regard and conformity under the high rein-forcement-for-conformity condition. By contrast, the Venkatesan experiment, which yielded null associations between self-regard and conformity scores, involved only one response per subject. Accordingly, one might reasonably expect the conformity scores in the first two experiments to have higher reliability than the conformity scores in the Venkatesan experiment. Of course, if self-regard and conformity variables are "really" related, the obtained correlation of conformity scores with self-regard scores will not reveal this if either measure is highly unreliable. The fact that we can only speculate on this point is a good example of why it is necessary to report psychometric information about both the self-regard and conformity measures if one wishes one's experiment to stand a chance of being interpretable by itself or in comparison with other experiments.

b. Chronic Self-Regard and Persuasibility

I have examined 22 studies which fall into this category, as the 2 terms, chronic self-regard and persuasibility were defined at the beginning of this section. Sixteen of these varied chronic self-regard only, and 6 involved both chronic and manipulated self-regard.

Regarding the latter 6, I consider here only that aspect of the study involving chronic self-regard.

In general, the group of published results is characterized either by weak or null associations between self-regard and persuasibility scores, or by complex and unreplicated interactions. However, in my opinion, none of them with the possible exception of Deaux's (1972) second study will sustain a psychological interpretation of its reported results. Naturally, then, no meaningful comparison or synthesis of these can be made. Some of my reasons for this disheartening evaluation follow.

Of these 22 studies 13 used the Janis-Field Scales or some modification thereof, with the intrinsic sources of artifact and the undeveloped evidence for construct validity described earlier in this section. The other studies used idiosyncratic instruments to measure self-regard, providing no adequate information in support of their construct validity or other relevant psychometric properties. Many used only 2 levels of the self-regard measure, precluding a search for curvilinearity, or they presented rs without looking into the question of curvilinearity. If curvilinearity of functions obtains, this could account for the null findings, but these limitations of design and analysis preclude evaluating this particular possible interpretation of the null findings. There was virtually no overlap between studies so far as the persuasion manipulation is concerned or in the influence-response scoring used. In almost every case, no or extremely inadequate information was given about the relevant psychometric properties of the influence measures. The possibility of common susceptibility to extreme response sets or acquiescent response sets between the self-regard and the influence measures occurred frequently. All but 2 of these studies used a pre-post design and some type of change score. Naturally, then, the problems of pretest effects on influence reactions, the unreliability of change scores, and most important, the invalidity of change scores characterize these studies. Two of the studies had a no-influence control group, but in one of them it was not used properly to evaluate the association between self-regard and influence scores in the absence of experimentally manipulated influence. Deaux (1972), in her second experiment, used two issues, one subjected to forewarning of influence procedures, one not. Each issue served as a no-influence control issue for half the subjects. Although she did not compute change scores from a pre-post design, her computed persuasion scores are not entirely clear. Having found that the variance [sic] for control issue scores did not differ "between groups" (presumably between self-regard groups), she subtracted the *mean* control-issue score from the influence-issue score of each subject to obtain that subject's persuasibility score (anticipatory change score). Since this amounts to subtracting a constant from each influence-issue score, it appears that the usual problems with difference scores do not obtain here. In any case, she found no significant association between chronic self-regard and anticipatory opinion change across three levels of chronic self-regard.

A number of investigators were concerned with interactions between self-regard variables and other variables in determining influence responses. Unfortunately, since other aspects of their procedure were so flawed as to preclude interpretation, their search for such refinements was not fruitful. A possible exception to this is Deaux's (1972) second study, discussed below in the section which examines interactions between manipulated and chronic self-regard in determining influence behavior.

Applying the criteria outlined earlier in this section, I could list other common flaws in these studies, but the ones already cited preclude interpretations of the reported results even if the unmentioned flaws were not thought to be serious.

The 13 excluded studies varying only chronic self-regard are: Bither and Wright (1973); Dabbs (1964); Dabbs and Leventhal (1966); Glass, Lavin, Henchy, Gordon, Mayhew, and Donohoe (1969); Janis (1954); Janis (1955); Janis and Field (1959); Janis and Rife (1959); Kumpf and Götz-Marchand (1973); Leventhal and Perloe (1962); Levonian (1968); Linton and Graham (1959); Silverman, Ford, and Morganti (1966).

The three excluded studies which varied not only chronic self-regard but also chronic specific self-evaluation are: T. Bell (1967); Cox and Bauer (1964); Lehmann (1970).

The five excluded studies which varied not only chronic self-regard but also manipulated over-all self-regard are: Gollob and Dittes (1965); C. W. Greenbaum (1966); Nisbett and Gordon (1967); Stimpson (1970); and Zellner (1970).

The studies by Janis (1954, 1955); Janis and Field (1959); Janis and Rife (1959); and Linton and Graham (1959) have been criticized in detail in Wylie (1961, pp. 153–154 and 157–159).

c. Manipulated Self-Regard and Conformity

In Gelfand's (1962) study, over-all self-regard was ostensibly manipulated by making subjects either fail or succeed on a variety of tasks. Control subjects did no tasks. Postmanipulation ratings of self-favorability confirmed the effectiveness of the manipulation. In the conformity task, the child subjects expressed preferences for one picture in each of a series of pairs of pictures. On each trial, the subject chose after a confederate peer had expressed a preference for the member of the pair previously shown to be the less preferred picture. Significantly more conformity responses were shown by the low self-regard (failure) subjects.

Another study which might conceivably be classifiable in this category is McMillen's (1971) experiment. The classification may be questionable since the two behaviors I have taken to be conformity behaviors are: (a) use of a tip that a B response on an important multiple choice examination is the most frequently correct response; and (b) the subjects "compliant behavior" at the end of the experiment, measured in terms of whether the subject agreed to do the experimenter a favor by staying afterwards to grade other multiple choice examinations ostensibly completely unrelated to the experiment.

If one is willing to accept either of these operations as falling within the definition of conformity procedures, then one must consider the question of whether the chronic self-regard of the groups was held constant when varying manipulated self-regard. The latter was done by assigning subjects randomly to one of two groups (a) those receiving bogus feedback from some CPI Scales to the effect that their personality characteristics were very favorable; (b) those receiving no feedback. Since random assignment to these groups was done, chronic self-regard was supposedly equated between the groups; yet, with Ns of 22 per self-esteem group, this is open to doubt, and no information from actual CPI scores is given to enable one to check this point. Moreover, there is no reported check on the effectiveness of the manipulation of self-regard.

In any event, manipulated self-regard was unrelated to the number of B responses the subject made on the psychology-information test. Also, there were no significant differences in compliance (agreement to help the experimenter) between groups having or not having experienced self-esteem manipulation. However, subjects who had received no special bogus "boost" to their self-regard tended to comply (agree to help the experimenter) when they had received the tip on how to succeed on the test, but not to comply (not to agree to help the experimenter) when they had not received tips. The author wishes to infer from this that compliance is a mechanism by which subjects not having specially high self-esteem can restore their self-esteem after transgression by complying with the experimenter's request to do him a favor. However, the procedure and data analyses do not preclude several alternate explanations, as the author points out.

Obviously, the above two studies are not open to comparison or synthesis.

d. MANIPULATED SELF-REGARD AND PERSUASIBILITY

Five of the studies I have examined appear to fall into this category. One of these used the questionable pre-post design to look at change scores as a function of presented arguments (Gollob & Dittes, 1965). This study has already been evaluated above under "Chronic Self-Regard and Persuasibility," where it was judged to be uninterpretable due to many methodological flaws enumerated there. The remaining four studies involve either anticipatory attitude change procedures (Dinner, Lewkowicz, & Cooper, 1972) or inducing subjects to engage in counterattitudinal behavior (two studies by Deaux, 1972; one by Cooper & Duncan, 1971).

All four tried to manipulate the subjects' over-all self-regard by giving bogus feedback on the basis of self-report personality tests. Cooper and Duncan (1971) and Dinner, Lewkowicz, and Cooper (1972) made a check on this manipulation and presented some evidence that the procedure had been effective. However, the means used to check were either idiosyncratic, with no psychometric information given, or of questionable relevance. Deaux (1972) gives no data relevant to this point. All the studies used a no-self-esteem manipulation control group, but only Deaux (1972) in her first study tried to establish three levels of manipulated self-regard as well; so only her data would lend themselves to a search for curvilinear relationships between self-regard and persuasibility.

All but one (Deaux's second experiment) used some form of no-influence control group. Unfortunately, however, these groups could be employed only to evaluate what opinion reports would be expected in the absence of influence procedures. These control groups do not enable one to evaluate whether *attitudes and self-regard levels are correlated in the absence of influence procedures,* since the no-influence control groups were not subdivided with regard to manipulated self-esteem levels. Thus, no firm conclusions can be drawn as to whether the influence procedure used in the experiment played a part in whatever relationship, null or significant, was obtained between manipulated self-regard and opinion scores. This very seriously limits the worth of all four studies.

A good feature of these experiments is that they avoided the pitfalls of the pre-post design, fully described above in the section on problems of research design and procedure. Two of them commendably used attitude ratings per se as their dependent variable measure of persuasibility, but Dinner, Lewkowicz, and Cooper (1972) and Deaux (1972) in her second experiment used a discrepancy score. That is, Dinner et al. subtracted each experimental subject's score on a given attitude scale from the mean attitude score on that scale made by the no-influence control group, whereas Deaux subtracted each subject's score on the experimental issue from the *mean* score of all subjects on the control issues (i.e., the issues not related to the experimental manipulation). This type of discrepancy score does not appear to be subject to the same interpretational ambiguities as the pre-post difference scores, since each subject's score had, in effect, a constant subtracted from it. At the same time, one wonders why the subtraction procedure was used at all, inasmuch as the results of data analysis should have been the same for the original experimental attitude scores as for the discrepancy scores.

So far as *main effects of manipulated self-regard on influenceability scores* are concerned, the studies are in agreement: No such effects were reported from any of the four experiments, each researcher using a different means of manipulating self-regard, and each a different influence procedure. Curvilinearity cannot be ruled out as an explanation of null results in the three studies which used only two levels of manipulated self-regard, but there is no evidence of curvilinearity in the results of Deaux's first experiment which used three levels of self-regard.

Pending further search for curvilinearity using self-regard and attitude measures with better demonstrated psychometric properties, it appears that there is probably no relationship between "over-all" self-regard and influence behavior following forewarning or counterattitudinal behavior. If null results continue to be reported when experimental methods are improved, two plausible interpretations might be offered: Perhaps the manipulation of "over-all" self-regard has not resulted in a sufficiently wide range of individual differences in self-regard, precluding the obtaining of significant relationships with influence behavior scores. Or perhaps the sort of over-all self-regard which is supposedly being manipulated is of little relevance to influence behavior regarding particular opinion issues. Instead, self-perceived competency to judge the particular issues, or self-perceived ideas as to how demeaning it would be to be swayed by arguments might have more to do with influence behavior under anticipatory or counterattitudinal manipulation conditions.

If main effects are not significant, what about interactions? Actually, it was *interactions which were the focus of interest* of these experimenters. Deaux (1972) reports that, in her first experiment, there was a significant interaction between source prestige and manipulated self-regard, with low self-regard subjects showing greater effects from high- than from low-prestige sources. However, in her second experiment, this interaction was not replicated. Deaux also looked at interactions between chronic and manipulated self-regard and her results are reported in the section dealing with this topic below.

Cooper and Duncan (1971) based their experiment on Aronson's (1969) view that cognitive dissonance per se does not affect attitudinal behavior; the dissonance will be effective only if it involves a discrepancy between the counterattitudinal behavior and the person's favorable self-concept. Aronson further assumes that, in the absence of self-regard manipulation, most persons have chronic favorable levels of self-regard. Cooper and Duncan said that Aronson's theory would predict that the amount of incentive offered the subject for counterattitudinal behavior would interact with the subject's manipulated self-regard level in determining the subject's attitudinal reports, with high self-regard subjects showing most influence effects when operating under low incentives for making a counterattitudinal speech. Their own prediction was that their results would *not* support Aronson's view, i.e., would not show this interaction. Although they obtained the negative main effect of size of incentive, their results did fail to support Aronson's idea, because they obtained no interaction between manipulated self-regard level and size of incentive. Cooper and Duncan (1971) themselves point out, however, that this failure to find the interaction does not definitely refute Aronson's theoretical point inasmuch as there was no direct measure of how the subjects felt about their level of personal integrity, the aspect of self-concept Aronson had thought would be especially implicated in dissonances which lead to larger attitude changes under lower incentives for performing counterattitudinal behaviors.

Using the anticipatory attitude change technique, Dinner, Lewkowicz, and Cooper (1972) based their hypotheses on McGuire and Millman's (1965) self-esteem explanations of subjects' behaviors in such situations. Dinner et al. predicted that manipulated self-regard would interact with familiarity of issue in the following way: high self-regard subjects were expected to show more anticipatory attitude change on familiar than on unfamiliar issues because this would enable them to protect their self-esteem by not having to succumb to the expected pressure regarding familiar issues (issues about which they feel they should already have well-founded opinions). The low self-regard subjects, on the other hand, were expected to show more anticipatory attitude change on unfamiliar rather than familiar issues, since, having less self-regard to protect, they would not mind the possibility of later giving in on a familiar issue. The predicted interaction was obtained.

In summary, so far as interactions are concerned, the above experiments showed one which was not able to be replicated, one which was obtained as predicted but which has not yet been replicated, and one which was predicted by Aronson's theory but was not obtained. Thus, essentially nothing can be said about interactions of manipulated self-regard and influence manipulations in determining attitude expressions. Again, this yield of null or unreplicated interactions may be a function of psychometrically inadequate or inappropriate instruments, as just explained in discussing the possible explanations of null main effects.

e. Chronic Specific Self-Evaluation and Conformity

In section B-1-a on chronic self-regard and conformity, section B-1-c on manipulated self-regard and conformity, and section B-1-g on manipulated specific self-evaluation and conformity, I make the point that conformity as a function of self-evaluation might more sensibly be expected to occur when the type of self-evaluation being examined in the research is not over-all self-regard but rather a type of self-evaluation specifically relevant to the type of task in which conformity behavior is supposed to occur. The findings from the three sections above suggest that these expectations have merit, inasmuch as conformity was not found to be associated with chronic or manipulated over-all self-regard, but was found in some studies to be negatively related to manipulated self-evaluation along specific dimensions which were relevant to the characteristics of the conformity task. Thus, one might expect that *chronic specific* dimensions of self-evaluation might be associated with conformity behaviors if the specific self-evaluation dimension under consideration is relevant to the conformity task.

As it happens, the studies in the section on manipulated specific self-evaluation and conformity are all concerned with manipulating specific self-evaluations of *abilities* presumably relevant to the conformity task. By contrast, the studies in the present section do not concern themselves with chronic specific self-evaluations of ability, but rather with chronic specific self-evaluation of restricted personality predispositions such as "tolerance" or "responsibility" (Crutchfield, 1955), or Murray needs (McDavid & Sistrunk, 1964), or adjectival self-descriptions from the ACL (F. Barron, 1953, 1968).

Unfortunately, the eight studies in this category which have come to my attention have too many methodological shortcomings to allow determining whether some kind(s) of chronic specific self-evaluations are associated with conformity behavior. For example, in Crutchfield's (1955) historic paper, he showed that reliable individual difference scores in conformity behavior could be obtained with his apparatus and procedure using a wide variety of stimuli, and he used a no-influence control group to evaluate the degree to which conformity pressures had determined the answers of subjects operating under such pressures. Unfortunately, he does not give any information as to whether individual differences in chronic specific self-evaluation are associated with performance in the tasks under no-influence conditions. For reasons explained in section A-4 above, this sort of control is essential for evaluating the correlations between specific self-report scores and conformity scores obtained under influence conditions when 100% accuracy cannot be expected in the absence of influence. Moreover, Crutchfield is vague about the way he checked on his manipulations and the suspicions of his subjects. Most damaging to the interpretibility of his findings, however, is the fact that he obviously correlated his conformity scores with scores from numerous personality dimensions—both self-report and observer-evaluated personality scores. He reports a few samples of these correlations which sound psychologically plausible. But there is no way of knowing how many correlation coefficients he computed and to what degree the variables involved in each were mutually overlapping; hence there is no way of evaluating whether the "significant" ones he reports by way of "examples" should be interpreted as meeting satisfactory standards of statistical significance.

Barron (1953, 1968), Tuddenham (1959), DiVesta and Cox (1960), Endler (1961b), Moeller and Applezweig (1957), and Appley and Moeller (1963) (the latter 2 publications reporting on the same 41 subjects)—all examined Asch-type conformity scores in relation to specific self-evaluations. When 100% accuracy could reasonably be expected in the absence of influence, there was no need to run no-influence control groups; but this expectation was not appropriate in every study. Only Moeller and Applezweig (1957) and DiVesta and Cox (1960) attempted to take account of the subjects' suspicions, and all of the researchers made many significance tests using the same subjects without regard to correlations among the variables used in the significance tests and without cross-validation. Izard's (1960c) study employing a somewhat different "conformity" procedure (in some ways more akin to suggestion techniques) is also open to the above criticisms. Moeller and Applezweig (1957) reported on associations between yielding and score patterns on their Behavior Interpretation Inventory which is (according to a personal communication from Applezweig) intended to measure aspects of the unconscious self-concept. (See Wylie, 1961, pp. 157 and 261; and Wylie, 1974, pp. 259-260, regarding this instrument.) Their results relating scores from this instrument to yielding behavior have not been replicated. Appley and Moeller (1963) compared the essentially null results reported in their 1963 publication with findings reported by Tuddenham, DiVesta and Cox, Endler, and Izard, insofar as the self-evaluation instruments used (EPPS, CPI) permitted tentative comparisons. They also noted that only 10 out of 105 reported correlations in the compared studies differed significantly from zero, and they conclude, "It must be expected that attempts to replicate successful predictions of acquiescence from measures of supposedly enduring personality characteristics must meet with only occasional and adventitious success" (p. 290).

McDavid and Sistrunk (1964) also correlated Asch-type conformity scores with 15 Edwards Personal Preference Schedule scores, 6 Gordon Survey of Interpersonal Values scores, 10 Guilford-Zimmerman Temperament Survey scores, 8 Leary Interpersonal Check List scores and 1 "social reinforcement scale" score. (See Wylie, 1974, pp. 213-223, for an evaluation of the Interpersonal Check List.) Coefficients are presented separately for soluble conformity tasks and insoluble conformity tasks. Each of the preceding coefficients was computed separately for the male sample, the female sample, and the combined male and female sample. They give extensive psychological discussion of the correlations of the self-report variables with conformity scores, paying no attention to the fact that only 16% of the 79 combined coefficients were significant at the .05 level or better. Obviously, there is no way of evaluating without cross-validation which of these was "significant" by chance alone, especially given the fact that many of the self-report variables were undoubtedly intercorrelated.

Thus I conclude that the question of the relationship, if any, between chronic specific self-evaluation and conformity behavior remains inadequately explored, but the possibilities of obtaining replicable nonnull associations are slight, at least with the specific self-evaluation scores used thus far.

f. Chronic Specific Self-Evaluation and Persuasibility

It seems reasonable that one's specific self-evaluations of personality aspects relevant to evaluating certain types of issues would influence one's willingness to be persuaded by arguments presented by an expert source. This is even more plausible than to expect over-all chronic self-regard to show a relation to persuasibility regarding a wide variety of issues—the assumption made by researchers whose studies are classified in the section on chronic self-regard and persuasibility.

Four studies classifiable in this category have come to my attention: Bell (1967), Berkowitz and Lundy (1957), Cox and Bauer (1964), and Lehmann (1970). Unfortunately, as I explained in the section on chronic self-regard and persuasibility, where part of the Cox and Bauer study was also considered, their experiment was so seriously flawed as to be uninterpretable. The psychometric properties of the instruments used, the use of pre-post design and ambiguous change scores, and the absence of an appropriate no-influence control group, are among the reasons this study cannot sustain interpretation. Lehmann (1970), also listed in the section on chronic self-regard and persuasibility, involved a measure of chronic specific self-evaluation (predispositional anxiety) as well as a measure of chronic self-regard. However, this study was characterized by all the flaws of the Cox and Bauer study. (Although Lehmann did run a no-influence control group, it was not used to examine the relationships between self-reported predispositional anxiety and opinion shifts among subjects receiving no message.) In Bell's (1967) study of 234 car buyers, an idiosyncratic self-report index of customers' "specific self-confidence" about their car-buying ability was correlated with a persuasibility score comprised of a combination of their own and their salesmen's estimates of how much influenced they were by their salesmen. The obtained null association is uninterpretable and is actually surprising in view of the opportunity for contamination between the measures of specific self-evaluation and persuasibility.

Berkowitz and Lundy's (1957) study is also open to so many criticisms that it does not seem to warrant summary or interpretation; for example, the use of pre-post design and uninterpretable change scores, the absence of a no-influence control, the possibilities of influence of suspicion plausibly aroused by concomitant administration of self-report measures and the attitude items later to be used in the influence manipulation. In addition, a number of crucial items of their procedure are not described or are vaguely described, so that other possible sources of artifact cannot be evaluated.

I must conclude that, so far as I know, the question of the relationship between chronic specific self-evaluations and persuasibility are still unexplored by scientifically defensible research.

g. Manipulated Specific Self-Evaluation and Conformity

In the section on conformity behavior as a function of chronic self-regard level, all of the studies reported no association between chronic self-regard scores and conformity scores. As I said there, this null trend could be due to unreliability or invalidity of the instruments used to measure the self-regard variables; or it could be due to curvilinear relationships obtaining, but not being discernible, given the two-step division of manipulated self-regard characteristics of the experiments; or it could be indicative of the fact that a person's over-all level of self-regard is psychologically irrelevant to his conforming behavior on very specific tasks such as conformity experiments employ. That the latter interpretation may be correct is strongly suggested by the group of studies which look at manipulations of specific aspects of the subjects' self-evaluations in relation to conformity behavior on tasks which are obviously relevant to the manipulated specific aspect of self-evaluation. The methodologically more adequate studies of this kind tend to yield some type of negative relationships between level of manipulated specific self-evaluation and conformity behavior, although these effects may appear as interactions rather than main effects.

Of the eight relevant studies which have come to my attention, six seem to be sufficiently sound methodologically to warrant some substantive summarizing: deCharms and Rosenbaum (1960); Endler, Wiesenthal, and Geller (1972); Ettinger, Marino, Endler, Geller, and Natziuk (1971); Fagen (in Diggory, 1966); R. L. Klein and Birren (1973); and Misra (1973). Each of these attempted to manipulate a different specific kind of self-evaluation, and each used a different task.

All but R. L. Klein and Birren (1973) reported some indication from a post-manipulation check that the groups of subjects given different specific self-evaluation manipulations did differ regarding their specific self-evaluations.

In four of the six studies summarized below, the task used in the procedure for manipulating specific self-evaluation was the same or closely related to the conformity task. However, Misra (1973) used a star-point-counting task to manipulate specific self-evaluation and an Asch line-judging task for the conformity procedure, while deCharms and Rosenbaum (1960) manipulated self-evaluated leadership ability and judgments of airplane silhouettes in an Asch-type situation. Obviously maximum similarity between the self-evaluation task and the conformity task gives the greatest chance for manipulated specific self-evaluation to be relevant to conformity task performance. On these grounds, Misra's and deCharms and Rosenbaum's findings would be least expected to show a significant relationship between level of manipulated specific self-evaluation and conformity behavior, and they are the only ones which report null findings. High similarity also means that suspiciousness would be expected to be maximum. Suspiciousness was evaluated to some extent in all the studies, and it does not seem plausible that uncontrolled suspicions could account for the significant findings.

An Asch-type or Crutchfield-type influence procedure was used in each of the studies. The adequacy of no-influence control data is important in this technique as in any influence procedure. What association is there between the relevant specific self-evaluation and conformity scores in the absence of any influence manipulations? None of the studies is entirely satisfactory in regard to answering this question. Accordingly, all have their interpretibility limited to a greater or lesser degree. Ettinger et al. (1971) had previously established that 95% accuracy should be expected on their manipulation and critical trials unless influence manipulations intervened, and deCharms and Rosenbaum (1960) reported 100% accuracy under no-influence conditions. Thus it seems unlikely that there could be any intrinsic relationships between conformity (accuracy) scores and differences in specific self-evaluation in a no-influence control group. Fagen (in Diggory, 1966) ran his subjects through alternate subject-alone and subject-in-a-group sessions. He showed that there was clearly more conformity (wrong answers) in the group situation. It is not possible from his published report, however, to say whether self-evaluation correlates differently with conformity (accuracy) within each no-influence situation as compared to within each influence session. R. L. Klein and Birren's (1973) report is too brief to permit evaluation of the adequacy of their control observations on this point. Endler et al. (1972) did not run a no-influence control; so it is impossible to evaluate the extent to which subjects' answers to their critical questions would have been in error and whether these error levels would correspond to levels of manipulated self-evaluation among subjects not receiving group pressure toward the wrong response. Misra (1973) ran no no-influence control, but since he used the Asch lines, one would expect 100% accuracy in the absence of influence, and, therefore, probably no correlation between manipulated self-evaluation and conformity in the absence of influence procedures would be likely.

As for the results of these studies, three of them report significant main effects of manipulated specific self-evaluation on conformity behavior, i.e., high specific self-evaluation was associated with less conformity behavior. These three are Ettinger et al. (1971), R. L. Klein and Birren (1973), and Fagen (in Diggory, 1966). Fagen's study is particularly interesting in that he not only manipulated the feedback given to subjects about their ability on the spatial relations task to be used in the conformity procedure, but he selected subjects who had actually obtained high and low scores on one form of this task on a previous occasion. Thus he had groups high and low on actual ability, with half of each group being told their abilities were high, half low. From his figure it appears that conformity behavior (number of wrong answers in agreement with the false feedback majority) was a negative function of both the actual ability level and the manipulated specific self-evaluation of this ability. Unfortunately, sufficient information about significance levels of the mean differences in conformity behavior among the four groups is not given.

A number of the studies yielded significant interactions. Endler, Wiesenthal, and Geller (1972) found that, in Grades 8, 9, and 10, conformity was a negative function of level of manipulated specific self-evaluation, but that in Grades 11, 12, and 13, manipulated self-competence had no influence on conformity. R. L. Klein and Birren (1973) also report a significant interaction between age and specific manipulated self-evaluation in determining degree of conformity behavior. The interaction was determined by the fact that, at the high self-evaluation levels, there were no age differences in conformity behavior, even though the main effect of age was significant.

Only Misra (1973) and deCharms and Rosenbaum (1960) failed to find a significant effect involving mean manipulated specific self-evaluation and conformity scores. This might be because their self-evaluation manipulation was done with respect to a different variable from the one involved in conformity behavior. Misra manipulated not only mean level of specific self-evaluation, but also manipulated variability or consistency from trial to trial in the self-evaluation task. This manipulated variability he found related to conformity behavior, with the subjects who were given to understand that their abilities were variable from trial to trial being more conforming.

Two of the studies seemed seriously enough flawed as not to merit inclusion in the above substantive summary. In one of these (K. H. Smith, 1961), uninterpretable pre-post change scores were used as a measure of conformity, and there was no check on the manipulation of "perceived competence." In the other, a study by Croner and Willis (1961), the method of manipulating specific self-esteem was so extreme as possibly to induce hostility and humiliation as well as lower levels of specific self-evaluation; there was no check on the effects of this manipulation or on suspiciousness, and scores on the influence task were computed in a very complex and not clearly interpretable manner. In addition, there was no no-influence control group.

h. MANIPULATED SPECIFIC SELF-EVALUATION AND PERSUASIBILITY

Rule and Rehill (1970) attempted to manipulate self-evaluation of intellectual ability (which they called self-esteem) by giving their subjects a perceptual-motor task described as part of an intelligence test. Some subjects were led to believe they had been very successful, others very unsuccessful, in this task. Prior to the experiment, all the subjects had expressed a negative opinion concerning the use of television for teaching purposes in the high school. After receiving the feedback on their performance on the IQ test, they were given (under distracting and nondistracting conditions) a one-sided argument for the use of television in teaching. They were then asked again for their opinion on the use of television for teaching purposes. The reported findings are uninterpretable, however, due to the following methodological flaws: a pre-post design; the use of change scores; the use of only two levels of manipulated self-evaluation, thus precluding a search for curvilinear relationships; lack of checks on the self-evaluation manipulation or on the suspiciousness of the subjects; and lack of a no-influence control group.

The only other study which might be considered in this section has already been evaluated in the section concerning chronic self-regard and persuasibility (Greenbaum, 1966). Specific self-evaluation was manipulated by giving one of five levels of reinforcement from strongly negative through strongly positive for the quality of a counterattitudinal speech made by the subject. However, for reasons fully explained there, the methodological flaws in the experiment render the reported findings uninterpretable.

i. CHRONIC SELF-REGARD AND MANIPULATED SELF-REGARD AND CONFORMITY

The only study I have examined which falls into this category is one reported by Gelfand (1962) and described in the sections on chronic self-regard and conformity and manipulated self-regard and conformity above. As reported there, chronic self-regard as measured by Sears's test did not show a significant association with conformity behavior, whereas manipulated self-regard did. The interaction between the two ways of varying self-regard was not significant, and no information is given as to whether there was any correlation between the two ways of varying self-regard.

j. CHRONIC SELF-REGARD AND MANIPULATED SELF-REGARD AND PERSUASIBILITY

McGuire (1968) pointed out that it is important to vary both chronic and manipulated self-regard in the same study in order to find out whether they are interchangeable ways of varying the same self-regard construct, and whether the two ways of varying self-regard interact in determining conformity behavior.

The available studies have already been evaluated in section B-1-b regarding the chronic self-regard variable and persuasibility, and section B-1-d regarding the manipulated self-regard variable and persuasibility. These studies are: Deaux (1972); Gollob and Dittes (1965); Nisbett and Gordon (1967); Stimpson (1970); and Zellner (1970). As explained fully in the section regarding chronic self-regard and persuasibility, only one of these studies is methodologically adequate enough to sustain psychological interpretation of the relationship of self-regard variables to influence behaviors (Deaux, 1972).

So far as interactions are concerned, Deaux reports a significant interaction between chronic and manipulated self-regard. The major contributions to this effect were the relatively large change shown by subjects with high chronic self-regard and low manipulated self-regard, and the virtual absence of change among subjects with low chronic self-regard and low negative manipulated self-regard.

Even though the studies as a group will not sustain psychological interpretations of self-regard relationships to persuasibility, it might be thought they would furnish information about the correlation between the two kinds of self-regard indices. Unfortunately, none of them provides any information germane to this point.

k. Chronic Self-Regard and Manipulated Specific Self-Evaluation and Conformity

The only experiment with this combination of independent variables which has come to my attention is that of deCharms and Rosenbaum (1960). As explained in some detail in section B-1-a on chronic self-regard and conformity, and section B-1-g on manipulated specific self-evaluation and conformity, low chronic self-regard was found to be associated with Asch-type conformity behavior, while manipulated specific self-evaluation of leadership ability was not found to be related to these conformity scores. The interaction between these two varieties of self-regard measures was not significant.

l. Chronic Self-Regard and Manipulated Specific Self-Evaluation and Persuasibility

Greenbaum's (1966) study is the only one I examined which fell into this category. For reasons fully explained in section B-1-b regarding chronic self-regard and persuasibility, methodological flaws in this study render its results uninterpretable.

2. Overview of Associations between Influenceability and Self-Concept Variables

In this chapter, influenceability is defined to include both conformity and persuasibility, while self-evaluation includes (a) over-all self-regard, either predispositional ("chronic") or experimentally manipulated ("acute"); and (b) self-evaluation along specific dimensions, such self-evaluations being either predispositional ("chronic") or experimentally manipulated ("acute"). Thus, 8 categories of studies could result from combinations of the 2 kinds of influence measures and the 4 categories of self-evaluations mentioned in (a) and (b). Actually, some investigators looked at more than one self-concept variable, e.g., both manipulated and predispositional self-regard, so that 12 different classes of investigation occurred among the publications examined. Some of these classes had only one or two exemplars.

The methodological adequacy of the entire group of researches is open to serious question on a number of grounds. Moreover, instrumentation and other aspects of procedure varied greatly among studies. Accordingly, no firm conclusions can be reached. Rather, a few hypotheses may be suggested as a result of this overview of research on influenceability as a function of self-concept variables.

a. CONFORMITY

With respect to conformity as a function of either chronic or manipulated over-all self-regard: weak, often insignificant trends are reported for low self-regard scores to be associated with high conformity scores. No evidence is presented that nonmonotonic relationships obtain. However, not all studies permitted one to look for nonlinearity. Only one author looked for interactions between chronic self-regard and manipulated self-regard, and no significant interaction is reported.

In attempting to explain these weak or null trends involving chronic and manipulated over-all self-regard, one might suggest that relationships are curvilinear and are therefore not revealed by analyses based on extreme groups (the method most commonly used). Sufficient evidence is not at hand to evaluate that possibility. It is also possible that the range of self-regard levels was too narrow to bring out strong positive trends. Information provided in the publications does not suffice to evaluate this possibility.

Another speculative possible interpretation of these weak or null findings is that self-evaluations which are not specifically relevant to the experimental conformity behaviors will be unrelated to degrees of conformity. This suggestion is given some support by a group of studies in which the task used in the procedure for manipulating specific self-evaluations was the same or closely related to the conformity task. That is, subjects were supposedly led to believe they were more or less capable with respect to the conformity task itself. Significant associations between low specific self-evaluations and high conformity are reported by these authors, whereas null results are reported by researchers manipulating specific self-evaluations apparently less relevant to the behavior required on the conformity task (e.g., manipulating self-conceptions of leadership ability and testing for conformity on a perceptual recognition task).

It is noteworthy that all the manipulated specific self-evaluations concerned some kind of ability. By contrast, researchers who looked for associations between conformity and chronic specific self-evaluations dealt with self-evaluations along other dimensions such as "tolerance" or "responsibility." These studies are few in number, methodologically inadequate, and yielded null findings. The relationships between chronic specific self-evaluations and conformity behavior remain to be explored by appropriate methods.

b. Persuasibility

I turn now to the possible associations between persuasibility and chronic or manipulated over-all self-regard. Most of the studies which varied self-regard in either way are inadequate methodologically. They yielded either weak or null associations, or complex and unreplicated interactions. As a group, they provide no obvious hints as to possible explanations of their weak or null findings. The general weakness of relationships seems similar to that just summarized from the research on conformity and over-all self-regard.

Insufficient evidence is available to rule out the possibility that curvilinearity of relationships may explain some of these null results coming mostly from comparisons of extreme groups. There are still possibilities that too narrow a range of over-all self-regard has been used and/or the type of self-evaluation which was varied is too global to be specifically relevant to persuasibility on particular issues. Regarding the latter point, the few studies of chronic or manipulated specific self-evaluation are extremely flawed and inconclusive. Thus, the possibility remains that, as with conformity behaviors, highly task-relevant or issue-relevant self-evaluations might predict persuasibility.

10
Authoritarianism/ Dogmatism and Self-Concept Variables

On the theoretical side, one needs to know first what is intended conceptually by the terms dogmatism and authoritarianism. Next, the question arises as to what theoretical predictions have been stated or assumed regarding associations between either of these constructs and self-concept characteristics. Some of these predictions might be concerned with over-all self-regard, whereas others might involve subjects' self-descriptions along more specific trait dimensions.

When one looks at the literature in search of answers to the above questions, two things become immediately apparent: (a) It is difficult to pin down just what the authors of the F scale and/or D scale might predict about subjects' self-descriptions as a function of their authoritarian or dogmatic scale scores. (b) Perhaps because of this lack of clarity, very few of the authors who have attempted to study empirical relationships in this area have prefaced their reports with any "derivation" of their hypotheses from the theoretical writings of Adorno, Frenkel-Brunswik, Levinson, and Sanford (1950) or of Rokeach (1960, 1968, 1973).

1. Theoretical and Operational Definitions of Terms

In examining the questions raised in the first paragraph I consider first the conceptual meaning(s) of the terms dogmatism and authoritarianism. For Rokeach (1954) dogmatism is "(a) a relatively closed cognitive organization of beliefs and disbeliefs about reality, (b) organized around a central set of beliefs about absolute authority which, in turn (c) provides a framework for patterns of intolerance and qualified tolerance toward others" (p. 195).

As Vacchiano, Schiffman, and Strauss (1967) point out, researchers using the Dogmatism scale often seem implicitly to assume that individual differences in D scores represent variations with respect to a unidimensional dogmatism construct. However, their internal factor analysis of 40 D-scale *items* suggests that the D scale is not unidimensional and that it may be measuring different dimensions for males and females. The interpretation of this study is moot in view of the small Ns in relation to the number of items, and the need for replication with more heterogeneous groups of subjects.

Although Adorno et al. (1950) and Rokeach (1960) both purport to deal with authoritarianism, Kerlinger and Rokeach (1966) point out

603

that authoritarianism, as conceptualized by Adorno et al., includes not only "closedness" of belief systems but a fascist ideological content as well, whereas the dogmatism about which Rokeach wrote referred to a "general authoritarianism regardless of ideological content" (Kerlinger & Rokeach, 1966, p. 391). The idea that somewhat different, although related or overlapping, constructs must be the referents for Adorno's term authoritarianism and Rokeach's term dogmatism (or general authoritarianism) is suggested by noting: (a) the items included in the scales intended to operationalize the respective constructs (i.e., the F and D scales); and (b) the fact that the two scales, while correlating to some degree, do not correlate as highly as one would expect if they were, in effect, alternate forms of one test. (Kerlinger and Rokeach [1966], for example, report rs of .54 to .77 in various groups; Rule and Hewitt [1970] report rs of .45 and .56). Moreover, the results of a factor analysis involving the F scale, several *subscales* of the D scale, and scales of political-economic conservatism, left opinionation, and right opinionation (Rokeach & Fruchter, 1956) suggested that dogmatism, as conceived and represented, measures something similar to authoritarianism, but independently of the left-right dimension and that it is also discriminable from rigidity and ethnocentrism. Supporting this view with their factor analysis of F and D *items* combined, Kerlinger and Rokeach (1966) obtained one factor which seemed to earn the label dogmatism or general authoritarianism that is independent of particular ideological content, whereas two other factors most associated with the F-scale items represented a "fascistic brand of authoritarianism." Although the F-D correlations are not large, they are fairly substantial, as indicated above, and Kerlinger and Rokeach thought this represented cumulative effects of a general authoritarian factor upon the total scores of each scale.

2. Theoretical Predictions

Regarding our second question (about what the Adorno et al. theory implies regarding associations between self-descriptions and F-scale scores), Singer and Feshbach (1959) pointed out that it is possible to draw diverse inferences about the nature and extent of these relationships, depending upon which statements of the authors of *The Authoritarian Personality* one reads. Masling (1954) summarized the alleged personality traits of the high-F scorer as follows, basing his list upon published writings of Adorno et al. (1950) and F. N. Sanford (1950): conventional, aggressive toward unconventional individuals, antiintraceptive, superstitious, stereotyped in thinking, cynical, destructive, concern with sexual identification, sado-masochistic, ambivalent toward authority, compulsive, anal sadistic, punitive, cold, directive, maladaptive. If one assumes, as Wrightsman (1962) does, that the high-F person has some awareness of these characteristics, one might predict that self-descriptions along each of these dimensions would correlate with F-scale scores. Moreover, since many of these are traits which surely have low stereotypic social-desirability values, one would expect that subjects perceiving themselves as high on a number of them would report poor over-all self-regard. On the other hand, Frenkel-Brunswik (1954), in her reply to Masling's article seems clearly to imply that one should not expect systematically unfavorable self-reports from high-F scorers because such persons were shown on initial interview to profess self-assurance which is based on repression of recognition of their "true" characteristics which were manifest only through depth interviews and/or projective techniques.

So far as Rokeach's dogmatic person is concerned, it seems clear that Rokeach regards belief subsystems about the self to be one among a number of belief systems about which a person can have an open or closed mind (Rokeach, 1960). Also, because a self-rejection subscale is included as part of the dogmatism scale, it is apparent that self-derogation is involved in a high degree of dogmatism. Evidently, then, one would expect to have negative correlations between dogmatism and reports of self-regard from other instruments, that is, the dogmatic person would have lower self-regard. However, nowhere in his three books (Rokeach, 1960, 1968, 1973) does Rokeach clarify his theoretical views as to why low self-regard should be characteristic of the dogmatic person. However, one might infer from general reading of his works that dogmatism in thinking arises partly as a protection against the anxiety associated with low self-regard.

Considering the sparsity and/or ambiguity of theorizing about authoritarianism and self-regard, it seems clear why researchers have mostly tended to be cautious or atheoretical in their approach to the empirical study of association between self-concept reports and measured authoritarianism or dogmatism.

B. METHODOLOGICAL QUESTIONS

1. Instruments Used: Reliability, Sources of Artifact

Consideration of the meaning of the constructs authoritarianism and dogmatism has necessarily already taken us into consideration of some of the methodological questions, especially into some of those concerning the construct validity of the *F* and *D* scales. Vacchiano, Strauss, and Hochman (1969) have cited some additional psychometric information relevant to interpreting the results of studies relating authoritarianism/dogmatism and self-concept reports. For the *D* scale, reliability is generally high for adults, and the scale appears to be unrelated to the Marlowe-Crowne Social Desirability Scale. Unfortunately, all *D* items are worded positively, leaving open the possibility that acquiescent response set could account for some of the correlations between *D*-scale scores and self-concept scores when the latter have not controlled for acquiescent response set (and for some of the correlations between the *F*-scale and *D*-scale scores, since the *F* scale also does not control for the acquiescent response set). In support of this possibility, Vacchiano, Strauss, and Hochman (1969) report positive *rs* between *D*-scale scores and the Minnesota Multiphasic Personality Inventory Total True Scores and the Couch/Keniston Scales.

On the other hand, Rokeach (1963, 1967) has published both hypothetical and empirical reasons to support his contention that the acquescent response set is *not* a determinant of indĭvidual differences in *F*-scale and *D*-scale scores.

A very important methodological point is related to the fact that the *D* scale contains within it items intended to elicit self-derogation. Therefore, any correlations between *D*-scale scores and self-regard scores might be artifacts of the overlapping content of the self-referent *D* subscale and any self-regard instrument. This was pointed out by K. A. Hess and Lindner (1973) who purported to examine the relationship between self-esteem (as supposedly indicated by the California Personality Inventory Sense of Well-Being Scale) and the Rokeach Dogmatism Scale, Forms D and E, with the self-referent items removed. Since they found correlations of -.51 and -.53 (involving Forms D and E respectively), they concluded that Dogmatism scores correlate with self-regard scores for reasons other than artifactual ones. Unfortunately, their study is based on an extremely small number of subjects ($N = 19$).

2. Possibility of Nonlinear Relationships between Authoritarianism/Dogmatism and Self-Regard

A further methodological caution involves the possibility that the constructs authoritarianism/dogmatism may be related curvilinearly rather than linearly to self-reports concerning self-regard. For example, high-*F* scorers may present a favorable self-report because of their tendencies toward repression; low-*F* scorers may present a favorable self-report if they recognize that they are characterized by the usually mentioned favorable characteristics of a low-authoritarian person, whereas middle-*F* scorers might have neither the extreme tendencies of the high-*F* person to repress recognition of unfavorable self-characteristics nor the realistic reasons of the low-*F* person to give a favorable self-report.

In any case, since so little can be said definitely about what the theorists in this area expect, it is important that data not be analyzed only with Pearson *r*s or comparison of extreme groups and that a wide range of scores should be examined. This is especially important in trying to interpret the apparent lack of association between *F*-scale scores and self-regard scores, which we report later on.

3. Methodological Criteria for Exclusion of Studies

Most of the studies I examined in this area are so flawed methodologically that they do not seem to me to merit substantive summarizing here. In fact, if one sets really adequate standards, even the individually cited studies in the substantive summaries have to be questioned for reasons indicated there. The chief faults have been as follows: use of a very small number of subjects, or (in some cases) such a large number of subjects that extremely small *r*s are "significant" and "interpreted" psychologically; use of idiosyncratic instruments to measure either the authoritarian/dogmatism or self-concept variables or both without giving enough information about the psychometric properties of the instruments to enable one to evaluate the results obtained with them; uncontrolled experimenter effects (i.e., one black and one white experimenter to vary race-of-experimenter as an independent variable); lack of interviewing or postmanipulation check to see whether the subject construed the meaning of the research as the experimenter intended; making of multiple significance tests especially when they involve variables which themselves are correlated, or involve overlapping items (i.e., scales of the California Personality Inventory, Minnesota Multiphasic Personality Inventory), so that one cannot evaluate how many of the "significant" findings could have occurred by chance. The excluded articles sometimes involve scales supposedly related to authoritarianism or dogmatism, but not the *F* or *D* scales. For example, a few studies looked at intolerance of ambiguity, prejudice toward minority groups or other countries, personal space used in interacting with minority groups.

C. Findings Regarding the Association of the California F Scale and Self-Concept Variables

1. Traits of the Authoritarian Personality

As I have said, it is not entirely clear whether subjects having the traits characteristic of the authoritarian personality are expected to repress recognition of these traits or be able to recognize the traits in themselves and rate themselves accordingly on appropriate self-rating scales. Apparently the only study which tried to look at this question empirically is one by Wrightsman (1962), who constructed 11 self-rating scales respectively describing 11 authoritarian-personality traits, which are considered on pages 228–241 of Adorno et al. (1950). Wrightsman attempted to describe each of the 11 self-rating scales in words which avoided the language of the actual F-scale items. Subjects were divided into high, medium, and low scorers on the F scale, and mean self-ratings were computed for each of the 11 trait scales for each F-scale group. Thus he allowed for the possibility of finding nonmonotonic relationships. In general, however, the trend was for the self-report means of the low-F subjects to be lowest on any authoritarian trait, the medium-F subjects' means to be next, and the high-F subjects' means to be highest on that self-rated authoritarian trait. The summed rating-scale scores correlated .61 with the F-scale scores. In other words, the trend was the opposite of what one would expect if high-F persons repress recognition of their authoritarian personality traits. But a number of reservations about this study must be borne in mind. No psychometric information is provided about the self-rating scales, and, in particular, we are not told whether they intercorrelate. If they do, this would make interpretation of the many significance tests presented even more indeterminate than is the case with research where many significance tests are presented without cross-validation. The interpretation of the r between the two total scores appears least subject to the latter reservation.

2. Over-all Self-Regard

The relatively more methodologically adequate studies do not seem to reveal any trend for F-scale scores to be associated with *over-all self-*

evaluation. Kayser (1972), in a factor analysis involving an idiosyncratic semantic-differential self-rating instrument and the *F* scale found that actual-self "potency" and *F* loaded on the same factor. Self-perceptions of being hard as opposed to soft, heavy as opposed to light, severe as opposed to lenient, and tenacious as opposed to yielding tended to go with high *F*. There was no trend for the *evaluative* factor of the semantic differential to go with *F*-scale scores (i.e., high *F* was unrelated to self-descriptions on the good-bad, wise-foolish, or successful-unsuccessful scales). Koutrelakos (1968), using self-ideal similarity from another idiosyncratic scale involving 100 Edwards Personal Preference Schedule items, obtained no correlation of self-ideal similarity and scores on a 28-item form of the *F* scale. Pedersen (1969), using yet another idiosyncratic semantic differential self-rating instrument, obtained no significant association between *F* and self-evaluation on 25 bipolar adjective scales. He found that the Self-Acceptance Scale of the Adjective Check List did correlate positively with *F* for females, but not for males. However, since Pedersen computed numerous correlations involving overlapping and intercorrelated scales, one can put no interpretation on this one significant positive *r*. Rule and Hewitt (1970) correlated 4 Index of Adjustment and Values scores (Self, Self-Acceptance, Ideal Self, and [Self—Ideal] discrepancies) with the *F* scale, and found only one significant *r* out of 8 computed (4 *r*s for males, 4 *r*s for females). Pilisuk (1963) reported a correlation of -.26 between self-ideal scores from a modified version of the Butler-Haigh *Q* sort and a scale of 23 items chosen from the *F* scale as alleged "indicators of defensive attitudes." (Applicable to one or more of the above studies are the following methodological cautions. The semantic differential format for measuring self-concept dimensions is open to considerable criticism [see Wylie, 1974, pp. 224-230], and, of course, idiosyncratic versions of any test are of even more dubious interpretability. The Adjective Check List has also been criticized by Wylie [1974, pp. 200-213]. And, finally, there is no way of telling whether the essentially zero *r*s obtained may be due to the fact that curvilinear relationships occur between self-regard and authoritarian attitudes.)

Let us assume for the moment that the provisional generalizations stated above are accurate, namely (a) high authoritarian persons tend to recognize the presumably socially undesirable personality traits within themselves, but (b) do not have or do not acknowledge poor over-all self-regard despite having and recognizing these traits (i.e., the correlations are zero and not negative between *F* scale and over-all self-regard scores). How could this be if one accepts the ideas of the authors of *The Authoritarian Personality* that these are undesirable traits? One suggestion might be that persons who have these characteristics take a different view of their desirability value than do the sophisticated psychologists who invented and assigned desirability values to the characteristics of the authoritarian personality. This possibility remains to be explored. Another interpretation might be, of course, that the particular self-regard instruments used in these studies are of very limited validity and would not be expected to reveal relationships which are actually there.

3. Excluded Studies

The *F*-scale studies judged to be even more methodologically flawed than those substantively considered above are simply listed below. Even if one were to accept their reported results as interpretable, they would not change the generalizations stated above. Bookbinder (1963); Boshier (1969); Brodbeck and Perlmutter (1954); J. E. Crandall (1969); DeSoto, Kuethe, and Wunderlich (1960); Eisenman (1970); Eisenman and Townsend (1970); Frankel and Barrett (1971); T. Gordon and Cartwright (1954); Pannes (1963); Pearl (1954); Maliver (1965); Marcia and Friedman (1970); Moore and Krupat (1971); Musella (1969); Noel (1964); Oskamp (1968); Perlmutter (1954); Rubinstein and Lorr (1956); Trotzer and Sease (1971).

D. FINDINGS REGARDING THE ASSOCIATION OF DOGMATISM (*D*-SCALE SCORES) AND SELF-CONCEPT VARIABLES

Of the 7 available studies 4 tend to agree in finding a significant though not strong trend for low self-regard scores to be associated with high Dogmatism scores. A fifth study (Foulkes & Foulkes, 1965) yielded a nonsignificant correlation of $-.12$ between Dogmatism scores and self-ideal *r*s from a variant of the Corsini Chicago *Q* sort. Correlations ranged from $-.18$ to $-.53$ in the studies by Hess and Lindner (1973); K. S. Larsen and Schwendiman (1969); Lee and Ehrlich (1971); Vacchiano, Strauss, and Schiffman (1968). The negative trends in the correlations in these 5 studies appear to accord with Rokeach's expectations. Each of the 5 researches yielding significant or nonsignificant negative *r*s has used a different self-regard instrument (altogether, 6 alleged self-regard scales were used in the 5 studies, 2 of which were idiosyncratic). One of the 5 studies (Hess & Lindner, 1973) used only 19 subjects. Only one of the studies (Hess & Lindner, 1973) removed the self-derogation items from the D scale to see whether the other parts of the scale would correlate with outside measures of self-derogation. They report that removal of these items had little effect on the relationship between the remaining D-scale items and the outside measure of self-derogation.

Two studies do not follow the above trend. Rule and Hewitt (1970) found positive, but insignificant rs between the Index of Adjustment and Values scores for Self, Self-Acceptance, and [Self—Ideal] discrepancies and Dogmatism scores based on the D scale with self-derogation items left in. This was true for both male and female samples. As one aspect of his multitrait-multimatrix study involving different kinds of measurement of dogmatism, self-esteem, and dominance, Hamilton (1971) correlated Rokeach's Dogmatism scale with self-esteem scores from the California Psychological Inventory, self-esteem scores from the Janis-Field Scale, [Self—Ideal] discrepancy scores from Leary's Interpersonal Check List, and self-ratings of self-esteem. Out of the 4 correlations, the only significant one was a *positive* $r = .39$ between Janis-Field self-esteem scores and Rokeach Dogmatism scores. The other 3 correlations were also positive rather than negative, but they were extremely small.

There is no obvious speculative reason why the six different self-regard scores involved in the first-mentioned studies should yield negative correlations with D scores while seven other self-regard scores mentioned in the immediately preceding paragraph should yield zero or positive correlations. At least one can say that the essentially zero correlations cannot be laid to the unreliability of such tests as Bills's Index of Adjustment and Values, the California Psychological Inventory, or the Interpersonal Check List.

If we assume without sufficient assurance that the significant negative correlations from the first mentioned studies represent some kind of replicable trend and are not artifactual, we are then faced with the question as to how Rokeach would interpret these findings, since his original statement is not fully developed and clear.

E. Conclusion

Altogether, the considerable effort expended in this area has not yielded research which would encourage one to think that this is a fruitful topic for future work unless theoretical ambiguities are first resolved and the quality of method is greatly improved.

11

Psychotherapy and Self-Concept Variables

1. Defining Characteristics of Psychotherapy
and Related Activities

This chapter looks at relationships between self-concept variables and a group of activities referred to as individual psychotherapy and/or counseling, group psychotherapy and/or counseling, sensitivity training, encounter group experience, marathon group experience, growth group experience, and T-group training. From an overview of the literature it is clear that some who engage in these differently labeled activities see them as not only somewhat different from each other, but also as exemplars of some common concept. But can this concept be defined in such a way as to encompass all the exemplars while distinguishing them as a group from other concepts?

Among the very few who even attempt an explicit definition of any of the terms just listed are Meltzoff and Kornreich (1970) in their volume on research in psychotherapy.

> The basic concern of our discussion is with the intentional, causal, predictable modification of pathological behavior by methods generically known as psychotherapy. Psychotherapy is taken to mean the informed and planful application of techniques derived from established psychological principles, by persons qualified through training and experience to understand these principles and to apply these techniques with the intention of assisting individuals to modify such personal characteristics as feelings, values, attitudes and behaviors which are judged by the therapist to be maladaptive or maladjustive. . . . [The psychological principles] include the entire systematic body of knowledge that comprises the science of psychology and all aspects of basic and clinical psychiatry exclusive of the so-called organic methods. [Pp. 3-4]

Three things especially stand out in the above definitional statement: (a) The authors' emphasis is on modification of "pathological behavior" or "maladaptive behavior." (b) The therapist is to be the judge of what is maladaptive. (c) The entire field of psychology is involved as a source of principles.

Others (e.g., Patterson, 1966; Lieberman, 1976) have pointed to the impossibility of using the first of these points to distinguish activities traditionally labeled psychotherapy from other activities such as counseling and group experiences. For example, Lieberman (1976) notes that psychotherapy and the activities assigned the other labels are sought by the same range of clients (i.e., from those with varying

615

degrees of subjective distress or clinically diagnosed pathology through those who are essentially seeking "growth" or further "education" rather than "repair"). Thus, although some form of change may be sought through any of the listed activities, psychotherapy cannot be separated from the others on the ground of repair of pathology or maladjustment as opposed to additional growth along constructive lines.

Regarding the second point from the Meltzoff-Kornreich definition, one must note that there are both individual psychotherapists and growth-group leaders who try to let the client, patient, or group member share or shoulder the decision as to what modifications should be sought. Thus, this criterion cannot be used for dividing psychotherapy experiences from the other listed types of activities.

As implied in Meltzoff and Kornreich's third point listed above, it has become increasingly recognized that one cannot distinguish psychotherapy from other activities considered in this chapter by saying that each is based in respectively different principles, peculiar to some domain of psychology. Experts speak of the area of psychotherapy and all other activities listed above as involving many areas of psychology, especially social psychology and learning psychology. For example, D. Cartwright (1968) says:

> One major impression, which is inescapable to the person who surveys the current literature, is that psychotherapy as a field of inquiry no longer forms a distinctive problem area for which special theories and techniques need to be devised. More and more it is apparent that the present perspective is that psychotherapy represents one kind of dyadic relationship to which the findings from the study of other social relationships are relevant. [P. 387]

This viewpoint is also expressed by D. J. Kiesler (1973) who states:

> Therapist-patient interaction in psychotherapy interviews are [sic] but restricted instances of more general human dyadic communication and interpersonal interaction. . . . By adopting the communication model, psychotherapy process researchers can thereby use the concepts and methodology of the science of linguistics and psycholinguistics to achieve greater precision and replicability of their efforts. [P. 20]

Also noting possible connections with social psychology are A. P. Goldstein, Heller, and Sechrest (1966), who speak of "fusions" with attitude studies, e.g., regarding cognitive consistency and inoculation. These authors also suggest another important and relevant "fusion," namely with learning, e.g., principles of transfer or concept attainment.

Actually, the first extensive and systematic attempt to conceptualize psychotherapy in terms of learning principles was Dollard and Miller's (1950) book. According to Matarazzo (1965) and Ford and Urban (1967), the psychoanalyst Franz Alexander concluded in 1963 that learning theory is the best way to conceptualize therapy. More recently several others, both in and out of the psychoanalytic tradition, have assumed that psychotherapy may be best conceptualized as learning. For example, Urban and Ford (1971) propose an analysis of psychotherapy as problem-solving. Also, according to K. I. Howard and Orlinsky (1972), both Rioch and Carkhuff "propose that therapy be viewed as education in interpersonal living, with therapists as teachers of interpersonal skills" (p. 637). Strupp, Fox, and Lessler (1969) liken psychoanalysis to "graduate education." Howard and Orlinsky (1972) conclude their systems-analysis approach to psychotherapy by saying,

it begins to appear that the major de facto function of our therapeutic activity system is *as a kind of "higher education," in the development of interpersonal skills and emotional capacities*. . . . It parallels the function of collegiate education, in which occupational skills and instrumental capacities are developed to the high level required by our socioeconomic system. . . . Psychotherapeutic "education" is tutorial in form, and often requires remedial work to correct dysfunctional interpersonal and emotional patterns learned in the course of family and peer group socialization, but it characteristically includes more advanced work as well (intimacy, spontaneity, self-disclosure, etc.). [P. 658]

By putting more traditional psychotherapies into the framework of general psychology, especially the psychology of learning, contemporary writers have clearly provided grounds for including such activities as sensitivity training, encounter groups, and T-groups in the same conceptual rubric as psychotherapy. They have also thereby revealed the futility of trying to make a definition which will include them all in one category while also conceptually differentiating them collectively from other classes of behavior. Accordingly, I consider these activities in one chapter because of certain common conceptual features indicated above. However, I make no attempt to state criteria which could clearly demarcate these denoted activities from repair or growth activities which undoubtedly go on intentionally and unintentionally in other settings and other ways.

2. Theoretical Predictions about Psychotherapy Effects

a. GENERAL RELATIONSHIPS OF PERSONALITY THEORY TO PSYCHOTHERAPY RESEARCH

Despite the contemporary view that therapeutic activities are primarily educational enterprises, psychotherapy has been historically linked far more strongly with a variety of personality theories. It is to this class of theories, then, that we must turn when seeking a rationale for research relating self-concept variables to therapy. A historical and broad-gauge view of relationships between theory and research puts the current state of affairs into perspective.

Personality theories grew out of clinicians' observations in psychotherapeutic situations. Moreover, it is common knowledge that many clinicians have assumed that the psychotherapeutic situation is the best, if not the only appropriate, setting in which to test such theories. On this ground one might expect close links between personality theory and research — in the present case, self-concept research. However, when one attempts to examine the mutual relevance of personality theories and research, one immediately encounters an exceedingly confused and nebulous situation.

More than six decades after Freud began theorizing on the basis of his psychoanalytic experience, Meehl (1955) noted, "The state of theory and its relation to technique is obviously chaotic whatever our pretensions" (p. 375).

Two years later, Rogers (1957) attempted to systematize the relevance of his theoretical views to predictions about the necessary and sufficient conditions of therapeutic personality change. A number of studies included in this chapter were addressed to some of these statements, e.g., assertions concerning the beneficial influences of such therapist conditions as empathic understanding, unconditional regard, and congruence. Although he formulated his predictions from his own theory, he considered them applicable to any therapeutic situation — "classical psychoanalysis, or any of its modern offshoots, or Adlerian psychotherapy, or any other" (p. 101). Accordingly, he did not expect research on these conditions to yield outcomes discriminantly supportive of one personality theory as opposed to another.

In 1961, a symposium edited by Stein considered the relevance to psychotherapy of Adlerian, client-centered, existential, interactional, interpersonal, psychoanalytic, and transactional theories, among others. Stein attributes the proliferation of theories and their lack of comparability or integration partly to the "differences in types of patients on which the founders of the different schools based their initial observations" (pp. 6-7), partly to the ego-involvement of each charismatic leader in the development and promotion of his own views. In any event, the contributors to this symposium made no attempts to state psychotherapy hypotheses distinctively appropriate to their respective theories. And, despite Stein's impression that there is much "duplication of effort," the participants made no attempt to distill any commonly shared testable implications of their theories.

Nevertheless, in 1963, Rogers expressed hope that, when therapists of different schools of thought examined therapy records from the same cases, they would be found to have some common goals and interpretations, in spite of what he assumed to be semantic differences among theories. His optimism was severely dashed by the outcomes of such explorations.

If variously oriented therapists could not agree in interpreting the same therapy protocol, might they at least be assumed to conduct therapy in different ways respectively appropriate to their theoretical orientations? Apparently not. D. J. Kiesler noted in 1966 that with "the advent of general tape-recording . . . it has become apparent that differences in technique and personality exist, even within schools, and that disagreement prevails" (p. 112). In reporting a formal study made by him and his colleagues, Lieberman (1976) states, "experienced therapists sharing identical theoretical orientations" did not "behave similarly with comparable populations" (p. 228). In DiLoreto's (1971) study, experienced therapists thought they had conducted therapy by three different methods respectively appropriate to their three different theoretical orientations. However, experienced judges from each respective school believed the therapy tapes showed the therapists had not behaved according to the respective schools of thought. Thus one cannot assume that the therapist's self-assigned theoretical label will indicate how he acts in the therapy situation.

More directly pertinent to the present attempts to relate psychotherapy research to theory are the analyses of Kiesler. Among his "myths of psychotherapy research," he includes "The Myth that Present Theories Provide Adequate Research Paradigms" (p. 120). He argues that Freudian, Rogerian, and behavior theories of therapy "do not explicitly deal with the problem of confounding variables; and do not specify the network of independent, dependent, and confounding variables in sufficient enough detail to permit researchers to solve sampling and other methodological problems" (p. 125). He also notes that some empirical findings which appear to have emerged from psychotherapy research have "not been incorporated into any theoretical system" (p. 128).

Possibly because of the complexities, inadequacies, and confusions described above, psychotherapy research has tended to become atheoretical (Gendlin & Rychlak, 1970).

b. PERSONALITY-THEORY PREDICTIONS ABOUT SELF-CONCEPT CHANGES AS A FUNCTION OF PSYCHOTHERAPY

Self-Regard

Despite the current atheoretical trend, it appears plausible that one very general theoretical point relevant to this chapter is implied by many of the theoretical and common-sense views of therapy, viz., that changes in conceptions and evaluations of self are among the goals of therapy. Thus, although each theory's statements are fuzzy, it would be broadly germane to look for this class of outcomes, their correlates, consequents, and antecedents.

The reader of Adler, Jung, Horney, Rogers, Maslow, and Sullivan among others will realize the ubiquity of the assertion that changes in cognitions and evaluations of self should occur as a function of therapy. Also relevant are two studies of therapists made by Seward (1962) and by R. K. Goldman and Mendelsohn (1969), who surveyed psychotherapists of varying theoretical persuasions. Seward's interviewees were comprised of 19 classical Freudians, 14 Neo-Freudians, 13 Horneyans, and 19 others including Jungians, Sullivanians, and existentialists. It was found that the open-ended interviews could be reliably coded for 4 categories of desired therapeutic change, including "self acceptance and expression." Although there were differences among the schools of thought, 45% of all therapists spontaneously affirmed this goal, ranging from 77% of the Horneyans to 16% of the Freudians.

Goldman and Mendelsohn (1969) surveyed a national sample of 1,200 psychotherapists of whom 35% responded, about one-third being psychiatrists, one-third psychologists, and one-third social workers. The sample was said to be "quite heterogeneous" with respect to "theoretical persuasions," which were categorized roughly as 63% psychoanalytic, 25% interpersonal, and 12% eclectic. The therapists were instructed to choose from the 300 adjectives in Gough's Adjective Check List those which describe "the kind of adult male patient that you work with best . . . , an adult male patient who has terminated therapy successfully, and . . . an adult male who has a satisfactory adaptation to himself and his environment" (p. 165). The adjectives *confident* and *self-confident* were among the 25 most often chosen to describe the normal person and the successfully terminated patient; they also were among the 12 adjectives which differentiated the patient from either the normal or the successfully terminated patient. The percent of clinicians applying these terms to the normal, the successfully terminated patient, and the patient respectively were: confident 86%, 75%, 29%; self-confident 78%, 71%, 30%. Thus considerable agreement was reached despite theoretical diversity of the therapists.

The term *mental health* would not be favored by many modern therapists who decry the "medical model." Nevertheless, Jahoda's (1958) extensive search of the literature and her discussions with experts from various fields resulted in a proposed set of criteria for mental health which are germane to the present argument. Jahoda states:

A recurring theme in many efforts to give meaning to the concept of mental health is the emphasis on certain qualities of a person's self. . . . [P. 24]

A number of different dimensions or components appear to run through the various proposals. Those aspects of the self-concept that stand out most clearly are: (1) accessibility to consciousness, (2) correctness, (3) feelings about self, and (4) sense of identity. Although not all of these components are made explicit by the writers who use attributes of the self as criteria for mental health, they are implicit in many of their contributions. . . . [P. 25]

The mentally healthy attitude toward the self is described by terms such as self-acceptance, self-confidence, or self-reliance, each with a slightly different connotation. Self-acceptance implies that a person has learned to live with himself, accepting both the limitations and possibilities he may find in himself. Self-confidence, self-esteem, and self-respect have a more positive slant; they express the judgment that in balance the self is "good," capable, and strong. . . . [P. 24]

The distinguishing mark of [the sense of identity] as compared to self-acceptance is its more cognitive emphasis on the *clarity* of self-image. [P. 29]

In short, it seems clear that properly conducted studies yielding increases in valid self-reports would be supportive of a wide variety of personality theories, although not constituting a discriminant test among theories.

Such increments might be inferred from tests purporting to measure over-all self-regard. For example, one might use Rosenberg's Self-Esteem Scale. Shlien (1966) proposed that a content-free, abstract measure of self-ideal congruence should be acceptable to a wide variety of theorists. Alternately, increments might be measured on a test from which one sums across a number of factorially clustered self-descriptions (e.g., a group of evaluative semantic differential scales, or a group of potency semantic differential scales).

Restricted Aspects of Self-Conception

If we follow Jahoda's suggestion that correctness of self-concept and sense of identity are criteria of mental health (hence, by implication, a possible goal of psychotherapy), then any behavioral change which is accomplished might be expected to be reflected in a corresponding self-description. For example, a person with a high level of self-reported predispositional anxiety might actually shift on this behavioral dimension as a function of therapy and then give a correspondingly changed self-report. This implies an indefinitely large number of possible hypothesis-testing studies involving self-descriptions, depending on the goals of client and therapist.

Self-Reports and Behaviors

Of more restricted relevance to phenomenological theories is the relationship of self-descriptions to behaviors. Thus, do self-descriptions simply index recognized behavior characteristics and changes? Are the behavior changes actually mediated by the changes in phenomenal self? Or do both relationships obtain? Although this issue is central to phenomenological theories, no specific ways to test it have been proposed.

3. Methodological Criteria

Even more than with other areas covered in this book, I was struck by two strong, paradoxical trends in the literature on psychotherapy research. On the one hand, there is a continual outpouring of literature reviews, e.g., one or two reviews every year in the *Annual Review of Psychology,* several in Bergin and Garfield (1971); and separate reviews by Back (1972); Kelley, Smits, Leventhal, and Rhodes (1970); Luborsky, Chandler, Auerbach, Cohen, and Bachrach (1971); and

Meltzoff and Kornreich (1970), who devoted an entire book to the subject. These reviews tended justifiably to be severely critical of the methodological adequacy of the extant psychotherapy research publications. On the other hand, excellent, specific advice about methodological standards for psychotherapy research continued to be published, but were largely unheeded. Among the latter sources, D. T. Campbell and Stanley (1963); Fiske, Hunt, Luborsky, Orne, Parloff, Reiser, and Tuma (1970); Goldstein, Heller, and Sechrest (1966); D. J. Kiesler (1966, 1971, 1973); and Meltzoff and Kornreich (1970) appear to be especially useful.

As was true in preparing each chapter, I kept in mind certain criteria by which to evaluate the methodological adequacy, hence the interpretability, of each study. Space precludes elaborating on these points, but sources of fuller explanations and discussions are cited. In sections B-1 and C-1, I summarize the degree to which group psychotherapy research and individual psychotherapy research respectively meet these criteria.

1. *Are all aspects of procedure described clearly enough* to permit evaluation of the reported results?

2. (a) Is the *sample* adequately described? From what population was it drawn, and by what criteria?

(b) Was the sample large enough to justify looking at the variable of concern? Adequacy in sample size must be judged in relationship to the heterogeneity of the sample on variables relevant to the dependent variable measures.

3. (a) In the case of outcome research, *were subjects assigned randomly to conditions?* Did this result in initially comparable groups? Or were the groups matched? If the latter, was matching adequately done with respect to subject variables which influence the dependent variable?

Of course, it is generally accepted that random assignment to groups is the only completely defensible procedure from the methodological standpoint. However, with small Ns, incomparable groups may nevertheless result. And even with large groups, error variance introduced by subject variables will be large (D. J. Kiesler, 1966). On the other hand, matching on a few variables of known or plausible importance may render the groups incomparable with respect to some other equally relevant subject variables (Underwood, 1957). Therefore matching cannot safely be used to compensate for small sample size.

Much has been written about the ethical problems of randomly assigning subjects to wait control groups or even to placebo control groups (e.g., J. M. Butler & Haigh, 1954; Kelley, Smits, Leventhal, & Rhodes, 1970; Goldstein, Heller, & Sechrest, 1966). However, one can argue that psychotherapy has not been scientifically demonstrated to be effective and may even be harmful. Therefore, one cannot say that witholding it from someone who has agreed to these research conditions is necessarily denying that person a benefit. Moreover, in order to learn more about the effects of psychotherapy and the variables which influence its course so that we can provide more helpful treatment to more persons in the long run, research using such methodological standards must be followed in psychotherapy research just as they are in medicine.

(b) *Was attrition from groups taken into account,* insofar as this might create incomparability among groups with respect to important subject variables (Back, 1974).

(c) Does the study examine groups formed ad hoc? For example, does it look at self-reports of groups which differ on the basis of some other measure of improvement? If so, were the ad hoc groups initially comparable in regard to variables relevant to improvement? Is there an opportunity for contamination between improvement measures and self-report indices?

4. Does the *treatment of the control groups* enable us to make the interpretive comparisons suggested by the researchers? Over and above the ethical problems with wait control assignments, a number of possible ambiguities obtain in interpreting the data from subjects in such groups (Subotnik, 1972; Goldstein, Heller & Sechrest, 1966). For example, waiting subjects may feel rejected or "pushed out." This might keep their self-regard low during the waiting period, whereas it might otherwise have risen spontaneously to some extent during that time. Or, despite some subjective improvement in self-regard during the waiting period, these subjects may repeat their self-report of poor self-regard in order to assure the therapist that they still need the promised therapy. Alternately, if there is any attrition in the wait-control group, it could selectively involve those subjects whose subjective state improved "spontaneously" or due to alternate helpful experiences during the wait period, or those whose scores increased due to statistical regression. All these possibilities could lead one to underestimate the degree to which score changes occur without the kind of therapy under study. Possibly operating in the opposite direction is a positive influence of expecting to get help or of having made a commitment to change. Or, as Subotnik (1972) suggests, controls may deal with the cognitive dissonance created

by their wait-list assignment by reporting that their self-regard has increased without therapy. Of course, it is difficult or impossible to make the waiting period as long as the therapy period in the case of research on long-term psychotherapy, since the possibilities of wait-group attrition mount with time. This leads to yet another ambiguity in comparing wait groups with therapy groups.

Much has also been written about the inappropriateness of normal, no-therapy controls. Obviously they differ in motivation from therapy volunteers (i.e., they do not wish to be treated and have no expectations of change from treatment). On these grounds, little change might be expected from them. Moreover, they have initially quite different standing on such variables as self-ideal congruence and self-reported trait anxiety. (See section D of this chapter.) Accordingly, there is statistically less room for their self-reports to move upward upon posttesting.

The need for attention-placebo controls has been noted (e.g., by Bergin, 1971; DiLoreto, 1971; Lieberman, 1976; McCardel & Murray, 1974; Strupp & Bergin, 1969). Such groups would help to separate expectation and other nonspecific effects from those supposedly induced by psychotherapy per se.

Lieberman (1976) has argued for the use of several groups receiving strongly contrasting treatments within the same research context. One point of this, of course, is to help to evaluate nonspecific effects.

We do not know the role of volunteering attitudes in producing therapeutic changes in those who spontaneously present themselves for therapy and are then induced to participate in research. Perhaps they expect success, and this facilitates increases in such measures as self-regard indices (Lieberman, 1976). Accordingly, one needs invited remedial treatment groups, as Goldstein, Heller, and Sechrest (1966) have pointed out.

Since the very fact of participating in psychotherapy research may have some effects on subjects in all the above-suggested control conditions, it is highly desirable to have groups who are tested on dependent-variable measures without knowing that their research treatment has anything to do with psychotherapy research (DiLoreto, 1971).

In general, one looks for information about how the various kinds of nontreated controls construed their role in the research and what they did during the period of time covered by the study. For example, unless the experimenter specifically rules this out, it is possible that the nontreated controls may be taking tranquilizing or antidepressant medication, or may be seeking counseling from a minister. Such lack of information is equivalent to a drug research study in which no check is kept on the nonexperimental drugs ingested by the no-drug control subjects (Luborsky et al., 1971).

5. (a) What is told about the *number, theoretical orientation, and level of experience of the therapists?* How were therapists assigned to conditions and groups? May null results perhaps be attributed to the use of inexperienced therapists? If there are very few therapists, therapist personality is at least partially confounded with experimental condition, precluding interpretability. Also, if the number of therapists is very small, generalizability of results is precluded.

(b) If the influence of therapist characteristics is under study, were such characteristics appropriately measured and were therapist characteristics unconfounded with subject and treatment variables?

6. What information is given about *what actually went on during therapy sessions?* Did the therapist follow a particular, designated *theoretical orientation?* Was the therapist's belief in a particular orientation confounded with his or her use of theoretical techniques, or did each therapist use more than one technique? It can be argued that therapists cannot function effectively with a theoretically oriented technique for which their beliefs and experience disqualify them. Thus, contrasting treatments would be given their best chance to show positive results by choosing therapists for each condition who are respectively highly qualified in and committed to the therapeutic technique being used in that condition. However, if one follows this dictum, the influences of belief and of therapeutic techniques per se are inevitably confounded.

7. Was the *design multivariate,* as demanded by the complex nature of the probable determinants of self-concept reports, and as necessary to bring out interaction effects? (A. L. Edwards & Cronbach, 1952; D. J. Kiesler, 1966; Luborsky et al., 1971).

8. What, if anything, is told by the researcher or known through other published sources about the content, reliability, and validity of the self-concept measures used? Was the scoring of the self-concept measure or the improvement measure done by the therapist or by the investigator who knew the hypotheses and the subjects' group assignments? Ford and Urban (1967) argue that the use of nonparticipant observers represents the "required methodological approach" (p. 354). In 1975, Bergin and Suinn criticized continued reliance on therapist-dominated measures.

9. In process studies, have the psychometric problems of content analysis been appropriately handled and reported (Kiesler, 1973)? Is there possibility of confounding between sequential self-report measures and other sequential indices of process which are supposedly conceptually separate, although related according to theory, e.g., increases in acceptance of self and others, or expressions of unconditional regard and increases in number of self-relevant statements?

In his proposal to apply stochastic process analyses to the study of psychotherapeutic processes, Hertel (1972) has pointed to the inadequacy of the following operational definitions of process: (a) changes in frequency (or relative frequency) of occurrence of patient-initiated and/or therapist-initiated events; (b) "counting contingencies of two events occurring during therapy, for example, how often a certain kind of patient response follows a certain kind of therapist response" (p. 422). He argues for a method which would enable one to measure the "many larger, more complex temporal relationships that exist in the data" (p. 422). Moreover, he has pointed out that it is "impossible to explicate [the process of change referred to as the 'therapeutic process'] until one has reliably delineated the initial or base-line sampling of patient and therapist processes in such a manner that any subsequent change can be detected" (p. 423).

10. Were *uninterpretable discrepancy scores* for individuals used as independent, dependent, or correlated variables? For example, did the research involve insight scores, certain two-part empathy scores, or patient-therapist similarity scores? (See Wylie, 1974, pp. 89-95, 304-309; Cronbach & Furby, 1970; and Luborsky, Chandler, Auerbach, Cohen, & Bachrach, 1971).

11. *When was testing done?*

(a) If pre-post testing was used, was the possible *reactivity to testing* properly taken into account (Goldstein, Heller, & Sechrest, 1966)? If more than one test was given, were there enough testing times to permit one to look for a *nonlinear function* (D. J. Kiesler, 1966), for *fluctuations* (Subotnik, 1972), or *cyclical processes* (Strupp & Bergin, 1969)?

(b) Was the *final test delayed* long enough to evaluate whether any treatment effects were lasting?

12. Were *multiple significance tests* made, precluding evaluation of the significance level of any particular comparison? Was this difficulty compounded by making these multiple significance tests on scores based on overlapping items or on scores which were intercorrelated?

B. Group Psychotherapy Studies

1. General Characteristics of Group Psychotherapy Studies

Altogether I have closely examined 89 references reporting results on one or more "experiments" which involved one or more self-reports as a function of some kind of experience in small groups. The types of experience include T-groups, sensitivity groups, group counseling (exclusive of vocational counseling), group therapy done from a variety of theoretical approaches, and leaderless groups following tape-recorded guidance.

In keeping with the topic of this book, I include only investigations which involved some kind of self-report measures which could plausibly be construed as indicants of some aspect(s) of self-conception. This includes purported measures of self-regard (the most frequently used kind of measure), and self-reports about more specific aspects of self-concept such as dependency or aggression. It excludes studies which used only self-rated improvement or check lists of symptoms marked by patients.

Of course it is well known that there is a poor correlation among various kinds of outcome measures, including self-report indices (Bergin & Suinn, 1975; Ford & Urban, 1967; Garfield, Prager, & Bergin, 1971; Luborsky, 1971; Luborsky, Chandler, Auerbach, Cohen, & Bachrach, 1971). Nevertheless, self-report measures are of particular relevance to studies of therapy because (a) dissatisfaction with self is a frequently stated reason for undertaking therapy; (b) a wide variety of theories predict changes in self-conception as a function of therapy, as discussed above; and (c) there is some empirical support for the idea that changes in self-image are among clients' commonest expectations about therapy. (In a small study of 65 consecutive clinic applicants, Begley and Lieberman [1970] found that 90.7% of patients endorsed the statement: "One major benefit of therapy will be that the patient will have a new and different picture of himself and his personality." This was one of the 12 most agreed-upon statements among 48 statements of expectation in their questionnaire.)

a. Reports of Procedure

With rare exceptions, the procedures in these studies are not adequately described.

b. Adequacy of Control Groups

These studies were devoted to examining outcomes rather than processes. Unfortunately, few investigators proceeded in an adequate fashion to establish control groups which were appropriate to their purposes. In fact, one fifth had no control groups at all, with completely inconclusive results. Another fifth provided so little information that one could not judge whether subjects had been assigned to conditions in a manner which would control subject variables. From the information given, I judged that about another third of the studies had clearly failed to establish comparable groups, e.g., when volunteers for "a psychological experiment" comprised the untreated control group, while volunteers for a marathon experience served as experimental subjects (Guinan & Foulds, 1970); or when a group experience was given to volunteers who indicated a high interest in participating, and their results were compared to those from a nontreated group of nonvolunteers who had said they were not interested in participating (Gilligan, 1974). About a third used the most desirable procedure, i.e., they assigned their subjects randomly to conditions. However, this cannot assure comparability when small Ns are used (as is typically the case), or when no information is given regarding pretreatment comparability of groups. Most authors give no information on the latter point. A number of those who do give such an analysis show that, despite their intentions, random division yielded groups who were incomparable at pretest.

In addition to problems of establishing comparable groups at the outset, many questions can be raised about the appropriateness of the handling of the control groups. All too often one cannot tell whether they knew they were participating in research, how they construed their activity (or lack thereof), or exactly what they did during the research and/or outside of the research setting during the time span when the experimental subjects were having a group experience.

c. Theoretical Orientations

While, for reasons already explained, no therapy study can be a critical test of the assertions of any particular personality theory, it is of some interest to note the therapists' theoretical orientations and corresponding practices in these researches. More than half the publications I examined provided so little information relevant to this question that a theoretical classification could not be determined. About a fifth stated or appeared to imply a Rogerian orientation, and about a tenth seemed to have a gestalt-experiential basis for their group activities and research hypotheses. Another tenth of the publications explicitly claimed a variety of other theoretical bases including psychoanalytic, Adlerian, or eclectic. Whether the leaders or therapists actually carried out the procedures in a manner acceptable to the respective theorists cannot often be ascertained from published information.

d. NUMBERS AND CHARACTERISTICS OF THERAPISTS

More than one-third of the reports failed to make clear how many therapists or group leaders participated. Approximately another third used only one or two leaders or therapists, whereas another sixth involved three or four. Obviously, generalizability is thereby limited. In addition, experimental conditions and leaders' characteristics are often confounded. It is sometimes clear that the author was not only the researcher but was also the only therapist or one of two therapists (e.g., Foulds, 1970, 1973; Foulds & Hannigan, 1974; Guinan & Foulds, 1970; Guinan, Foulds, & Wright, 1973). Since this crucial point is left unclear in many publications, this serious fault may well have occurred often.

About half the reports give no information or are extremely vague about the training and experience of the therapists. About a fifth used graduate students or paraprofessionals, and perhaps only about one third of the researches involved fully trained and experienced practicing professionals.

Almost never is one given enough concrete information about what went on during therapy and whether independent judges were convinced that the therapist-patient interactions were as the therapist intended, described, or construed them.

e. LIMITATIONS OF DESIGN

Although everyone would agree that psychotherapy outcomes in general and self-concept reports in particular are multiply determined, the present area is notable for the absence of controlled multivariate research.

Almost three-fourths of the publications were based on a pretest-posttest design. Aside from interpretive problems introduced by possible reactivity to pretesting, the use of only two test times precludes looking for nonlinear relationships and/or fluctuations. Since no posttest was done much later than the group experience, one can learn nothing about possibly lasting effects of treatment.

About a fifth of the researchers tested their subjects at three or more times, usually at pre-, post-, and follow-up-points. Nevertheless, a search for nonlinear relationships was rarely made by these workers and never under conditions which were otherwise methodologically adequate.

About a tenth of the investigators looked at post-only data. If large enough randomly formed groups had been employed, and other variables properly controlled, such post-only data could have been useful to circumvent or evaluate possible reactivity from pretesting.

f. Construct Validity of Self-Concept Measures

The construct validity of the self-concept measure is, of course, of paramount importance in these investigations. Most of the studies were concerned with over-all self-regard, but a few purported to look at specific aspects of self-concept. Unfortunately, more than a third of the references I examined were based on the use of idiosyncratic instruments about which little or no information is available. Presumably because of the gestalt-experiential or Rogerian orientation of many of the researchers, Shostrom's (1964, 1966) Personal Orientation Inventory (POI) was used in one-fifth of the studies. The Tennessee Self Concept Scale (TSCS) and the Butler-Haigh Q sort (BHQ) were each used in about a tenth of the researches, with one to four studies each using the Adjective Check List (ACL), the Berger Scales of Acceptance of Self and Others (SA and AO), California Psychological Inventory (CPI), the Edwards Personal Preference Scale (EPPS), Bills's Index of Adjustment and Values (IAV), Leary's Interpersonal Check List (ICL), the Lipsitt Self-Concept Scale for Children, the Piers-Harris Self-Concept Scale for Children (PH), Minnesota Multiphasic Personality Inventory (MMPI), Minnesota Counseling Inventory (MCI), and the Cattell Sixteen Personality Factor Questionnaire (16 PF). (Of these, I have extensively reviewed and criticized the following in my 1974 book: ACL, BHQ, IAV, ICL, Lipsitt's scale, PH, TSCS.)

Regarding Shostrom's Personal Orientation Inventory, one must note the following cautions. There is a great deal of item overlap among the 12 scales. On this ground alone, discriminant validity of each scale is impaired, and scale intercorrelations are not interpretable. No detailed rationale for assigning items to scales is given nor is there information about interjudge agreement about such assignments. The intercorrelation between the Self-Regard (*Sr*) and Self-Acceptance (*Sa*) scales, based on 138 college students, = .21. This value is among the lowest one-fifth of the scale intercorrelations. Presumably this could occur because there is only one overlapping item and because the *Sr* items purport to represent "the ability to like oneself *because of one's strength as a person,*" while *Sa* items purport to indicate "acceptance of one's self *in spite of one's weaknesses or deficiencies*" [emphasis added] (p. 20). In any event, multiple significance tests from the 12 scales—the usual procedure in studies using the test—result in uninterpretable *P* values. The only test-retest reliability information given in the manual is based on 48 undergraduate students and a one-week interval. Obviously, this amount of information does not enable one to evaluate the possible role of test unreliability in leading to null results. Also, this amount of information is insufficient for drawing comparative conclusions about scale differences which are said to be respectively significant and insignificant in a particular study.

g. Use of Dyadic Scores

Some of the reports were necessarily inconclusive, regardless of their other merits, because their data analyses were based on psychometrically indefensible and uninterpretable gain, change, discrepancy, or similarity scores for individuals.

h. Multiple Significance Tests

With respect to the dependent variable, more than 80% of the authors looked at numerous self-report scores and occasionally at other types of measures. Many of these indices were based on overlapping items and/or components (e.g., TSCS scales or POI scales); other indices were probably intercorrelated, although not overlapping. Thus, significance levels for any given score cannot be evaluated, especially when no cross-validation was undertaken, as is almost always the case.

2. Substantive Summaries of Studies

If one applied rigorously the appropriate methodological screening criteria, one could find no study which fulfilled all the desiderata. However, I have chosen to summarize a few which seem to me to be relatively more adequate than the others. The latter are listed at the end, as they do not appear to warrant substantive summary.

a. STUDIES OF NONPATIENT ADULTS

It seems salutary to begin with the only study I found which introduced any control for the possibly nonspecific effects of group experience, e.g., leaders' or participants' expectancy of favorable outcome, group enthusiasm, and the possibly reactive nature of outcome measures (McCardel & Murray, 1974). Volunteer adults recruited through a campus newspaper advertisement were randomly divided into five groups. Four groups were provided weekend experiences simultaneously at the same retreat: Group I (high structure) participated in lectures and in exercises "widely used in encounter groups"; Group II (medium structure) spent about six hours in activities similar to Group I, with the remainder of the weekend spent in unstructured T-group meetings focusing mainly on group process; Group III (low structure) spent the entire time sitting in a circle, verbalizing hopes and fears with "no exercises or gimmicks"; Group IV (on-site control) participated in recreational activities such as ballroom dancing, charades, boat trips, and party games, with "no meaningful or therapeutically oriented discussion." Members of the latter group believed they were participating in a kind of encounter-group activity. Group V (at-home control) had a group experience after the follow-up testing of all five groups. Unfortunately, a different leader with respectively different training was used for each group; so specific leader characteristics and training were confounded with type of treatment. However, all four leaders were women in their thirties who were said on an unspecified basis to be "attractive, warm, and enthusiastic." The leader of each of the first three groups was an "experienced practitioner and enthusiastic proponent of the type of group that she conducted" (p. 339). Thus, some leader comparability obtained across groups. The on-site control-group leader, a secretary and former dance teacher, had no training relevant to encounter groups. However, this uncontrolled factor should have operated against rather than artifactually in favor of the reported findings of essentially similar outcomes among the first four groups.

Shostrom's POI and other measures were used 4 days before, 3 days after, and 10 weeks after the encounter weekend. Despite random division, the groups differed significantly at pretest on 2 POI scales; so

ANCOVAs were performed on posttest scores, using pretest scores as covariates. The repeated use of ANCOVAs on each of the 12 POI scales makes any significant findings uninterpretable without cross-validation. However, 3 days after the weekend no significant differences were reported among the 3 encounter groups, and the on-site control group differed significantly from the 3 encounter groups on only 1 scale. Of the 12 scales, 7 showed significant differences between the at-home control group and the other 4 groups. (The Self-regard scale, but not the Self-Acceptance scale was among the 7.)

These results lend support to the idea that positive effects on self-reports obtained in some encounter group studies may plausibly represent the operation of nonspecific factors, as opposed to purportedly beneficial activities peculiar to encounter groups. On the 10-week follow-up measures, the on-site control group showed no significant differences from the 3 encounter groups on any POI scale. The at-home controls differed significantly from the other 4 groups on 6 scales, but not exactly the same scales as at post test. (I omit reference to a self-perception accuracy score, as it appears to be psychometrically undefensible.)

Another investigation using several groups and measures was carried out by Dye (1974), who randomly divided 56 freshman nursing students into 5 groups, all of whom responded to the TSCS and Taylor's Manifest Anxiety Scale (TMAS) before, immediately after, and 1 month after their 7-week experience in the study (1-1/2 hours per week). Group I used Bell and Howell Encountertapes with a facilitator present but not leading the activities ($N = 10$); Group II underwent sensitivity training under "an experienced trainer" ($N = 9$); Group III underwent human relations training led by "an experienced doctoral candidate" ($N = 10$); Group IV, the placebo subjects, met the same number of times as groups I–III, but, instead of being treated, they kept journal notebooks of critical incidents in their lives as nursing students ($N = 10$). Group V, the no-treatment subjects, were only tested ($N = 17$). Published information about the nature of the group treatments is very scanty. Apparently leader and treatment were confounded, which would render significant between-group findings uninterpretable. Likewise, multiple significance tests would render uninterpretable any significant between-group score differences. However, we are not asked to accept such between-group differences, inasmuch as there were no such differences on any TSCS score or on the TMAS. It is of some interest (although not clearly interpretable due to multiple significance testing) that *all* groups showed a significant increase in Total Positive score on the TSCS. Thus, one could not even argue for a nonspecific effect of group participation.

In a less well-controlled and described study of 61 nursing students (including 1 male), M. Coleman and Glofka (1969) used the TSCS immediately before and after the 30 experimental subjects underwent a 10-week experiment in an undescribed kind of "group therapy." ($N =$ 10 per group; control $N = 31$.) Although the 2 groups did not differ on any TSCS scale at pretest, 9 out of 12 scales appear to favor the control group at that time. Of 14 posttest comparisons, including Total Positive scores, 7 were said to favor significantly the experimental group. Aside from the ambiguity introduced by multiple significance testing, however, one must note that experimental and control subjects came from different hospitals, so that the comparability of the groups' extraexperimental experience may be questioned.

Like Dye (1974) and McCardel and Murray (1974), Trotzer and Sease (1971) established several groups of young adults in several levels of treatment. A total of 90 volunteers from university residence halls was randomly allotted by sex into 7 groups: 3 "basic encounter" groups (whose general goals and reference frame are vaguely described); 3 "placebo discussion" groups (who discussed specific topics such as the Vietnam War, religion, and student unrest); and 1 "no treatment" control group. Groups were randomly assigned to 1 of 3 leaders, each leader having 1 of each kind of group. Qualifications and orientations of leaders are not indicated, but tape-recorded excerpts of the group sessions were used as a basis for judging the leaders' behaviors in terms of the Truax Scales which purport to index accurate empathy and unconditional positive regard.

Use of a Campbell-Stanley posttest-only design obviated reactive effects of pretesting. Scores from the TSCS, Berger's SA and AO, Bills's IAV, and Rokeach's Dogmatism Scale were examined. This, of course, led to multiple significance tests. Accordingly, had significant results been obtained, they would have been uninterpretable without cross-validation. However, the following scores showed nonsignificant differences across all levels: IAV ideal self and self-ideal congruence, Berger's SA and AO, TSCS Total Positive, Self-criticism, and Self-satisfaction. These null differences occurred even though three-fourths of the Truax ratings of leaders differed between the two types of groups.

In a much less methodologically adequate study, Weissman, Goldschmid, Gordon, and Feinberg (1972) randomly divided 20 undergraduate volunteers into 1 encounter and 1 wait-control group whose activities are undescribed. Audio encounter tapes gave directions for group activities to be followed in the 10, biweekly, 1-1/2-hour, leaderless encounter sessions. Mean self-ideal *rhos* obtained from an idiosyncratic semantic-differential instrument showed no pre-post change in the wait-control group and a significant change in the encounter group. However, the encounter group had a lower mean *rho* at pretest (.065 vs. .26), and the level of significance of this intergroup pretest difference is not mentioned.

K. R. White (1974) reports yet another study using several groups and measures. Volunteers for a Boston University T-group program were randomly sampled and divided in an unspecified way into 5 groups of approximately 10 each: 2 regular T-groups, 2 fish-bowl T-groups, and 1 untreated group whose instructions and activities are not described. Total group time was 24 hours in 7 weekly meetings. Trainer teams were different for each group, leaving open some possibility of confounding of treatment and trainer-team characteristics, but at least the trainers had received roughly equivalent ratings on dimensions of congruence, empathy, positive regard, and unconditionality of regard. Seventeen self-concept scores were compared, including TSCS Total Positive and 8 other undesignated TSCS scales and 8 octant scores from the ICL. Thus, significant effects would have been uninterpretable without replication. However, the groups were said not to differ at the outset, and none of the 17 scores differentiated significantly between conditions on posttesting.

Both of the following publications (D. S. Jones & Medvene, 1975, and Kimball & Gelso, 1974) are based on volunteers for marathon experiences who were randomly divided into two conditions—marathon (each study had more than one such group) and wait (each study had one such group). Both employed a different expert leader for each group, and both used three testing times: pregroup, postgroup, and follow-up. Little or no information about group procedures is given in either reference. On the posttest, but not at follow-up, Kimball and Gelso (1974) report significant differences in Self-regard and Self-acceptance scales of the TSCS. However, multiple significance testing makes interpretation of these significance levels (as well as their other significant results) moot. Also, some of their other data involve psychometrically undefensible change scores.

D. S. Jones and Medvene (1975) analyzed each POI scale at each of three levels of Barron's Ego Strength. Multiple significance testing precludes interpreting their few significant main effects and interactions. In any event, no main effect on Self-regard or Self-acceptance scales is reported.

In a study of counseling directed particularly toward the "anxieties" of college-bound high school seniors, Clements (1966) commendably used a large number of subjects divided randomly into experimental and control groups, and he based some of his analyses on post-only test scores, obviating the effects of test reactivity. Only 2 counselors were involved (both "doctoral students"); each handled 3 groups of 10 in a briefly described manner, for 6 50-minute weekly sessions in the spring of the high school students' senior year. No information is given about the instructions to or the activities of the 120 control subjects, half of whom were tested in the spring, half of whom were tested in college the following fall. Self-ideal discrepancies from an idiosyncratic version of the IAV and an idiosyncratic new Self-Concept Inventory were said to index "anxiety." The psychometric characteristics of these scores are unreported. In the comparison which seems most defensible, the 60 counseled subjects were said to have significantly smaller self-ideal discrepancies on both instruments compared to the 60 contemporaneously tested controls. No specific information is given about these particular significance tests, however.

b. STUDIES OF PERSONS WITH DIAGNOSED OR SELF-REPORTED PROBLEMS

The group of studies summarized immediately below involved retarded persons or persons with some sort of diagnosed or self-reported behavior problem. All of these investigations are seriously limited and/or flawed. Three of them may suggest the possibility that group counseling improves self-ideal congruence among adolescents with serious behavior problems. One suggests that group treatment may improve self-reported predispositions toward interpersonal and/or general anxiety. However, none has a suitable control for nonspecific effects; so one must withhold any interpretations that counseling per se was a factor in the reported improvements.

Humes, Adamczyk, and Myco (1969) randomly divided 28 educable retarded adolescents into 2 counseled groups and 2 control groups. Each of "two experienced school counselors" handled 1 counseled and 1 control group. While the 2 counseled groups met 1 hour per week for 12 weeks to be counseled by a briefly described method, the 2 control groups met to receive vocational and occupational information.

Counselors were uninformed about the hypotheses of the experiment. A number of self-concept and behavioral posttest measures were analyzed, pretest data being used only to check for the equalizing effects of random assignment to groups. Unfortunately, the use of multiple significance tests (especially since they involved intercorrelated variables) mars the interpretability of obtained "significant" p values. In any event, neither Lipsitt's Self-Concept Scale for Children nor the Piers-Harris Self-Concept Scale for Children revealed any significant intergroup differences. An unspecified score from the California Test of Personality significantly differentiated the experimental and control subjects.

From 112 fourth- and fifth graders in one school, English and Higgins (1971) chose the 20 most maladjusted children (as inferred from the teachers' reports on a School Adjustment Scale). These 20 were randomly assigned to an experimental group (which received 45 minutes of client-centered counseling once a week for 10 weeks from an experienced school psychologist) and a control group (which had a corresponding schedule of teacher-supervised activity periods with a choice of such things as games, free reading, or schoolwork). Obviously, leader and treatment were confounded. Groups were virtually identical with respect to mean scores on an idiosyncratic Feelings of Inadequacy Scale administered 4 weeks before counseling. They continued to differ nonsignificantly on a posttest 2 weeks after counseling. The fact that all the children expressed willingness to participate suggests that resistance to counseling probably did not play a part in the lack of change. The authors speculate that their null results may have occurred because the counseling method may be inappropriate to the age group.

In a very sketchily reported study, Arbuckle and Boy (1961) also used client-centered therapy, but with a slightly older group—junior high school students classified by both teachers and administrators as major behavior problems. Three groups, matched with respect to mean and SD of age, grade, IQ, Stanford Achievement Test, and teachers' behavior ratings were treated as follows: (a) release from after-school detention plus 12 sessions of client-centered counseling; (b) a continuation of after-school detention; (c) a release from after-school detention. Unfortunately, no information is given regarding the instrument used or even the mean values of self-ideal rs. We are simply told that the groups did not differ significantly at pretest and that only the counseled group showed a significantly higher mean r at posttest.

From a large junior high school, Caplan (1957) chose 34 boys, aged 12–15, with "records of long-term, frequent conflict with school authorities and regulations" (p. 124). The experimental and control groups (each containing 17 subjects) were "roughly matched for economic satus, intelligence, age, and school record" (p. 124). Three pairs of comparison subgroups were formed from seventh, eighth, and ninth grades, respectively. The 3 counseled groups had 10 50-minute weekly counseling sessions, the nature of which is vaguely described. It is unclear what the controls did and whether they knew they were part of the research, i.e., whether they might have felt "pushed out." A vaguely described, idiosyncratic Q sort, used before and after counseling, yielded no experimental-control difference at pretesting. Each of the 3 counseled groups showed a significant increase in mean z after the counseling sessions, whereas none of the 3 control groups did.

Truax, Wargo, and Silber (1966) randomly divided a group of institutionalized, delinquent girls into a therapy group ($N = 40$) and a control group ($N = 30$). Four therapy subgroups of 10 each met twice a week for 24 sessions. Only 2 therapists were involved, but both had been previously judged (and were judged again in this study) to be "above average" on accurate empathy and nonpossessive warmth. The orientation of the therapists and exactly what transpired in therapy sessions are not described, nor do the authors tell what the control subjects did or even whether they knew they had been so designated. A modified Butler-Haigh Q sort was used before and after counseling and was scored several ways, leading to numerous significance tests involving overlapping components. Thus, the interpretability of all the significance tests is questionable. Considering only the self-ideal z, one sees that the controls' mean z at pretest was .52, while the therapy-group mean z was .44. (It is not said whether this difference is significant.) The authors attempted to justify the use of between-condition comparisons of pre-post change scores by the use of ANCOVA which yielded a significant difference. The posttherapy mean $z = .70$; posttest control mean $z = .44$.

A study reported by Fairweather, Simon, Gebhard, Weingarten, Holland, Sanders, Stone, and Reahl (1960) involved both individual and group therapy. It is summarized in the section of this chapter concerned with individual therapy. They obtained no evidence for self-concept change as a function of group therapy in hospitalized non-psychotic, short-term psychotic, and long-term psychotic patients.

By an unspecified method, Ends and Page (1957) divided 69 male, hospitalized inebriates into 16 groups. Only 63 subjects completed the research program, and one cannot evaluate attrition effects, if any. Four groups were assigned by an unspecified method to each of 4 conditions: (a) therapy based on Mowrer's learning theory, (b) client-centered therapy, (c) psychoanalytic therapy, and (d) social discussion (control). Each of 4 therapists took 1 group under each of the 4 conditions. Each therapist had at least 2 years of experience and had trained at least 1 year in methods other than his own. Sessions were held 3 times per week for 5 weeks. Patients' mean pretest and posttest self-ideal zs from the Butler-Haigh Q sort are presented for each of the 4 conditions. Although it appears that the pretest mean zs are unequal between conditions, no ANOVAs are provided to enable one to evaluate the significance of these differences. Analysis of covariance was not used in analyzing posttest differences. Instead, the pre-post mean change within each condition was separately tested for significance. Client-centered, psychoanalytic, and social discussion (control) mean zs were all higher at posttest than at pretest, but none was significantly higher. The mean posttest z under the learning theory condition was significantly lower than the pretest z.

DiLoreto's (1971) research is notable for a number of methodological points, including an attempt to direct group therapy toward a relatively restricted aspect of self-conception and behavior, as opposed to directing it toward over-all self-regard. As I have noted in a number of places in this book, it appears that research on global self-regard constructs may yield fewer strong relationships with other variables than does research involving more restricted aspects of self-concept.

Out of approximately 600 introductory psychology students who were told about a program which might lower their self-reported "interpersonal anxiety," 217 volunteered to take the author's test battery, including an idiosyncratic Interpersonal Anxiety Scale (IPAS), other anxiety measures, and the Myers-Briggs Type Indicator which purports to measure introversion-extraversion. From 149 students meeting stated selection criteria, 100 were assigned randomly, within stratified blocks, to one of 10 introvert and 10 extravert groups. The modal composition of the 20 groups of 5 subjects each was 2 males and 3 females, and each 5-person group was assigned randomly to one of the 5 conditions listed below.

The items in the two forms of the specially developed Interpersonal Anxiety Scale are published, along with some psychometric information based on a pilot study. Also used as a measure of interpersonal anxiety was the Interpersonal subsection of the S-R Inventory of Anxiousness (Endler, Hunt, & Rosenstein, 1962). "General anxiety" predispositions were indexed by Endler et al.'s Fear of the Unknown subsection and the Spielberger and Gorsuch (1966) Trait Anxiety Inventory. Although both trait and state anxiety indices were employed in this study, I consider here only the former, because self-reported trait anxiety seems more appropriately classifiable as a specific aspect of self-conception.

There were 5 conditions: 11 hours of group therapy by (a) systematic desensitization; or (b) Ellis's rational approach; or (c) Rogers's client-centered approach; (d) 11 hours of "attention" (placebo); (e) no contact (these subjects were unaware they were in the study, posttest and follow-up data being secured by mail under the guise of a "random sampling" for test validation). DiLoreto chose the 3 therapy approaches because all of them have dealt theoretically with interpersonal anxiety and have allegedly been therapeutically successful with this characteristic. The 5 major groups listed above did not differ at pretest on IPAS or any of the other measures used.

The six therapists were advanced graduate students who were experienced in and committed to one of the above three therapeutic orientations. DiLoreto argues that a particular kind of therapy will have the best opportunity to show an effect if it is carried out by an experienced and convinced advocate. On these grounds, he believed it inappropriate to control therapist orientation across therapy groups.

Data are available from a pretest battery, a posttest battery, and a 13-week follow-up battery. ANOVAs with Scheffé post hoc comparisons were performed on posttest and follow-up data. So many comparisons are made that the significance level of any particular outcome cannot be evaluated. Nevertheless, DiLoreto concluded: (a) Each of the therapy conditions produced a significantly greater reduction in interpersonal anxiety and in general anxiety than either of the control conditions. (b) The no-treatment (placebo) control condition produced a significantly greater reduction in interpersonal anxiety and in general anxiety than the no-contact control condition.

I note that inspection of the means reveals the following points of interest: (a) When pre-post differences in anxiety means occurred, they tended to be large, with less change or no further change occurring at follow-up. (b) In the no-contact control condition, extraverts' anxiety means are somewhat lower at posttest and follow-up than at pretest, whereas introverts' anxiety means tend to be more nearly the same across all three points. This observation is of some suggestive interest in the light of the fact that the pretest anxiety means of introverts appear to be considerably above those of the extraverts. Accordingly, more regression to the mean would be expected among the introverts, and the results among the no-contact controls fall opposite to what would be expected on the basis of the regression artifact. (c) In contrast to the situation with the no-contact controls, pretest to follow-up changes in anxiety means in the placebo-control groups are larger in the introvert groups than in the extravert groups. This finding *is* congruent with what one might expect on the basis of statistical regression to the mean. However, since no tendency toward statistical regression was observable in the no-contact introverts, it seems questionable whether the introverts' greater change in anxiety means in the placebo-control conditions is attributable simply to statistical regression.

DiLoreto took the precaution of having records of the therapy sessions evaluated by expert judges who had theoretical commitments and experience relevant to the three therapy approaches, respectively. Unfortunately, these experts did not think that the therapy had been conducted according to the respective approach each purportedly represented. For this reason and because therapists were not counterbalanced across techniques, I omit consideration of results comparing the three treatment conditions.

In summary, results of this research do suggest that activity which is labeled group therapy created a greater difference in self-reported predispositional anxiety than occurred in placebo or no-contact control groups. So far as one can discern, the placebo group did not construe their "attention" as therapy; therefore there is no control in this study for the nonspecific therapy effects suggested by the results of McCardel and Murray (1974) whose work is summarized at the beginning of this section.

It is interesting that therapy directed toward predispositional interpersonal anxiety appeared to affect more general predispositional anxiety as well.

c. Overview of Substantively Summarized Studies

An overview of all the substantively summarized research gives no support for the belief that allegedly therapeutic or growth-producing group experiences affect the over-all level of self-regard of volunteer "normal," young adult participants. Null findings are by far the most common. This is true even in those studies in which nonspecific influences such as leaders' or participants' belief in the potential efficacy of the experience could have induced apparently positive effects, inasmuch as such nonspecific influences were not controlled. Results from one study suggest that it is necessary to control for such nonspecific effects.

While a "box score" count of outcomes from all the publications I examined might have pointed toward a bit more optimistic conclusion, serious methodological flaws make such a box score approach undefensible.

Perhaps counseling directed toward specific sources of anxiety may increase reported self-regard and/or change self-reported predispositional anxiety. However, controls for nonspecific effects were not adequate.

The most consistently positive outcomes involved subjects who manifested problems at pretest, i.e., subjects observed to show serious behavior problems or delinquency, and subjects selected for their high levels of self-reported predispositional anxiety. Since these investigations did not provide control of nonspecific effects, their results, too, must be viewed with reservations. Two studies of hospitalized adults (alcoholics and psychotics) yielded null results.

3. List of Studies Not Substantively Summarized

Following is a list of those investigations which seemed so seriously flawed as not to warrant substantive summaries. Adesso, Euse, Hanson, Hendry, and Choca (1974); N. E. Adler and Goleman (1975); Apostal and Muro (1970); Barrett-Lennard, Kwasnik, and Wilkinson (1973/74); F. Barron and Leary (1955); Baymurr and Patterson (1960); Bebout (1971/72); Berzon, Reisel, and Davis (1969); R. L. Burke and Bennis (1961); J. V. Clark, Culbert, and Bobele (1969); Culbert, Clark, and Bobele (1968); Eiben and Clack (1973); Ends and Page (1959); Foulds (1970, 1973); Foulds, Girona, and Guinan (1970); Foulds and Hannigan (1974); Fromme, W. H. Jones, and J. O. Davis (1974); Gassner, J. Gold, and Snadowsky (1964); Gilligan (1974); Guinan and Foulds (1970) (see Marks, Conry, and Foster [1973] for a critique of this study); Guinan, Foulds, and Wright (1973), covering the same study as Guinan and Foulds (1970); Hansen, Moore, and Carkhuff (1968);

Hewitt and Kraft (1973); Hurst, Delworth, and Garriott (1973); Insel and Moos (1972); Jacobson and Smith (1972); Kelman and Parloff (1957); King, Payne, and W. G. McIntire (1973); Koile and Draeger (1969); Levinson and Kitchener (1966); Mann (1969); Mann, Beaber, and Jacobson (1969), covering the same study as Mann (1969); McCardel and Murray (1974); McGinnis (1963); W. G. McIntire (1973); F. E. McLaughlin, M. L. Davis, and Reed (1972); Muzekari, Weinman, and Kreiger (1973); Myrick and Pare (1971); O'Connell and Hanson (1970); Osborne and Swenson (1972); Parloff, Kelman, and Frank (1954); D. R. Peters (1970); Pleck (1972); Reddy (1972, 1973); Ritter (1968); I. M. Rubin (1967a, 1967b) which cover the same study; Sakowitz and Hirschman (1975); Satz and Baraff (1962); Schatt, Burtness, and K. W. Wilson (1973); Schwartz and Dubitzky (1968); Seeman, Nidich, and Banta (1972); Sherwood (1965, 1967) which analyze the same data; W. R. Thompson and Randolph (1973); Treppa and Fricke (1972); Truax, Schuldt, and Wargo (1968); Truax and Wargo (1969); University of Massachusetts Counseling Center Staff (1972); Vicino, Krusell, Bass, Deci, and Landy (1973); Walton (1973); Weigel and Warnath (1968); Weinstein and Hanson (1975); H. N. Weissman, Seldman, and Ritter (1971); J. White (1974); M. Williams, McGee, Kittleson, and Halperin (1962); Winkler, Munger, Gust, and Teigland (1963); Woody (1971); Young and Jacobson (1970).

C. STUDIES OF INDIVIDUAL PSYCHOTHERAPY

1. General Characteristics of Individual Psychotherapy Studies

This section is based on a close examination of 77 research reports concerning individual psychotherapy. Apparently only about 61 different sets of data are involved, as some studies have been reported piecemeal or repeatedly in 2 to 8 publications each. I include only investigations which involved some kind of self-report measures which could plausibly be construed as indicants of some aspect(s) of self-conception. This section excludes studies which used only self-rated improvement or check lists of symptoms marked by patients.

a. REPORTS OF PROCEDURES

With rare exceptions, the studies considered here are not adequately described.

b. Use and Adequacy of Control Groups

As in the research on group psychotherapy, the present investigations were aimed mostly at studying outcomes. Unfortunately, about half of them had no nontherapy control group. (This includes several in which different groups were given various kinds of therapy.) Another third of the publications either gave insufficient information about the characteristics of the control groups or they made it obvious that the characteristics of control and therapy groups were definitely not comparable. Uncontrolled effects of attrition seem plausibly important in these studies, but cannot be evaluated from the information given.

Aside from the adequacy of equating personal characteristics and motivations of control and therapy subjects, one needs to know whether the instruction and activities of these persons were appropriate to the experimenters' purposes. All the publications are extremely weak on these points.

c. Theoretical Orientations

As already stated, the psychotherapy situation is not satisfactory for definitive testing of the tenets of any particular personality theory. Nonetheless, it is of interest to see the stated theoretical predilections of the researchers as these partially determined their hypotheses and procedures. Research on individual psychotherapy was initiated by self-concept theorists, and this orientation is the most common one underlying the studies considered here. However, more than one-third of the studies considered here gave an extremely vague statement or no information at all about the underlying theoretical orientation. Regardless of quality of method and statistical interpretability of results, then, the group of studies as a whole cannot be said to advance our knowledge of the relative merits of various personality theories.

d. Numbers and Characteristics of Therapists

More than one-third of the publications give no information about the number of therapists involved. In 17 studies, 11 or more therapists participated; in the remainder, 1 to 10 therapists were used. It is impossible to estimate the extent to which therapist characteristics were confounded with treatment conditions, or the extent to which the therapists knew the hypotheses or even planned the research, and therefore had a vested interest in its outcome.

Published information provides no basis for a precise evaluation of the level of experience of therapists involved in the researches. Nearly half the reports give no such information, and the remainder are often vague. Of those that give any information, apparently half (i.e., only about one-fourth of all studies) used "professional," "experienced," or "Ph.D. level" counselors; almost as many used students, including graduate students, "journeymen," and medical students with unspecified or no previous experience in giving psychotherapy. Thus, one cannot evaluate the likelihood that null outcomes may be accounted for in part by the use of inexperienced therapists. With extremely rare exceptions, the publications stand silent about what actually transpired in the therapy sessions.

e. Construct Validity of Self-Concept Measures

Of course the construct validity of the self-report measures is very important in trying to interpret reported results. Unfortunately, almost one-third of the results are based on idiosyncratic scales about which little or no psychometric information is presented, precluding a thorough evaluation and psychological interpretation of the results.

In addition to self-concept tests or scales, a number of persons have developed ways of coding self-referent constructs from therapy interviews themselves, and they have presented some psychometric information about their schemes: Braaten (1961), Bugental (1952), Lipkin (1954), Raimy (1948), Raskin (1952), Rosenman (1955), Scheerer (1949), Stock (1949), Todd and Ewing (1961), Vargas (1954). Such schemes could conceivably be useful in looking at processes within therapy as well as in examining outcomes. In the absence of control groups, the application of none of these coding procedures permits conclusions about outcomes, of course. Even changes across the therapy period cannot be interpreted as a function of therapy per se in the absence of a control series of interviews which do not purport to be therapeutic and/or comparable sets of interviews conducted by supposedly contrasting therapeutic approaches. As the publication dates show, research of this type seems to have died out. Although content of interviews continues to be a live issue (see Kiesler, 1973, for an excellent methodological overview), I have not found recent applications of the technique to process or outcome research concerning self-referent constructs such as self-regard or particular aspects of self-description and evaluation.

As befits a research area which was started by the Rogerian group, the Butler-Haigh Q sort (BHQ) or Dymond's modification thereof was the most commonly used well-known instrument (Butler and Haigh, 1954; Dymond, 1954). Eight studies used one or more MMPI scales, while one or two used each of the following: the California Psychological Inventory, the Willoughby Emotional Maturity Scale, the Edwards Personal Preference Scale, the Gordon Personal Profile and Gordon Personal Inventory, the Hilden Q set, Interpersonal Check List (ICL), Myers-Briggs Type Indicator, the Miskimins Self-Goal-Other Inventory, Cattell's 16 PF Inventory, Shostrom's Personal Orientation Inventory (POI), Kelly's Role Construct Repertory Test, and the Welsh Anxiety Scale. (In my 1974 book, I have extensively evaluated the BHQ, Hilden Q, and ICL. Relevant comments on POI may be found in section B-1 of this chapter.)

f. COMMON USE OF DYADIC SCORES

Unfortunately, many of the outcome studies are uninterpretable because of the use of dyadic scores. Although it is now generally accepted (see Wylie, 1974, pp. 89-95, 304-309; and Cronbach and Furby, 1970) that such scores are psychometrically indefensible, many of these publications appeared before that methodological point was recognized. Consequently, use of change scores, discrepancy scores, client-therapist similarity scores, insight scores (see Wylie, 1974, chap. 6), and certain empathy scores vitiate the interpretability of a great many of the results in this area.

g. LIMITATIONS OF DESIGN

All but two of the studies which purported to look at outcome used a pre-post design. Thus, possible reactivity from pretesting could not be evaluated. Also, one could not see whether the obtained function might be nonlinear or whether fluctuations or cycles occur. Moreover, there is no indication as to whether lasting changes in self-conception were produced.

While it is commonly accepted that self-reports have many determinants, this research area is notable for the lack of controlled multivariate research designs.

h. Multiple Significance Tests

With respect to dependent variables, at least two-thirds of the publications present multiple significance tests typically based on scores which either are comprised of overlapping components or are probably intercorrelated for other reasons. Thus, the significance of any one of the reportedly significant findings cannot be evaluated, especially in the absence of cross-validation which is lacking in this area.

2. Intercorrelations among Self-Report Measures

Some of the researches which used no control groups attempted to look at relationships among self-report variables within the therapy situation. Some of these investigations intercorrelated or factor-analyzed self-reports of clients or patients. These include Braaten (1961); D. S. Cartwright and Roth (1957); D. S. Cartwright, Kirtner, and Fiske (1963); Forsyth and Fairweather (1961) (although there was a no-therapy control group in this study, all cases were thrown together for the cluster analysis); Garfield, Prager, and Bergin (1971) (see Fiske, 1971, and Luborsky, 1971, for a critique of this study); Gibson, Snyder, and Ray (1955); Raskin (1952).

This approach, if properly applied, might conceivably reveal fragmentation or patterning in self-reports in therapy. Such findings could be of methodological relevance to future, properly controlled research on outcomes or process. However, the present studies, lacking control groups, cannot shed light on whether therapy influenced these correlations. (The researches are characterized by other methodological flaws as well.)

3. Psychotherapy Success and Self-Report

Studies of other researches without control groups, as well as some with such groups, correlated judgments of psychotherapeutic "success" or "change" against self-report measures. About a fifth of all the examined reports fell in this category: J. M. Butler (1968); J. M. Butler and Haigh (1954); R. D. Cartwright (1957, 1961); R. D. Cartwright and Lerner (1963); Endler (1961a); Ewing (1954); Haigh (1949); Hollon and Zolik (1962); Lipkin (1954); Raimy (1948); Rosenman (1955); Varble and Landfield (1969); Vargas (1954). Among other methodological shortcomings, a very serious problem with many of these is that the therapist was at least one of the judges of improvement. Thus, it appears that there could be contamination between the subject's written self-reports and therapists' judgments, insofar as the latter are affected by the subject's oral self-references during therapy interviews.

4. Therapist and Client Characteristics Related to Outcome

Almost a tenth of all studies attempted to relate self-concept outcome variables to: (a) therapist characteristics (e.g., therapist competence, therapist empathy, therapist expectations), or (b) client characteristics (e.g., repressor-sensitizer scores), or (c) therapist-client similarity in self-reported personality characteristics. The results of these researches are uninterpretable for one or more of the reasons, given below, among others.

a. THERAPIST CHARACTERISTICS

As K. I. Howard and Orlinsky (1972) have pointed out, serious psychometric limitations or problems characterize the measurement of therapist characteristics. For example, in two studies, therapist characteristics were judged partly in terms of subjects' reports about the therapist, implying possible contamination between measures of therapeutic competence and subjects' self-concept scores (Barrett-Lennard, 1962; Kurtz & Grummon, 1972). In other studies, the highly debatable Accurate Empathy score is involved (e.g., Rogers, Gendlin, Kiesler, & Truax, 1967). Among the questions which may be raised about this score is the following: if empathy is judged from tapes which include the subjects' remarks or paraphrases of them by the therapist, is it not possible, even likely, that there is a contamination between self-concept outcome scores and therapist empathy scores? (See Chinsky & Rappaport, 1970; Truax, 1972; and J. Rappaport & Chinsky, 1972, regarding the controversy surrounding this score. See Kurtz and Grummon [1972] for lack of correlation among alternate purported measures of "therapist empathy.")

(Two researchers looked for associations between therapists' evaluations of self [and/or others] and their rated therapeutic competence. Maskin [1974] related therapists' Self-confidence and Self-control scores taken from Gough's Adjective Check List to their clients' evaluations of their therapeutic effectiveness on Cottle's Client

Evaluation Form. Very small Ns and the use of an insufficiently described, idiosyncratic instrument preclude interpretations. Streitfeld [1959] reported a null relationship between therapists' scores on Berger's Self Acceptance and Acceptance of Others scales and supervisors' ratings of their therapeutic competence. It appears that the ability-scale ratings actually assigned must have fallen within a range of less than one step on a scale from 1–6; and no information about reliability is given. Thus, these null findings may be attributable partly to psychometric characteristics of the instrument, but as things stand, the results are uninterpretable.)

b. SELF-REPORTED CHARACTERISTICS OF THE CLIENT

With respect to predicting self-report outcomes from pretherapy self-reports, the possibility of contamination between predictor and predicted variables seems obvious. Moreover, correlations of self-report outcomes and initial self-report status may be artifactually influenced by the fact that only those with initially unfavorable self-reports could show much upward change (e.g., as in Barrett-Lennard's 1962 study).

c. CLIENT-THERAPIST SIMILARITY

The whole group of researches involving client-therapist similarity in self-reports is uninterpretable for two reasons. First, despite occasional recognition of the psychometric weaknesses of dyadic scores, the problem was not adequately resolved methodologically. Second, since part of this particular kind of dyadic score is a subject's self-report, one is in some studies dealing with a correlation between two subject-self-report variables, namely a self-report measure of outcome and a similarity index also involving the subject's self-report.

Studies involving similarity between client and therapist self-reports include Bare (1967); Carson and Heine (1962); Carson and Llewellyn (1966); Lichtenstein (1966); Mendelsohn (1966); Mendelsohn and Geller (1963, 1965, 1967).

5. Substantive Summaries of Outcome Studies

If one chose for substantive summary those publications which meet reasonably rigorous standards of methodological and reporting adequacy, one could not justify summarizing any studies of the effects of individual psychotherapy on self-concept reports. However, I have chosen a few which are of historical importance or seem to be relatively more adequate than the rest.

A historical landmark was set by the research on the effects of individual nondirective psychotherapy which is extensively reported in Rogers and Dymond's (1954) book. The research team showed commendable scientific intentions in their proposal to apply theoretically relevant measurements to subjects undergoing therapy and various control conditions. However, the research yielded inconclusive results, for reasons explained below.

Among numerous measurements taken, those most relevant to the self-concept were self-descriptions on the Butler-Haigh Q sort and a modified Willoughby's Emotional Maturity Scale. (The BHQ is extensively described and evaluated in Wylie, 1974.) Several scores were obtained from each individual's Q sort: self-ideal r, self-self r over time, ideal-ideal r over time, and Dymond's specially devised adjustment score based on 74 of the 100 items. Naturally, then, multiple significance testing was entailed, in some instances involving overlapping items or scores. Thus, significance levels are uninterpretable.

Although the research team planned to sample randomly all adult applicants to the University of Chicago Counseling Center, stratifying only according to sex and student-nonstudent status, many factors prevented their doing so (Grummon, 1954a). For a variety of reasons, about half the persons who were requested to participate refused to do so. For humanitarian reasons, research participants were not always randomly assigned to the wait or immediate treatment groups, leading to unknown sources of lack of comparability between these groups. Only those therapy clients who completed six or more interviews were retained. Because nine cases could not be posttested, they were dropped from the therapy group. Some of them were dropped because they refused posttesting, and the dropped group was also judged to be less successful than the average case (Grummon, 1954a). Altogether, the preceding three sources of attrition in the experimental group imply that the experimental findings are probably biased in favor of finding the predicted improvements in self-report as a function of therapy.

The over-all plan called for 4 groups: (a) a wait group tested at 4 times—pre-wait, before therapy (after a 60-day wait period), after therapy, after a 6-12 month follow-up; (b) a no-wait group tested 3 times—before therapy, after therapy, after a 6-12 month follow-up period; (c) a control group of subjects who volunteered to serve as subjects for "research on personality," these persons matched on sex, student status, age, and approximate socioeconomic status with the subjects in the first group and tested 4 times at comparable points; (d) a control group of subjects who also volunteered to serve as subjects for "research on personality," these persons matched on sex, student status, age, and approximate socioeconomic level with the second group and tested at comparable times. Groups 1 and 2 comprised 29 persons, Groups 3 and 4 comprised 23 persons. However, not all subjects in all groups were used for various comparisons.

Some of the problems in establishing the first two groups have already been mentioned. In addition, the following difficulties must be noted.

J. M. Butler and Haigh (1954) report that the 15 wait-control clients who later went on to therapy showed no improvement in self-ideal congruence over the waiting period (mean rs were -.01 and -.01). Grummon (1954b) says that 8 no-therapy controls (presumably those matched to the wait controls) also showed no change between the first and second administration of the test (mean rs were .79 and .82). This type of comparison is not appropriate on several grounds. First, it does not tell us what changes would have occurred in the waiting subjects if they had not expected to get therapy eventually. Perhaps they felt rejected by having to wait, counteracting any tendencies for self-ideal r to rise as it might in a comparable time period when they were not experiencing rejection. Or perhaps they made less effort to solve their own problems in the interim than would subjects not having expectation of forthcoming help. Alternately, they may have wished to indicate just before therapy that they were still in need of help, thus producing a low self-ideal r at pretherapy despite changes which had actually occurred in their self-concepts.

J. M. Butler and Haigh (1954) say that 23 clients (evidently all those who did not terminate in 6 interviews) moved from a mean pretherapy r of -.01 to a follow-up r of .31. By contrast, 16 no-therapy control subjects (evidently those matched to nonterminating clients) moved only from .58 at precounseling to .59 at follow-up.

It is clear that the no-therapy controls were not comparable to the therapy clients with respect to motivation for therapy and self-ideal congruence. As Calvin (1954) has pointed out, the pretherapy-follow-up comparison does not specifically indicate what would have happened over this long period to noncounseled controls who started out with self-ideal rs as low as the therapy patients. One should note, too, that on purely statistical grounds, there is less room for upward change from a value of + .58 than from -.01.

The Butler-Haigh Q sorts made by the subjects in this research were also assigned an "adjustment score" developed by Dymond (1954). The results concerning the effects of counseling on the adjustment score parallel those reported by Butler and Haigh in terms of self-ideal congruence. However, the fact that the adjustment score and the self-ideal rs were derived from the same instrument and correlated + .8 with each other indicates that these findings are not independent tests of a hypothesis concerning the effects of therapy on the self-concept.

In the same research, Rogers (1954) found no change in the subjects' self-reports on a modified Willoughby Emotional Maturity Scale during the pretherapy waiting period, and no change in the no-therapy control subjects. But there was a significant change toward reports of greater maturity from pretherapy to posttherapy in subjects who received therapy. Thus, his data using self-reports from the same subjects as those studied by Butler and Haigh and by Dymond gave results parallel to theirs. It seems plausible that the Emotional Maturity Scale correlates with both types of scores from the Butler-Haigh Q sort. Therefore, the three sets of trends cannot be independently evaluated for significance. (Interestingly enough, Emotional Maturity ratings of therapy patients made by their friends and judgments of therapy success made by the counselor did not relate to each other or to the subjects' self-reports on the Emotional Maturity Scale in any simple fashion.)

In yet another analysis of the Q-sort data (based on only 8 of the wait-control subjects), Rudikoff (1954) pointed out that the following held true for each case: (a) the self-self correlations based on prewait and pretherapy testing were larger than were the self-self correlations based on pretherapy and posttherapy testing, suggesting that more changes in self-description occurred during the therapy period; (b) the ideal-ideal correlations based on pretherapy and posttherapy testing were higher than the self-self correlations based on these testing points, suggesting that shifts in self-ideal r in therapy might be more attributable to shifts in self-description than to shifts in ideal-self description.

It appears that reports by Shlien, Mosak, and Dreikurs (1962) and J. M. Butler (1968) involve almost entirely overlapping sets of subjects and that Butler's report gives again the data for normal controls published in J. M. Butler and Haigh (1954). Unfortunately, extremely vague and incomplete reporting in the two articles makes it impossible to evaluate precisely the degree of overlap among the three reports. Butler (1968) says nothing about the number and experience of the therapists, Shlien et al. (1962) say only that 15 client-centered and 8 Adlerian therapists were involved.

Apparently 6 different groups were involved in the 2 articles as follows: (a) *Normal, no-therapy controls* (Shlien et al. give no other information, but it appears that these subjects may be the same as those reported by Butler (1968). From Butler's *N*s and self-ideal *r* values, one must infer that his normal-group data are the same as those reported earlier by J. M. Butler and Haigh (1954). (b) 20 patients given *limited client-centered therapy*, i.e., according to a pretherapy agreement, no more than 20 interviews would be held. Apparently data from this group are given in both articles. (c) 20 patients given *limited Adlerian therapy*, i.e., according to a pretherapy agreement, no more than 20 interviews would be held. Apparently data from this group are given in both articles, although Shlien et al. give no *N*. (d) 29 or 30 patients given *unlimited client-centered therapy*, the average number of interviews = 37. Shlien et al. mention 30 such patients, Butler 29, but the self-ideal *z* values are exactly the same in the 2 publications; so one assumes they come from the same group. (e) 43 patients given *10 weeks of client-centered therapy*. Apparently this group is unique to the Butler (1968) report. (6) *wait controls*—20 who waited 10 weeks, according to Butler's report; an unspecified number who waited 3 months, according to Shlien et al.'s report.

Obviously the criticisms of the Rogers and Dymond control groups (explained in detail above) must be applicable here as well. Thus, no clear inference can be drawn from the fact that the wait-control group (or groups) show essentially zero mean self-ideal *r* at prewait and pretherapy. (How Shlien et al. obtained their reported zero *r* for the wait controls at follow-up as well is not clear, since the wait controls presumably got therapy after three months.) Both the motivation of the normal controls and their self-ideal *r*s were quite different from the therapy groups, as was the case in the Rogers and Dymond (1954) study.

From J. M. Butler's (1968) report one gleans that all therapy groups showed a significant increase in self-ideal *r* from pretherapy to posttherapy. From Shlien et al.'s report one sees that the three therapy groups they mention apparently held their gains at follow-up. It does not appear that the three therapy groups in the Shlien et al. report differed among themselves, but insufficient information is given to be sure. Shlien et al. state that the greater efficiency of the limited type of therapy is suggested by the similarity among therapy groups. However, direct comparisons are dubious because, according to Butler (1968), Group 1 was given the usual 100-item BHQ, while Groups 2 and 3 were given a "very similar form"; whereas Shlien et al. say that Groups 1, 2, and 3 were all given an 80-item form of the BHQ!

It seems possible that Rogers and Dymond's (1954) book and these two articles combined involved five therapy groups altogether and that each showed a significant increase in mean self-ideal r across the therapy period. However, the problems with the control groups preclude attributing these significant increases specifically to psychotherapy.

While the University of Chicago work just discussed used student and community outpatients, Fairweather, Simon, Gebhard, Weingarten, Holland, Sanders, Stone, and Reahl (1960) used patients in a veterans' neuropsychiatric hospital. Up to a point, new patients were randomly assigned to 1 of 4 treatment groups, after which further placements were made by matching across treatments according to age, diagnosis, and length of hospitalization. Further arrivals not meeting the matching criteria were randomly assigned to 1 of the 4 treatment groups, until there were 24 patients in each treatment group and 32 patients in each of 3 diagnostic groups.

Treatment groups were as follows: (a) A *no-therapy control* group receiving an individual work assignment and consultation about posthospital living. (b) An *individual therapy group* receiving an individual work assignment, consultation about departure plans, and also psychoanalytically oriented individual therapy sessions 2 to 4 times per week. (c) A *group therapy group* receiving an individual work assignment, consultation regarding departure plans, and also psychoanalytically oriented group therapy twice a week. (d) A *group therapy, group-living* group who received a group work assignment, a group-living assignment, and group psychotherapy. They apparently received no consultation concerning posthospital plans.

Treatment groups were "quite homogeneous with respect to diagnosis, amount of drugs received, age, education, race, length of previous hospitalization, pensions for NP illness, age of first hospitalization, employment history, occupational status, and marital status" (p. 4). The three diagnostic groups within each of the four treatment groups were (a) nonpsychotic, (b) short-term psychotic, and (c) long-term psychotic.

Only 2 group therapists participated, each having postdoctoral

656

THE SELF-CONCEPT

experience, and each assigned to 24 patients. Individual therapy was administered by 15 individual therapists with a "wide range of experience."

Among numerous items of data available for each subject are self-ideal rs for an idiosyncratic 100-item Q sort. The items and sufficient psychometric information are not published. Five different subscores as well as an over-all self-ideal r were analyzed by Fairweather et al.

Unfortunately, the authors performed their ANOVAs on individual pre-post *change* scores. Thus, these results are uninterpretable. Fortunately, they also published initial and terminal self-ideal rs for each case for the total set of 100 Q-sort items. From computations on these data, one can see the following: (a) Within each of the 3 diagnostic subgroups, initial mean rs for the controls were the highest of the 4 treatment groups. (b) In each of the 4 treatment groups of 24 persons, about half the subjects showed a higher terminal than initial self-ideal r. Specifically, the numbers of such upward changes were: no-therapy controls = 12; individual therapy subjects = 12; group therapy subjects = 12; group therapy, group living = 11. Thus, there is no evidence for effects of therapy on self-ideal congruence. (This agrees with the conclusion reached by the authors from their analysis of change scores.)

Unfortunately, their change-score analyses involving five subscales of the Q sort are uninterpretable, and individual data are not published to enable one to make alternate analyses.

Since there are several points of differences between the outpatient and inpatient studies discussed thus far, one cannot guess which of these method variations led to the contrasting findings: hospitalization status, severity of patient disturbance, psychoanalytic as opposed to client-centered or Adlerian therapy, or use of two different Q sorts having possibly different psychometric properties.

No light is thrown on this question by the study of Rogers, Gendlin, Kiesler, and Truax (1967) in which each of 8 therapists gave individual therapy to a randomized triad of persons comprised of one "more chronic schizophrenic," one "more acute schizophrenic," and one "normal person." Corresponding to each of these 24 treated persons was an untreated control person of comparable age, sex, and educational level and (among psychotic subjects) degree of psychological disturbance. Within each pair of corresponding subjects the assignment to treatment or no-treatment was decided randomly.

Among many other measures, self sorts on 80 unspecified items from the BHQ were obtained. The subjects' individual ideal-self descriptions were not obtained, however. Instead, an "ideal standard sort reflecting the conception of clinical psychologists as to the theoretically well-adjusted person" (p. 265) was used as the basis for getting self-ideal rs for each subject. Dymond's adjustment scoring procedure was also applied to the self sorts.

For the therapy patients as a group versus the controls as a group, repeated measures ANOVAs of initial and terminal scores were computed for Q-sort r, Q-sort adjustment score, and MMPI scale scores. No group effects were significant; only three MMPI scales showed significant trials effects, and no groups × trials interactions were significant.

The many ANOVAs were applied to intercorrelated variables. Thus, if significant F ratios had been obtained, they would have been uninterpretable.

In an effort to see whether the therapists' Accurate Empathy ratings predicted self-report changes, Rogers et al. divided all treated patients into those experiencing therapy conditions judged to be high and low on Accurate Empathy. No significant differences in improvement rate (Q-sort r or Q-sort adjustment) were found for the high empathy–low empathy therapy conditions. It is apparent from figure 11.5, p. 272, that extremely low self-ideal rs (.08 to .12) characterized all groups at both initial and terminal tests.

One might suggest that both Fairweather et al. and Rogers et al. obtained null results because they were dealing mostly or entirely with severely disturbed patients. However, the two studies cannot be directly compared since each used a different therapeutic orientation and different self-regard measures.

The reader will remember from the group therapy section that McCardel and Murray (1974) reported significant improvement in self-regard among persons who thought they were in a marathon group but were actually in a nontechnically led recreational-social group (improvement in this group did not differ from 2 others who actually were in encounter groups.) It is interesting and ironic to note that the one study reporting significant increases in self-regard among individually handled psychotic, neurotic, and character-disordered hospitalized patients apparently obtained these results from 5 to 10 minutes of daily conversation which were nondirective and purportedly friendly, chatty, and informal (i.e., not specifically therapeutic) (Dreiblatt & Weatherley, 1965). One must note that these results were significant on a one-tail test, however.

After obtaining an encouraging outcome from preliminary work with only 1 therapist, Dreiblatt and Weatherley (1965) performed a second experiment involving 74 patients divided as follows: (a) 21 persons who received 6 nonsymptom-oriented brief contacts each week during a 2-week period; (b) 20 persons who received 6 symptom-oriented brief contacts each week; (c) 17 persons contacted 6 times each week to participate in a control task (a guessing game); (d) 16 persons exposed only to the regular ward routine to which all groups were exposed. Patients were randomly assigned to the first 3 groups. The non-contacted controls (Group 4) were drawn from patients admitted either before or after the treatment period so as to insure their not feeling rejected by observing others being contacted.

Self-esteem was defined in terms of self-ideal rs on one of Hilden's Q-sort decks. (See Wylie, 1974, for an evaluation of this set of Q sorts.) Self-concept adjustment scores were obtained by scoring each persons' self-sort in terms of an ideal standard. Testing was done by persons other than those who conversed with the patients. (Symptom check lists, the Welsh A Scale, and length of hospitalization were also analyzed.)

Group 1 (having nonsymptom-oriented conversations) showed a significantly greater increment in self-esteem and self-concept adjustment scores than did either of the control groups. One-tail p values were used in these comparisons, however. Group 2 (having symptom-oriented conversations) did not differ from either the controls or from Group 1 (2-tailed test). The two control groups did not differ from each other, implying that mere contact with a staff member did not have any effect over and above that of ward routine.

In evaluating these results, one must remember that significance tests on obviously intercorrelated dependent-variable measures cannot be adequately interpreted and that the most interesting finding was significant on a one-tail test only. Strengthening this finding somewhat is the fact that results from the pilot study had pointed in the same direction.

In summary, among the substantively discussed studies it appears that five therapy groups showed some improvement in self-regard. However, control problems render the interpretation of even these findings moot. There is some possibility that severity of the patients' disorder may be a limiting factor, since these five groups were all independent, functioning adults, whereas two studies with severely disturbed, hospitalized patients yielded null results. However, this hypothesis cannot be confidently suggested. In fact, one study points to the possibility that brief, nontherapeutically oriented conversational contacts may have had a beneficial influence on self-esteem of patients who were as severely disturbed as those who showed no effects in the major researches which attempted rather extensive therapeutic intervention.

It seems almost unbelievable that more than 20 years of research on the effects of individual psychotherapy on self-concept variables have yielded such meager and ambiguous outcomes. The burden of proof is still on those who claim such effects.

6. List of Studies Not Substantively Summarized

Throughout this section on individual psychotherapy I have simply listed studies which purportedly bore on various topics respectively, but which seemed to me to be methodologically inadequate to sustain conclusions. In addition to those already so listed, the following also seem to me to be too methodologically flawed to merit substantive summaries: Altrocchi, Parsons, and Dickoff (1960); Ashcraft and Fitts (1964); Barron and Leary (1955); Baymurr and Patterson (1960); Cardillo (1971); R. D. Cartwright and Vogel (1960); Dymond (1955); Ewing (1964); Farson (1961); Fiedler and Senior (1952); Fiske, Cartwright, and Kirtner (1964); Fiske and Goodman (1965); A. P. Goldstein (1960); Guller (1969); Hartlage (1970); Heller and Goldstein (1961); J. Hunt, Ewing, LaForge, and Gilbert (1959); Leary and Harvey (1956); M. Lesser (1961); Lorr, Katz, and Rubenstein (1958); Luria (1959); Nichols and Beck (1960); Pearl (1954); E. L. Phillips, Raiford, and El-Batrawi (1965); Rehm and Marston (1968); Rice (1965); Rubinstein and Lorr (1957); Schwartz and Dubitzky (1968); Seitz (1971); Shostrom and Knapp (1966); Strupp, Fox, and Lessler (1969); Strupp, Wallach, and Wogan (1964).

D. Overview of Research Situation in Individual and Group Psychotherapy

Although personality theories are vague and incomplete on many points, it appears that most therapists and patients expect therapy to improve the clients' self-regard and perhaps to effect changes in other aspects of self-concept as well. If positive findings had been reported from the better controlled studies reviewed in this chapter, such trends would have been hailed as supportive of theory and indicative of one kind of benefit to be derived from therapy. Even so, such welcome findings would have had to be regarded with extreme caution. For one thing, they might have stemmed from clients' desires to reduce cognitive dissonance by believing they had been helped by the strenuous regime to which they had committed themselves. Or they might represent the clients' wishes to express gratitude to the therapist by reporting those self-concept changes which were apparently desired by the therapist. (This could occur whether or not the client really experienced changes in self-conception.) Moreover, positive results, had they occurred, might have been partly or wholly attributable to the subjects' expectations or hopes (the placebo effect), rather than to any activity or relationship specific to the therapy situation. Nothing in even the better controlled studies rules out any of the above alternate explanations of positive findings.

By and large, however, the trends are not positive — they are weak or null. This puts us in an even more ambiguous situation. We cannot logically retreat at this point into the position that self-reports are irrelevant or trivial after all and that other criteria are the "correct" measures of therapy change and outcome. This is so because, no matter how desirable or expected other behavior changes may also be, theorists, therapists, and clients seem clearly to agree that self-concept changes should be among the changes brought about by therapy.

If one wishes to retain the original theoretical position, one might perhaps argue that the measures of self-concept were somehow too unreliable or invalid to monitor the clients' initial states and the theory-supportive changes which were actually occurring. Can we lay null results to the inadequacies of the self-report about self-regard or other aspects of self-concept? Certainly all measurement in this area is in its infancy, and the validity and reliability of many instruments, especially the idiosyncratic ones, are highly questionable.

But it seems unlikely that this is the whole story. For one thing, using a variety of self-regard measures, many authors report that patients entering therapy or living in a psychiatric hospital tend to obtain low self-regard scores as compared to subjects not applying for therapy or not hospitalized. (See, for example, J. M. Butler & Haigh, 1954; Chase, 1957; Fitts, 1965; Jaskar & Reed, 1963; Kogan, Quinn, Ax, & Ripley, 1957; Sarbin & Rosenberg, 1955; Shlien, Mosak, & Dreikurs, 1962; Tamkin, 1957; Zuckerman, Baer, & Monashkin, 1956.) This is what theorists and therapists would expect from instruments with some validity for indicating self-regard.

Moreover, it seems clear that low self-regard scores are associated with subjective discomfort of the type that brings patients to therapy. Many authors have obtained associations between self-regard and self-reported trait anxiety and/or depression. (For examples involving a variety of self-regard measures and a variety of *depression* measures such as the MMPI *D*-scale, Rosenberg's Guttman Scale of Depressive Affect, Wessman and Ricks's Mood Scales and the Multiple Affect Adjective Check List, see the following: Bachman, 1970; E. M. Berger, 1955; Block and Thomas, 1955; Engel, 1959; Heath, 1965; Kaplan and Pokorny, 1969; Luck and Heiss, 1972; Mackeen and Herman, 1974; Rosenberg, 1965; Zuckerman, Baer, and Monashkin, 1956. For examples involving a variety of self-regard measures and a variety of measures of *manifest anxiety:* Bass and Fiedler, 1961; Coopersmith, 1967; Cowen, Heilizer, Axelrod, and Alexander, 1957; Fiedler, Hutchins, and Dodge, 1959; Frankel and Barrett, 1971; Heath, 1965; F. D. Horowitz, 1962; Hughes, 1968; L. C. Johnson, 1956; Lekarczyk and Hill, 1969; J. Lewis and Adank, 1975; Lipsitt, 1958; Luck and Heiss, 1972; Mackeen and Herman, 1974; Marcia and Friedman, 1970; Ohnmacht and Muro, 1967; L. B. Parsons, Peterson, and Davids, 1968; B. N. Phillips, Hindsman, and Jennings, 1960; Pilisuk, 1963; Sinha and Sinha, 1968; Truax, Schuldt, and Wargo, 1968; Weitzner, Stallone, and Smith, 1967; Winkler and Myers, 1963; Worchel, 1957.)

Of course one can suggest that such associations between low self-regard and self-reported anxiety and depression represent partly the influence of construct-irrelevant response sets upon the scores from each of the correlated instruments. But such findings are ubiquitous and based on a wide variety of instruments of varying formats. This suggests that response set cannot be the whole explanation of these obtained associations, then. Some may argue that this kind of correlation is obtained because some persons are more willing than others to *admit* both their low self-regard and their predispositional anxiety and depression. This may well be. But, by the same token, one would then expect such frank persons to be influenceable by therapy insofar as they are willing to admit that, by their own standards, they are uncomfortable and in need of change. Moreover, on purely statistical grounds, the initially low level of self-regard scores leaves room for change as a function of therapy, i.e., null findings cannot be due to a ceiling effect. If anything, one would have needed to interpret improvements with caution, owing to the possibility for operation of the statistical regression artifact.

Could the puzzling null findings be attributed to some characteristics of the therapists and/or of the therapies used in these studies? Since we are told virtually nothing specific about the qualifications and behaviors of the therapists and the actual transactions taking place during therapy, we cannot even guess to what extent null findings might be attributable to factors in these areas. About the only hint we get here is that experience per se does not suffice to yield positive results, since null trends occurred in studies involving highly trained and experienced therapists.

Thus we have arrived at a dilemma. As one alternative we could abandon the popular and plausible idea that therapy should improve self-regard and also change other aspects of self-concept. Alternately, we could assert that this notion is too intuitively plausible to abandon on the basis of null findings from inadequately conceived, executed, or reported research. Those who choose the latter alternative obviously have much methodological spadework to do before trying to grow a viable crop of theory-supportive experiments.

12

Self-Favorability Biases
in Self-Reports

Common sense and numerous personality theories agree that human beings have a strong, lifelong need to maintain a favorable self-concept. In one sense, a favorable self-concept could mean simply that one's self-characteristics, acknowledged faults included, make one a person worthy of love and respect from self and others. But in our culture, at least, having a favorable self-concept clearly implies that one experiences a rewarding sense of competence in manipulating the physical environment and that one thinks one has relative superiority to others on a variety of salient traits (the particular traits which are salient differing from person to person). Unless the need to maintain a favorable self-concept in the latter sense is counteracted by some other typically rarer or weaker need (e.g., the need to reduce purely cognitive dissonance, or the need to expiate guilt through self-punishment, or the need to use self-denigration to avoid threatening an important other person), one would expect the need for self-enhancement to lead to a favorability bias in the self-concept and the corresponding self-reports. Thus, a trend toward self-favorability would be expected to hold true for groups of persons.

Self-concept theorists among others have posited that, in order to maintain a favorable self-concept, persons use selective perception, interpretation, and memory of feedback regarding their characteristics. That is, theorists expect that unfavorable feedback will tend to be distorted, minimized, ignored, or forgotten to some degree, whereas favorable information will be exaggerated and remembered longer or more clearly.

The feedback which the subject processes selectively comes from two general sources: nonsocial and social. Exemplifying the former are tangible and visible physical characteristics and the degree of success one has in manipulating the physical environment. If Adler is correct in emphasizing the phenomenal side of biological "inferiorities," some of this kind of nonsocial information may be very discouraging, and children and old persons may be especially likely to encounter this kind of unfavorable information. However, one can speculate that children may be less vulnerable for two reasons: (a) They do not have the standards of perfection which they will later learn, whereas old persons have learned standards for evaluating their physical characteristics and competencies in manipulating the physical environment. (b) Given that children typically improve in physical strength and skills, they would tend to be encouraged despite momentary poor nonsocial feedback, while this would not be true for old people, who cannot help sensing their decline in nonsocial characteristics and skills.

So far as social feedback is concerned, there seem to be certain commonly known practices in our culture which would supplement the selective mechanisms used by the typical person to enhance or maintain the favorability of the self-concept. First, it appears that most parents and teachers have a tendency to react favorably to desired behaviors or other characteristics in children, without necessarily making comparisons with other children. Although parents and teachers must also draw some attention to undesirable behavior, they are often advised to make clear to the child that it is a particular characteristic which is to be modified, while the child as a whole is acceptable. Given the child's need for self-concept enhancement and his selective processing mechanisms, these very early treatments should lead eventually to strongly persistent trends toward feeling one is at least average or above in most important respects. This effect seems all the more plausible when one considers what a narrow frame of reference the child has for evaluating himself, so that he could not grasp the range of possible comparisons which can eventually imply that he is below average. Secondly, when adults interact, the socially acceptable practice of ingratiating oneself with others (E. E. Jones, 1964) by being tactful and/or hypocritical would tend to lead to each individual's receiving more positive feedback than realistically represents others' opinions of him.

When one enters old age, the nonsocial feedback about physical characteristics and capabilities is probably increasingly negative, as I suggested. Although the older person's self-favorability is socially fostered to some extent by others' tact and ingratiating behaviors, these positive social influences are probably counteracted to some degree by the old person's knowledge that the elderly are poorly regarded in our culture. Thus, one might speculate that self-favorability biases would further diminish between middle and old age.

I have spoken about the possible effect of "reality" in counteracting successively older persons' tendencies to maintain self-favorability biases through selective processing or distortion of feedback regarding self characteristics. Focusing on this point in particular, one might speculate that, at any age, less self-favorability bias will be encountered in regard to dimensions in which subjects have been given unmistakably clear information about themselves. I give below some information relevant to this point.

B. Methodological Criteria for Acceptable Studies

To state reasons why one might theoretically expect to find a self-favorability bias in self-reports is much easier than to marshal unequivocal evidence that such a bias occurs for one or more self-concept characteristics. It is fairly commonplace to read that data have been found to support the inference of such a bias, but, unfortunately, insufficiently close analysis has been made of the methodological characteristics of the studies which are supposedly supportive. For example, in my earlier book (Wylie, 1961), I accepted nine reports as indicative of self-favorability bias, but reexamining their method more closely has led me to conclude that six of them are not interpretable after all.

There are many complex methodological problems which must be resolved before we can safely interpret findings as indicative of group trends toward overestimation bias, underestimation bias, or absence of bias in self-concept reports.

The reader will recognize that the question of self-favorability bias is but one aspect of the general area of research which has gone under the names of "accuracy of self-perception" or "insight." Elsewhere (Wylie, 1974, chap. 6) I have dealt in great detail with the methodological problems and pitfalls in the entire area of research on "insightfulness" of the self-concept. There I concluded that most of the studies I examined could not pass muster and must be listed as uninterpretable for a variety of reasons. In taking up here only one question in the area of "insight" (group trends toward self-favorability biases), I do not repeat my detailed analysis of method problems. Instead, I simply list here the questions I asked about each possible pertinent study before deciding whether it can provide any interpretable information relevant to the hypothesis that self-favorability biases are the rule.

1. Appropriate Type of Self-Concept Report

Is the subject asked to give an appropriate type of self-concept report in this study? It is obvious that, if one is going to speak of self-favorability bias, one must have some standard against which to judge whether the subjects' responses are unbiased, unwarrantedly favorably biased, or unwarrantedly unfavorably biased. Thus, the first question one must ask is whether the subject has been instructed to give his self-report in terms of the standard to which he will be compared. Consider the trait friendliness, for example. A person might privately feel he is friendly in his attitude toward others (and might say this in his so-called private-self-concept report), but he might also recognize that others do not consider him to be a particularly friendly person (and this he could say if he were asked for a social-self-concept report). If one is going to compare his self-concept report with the expressed opinions of others regarding his friendliness, it is patently inappropriate to use the private self-concept report for such a comparison. The only defensible comparison is between his social-self-concept report and the reports of others. Or consider, as another example, the characteristic "academic ability." The individual may feel that he is not particularly able (and so indicate when instructed to give his private self-concept report), but he may also realize that his teachers seem to think fairly well of his academic ability (and this, too, he could report, if the question were phrased to elicit a social-self-concept report). Thus, if the standard with which his self-report is to be compared is teachers' rankings on an academic ability dimension, a social-self-concept report would be the only appropriate one to use to see whether he gives an unbiased, unduly favorably biased, or unduly unfavorably biased answer.

The investigators in many studies instruct the subject in such a way as to elicit an inappropriate self-report, i.e., a private-self-concept report, or they give so little information that one cannot be assured that this point has been adequately handled.

2. Appropriate Instructions to the Subject

Has the subject been instructed in such a way as to assure that he is addressing his self-concept report to the same dimension as will be inferred from the measure to which his self-concept report is to be compared?

For example, suppose a subject's sorority sisters have been asked to rank her among themselves with respect to generosity, and she has been asked to state where she thinks they will rank her with respect to this trait. Has the term been adequately defined for both subject and rankers so that everyone is directing her ranking efforts toward the same construct? Or, to take another example, if the self-report is supposed to indicate where the subject thinks she ranks in academic ability in her homeroom, has the experimenter explained to her the nature of the academic ability measure which will be used to evaluate the accuracy of her self-ranking?

Again, most studies have not dealt with this problem adequately or have not reported how they dealt with it; so their results are uninterpretable.

3. Appropriate, Specified Reference Group

If a subject's social-self-concept report is to be compared to his standing within a reference group, has the reference group to which he is to address his self-concept report been adequately described to him? For example, is he told to report his academic ability ranking within the students in his homeroom, the students in his high school, all high school students in the United States, or "students in general"? One cannot hope to evaluate the accuracy of his self-reported ranking within a group unless one uses the same group the subject is using as a basis for his self-ranking. Although this point is obvious, it is one which is often overlooked or vaguely glossed over in instructions given to the subjects, with consequent uninterpretability of results.

4. Subject's Knowledge of Instrument's Psychometric Properties

Even if one assumes that the subject has been led to understand that he is to give a social-self-concept report regarding an adequately defined construct, with respect to a particular reference group, does the subject know all he needs to know in order to produce self-reports which are interpretable in terms of degree of favorability bias? Not unless he has an accurate idea of the psychometric properties of the experimenter's measure. Suppose, for example, the subject is asked to guess his *score* on a standard intelligence test. Suppose that the test's underlying constructs have been at least fairly well explained to him, but he still does not know the psychometric information about the test which he will need in order to make a usable self-rating. Unless he has some idea of the mean and standard deviation of the reference group against which he is to be evaluated, his inaccuracies in guessing his score might stem from wrong assumptions about these matters rather than from wrong assumptions about himself, or his "accuracies" might be a matter of sheer luck. To take another example, suppose that ratings are used as a basis for evaluating the subject's social-self-concept reports regarding his friendliness. Unless the subject knows about the ways his raters use rating scales, his supposed *self*-favorability may simply be a matter of his making the wrong assumptions about how all the ratings, including his own, are distributed.

A large number of studies yield uninterpretable results because they have compared estimated scores with obtained scores (or estimated ratings with obtained ratings) without regard to the above-described pitfalls in this kind of procedure.

a. Self-Rankings Versus Others' Rankings

This problem can be surmounted to a certain extent by having the subject *rank* himself in a *specified* group. Of course, others' evaluations should also be in terms of ranking of subjects within the same specified group. Only then can one appropriately compare the subject's social-self-concept report with the others' evaluations of the subject. This procedure rules out one possible source of irrelevant determiners of whether subjects' self-report scores turn out to be unbiased, favorably biased, or unfavorably biased, namely the possibility that others' evaluations will vary from the subjects' self-evaluations in elevation of all their ratings, as can happen with the use of rating scales. This procedure also minimizes, although it does not eliminate, the irrelevant effects upon the subjects' bias scores of intrasubject and intersubject differences in the knowledge of the characteristics of the others' scores or ratings for the subjects on various dimensions.

Even with the use of ranking procedures, problems remain: If several others are used to rank each subject, the others' score for that subject will necessarily be a mean or median rank. That is, 3 others may differ among themselves in ranking a certain subject, and the 3 others' rankings of the subject must be combined in some way, either by computing a mean or median others' rank for the subject. In a group of 10 persons, for example, a subject's ranks of self among others could run from 1 to 10. The range of mean others' ranks obtained by the 10 subjects may well range only from, say, 2.0 to 7.5. Therefore, the size of discrepancies between a subject's social-self-concept rank and the others' "rank" of that subject will necessarily be determined in part by the fact that the mean or median others' ranks have a smaller dispersion than the ranks to which each subject is referring his self report. One way to get around this difficulty is to rank the subjects (in the above example, from 1 to 10) according to their mean or median others' ranks.

b. SELF-RANKINGS VERSUS MAXIMUM POSSIBLE NUMBER PER RANK

Alternately, instead of trying to use predicted self-ranks as compared to attained ranks, the following method may be used, provided of course that the procedure is accurate in terms of criteria 1, 2, and 3 above: If subjects are asked to state some range of ranks within which they expect others will rank them, or within which test scores will rank them, then one can see, for the group, whether the social-self-concept ranks depart significantly from what would be possible by definition. For example, suppose that subjects are asked whether their teachers would rank their academic ability in the top or the bottom half of the students in their home room. If 75% of students report they believe they would be ranked in the top 50%, then there must be more favorability in the group than would be expected if all errors in self-judgment were random. Or, suppose subjects are asked whether they are in the top tenth, the next to the top tenth, etc. and suppose that subjects' self-rankings place them preponderantly in the top three-tenths, with few ranking themselves in the bottom two-tenths. Such results would, if statistically significant, indicate self-favorability bias in the group.

5. Summary of Acceptance Criteria

With the above methodological criteria in mind, I examined 150 studies which purported explicitly or implicitly to look at "insight" or "accuracy of self-perception." From this group, I first eliminated from further consideration all those reports which presented their data only in correlational terms, giving no published basis for inferring self-favorability biases. This eliminated group contained a few studies which were relatively adequate for drawing correlational conclusions. However, most of them were so flawed that, even if they had given information possibly relevant to self-favorability biases, the results would not have been interpretable. (Most of this eliminated group has already been evaluated and listed in Wylie, 1974.) Next I looked at the remaining studies, those which either reported results in terms of self-favorability biases or provided information enabling the reader to estimate the occurrence of such biases. Most of these fell so far short of fulfilling the above-stated criteria for methodological adequacy that they, too, had to be eliminated. The substantive summary below, then, is based on 19 studies which were judged probably to merit interpretation. Even some of these are somewhat equivocal, as I show below.

C. FINDINGS REGARDING SELF-FAVORABILITY BIASES

Most of the reports which survived the winnowing process are concerned with self-estimates of cognitive performances or abilities. The measures used may be classified as follows: (a) reported memories or estimates of the subjects' actual attainments as previously reported to them; (b) the subjects' estimates of their future performances on clearly described cognitive tasks, for example, an arithmetic test; (c) the subjects' estimates of their standings in more or less vaguely described abilities such as their abilities to do schoolwork. Obviously, in each successive class of studies, there is relatively less room for realistic knowledge to influence subjects' self-rankings and, therefore, relatively more room for either random or systematic errors, such as self-favorability biases, to occur in the subjects' self-estimates. As one might expect, the studies in the first category show no or trivial indications of self-favorability in self-reports, with stronger trends toward self-favorability in the second and third categories.

1. Remembering or Estimating School Grades

The first group of studies comprises four which looked at the subjects' accuracy in remembering or estimating school grades. Three of these yielded trivial or no evidence of a self-favorability bias in self-reporting, while the interpretability of the fourth is moot.

In Kirk and Sereda's (1969) study, architecture students were asked to state their "cumulative grade point average at Berkeley" and were assured that their answers would be used only in group form, for research purposes. Discrepant reporting was defined as $\geq$ .1 grade-point difference between reported and attained grade-point average on a scale running from 0.0 to 4.0. Discrepant reporting defined in this way characterized 56.8% of the 338 male subjects' reports. Overestimating discrepancies occurred among 43.8%, whereas underestimating discrepancies occurred among 13.0%. The difference between these two percent values is significant. For 4 out of 5 subgroups, the mean estimated grade-point average slightly exceeded the mean obtained grade-point average, but each mean difference is very small, the largest being +.08; so no significance tests seem warranted. Thus, there may be a very slight self-favorability bias in these self-reports of memories of actually obtained grade-point averages, but the absolute magnitude of overestimation seems trivial.

In studies by Wylie (1963) and Wylie and Hutchins (1967), 2 groups of subjects were asked to tell whether their grades for the year were probably in the top or bottom half of their homeroom group. Each homeroom group had been together for at least a year before being tested in May; the subjects were guaranteed anonymity, and they were assured of the research nature of the data collection process. Only 53% of 712 junior high school pupils and 55% of 1,163 senior high school pupils in the respective groups reported thinking that their grades fell in the top half of the grades received in their homeroom group; so no strong self-favorability bias can be inferred here even though the 55% differs significantly from 50%, given the very large number of subjects.

In St. John's (1971) study of 957 pupils from 36 Boston sixth-grade rooms, classrooms were categorized according to social context into the following 4 types: I, predominantly black, lower and middle class; II, majority black, lower class; III, majority white, lower class; IV, majority white, middle class. St. John classified blacks and whites from each of the 4 types of classrooms according to whether they overestimated, underestimated, or accurately estimated their grade-point averages for the sixth grade. No information is provided about the instructions given to each subject for making these estimations or about the cutoff points used to classify these estimations into overestimations and underestimations. In all 4 types of classroom, a greater percentage of blacks overestimated than underestimated their grade-point averages. However, blacks in Type IV classrooms overestimated less and underestimated more than did blacks in any of the other 3 types of classrooms. Also, in Type II and Type III classrooms, a greater percentage of whites overestimated than underestimated their grade-point averages. Apparently there were few whites in Type I classrooms, since no data are reported for them. The whites in Type IV classrooms are the only group in which a greater percentage of students un-derestimated their grade-point average than overestimated them. Although St. John does provide some evidence to support a self-favorability bias in reporting grade-point averages in classrooms with certain types of social contexts, results from this study are not conclusive due to insufficiently detailed reporting and lack of significance tests.

2. Making Specific Task Estimates

Two studies fall into the second category, that is, the examination of subjects' specific task estimates. In Brandt's (1958) study of 2 groups of sixth-grade children (Ns = 27 and 31), pupils estimated for each of 3 forthcoming tests whether their scores would fall in the first, second, third, or fourth quarter of scores made by classmates who were well known to them. Anonymity and the research nature of the project were stressed, and the nature of each test (arithmetic, spelling, vocabulary) was clearly described to the children before they were tested. The results show strong self-favorability biases. For example, in the raw data made available to me by Brandt, 66% of the children estimated that their arithmetic scores would fall in the top 50% of the arithmetic test; 73% that their spelling scores would fall in the top 50%; and 74% that their vocabulary scores would fall in the top 50%. Each of these percent values is significantly different from 50. When estimated and obtained quarter standings were compared, percents of overestimating, accurate, and underestimating pupils were as follows: arithmetic — 35% overestimators, 43% accurate estimators, 22% underestimators; spelling — 45% overestimators, 39% accurate estimators, 16% un-derestimators; vocabulary — 45% overestimators, 36% accurate estimators, 19% underestimators.

Using a different task and college subjects, DeSoto, Coleman, and Putnam (1960) also obtained clear evidence of self-favorability. Each control subject was told the associations allegedly made to each of several words by another person. The control subject was led to believe that there was a rule by which the other person's associations could be judged to be correct or incorrect. However, there was no such rule. The control subject was asked to guess, for each word, whether the other's association had been "correct" in the light of the supposedly applicable rule for correct associations. Actually, the control subject who was guessing the "correctness" of the other's response was informed on a preprogrammed schedule whether the other's association had been "correct." Under this control condition, the control subjects showed the usual probability matching between the percent of the time their guesses about the correctness of the other's responses was positively reinforced and the percent of the time they predicted that the other's association was correct. In the experimental condition, exactly the same task was used, but each experimental subject was to make his own association and guess whether his association was or was not correct according to the supposed but actually nonexistent rule. For each word, experimental subjects made an association, then predicted whether or not it would be correct according to the supposed rule. Different groups of experimental subjects received positive reinforcement for their guesses according to the following respective reinforcement schedules: 5, 10, 15, 20, or 25 times in each block of 30 associations, their guesses about their correctness were positively reinforced. When probability matching as shown by control subjects was taken as the expected baseline, subjects "persistently overpredicted success in most of these (reinforcement) conditions; they predicted it far more often than they obtained it. This overprediction was greatest for the least successful conditions, lessening as the proportion of actual successes increased, until in the 5/6 condition subjects actually slightly underpredicted their success." (DeSoto et al., 1960, p. 43).

3. Estimating Intellectual Abilities

In the third group of studies involving cognitive performances or abilities, subjects were asked to estimate their relative standings on a variety of fairly vaguely defined intellectual abilities. In each report, strong evidence of self-favorability bias is given.

Brim, Neulinger, and Glass (1965) examined self-estimates of intelligence in a sample of 1,500 United States adults ranging in age from their twenties to their seventies. Subjects were asked, "How do you think you compare to other people in intelligence?" The 10 "other people" or classes of people to whom they were to compare themselves included father, mother, brother, sister, spouse, children, the average person in the United States today, people who do the same kind of work as themselves, people who went to school with them, and most of their friends today. Subjects were instructed to indicate whether they considered themselves much higher, higher, the same, lower, or much

lower in intelligence as compared to each "other." In the case of each of
8 others listed above, the percent of respondents reporting that they felt
they were much higher or higher exceeded the percent reporting that
they felt they were much lower or lower than the other. The percent
reporting they considered themselves to be lower or much lower than
spouse or children exceeded the percent stating that they considered
themselves to be much higher or higher than these 2 others. Although
the contradictory finding for the view of the spouse is not explained,
Brim et al. feel that the parents' view of themselves as lower in intelligence than their children can be explained by the parents'
aspirations and hopes for the future of their children.

In Uhrbock's (1926) research, all freshmen at the University of
Wyoming were asked to indicate "whether they considered themselves
above or below average in intelligence, so far as their immediate group
was concerned" (p. 495). Of 293 subjects, 71% estimated that they were
above average of the "immediate group." This is highly significantly
different from 50%; so, if one is willing to assume that the subjects had
"top 50%" in mind when calling themselves "above average," this study
indicates a strong self-favorability bias in this group of subjects.

Torrance (1954a, 1954b) reports that 1,215 "Kansas State College
Freshmen (September, 1949) [were asked to] give self-estimates of how
they thought they would stand in relation to their classmates on tests of
scholastic ability and achievement (American Council on Education
Psychological Examination, Cooperative English Achievement, and
Cooperative Reading Achievement" [1954a, pp. 211–212]). Presumably
they stated their predicted standings in rank terms, but Torrance's
description is not clear on this point. He reports that "over 65% of the
total group placed themselves in the upper fourth in scholastic ability
and 95% placed themselves in the upper half" (1954a, p. 212).

In a study by Brim (1954), 103 students in an advanced social
psychology class were asked to estimate their rank among 100 students
taken at random from their class and given a series of intelligence tests.
He found the mean estimated rank to be 39. Since by definition the
mean rank of 100 persons is 50.5, a trend to self-favorability is evident.
No statistical significance test is given for the difference between 39 and
50.5.

Bachman (1970) found evidence of self-favorability in self-concept of
intellectual and schoolwork ability in his representative national
probability sample of 2,213 tenth-grade boys in United States public

high schools in 1966. In answer to the question, "How do you rate yourself in school ability compared with those in your grade in school?" 83% of the sample placed themselves in either the far above, above, or slightly above average categories. In answer to the question, "How intelligent do you think you are, compared with other boys your age?" 84% placed themselves in the far above, above, or slightly above average categories. And, in answer to the question, "How good a reader do you think you are compared with other boys your age?" 67% placed themselves in 1 of 3 categories above.

In Kranzler's (1970) research, high school sophomores who had taken the School and College Ability Test (SCAT), but had not received their scores, were reminded of that test and its two parts. They were then asked to estimate whether their "ability to deal with words (verbal ability)" and "ability to deal with numbers (quantitative ability)" was in the "top one-fourth of your class, second one-fourth of your class, third one-fourth of your class, lowest one-fourth of your class" (p. 222). Among subjects who actually had fallen below the local SCAT median, there were 4 underestimators, 3 accurate estimators, and 34 overestimators when accuracy was defined as having the same quarter standing for estimated and obtained scores. Obviously, an extreme self-favorability bias operated among those who actually scored below the local median. Unfortunately, no data are presented about above-median scorers.

Wylie (1963) and Wylie and Hutchins (1967) explained to their subjects, "By ability we don't necessarily mean how well you *actually* do your school work but rather how well you *could* do school work if you tried your best . . . decide whether you would probably belong in the top half of the students in your homeroom, or . . . somewhere below the top half" (Wylie & Hutchins, 1967, p. 787). The subject's privacy and the research nature of the data collection were stressed. Members of the homeroom groups had been together at least one academic year. The results were as follows for the two junior high school and two senior high school groups: 59% of 823 junior high school subjects, 66% of 712 junior high school subjects, 70% of 1,163 senior high school subjects, and 77% of 731 senior high school subjects reported their ability to do schoolwork as probably in the top half of the students in their homerooms. All these obtained percent values depart significantly from 50. It should be noted that the instructions to these subjects explicitly encouraged them not to say how well they were actually performing, but how well they could do schoolwork if they tried their best. They must have made some sort of distinction between performance and ability since, as stated earlier, there was virtually no self-favorability bias in reporting whether recently attained grades fell in the top half of the homeroom, whereas there was, as just shown, considerable self-favorability bias in reporting what they *could* do.

4. Estimating Personality Characteristics

The remaining possibly interpretable studies of self-favorability dealt with a variety of personality characteristics. In general, they support the idea that self-favorability biases obtain with reference to these traits.

In each of 2 groups of 11 nursery-school children (ages 47–62 months), Weiner (1964) asked each child individually to compare himself or herself with each other child regarding a variety of characteristics. This method of paired comparisons enabled Weiner to infer the child's self-perceived rank order with respect to each characteristic. The items about which he inquired were drawing skill, skill in dressing self, climbing skill, size, friendliness, strength, intelligence, frequency of fighting, and how well each teacher liked the child. Before interviewing the children and asking the paired-comparison questions, he worked with the teachers to develop understandable and appropriate wording. With the possible exception of friendliness, he felt that the children seemed to understand the questions and the idea of the paired-comparison task. If there were no self-favorability bias, the median self-rank on any one of the above dimensions would be 5.5. The obtained median self-rankings were: drawing skill = 2.25; skill in dressing self = 3.0; climbing skill = 5.25; size = 3.75; friendliness = 2.75; strength = 4.0; intelligence = 2.0; frequency of fighting = 5.0; liking by all teachers combined = 3.25. Weiner gives no significance tests for these as compared to the expected median of 5.5, but the visual trend toward self-favorability appears to be marked.

Wylie (1965) asked each airman subject to rate randomly selected members of his living group on each of 5 rating scales and to state for each scale where he thought the others in his living group would rate him. The 5 scales were friendliness, likability, generosity, intelligence, and sense of humor. Along each scale, the rating points were defined by a brief description which was intended to maximize uniformity of understanding of the dimension and the scale subdivisions. Since the subject placed his social-self-concept rating among those he assigned to a random sample of his living group, one can infer his perception of his relative standing in his living group by seeing whether he placed the social-self-concept rating in the top or bottom half of the ratings he assigned to others. If each subject realistically perceives the rank order of his own social stimulus value for the members of his group, one should find that 50% of the subjects placed their self-ratings in each of the two halves. Random errors made by subjects in perceiving their rank-order standing accurately should not systematically affect the expectations that subjects will distribute themselves approximately equally into the two halves. The actually obtained proportions of subjects placing their self-ratings in the top half are: for friendliness, p = .48; for likability p = .71; for generosity, p = .73; for intelligence, p = .66; for sense of humor, p = .76. The obtained proportions differ from .50 to a highly significant degree on each of the last 4 traits. Thus, even when one holds constant the factor of stereotype accuracy (i.e., the absolute range of the scale which the subject uses in rating himself and others), one finds significant evidence that the more frequent tendency among these subjects is to see themselves in a favorable light, more favorable than the reality situation warrants.

The data analyzed by Heiss and Owens (1972) were obtained from Crain and Weisman's (1972) block quota sample of black northern metropolitan males and females aged 21–45, whose data are weighted to reflect the actual population, and from another sample of northern metropolitan whites aged 21–45 from a National Opinion Research Center (NORC) study done at about the same time. Although the weighted N for blacks was 4,286, the actual N was about 40% of this number. They and 343 whites were asked to rate themselves as above average, about average, or below average in the following areas: as a son or daughter, as a parent, as a spouse, as a conversationalist, as an athlete, in attractiveness, in willingness to work hard, in trustworthiness, in intelligence, and in mechanical ability. For 6 out of these 10 areas, only 2% of the subjects rated themselves as below average. And on ratings of being a conversationalist and attractiveness, only about 10% rated themselves below average. The only areas in which a greater percentage of subjects considered themselves below average than above average were athletic and mechanical ability. Thus, both blacks and whites showed a self-favorability bias in that they rated themselves average or above average rather than below average in 8 out of the 10 areas studied.

It is worthy of note that, in these two studies, as in the earlier ones cited, intelligence is a trait on which subjects showed a self-favorability bias.

As part of a lengthy questionnaire sent to 5,000 executives, questions about ethical behaviors were included (Baumhart, 1961). A random half of the respondents was given each of 4 hypothetical situations (e.g., concerning padding expense accounts) and asked "What would you do?" while the other random half was asked "What would the average executive do?" Since 1,700 replies were received and the comparability of the two random halves was demonstrated on a number of points, it seems safe to assume that answers concerning the average executive would have been about the same in the half which answered the question "What would you do?" as they were in the half which actually described the behavior of the average executive. For each of the 4 hypothetical cases, a much larger percent of the executives imputed to themselves more ethical behavior choices than were said to characterize the "average business executive." Although no significance tests are presented, the visual trends in the data appear to be extremely strong.

A study by Gustafson and Gaumnitz (1972) was concerned with the effect of including as opposed to excluding self-rankings in the consensus rankings of 50 small groups of 4 to 6 undergraduate students each, who discussed case situations involving the content of their classwork. The subjects were asked to rank the members of their group including themselves according to the following variables: participation in the discussion, contributions of the best ideas to the discussion, guiding the discussion, keeping the group moving effectively, and taking a leadership role during the discussion. Mean coefficients of concordance for these 4 variables were found to be significantly higher with self-rankings excluded than they were with self-rankings included. In their comparisons of self-rankings with rankings of each individual by the others in the group, Gustafson and Gaumnitz found that the mean self-rankings were significantly higher than the average rankings by the other members of the group for all 4 variables. However, one major criticism of this study is that subjects were apparently not instructed when giving their self-rankings to rank themselves in terms of how others would see them. This limits the interpretability of the results.

D. Summary

In summary, there appears to be considerable consistency among the methodologically more adequate studies in showing trends toward self-favorability biases regarding evaluative characteristics. This was least true or not true in the case of reported memories of grade-point averages and more true with respect to characteristics which would be more open to self-favorable distortion. The preceding generalizations are congruent with the theoretical arguments developed at the beginning of this section that self-favorable biases occur and that the amount of bias should depend in part on the opportunities for the subject to distort recognition of his own status.

The largest number of researches concerned self-estimates of cognitive and intellectual characteristics, with only a few concerning a miscellaneous assortment of noncognitive traits. Thus much more research is needed to establish the generality of self-favorability biases across traits.

Although I postulated at the outset that age trends in self-favorability biases seemed theoretically plausible, no data appear to be available relevant to this proposition.

E. List of Studies Not Substantively Summarized

Most remarkable was the large volume of work which could not be considered because of methodological shortcomings so serious that the reported results could not sustain interpretable answers about self-favorability bias. These studies are partially listed below. The list given here does not contain the studies which were excluded because they offered information only in correlational terms, although many of these were too flawed to sustain even the correlational conclusions they purported to support, nor does it repeat all the criticized studies already listed in Wylie (1974).

T. B. Anderson and Olsen (1965); Arbuckle (1958); Arsenian (1942); Bailey (1971); R. C. Bailey and K. G. Bailey (1971); K. G. Bailey and Gibby (1971); Bailey and Shaw (1971); Barrett (1968); Borgatta (1960a, 1960b); Crook (1937); Crook (1938); Freese and West (1972); Goslin (1962); Groff (1961); Jervis (1959); Kasl (1972); Kemp (1964); W. K. Kirchner (1965); G. S. Klein (1948); Kreines and Bogart (1974); Lehner

(1956, 1960); Maguire (1973); Michael, Plass, and Lee (1973); Morrison, Thomas, and Weaver (1973); Nebergall, Angelino, and Young (1959); Preiss (1968); Reed (1953); Renzaglia, Henry, and Rybolt (1962); Russell (1953); Rychlak (1970); Shen (1925); Siegenthaler and Flamm (1961); A. Soares and L. Soares (1970a, 1971); L. Soares and A. Soares (1971); Spiegel (1970); Start (1963); Steger, Simmons, and Lavelle (1973); Sumner (1932); Thornton (1968); Touhey (1971); Trent (1957).

13

Overview and Recommendations

Little purpose could be served by attempting to distill here the summaries and conclusions presented at the end of each topic or subtopic of this book. This is so for several reasons. The contents of the chapters are so disparate, and, within each, the summaries are easy to locate. Moreover, presentation of condensations of summaries would only create a misleadingly simplified idea of topics which are exceedingly complex, and mere juxtaposition of such simplified summaries would serve only to create an impression of miscellany and disjointedness. By contrast, from a broader comparative view of all the chapters, one can see some extremely interesting and provocative trends and patterns emerging.

It is fascinating that hundreds of thousands of research hours have been devoted to studying self-concept variables, especially over-all self-regard, and that both lay persons and professional individuals from many disciplines evidently continue to be impressed with the importance of the topic despite the paucity of definitive findings and, indeed, despite numerous resounding failures to obtain support for some of their most strongly held hypotheses. One may notice here an analogy to the state of affairs in the study of certain other constructs in psychology, such as "intelligence," or "motivation." That is, the elusiveness of adequate conceptual and operational definitions and difficulties in relating the constructs to other variables have not convinced self-concept investigators any more than intelligence or motivation researchers that we are groping with a phantom topic or an unimportant set of questions.

What suggestions can one draw from an over-all view of this book which might justify this refusal to give up in the face of the state of available research findings? More positively, is there a view of the null findings coupled with the patterning of the significant associations which might be seen with hindsight to be congruent with the importance attached to self-regard and other self-concept variables and might be seen with foresight as indicative of ways in which our further theorizing and research should move?

In addressing myself to these questions, I group my remarks into the following categories: (a) the status and interrelationships of theory and methodology, and the implications of these points for future research; (b) the upward or downward trends in topical emphases in the past two decades and their implications for future research; (c) the widespread occurrence of null or weak findings in areas where strong predictions have been made, and the possible theoretical and research implications of this; (d) the likelihood that, if self-concept research is to prove to be scientifically or practically useful, investigations involving more specific aspects of self-concept will be fruitful in their own right and for the light they throw on over-all self-regard and its relationships with other variables. Although (c) and (d) are separated for convenience, they are closely interrelated, even in some ways complementary.

A. Theory, Methodology, and Implications for Future Research

Many of my 1974 conclusions about theory, methodology, and their implications for future research were reinforced by my experience in preparing this volume. Accordingly, this section comprises a brief summary of the conclusions from volume 1, whereas sections B, C, and D include additional points on this topic, based on an overview of volume 2.

In 1974 I argued that the theoretical, methodological, and empirical situation in self-concept research implied only two alternatives: abandon theorizing and research involving self-referent constructs or make whatever theoretical and methodological improvements are necessary in order to put such work on a more scientifically respectable base. I argued then and would still argue for the second alternative because I believe that the possible usefulness of self-referent constructs has not as yet been adequately tested, and therefore such constructs deserve further consideration in the light of more sophisticated hypothesizing and research methods.

Everyday introspection has suggested to many that self-referent constructs, as opposed to more behavioristic analyses, may be useful or necessary in order to account for some human actions, especially the complex patterns observed in the clinic, school, and other "everyday life" situations. Moreover, it has seemed to some that the complex patterning of behaviors requires the invocation of phenomenal constructs (especially self-referent constructs) which have gestalt characteristics. But the proposed constructs have been so vague and have been stretched to cover so many inferred cognitive and motivational processes that their utility for analytic and predictive purposes has been greatly diminished. Such broad, amorphous constructs as self-actualization, phenomenal self-differentiation, and self-consistency have not led to enlightening research regarding their measurement, their relationships to alleged antecedents or consequents, or their relationships with plausibly covarying constructs. Self-esteem and self-acceptance, although still vague and broad, have led to somewhat more manageable and fruitful research suggestive of the importance of refining and extending the study of this kind of variable. And it seems plausible that studies of even more restricted aspects of self-conception which are intuitively relevant to respective input variables, correlated inferred variables, and output variables may also be theoretically appropriate, operationally manageable, and empirically fruitful.

The low yield of interpretable empirical findings based on purported indices of self-concept variables could suggest that any kind of phenomenal variables may well be insufficient or even unnecessary to account for behavior. Some have suggested that nonphenomenal variables such as unconscious self-evaluation or unconscious motivation must be included in order to account for the behaviors to which phenomenological theorists have addressed themselves. This may be the case. However, it is still possible that weak findings involving phenomenological variables may be attributable in unknown degree to shortcomings in phenomenological theory, measurement, and research methods. Certainly, the delineation, measurement, and empirical usefulness of possibly supplemental nonphenomenal intrasubject variables (e.g., aspects of the unconscious self-concept) and objective factors (both personal and situational) remain to be adequately explored.

B. Trends in Topical Emphases

In the 1961 edition of this book, I attempted to organize the available substantive researches according to whether they purported to deal with (a) descriptive development of self-conceptions; (b) supposed relations of antecedent variables to self-concept variables; (c) supposed relationships between self-concept variables and behaviors, when behaviors were either postulated consequents of the self-concept variables, or merely correlated with them because no one temporal or sequential ordering could be or was hypothesized. I noted that almost all available researches were correlational, even when linear antecedent → self-concept → consequent relationships were at issue in the hypotheses.

In this volume, one again sees a very great preponderance of correlational researches, even when the investigators' hypotheses involve cause-effect or sequential relationships. It appears that the bulk of the studies reviewed here has been directed toward supposed antecedents of self-conceptions, e.g., age-related influences, socioeconomic class, racial/ethnic status, sex, family influences, sociometric status, and psychotherapy. Relatively few have been directed toward behavioral consequents of self-conceptions or correlations involving possibly reciprocal or circular relationships between self-conception and other inferred or observed variables. This relative emphasis is especially interesting in view of the fact that theorists' major purpose in introducing phenomenal variables such as self-referent constructs was to account for behavior. Obviously, this imbalance of emphasis needs to be redressed in future work.

In this volume I do not attempt to divide the researches according to the three classes listed above, but rather have grouped them according to substantive topics without particular regard to these classes.

So far as trends in emphases on these particular substantive topics are concerned, I have been struck with the recent burgeoning literature in some areas which received no attention or proportionately little attention in the publications reviewed for the 1961 edition of this book. Prime examples of these newly developed or emphasized topics are associations between persons' self-conceptions and such factors as age or developmental level; sex; socioeconomic class; racial/ethnic status; achievement, ability, and creativity indices; and influenceability and expressions of interpersonal attraction, especially in laboratory situations.

It appears that the accelerated output on some of these topics has been partly a manifestation of researchers' concerns with social action. These concerns reflect the contemporary public preoccupations with the need to improve the educational system, to equalize opportunities for self-development, and to increase the well-being of disadvantaged persons and groups. Indeed, such social-action interests often seemed to play a stronger role than formal theorizing in determining research predictions, topics, and procedures. (Parenthetically, one may speculate whether the desire to move as quickly as possible to socially relevant generalizations has led many researchers to oversimplify their conceptualizations and research operations, thus leading inadvertently to some of the oft-repeated null findings and, in the minds of some, to disenchantment with the theoretical usefulness of self-referent constructs.)

Then there may be another reason why some substantive topics have received proportionately so much emphasis. The idea of the importance of self-esteem or "self-enhancement" tendencies has been taken up by social psychologists whose main theoretical heritage and focus were not in the phenomenological personality theories. These psychologists have envisaged ways which they thought would bring the study of self-esteem into the laboratory and relate it to variables of interest to social psychologists. Thus we have, for example, many relatively brief and delimited laboratory studies of influenceability and interpersonal attraction as a function of self-esteem.

In contrast to the rapid growth of publication on some topics, a noticeable stagnation has characterized the past two decades of research on others. For example, psychotherapy was the biggest single area covered in the 1961 edition of this book. This was consonant with the facts that self-concept theory came largely from experiences of client-centered therapists and that Rogers was a pioneer in attempting to apply scientific methods to the study of process and outcome in psychotherapy. Although considerable psychotherapy research is still being done and studies of group experiences of all kinds are now fairly common, psychotherapy is by no means the most popular topic in self-concept research today. Moreover, one gets the impression that both theory and research in this area have foundered. Older techniques (e.g., interview coding) have not been further developed and used. And, despite agreement that methodological innovation and increasing methodological sophistication are needed, only a very few researches have exemplified such improvements.

Another example of a currently undeveloped topic which was proportionately prominent among self-concept research publications two decades ago is the influence of family variables on the self-concept.

It appears that both theorists and practitioners still accord great importance to both family influences and psychotherapy in development or change of self-conceptions and self-evaluations. Therefore, research stagnation in these areas cannot be laid to changing theoretical opinions about the probable strength of these influences. Instead, it seems likely that recognition of the complexity and time requirements of what must be done to frame and test researchable, worthwhile questions in these areas may well have stymied research efforts.

A third example of a topic less stressed now than formerly is the relationships between authoritarianism and/or dogmatism on the one hand and self-concept variables on the other. The decline may be partly attributable to the fact that theoretical expectations were never clarified and research involving these relationships has not been particularly fruitful. In part it may be due to a lessening of emphasis on authoritarianism and/or dogmatism in the area of social psychology, perhaps related to a growing recognition of the psychometric limitations and obsolescence of the California F scale (Cronbach, 1975).

C. Widespread Occurrence of Null or Weak Findings

The most impressive thing which emerges from an overview of this book is that null or weak findings have been obtained many times in each of a number of areas in which theory and conventional wisdom very confidently predicted strong trends. (When I say null, I refer to situations in which only null findings have been obtained, or mostly null findings along with approximately equal number of positive and negative weak trends.)

The most striking examples of null findings occur in the researches involving over-all self-regard, where such scores have not been shown to be related to such proposed antecedents as age, race, sex, socioeconomic level, or psychotherapy or to such proposed correlates as creativity indices and persuasibility. Other examples of null findings incongruent with predictions occur in the area of interpersonal attraction where the actual similarity between self-concept profiles of friends or marital pairs does not exceed the actual similarity between self-concept profiles of randomly paired subjects. There are many null findings involving specific aspects of self-conception as well, but, generally speaking, one can see some sensible patterns beginning to emerge in some such studies. Therefore this section focuses primarily on over-all self-regard, with consideration of research on specific aspects of self-concept given in section D below.

So far as weak findings are concerned, one sees these resulting from studies of relationships of over-all self-regard scores to such proposed correlates as ability scores, achievement scores, and sociometric status. Here the associations, although tending to be positive, are not only relatively small in absolute terms, but are by no means always significant.

Of course, null results are always ambiguous, but one feels the need to speculate when they are so repeatedly obtained from a variety of approaches to the study of a number of variables for each of which many persons have expressed strong expectations of finding significant associations of large enough size to have psychological importance.

Are these null findings indicative that over-all self-regard is, after all, not a theoretically useful construct? Or do they to some degree at least reflect gross psychometric inadequacies in purported self-regard measures or the way in which these instruments were applied in these researches? Are they perhaps partly attributable to design problems? And do deficiencies in instrumentation and design stem most basically from neglect of some very plausible and important psychological considerations about the construct, over-all self-regard?

My speculations begin with some of the simpler methodological possibilities and proceed to psychological considerations and their methodological implications.

1. Some Possible Methodological Explanations

Assuming for the moment that over-all self-regard is a plausible construct (or closely related group of constructs), one might propose that the null results from so many researches may reflect the lack of construct validity of purported self-regard indices. For example, such instruments may be too insensitive to reflect the actually occurring effects or associations with these other variables. Or perhaps respondents are sometimes deliberately not revealing their global self-evaluations, as might happen if black respondents do not wish to reveal their actually low self-evaluations. These proposals may be true. There are, however, other possibilities to be considered, especially in light of the fact that some of the instruments have good reliability; scores from them do intercorrelate significantly, and the creators of some have presented some other preliminary evidence supportive of their purported construct validity.

Two other methodological possibilities relevant to null results are that (a) too narrow a range of over-all self-regard has been examined to enable sizeable associations with other variables to be obtained, (b) too few steps on the self-regard range have been used, or inappropriate statistical analyses have been made, leading researchers to overlook nonlinear associations.

Still other methodological explanations are considered below after a more detailed discussion of possible psychological explanations which have methodological implications.

2. Possible Psychological Explanations and Their Methodological Implications

I turn now to a speculative argument that the striking incidence of null findings we are trying to explain does not stem from the unimportance of self-regard, but rather may be attributable to two factors: the maintenance of self-regard, far from being unimportant, is psychologically crucial; and researchers have overlooked many of the psychological subtleties which must be considered in designing and interpreting research concerning the relationship of self-regard with other variables.

Certainly, many theorists, researchers, professionals, and lay persons would agree with the assumption that the need to maintain and enhance the level of conscious over-all self-regard is extremely important. In addition, we need to introduce the following assumptions into this speculative argument. Over-all self-regard is multiply determined. Secondly, so far as race, sex, socioeconomic level, and age are concerned, each person is exposed to many influences other than the advantageous or disadvantageous ones associated with his or her demographic classification. This implies the possibility of wide individual variations occurring with respect to these other factors. Thirdly, persons have considerable latitude in "choosing" the attributes they consider salient for their self-regard, the reference groups to which they compare themselves, and the persons whom they consider to be "significant others." Then one must couple all these assumptions with the evidence for widespread occurrence of self-favorability biases in conscious self-evaluations (chap. 12). This line of thinking leads to the suggestion that whatever devaluating pressures are experienced as a result of age, race, sex, socioeconomic level, achievement/ability level, creativity level, or sociometric status may well be overridden by a tendency to enhance the self by one or more of the following strategies. It is possible that a person will not experience his or her group membership as salient for self-evaluation. Alternately, one may play down the derogatory and handicapping influences associated with one's group membership, or except oneself from unfavorable attributes supposedly characterizing the typical member of one's group. Moreover, instead of evaluating oneself in terms of the standards held by "society at large," as many researchers have assumed people do, one may evaluate oneself in terms of restricted "realistic" reference groups and attainable goals. It is also possible to emphasize the importance of whatever good qualities one sees oneself as having, and one can selectively attend to those particular others who emphasize one's strengths and/or give unconditional acceptance. Such ideas have been repeatedly suggested in the chapters on racial status, socioeconomic level, sex, age, and ability/achievement.

If the above suggestions are true, we must conclude that over-all self-regard is an important area for study, but that it has been approached too simplistically, both in theory and research.

But now suppose we accept the general idea of a multipronged explanation of why null or weak relationships obtain between self-regard and age, race, sex, socioeconomic level, and achievement scores. This still leaves us with a puzzle. If people are so successful in using these available strategies for maintaining and enhancing self-regard in the face of objectively disadvantageous facts about themselves or their groups, then why do individuals differ reliably on purported measures of over-all self-regard? If the scores from these measures even roughly indicate individual differences in inferred over-all self-regard, how does one account for this variance, if not in terms of such "obvious" influences as ascribed group membership, achievement levels, or popularity levels?

An overview of this book provides no answers, but furnishes a few hints for future consideration.

One such hint is provided by the fact that we know very little about parental influences which seem intuitively to be so crucial (see chap. 6). In view of the undeveloped state of that research area, however, we can only raise the question whether a variety of parental characteristics or treatments might partially account for stable individual differences in over-all self-regard scores (as well as more specific aspects of self-concept) regardless of demographic status or levels of ability and achievement.

Another hint is provided by some of the very few available multivariate studies. If it is reasonable to presume that over-all self-regard is multiply determined, then perhaps there is a summative effect of many influences, each of which accounts for only a small increase or decrease in self-regard. As a hypothetical example, favorable parental treatment, a respected socioeconomic family status, high individual educational achievement, healthy and attractive bodily characteristics, and popularity with peers might conjointly lead to a level of self-regard reliably above average.

Or multiple determination may also imply that many unexplored

THE SELF-CONCEPT

interactions occur among such variables as sex, socioeconomic level, parental variables, and school success, as well as among these variables and situations which promote or minimize the likelihood of a subject's using one or more of the self-enhancing strategies mentioned above. As a relatively simple hypothetical example suggested partially by Rosenberg's (1965) work, the self-evaluative advantages of being an only child may be particularly augmented if one is also a Jewish male in a Jewish neighborhood.

Given the sparsity of the data and the inability to compare the results of the few extant multivariate studies of over-all self-regard, this hint cannot be said to be well grounded in the outcomes of the presently reviewed research. It is, however, consonant with the relatively recent trend of thought represented in Cronbach's (1975) argument that social scientists must turn to the search for complex higher order interactions (including those involving "the times" and relatively restricted situational contexts) if they wish to enhance their ability to predict outcomes.

Although I share Cronbach's recommendations that we search for higher order interactions, I am not ready to share his pessimistic view that even such complex approaches are unlikely ever to yield any relatively enduring, systematic theories about "man in society" (in the present case, about determinants, correlates, and consequents of self-regard, and, for that matter, other self-concept variables). Rather, I would share Schlenker's (1974) view that

> it is the case in the social sciences that many contemporary principles formulated through social research are empirical generalizations which incorporate numerous specifics. . . . Without the compilation of systematic information about social behavior, construction of higher-order theories would be rendered near impossible. However, a myopic focus on such particulars only promotes undue pessimism and does not imply that underlying abstract regularities cannot and have not been formulated. [P. 3]

My hunch is that we should attend to McGuire's (1973) recommendations for a new paradigm in order to envisage multivariate analyses more likely to uncover some transhistorical, abstract scientific generalizations.

> On the creative side, [a radically different new paradigm for social psychology] will involve theoretical models of the cognitive and social systems in their true multivariate complexity, involving a great deal of parallel

processing, bidirectional relationships, and feedback circuits. Since such complex theoretical formulations will be far more in accord with actual individual and social reality than our present a-affects-b linear models, it follows that theory-derived hypotheses will be similar to hypotheses selected for their relevance to social issues. Correspondingly, the critical aspect of this new paradigm involves hypothesis testing by multivariate time series designs that recognize the obsolescence of our current simplistic a-affects-b sequential designs with their distinctions between dependent and in-dependent variables. . . . [the] radically different paradigm . . . will be hammered out by theoretically and empirically skilled researchers in a hundred eyeball-to-eyeball confrontations of thought with data, all the while obscured by a thousand mediocre and irrelevant studies which will constitute the background noise in which the true signal will be detected only gradually. [P. 450]

I agree with both Cronbach (1975) and McGuire (1973) that improved multivariate analyses will probably be most useful in generating understanding and in yielding successively more fruitful research if they are supplemented by suggestions obtained from direct observations. Cronbach (1975) states:

As results accumulate, a person who seeks understanding will do his best to trace how the uncontrolled factors could have caused local departures from the modal effect. That is, generalization comes late, and the exception is taken as seriously as the rule. . . . The two scientific disciplines, experimental control and systematic correlation, answer formal questions stated in advance. Intensive local observation goes beyond discipline to an open-eyed, open-minded appreciation of the surprises nature deposits in the investigative net. [P. 125]

In a similar vein, McGuire (1973) argues for the theory-creative usefulness of trying to account for paradoxical findings and "for observing people, not data."

In our holy determination to confront reality and put our theory to the test of nature, we have plunged through reality, like Alice through the mirror, into a never-never land in which we contemplate not life but data. All too often, the scientific psychologist is observing not mind or behavior but summed data and computer printout. [P. 453]

Taking yet another view of the research reviewed in this book yields a third hint about how we might account for stable individual differences in over-all self-regard coupled with unexpectedly weak or null associations between self-regard and many of the variables thus far explored. This hint comes from considering where one does find relatively strong relationships with self-regard scores.

The strongest associations involving self-regard scores tend to occur when the self-regard scores are correlated with other self-report scores. For example, we may very tentatively suggest that there appear to be somewhat larger correlations between over-all self-regard and perceived sociometric status than actual sociometric status (chap. 8). Likewise, correlations of self-regard scores are higher with self-conceptions of schoolwork ability than with "objective" ability or achievement indices (chap. 7). Also, from very incomplete and essentially incomparable data, we might risk a guess that correlations are closer between self-regard scores and subjects' perceived parental treatments and attitudes than between self-regard scores and parental treatment as inferred from parental report or observers' records of parental behavior (chap. 6).

Along this same vein, it is interesting to note that assumed similarity between self and friend is more apt to be significant than is the actual similarity between self-concept reports of friends (chap. 8). And it is well known that self-regard scores correlate substantially with self-reported acceptance of others (chap. 8), self-reported depression, and self-reported anxiety (chap. 11).

Of course it is both parsimonious and plausible to be very suspicious of the interpretability of correlations between self-reports. They may represent mainly or entirely the common influence of some irrelevant response set. Or the self-report measures may correlate because they do not have respectively discriminant validity for their purportedly different purposes, being instead alternate indices of a very general favorability/unfavorability of outlook.

But there is also another way of looking at the fact that self-regard scores seem to correlate more highly with other self-report scores than with objective indices. In this view, the higher correlations are not necessarily artifacts, but rather what phenomenological theorists should expect. That is, assuming for the moment that popularity is an important antecedent of a child's self-regard, the phenomenologist would expect that it is not the child's actual popularity but his perception of his popularity which should have the immediate impact upon over-all self-regard. Likewise, insofar as academic achievement is important to an individual's self-regard, it should not be her objectively measured achievement, but her perception of her achievement which should have the immediate impact on self-regard. Similarly, not the parents' actions, but children's perceptions and interpretations of their actions should affect over-all self-regard. (An analogous interpretation could be made of the probable fact that assumed interpersonal similarity is more closely related to expressed interpersonal attraction than is actual interpersonal similarity between self-concept reports.) Of course the "objective" input and reinforcement history would be expected to play some role both in determining the importance attached to popularity, achievement, or parental behaviors as determiners of self-regard and in determining the child's phenomenal evaluation of his or her popularity, achievement level, or status in the parents' affections. But the point at issue here is that there are always psychometric, situational, and strategic reasons to expect considerable lack of correspondence between such input and the receiver's phenomenal view. Hence it is entirely congruent with phenomenal theory that the most immediate connections should be between the phenomenal view of the particular characteristic or situation and the phenomenal over-all self-regard which is presumably reflected in turn in the self-regard index. Obviously, relationships between input and the receiver's phenomenological views of particular characteristics and situations are important and should be explored as one kind of link in the chains or loops of events involving antecedents, mediating constructs, and behavior, as postulated by phenomenologists.

Indeed, not only phenomenological theorists but also social learning theorists have averred that predictions cannot be made only on the basis of the "objective" stimulus input and that self-reports are one important way of indexing the behavior-determining constructions which persons put on stimulus situations and their own characteristics. For example, Mischel (1968) argues, "one must know the properties or meaning that the stimulus has acquired for the subject. If the history is unknown, the response has to be assessed directly" (p. 190). And in 1973, he went on to say that "the acquired meanings of a stimulus can only be known by determining what the person does with it verbally and behaviorally. . . . Considerable evidence suggests that in this assessment enterprise, direct information from the person is the best source of data" (p. 261).

We must, of course, remember that, if self-reports and correlations between them are to become more clearly psychologically interpretable, as opposed to being explainable in terms of artifactual influences, improvements in measurement techniques and their construct validation must be effected.

Still another way of accounting for many of the null relationships involving over-all self-regard is to suggest that it is unconscious self-regard rather than conscious self-regard which is affected by these variables. On this view, women, blacks, old people, members of lower socioeconomic classes, and mentally retarded persons "really do" have "low self-regard," but it would take measures of nonphenomenal or unconscious self-regard to show this. Such a possibility cannot now be refuted and it should be left open. However, two replies may be made to this suggestion. First, it is by no means apparent that the strong a priori predictions made by social scientists referred to unconscious as opposed to conscious self-regard, and this weakens the force of any ad hoc formulations made in terms of unconscious self-regard. Second, to test hypotheses about unconscious self-regard, we must have instruments to index this construct. In volume 1, I present a detailed examination of proposed indices of unconscious self-concept and conclude, as mentioned above, that there is no evidence for the appropriate kind of construct validity of any of the extant instruments for which published information is available. Thus, following up this hint takes one onto the very beginning of an extremely arduous and risky path.

D. Scientific Usefulness of Studying Specific Aspects of Self-Conception

Some of the speculative points just made about relationships of self-regard with other variables imply the possible scientific fruitfulness of looking for relationships between more specific aspects of self-concept on the one hand and supposed antecedent, consequent, and correlated variables on the other, as suggested in my 1974 over-all conclusions summarized in section A. For one thing, if "over-all self-regard" is comprised of various subevaluations which are assigned different salience by different persons, it is clearly important to direct research attention to these specific aspects, their differing saliences, and how these differences in salience are acquired. Moreover, as already argued, one might expect much closer correlations between specific aspects of self-conception and respectively relevant specific input, output, and correlated variables than between over-all self-regard and these same specific variables. An overview of this book suggests that the latter expectation may be borne out and in those very areas in which null or weak associations with over-all self-regard occur. Thus, the applicability of self-concept theory might be enhanced by more research on specific aspects of self-conceptions. Examples from various chapters of the book may be cited. (Three points about these examples must be stressed. It is by no means true that significant, let alone strong, relationships obtain between specific self-concept variables and all kinds of input or output variables. Rather, it is suggested that the significant associations involve specific self-concept variables which might intuitively be appropriately related to specified other variables. Secondly, comparisons suggested in the examples must be regarded very tentatively, as they do not necessarily come from clearly comparable researches. Thirdly, these examples should not be construed as one-sentence summaries of the contents of the indicated chapters.)

As one class of examples of fruitful study of relatively specific self-conceptions, I note that some progress has been made in the study of self-conceptions of age, socioeconomic level, race, and gender as a function of age and other variables (chaps. 2, 3, 4). While self-regard does not appear to be a function of the subject's sex, self-reported affiliative predispositions have shown some tendency to differentiate the sexes (chap. 5). And although self-regard does not appear to be a function of the subject's socioeconomic level, it seems likely that there is a positive relationship between socioeconomic level and self-conceptions of schoolwork ability with IQ and/or GPA controlled (chap. 3). Despite methodological shortcomings which should attenuate the correlations, fairly substantial associations do occur between achievement scores and concepts of schoolwork ability with IQ scores controlled (chap. 7). Likewise, the small amount of available evidence tentatively suggests that self-conceptions of personal characteristics congruent with academic success do correlate with achievement scores more predictably than do less plausibly relevant ones (chap. 7). Although creativity seems unrelated to over-all self-regard, a number of specific self-conceptions have been associated with creativity indices in several studies (chap. 7). Self-conceptions of abilities specifically relevant to the respective requirements of conformity tasks tend to be associated with conformity behavior on these tasks, while no satisfactory evidence of a main effect of over-all self-regard on conformity behavior has thus far been published (chap. 9). In one of the better studies, changes in self-reported predispositional anxiety seemed to change as a function of psychotherapy specifically directed toward that characteristic, whereas many null (or otherwise uninterpretable) results have been reported concerning over-all self-regard changes as a function of psychotherapy (chap. 11). And while over-all self-regard has not been shown to be related to F-scale scores of authoritarianism, subjects' self-reports about their own standing on those particular characteristics which supposedly typify authoritarian persons were reported to correlate with F-scale scores (chap. 10).

As I say at the beginning of this chapter, some of the points made in this section and the immediately preceding one are closely interrelated, in some respects complementary. That is, it is possible to make speculative psychological sense out of the combined facts that (a) stable individual differences in self-regard scores have repeatedly been found; (b) null results have repeatedly been obtained between self-regard scores and certain other "objective" variables (especially alleged antecedents); (c) more frequent and/or substantial associations tend to be found between specific aspects of self-conception and respectively relevant specific input and output variables as well as over-all self-regard. Perhaps pursuing the implications of these facts and the suggested integrative explanation may suggest some of the paths toward fruitful further research.

E. Conclusions

Looked at from one perspective, the yield from the very large number of researches considered in this book is very disappointing and ambiguous. The extremely high incidence of avoidable methodological flaws is especially dismaying. And since we have not yet found what would result when extant methodological standards are rigorously and consistently applied, it is all the riskier to speculate about the possible fruitfulness of following any of the suggestions for improving or radically changing our theoretical and methodological paradigms.

From another perspective, our research overview may suggest that some values have accrued, especially in regard to future work. It appears that we have sufficiently explored some simplistic hypotheses predicting strong relations which were consistently unsupported by research results. The analysis presented in this chapter implies that we may have gotten some glimpses of the beginnings of possibly useful, more complex new paths. And throughout the book, attention is called not only to what appear to be the most interpretable results to date, but also to important particular topics and issues which are virtually or completely unexplored.

Of course one can offer no assurances as to the ultimate usefulness of pursuing theory and research on self-referent constructs. I still agree with my final statement in volume 1 (1974): "Continuing to spawn and subsequently publish numerous researches with avoidable conceptual and methodological flaws would be a most unfortunate waste of professional time and energy and would harm the development of scientific personality study" (p. 331). However, an overview of volume 2 reaffirms my belief that self-referent constructs are potentially very important to theoretical understanding and practical application. One can adequately test this idea only by approaching one's inquiry with the sophistication of thought and method appropriate to the subtlety and complexity of these constructs, their hypothetical relationships among themselves, and their hypothetical relationships with other variables.

Bibliography

Abate, M., & Berrien, F. K. Validation of stereotypes: Japanese versus American students. *Journal of Personality and Social Psychology*, 1967, 7, 435-438.

Achord, C. D., & McCary, P. The impact of attrition on the self-concept and anxiety level of freshman nursing students at the University of Northern Colorado. *Colorado Journal of Educational Research*, 1975, 14, 25-26.

Adesso, V. J.; Euse, F. J.; Hanson, R. W.; Hendry, D.; & Choca, P. Effects of a personal growth group on positive and negative self-references. *Psychotherapy: Theory, Research and Practice*, 1974, 11, 354-355.

Adler, A. Sex. In J. B. Miller (Ed.), *Psychoanalysis and women*. Baltimore, Md.: Penguin Books Inc., 1973. Pp. 40-50.

Adler, N. E., & Goleman, D. Goal setting, T-group participation, and self-rated change: An experimental study. *Journal of Applied Behavioral Science*, 1975, 11, 197-208.

Adorno, T. V.; Frenkel-Brunswik, E.; Levinson, D. J.; & Sanford, R. N. *The authoritarian personality*. New York: Harper & Row, 1950.

Ageton, S. S., & Elliott, D. S. The effects of legal processing on delinquent orientations. *Social Problems*, 1974, 22, 87-100.

Ahammer, I. M. Actual versus perceived age differences and changes: Young adults and older people view themselves and each other. *Proceedings of the 79th Annual Convention of the American Psychological Association*, 1971, 6, 593-594.

Aisenberg, R. What happens to old psychologists? A preliminary report. In R. Kastenbaum (Ed.), *New thoughts on old age*. New York: Springer, 1964. Pp. 116-135.

Alexandra, Sister M. Personality adjustment and leadership. *Education*, 1946, 66, 584-590.

Alfert, E. Two components of assumed similarity. *Journal of Abnormal and Social Psychology*, 1958, 56, 135-138.

Allport, G. W. *Pattern and growth in personality*. New York: Holt, Rinehart, & Winston, 1961.

703

Altrocchi, J.; Parsons, O. A.; & Dickoff, H. Changes in self-ideal discrepancy in repressors and sensitizers. *Journal of Abnormal and Social Psychology*, 1960, 61, 67–72.

Amatora, Sister, M. Developmental trends in pre-adolescence and in early adolescence in self-evaluation. *Journal of Genetic Psychology*, 1957, 91, 89–97.

Ames, L. B. The sense of self of nursery school children as manifested by their verbal behavior. *Journal of Genetic Psychology*, 1952, 81, 193–232.

Amsterdam, B. Mirror self-image reactions before age two. *Developmental Psychobiology*, 1972, 5, 297–305.

Anastasi, A. *Differential psychology: Individual and group differences in behavior.* New York: Macmillan Co., 1937.

Anastasi, A. *Differential psychology: Individual and group differences in behavior.* (3rd ed.) New York: Macmillan Co., 1958.

Anastasi, A. *Psychological testing.* (3rd ed.) London: Macmillan Co., 1968.

Anastasiow, N. J. Sex differences in self-concept scores of high and low ability elementary students. *Gifted Child Quarterly*, 1967, Summer, 112–116.

Anderson J. G. & Johnson, W. H. Stability and change among three generations of Mexican-Americans: Factors affecting achievement. *American Education Research Journal*, 1971, 8, 285–309.

Anderson, N. N. Effects of institutionalization on self-esteem of older people. *Journal of Gerontology*, 1967, 22, 313–317.

Anderson, T. B., & Olsen, L. C. Congruence of self and ideal-self and occupational choices. *Personnel and Guidance Journal*, 1965, 44, 171–176.

Angyal, A. *Foundations for a science of personality.* New York: Commonwealth Fund, 1941.

Ansbacher, H. L., & Ansbacher, R. R. (Eds.). *The individual psychology of Alfred Adler.* New York: Basic Books, 1956.

Antley, M. A.; Antley, R. M.; & Hartlage, L. C. Effects of genetic counseling on parental self-concepts. *Journal of Psychology*, 1973, 83, 335–338.

Antonovsky, A. Aspirations, class and racial-ethnic membership. *Journal of Negro Education*, 1967, 36, 385–393.

Antonovsky, A. & Lerner, M. J. Occupational aspirations of lower class Negro and white youth. *Social Problems*, 1959, 7, 132–138.

Antonovsky, A. & Lorwin, L. (Eds.). *Discrimination and low incomes.* New York: New York State Commission Against Discrimination, 1959.

Apostal, R. A., & Muro, J. J. Effects of group counseling on self-reports and on self-recognition abilities of counselors in training. *Counselor Education and Supervision*, 1970, 10, 56–63.

Appley, M. H., & Moeller, G. Conforming behavior and personality variables in college women. *Journal of Abnormal and Social Psychology*, 1963, 66, 284–290.

Arbuckle, D. S. Self-ratings and test scores on two standardized personality inventories. *Personnel and Guidance Journal*, 1958, 37, 292–293.

Arbuckle D. S., & Boy, A. Client-centered therapy in counseling students with behavior problems. *Journal of Counseling Psychology*, 1961, 8, 136–139.

Archibald, W. P. Self-esteem and balance with impersonal attitude objects. *Psychonomic Science: Section on Human Experimental Psychology*, 1970, 21, 363–364.

Arkoff, A., & Weaver, H. B. Body image and body dissatisfaction in Japanese-Americans. *Journal of Social Psychology*, 1966, 68, 323–330.

Aronson, E. The theory of cognitive dissonance: A current perspective. In L. Berkowitz (Ed.), *Advances in experimental social psychology*. Vol. 4. New York: Academic Press, 1969. Pp. 1–34.

Aronson, E., & Linder, D. Gain and loss of esteem as determinants of interpersonal attractiveness. *Journal of Experimental Social Psychology*, 1965, 1, 156–171.

Aronson, E.; Willerman, B.; & Floyd, J. The effect of a pratfall on increasing interpersonal attractiveness. *Psychonomic Science*, 1966, 4, 227–228.

Aronson, E., & Worchel, P. Similarity versus liking as determinants of interpersonal attractiveness. *Psychonomic Science*, 1966, 5, 157–158.

Arrowood, A. J., & Short, J. A. Agreement, attraction and self-esteem. *Canadian Journal of Behavioural Science*, 1973, 5, 242–252.

Arsenian, S. Own estimate and objective measurement. *Journal of Educational Psychology*, 1942, 33, 291–302.

Ashcraft, C., & Fitts, W. H. Self-concept change in psychotherapy. *Psychotherapy: Theory, Research & Practice*, 1964, 1, 115–118.

Attenborough, R. E., & Zdep, S. M. Self-image among a national probability sample of girls. *Proceedings of the 81st Annual Convention of the American Psychological Association*, 1973, 8, 237–238.

Ausubel, D. P. Ego development among segregated Negro children. *Mental Hygiene*, 1958, 42, 362–369.

Bachman, J. G. *Youth in transition*. Vol. 2. *The impact of family background and intelligence on tenth-grade boys*. Ann Arbor, Mich.: Survey Research Center, Institute for Social Research, 1970.

Bachman, J. G., & O'Malley, P. M. Self-esteem in young men: A longitudinal analysis of the impact of educational and occupational attainment. *Journal of Personality and Social Psychology*, 1977, 35, 365–380.

Back, K. W. *Beyond words*. New York: Russell Sage, 1972.

Back, K. W. Intervention techniques: Small groups. In M. R. Rosenzweig & L. W. Porter (Eds.), *Annual review of psychology*. Palo Alto, Calif.: Annual Reviews, Inc., 1974, Pp. 367–387.

Back, K. W. & Gergen, K. J. The self through the latter span of life. In C. Gordon & K. J. Gergen (Eds.), *The self in social interaction*. Vol. 1. *Classic and contemporary perspectives*. New York: Wiley, 1968. Pp. 241–250.

Back, K. W. & Guptill, C. S. Retirement and self-ratings. In I. H. Simpson & J. C. McKinney (Eds.), *Social aspects of aging*. Durham: Duke University Press, 1966. Pp. 120–129.

Back, K. W., & Paramesh, C. R. Self-image, information exchange and social character. *International Journal of Psychology*, 1969, 4, 109-117.

Backman, C. W., & Secord, P. F. Liking, selective interaction, and misperception in congruent interpersonal relations. *Sociometry*, 1962, 25, 321-335.

Badgett, J. L.; Hope, L. H.; & Kerley, S. A. The relationship between self-concept and academic aptitude of entering male college freshmen. *Psychology*, 1971, 8, 43-47.

Bagley, C., & Evan-Wong, L. Neuroticism and extraversion in responses to Coopersmith's Self-Esteem Inventory. *Psychological Reports*, 1975, 36, 253-254.

Bailey, K. G. & Gibby, R. G. Developmental differences in self-ratings on intelligence. *Journal of Clinical Psychology*, 1971, 27, 51-54.

Bailey, R. C. Self-concept differences in low and high achieving students. *Journal of Clinical Psychology*, 1971, 27, 188-191.

Bailey, R. C., & Bailey, K. G. Perceived ability in male and female college students. *Perceptual and Motor Skills*, 1971, 32, 293-294.

Bailey, R. C.; Finney, P.; & Bailey, K. G. Level of self-acceptance and perceived intelligence in self and friend. *Journal of Genetic Psychology*, 1974, 124, 61-67.

Bailey, R. C., & Shaw, W. R. Direction of self-estimate of ability and college-related criteria. *Psychological Reports*, 1971, 29, 959-964.

Baird, L. L. Prediction of accomplishment in college: A study of achievement. *Journal of Counseling Psychology*, 1969, 16, 246-253.

Baker, G. P. The effectiveness of nursery school on affective and conceptual development of disadvantaged and nondisadvantaged children. *Developmental Psychology*, 1973, 9, 140.

Baldwin, J. M. *Social and ethical interpretations in mental development.* New York: Macmillan, 1899.

Baltes, P. B., & Nesselroade, J. R. Cultural change and adolescent personality development: An application of longitudinal sequences. *Developmental Psychology*, 1972, 7, 244-256.

Bandura, A. Social-learning theory of identificatory processes. In D. A. Goslin (Ed.), *Handbook of socialization theory and research.* Chicago: Rand McNally, 1969. Pp. 213-262.

Banta, T. J., & Hetherington, M. Relations between needs of friends and fiancés. *Journal of Abnormal and Social Psychology*, 1963, 66, 401-404.

Barber, T. X. Hypnotizability, suggestibility, and personality: V. A critical review of research findings. *Psychological Reports*, 1964, 14, 299-320.

Bardwick, J. M. *Psychology of women: A study of bio-cultural conflicts.* New York: Harper and Row, 1971.

Bare, C. E. Relationship of counselor personality and counselor-client similarity to selected counseling success criteria. *Journal of Counseling Psychology*, 1967, 14, 419-425.

Barnes, E. J. The black community as the source of positive self-concept for black children: A theoretical perspective. In R. L. Jones (Ed.), *Black psychology*. New York: Harper & Row, 1972. Pp. 166–192.

Barrett, R. L. Changes in accuracy of self-estimates. *Personnel and Guidance Journal*, 1968, 47, 353–357.

Barrett-Lennard, G. T. Dimensions of therapist response as causal factors in therapeutic change. *Psychological Monographs: General and Applied*, 1962, 76 (43, Whole No. 562).

Barrett-Lennard, G. T.; Kwasnik, T. P.; & Wilkinson, G. R. Some effects of participation in encounter group workshops: An analysis of written follow-up reports. *Interpersonal Development*, 1973/74, 4, 35–41.

Barron, F. Some personality correlates of independence of judgment. *Journal of Personality*, 1953, 21, 287–297.

Barron, F. The disposition toward originality. *Journal of Abnormal and Social Psychology*, 1955, 51, 478–485.

Barron, F. Originality in relation to personality and intellect. *Journal of Personality*, 1957, 25, 730–742.

Barron, F. *Creativity and personal freedom*. Princeton, N. J.: D. Van Nostrand, 1968.

Barron, F. *Creative person and creative process*. New York: Holt, Rinehart, and Winston, 1969.

Barron, F., & Leary, T. F. Changes in psychoneurotic patients with and without psychotherapy. *Journal of Consulting Psychology*, 1955, 19, 239–245.

Barron, M. L. *The aging Americans: An introduction to social gerontology and geriatrics*. New York: Crowell, 1961.

Baruch, G. K. Feminine self-esteem, self-ratings of competence, and maternal career commitment. *Journal of Counseling Psychology*, 1973, 20, 487–488.

Bass, A. R., & Fiedler, F. E. Interpersonal perception scores and their components as predictors of personal adjustment. *Journal of Abnormal and Social Psychology*, 1961, 62, 442–445.

Bauer, N. J. Differences in personality traits among most preferred and least preferred students in grades 10, 11, and 12. *Journal of Educational Research*, 1971, 65, 65–70.

Baughman, E. E. *Black Americans: A psychological analysis*. New York: Academic Press, 1971.

Baughman, E. E., & Dahlstrom, W. G. *Negro and white children: A psychological study in the rural South*. New York: Academic Press, 1968.

Baumhart, R. How ethical are businessmen? *Harvard Business Review*, 1961, 39, 61–67.

Baumrind, D. Current patterns of parental authority. *Developmental Psychology Monographs*, 1971, No. 1, Part 2, 1–103.

Baymurr, F. B., & Patterson, C. H. A comparison of three methods of assisting underachieving high school students. *Journal of Counseling Psychology*, 1960, 7, 83–89.

Bayton, J. A.; Austin, L. J.; & Burke, K. R. Negro perception of Negro and white personality traits. *Journal of Personality and Social Psychology*, 1965, 1, 250-253.

Bayton, J. A.; McAlister, L. B.; & Hamer, J. Race-class stereotypes. *Journal of Negro Education*, 1956, 25, 75-78.

Bayton, J. A., & Muldrow, T. W. Interacting variables in the perception of racial personality traits. *Journal of Experimental Research in Personality*, 1968, 3, 39-44.

Bebout, J. The use of encounter groups for interpersonal growth: Initial results of the TIE Project. *Interpersonal Development*, 1971-72, 2, 91-104.

Becker, G. The complementary-needs hypothesis, authoritarianism, dominance, and other Edwards Personal Preference Schedule scores. *Journal of Personality*, 1964, 32, 45-46.

Becker, G., & Dileo, D. T. Scores on Rokeach's Dogmatism Scale and the response set to present a positive social and personal image. *Journal of Social Psychology*, 1967, 71, 287-293.

Becker, W., & Krug, R. S. Parent attitude research instrument: A research review. *Child Development*, 1965, 36, 329-365.

Begley, C. E.; & Lieberman, L. R. Patients' expectations of therapists' techniques. *Journal of Clinical Psychology*, 1970, 26, 112-118.

Beier, E. G., & Ratzeburg, F. The parental identifications of male and female college students. *Journal of Abnormal and Social Psychology*, 1953, 48, 569-572.

Beier, E. G.; Rossi, A. M.; & Garfield, R. L. Similarity plus dissimilarity of personality: Basis for friendship? *Psychological Reports*, 1961, 8, 3-8.

Bell, G. D. Self-confidence and persuasion in car buying. *Journal of Marketing Research*, 1967, 4, 46-52.

Bell, T. The relationship between social involvement and feeling old among residents in homes for the aged. *Journal of Gerontology*, 1967, 22, 17-22.

Bene, E., & Anthony, J. *Family relations test*. London: National Foundation for Educational Research in England and Wales, 1957.

Bennett, L. A.; Sorensen, D. E.; & Forshay, H. The application of self-esteem measures in a correctional setting: I. Reliability of the scale and relationship to other measures. *Journal of Research in Crime and Delinquency*, 1971, 8, 1-9.

Bennett, V. D. C. Development of a self-concept Q sort for use with elementary age school children. *Journal of School Psychology*, 1964, 3, 19-25.

Berger, C. R. Attributional communication, situational involvement, self-esteem and interpersonal attraction. *Journal of Communication*, 1973, 23, 284-305.

Berger, E. M. The relation between expressed acceptance of self and expressed acceptance of others. *Journal of Abnormal and Social Psychology*, 1952, 47, 778-782.

Berger, E. M. Relationships among acceptance of self, acceptance of others, and MMPI scores. *Journal of Counseling Psychology*, 1955, 2, 279-284.

Bergin, A. E. The evaluation of therapeutic outcomes. In A. E. Bergin & S. L. Garfield (Eds.), *Handbook of psychotherapy and behavior change: An empirical analysis*. New York: Wiley, 1971. Pp. 217-270.

Bergin, A. E., & Garfield, S. L. (Eds.). *Handbook of psychotherapy and behavior change: An empirical analysis*. New York: Wiley, 1971.

Bergin, A. E., & Suinn, R. M. Individual psychotherapy and behavior therapy. In M. R. Rosenzweig & L. W. Porter (Eds.), *Annual review of psychology*. Palo Alto, Calif.: Annual Reviews, Inc., 1975. Pp. 509-556.

Bergum, B. O. Selection of specialized creators. *Psychological Reports*, 1973, 33, 635-639.

Bergum, B. O. Self-perceptions of members of a graduate faculty whose publication rates are high or low. *Psychological Reports*, 1974, 35, 857-858.

Bergum, B. O. Self-perceptions of creativity among academic inventors and non-inventors. *Perceptual and Motor Skills*, 1975, 40, 78.

Berkowitz, L., & Lundy, R. M. Personality characteristics related to susceptibility to influence by peers or authority figures. *Journal of Personality*, 1957, 25, 306-316.

Berlyne, D. E. *Conflict, arousal, and curiosity*. New York: McGraw-Hill, 1960.

Berman, J. J., & Brickman, P. Standards for attribution of liking: Effects of sex, self esteem, and other's attractiveness. *Proceedings of the 79th Annual Convention of the American Psychological Association*, 1971, 6, 271-272.

Berzon, B.; Reisel, J.; & Davis, D. P. Peer: An audiotape program for self-directed small groups. *Journal of Humanistic Psychology*, 1969, 9, 71-86.

Bieri, J., & Lobeck, R. Self-concept differences in relation to identification, religion, and social class. *Journal of Abnormal and Social Psychology*, 1961, 62, 94-98.

Bieri, J.; Lobeck, R.; & Galinsky, M. D. A comparison of direct, indirect, and fantasy measures of identification. *Journal of Abnormal and Social Psychology*, 1959, 58, 253-258.

Bigner, J. J. Sibling position and definition of self. *Journal of Social Psychology*, 1971, 84, 307-308.

Biller, H. B., & Bahm, R. M. Father absence, perceived maternal behavior and masculinity of self-concept among junior high school boys. *Developmental Psychology*, 1971, 4, 178-181.

Billingsley, A. *Black families in white America*. Englewood Cliffs, N. J.: Prentice-Hall. 1968.

Bills, R. E. *Index of Adjustment and Values. Manual*. University, Alabama: Mimeographed, n. d.

Bills, R. E. *Index of Adjustment and Values. Forms: Elementary, Junior High School, and High School. Manual*. University, Alabama; Mimeographed, n.d.

Bills, R. E. Acceptance of self as measured by interviews and the Index of Adjustment and Values. *Journal of Consulting Psychology*, 1954, 18, 22.

Binder, D. M.; Jones, J. G.; & Strowig, R. W. Non-intellective self-report variables as predictors of scholastic achievement. *Journal of Educational Research*, 1970, 63, 364-366.

Birren, J. E. Principles of research on aging. In J. E. Birren (Ed.), *Handbook of aging and the individual*. Chicago: University of Chicago Press, 1959. Pp. 3-42.

Bither, S. W. & Wright, P. L. The self-confidence-advertising response relationship: A function of situational distraction. *Journal of Marketing Research*, 1973, 10, 146-152.

Black, F. W. Self-concept as related to achievement and age in learning-disabled children. *Child Development*, 1974, 45, 1137-1140.

Blau, Z. S. Changes in status and age identification. *American Sociological Review*, 1956, 21, 198-203.

Bledsoe, J. C. Self concepts of children and their intelligence, achievement, interests, and anxiety. *Journal of Individual Psychology*, 1964, 20, 55-58.

Bledsoe, J. C. Sex differences in self-concept: Fact or artifact? *Psychological Reports*, 1973, 32, 1253-1254.

Bledsoe, J. C., & Khatena, J. Factor analytic study of Something About Myself. *Psychological Reports*, 1973, 32, 1176-1178.

Bledsoe, J. C., & Khatena, J. Factor analytic study of the test, What Kind of Person Are You? *Perceptual and Motor Skills*, 1974, 39, 143-146.

Bledsoe, J. C., & Wiggins, R. G. Congruence of adolescents' self-concepts and parents' perceptions of adolescents' self-concepts. *Journal of Psychology*, 1973, 83, 131-136.

Block, J. An unprofitable application of the semantic differential. *Journal of Consulting Psychology*, 1958, 22, 234-236.

Block, J., & Thomas, H. Is satisfaction with self a measure of adjustment? *Journal of Abnormal and Social Psychology*, 1955, 51, 254-259.

Block, J. H. Conceptions of sex role: Some cross-cultural and longitudinal perspectives. *American Psychologist*, 1973, 28, 512-526.

Bloom, K. L. Age and the self concept. *American Journal of Psychiatry*, 1961, 118, 534-538.

Bonney, M. E. A study of the relation of intelligence, family size, and sex differences with mutual friendships in the primary grades. *Child Development*, 1942, 13, 79-100.

Bonney, M. E. The constancy of sociometric scores and their relationship to teacher judgments of social success, and to personality self-ratings. *Sociometry*, 1943, 6, 409-424.

Bonney, M. E. A sociometric study of the relationship of some factors to mutual friendships on the elementary, secondary, and college levels. *Sociometry*, 1946, 9, 21-47.

Bookbinder, L. J. Perception of others, self perception, and response sets in high and low authoritarians. *Perceptual and Motor Skills*, 1963, 17, 694.

Bordeau, E.; Dales, R.; & Connor, R. Relation of self-concept to 4-H club leadership. *Rural Sociology*, 1963, 28, 413-418.

Borgatta, E. F. The stability of interpersonal judgments in independent situations. *Journal of Abnormal and Social Psychology*, 1960, 60, 188-194. (a)

Borgatta, E. F. Rankings and self-assessments: Some behavioral characteristics replication studies. *Journal of Social Psychology*, 1960, 52, 279-307. (b)

Borislow, B. Self-evaluation and academic achievement. *Journal of Counseling Psychology*, 1962, 9, 246-254.

Boshier, R. A study of the relationship between self-concept and conservatism. *Journal of Social Psychology*, 1969, 77, 139-140.

Boshier, R. The effect of academic failure on self-concept and maladjustment indices. *Journal of Educational Research*, 1972, 65, 347-351.

Boshier, R. Educational participation and dropout: A theoretical model. *Adult Education*, 1973, 23, 255-282.

Boshier, R. W., & Hamid, P. N. Academic success and self concept. *Psychological Reports*, 1968, 22, 1191-1192.

Bossom, J., & Maslow, A. H. Security of judges as a factor in impressions of warmth in others. *Journal of Abnormal and Social Psychology*, 1957, 55, 147-148.

Botwinick, J. Age differences in self-ratings of confidence. *Psychological Reports*, 1970, 27, 865-866.

Bowerman, C. E., & Day, B. R. A test of the theory of complementary needs as applied to couples during courtship. *American Sociological Review*, 1956, 21, 602-605.

Bowman, D. O. A longitudinal study of selected facets of children's self concepts as related to achievement and intelligence. *The Citadel: Monograph Series: Number XII*, 1974, 1-16.

Boyd, G. F. The levels of aspiration of white and Negro children in a non-segregated elementary school. *Journal of Social Psychology*, 1952, 36, 191-196.

Boyd, R. E. Conformity reduction in adolescence. *Adolescence*, 1975, 10, 297-300.

Braaten, L. J. The movement from non-self to self in client-centered psychotherapy. *Journal of Counseling Psychology*, 1961, 8, 20-24.

Bradley, F. O., & Newhouse, R. C. Sociometric choice and self perceptions of upper elementary school children. *Psychology in the Schools*, 1975, 12, 219-222.

Brandt, R. M. The accuracy of self estimate: A measure of self-concept reality. *Genetic Psychology Monographs*, 1958, 58, 55-99.

Brazziel, W. F. Correlates of southern Negro personality. *Journal of Social Issues*, 1964, 20, 46-53.

Brigham, J. C. Ethnic stereotypes. *Psychological Bulletin*, 1971, 76, 15-38.

Brigham, J. C. Views of black and white children concerning the distribution of personality characteristics. *Journal of Personality*, 1974, 42, 144-158.

Brim, O. G., Jr. College grades and self-estimates of intelligence. *Journal of Educational Psychology*, 1954, 45, 477-484.

Brim, O. G., Jr.; Neulinger, J.; & Glass, D. C. Experiences and attitudes of American adults concerning standardized intelligence tests. Technical Report No. 1 on the Social Consequences of Testing. New York: Russell Sage Foundation, 1965.

Brim, O. G., Jr., & Wood, N. Self and other conceptions in courtship pairs and marriage pairs. *Marriage and Family Living*, 1956, 18, 243-248.

Brodbeck, A. J., & Perlmutter, H. V. Self-dislike as a determinant of marked ingroup-outgroup preferences. *Journal of Psychology*, 1954, 38, 271-280.

Bronfenbrenner, U. Freudian theories of identification and their derivatives. *Child Development*, 1960, 31, 15-40.

Brookover, W. B.; Erickson, E. L.; & Joiner, L. M. *Self-concept of ability and school achievement: Relationship of self-concept to achievement in high school.* U.S. Office of Education, Cooperative Research Project No. 2831, Michigan State University, 1967.

Brookover, W. B. LePere, J. M.; Hamachek, E. D.; Thomas, S.; & Erickson, E. L. *Self-concept of ability and school achievement. II: Improving academic achievement through students' self-concept enhancement.* U.S. Office of Education, Cooperative Research Project No. 1636. East Lansing: Educational Publication Services, Michigan State University, 1965.

Brookover, W. B.; Paterson, A.; & Thomas, S. *Self-concept of ability and school achievement.* U.S. Office of Education, Cooperative Research Project No. 845. East Lansing: Educational Publication Services, Michigan State University, 1962.

Brookover, W. B.; Thomas, S.; & Paterson, A. Self-concept of ability and school achievement. *Sociology of Education,* 1964, 37, 271-278.

Brooks, M., & Hillman, C. Parent-daughter relationship as factors in non-marriage studied in identical twins. *Journal of Marriage and the Family,* 1965, 27, 383-385.

Broverman, I. K.; Broverman, D. M.; Clarkson, F. E.; Rosenkrantz, P. S.; & Vogel, S. R. Sex-role stereotypes and clinical judgments of mental health. *Journal of Consulting and Clinical Psychology,* 1970, 34, 1-7.

Broverman, I. K.; Vogel, S. R.; Broverman, D. M.; Clarkson, F. E.; & Rosenkrantz, P. S. Sex-role stereotypes: A current appraisal. *Journal of Social Issues,* 1972, 28, 59-78.

Brown, S. R., & Hendrick, C. Introversion, extraversion and social perception. *British Journal of Social and Clinical Psychology,* 1971, 10, 313-319.

Broxton, J. A. A test of interpersonal attraction predictions derived from balance theory. *Journal of Abnormal and Social Psychology,* 1963, 66, 394-397.

Brozek, J. Personality of young and middle-aged normal men: Item analysis of a psychosomatic inventory. *Journal of Gerontology,* 1952, 7, 410-418.

Brozek, J. Personality changes with age: An item analysis of the Minnesota Multiphasic Personality Inventory. *Journal of Gerontology,* 1955, 10, 194-206.

Brunkan, R. J., & Shen, F. Personality characteristics of ineffective, effective, and efficient readers. *Personnel and Guidance Journal,* 1966, 44, 837-843.

Bugental, J. F. T. A method of assessing self and non-self attitudes during the therapeutic series. *Journal of Consulting Psychology,* 1952, 16, 435-439.

Buhler, C. Genetic aspects of the self. *Annals of the New York Academy of Sciences,* 1962, 96, 730-764.

Burgess, E. W.; Cavan, R. S.; & Havighurst, R. J. *Your activities and attitudes.* Chicago: Science Research Associates, 1948.

Burke, D. A., & Sellin, D. F. Measuring the self concept of ability as a worker. *Exceptional Children,* 1972, 39, 126-132.

Burke, R. L., & Bennis, W. G. Changes in perception of self and others during human relations training. *Human Relations,* 1961, 14, 165-182.

Buros, O. K. (Ed.), *Personality tests and reviews.* Highland Park, N. J.: Gryphon Press, 1970.

Busk, P. L.; Ford, R. C.; & Schulman, J. L. Stability of sociometric responses in classrooms. *Journal of Genetic Psychology,* 1973, 123, 69-84.

Busse, E. W. Theories of aging. In E. W. Busse & E. Pfeiffer (Eds.), *Behavior and adaptation in late life.* Boston: Little Brown, 1969. Pp. 11-32.

Butler, J. M. Self-ideal congruence in psychotherapy. *Psychotherapy: Theory, Research, and Practice,* 1968, 5, 13-17.

Butler, J. M., & Haigh, G. V. Changes in the relation between self-concepts and ideal concepts consequent upon client-centered counseling. In C. R. Rogers & R. F. Dymond (Eds.), *Psychotherapy and personality change.* Chicago: University of Chicago Press, 1954. Pp. 55-75.

Butler, R. N. Aspects of survival and adaptation in human aging. *American Journal of Psychiatry,* 1967, 123, 1233-1243.

Butts, H. F. Skin color perception and self-esteem. *Journal of Negro Education,* 1963, 32, 122-128.

Byrne, D. *The attraction paradigm.* New York: Academic Press, 1971.

Byrne, D., & Clore, G. L. A reinforcement model of evaluative responses. *Personality,* 1970, 1, 103-129.

Byrne, D.; Clore, G. L.; & Worchel, P. Effect of economic similarity-dissimilarity on interpersonal attraction. *Journal of Personality and Social Psychology,* 1966, 4, 220-224.

Byrne, D.; Ervin, C. R.; & Lamberth, J. Continuity between the experimental study of attraction and real-life computer dating. *Journal of Personality and Social Psychology,* 1970, 16, 157-165.

Byrne, D., & Griffitt, W. Similarity versus liking: A clarification. *Psychonomic Science,* 1966, 6, 295-296.

Byrne, D., & Griffitt, W. Interpersonal attraction. *Annual Review of Psychology*, 1973, 24, 317–336.

Byrne, D.; Griffitt, W.; & Stefaniak, D. Attraction and similarity of personality characteristics. *Journal of Personality and Social Psychology*, 1967, 5, 82–90.

Byrne, D., & Nelson, D. Attraction as a linear function of proportion of positive reinforcements. *Journal of Personality and Social Psychology*, 1965, 1, 659–663.

Byrne, D., & Rhamey, R. Magnitude of positive and negative reinforcements as a determinant of attraction. *Journal of Personality and Social Psychology*, 1965, 2, 884–889.

Calvin, A. D. Some misuses of the experimental method in evaluating the effect of client-centered counseling. *Journal of Counseling Psychology*, 1954, 1, 249–251.

Campbell, D. T. Factors relevant to the validity of experiments in social settings. *Psychological Bulletin*, 1957, 54, 297–312.

Campbell, D. T. Conformity in psychology's theories of acquired behavioral dispositions. In I. A. Berg & B. M. Bass (Eds.), *Conformity and deviation*. New York: Harper, 1961. Pp. 101–142.

Campbell, D. T., & Fiske, D. W. Convergent and discriminant validation by the multitrait-multimethod matrix. *Psychological Bulletin*, 1959, 56, 81–105.

Campbell, D. T., & Stanley, J. C. Experimental and quasi-experimental designs for research on teaching. In N. L. Gage (Ed.), *Handbook of research on teaching*. Chicago: Rand McNally, 1963. Pp. 171–246.

Campbell, J. D.; Yarrow, L. J.; & Yarrow, M. R. A study of adaptation to a new social situation. *Journal of Social Issues*, 1958, 14, 3–7.

Campbell, P. B. School and self concept. *Educational Leadership*, 1967, 24, 510–515.

Cantril, H. Identification with social and economic class. *Journal of Abnormal and Social Psychology*, 1944, 38, 74–80.

Caplan, S. W. The effect of group counseling in junior high school boys' concepts of themselves in school. *Journal of Counseling Psychology*, 1957, 4, 124–128.

Caplin, M. D. Self-concept, level of aspiration, and academic achievement. *Journal of Negro Education*, 1968, 37, 435–439.

Caplin, M. D. The relationship between self concept and academic achievement. *Journal of Experimental Education*, 1969, 37, 13–16.

Cardillo, J. P. The effects of teaching communication roles on interpersonal perception and self-concept in disturbed marriages. *Proceedings of the 79th Annual Convention of the American Psychological Association*, 1971, 6, 441–442.

Carlson, R. Identification and personality structure in preadolescents. *Journal of Abnormal and Social Psychology*, 1963, 67, 566–573.

Carlson, R. Stability and change in the adolescent's self-image. *Child Development*, 1965, 36, 659-666.

Carlson, R. On the structure of self-esteem: Comments on Ziller's formulation. *Journal of Consulting and Clinical Psychology*, 1970, 2, 264-268.

Carlson, R. Sex differences in ego functioning: Exploratory studies of agency and communion. *Journal of Consulting and Clinical Psychology*, 1971, 37, 267-277.

Carlson, R., & Levy, N. Brief method for assessing social-personal orientation. *Psychological Reports*, 1968, 23, 911-914.

Carlson, R., & Levy, N. Self, values, and affects: Derivations from polarity theory. *Journal of Personality and Social Psychology*, 1970, 16, 338-345.

Carpenter, T. R., & Busse, T. V. Development of self concept in Negro and white welfare children. *Child Development*, 1969, 40, 935-939.

Carson, R. C., & Heine, R. W. Similarity and success in therapeutic dyads. *Journal of Consulting Psychology*, 1962, 26, 38-43.

Carson, R. C., & Llewellyn, C. E., Jr. Similarity in therapeutic dyads: A reevaluation. *Journal of Consulting Psychology*, 1966, 30, 458.

Carter, T. P. The negative self-concept of Mexican-American students. *School and Society*, 1968, 96, 217-219.

Cartwright, D. S. Emotional dimensions of group life. In M. L. Reymert (Ed.), *Feelings and emotions*. New York: McGraw-Hill, 1950.

Cartwright, D. S.; Kirtner, W. L.; & Fiske, D. W. Method factors in changes associated with psychotherapy. *Journal of Abnormal and Social Psychology*, 1963, 66, 164-175.

Cartwright, D. S., & Roth, I. Success and satisfaction in psychotherapy. *Journal of Clinical Psychology*, 1957, 13, 20-26.

Cartwright, R. D. Effects of psychotherapy on self-consistency. *Journal of Counseling Psychology*, 1957, 4, 15-22.

Cartwright, R. D. The effects of psychotherapy on self-consistency: A replication and extension. *Journal of Consulting Psychology*, 1961, 25, 376-382.

Cartwright, R. D. Psychotherapeutic processes. In P. R. Farnsworth; M. R. Rosenzweig; & J. T. Polefka (Eds.), *Annual Review of Psychology*. Palo Alto, Calif.: Annual Reviews, Inc., 1968. Pp. 387-416.

Cartwright, R. D., & Lerner, B. Empathy, need to change, and improvement with psychotherapy. *Journal of Consulting Psychology*, 1963, 27, 138-144.

Cartwright, R. D., & Vogel, J. L. A comparison of changes in psychoneurotic patients during matched periods of therapy and no therapy. *Journal of Consulting Psychology*, 1960, 24, 121-127.

Cashdan, S., & Welsh, G. S. Personality correlates of creative potential in talented high school students. *Journal of Personality*, 1966, 34, 445-455.

Cass, L. K. An investigation of parent-child relationships in terms of awareness, identification, projection, and control. *American Journal of Orthopsychiatry*, 1952, 22, 305-313. (a)

Cass, L. K. Parent-child relationships and delinquency. *Journal of Abnormal and Social Psychology*, 1952, 47, 101-104. (b)

Cattell, R. B. *The scientific analysis of personality*. Chicago: Aldine, 1966.

Cavan, R. S. Self and role in adjustment during old age. In A. Rose (Ed.), *Human behavior and social processes*. Boston: Houghton Mifflin, 1962.

Centers, R. *The psychology of social classes*. New York: Russell and Russell, 1949.

Chang, J., & Block, J. A study of identification in male homosexuals. *Journal of Consulting Psychology*, 1960, 24, 307-310.

Chase, P. H. Self concepts in adjusted and maladjusted hospital patients. *Journal of Consulting Psychology*, 1957, 21, 495-497.

Chesler, P. *Women and madness*. Garden City, N.Y.: Doubleday, 1972.

Chinsky, J. M., & Rappaport, J. Brief critique of the meaning and reliability of "accurate empathy" ratings. *Psychological Bulletin*, 1970, 73, 379-382.

Chodorow, N. Family structure and feminine personality. In M. Z. Rosaldo & L. Lamphere (Eds.), *Woman, culture, and society*. Stanford, Calif.: Stanford University Press, 1974. Pp. 43-67.

Christmas, J. J. Self-concept and attitudes. In K. S. Miller & R. M. Dreger (Eds.), *Comparative studies of blacks and whites in the United States*. New York: Seminar Press, 1973. Pp. 249-272.

Clark, J. V.; Culbert, S. A.; & Bobele, H. K. Mutually therapeutic perception and self-awareness under variable conditions. *Journal of Applied Behavioral Science*, 1969, 5, 65-72.

Clark, K. B. Color, class, personality, and juvenile delinquency. *Journal of Negro Education*, 1959, 28, 240-251.

Clark, K. B. *Prejudice and your child*. (2nd ed.) New York: Beacon Press, 1963.

Clark, K. B. *Dark ghetto: Dilemmas of social power*. New York: Harper and Row, 1965.

Clark, K. B., & Clark, M. K. The development of consciousness of self and the emergence of racial identification in Negro preschool children. *Journal of Social Psychology*, 1939, 10, 591-599.

Clark, K. B., & Clark, M. K. Skin color as a factor in racial identification of Negro preschool children. *Journal of Social Psychology*, 1940, 11, 159-169.

Clark, K. B., & Clark, M. K. Racial identification and preference in Negro children. In T. M. Newcomb & E. L. Hartley (Eds.), *Readings in social psychology*. New York: Holt, Rinehart, & Winston, 1947. Pp. 169-178. Also in H. Proshansky & B. Seidenberg (Eds.), *Basic studies in social psychology*. New York: Holt, Rinehart, & Winston, 1965. Pp. 308-317.

Clarkson, F. E.; Vogel, S. R.; Broverman, I. K.; Broverman, D. M.; & Rosenkrantz, P. S. Family size and sex-role stereotypes. *Science*, 1970, 167, 390-392.

Clements, B. E. Transitional adolescents, anxiety, and group counseling. *Personnel and Guidance Journal*, 1966, 45, 67-71.

Coe, R. M. Self-conception and institutionalization. In A. M. Rose & W. A. Peterson (Eds.), *Older people and their social world*. Philadelphia: Davis, 1965. Pp. 225-243.

Cohen, H. A., & Miller, R. Mobility as a factor in adolescent identity problems. *Psychological Reports*, 1969, 25, 775-778.

Coleman, J. S.; Campbell, E. Q.; Hobson, C. J.; McPartland, J.; Mood, A. M.; Weinfeld, F. D.; & York, R. L. *Equality of educational opportunity*. Washington, D.C.: U.S. Government Printing Office, 1966.

Coleman, J. S.; Campbell, E. Q.; Hobson, C. J.; McPartland, J.; Mood, A. M.; Weinfeld, F. D.; & York, R. L. The locus of control and academic performance among racial groups. In S. S. Guterman (Ed.), *Black psyche: The modal personality patterns of black Americans*. Berkeley, Calif.: Glendessary, 1972. Pp. 273-290.

Coleman, M., & Glofka, P. T. Effect of group therapy on self-concept of senior nursing students. *Nursing Research*, 1969, 18, 274-275.

Coller, A. R. *Report for ERIC/TM: An annotated bibliography of self concept measures for the early childhood years*. Mimeographed. Urbana-Champaign, Ill.: University of Illinois, 1970.

Collins, H. A.; Burger, G. K.; & Doherty, D. Self-concept of EMR and nonretarded adolescents. *American Journal of Mental Deficiency*, 1970, 75, 285-289.

Constantinople, A. An Eriksonian measure of personality development in college students. *Developmental Psychology*, 1969, 1, 357-372.

Cooley, C. H. *Human nature and the social order*. New York: Scribners, 1902.

Cooley, C. H. *The two major works of Charles H. Cooley: Social organization, and Human nature and the social order*. Glencoe, Ill.: The Free Press, 1956.

Coombs, R. H., & Davies, V. Self-conception and the relationship between high school and college scholastic achievement. *Sociology and Social Research*, 1966, 50, 460-471.

Coons, W. H.; McEachern, D. L.; & Annis, H. Self-acceptance, acceptance-of-others, and verbal conditioning with mental hospital patients. *Canadian Journal of Behavioural Science*, 1973, 5, 290-296.

Cooper, J., & Duncan, B. L. Cognitive dissonance as a function of self-esteem and logical inconsistency. *Journal of Personality*, 1971, 39, 289-302.

Coopersmith, S. A method for determining types of self-esteem. *Journal of Abnormal and Social Psychology*, 1959, 59, 87-94.

Coopersmith, S. *The antecedents of self-esteem*. San Francisco: W. H. Freeman, 1967.

Corsini, R. J. Understanding and similarity in marriage. *Journal of Abnormal and Social Psychology*, 1956, 52, 327-332.

Costantini, E., & Craik, K. H. Women as politicians: The social background, personality, and political careers of female party leaders. *Journal of Social Issues*, 1972, 28, 217-236.

Costanzo, P. R. Conformity development as a function of self-blame. *Journal of Personality and Social Psychology*, 1970, 14, 366–374.

Cotler, S., & Palmer, R. J. The relationships among sex, sociometric, self, and text anxiety factors and the academic achievement of elementary school children. *Psychology in the Schools*, 1970, 7, 211–216.

Couch, C. J. Family role specialization and self-attitudes in children. *Sociological Quarterly*, 1962, 3, 115–121.

Cowan, M. L.; Weiner, E. A.; & Weiner, B. J. Therapist perceptions of clients and client self-report. *Journal of Clinical Psychology*, 1974, 30, 227–230.

Cowen, E. L.; Heilizer, F.; Axelrod, H. S.; & Alexander, S. The correlates of manifest anxiety in perceptual reactivity, rigidity, and self concept. *Journal of Consulting Psychology*, 1957, 21, 405–411.

Cox, D. F., & Bauer, R. A. Self-confidence and persuasibility in women. *Public Opinion Quarterly*, 1964, 28, 453–466.

Crain, R. L., & Weisman, C. S. *Discrimination, personality, and achievement: A survey of northern blacks.* New York: Seminar Press, 1972.

Crandall, J. E. Self-perception and interpersonal attraction as related to tolerance-intolerance of ambiguity. *Journal of Personality*, 1969, 37, 127–140.

Crandall, V. J., & Bellugi, U. Some relationships of interpersonal and intrapersonal conceptualizations to personal-social adjustment. *Journal of Personality*, 1954, 23, 224–232.

Cratty, B. J. *Perceptual and motor development in infants and children.* London: Macmillan, 1970.

Cronbach, L. J. Beyond the two disciplines of scientific psychology. *American Psychologist*, 1975, 30, 116–127.

Cronbach, L. J., & Furby, L. How we should measure "change" — or should we? *Psychological Bulletin*, 1970, 74, 68–80.

Croner, M. D., & Willis, R. H. Perceived differences in task competency and asymmetry of dyadic influence. *Journal of Abnormal and Social Psychology*, 1961, 62, 705–708.

Crook, M. N. The constancy of neuroticism scores and self-judgments of constancy. *Journal of Psychology*, 1937, 4, 27–34.

Crook, M. N. A further note on self-judgments of constancy in neuroticism scores. *Journal of Social Psychology*, 1938, 9, 485–487.

Crutchfield, R. S. Conformity and character. *American Psychologist*, 1955, 10, 191–198.

Culbert, S. A.; Clark, J. V.; & Bobele, H. K. Measures of change toward self-actualization in two sensitivity training groups. *Journal of Counseling Psychology*, 1968, 15, 53–57.

Curry, T. J., & Emerson, R. M. Balance theory: A theory of interpersonal attraction? *Sociometry*, 1970, 33, 216–238.

Curtis, L. Digest of research studies on self-concept. *Graduate Research in*

Education and Related Disciplines, 1963-67, 3, 82-88.

Dabbs, J. M., Jr. Self-esteem, communicator characteristics, and attitude change. *Journal of Abnormal and Social Psychology*, 1964, 69, 173-181.

Dabbs, J. M., Jr., & Leventhal, H. Effects of varying the recommendations in a fear-arousing communication. *Journal of Personality and Social Psychology*, 1966, 4, 525-531.

Dai, B. Some problems of personality development among Negro children. In C. Kluckhohn; H. A. Murray; & D. M. Schneider (Eds.), *Personality in nature, society, and culture.* (2nd ed.) New York: Knopf, 1953. Pp. 545-566.

Dales, R. J., & Keller, J. F. Self-concept scores among black and white culturally deprived adolescent males. *Journal of Negro Education*, 1972, 41, 31-34.

Dauw, D. C. Personality self-descriptions of original thinkers and good elaborators. *Psychology in the Schools*, 1966, 3, 78-79.

David, K. H. Ego-strength, sex differences, and description of self, ideal and parents. *Journal of General Psychology*, 1968, 79, 79-81.

Davids, A. Self-concept and mother-concept in black and white preschool children. *Child Psychiatry and Human Development*, 1973, 4, 30-43.

Davids, A., & Lawton, M. J. Self-concept, mother concept, and food aversions in emotionally disturbed and normal children. *Journal of Abnormal and Social Psychology*, 1961, 62, 309-314.

Davidson, H. H., & Lang, G. Children's perceptions of their teachers' feelings toward them related to self-perception, school achievement and behavior. *Journal of Experimental Education*, 1960, 29, 107-118.

Davis, A., & Dollard, J. *Children of bondage.* Washington, D.C.: American Council on Education, 1940.

Davis, J. H. *Great aspirations.* Vol. 1. Chicago, Ill.: National Opinion Research Center, 1964.

Davis, R. W. The relationship of social preferability of self-concept in an aged population. *Journal of Gerontology*, 1962, 17, 431-436.

Davitz, J. R. Social perception and sociometric choice of children. *Journal of Abnormal and Social Psychology*, 1955, 50, 173-176.

Day, B. R. A comparison of personality needs of courtship couples and same-sex friendships. *Sociology and Social Research*, 1961, 45, 435-440.

Deaux, K. Anticipatory attitude change: A direct test of the self-esteem hypothesis. *Journal of Experimental Social Psychology*, 1972, 8, 143-55.

Deaux, K. K., & Coppess, C. Partner preferences for cooperative and competitive tasks: The effect of self-esteem. *Psychological Record*, 1971, 21, 265-268.

de Beauvoir, S. *The second sex.* New York: Bantam Books, 1949.

de Charms, R., & Rosenbaum, M. E. Status variables and matching behavior. *Journal of Personality*, 1960, 28, 492-502.

Deitz, G. E. A comparison of delinquents with nondelinquents on self-concept, self-acceptance, and parental identification. *Journal of Genetic Psychology,* 1969, 115, 285-295.

de Jung, J. E., & Gardner, E. F. The accuracy of self-role perception: A developmental study. *Journal of Experimental Education,* 1962, 31, 27-41.

Denmark, F. L. The effect of integration on academic achievement and self-concept. *Integrated Education,* 1970, 8, 34-42.

Dennis, W. Racial change in Negro drawings. *Journal of Psychology,* 1968, 69, 129-130.

Denzin, N. K. The genesis of self in early childhood. *Sociological Quarterly,* 1972, 13, 291-314.

Deo, P., & Sharma, S. Self-ideal discrepancy and school achievement. *Adolescence,* 1970, 5, 353-360.

DeSoto, C. B.; Coleman, E. B.; & Putnam, P. L. Predictions of sequences of successes and failures. *Journal of Experimental Psychology,* 1960, 59, 41-46.

DeSoto, C. B.; Kuethe, J. L.; & Wunderlich, R. Social perception and self-perception of high and low authoritarians. *Journal of Social Psychology,* 1960, 52, 149-155.

Deutsch, M. Minority group and class status as related to social and personality factors in scholastic achievement. *Monograph No. 2, Society of Applied Anthropology,* 1960.

Deutsch, M. Minority group and class status as related to social and personality factors in scholastic achievement. In M. M. Grossack (Ed.), *Mental health and segregation.* New York: Springer, 1963. Pp. 64-75.

Deutsch, M., & Solomon, L. Reactions to evaluations by others as influenced by self-evaluations. *Sociometry,* 1959, 22, 93-112.

Dien, D. S., & Vinacke, W. E. Self-concept and parental identification of young adults with mixed Caucasian-Japanese parentage. *Journal of Abnormal and Social Psychology,* 1964, 69, 463-466.

Diener, E. Maternal child-rearing attitudes as antecedents of self-actualization. *Psychological Reports,* 1972, 31, 694.

Diggory, J. C. *Self-evaluation: Concepts and studies.* New York: Wiley, 1966.

DiLoreto, A. O. *Comparative psychotherapy: An experimental analysis.* Chicago: Aldine-Atherton, 1971.

Dinner, S. H.; Lewkowicz, B. E.; & Cooper, J. Anticipatory attitude change as a function of self-esteem and issue familiarity. *Journal of Personality and Social Psychology,* 1972, 24, 407-412.

Dittes, J. E. Attractiveness of group as a function of self-esteem and acceptance by group. *Journal of Abnormal and Social Psychology,* 1959, 59, 77-82.

Dittes, J. E. On the need for control in persuasive scientific communications. *Psychological Reports,* 1970, 27, 672.

DiVesta, F. J., & Cox, L. Some dispositional correlates of conformity behavior. *Journal of Social Psychology,* 1960, 52, 259-268.

Dixon, J. C. Development of self recognition. *Journal of Genetic Psychology,* 1957, 91, 251-256.

Dodge, J. S. Changes in the self-percept with age. *Perceptual and Motor Skills,* 1961, 13, 88.

Dollard, J., & Miller, N. E. *Personality and psychotherapy: An analysis in terms of learning, thinking, and culture.* New York: McGraw-Hill, 1950.

Donahue, W. Relationship of age of perceivers to their social perceptions. *Gerontologist,* 1965, 5, 241-245, 276.

Donnenwerth, G. V.; Teichman, M.; & Foa, U. G. Cognitive differentiation of self and parents in delinquent and non-delinquent girls. *British Journal of Social and Clinical Psychology,* 1973, 12, 144-152.

Doyle, J. A. Field-independence and self-actualization. *Psychological Reports,* 1975, 36, 363-366.

Dreger, R. M. Temperament. In K. S. Miller & R. M. Dreger (Eds.), *Comparative studies of blacks and whites in the United States.* New York: Seminar Press, 1973. Pp. 231-248.

Dreger, R. M., & Miller, K. S. Comparative psychological studies of Negroes and whites in the United States. *Psychological Bulletin,* 1960, 57, 361-402.

Dreger, R. M., & Miller, K. S. Comparative psychological studies of Negroes and whites in the United States: 1959-1965. *Psychological Bulletin Monograph Supplement,* 1968, 70, No. 3, Part 2.

Dreiblatt, I. S., & Weatherley, D. An evaluation of the efficacy of brief-contact therapy with hospitalized psychiatric patients. *Journal of Consulting Psychology,* 1965, 29, 513-519.

Dreyer, A. S., & Haupt, D. Self-evaluation in young children. *Journal of Genetic Psychology,* 1966, 108, 185-197.

Drummond, R. J., & McIntire, W. G. Note on test-retest reliability of the Self-Concept and Motivation Inventory. *Psychological Reports,* 1975, 36, 563-566.

Duncan, O. T. A socioeconomic index for all occupations. In A. J. Reiss; O. D. Duncan; P. K. Hatt; & C. C. North. *Occupations and social status.* New York: Free Press, 1961. Pp. 109-138.

Durr, W. K., & Schmatz, R. R. Personality differences between high-achieving and low-achieving gifted children. *Reading Teacher,* 1964, 17, 251-254.

Dutton, D. G., & Arrowood, A. J. Situational factors in evaluation congruency and interpersonal attraction. *Journal of Personality and Social Psychology,* 1971, 18, 222-229.

Dye, C. A. Self-concept, anxiety, and group participation as affected by human relations training. *Nursing Research,* 1974, 23, 301-306.

Dymond, R. F. Adjustment changes over therapy from self-sorts. In C. R. Rogers & R. F. Dymond (Eds.), *Psychotherapy and personality change.* Chicago: University of Chicago Press, 1954. Pp. 76-84.

Dymond, R. F. Adjustment changes in the absence of psychotherapy. *Journal of Consulting Psychology,* 1955, 19, 103-107.

Eagleson, O. W. A racial comparison of personality traits. *Journal of Applied Psychology*, 1938, 22, 271-274.

Eagly, A. Sex differences in the relationship between self-esteem and susceptibility to social influence. *Journal of Personality*, 1969, 37, 581-591.

Eagly, A. H., & Whitehead, G. I. III. Effect of choice on receptivity to favorable and unfavorable evaluation of oneself. *Journal of Personality and Social Psychology*, 1972, 22, 223-230.

Eberlein, L.; Park, J.; & Matheson, W. Self-ideal congruence in five occupational groups. *Alberta Journal of Educational Research*, 1971, 17, 95-103.

Edwards, A. A social and economic grouping of the gainful workers of the United States. *Journal of the American Statistical Association*, 1933, 28, 337-387.

Edwards, A. L. *Edwards Personal Preference Schedule Revised Manual.* New York: The Psychological Corp., 1959.

Edwards, A. L., & Cronbach, L. J. Experimental design for research in psychotherapy. *Journal of Clinical Psychology*, 1952, 8, 51-59.

Edwards, D. W. Blacks versus whites: When is race a relevant variable? *Journal of Personality and Social Psychology*, 1974, 29, 39-49.

Eiben, R., & Clack, R. J. Impact of a participatory group experience on counselors in training. *Small Group Behavior*, 1973, 4, 486-495.

Eisenman, R. Birth order, sex, self-esteem, and prejudice against the physically disabled. *Journal of Psychology*, 1970, 75, 147-155.

Eisenman, R., & Grove, M. S. Self-ratings of creativity, semantic differential ratings, and preferences for polygons varying in complexity, simplicity, and symmetry. *Journal of Psychology*, 1972, 81, 63-67.

Eisenman, R., & Townsend, T. D. Studies in acquiescence; I Social Desirability; II Self-Esteem; III Creativity; and IV Prejudice. *Journal of Projective Techniques and Personality Assessment*, 1970, 34, 45-54.

Eiser, J. R., & Smith, A. J. Preference for accuracy and positivity in the description of oneself by another. *European Journal of Social Psychology*, 1972, 2, 199-201.

Ellis, L. J., & Bentler, P. M. Traditional sex-determined role standards and sex stereotypes. *Journal of Personality and Social Psychology*, 1973, 25, 28-34.

Elman, J.; Press, A.; & Rosenkrantz, P. Sex roles and self-concepts: Real and ideal. *Proceedings of the 78th Annual Convention of the American Psychological Association*, 1970, 5, 455-456.

Endler, N. S. Changes in meaning during psychotherapy as measured by the semantic differential. *Journal of Counseling Psychology*, 1961, 8, 105-111. (a)

Endler, N. S. Conformity analyzed and related to personality. *Journal of Social Psychology*, 1961, 53, 271-283. (b)

Endler, N. S.; Hunt, J. McV.; & Rosenstein, A. J. An S-R Inventory of Anxiousness. *Psychological Monographs,* 1962, 76 (17, Whole No. 536).

Endler, N. S.; Wiesenthal, D. L.; & Geller, S. H. The generalization of the effects of agreement and correctness on relative competence mediating conformity. *Canadian Journal of Behavioral Science,* 1972, 4, 322-329.

Ends, E. J., & Page, C. W. A study of three types of group psychotherapy with hospitalized male inebriates. *Quarterly Journal of Studies on Alcohol,* 1957, 18, 263-277.

Ends, E. J., & Page, C. W. Group psychotherapy and concomitant psychological change. *Psychological Monographs,* 1959, 73 (Whole No. 480).

Engel, M. The stability of the self-concept. *Journal of Abnormal and Social Psychology,* 1959, 58, 211-215.

Engle, T. L. Personality adjustments of children belonging to two minority groups. *Journal of Educational Psychology,* 1945, 36, 543-560.

English, R. W., & Higgins, T. E. Client-centered group counseling with pre-adolescents. *Journal of School Health,* 1971, 41, 507-510.

Epps, E. G. Correlates of academic achievement among Northern and Southern urban Negro students. *Journal of Social Issues,* 1969, 25, 55-70.

Erikson, E. H. Identity and the life cycle: Selected papers. *Psychological Issues,* 1959, 1, 1-171.

Erikson, E. H. *Childhood and society.* (2nd ed.) New York: Norton, 1963.

Erikson, E. H. The concept of identity in race relations: Notes and queries. *Daedalus,* 1966, 95, 145-171.

Ettinger, R. F.; Marino, C. J.; Endler, N.S.; Geller, S. H.; & Natziuk, T. Effects of agreement and correctness on relative competence and conformity. *Journal of Personality and Social Psychology,* 1971, 19, 204-212.

Ewing, T. N. Changes in attitude during counseling. *Journal of Consulting Psychology,* 1954, 1, 232-239.

Ewing, T. N. Changes during counseling appropriate to the client's initial problem. *Journal of Counseling Psychology,* 1964, 11, 146-150.

Fairweather, G. W.; Simon, R.; Gebhard, M. E.; Weingarten, E.; Holland, J. L.; Sanders, R.; Stone, G. B.; & Reahl, J. E. Relative effectiveness of psychotherapeutic programs: A multicriteria comparison of four programs for three different patient groups. *Psychological Monographs,* 1960, 74 (Whole No. 492).

Fannin, L. F., & Clinard, M. B. Differences in the conception of self as a male among lower- and middle-class delinquents. *Social Problems,* 1965, 13, 205-214.

Farley, J. Maternal employment and child behavior. *Journal of Social Relations,* 1968, 3, 58-71.

Farson, R. E. Introjection in the psychotherapeutic relationship. *Journal of Counseling Psychology,* 1961, 8, 337-342.

Fein, D.; O'Neill, S.; Frank, C.; & Velit, K. M. Sex differences in preadolescent self-esteem. *Journal of Psychology*, 1975, 90, 179–183.

Feldman, J. J., & Coleman, J. S. Appendix B: Methodology. In E. Shanas, *The health of older people: A social survey*. Cambridge, Mass.: Harvard University Press, 1962.

Felker, D. W. Relationship between self-concept, body build, and perception of father's interest in sports in boys. *Research Quarterly*, 1968, 39, 513–517.

Felker, D. W., & Kay, R. S. Self-concept, sports interest, sports participation, and body type of seventh- and eighth-grade boys. *Journal of Psychology*, 1971, 78, 223–228.

Felker, D. W., & Stanwyck, D. J. General self-concept and specific self-evaluations after an academic task. *Psychological Reports*, 1971, 29, 60–62.

Festinger, L. *A theory of cognitive dissonance*. Evanston, Ill.: Row, Peterson, 1957.

Fey, W. F. Acceptance of self and others, and its relation to therapy readiness. *Journal of Clinical Psychology*, 1954, 10, 269–271.

Fey, W. F. Acceptance by others and its relation to acceptance of self and others. *Journal of Abnormal and Social Psychology*, 1955, 50, 274–276.

Fey, W. F. Correlates of certain subjective attitudes towards self and others. *Journal of Clinical Psychology*, 1957, 13, 44–49.

Fiedler, F. E. Assumed similarity measures as predictors of team effectiveness. *Journal of Abnormal and Social Psychology*, 1954, 49, 381–388.

Fiedler, F. E.; Dodge, J. S.; Jones, R. E.; & Hutchins, E. B. Interrelations among measures of personality adjustment in nonclinical populations. *Journal of Abnormal and Social Psychology*, 1958, 56, 345–351.

Fiedler, F. E.; Hutchins, E. B.; & Dodge, J. S. Quasi-therapeutic relations in small college and military groups. *Psychological Monographs*, 1959, 73, 1–28.

Fiedler, F. E., & Senior, K. An exploratory study of unconscious feeling reactions in fifteen patient-therapist pairs. *Journal of Abnormal and Social Psychology*, 1952, 47, 446–453.

Fiedler, F. E.; Warrington, W. G.; & Blaisdell, F. J. Unconscious attitudes as correlates of sociometric choice in a social group. *Journal of Abnormal and Social Psychology*, 1952, 47, 790–791.

Fink, M. B. Self concept as it relates to academic underachievement. *California Journal of Educational Research*, 1962, 13, 57–62.

Fishman, C. G. Need for approval and the expression of aggression under varying conditions of frustration. *Journal of Personality and Social Psychology*, 1965, 2, 809–816.

Fiske, D. W. The shaky evidence is slowly put together. *Journal of Consulting and Clinical Psychology*, 1971, 37, 314–315.

Fiske, D. W.; Cartwright, D. S.; & Kirtner, W. L. Are psychotherapeutic changes predictable? *Journal of Abnormal and Social Psychology*, 1964, 69, 418–426.

Fiske, D. W., & Goodman, G. The posttherapy period. *Journal of Abnormal Psychology*, 1965, 70, 169-179.

Fiske, D. W.; Hunt, H. F.; Luborsky, L.; Orne, M. T.; Parloff, M. B.; Reiser, M. F.; & Tuma, A. H. Planning of research on effectiveness of psychotherapy. *Archives of General Psychiatry*, 1970, 22, 22-32.

Fitts, W. H. *Tennessee Self Concept Scale: Manual.* Nashville, Tenn.: Counselor Recordings and Tests, 1965.

Fitzgerald, M. P. The relationship between expressed self-esteem and assumed similarity. *Journal of Psychology*, 1965, 60, 181-191.

Flammer, D. P., & Matas, L. An exploratory investigation of three self-other orientation measures. *Journal of Personality Assessment*, 1972, 36, 447-450.

Flemming, E. G. Best friends. *Journal of Social Psychology*, 1932, 3, 385-390.

Ford, D. H., & Urban, H. B. Psychotherapy. In P. R. Farnsworth; O. Mc-Nemar; & Q. McNemar (Eds.), *Annual review of psychology.* Palo Alto, Calif.: Annual Reviews, Inc., 1967. Pp. 333-372.

Forsyth, R. P., & Fairweather, G. W. Psychotherapeutic and other hospital treatment criteria: The dilemma. *Journal of Abnormal and Social Psychology*, 1961, 62, 598-604.

The Fortune Survey: XXVII. The people of the U.S.A.: A self portrait. *Fortune*, 1940, 14-136.

Foulds, M. L. Effects of a personal growth group on a measure of self-actualization. *Journal of Humanistic Psychology*, 1970, 10, 33-38.

Foulds, M. L. Effects of a personal growth [sic] on ratings of self and others. *Small Group Behavior*, 1973, 4, 508-512.

Foulds, M. L.; Girona, R.; & Guinan, J. F. Changes in ratings of self and others as a result of a marathon group. *Comparative Group Studies*, 1970, 1, 349-355.

Foulds, M. L., & Hannigan, P. S. Effects of psychomotor group therapy on ratings of self and others. *Psychotherapy: Theory, Research, and Practice*, 1974, 11, 351-353.

Foulkes, D., & Foulkes, S. Self-concept, dogmatism, and tolerance of trait inconsistency. *Journal of Personality and Social Psychology*, 1965, 2, 104-110.

Frankel, A. S., & Barrett, J. Variations in personal space as a function of authoritarianism, self-esteem, and racial characteristics of a stimulus situation. *Journal of Consulting and Clinical Psychology*, 1971, 37, 95-98.

Frease, D. E. The schools, self-concept, and juvenile delinquency. *British Journal of Criminology*, 1972, 12, 133-146.

Freeman, H. R. Effects of positive and negative feedback and degree of discrepancy on responses to test results. *Journal of Counseling Psychology*, 1973, 20, 571-572.

Freese, G. T., & West, C. K. Congruence, empathy, and regard: A comparison of adolescent ratings with teacher self-ratings. *Adolescence*, 1972, 7, 525-529.

Frenkel-Brunswik, E. Social research and the problem of values: A reply. *Journal of Abnormal and Social Psychology*, 1954, 49, 466–471.

Frerichs, M. Relationship of self-esteem and internal-external control to selected characteristics of associate degree nursing students. *Nursing Research*, 1973, 22, 350–352.

Freud, S. Some psychological consequences of the anatomical distinction between the sexes. *International Journal of Psychoanalysis*, 1927, 8, 133–142.

Freud, S. Female sexuality. *International Journal of Psychoanalysis*, 1932, 13, 281–297.

Freud, S. The psychology of women. In *New introductory lectures on psychoanalysis*. New York: W. W. Norton, 1933.

Freyberg, J., & Shapiro, N. Digest of research studies on the relation of socioeconomic status to personality variables (1962–1965). *Graduate Research in Education and Related Disciplines*, 1966, 2, 102–107.

Friedman, H. S. Effects of self-esteem and expected duration of interaction on liking for a highly rewarding partner. *Journal of Personality and Social Psychology*, 1976, 33, 686–690.

Friedman, S.; Rogers, P. P.; & Gettys, J. Project Re-ed: Increase in self-esteem as measured by the Coopersmith Inventory. *Perceptual and Motor Skills*, 1975, 40, 165–166.

Friedsam, H. J., & Martin, H. W. A comparison of self and physicians' health ratings in an older population. *Journal of Health and Human Behavior*, 1963, 4, 179–183.

Fromm, E. Selfishness and self-love. *Psychiatry*, 1939, 2, 507–523.

Fromm, E. *Man for himself*. New York: Rinehart, 1947.

Fromm, E. Sex and character. In R. Anshen (Ed.), *The family: Its function and destiny*. New York: Harper, 1949. Pp. 375–392.

Fromme, D. K.; Jones, W. H.; & Davis, J. O. Experimental group training with conservative populations: A potential for negative effects. *Journal of Clinical Psychology*, 1974, 30, 290–296.

Furst, E. J. Validity of some objective scales of motivation for predicting academic achievement. *Educational and Psychological Measurement*, 1966, 26, 927–933.

Gadzella, B. M., & Fournet, G. P. Differences and changes among college classes (freshman through graduate levels) in self-ratings of a quality student. *Journal of Educational Psychology*, 1975, 67, 243–252.

Gaier, E. L., & Wambach, H. S. Self-evaluation of personality assets and liabilities of southern white and Negro students. *Journal of Social Psychology*, 1960, 51, 135–143.

Gallup, G. P., Jr. Chimpanzees: Self recognition. *Science*, 1970, 167, 86–87.

Garai, J. E., & Scheinfeld, A. Sex differences in mental and behavioral traits. *Genetic Psychology Monographs*, 1968, 77, 169–299.

Garfield, S. L.; Prager, R. A.; & Bergin, A. E. Evaluation of outcome in psychotherapy. *Journal of Consulting and Clinical Psychology*, 1971, 37, 307-313.

Garretson, W. S. The consensual definition of social objects. *Sociological Quarterly*, 1962, 3, 107-113.

Gartner, D., & Goldstein, H. S. Leary's Interpersonal diagnosis in mothers of severely disturbed children attending a therapeutic nursery. *Psychological Reports*, 1973, 32, 693-694.

Garwood, D. S. Personality factors related to creativity in young scientists. *Journal of Abnormal and Social Psychology*, 1964, 68, 413-419.

Gassner, S. M.; Gold, J.; & Snadowsky, A. M. Changes in the phenomenal field as a result of human relations training. *Journal of Psychology*, 1964, 58, 33-41.

Gebel, A. S. Self-perception and leaderless group discussion status. *Journal of Social Psychology*, 1954, 40, 309-318.

Gecas, V. Parental behavior and dimensions of adolescent self-evaluation. *Sociometry*, 1971, 34, 466-482.

Gecas, V. Parental behavior and contextual variations in adolescent self-esteem. *Sociometry*, 1972, 35, 332-345.

Gecas, V.; Calonico, J. M.; & Thomas, D. L. The development of self-concept in the child: Mirror theory *versus* model theory. *Journal of Social Psychology*, 1974, 92, 67-76.

Gelfand, D. M. The influence of self-esteem on rate of verbal conditioning and social matching behavior. *Journal of Abnormal and Social Psychology*, 1962, 65, 259-265.

Gellert, E. Children's constructions of their self-images. *Perceptual and Motor Skills*, 1975, 40, 307-324.

Gendlin, E. T., & Rychlak, J. F. Psychotherapeutic processes. In P. H. Mussen & M. R. Rosenzweig (Eds.), *Annual review of psychology*. Palo Alto, Calif.: Annual Reviews, Inc., 1970. Pp. 155-190.

Gergen, K. J., & Back, K. W. Aging and the paradox of somatic concern. In I. H. Simpson & J. C. McKinney (Eds.), *Social aspects of aging*. Durham, N.C.: Duke University Press, 1966.

Gergen, K. J., & Bauer, R. A. Interactive effects of self-esteem and task difficulty on social conformity. *Journal of Personality and Social Psychology*, 1967, 6, 16-22.

Getsinger, S. H.; Kunce, J. T.; Miller, D. E.; & Weinberg, S. R. Self-esteem measures and cultural disadvantagement. *Journal of Consulting and Clinical Psychology*, 1972, 38, 149.

Gibby, R. G., & Gabler, R. The self-concept of Negro and white children. *Journal of Clinical Psychology*, 1967, 23, 144-148.

Gibson, R. L.; Snyder, W. U.; & Ray, W. S. A factor analysis of measures of change following client-centered therapy. *Journal of Counseling Psychology*, 1955, 2, 83-90.

Gill, M. P., & D'Oyley, V. R. Research note: The construction of an objective measure of self-concept. *Interchange,* 1970, 1, 110-113.

Gilligan, J. F. Sensitivity training and self-actualization. *Psychological Reports,* 1974, 34, 319-325.

Ginn, R. O. Defensive and nondefensive repressors and sensitizers and self-actualization. *Journal of Clinical Psychology,* 1974, 30, 82-83.

Gist, N. P., & Bennett, W. S. Aspirations of Negro and white students. *Social Forces,* 1963, 42, 40-48.

Gitter, A. G., & Satow, Y. Color and physiognomy as variables in racial misidentification among children. *Proceedings of the 77th Annual Convention of the American Psychological Association,* 1969, 4, 677-678.

Glass, D. C. Changes in liking as a means of reducing cognitive discrepancies between self-esteem and aggression. *Journal of Personality,* 1964, 32, 531-549.

Glass, D. C.; Lavin, D. E.; Henchy, T.; Gordon, A.; Mayhew, P.; & Donohoe, P. Obesity and persuasibility. *Journal of Personality,* 1969, 37, 407-414.

Glenn, N. D. Negro prestige criteria: A case study in the bases of prestige. *American Journal of Sociology,* 1963, 68, 645-657.

Golann, S. E. Psychological study of creativity. *Psychological Bulletin,* 1963, 60, 548-565.

Gold, S. R., & Coghlan, A. J. Effect of residential treatment on adolescent drug abusers: A preliminary report. *Proceedings of the 81st Annual Convention of the American Psychological Association,* 1973, 8, 395-396.

Goldfried, M. R. Feelings of inferiority and the depreciation of others: A research review and theoretical reformulation. *Journal of Individual Psychology,* 1963, 19, 27-48.

Golding, S. L., & Lichtenstein, E. Confession of awareness and prior knowledge of deception as a function of interview set and approval motivation. *Journal of Personality and Social Psychology,* 1970, 14, 213-223.

Goldman, R. D.; Hudson, D.; & Daharsh, B. J. Self-estimated task persistence as a nonlinear predictor of college success. *Journal of Educational Psychology,* 1973, 65, 216-221.

Goldman, R. K., & Mendelsohn, G. A. Psychotherapeutic change and social adjustment: A report of a national survey of psychotherapists. *Journal of Abnormal Psychology,* 1969, 74, 164-172.

Goldman, W. J., & May, A. Comparison of the self-concept of nonretarded and retarded children matched for chronological age and environmental background. *Training School Bulletin,* 1972, 69, 136-140.

Goldstein, A. P. Therapist and client expectation of personality change in psychotherapy. *Journal of Counseling Psychology,* 1960, 7, 180-184.

Goldstein, A. P.; Heller, K.; & Sechrest, L. B. *Psychotherapy and the psychology of behavior change.* New York: Wiley, 1966.

Goldstein, J. W., & Rosenfeld, H. M. Insecurity and preference for persons similar to oneself. *Journal of Personality*, 1969, 37, 253-268.

Gollob, H. F., & Dittes, J. E. Effects of manipulated self-esteem on persuasibility depending on threat and complexity of communication. *Journal of Personality and Social Psychology*, 1965, 2, 195-201.

Good, L. R., & Good, K. C. A measure of self-esteem. *Psychology*, 1975, 12, 32-34.

Goodman, M. E. Evidence concerning the genesis of interracial attitudes. *American Anthropologist*, 1946, 48, 624-630.

Goodman, M. E. *Race awareness in young children*. New York: Collier, 1964.

Gordon, C. *Looking ahead: Self-conceptions, race and family as determinants of adolescent orientation to achievement*. Washington, D.C.: American Sociological Association, 1972.

Gordon, J. E. Interpersonal predictions of repressors and sensitizers. *Journal of Personality*, 1957, 25, 686-698.

Gordon, S. K., & Vinacke, W. E. Self- and ideal self-concepts and dependency in aged persons residing in institutions. *Journal of Gerontology*, 1971, 26, 337-343.

Gordon, T., & Cartwright, D. The effect of psychotherapy upon certain attitudes toward others. In C. R. Rogers and R. F. Dymond (Eds.), *Psychotherapy and personality change*. Chicago: University of Chicago Press, 1954. Pp. 167-195.

Gorlow, L.; Butler, A.; & Guthrie, G. M. Correlates of self-attitudes of retardates. *American Journal of Mental Deficiency*, 1963, 67, 549-555.

Gormly, J.; Gormly, A.; & Johnson, C. Consistency of sociobehavioral responses to interpersonal disagreement. *Journal of Personality and Social Psychology*, 1972, 24, 221-224.

Goslin, D. A. Accuracy of self perception and social acceptance. *Sociometry*, 1962, 25, 283-296.

Gough, H. G. The relationship of socio-economic status to personality inventory and achievement test scores. *Journal of Educational Psychology*, 1946, 37, 527-540.

Gough, H. G. A new dimension of status: I. Development of a personality scale. *American Sociological Review*, 1948, 13, 401-409.

Gough, H. G. A short social status inventory. *Journal of Educational Psychology*, 1949, 40, 52-56. (a)

Gough, H. G. A new dimension of status: III. Discrepancies between the *St* scale and "objective" status. *American Sociological Review*, 1949, 14, 275-281. (b)

Gough, H. G. *Manual for the California Psychological Inventory*. Palo Alto, Calif.: Consulting Psychologists Press, 1957.

Gough, H. G. *California Psychological Inventory Manual*. Palo Alto, Calif.: Consulting Psychologists Press, 1969.

Gough, H. G., & Heilbrun, A. B. *The Adjective Check List Manual.* Palo Alto, Calif.: Consulting Psychologists Press, 1965.

Gough, H. G., & Woodworth, D. G. Stylistic variations among professional research scientists. *Journal of Psychology,* 1960, 49, 87–98.

Graham, J. R., & Barr, K. G. Q-sort study of the relationship between students' self-acceptance and acceptance of their college. *Psychological Reports,* 1967, 21, 779–780.

Grant, C. A. Black studies materials do make a difference. *Journal of Educational Research,* 1973, 66, 400–404.

Grant, C. H. Age differences in self-concept from early adulthood through old age. *Proceedings of the 77th Annual Convention of the American Psychological Association,* 1969, 4, 717–718.

Gray, S. A note on the values of Southern college women, white and Negro. *Journal of Social Psychology,* 1947, 25, 239–241.

Gray, S. W. Perceived similarity to parents and adjustment. *Child Development,* 1959, 30, 91–107.

Green, R. A., & Murray, E. J. Instigation to aggression as a function of self-disclosure and threat to self-esteem. *Journal of Consulting and Clinical Psychology,* 1973, 40, 440–443.

Greenbaum, C. W. Effect of situational and personality variables on improvisation and attitude change. *Journal of Personality and Social Psychology,* 1966, 4, 260–269.

Greenbaum, J. J., & Wang, D. D. A semantic-differential study of the concepts of mental retardation. *Journal of General Psychology,* 1965, 73, 257–272.

Greenberg, J. S. The masturbatory behavior of college students. *Psychology in the Schools,* 1972, 9, 427–432.

Greenberg, J. S., & Archambault, F. X. Masturbation, self-esteem, and other variables. *Journal of Sexual Research,* 1973, 9, 41–51.

Greenberg, J. W.; Gerver, J. M.; Chall, J.; & Davidson, H. H. Attitudes of children from a deprived environment toward achievement related concepts. *Journal of Educational Research,* 1965, 59, 57–62.

Greenberger, E.; Campbell, P.; Sorensen, A. B.; & O'Connor, J. Report No. 110, *Toward the measurement of psychosocial maturity.* Center for Social Organization of Schools, Johns Hopkins University, July, 1971.

Greenberger, E., & Marini, M. M. Report No. 136, *Black-white differences in psychosocial maturity: A further analysis.* Center for Social Organization of Schools, Johns Hopkins University, September, 1972.

Greene, J. F., & Zirkel, P. A. Academic factors relating to the self-concept of Puerto Rican pupils. *Catalog of Selected Documents in Psychology,* 1971, 1, 20–21.

Greenwald, H. J., & Oppenheim, D. B. Reported magnitude of self-misidentification among Negro children: Artifact? *Journal of Personality and Social Psychology,* 1968, 8, 49–52.

Gregor, A. J., & McPherson, D. A. Racial attitudes among white and Negro children in a deep-South standard metropolitan area. *Journal of Social Psychology*, 1966, 68, 95-106.

Griffitt, W. B. Interpersonal attraction as a function of self-concept and personality similarity-dissimilarity. *Journal of Personality and Social Psychology*, 1966, 4, 581-584.

Griffitt, W. B. Personality similarity and self-concept as determinants of interpersonal attraction. *Journal of Social Psychology*, 1969, 78, 137-146.

Griffitt, W.; Byrne, D.; & Bond, M. Proportion of positive adjectives and personal relevance of adjectival descriptions as determinants of attraction. *Journal of Experimental Social Psychology*, 1971, 7, 111-121.

Groff, P. The personality self-images of student teachers. *Journal of Teacher Education*, 1961, 4, 433-436.

Gross, N. Social class identification in the urban community. *American Sociological Review*, 1953, 18, 398-404.

Grossack, M. M. Group belongingness among Negroes. *Journal of Social Psychology*, 1956, 43, 167-180.

Grossack, M. M. Some personality characteristics of Southern Negro students. *Journal of Social Psychology*, 1957, 46, 125-131.

Grummon, D. L. Design, procedures, and subjects for the first block. In C. R. Rogers and R. F. Dymond (Eds.), *Psychotherapy and personality change.* Chicago: University of Chicago Press, 1954. Pp. 35-52. (a)

Grummon, D. L. Personality changes as a function of time in persons motivated for therapy. In C. R. Rogers and R. F. Dymond (Eds.), *Psychotherapy and personality change.* Chicago: University of Chicago Press, 1954. Pp. 238-255. (b)

Grupp, S.; Ramseyer, G.; & Richardson, J. The effect of age on four scales of the California Psychological Inventory. *Journal of General Psychology*, 1968, 78, 183-187.

Guardo, C. J. Self revisited: The sense of self-identity. *Journal of Humanistic Psychology*, 1968, 8, 137-142.

Guardo, C. J. Sociometric status and self-concept in sixth-graders. *Journal of Educational Research*, 1969, 62, 319-322.

Guardo, C. J., & Bohan, J. B. Development of a sense of self-identity in children. *Child Development*, 1971, 42, 1909-1921.

Guerney, B., Jr., & Burton, J. L. Comparison of typical peer, self, and ideal percepts related to college achievement. *Journal of Social Psychology*, 1967, 73, 253-259.

Guggenheim, F. Self-esteem and achievement expectations for white and Negro children. *Journal of Projective Techniques and Personality Assessment*, 1969, 33, 63-71.

Guilford, J. P. Creative abilities in the arts. *Psychological Review*, 1957, 64, 110-118.

Guilford, J. P.; Christensen, P. R.; Frick, J. W.; & Merrifield, P. R. *The relations of creative-thinking aptitudes to non-aptitude personality traits.* Reports from the Psychological Laboratory, No. 20. Los Angeles: University of Southern California, 1957.

Guilford, J. P., & Merrifield, P. R. *The structure of intellect model: Its uses and implications.* Reports from the Psychological Laboratory, No. 24. Los Angeles: University of Southern California, 1960.

Guinan, J. F., & Foulds, M. L. Marathon group: Facilitator of personal growth? *Journal of Counseling Psychology,* 1970, 17, 145-149.

Guinan, J. F.; Foulds, M. L.; & Wright, J. C. Do the changes last? A six-month follow-up of a marathon group. *Small Group Behavior,* 1973, 4, 177-180.

Guller, I. B. Increased stability of self-concept in students served by a college counseling center. *Personnel and Guidance Journal,* 1969, 48, 546-551.

Gump, J. P. Sex-role attitudes and psychological well-being. *Journal of Social Issues,* 1972, 28, 79-92.

Gunderson, E. K. E., & Johnson, L. C. Past experience, self-evaluation, and present adjustment. *Journal of Social Psychology,* 1965, 66, 311-321.

Guptill, C. S. A measure of age identification. *Gerontologist,* 1969, 9, 96-102.

Gurin, G.; Veroff, J.; & Feld, S. *Americans view their mental health.* New York: Basic Books, 1960.

Guskin, S. Social psychologies of mental deficiency. In N. R. Ellis (Ed.), *Handbook of mental deficiency.* New York: McGraw-Hill, 1963. Pp. 325-352.

Gustafson, D. P., & Gaumnitz, J. E. Consensus rankings in small groups: Self-rankings included and excluded. *Sociometry,* 1972, 35, 610-618.

Gustav, A. Comparison of college grades and self-concept. *Psychological Reports,* 1962, 11, 601-602.

Guthrie, G. M.; Butler, A.; & Gorlow, L. Patterns of self-attitudes of retardates. *American Journal of Mental Deficiency,* 1961, 66, 222-229.

Guthrie, G. M.; Butler, A.; & Gorlow, L. Personality differences between institutionalized and non-institutionalized retardates. *American Journal of Mental Deficiency,* 1963, 67, 543-548.

Haan, N. The relationship of ego functioning and intelligence to social status and social mobility. *Journal of Abnormal and Social Psychology,* 1964, 69, 594-605.

Hacker, H. M. Women as a minority group. *Social Forces,* 1951, 30, 60-69.

Hacker, H. M. Women as a minority group twenty years later. In R. K. Unger and F. L. Denmark (Eds.), *Woman: Dependent or independent variable.* New York: Psychological Dimensions, Inc., 1975.

Haigh, G. V. Defensive behavior in client-centered therapy. *Journal of Consulting Psychology,* 1949, 13, 181-189.

Hall, J. E.; Morris, H. L.; & Barker, H. R. Sexual knowledge and attitudes of mentally retarded adolescents. *American Journal of Mental Deficiency,* 1973, 77, 706-709.

Hall, W. B., & MacKinnon, D. W. Personality inventory correlates of creativity among architects. *Journal of Applied Psychology*, 1969, 53, 322-326.

Hall, W. S.; Cross, W. E., Jr.; & Freedle, R. Stages in the development of black awareness: An exploratory investigation. In R. L. Jones (Ed.), *Black psychology*. New York: Harper & Row, 1972. Pp. 156-165.

Haller, A. O., & Thomas, S. Personality correlates of the socioeconomic status of adolescent males. *Sociometry*, 1962, 25, 398-404.

Hamilton, D. L. Responses to cognitive inconsistencies: Personality, discrepancy level, and response stability. *Journal of Personality and Social Psychology*, 1969, 11, 351-362.

Hamilton, D. L. Personality attributes related to response preferences in resolving inconsistencies. *Journal of Personality*, 1970, 38, 134-145.

Hamilton, D. L. A comparative study of five methods of assessing self-esteem, dominance, and dogmatism. *Educational and Psychological Measurement*, 1971, 31, 441-452.

Hammond, S. B. The self and society. In O. A. Oeser & S. B. Hammond (Eds.), *Social structure and personality in a city*. New York: Macmillan, 1954. Pp. 261-278. (a)

Hammond, S. B. The boundaries of perceived strata. In O. A. Oeser & S. B. Hammond (Eds.), *Social structure and personality in a city*. New York: Macmillan, 1954. Pp. 279-285. (b)

Hammond, S. B. Attitudes towards perceived social strata. In O. A. Oeser & S. B. Hammond (Eds.), *Social structure and personality in a city*. New York: Macmillan, 1954. Pp. 286-303. (c)

Hannerz, U. The rhetoric of soul: Identification in Negro society. *Race*, 1968, 9, 453-465.

Hansen, J. C.; Moore, G. D.; & Carkhuff, R. R. The differential relationships of objective and client perceptions of counseling. *Journal of Clinical Psychology*, 1968, 24, 244-246.

Harootunian, B. *Self-other relationships of segregated and desegregated ninth graders*. (ED 023765) Arlington, Virginia: ERIC Document Reproduction Service, 1968.

Harper, D. G. The reliability of measures of sociometric acceptance and rejection. *Sociometry*, 1968, 31, 219-227.

Harris, S., & Braun, J. R. Self-esteem and racial preference in black children. *Proceedings of the 79th Annual Convention of the American Psychological Association*, 1971, 6, 259-260.

Harrison, R. H., & Budoff, M. Demographic, historical, and ability correlates of the Laurelton Self-Concept Scale in an EMR sample. *American Journal of Mental Deficiency*, 1972, 76, 460-480. (a)

Harrison, R. H., & Budoff, M. A factor analysis of the Laurelton Self-Concept Scale. *American Journal of Mental Deficiency*, 1972, 76, 446-459. (b)

Harrison, R. H., & Kass, E. H. Differences between Negro and white pregnant women on the MMPI. *Journal of Consulting Psychology*, 1967, 31, 454-463.

Harrison, R. H., & Kass, E. H. MMPI correlates of Negro acculturation in a northern city. *Journal of Personality and Social Psychology*, 1968, 10, 262–270.

Hart, R. J. Evaluations of self and others and aggression. *Proceedings of the 81st Annual Convention of the American Psychological Association*, 1973, 8, 233–234.

Hartlage, L. C. Subprofessional therapists' use of reinforcement versus traditional psychotherapeutic techniques with schizophrenics. *Journal of Consulting and Clinical Psychology*, 1970, 34, 181–183.

Hartnagel, T. F. Father absence and self conception among lower class white and Negro boys. *Social Problems*, 1970, 18, 152–163.

Harvey, O. J. Personality factors in resolution of conceptual incongruities. *Sociometry*, 1962, 25, 336–352.

Harvey, O. J.; Kelley, H. H.; & Shapiro, M. M. Reactions to unfavorable evaluations of the self made by other persons. *Journal of Personality*, 1957, 25, 393–411.

Hasler, K. R., & Clarke, W. V. AVA norms and scores from general population and Negro population samples. *Psychological Reports*, 1967, 21, 661–677.

Hassell, J., & Smith, E. W. L. Female homosexuals' concepts of self, men, and women. *Journal of Personality Assessment*, 1975, 39, 154–159.

Havighurst, R. J. Successful aging. In R. H. Williams; C. Tibbitts; & W. Donahue (Eds.), *Processes of aging: Social and psychological perspectives*. Vol. 1. New York: Atherton, 1963. Pp. 299–320.

Havighurst, R. J., & Albrecht, R. *Older people*. New York: Longmans Green, 1953.

Havighurst, R. J.; Robinson, M. Z.; & Dorr, M. The development of the ideal self in childhood and adolescence. *Journal of Educational Research*, 1946, 40, 241–257.

Healey, G. W., & deBlassie, R. R. A comparison of Negro, Anglo, and Spanish-American adolescents' self concepts. *Adolescence*, 1974, 9, 15–24.

Healy, C. C. The relation of esteem and social class to self-occupational congruence. *Journal of Vocational Behavior*, 1973, 3, 43–51.

Heath, D. H. *Explorations of maturity: Studies of mature and immature college men*. New York: Appleton-Century-Crofts, 1965.

Heider, F. *The psychology of interpersonal relations*. New York: Wiley, 1958.

Heiss, J., & Owens, S. Self-evaluation of blacks and whites. *American Journal of Sociology*, 1972, 78, 360–370.

Heller, K., & Goldstein, A. P. Client dependency and therapist expectancy as relationship maintaining variables in psychotherapy. *Journal of Consulting Psychology*, 1961, 25, 371–375.

Helmreich, R.; Aronson, E.; & LeFan, J. To err is humanizing—sometimes: Effects of self-esteem, competence, and a pratfall on interpersonal attraction. *Journal of Personality and Social Psychology*, 1970, 16, 259–264.

Helper, M. M. Learning theory and the self-concept. *Journal of Abnormal and Social Psychology*, 1955, 51, 184-194.

Helper, M. M. Parental evaluations of children and children's self-evaluations. *Journal of Abnormal and Social Psychology*, 1958, 56, 190-194.

Helson, R. Personality characteristics and developmental history of creative college women. *Genetic Psychology Monographs*, 1967, 76, 205-256. (a)

Helson, R. Sex differences in creative style. *Journal of Personality*, 1967, 35, 214-233. (b)

Helson, R. Women mathematicians and the creative personality. *Journal of Consulting and Clinical Psychology*, 1971, 36, 210-220.

Helson, R., & Crutchfield, R. S. Creative types in mathematics. *Journal of Personality*, 1970, 38, 177-197. (a)

Helson, R., & Crutchfield, R. S. Mathematicians: The creative researcher and the average Ph.D. *Journal of Consulting and Clinical Psychology*, 1970, 34, 250-257. (b)

Henderson, E. H., & Long, B. H. Personal-social correlates of academic success among disadvantaged school beginners. *Journal of School Psychology*, 1971, 9, 101-113.

Hendrick, C., & Brown, S. R. Introversion, extraversion, and interpersonal attraction. *Journal of Personality and Social Psychology*, 1971, 20, 31-36.

Hendrick, C., & Page, H. A. Self-esteem, attitude similarity, and attraction. *Journal of Personality*, 1970, 38, 588-601.

Henry, A. F. Family role structure and self blame. *Social Forces*, 1956, 35, 35-38.

Henton, C. L., & Johnson, E. E. *Relationship between the self-concepts of Negro elementary-school children and their academic achievement, intelligence, interests and manifest anxiety.* (ED 003288) Arlington, Virginia: ERIC Document Reproduction Service, 1964.

Herbert, E. W.; Gelfand, D. M.; & Hartmann, D. P. Imitation and self-esteem as determinants of self-critical behavior. *Child Development*, 1969, 40, 421-430.

Herman, M.; Sadofsky, S.; Bensman, J.; Lilienfeld, R.; & Manos, C. *Study of the meaning, experience, and effects of the neighborhood youth corps on Negro youth who are seeking work.* New York: New York University Graduate School of Social Work, 1967.

Hernandez, N. G. Variables affecting achievement of middle school Mexican-American students. *Review of Educational Research*, 1973, 43, 1-39.

Hertel, R. K. Application of stochastic process analyses to the study of psychotherapeutic processes. *Psychological Bulletin*, 1972, 77, 421-430.

Hess, A. L., & Bradshaw, H. L. Positiveness of self-concept and ideal self as a function of age. *Journal of Genetic Psychology*, 1970, 117, 57-67.

Hess, K. A., & Lindner, R. Dogmatism and self-esteem: A negative relationship confirmed. *Psychological Reports*, 1973, 32, 158.

Hess, R. D. Social class and ethnic influences on socialization. In P. H. Mussen (Ed.), *Carmichael's manual of child psychology*. (3rd ed.) New York: Wiley, 1970.

Hetherington, E. M. Effects of father absence on personality development in adolescent daughters. *Developmental Psychology*, 1972, 7, 313-326.

Hewitt, J. Liking and the proportion of favorable evaluations. *Journal of Personality and Social Psychology*, 1972, 22, 231-235.

Hewitt, J., & Kraft, M. Effects of an encounter group experience on self-perception and interpersonal relations. *Journal of Consulting and Clinical Psychology*, 1973, 40, 162.

Heyns, B. Social selection and stratification within schools. *American Journal of Sociology*, 1974, 79, 1434-1451.

Hickey, T., & Kalish, R. Young people's perceptions of adults. *Journal of Gerontology*, 1968, 23, 215-219.

Hilgard, E. R. *Hypnotic susceptibility*. New York: Harcourt, Brace, & World, 1965.

Hill, D. The attitudes of West Indian and English adolescents in Britain. *Race*, 1970, 11, 313-321.

Hill, T. J. Attitudes toward self: An experimental study. *Journal of Educational Sociology*, 1957, 30, 395-397.

Hishiki, P. The self concepts of sixth grade girls of Mexican-American descent. *California Journal of Educational Research*, 1969, 20, 56-62.

Hodge, R. W.; Siegel, P. M.; & Rossi, P. H. Occupational prestige in the U.S., 1925-1963. *American Journal of Sociology*, 1964, 70, 286-302.

Hodgkins, B. J., & Stakenas, R. G. A study of self-concepts of Negro and white youths in segregated environments. *The Journal of Negro Education*, 1969, 38, 370-377.

Hoffman, L. R. Similarity of personality: A basis for interpersonal attraction? *Sociometry*, 1958, 21, 300-308.

Hoffman, L. R., & Maier, N. R. F. An experimental reexamination of the similarity-attraction hypothesis. *Journal of Personality and Social Psychology*, 1966, 3, 145-152.

Holland, J. L., & Nichols, R. C. Prediction of academic and extra-curricular achievement in college. *Journal of Educational Psychology*, 1964, 55, 55-65.

Hollander, E. P., & Marcia, J. E. Parental determinants of peer-orientation and self-orientation among preadolescents. *Developmental Psychology*, 1970, 2, 292-302.

Hollender, J. Sex differences in sources of social self-esteem. *Journal of Consulting and Clinical Psychology*, 1972, 38, 343-347.

Hollender, J. W. Self-esteem and parental identification. *Journal of Genetic Psychology*, 1973, 122, 3-7.

Hollingshead, A. B., & Redlich, F. C. *Social class and mental illness: A community study*. New York: Wiley, 1958.

Hollon, T. H., & Zolik, E. S. Self-esteem and symptomatic complaints in the initial phase of psychoanalytically oriented psychotherapy. *American Journal of Psychotherapy*, 1962, 16, 83–93.

Holly, K. A.; Purl, M. C.; Dawson, J. A.; & Michael, W. B. The relationship of an experimental form of the mathematics self-concept scale to cognitive and noncognitive variables for a sample of seventh-grade pupils in a middle-class Southern California community. *Educational and Psychological Measurement*, 1973, 33, 505–508.

Homall, G. M.; Juhasz, S.; & Juhasz, J. Differences in self-perception and vocational aspirations of college women. *California Journal of Educational Research*, 1975, 26, 6–10.

Horney, K. *The neurotic personality of our times.* New York: W. W. Norton, 1937.

Horney, K. *New ways in psychoanalysis.* New York: W. W. Norton, 1939.

Horney, K. *Our inner conflicts.* New York: W. W. Norton, 1945.

Horney, K. *Feminine psychology.* New York: W. W. Norton Co., 1967.

Horowitz, F. D. The relationship of anxiety, self-concept, and sociometric status among fourth, fifth, and sixth grade children. *Journal of Abnormal and Social Psychology,* 1962, 65, 212–214.

Horowitz, R. Racial aspects of self-identification in nursery school children. *Journal of Psychology,* 1939, 7, 91–99.

Horrocks, J. E., & Benimoff, M. Stability of adolescent's nominee status, over a one-year period, as a friend by their peers. *Adolescence*, 1966, 1, 224–229.

Howard, K. I., & Orlinsky, D. E. Psychotherapeutic processes. In P. H. Mussen & M. R. Rosenzweig (Eds.), *Annual review of psychology.* Palo Alto, Calif.: Annual Reviews, Inc., 1972. Pp. 615–668.

Howard, R. C., & Berkowitz, L. Reactions to the evaluators of one's performance. *Journal of Personality*, 1958, 26, 494–507.

Hughes, J. H., & Thompson, G. G. A comparison of the value systems of Southern Negro and Northern white youth. *Journal of Educational Psychology*, 1954, 45, 300–309.

Hughes, R. E., & Works, E. The self-concepts of black students in a predominantly white and in a predominantly black high school. *Sociology and Social Research*, 1974, 59, 50–54.

Hughes, T. M. The relationship of coping strength to self-concept, school achievement, and general anxiety level in sixth grade pupils. *Journal of Experimental Education*, 1968, 37, 59–64.

Hulbary, W. E. Race, deprivation, and adolescent self-images. *Social Science Quarterly*, 1975, 56, 105–114.

Humes, C. W., Jr.; Adamczyk, J. S.; & Myco, R. W. A school study of group counseling with educable retarded adolescents. *American Journal of Mental Deficiency*, 1969, 74, 191–195.

Hunt, D. E., & Hardt, R. H. The effect of upward bound programs on the attitudes, motivation, and academic achievement of Negro students. *Journal of Social Issues*, 1969, 25, 117–129.

Hunt, J. McV.; Ewing, T. N.; LaForge, R.; & Gilbert, W. M. An integrated approach to research on therapeutic counseling with samples of results. *Journal of Counseling Psychology,* 1959, 6, 46-54.

Hurlock, E. B. A study of self-ratings by children. *Journal of Applied Psychology,* 1927, 11, 490-502.

Hurst, J. C.; Delworth, U.; & Garriott, R. Encountertapes: Evaluation of a leaderless group procedure. *Small Group Behavior,* 1973, 4, 476-485.

Husaini, B. A. Achievement motivation and self-esteem: A cross-cultural study. *Indian Journal of Psychology,* 1974, 49, 100-108.

Inkeles, A. Industrial man: The relation of status to experience perception, and value. *American Journal of Sociology,* 1960, 66, 1-31.

Insel, P., & Moos, R. An experimental investigation of process and outcome in an encounter group. *Human Relations,* 1972, 25, 441-447.

Irvin, F. S. Sentence-completion responses and scholastic success or failure. *Journal of Counseling Psychology,* 1967, 14, 269-271.

Izard, C. E. Personality correlates of sociometric status. *Journal of Applied Psychology,* 1959, 43, 89-93.

Izard, C. E. Personality similarity, positive affect, and interpersonal attraction. *Journal of Abnormal and Social Psychology,* 1960, 61, 484-485. (a)

Izard, C. E. Personality similarity and friendship. *Journal of Abnormal and Social Psychology,* 1960, 61, 47-51. (b)

Izard, C. E. Personality characteristics associated with resistance to change. *Journal of Consulting Psychology,* 1960, 24, 437-440. (c)

Izard, C. E. Personality similarity and friendship: A follow-up study. *Journal of Abnormal and Social Psychology,* 1963, 66, 598-600.

Jackson, D. N. *Personality Research Form Manual.* Goshen, N. Y.: Research Psychologists Press, Inc., 1967.

Jackson, J. J. Family organization and ideology. In K. S. Miller & R. M. Dreger (Eds.), *Comparative studies of blacks and whites in the United States.* New York: Seminar Press, 1973. Pp. 405-445.

Jacobs, L.; Berscheid, E.; & Walster, E. Self-esteem and attraction. *Journal of Personality and Social Psychology,* 1971, 17, 84-91.

Jacobson, E. A., & Smith, S. J. Effect of weekend encounter group experience upon interpersonal orientations. *Journal of Consulting and Clinical Psychology,* 1972, 38, 403-410.

Jahoda, M. *Current concepts of positive mental health.* New York: Basic Books, 1958.

Janis, I. L. Personality correlates of susceptibility to persuasion. *Journal of Personality,* 1954, 22, 504-518.

Janis, I. L. Anxiety indices related to susceptibility to persuasion. *Journal of Abnormal and Social Psychology,* 1955, 51, 663-667.

Janis, I. L., & Field, P. B. Sex differences and personality factors related to persuasibility. In C. I. Hovland & I. L. Janis (Eds.), *Personality and persuasibility*. New Haven: Yale University Press, 1959. Pp. 55-68.

Janis, I. L., & Rife, D. Persuasibility and emotional disorder. In C. I. Hovland and I. L. Janis (Eds.), *Personality and persuasibility*. New Haven: Yale University Press, 1959. Pp. 121-137.

Jarrett, R. F., & Sherriffs, A. C. Propaganda, debate, and impartial presentation as determiners of attitude change. *Journal of Abnormal and Social Psychology*, 1953, 48, 33-41.

Jaskar, R. O., & Reed, M. R. Assessment of body image organization of hospitalized and nonhospitalized subjects. *Journal of Projective Techniques and Personality Assessment*, 1963, 27, 185-190.

Jeffers, F. C.; Eisdorfer, C.; & Busse, E. W. Measurement of age identification: A methodologic note. *Journal of Gerontology*, 1962, 17, 437-439.

Jellison, J. M., & Zeisset, P. T. Attraction as a function of the commonality and desirability of a trait shared with another. *Journal of Personality and Social Psychology*, 1969, 11, 115-120.

Jervis, F. M. The meaning of a positive self-concept. *Journal of Clinical Psychology*, 1959, 15, 370-373.

Joesting, J., & Joesting, R. Attitudes about sex roles, sex, and marital status of anti-war demonstrators. *Psychological Reports*, 1972, 31, 413-414.

Joesting, J., & Joesting, R. Sex differences in equalitarianism and anxiety in ninth grade students. *Adolescence*, 1975, 10, 59-60.

Johnson, C. D.; Gormly, J.; & Gormly, A. Disagreements and self-esteem: Support for the competence-reinforcement model of attraction. *Journal of Research in Personality*, 1973, 7, 165-172.

Johnson, C. S. *Growing up in the black belt*. New York: Shocken, 1967.

Johnson, H. H. Some effects of discrepancy level on responses to negative information about one's self. *Sociometry*, 1966, 29, 52-66.

Johnson, H. H., & Steiner, I. D. The effects of source on responses to negative information about one's self. *Journal of Social Psychology*, 1968, 74, 215-224.

Johnson, L. C. Body-cathexis as a factor in somatic complaints. *Journal of Consulting Psychology*, 1956, 20, 145-149.

Johnson, M. M. Sex role learning in the nuclear family. *Child Development*, 1963, 34, 319-333.

Joiner, L. M.; Erickson, E. L.; Crittenden, J. B.; & Stevenson, V. M. Predicting the academic achievement of the acoustically impaired using intelligence and self-concept of academic ability. *Journal of Special Education*, 1969, 3, 425-431.

Jones, D. S., & Medvene, A. M. Self-actualization effects of a marathon growth group. *Journal of Counseling Psychology*, 1975, 22, 39-43.

Jones, E. E. *Ingratiation*. New York: Appleton-Century-Crofts, 1964.

Jones, E. E.; Hester, S. L.; Farina, A.; & Davis, K. E. Reactions to unfavorable personal evaluations as a function of the evaluator's perceived adjustment. *Journal of Abnormal and Social Psychology*, 1959, 59, 363–370.

Jones, J. G., & Strowig, R. W. Adolescent identity and self-perception as predictors of scholastic achievement. *Journal of Educational Research*, 1968, 62, 78–82.

Jones, L. W. Personality and age. *Nature*, 1935, 136, 779–782.

Jones, R. L. Labels and stigma in special education. *Exceptional Children*, 1972, 38, 553–564.

Jones, S. C. Some determinants of interpersonal evaluating behavior. *Journal of Personality and Social Psychology*, 1966, 3, 397–403.

Jones, S. C. Self and interpersonal evaluations: Esteem theories versus consistency theories. *Psychological Bulletin*, 1973, 79, 185–199.

Jones, S. C., & Ratner, C. Commitment to self-appraisal and interpersonal evaluations. *Journal of Personality and Social Psychology*, 1967, 6, 442–447.

Jones, S. C., & Shrauger, J. S. Reputation and self-evaluation as determinants of attractiveness. *Sociometry*, 1970, 33, 276–286.

Jorgensen, E. C., & Howell, R. J. Changes in self, ideal-self correlations from ages 8 through 18. *Journal of Social Psychology*, 1969, 79, 63–67.

Joseph, M. P., & McDonald, A. S. Psychological needs and reading achievement. In E. L. Thurston & L. E. Hofman (Eds.), *Thirteenth yearbook of the national reading conference*. Milwaukee: National Reading Conference, 1964. Pp. 150–157.

Jourard, S. M. Identification, parent-cathexis, and self-esteem. *Journal of Consulting Psychology*, 1957, 21, 375–380.

Jourard, S. M., & Remy, R. M. Perceived parental attitudes, the self, and security. *Journal of Consulting Psychology*, 1955, 19, 364–366.

Kagan, J. The child's perception of the parent. *Journal of Abnormal and Social Psychology*, 1956, 53, 257–258.

Kagan, J. The concept of identification. *Psychological Review*, 1958, 65, 296–305.

Kagan, J. Acquisition and significance of sex typing and sex role identity. In M. Hoffman & L. Hoffman (Eds.), *Review of child development research*. Vol. 1. New York: Russell Sage, 1964. Pp. 137–167.

Kagan, J. On the need for relativism. *American Psychologist*, 1967, 22, 131–142.

Kagan, J.; Hosken, B.; & Watson, S. Child's symbolic conceptualization of parents. *Child Development*, 1961, 32, 625–636.

Kagan, J., & Lemkin, J. The child's differential perception of parental attributes. *Journal of Abnormal and Social Psychology*, 1960, 61, 440–447.

Kagan, J., & Moss, H. A. *Birth to maturity*. New York: Wiley, 1962.

Kahana, E., & Coe, R. M. Self and staff conceptions of institutionalized aged. *Gerontologist*, 1969, 9, 264–267.

Kahl, J. A., & Davis, J. A. A comparison of indexes of socioeconomic status. *American Sociological Review*, 1955, 20, 317–325.

Kaltsounis, B. Attitude patterns as providing validity evidence of "What Kind of a Person Are You?" *Perceptual and Motor Skills*, 1975, 40, 670. (a)

Kaltsounis, B. Further validity on "Something about Myself." *Perceptual and Motor Skills*, 1975, 40, 94. (b)

Kaplan, H. B. Self-derogation and childhood family structure. *Journal of Nervous and Mental Disease*, 1970, 151, 13–23.

Kaplan, H. B. Social class and self-derogation: A conditional relationship. *Sociometry*, 1971, 34, 41–64.

Kaplan, H. B. The self-esteem motive and change in self-attitudes. *Journal of Nervous and Mental Disease*, 1975, 161, 265–275. (a)

Kaplan, H. B. Sequelae of self-derogation: Predicting from a general theory of deviant behavior. *Youth and Society*, 1975, 7, 171–197. (b)

Kaplan, H. B. Antecedents of negative self attitudes: Membership group devaluation and defenselessness. *Social Psychiatry*, 1976, 11, 15–25.

Kaplan, H. B., & Pokorny, A. D. Self-derogation and psychosocial adjustment. *Journal of Nervous and Mental Disease*, 1969, 149, 421–434.

Kaplan, H. B., & Pokorny, A. D. Aging and self-attitude: A conditional relationship. *Aging and Human Development*, 1970, 1, 241–250.

Kaplan, H. B., & Pokorny, A. D. Self-derogation and childhood broken home. *Journal of Marriage and the Family*, 1971, 33, 328–337.

Kardiner, A., & Ovesy, L. *The mark of oppression: Explorations in the personality of the American Negro.* Cleveland, Ohio: World Publishing Company, 1951.

Kasl, S. V. Relationship of distortion in self-reports of grades and extracurricular activities to the Crowne-Marlowe measure of approval motive. *Psychological Reports*, 1972, 30, 252–254.

Kasl, S. V., & French, J. R. P., Jr. The effects of occupational status on physical and mental health. *Journal of Social Issues*, 1962, 18, 67–89.

Kastenbaum, R., & Durkee, N. Elderly people view old age. In R. Kastenbaum (Ed.), *New thoughts on old age.* New York: Springer, 1964. Pp. 250–262.

Katcher, A. The discrimination of sex differences by young children. *Journal of Genetic Psychology*, 1955, 87, 131–143.

Katz, I.; Glucksberg, S.; & Krauss, R. Need satisfaction and Edwards PPS scores in married couples. *Journal of Consulting Psychology*, 1960, 24, 205–208.

Katz, P., & Zigler, E. Self-image disparity: A developmental approach. *Journal of Personality and Social Psychology*, 1967, 5, 186–195.

Kauffman, J. M. Family relations test responses of disturbed and normal boys: Additional comparative data. *Journal of Personality Assessment*, 1971, 35, 128–138.

Kayser, B. D. Authoritarianism, self-esteem, emotionality and intelligence. *Perceptual and Motor Skills*, 1972, 34, 367–370.

Keislar, E. R. Experimental development of "like" and "dislike" of others among adolescent girls. *Child Development*, 1961, 32, 59-66.

Keller, S. The social world of the urban slum child: Some early findings. *American Journal of Orthopsychiatry*, 1963; 33, 823-831.

Kelley, J.; Smits, S. J.; Leventhal, R.; & Rhodes, R. Critique of the designs of process and outcome research. *Journal of Counseling Psychology*, 1970, 17, 337-341.

Kelly, E. L. Psychological factors in assortative mating. *Psychological Bulletin*, 1940, 37, 576.

Kelly, E. L. Marital compatibility as related to personality traits of husbands and wives as rated by self and spouse. *Journal of Social Psychology*, 1941, 13, 193-198.

Kelly, E. L. Consistency of the adult personality. *American Psychologist*, 1955, 10, 659-681.

Kelly, J. M. Self-concept development in parent deprived children: A comparative study. *Graduate Research in Education and Related Disciplines*, 1970, 6, 30-48.

Kelman, H. C., & Parloff, M. B. Interrelations among three criteria of improvement in group therapy: Comfort, effectiveness, and self-awareness. *Journal of Abnormal and Social Psychology*, 1957, 54, 281-288.

Kemp, C. G. Self-perception in relation to open-closed belief systems. *Journal of General Psychology*, 1964, 70, 341-344.

Kerlinger, F., & Rokeach, M. The factorial nature of the *F* and *D* scales. *Journal of Personality and Social Psychology*, 1966, 4, 391-399.

Kerr, W. A., & Remmers, H. H. *Manual for the American Home Scale.* Chicago: Science Research Associates, 1942.

Khatena, J. Something About Myself: A brief screening device for identifying creatively gifted children and adults. *Gifted Child Quarterly*, 1971, 15, 262-266. (a)

Khatena, J. *Something About Myself: Norms and technical manual research edition.* Huntington, W.Va.: Marshall University, 1971. (b)

Khatena, J. Attitude patterns as providing validity evidence of "Something About Myself." *Perceptual and Motor Skills*, 1972, 34, 563-564.

Khatena, J. Relationship of autonomous imagery and creative self-perceptions. *Perceptual and Motor Skills*, 1975, 40, 357-358. (a)

Khatena, J. Vividness of imagery and creative self perceptions. *Gifted Child Quarterly*, 1975, 19, 35-37. (b)

Kiesler, C. A., & Goldberg, G. N. Multi-dimensional approach to the experimental study of interpersonal attraction: Effect of a blunder on the attractiveness of a competent other. *Psychological Reports*, 1968, 22, 693-705.

Kiesler, D. J. Some myths of psychotherapy research and the search for a paradigm. *Psychological Bulletin*, 1966, 65, 110-136.

Kiesler, D. J. Experimental designs in psychotherapy research. In A. E. Bergin

& S. L. Garfield (Eds.), *Handbook of psychotherapy and behavior change: An empirical analysis.* New York: Wiley, 1971. Pp. 36-74.

Kiesler, D. J. *The process of psychotherapy: Empirical foundations and systems of analysis.* Chicago: Aldine, 1973.

Kiesler, S. B., & Baral, R. L. The search for a romantic partner: The effects of self-esteem and physical attractiveness on romantic behavior. In K. Gergen & D. Marlowe (Eds.), *Personality and social behavior.* Reading, Mass.: Addison-Wesley, 1970. Pp. 155-165.

Kimball, R., & Gelso, C. J. Self-actualization in a marathon growth group. *Journal of Counseling Psychology,* 1974, 21, 38-42.

King, M.; Payne, D. C.; & McIntire, W. G. The impact of marathon and prolonged sensitivity training on self-acceptance. *Small Group Behavior,* 1973, 4, 414-423.

Kipnis, D. M. Changes in self concepts in relation to perceptions of others. *Journal of Personality,* 1961, 29, 449-465.

Kirchner, E. P., & Vondracek, S. I. Perceived sources of esteem in early childhood. *Journal of Genetic Psychology,* 1975, 126, 169-179.

Kirchner, W. K. Relationships between supervisory and subordinate ratings for technical personnel. *Journal of Industrial Psychology,* 1965, 3, 57-60.

Kirk, B. A., & Sereda, L. Accuracy of self-reported college grade averages and characteristics of non and discrepant reporters. *Educational and Psychological Measurement,* 1969, 29, 147-155.

Kirkpatrick, J. J. Occupational aspirations, opportunities, and barriers. In K. S. Miller & R. M. Dreger (Eds.), *Comparative studies of blacks and whites in the United States.* New York: Seminar Press, 1973. Pp. 355-373.

Klaff, F. R., & Docherty, E. M. Children's self-concept and attitude toward school in open and traditional classrooms. *Journal of School Psychology,* 1975, 13, 97-103.

Klausner, S. Z. Social class and self concept. *Journal of Social Psychology,* 1953, 38, 201-205.

Kleemeier, R. W. Relation of body change to psychological aspects of aging. In E. W. Busse & F. C. Jeffers (Eds.), *Duke University Council on Gerontology, Proceedings of Seminars: 1961-65.* Durham, N.C.: Duke University, 1965.

Klein, G. S. Self-appraisal of test performance as a vocational selection device. *Educational and Psychological Measurement,* 1948, 8, 69-84.

Klein, R. L., & Birren, J. E. Age, perceived self-competence, and conformity: A partial explanation. *Proceedings of the 81st Annual Convention of the American Psychological Association,* 1973, 8, 775-776.

Klein, V. *The feminine character: History of an ideology.* (2nd ed.) London: Routledge & Kegan Paul, 1971.

Kleinfeld, J. The relative importance of teachers and parents in the formation of Negro and white students' academic self-concept. *Journal of Educational Research,* 1972, 65, 211-212.

Klett, C. J. Performance of high school students on the Edwards Personal Preference Schedule. *Journal of Consulting Psychology*, 1957, 21, 68–72.

Knight, O. B. Self-concept of Negro and white educable mentally retarded boys. *Journal of Negro Education*, 1969, 38, 143–146.

Knight, O. B. Some problems in measuring the self concept of the educable mentally retarded. *American Institute for Mental Studies Training School Bulletin*, 1970, 66, 178–180.

Kniss, J. T.; Butler, A.; Gorlow, L.; & Guthrie, G. M. Ideal self patterns of female retardates. *American Journal of Mental Deficiency*, 1962, 67, 245–249.

Koeck, R., & Guthrie, G. M. Reciprocity in impression formation. *Journal of Social Psychology*, 1975, 95, 67–76.

Koenig, F. Definitions of self and ordinal position of birth. *Journal of Social Psychology*, 1969, 78, 287–288.

Kogan, N., & Wallach, M. A. Age changes in values and attitudes. *Journal of Gerontology*, 1961, 16, 272–280.

Kogan, W. S.; Quinn, R.; Ax, A. F.; & Ripley, H. Some methodological problems in the quantification of clinical assessment by Q array. *Journal of Consulting Psychology*, 1957, 21, 57–62.

Kohlberg, L. A cognitive-developmental analysis of children's sex-role concepts and attitudes. In E. Maccoby (Ed.), *The development of sex differences*. Stanford, Calif.: Stanford University Press, 1966. Pp. 82–173.

Kohlberg, L. Stage and sequence: The cognitive-developmental approach to socialization. In D. A. Goslin (Ed.), *Handbook of socialization theory and research*. Chicago: Rand McNally, 1969. Pp. 347–480.

Kohn, A. R., & Fiedler, F. E. Age and sex differences in the perception of persons. *Sociometry*, 1961, 24, 157–163.

Kohn, M. L. Social class and parent-child relationships: An interpretation. *American Journal of Sociology*, 1963, 68, 471–480.

Kohn, M. L. *Class and conformity: A study in values*. Homewood, Ill.: Dorsey, 1969.

Kohn, M. L., & Schooler, C. Class, occupation, and orientation. *American Sociological Review*, 1969, 34, 659–678.

Koile, E. A., & Draeger, C. T-group member ratings of leader and self in a human relations laboratory. *Journal of Psychology*, 1969, 72, 11–20.

Kornreich, L. B.; Straka, J.; & Kane, A. Meaning of self-image disparity as measured by the Q sort. *Journal of Consulting and Clinical Psychology*, 1968, 32, 728–730.

Kosa, J.; Rachiele, L. D.; & Schommer, C. O. The self-image and performance of socially mobile college students. *Journal of Social Psychology*, 1962, 56, 301–316.

Koutrelakos, J. Authoritarian person's perception of his relationship with his father. *Perceptual and Motor Skills*, 1968, 26, 967–973.

Kranzler, G. D. Some effects of reporting scholastic aptitude test scores to high school sophomores. *School Counselor*, 1970, 17, 209-227.

Krauss, H. H., & Critchfield, L. L. Contrasting self-esteem theory and consistency theory in predicting interpersonal attraction. *Sociometry*, 1975, 38, 247-260.

Kreiger, M. H., & Worchel, P. A test of the psychoanalytic theory of identification. *Journal of Individual Psychology*, 1960, 16, 56-63.

Kreines, D. C., & Bogart, K. Defensive projection and the reduction of dissonance. *Journal of Social Psychology*, 1974, 72, 103-108.

Kubiniec, C. M. The relative efficacy of various dimensions of the self-concept in predicting academic achievement. *American Educational Research Journal*, 1970, 7, 321-336.

Kuhlen, R. G. Aging and life-adjustment. In J. E. Birren (Ed.), *Handbook of aging and the individual*. Chicago: University of Chicago Press, 1959. Pp. 852-897.

Kuhn, M. H. Self-attitudes by age, sex, and professional training. *Sociological Quarterly*, 1960, 9, 39-55.

Kumpf, M., & Götz-Marchand, B. Reduction of cognitive dissonance as a function of magnitude of dissonance, differentiation, and self-esteem. *European Journal of Social Psychology*, 1973, 3, 255-270.

Kunce, J. T.; Getsinger, S. H.; & Miller, D. E. Educational implications of self-esteem. *Psychology in the Schools*, 1972, 9, 314-316.

Kurtz, R. R., & Grummon, D. L. Different approaches to the measurement of therapist empathy and their relationship to therapy outcomes. *Journal of Consulting and Clinical Psychology*, 1972, 39, 106-115.

Kutner, B.; Fanshel, D.; Togo, A. M.; & Langner, T. S. *Five hundred over sixty*. New York: Russell Sage Foundation, 1956.

Lacey, L. A., & Erickson, C. E. Psychology of scientist: XXXI Discriminability of a creativity scale for the Adjective Check List among scientists and engineers. *Psychological Reports*, 1974, 34, 755-758.

Lacklen, R., & Harmon, L. R. Criterion Committee report. In C. W. Taylor (Ed.), *The second University of Utah research conference on the identification of creative scientific talent*. Salt Lake City: University of Utah, 1957. Pp. 243-248.

Lana, R. E. Pretest sensitization. In R. Rosenthal & R. L. Rosnow (Eds.), *Artifact in behavioral research*. New York: Academic Press, 1969. Pp. 119-141.

Landreth, C., & Johnson, B. C. Young children's responses to a picture and inset test designed to reveal reactions to persons of different skin color. *Child Development*, 1953, 24, 63-79.

Landy, D., & Aronson, E. Liking for an evaluator as a function of his discernment. *Journal of Personality and Social Psychology*, 1968, 9, 133-141.

Lane, B. Attitudes of youth toward the aged. *Journal of Marriage and the Family,* 1964, 26, 229-231.

Langford, L. M., & Alm, G. W. A comparison of parent judgment and child feelings concerning the self-adjustment and social adjustment of twelve-year old children. *Journal of Genetic Psychology,* 1954, 85, 39-46.

Langner, T., & Michael, S. *Life stress and mental health.* Glencoe, Ill.: Free Press (Macmillan), 1963.

Lansky, L. M.; Crandall, V. J.; Kagan, J.; & Baker, C. T. Sex differences in aggression and its correlates in middle-class adolescents. *Child Development,* 1961, 32, 45-58.

LaPlante, M. J., & Irvin, F. S. Sentence-completion responses and academic performance re-examined. *Journal of Projective Techniques and Personality Assessment,* 1970, 34, 219-222.

Larkin, R. W. Class, race, sex, and preadolescent attitudes. *California Journal of Educational Research,* 1972, 23, 213-223.

Larsen, K. S., & Schwendiman, G. Authoritarianism, self esteem and insecurity. *Psychological Reports,* 1969, 25, 229-230.

Larsen, S. C.; Parker, R.; & Jorjorian, S. Differences in self-concept of normal and learning disabled children. *Perceptual and Motor Skills,* 1973, 37, 510.

Lawrence, E. A., & Winschel, J. F. Self concept and the retarded: Research and issues. *Exceptional Children,* 1973, 39, 310-319.

Lazowick, L. M. On the nature of identification. *Journal of Abnormal and Social Psychology,* 1955, 51, 175-183.

League, B. J., & Jackson, D. N. Conformity, veridicality, and self-esteem. *Journal of Abnormal and Social Psychology,* 1964, 68, 113-115.

Leary, T. F., & Harvey, J. S. A methodology for measuring personality changes in psychotherapy. *Journal of Clinical Psychology,* 1956, 12, 123-132.

Lecky, P. *Self consistency: A theory of personality.* New York: Island Press, 1945.

Lee, D. E., & Ehrlich, H. J. Beliefs about self and others: A test of the dogmatism theory. *Psychological Reports,* 1971, 28, 919-922.

Lee, R. E. A note on the relationship of critical behavior and self-esteem in the hospitalized veteran. *Psychotherapy: Theory, Research, and Practice,* 1972, 9, 130-131.

Lefley, H. P. Effects of a cultural heritage program on the self-concept of Miccosukee Indian children. *Journal of Educational Research,* 1974, 67, 462-466.

Lehmann, S. Personality and compliance: A study of anxiety and self-esteem in opinion behavior and change. *Journal of Personality and Social Psychology,* 1970, 15, 76-86.

Lehner, G. F. J. Personal adjustment scores and assigned "average" scores. *Journal of Psychology,* 1956, 42, 227-236.

Lehner, G. F. J. Some relationships among personal adjustment self-ratings, self-scores, and assigned "average" scores. *Journal of Psychology*, 1960, 50, 333-337.

Lekarczyk, D. T., & Hill, K. T. Self-esteem, text anxiety, stress, and verbal learning. *Developmental Psychology*, 1969, 1, 147-154.

Leonard, R. L. Self-concept as a factor in the similarity-attraction paradigm. *Proceedings of the 81st Annual Convention of the American Psychological Association*, 1973, 8, 199-200.

Lepper, M. R. Dissonance, self-perception, and honesty in children. *Journal of Personality and Social Psychology*, 1973, 25, 65-74.

Lerner, M. J., & Becker, S. W. Interpersonal choice as a function of ascribed similarity and definition of the situation. *Human Relations*, 1962, 15, 27-34.

Lesser, G. S., & Abelson, R. P. Personality correlates of persuasibility in children. In C. I. Hovland & I. L. Janis (Eds.), *Personality and persuasibility*. New Haven: Yale University Press, 1959. Pp. 187-221.

Lesser, M. The relationship between counseling progress and empathic understanding. *Journal of Counseling Psychology*, 1961, 8, 330-336.

Levanway, R. W. The effect of stress on expressed attitudes toward self and others. *Journal of Abnormal and Social Psychology*, 1955, 50, 225-226.

Leventhal, H., & Perloe, S. I. A relationship between self-esteem and persuasibility. *Journal of Abnormal and Social Psychology*, 1962, 64, 385-388.

Levine, J. M.; Ranelli, C. J.; & Valle, R. S. Self-evaluation and reaction to a shifting other. *Journal of Personality and Social Psychology*, 1974, 29, 637-643.

Levinger, G. Note on need complementarity in marriage. *Psychological Bulletin*, 1964, 61, 153-157.

Levinson, R., & Kitchener, H. Treatment of delinquents: Comparison of four methods for assigning inmates to counselors. *Journal of Consulting Psychology*, 1966, 30, 364.

Levitt, E. E. A comparison of parental and self-evaluations of psychopathology in children. *Journal of Clinical Psychology*, 1959, 15, 402-404.

Levonian, E. Self-esteem and opinion change. *Journal of Personality and Social Psychology*, 1968, 9, 257-259.

Levonian, E. Need for control data in studies of self-esteem and persuasibility. *Psychological Reports*, 1970, 27, 527-544. (a)

Levonian, E. Comment on "Reply to Levonian." *Psychological Reports*, 1970, 27, 589-590. (b)

Levonian, E. Comment on Dittes' note. *Psychological Reports*, 1970, 27, 673-674. (c)

Levy, L. H. The meaning and generality of perceived actual-ideal discrepancies. *Journal of Consulting Psychology*, 1956, 20, 396-398.

Lewin, K. *Resolving social conflicts*. New York: Harper, 1948.

Lewis, C. N. Reminiscing and self-concept in old age. *Journal of Gerontology*, 1971, 26, 240–243.

Lewis, J., & Adank, R. Intercorrelations among measures of intelligence, achievement, self-esteem, and anxiety in two groups of elementary school pupils exposed to two different models of instruction. *Educational and Psychological Measurement*, 1975, 35, 499–501.

Lewis, M., & Brooks, J. Self, other, and fear: Infants' reactions to people. In M. Lewis & L. A. Rosenblum (Eds.), *Origins of fear*. New York: Wiley, 1974. Pp. 195–226.

Lewis, M., & Brooks, J. Infants' social perception: A constructivist view. In L. Cohen & S. Salapatek (Eds.) *Infant perception: From sensation to cognition*. Vol. 2. *Perception of space, speech, and sound*. New York: Academic Press, 1975. Pp. 102–143.

Lichtenstein, E. Personality similarity and therapeutic success: A failure to replicate. *Journal of Consulting Psychology*, 1966, 30, 282.

Lieberman, M. A. Change induction in small groups. In M. R. Rosenzweig & L. W. Porter (Eds.), *Annual review of psychology*. Palo Alto, Calif.: Annual Reviews, Inc., 1976. Pp. 217–250.

Lieberman, M.; Prock, V.; & Tobin, S. Psychological effects of institutionalization. *Journal of Gerontology*, 1968, 23, 343–353.

Lindzey, G., & Byrne, D. Measurement of social choice and interpersonal attractiveness. In G. Lindzey & E. Aronson (Eds.), *The handbook of social psychology*. Vol. 2. Reading, Mass.: Addison-Wesley, 1968. Pp. 452–525.

Lindzey, G., & Urdan, J. A. Personality and social choice. *Sociometry*, 1954, 17, 47–63.

Linton, H., & Graham, E. Personality correlates of persuasibility. In C. I. Hovland & I. L. Janis (Eds.), *Personality and persuasibility*. New Haven: Yale University Press, 1959. Pp. 69–101.

Lipkin, S. Clients' feelings and attitudes in relation to the outcome of client-centered therapy. *Psychological Monographs*, 1954, 68, 1–30.

Lipsitt, L. P. A self-concept scale for children and its relationship to the children's form of the Manifest Anxiety Scale. *Child Development*, 1958, 29, 463–472.

Lively, E. L.; Dinitz, S.; & Reckless, W. C. Self concept as a predictor of juvenile delinquency. *American Journal of Orthopsychiatry*, 1962, 32, 159–168.

Lockwood, D. H., & Guerney, B. Identification and empathy in relation to self-dissatisfaction and adjustment. *Journal of Abnormal and Social Psychology*, 1962, 65, 343–347.

Long, B. H. Critique of Soares and Soares' "Self-perceptions of culturally disadvantaged children." *American Educational Research Journal*, 1969, 6, 710–711.

Long, B. H., & Henderson, E. H. Self-social concepts of disadvantaged school beginners. *Journal of Genetic Psychology*, 1968, 113, 41–51.

Long, B. H., & Henderson, E. H. Social schemata of school beginners: Some demographic correlates. *Merrill-Palmer Quarterly*, 1970, 16, 305–324.

Long, B. H.; Henderson, E. H.; Gantcheff, H.; & Kastersztein, J. Self-other orientations of English and French adolescents in Europe and Canada. *International Journal of Psychology*, 1972, 7, 181–189.

Long, B. H.; Henderson, E. H.; & Platt, L. Self-other orientations of Israeli adolescents reared in kibbutzim and moshavim. *Developmental Psychology*, 1973, 8, 300–308.

Long, B. H.; Henderson, E. H.; & Ziller, R. C. Developmental changes in the self-concept during middle childhood. *Merrill-Palmer Quarterly*, 1967, 13, 201–215. (a)

Long, B. H.; Henderson, E. H.; & Ziller, R. C. Self-social correlates of originality in children. *Journal of Genetic Psychology*, 1967, 111, 47–57. (b)

Long, B. H.; Henderson, E. H.; & Ziller, R. C. *Manual for the Self-Social Symbols Tasks and the Children's Self-Social Constructs Test.* Mimeographed. Baltimore, Md.: Goucher College, 1970.

Long, B. H.; Ziller, R. C.; & Henderson, E. H. Developmental changes in the self-concept during adolescence. *The School Review*, 1968, 76, 210–230.

Lorenz, G. Aspirations of low-income blacks and whites: A case of reference group processes. *American Journal of Sociology*, 1972, 78, 371–398.

Lorge, I.; Tuckman, J.; & Abrams, A. R. Attitudes of junior and senior high school students toward aging. *Annual Report of the New York Joint Legislative Committee on the Problems of the Aging*, 1954, Pp. 59–63.

Lorr, M.; Katz, M. M.; & Rubenstein, E. A. The prediction of length of stay in psychotherapy. *Journal of Consulting Psychology*, 1958, 22, 321–327.

Lott, A. J., & Lott, B. E. *Negro and white youth: A psychological study in a border-state community.* New York: Holt, Rinehart, & Winston, 1963.

Lott, A. J., & Lott, B. E. A learning theory approach to interpersonal attitudes. In A. G. Greenwald; T. C. Brock; & T. M. Ostrom (Eds.), *Psychological foundations of attitudes.* New York: Academic, 1968. Pp. 67–88.

Lott, A. J.; Lott, B. E.; Reed, T.; & Crow, T. Personality-trait descriptions of differentially liked persons. *Journal of Personality and Social Psychology*, 1970, 16, 284–290.

Lowe, C. A., & Goldstein, J. W. Reciprocal liking and attributions of ability: Mediating effects of perceived intent and personal involvement. *Journal of Personality and Social Psychology*, 1970, 16, 291–297.

Luborsky, L. Perennial mystery of poor agreement among criteria for psychotherapy outcome. *Journal of Consulting and Clinical Psychology*, 1971, 37, 316–319.

Luborsky, L.; Chandler, M.; Auerbach, A. H.; Cohen, J.; & Bachrach, H. M. Factors influencing the outcome of psychotherapy: A review of quantitative research. *Psychological Bulletin,* 1971, 75, 145-185.

Luck, P. W., & Heiss, J. Social determinants of self-esteem in adult males. *Sociology and Social Research,* 1972, 57, 69-84.

Luckey, E. B. Implications for marriage counseling of self perceptions and spouse perceptions. *Journal of Counseling Psychology,* 1960, 1, 3-9. (a)

Luckey, E. B. Marital satisfaction and its association with congruence of perception. *Marriage and Family Living,* 1960, 22, 49-54. (b)

Luckey, E. B. Marital satisfaction and congruent self-spouse concepts. *Social Forces,* 1960, 39, 153-157. (c)

Luckey, E. B. Perceptional congruence of self and family concepts as related to marital interaction. *Sociometry,* 24, 1961, 234-250.

Ludwig, D. J. Evidence of construct and criterion-related validity for the self-concept. *Journal of Social Psychology,* 1970, 80, 213-223.

Lundgren, D. C., & Schwab, M. R. Sex differences in the social bases of self-esteem. Paper presented at the American Psychological Association Meetings, New Orleans, September, 1974.

Lundy, R. M. Self perceptions regarding masculinity-femininity and descriptions of same and opposite sex sociometric choices. *Sociometry,* 1958, 21, 238-246.

Lundy, R. M.; Katkovsky, W.; Cromwell, R. L.; & Shoemaker, D. J. Self acceptability and descriptions of sociometric choices. *Journal of Abnormal and Social Psychology,* 1955, 51, 260-262.

Lunneborg, P. W. Stereotypic aspect in masculinity-femininity measurement. *Journal of Consulting and Clinical Psychology,* 1970, 34, 113-118.

Luria, Z. A semantic analysis of a normal and a neurotic therapy group. *Journal of Abnormal and Social Psychology,* 1959, 58, 216-220.

Lyell, R. G. Adolescent and adult self-esteem as related to cultural values. *Adolescence,* 1973, 8, 85-92.

Lynd, H. M. *On shame and the sense of identity.* New York: Harcourt Brace, 1958.

Lynn, D. B. A note on sex differences in the development of masculine and feminine identification. *Psychological Review,* 1959, 66, 126-135.

Lynn, D. B. Sex-role and parental identification. *Child Development,* 1962, 33, 555-564.

Maccoby, E. E. (Ed.), *The development of sex differences.* Stanford, Calif.: Stanford University Press, 1966.

Maccoby, E. E., & Jacklin, C. N. *The psychology of sex differences.* Stanford, Calif.: Stanford University Press, 1974.

Mackeen, B. A., & Herman, A. Effects of group counseling on self-esteem. *Journal of Counseling Psychology,* 1974, 21, 210-214.

MacKinnon, D. W. The nature and nurture of creative talent. *American Psychologist,* 1962, 17, 484-495.

MacKinnon, D. W. Creativity and images of the self. In R. W. White (Ed.), *The study of lives.* New York: Atherton Press, 1963. Pp. 251-278.

MacKinnon, D. W. The creativity of architects. In C. W. Taylor (Ed.), *Widening horizons in creativity.* New York: Wiley, 1964. Pp. 359-378.

MacKinnon, D. W. Personality and the realization of creative potential. *American Psychologist,* 1965, 20, 273-281.

Maguire, Sister M. A self inventory scale of adolescent symptomatology based on Devereux Adolescent Behavior Scale. *Adolescence,* 1973, 8, 277-284.

Mahoney, J., & Hartnett, J. Self-actualization and self-ideal discrepancy. *Journal of Psychology,* 1973, 85, 37-42.

Maisonneuve, J. A. A contribution to the sociometry of mutual choices. *Sociometry,* 1954, 17, 33-46.

Maliver, B. Anti-Negro bias among Negro college students. *Journal of Personality and Social Psychology,* 1965, 2, 770-775.

Manis, M. Social interaction and the self concept. *Journal of Abnormal and Social Psychology,* 1955, 51, 362-370.

Manis, M. Personal adjustment, assumed similarity to parents, and inferred parental evaluations of the self. *Journal of Consulting Psychology,* 1958, 22 481-485.

Mann, P. H. Modifying the behavior of Negro educable mentally retarded boys through group counseling procedures. *Journal of Negro Education,* 1969, 38, 135-142.

Mann, P. H.; Beaber, J. D.; Jacobson, M. D. The effect of group counseling on educable mentally retarded boys' self concepts. *Exceptional Children,* 1969, 35, 359-366.

Mannheim, B. F. Reference groups, membership groups and the self image. *Sociometry,* 1966, 29, 265-279.

Marcia, J. E., & Friedman, M. L. Ego identity status in college women. *Journal of Personality,* 1970, 38, 249-263.

Marks, S. E.; Conry, R. F.; & Foster, S. F. The marathon group hypothesis: An unanswered question. *Journal of Counseling Psychology,* 1973, 20, 185-187.

Markson, E. & Grevert, P. Circe's terrible island of change: Self perceptions of incapacity. *Aging and Human Development,* 1972, 3, 261-271.

Marlowe, D., & Gergen, K. J. Personality and social interaction. In G. Lindzey & E. Aronson (Eds.), *Handbook of social psychology.* Vol. 3. Reading, Mass.: Addison-Wesley, 1968. Pp. 590-665.

Marsella, A. J.; Sanborn, K. O.; Kameoka, V.; Shizuru, L.; & Brennan, J. Cross-validation of self-report measures of depression among normal populations of Japanese, Chinese, and Caucasion ancestry. *Journal of Clinical Psychology,* 1975, 31, 281-287.

Martin, D. G. Consistency of self-descriptions under different role sets in neurotic and normal adolescents and adults. *Journal of Abnormal Psychology,* 1969, 74, 173-176.

Maskin, M. B. Differential impact of student counselors' self-concept on clients' perceptions of therapeutic effectiveness. *Psychological Reports*, 1974, 34, 967–969.

Maskin, M. B., & Flescher, B. E. Change in self-concept in work-oriented versus communication-oriented juvenile correction programs. *Psychological Reports*, 1975, 36, 460–462.

Masling, M. How neurotic is the authoritarian? *Journal of Abnormal and Social Psychology*, 1954, 49, 316–318.

Maslow, A. H. *Motivation and personality.* New York: Harper, 1954.

Mason, E. P. Some factors in self judgments. *Journal of Clinical Psychology*, 1954, 10, 336–340. (a)

Mason, E. P. Some correlates of self judgment of the aged. *Journal of Gerontology*, 1954, 9, 324–337. (b)

Mason, E. P.; Adams, H. L.; & Blood, D. F. Personality characteristics of gifted college freshmen. *Psychology in the Schools*, 1966, 3, 360–365.

Mason, E. P.; Adams, H. L.; & Blood, D. F. Further study of personality characteristics of bright college freshmen. *Psychological Reports*, 1968, 23, 395–400.

Matarazzo, J. D. Psychotherapeutic processes. In P. R. Farnsworth; O. Mc-Nemar; & Q. McNemar (Eds.), *Annual review of psychology.* Palo Alto, Calif.: Annual Reviews, Inc., 1965. Pp. 181–224.

Mayer, C. L. The relationship of early special class placement and the self-concepts of mentally handicapped children. *Exceptional Children*, 1966, 33, 77–81.

Mayer, C. L. Relationships of self-concepts and social variables in retarded children. *American Journal of Mental Deficiency*, 1967, 72, 267–271.

Mayer, K. B. *Class and society.* New York: Random House, 1955.

McAfee, R. O., & Cleland, C. C. The discrepancy between self-concept and ideal-self as a measure of psychological adjustment in educable mentally retarded males. *American Journal of Mental Deficiency*, 1965, 70, 63–68.

McCallon, E. L. Interpersonal perception characteristics of teachers. *Journal of Experimental Education*, 1966, 34, 97–100.

McCandless, B. R. *Children: Behavior and development.* (2nd ed.) Hinsdale, Ill.: Dryden, 1967.

McCardel, J., & Murray, E. J. Nonspecific factors in weekend encounter groups. *Journal of Consulting and Clinical Psychology*, 1974, 42, 337–345.

McCarthy, B. W., & Rafferty, J. E. Effect of social desirability and self-concept scores on the measurement of adjustment. *Journal of Personality Assessment*, 1971, 35, 576–583.

McCarthy, J., & Yancey, W. L. Uncle Tom and Mr. Charlie: Metaphysical pathos in the study of racism and personal disorganization. *American Journal of Sociology*, 1971, 76, 648–672.

McClain, E. W. Personality characteristics of Negro college students in the

South—a recent appraisal. *Journal of Negro Education,* 1967 Summer Yearbook, 36, 320-325.

McClelland, D. C. *Personality.* New York: William Sloane, 1951.

McConville, B. J.; Boag, L. C.; & Purohit, A. P. Three types of childhood depression. *Canadian Psychiatric Association Journal,* 1973, 18, 133-138.

McCormick, M., & Balla, D. Self-image disparity and attachment to ethnic subculture. *Journal of Psychology,* 1973, 84, 97-104.

McCoy, G. F. Some ego factors associated with academic success and failure of educable mentally retarded pupils. *Exceptional Children,* 1963, 30, 80-84.

McDavid, J. W., & Sistrunk, F. Personality correlates of two kinds of conforming behavior. *Journal of Personality,* 1964, 32, 420-435.

McDermid, C. D. Some correlates of creativity in engineering personnel. *Journal of Applied Psychology,* 1965, 49, 14-19.

McDonald, R. L. Nonintellectual factors associated with performance in medical school. *Journal of Genetic Psychology,* 1963, 103, 185-194.

McDonald, R. L. Effects of sex, race, and class on self, ideal-self and parental ratings in southern adolescents. *Perceptual and Motor Skills,* 1968, 27, 15-25.

McDonald, R. L., & Gynther, M. D. MMPI differences associated with sex, race, and class in two adolescent samples. *Journal of Consulting Psychology,* 1963, 27, 112-116.

McDonald, R. L., & Gynther, M. D. Relationship of self and ideal-self descriptions with sex, race, and class in southern adolescents. *Journal of Personality and Social Psychology,* 1965, 1, 85-88.

McGinnis, C. A. The effect of group-therapy on the Ego-Strength Scale scores of alcoholic patients. *Journal of Clinical Psychology,* 1963, 19, 346-347.

McGuire, W. J. Personality and susceptibility to social influence. In E. F. Borgatta & W. W. Lambert (Eds.), *Handbook of personality theory and research.* Chicago: Rand McNally, 1968. Pp. 1130-1187.

McGuire, W. J. Suspiciousness of experimenter's intent. In R. Rosenthal & R. L. Rosnow (Eds.), *Artifact in behavioral research.* New York: Academic Press, 1969. Pp. 13-57.

McGuire, W. J. The Yin and Yang of progress in social psychology: Seven koan. *Journal of Personality and Social Psychology,* 1973, 26, 446-456.

McGuire, W. J., & Millman, S. Anticipatory belief lowering following forewarning of a persuasive attack. *Journal of Personality and Social Psychology,* 1965, 2, 471-479.

McIntire, W. G. The impact of T-group experiences on level of self-actualization. *Small Group Behavior,* 1973, 4, 459-465.

McIntyre, C. J. Acceptance by others and its relation to acceptance of self and others. *Journal of Abnormal and Social Psychology,* 1952, 47, 624-626.

McKee, J. P., & Sherriffs, A. C. The differential evaluation of males and females. *Journal of Personality,* 1957, 25, 356-371.

McKee, J. P., & Sherriffs, A. C. Men's and women's beliefs, ideals, and self-concepts. *American Journal of Sociology*, 1959,64, 356-363.

McKenna, H. V.; Hofstaetter, P. R.; & O'Connor, J. P. The concepts of the ideal self and of the friend. *Journal of Personality*, 1956, 24, 262-271.

McKinley, D. G. *Social class and family life.* New York: Free Press, 1964.

McLaughlin, B. The WAI dictionary and self-perceived identity in college students. In P. J. Stone; D. C. Dunphy; M. S. Smith; & D. M. Ogilvie (Eds.), *The general inquirer: A computer approach to content analysis.* Cambridge, Mass.: M.I.T. Press, 1966. Pp. 548-566.

McLaughlin, B. Similarity, recall, and appraisal of others. *Journal of Personality*, 1970, 38, 106-116.

McLaughlin, B. Effects of similarity and likableness on attraction and recall. *Journal of Personality and Social Psychology*, 1971, 20, 65-69.

McLaughlin, F. E., Davis, M. L.; & Reed, J. L. Effects of three types of group leadership structure on the self-perceptions of undergraduate nursing students. *Nursing Research*, 1972, 21, 244-257.

McMillen, D. L. Transgression, self-image, and compliant behavior. *Journal of Personality and Social Psychology*, 1971, 20, 176-179.

McPartland, T. S., & Cumming, J. H. Self-conception, social class, and mental health. *Human Organization*, 1958, 17, 24-29.

Mead, G. H. *Mind, self, and society: From the standpoint of a social behaviorist.* Chicago: University of Chicago Press, 1934.

Medinnus, G. R. Adolescents' self-acceptance and perceptions of their parents. *Journal of Consulting Psychology*, 1965, 29, 150-154.

Medinnus, G. R., & Curtis, F. J. The relation between maternal self-acceptance and child acceptance. *Journal of Consulting Psychology*, 1963, 27, 542-544.

Mednick, S. A., & Mednick, M. T. An associative interpretation of the creative process. In C. W. Taylor (Ed.), *Widening horizons in creativity: The proceedings of the fifth Utah creativity research conference.* New York: Wiley, 1964. Pp. 54-68.

Meehl, P. E. Psychotherapy. In C. P. Stone & Q. McNemar (Eds.), *Annual review of psychology.* Palo Alto, Calif.: Annual Reviews, 1955. Pp. 357-378.

Mehlman, B. Similarity in friendships. *Journal of Social Psychology*, 1962, 57, 195-202.

Mehlman, M. R., & Fleming, J. E. Social stratification and some personality variables. *Journal of General Psychology*, 1963, 69, 3-10.

Mehta, P. H. The self-concept of bright underachieving male high school students. *Indian Educational Review*, 1968, 3, 81-100.

Meissner, A. L.; Thoreson, R. W.; & Butler, A. J. Relation of self-concept to impact and obviousness of disability among male and female adolescents. *Perceptual and Motor Skills*, 1967, 24, 1099-1105.

Meltzoff, J., & Kornreich, M. *Research in psychotherapy.* New York: Atherton, 1970.

Mendelsohn, G. A. Effects of client personality and client-counselor similarity on the duration of counseling: A replication and extension. *Journal of Counseling Psychology,* 1966, 13, 228-234.

Mendelsohn, G. A., & Geller, M. H. Effects of counselor-client similarity on the outcome of counseling. *Journal of Counseling Psychology,* 1963, 10, 71-77.

Mendelsohn, G. A., & Geller, M. H. Structure of client attitudes toward counseling and their relation to client-counselor similarity. *Journal of Consulting Psychology,* 1965, 29, 63-72.

Mendelsohn, G. A., & Geller, M. H. Similarity, missed sessions, and early termination. *Journal of Counseling Psychology,* 1967, 14, 210-215.

Messer, M. Race differences in selected attitudinal dimensions of the elderly. *Gerontologist,* 1968, 8, 245-249.

Mettee, D. R. Changes in liking as a function of the magnitude and affect of sequential evaluations. *Journal of Experimental Social Psychology,* 1971, 7, 157-172. (a)

Mettee, D. R. The true discerner as a potent source of positive affect. *Journal of Experimental Social Psychology,* 1971, 7, 292-303. (b)

Meyfrowitz, J. H. Self-derogations in young retardates and special class placement. *Child Development,* 1962, 33, 443-451.

Michael, J. J.; Plass, A.; & Lee, Y. B. A comparison of the self-report and the observed report in the measurement of the self-concept: Implications for construct validity. *Educational and Psychological Measurement,* 1973, 33, 433-439.

Miller, N.; Campbell, D. T.; Twedt, H.; & O'Connell, E. J. Similarity, contrast, and complementarity in friendship choice. *Journal of Personality and Social Psychology,* 1966, 3, 3-12.

Miller, T. W. Communicative dimensions of mother-child interaction as they affect the self-esteem of the child. *Proceedings of the 79th Annual Convention of the American Psychological Association,* 1971, 6, 241-242.

Mischel, W. A social-learning view of sex differences in behavior. In E. E. Maccoby (Ed.), *The development of sex differences.* Stanford, Calif.: Stanford University Press, 1966. Pp. 56-81.

Mischel, W. *Personality and assessment.* New York: John Wiley, 1968.

Mischel, W. Sex-typing and socialization. In P. H. Mussen (Ed.), *Carmichael's manual of child psychology.* New York: Wiley, 1970.

Mischel, W. Toward a cognitive social learning reconceptualization of personality. *Psychological Review,* 1973, 80, 252-283.

Miskimins, R. W., & Baker, B. R. Self-concept and the disadvantaged. *Journal of Community Psychology,* 1973, 1, 347-361.

Miskimins, R. W., & Simmons, W. L. Goal preference as a variable in involutional psychosis. *Journal of Consulting Psychology,* 1966, 30, 73-77.

Misra, S. Instability in self-evaluation, conformity, and affiliation. *Journal of Personality,* 1973, 41, 361-375.

Mitchell, J. V., Jr. Goalsetting behavior as a function of self-acceptance, over- and underachievement, and related personality variables. *Journal of Educational Psychology*, 1959, 50, 93–104.

Moeller, G., & Applezweig, M. H. A motivational factor in conformity. *Journal of Abnormal and Social Psychology*, 1957, 55, 114–120.

Monge, R. H. Developmental trends in factors of adolescent self-concept. *Developmental Psychology*, 1973, 8, 382–393.

Moore, A. B. Selected standardized noncognitive measures and their utility for the disadvantaged. *Adult Education*, 1972, 22, 110–121.

Moore, J. C., & Krupat, E. Relationships between source status, authoritarianism, and conformity in a social influence setting. *Sociometry*, 1971, 34, 122–134.

Morena, D. A., & Litrownik, A. J. Self-concept in educable mentally retarded and emotionally handicapped children. *Journal of Abnormal Child Psychology*, 1974, 2, 281–292.

Morland, J. K. Racial recognition by nursery school children in Lynchburg, Virginia. *Social Forces*, 1958, 37, 132–137.

Morland, J. K. Race awareness among American and Hong Kong Chinese children. In S. S. Guterman (Ed.), *Black psyche: The modal personality patterns of black Americans*. Berkeley, Calif.: Glendessary, 1972.

Morrison, R. F.; Owens, W. A.; Glennon, J. R.; & Albright, L. E. Factored life history antecedents of industrial research performance. *Journal of Applied Psychology*, 1962, 46, 281–284.

Morrison, T. L., & Thomas, M. D. Self-esteem and classroom participation. *Journal of Educational Research*, 1975, 68, 374–377.

Morrison, T. L.; Thomas, M. D.; & Weaver, S. J. Self-esteem and self-estimates of academic performance. *Journal of Consulting and Clinical Psychology*, 1973, 41, 412–415.

Morsbach, G. Auto- and heterostereotypes of Indian students in South Africa. *Journal of Behavior Science*, 1972, 1, 161–167.

Morse, R. J. Socioeconomic status and functioning in school: A symbolic interactionist interpretation. In W. B. Brookover; E. L. Erickson; & L. M. Joiner, *Self-concept of ability and school achievement: Relationship of self-concept to achievement in high school*. U.S. Office of Education, Cooperative Research Project No. 2831, Michigan State University, 1967. Pp. 211–229.

Morse, R. N., & Piers, E. V. *Variables affecting self-concept in black, disadvantaged boys*. Mimeographed. University Park, Pa.: Pennsylvania State University, undated.

Moses, E. G.; Zirkel, P. A.; & Greene, J. F. Measuring the self-concept of minority group pupils. *Journal of Negro Education*, 1973, 42, 93–98.

Mouton, J. S.; Blake, R. R.; & Fruchter, B. The reliability of sociometric measures. In J. L. Moreno (Ed.), *Sociometry reader*. Glencoe, Ill.: Free Press, 1960. Pp. 320–361. (a) Also in *Sociometry*, 1955, 18, 7–48. (a)

Mouton, J. S.; Blake, R. R.; & Fruchter, B. The validity of sociometric responses. In J. L. Moreno (Ed.), *Sociometry reader.* Glencoe, Ill.: Free Press, 1960. Pp. 362-387. (b) Also in *Sociometry,* 1955, 18, 181-206. (b)

Mowrer, O. H. Identification: A link between learning theory and psychotherapy. In O. H. Mowrer, *Learning theory and personality dynamics.* New York: Ronald Press, 1950. Pp. 573-616.

Mukherjee, B. N., & Sinha, R. Achievement values and self-ideal discrepancies in college students. *Personality: An International Journal,* 1970, 1, 275-301.

Mullener, N., & Laird, J. D. Some developmental changes in the organization of self-evaluations. *Developmental Psychology,* 1971, 5, 233-236.

Muller, D., & Leonetti, D. R. Self-concepts of primary level Chicano and Anglo students. *California Journal of Educational Research,* 1974, 25, 57-60.

Murray, H. A. *Explorations in personality.* Cambridge: Harvard University Press, 1938.

Murstein, B. I. Self and ideal self discrepancy and the choice of marital partner. *Proceedings of the 78th Annual Convention of the American Psychological Association,* 1970, 5, 459-460.

Murstein, B. I. Self-ideal-self discrepancy and the choice of marital partner. *Journal of Consulting and Clinical Psychology,* 1971, 37, 47-52. (a)

Murstein, B. I. (Ed.). *Theories of attraction and love.* New York: Springer, 1971. (b)

Musella, D. Perceptual-cognitive style as related to self-evaluation and supervisor rating by student teachers. *Journal of Experimental Education,* 1969, 37, 51-55.

Mussen, P. H., & Porter, L. W. Personal motivations and self-conceptions associated with effectiveness and ineffectiveness in emergent groups. *The Journal of Abnormal and Social Psychology,* 1959, 59, 23-27.

Muzekari, L. H.; Weinman, B.; & Kreiger, P. A. Self-experiential treatment in chronic schizophrenia. *Journal of Nervous and Mental Disease,* 1973, 157, 420-427.

Myrick, R. D., & Pare, D. D. A study of the effects of group sensitivity training with student counselor-consultants. *Counselor Education and Supervision,* 1971, 11, 90-96.

Nahinsky, I. D. The self-ideal correlation as a measure of generalized self satisfaction. *Psychological Record,* 1966, 16, 55-64.

National Council on the Aging, Inc. *The myth and reality of aging in America.* National Council on the Aging, Inc., 1975.

National Opinion Research Center (North, C. D., & Hatt, P. K.) Jobs and occupations: A popular evaluation. In R. Bendix & S. M. Lipset (Eds.), *Class, status, and power.* Glencoe, Ill.: Free Press, 1953. Pp. 411-426.

Neale, D. C., & Proshek, J. M. School-related attitudes of culturally disadvantaged elementary school children. *Journal of Educational Psychology,* 1967, 58, 238-244.

Nebergall, N. S.; Angelino, H.; & Young, H. H. A validation study of the The Self-Activity Inventory as a predictor of adjustment. *Journal of Consulting Psychology,* 1959, 23, 21–24.

Neugarten, B. L. Social class and friendship among school children. *American Journal of Sociology,* 1946, 51, 305–313.

Neugarten, B. L. *Middle age and aging.* Chicago: University of Chicago Press, 1968.

Neuringer, C., & Wandke, L. W. Interpersonal conflicts in persons of high self-concept and low self-concept. *Journal of Social Psychology,* 1966, 68, 313–322.

Newcomb, T. M. The prediction of interpersonal attraction. *American Psychologist,* 1956, 11, 575–586.

Nichols, R. C., & Beck, K. Factors in psychotherapy change. *Journal of Consulting Psychology,* 1960, 24, 388–399.

Nichols, R. C., & Holland, J. L. Prediction of the first-year college performance of high aptitude students. *Psychological Monographs,* 1963, 77 (7, Whole No. 570).

Nisbett, R. E., & Gordon, A. Self-esteem and susceptibility to social influence. *Journal of Personality and Social Psychology,* 1967, 268–276.

Nobles, W. W. Psychological research and the black self-concept: A critical review. *Journal of Social Issues,* 1973, 29, 11–31.

Noel, D. L. Group identification among Negroes: An empirical analysis. *Journal of Social Issues,* 1964, 20, 71–84.

Norfleet, M. W. Personality characteristics of achieving and underachieving high ability senior women. *Personnel and Guidance Journal,* 1968, 46, 976–980.

Norman, R. D., & Daley, M. F. The comparative personality adjustment of superior and inferior readers. *Journal of Educational Psychology,* 1959, 50, 31–36.

Northway, M. L. The sociometry of society: Some facts and fancies. *Canadian Journal of Behavioural Science,* 1971, 3, 18–36.

Northway, M. L., & Detweiler, J. I. Sociometry in education: Children's perception of friends and non-friends. *Sociometry and the Science of Man,* 1955, 18, 271–275.

O'Connell, W. E., & Hanson, P. G. Patients' cognitive changes in human relations training. *Journal of Individual Psychology,* 1970, 26, 57–63.

O'Connor, W. F. *The interrelationships of social perception, sociometric status, personality, and the ability to judge personality traits.* (Research Project MR005.13-5001, Subtask 2, No. 9). U.S. Naval School of Aviation Medicine, Florida: Bureau of Medicine and Surgery, November, 1960.

Oetzel, R. M. Annotated bibliography. In E. E. Maccoby (Ed.), *The development of sex differences.* Stanford, Calif.: Stanford University Press, 1966.

Ogletree, E. Skin color preference of the Negro child. *Journal of Social Psychology*, 1969, 79, 143-144.

O'Hara, R. P. Vocational self concepts and high school achievement. *Vocational Guidance Quarterly*, 1966, 15, 106-112.

Ohnmacht, F. W., & Muro, J. J. Self-acceptance: Some anxiety and cognitive style relationships. *Journal of Psychology*, 1967, 67, 235-239.

Olczak, P. V., & Goldman, J. A. The relationship between self-actualization and psychosocial maturity. *Journal of Clinical Psychology*, 1975, 31, 415-419.

O'Leary, V. E., & Hood, W. R. Latitudes of acceptance, rejection and non-commitment, and attitudes towards self: A factor analytic study. *Journal of Social Psychology*, 1969, 79, 283-284.

Omwake, K. The relation between acceptance of self and acceptance of others shown by three personality inventories. *Journal of Consulting Psychology*, 1954, 18, 443-446.

Osborne, D., & Swenson, W. M. Counseling readiness and changes in self-evaluation during intensive group psychotherapy. *Psychological Reports*, 1972, 31, 646.

Osgood, C. E.; Suci, G. J.; & Tannenbaum, P. H. *The measurement of meaning*. Urbana, Ill.: University of Illinois Press, 1957.

Oskamp, S. Relationship of self-concepts to international attitudes. *Journal of Social Psychology*, 1968, 76, 31-36.

Page, H. A., & Markowitz, G. The relationship of defensiveness to rating scale bias. *Journal of Psychology*, 1956, 41, 431-435.

Palermo, D. S. Racial comparisons and additional normative data on the Children's Manifest Anxiety Scale. *Child Development*, 1959, 30, 53-57.

Palmer, J., & Byrne, D. Attraction toward dominant and submissive strangers: Similarity versus complementarity. *Journal of Experimental Research in Personality*, 1970, 4, 108-115.

Palmer, R. J., & Masling, J. Vocabulary for skin color in Negro and white children. *Developmental Psychology*, 1969, 1, 396-401.

Pannes, E. D. The relationship between self-acceptance and dogmatism in junior-senior high school students. *Journal of Educational Sociology*, 1963, 36, 419-426.

Parker, S., & Kleiner, R. J. Status position, mobility, and ethnic identification of the Negro. *Journal of Social Issues*, 1964, 20, 85-102.

Parker, S., & Kleiner, R. J. *Mental illness in the urban Negro community*. New York: Free Press, 1966.

Parloff, M. B.; Datta, L.; & Handlon, J. H. Personality characteristics which differentiate creative male adolescents and adults. *Journal of Personality*, 1968, 36, 528-552.

Parloff, M. B.; Kelman, H. C.; & Frank, J. D. Comfort, effectiveness and self-awareness as criteria of improvement in psychotherapy. *American Journal of Psychiatry*, 1954, 3, 343-352.

Parsons, L. B.; Peterson, R. A.; & Davids, A. Manifest anxiety and self-concept in emotionally disturbed boys in residential treatment. *Journal of Clinical Psychology*, 1968, 24, 332–335.

Parsons, T. *Family, socialization, and the interaction process*. New York: Free Press, 1953.

Paschal, B. J. The role of self concept in achievement. *Journal of Negro Education*, 1968, 37, 392–396.

Paschal, B. J., & Williams, R. H. Some effects of participation in a summer upward bound program on the self-concept and attitude of the disadvantaged adolescent. *Journal of Negro Education*, 1970, 39, 34–43.

Passow, A. H., & Goldberg, M. The talented youth project: A progress report 1962. *Exceptional Children*, 1962, 28, 223–231.

Paterson, A. Reliability and validity of self-concept of ability scales. In W. B. Brookover; E. L. Erickson; & L. M. Joiner. *Self-concept of ability and school achievement: Relationship of self-concept to achievement in high school*. U.S. Office of Education, Cooperative Research Project No. 2381, Michigan State University, 1967. Pp. 155–172.

Patrick J. R., & Sims, V. M. Personality differences between Negro and white college students, North and South. *Journal of Abnormal and Social Psychology*, 1934, 29, 181–201.

Patterson, C. H. Counseling. In P. R. Farnsworth; O. McNemar; & Q. McNemar (Eds.), *Annual review of psychology*. Palo Alto, Calif.: Annual Reviews, Inc., 1966. Pp. 79–110.

Payne, D. A. The concurrent and predictive validity of an objective measure of academic self-concept. *Educational and Psychological Measurement*, 1962, 22, 773–780.

Payne, D. A., & Farquhar, W. W. The dimensions of an objective measure of academic self-concept. *Journal of Educational Psychology*, 1962, 53, 187–192.

Payne, D. E., & Mussen, P. H. Parent-child relations and father identification among adolescent boys. *Journal of Abnormal and Social Psychology*, 1956, 52, 358–362.

Pearl, D. Ethnocentrism and the self-concept. *Journal of Social Psychology*, 1954, 40, 137–147.

Pearlin, L. I., & Kohn, M. L. Social class, occupation, and parental values: A cross-national study. *American Sociological Review*, 1966, 31, 466–479.

Pechacek, T. F.; Bell, K. F.; Cleland, C. C.; Baum, C.; & Boyle, M. Self-recognition in profoundly retarded males. *Bulletin of the Psychonomic Society*, 1973, 1, 328–330.

Pedersen, D. M. Evaluation of self and others and some personality correlates. *Journal of Psychology*, 1969, 71, 225–244.

Pedersen, D. M., & Stanford, G. H. Personality correlates of children's self-esteem and parental identification. *Psychological Reports*, 1969, 25, 41–42.

Pepitone, A., & Wilpizeski, C. Some consequences of experimental rejection. *Journal of Abnormal and Social Psychology*, 1960, 60, 359-364.

Perkins, C. W., & Shannon, D. T. Three techniques for obtaining self-perceptions in preadolescent boys. *Journal of Personality and Social Psychology*, 1965, 2, 443-447.

Perkins, H. V. Teachers' and peers' perceptions of children's self-concepts. *Child Development*, 1958, 29, 203-220. (a)

Perkins, H. V. Factors influencing change in children's self-concepts. *Child Development*, 1958, 29, 221-230. (b)

Perlin, S., & Butler, R. N. Psychiatric aspects of adaptation to the aging experience. In J. E. Birren; R. N. Butler; S. W. Greenhouse; L. Sokoloff; & M. R. Yarrow (Eds.), *Human aging: A biological and behavioral study* (Public Health Service Publication No. 986). Washington, D.C.: U.S. Government Printing Office, n.d. Pp. 159-213.

Perlmutter, H. V. Relations between the self-image, the image of the foreigner, and the desire to live abroad. *Journal of Psychology*, 1954, 38, 131-137.

Pervin, L. A. Satisfaction and perceived self-environment similarity: A semantic differential study of student-college interaction. *Journal of Personality*, 1967, 35, 623-634.

Pervin, L. A., & Smith, S. H. Further test of the relationship between satisfaction and perceived self-environment similarity. *Perceptual and Motor Skills*, 1968, 26, 835-838.

Peters, D. R. Self-ideal congruence as a function of human relations training. *Journal of Psychology*, 1970, 76, 199-207.

Peters, G. R. Self-conceptions of the aged, age identification, and aging. *Gerontologist*, 1971, 11, 69-73.

Peterson, B., & Ramirez, M. Real ideal self disparity in Negro and Mexican-American children. *Psychology*, 1971, 8, 22-28.

Pettigrew, T. F. *A profile of the Negro American.* Princeton, New Jersey: Van Nostrand, 1964. (a)

Pettigrew, T. F. Negro American personality: Why isn't more known? *Journal of Social Issues*, 1964, 2, 4-23. (b)

Pettigrew, T. F. Social evaluation theory: Convergences and applications, In D. Levine (Ed.), *Nebraska symposium on motivation.* Lincoln, Nebr.: University of Nebraska Press, 1967. Pp. 241-311.

Pfautz, H. W. The current literature on social stratification: Critique and bibliography. *American Journal of Sociology*, 1953, 58, 391-418.

Phillips, B. N. Role change, subjective age, and adjustment: A correlational analysis. *Journal of Gerontology*, 1961, 16, 347-352.

Phillips, B. N. Age changes in accuracy of self-perceptions. *Child Development*, 1963, 34, 1041-1046.

Phillips, B. N.; Hindsman, E.; & Jennings, E. Influence of intelligence on anxiety and perception of self and others. *Child Development*, 1960, 31, 41-46.

Phillips, B. S. A role theory approach to adjustment in old age. *American Sociological Review*, 1957, 22, 212–217.

Phillips, E. L. Attitudes toward self and others: A brief questionnaire report. *Journal of Consulting Psychology*, 1951, 15, 79–81.

Phillips, E. L.; Raiford, A.; & El-Batrawi, S. The Q-sort reevaluated. *Journal of Consulting Psychology*, 1965, 29, 422–425.

Phillips, V. K. Creativity: Performance, profiles, and perceptions. *Journal of Psychology*, 1973, 83, 25–30.

Piaget, J., & Inhelder, B. *The psychology of the child.* New York: Basic Books, 1969.

Piers, E. V. *Manual for the Piers-Harris Children's Self Concept Scale (The Way I Feel About Myself).* Nashville, Tenn.: Counselor Recordings and Tests, 1969.

Piers, E. V. Parent prediction of children's self-concepts. *Journal of Consulting and Clinical Psychology*, 1972, 38, 428–433.

Piers, E. V., & Harris, D. B. Age and other correlates of self-concept in children. *Journal of Educational Psychology*, 1964, 55, 91–95.

Pilisuk, M. Anxiety, self-acceptance, and open-mindedness. *Journal of Clinical Psychology*, 1963, 19, 387–391.

Pintner, R.; Forlano, G.; & Freedman, H. Personality and attitudinal similarity among classroom friends. *Journal of Applied Psychology*, 1937, 21, 48–65.

Pleck, J. H. Self-referent accuracy in self-analytic groups. *Journal of Social Psychology*, 1972, 88, 289–296.

Plutchik, R.; Conte, H.; & Weiner, M. B. Body feelings as measured by the semantic differential. *Proceedings of the 80th Annual Convention of the American Psychological Association*, 1972, 7, 669–670.

Plutchik, R.; Weiner, M. B.; & Conte, H. Studies of body image: I. Body worries and body discomforts. *Journal of Gerontology*, 1971, 26, 344–350.

Pollack, M.; Karp, E.; Kahn, R. L.; & Goldfarb, A. I. Perception of self in institutionalized aged subjects: I. Response patterns to mirror reflection. *Journal of Gerontology*, 1962, 17, 405–408.

Ponzo, Z., & Strowig, R. Relations among sex-role identity and selected intellectual and non-intellectual factors for high school freshmen and seniors. *Journal of Educational Research*, 1973, 67, 137–141.

Porter, L. G., & Stacey, C. L. A study of the relationship between self-ratings and parent-ratings for a group of college students. *Journal of Clinical Psychology*, 1956, 12, 243–248.

Powell, G. J. Self-concept in white and black children. In C. V. Willie; B. M. Kramer; & B. S. Brown, *Racism and mental health.* Pittsburgh: University of Pittsburgh Press, 1973.

Powers, J. M.; Drane, H. T.; Close, B. L.; Noonan, M. P.; Wines, A. M.; & Marshall, J. C. A research note on the self-perception of youth. *American Educational Research Journal*, 1971, 8, 665–670.

Precker, J. A. Similarity of valuings as a factor in selection of peers and near-authority figures. *Journal of Abnormal and Social Psychology*, 1952, 47, 406-414.

Preiss, J. J. Self and role in medical education. In C. Gordon, & K. J. Gergen (Eds.), *The self in social interaction.* New York: Wiley, 1968. Pp. 207-218.

Preston, C. E. Self-perceptions among adolescents. *Psychology in the Schools*, 1967, 4, 254-256.

Preston, C. E., & Gudiksen, K. S. A measure of self perception among older people. *Journal of Gerontology*, 1966, 21, 63-71.

Primavera, L. H.; Simon, W. E.; & Primavera, A. M. The relationship between self-esteem and academic achievement: An investigation of sex differences. *Psychology in the Schools*, 1974, 11, 213-216.

Progoff, I. *Jung's psychology and its social meaning.* New York: Julian Press, 1953.

Proshansky, H., & Newton, P. Colour: The nature and meaning of Negro self-identity. In P. Watson (Ed.), *Psychology and race.* Chicago, Ill.: Aldine, 1973. Pp. 176-212.

Purkey, W. W. Measured and professed personality characteristics of gifted high school students and an analysis of their congruence. *Journal of Educational Research*, 1966, 60, 99-104.

Purkey, W. W.; Graves, W.; & Zellner, M. Self-perceptions of pupils in an experimental elementary school. *Elementary School Journal*, 1970, 71, 166-171.

Pushkin, I., & Veness, T. The development of racial awareness and prejudice in children. In P. Watson (Ed.), *Psychology and race.* Chicago: Aldine, 1973. Pp. 23-42.

Quimby, V. Differences in the self-ideal relationship of an achiever group and an underachiever group. *California Journal of Educational Research*, 1967, 18, 23-31.

Rabinowitz, M. The relationship of self regard to the effectiveness of life experiences. *Journal of Counseling Psychology*, 1966, 13, 139-143.

Radke, M.; Sutherland, J.; & Rosenberg, P. Racial attitudes of children. *Sociometry*, 1950, 13, 154-171.

Radke, M., & Trager, H. G. Children's perceptions of the social roles of Negroes and whites. *Journal of Psychology*, 1950, 29, 3-33.

Radke, M.; Trager, H.; & Davis, H. Social perceptions and attitudes of children. *Genetic Psychology Monographs*, 1949, 40, 327-447.

Raimy, V. C. Self-reference in counseling interviews. *Journal of Consulting Psychology*, 1948, 12, 153-163.

Rainwater, L. Crucible of identity: The Negro lower-class family. *Daedalus*, 1966, 95, 172-216.

Ramos, E. Adolescent nisei self-image. *Pakistan Journal of Psychology*, 1974, 7, 55-60.

Rappaport, A. F.; Payne, D.; & Steinmann, A. Perceptual differences between married and single college women for the concepts of self, ideal woman, and men's ideal woman. *Journal of Marriage and the Family*, 1970, 32, 441–442.

Rappaport, J., & Chinsky, J. M. Accurate empathy: Confusion of a construct. *Psychological Bulletin*, 1972, 77, 400–404.

Raskin, N. J. An objective study of the locus-of-evaluation factor in psychotherapy. In W. W. Wolff, & J. A. Precker (Eds.), *Success in psychotherapy*. New York: Grune and Stratton, 1952. Chapter 6.

Reader, N., & English, H. B. Personality factors in adolescent female friendships. *Journal of Consulting Psychology*, 1947, 11, 212–220.

Reddy, W. B. On affection, group composition, and self-actualization in sensitivity training. *Journal of Consulting and Clinical Psychology*, 1972, 38, 211–214.

Reddy, W. B. The impact of sensitivity training on self-actualization: A one-year follow-up. *Small Group Behavior*, 1973, 4, 407–413.

Reece, C. Black self-concept. *Children Today*, 1974, March–April, 24–26.

Reece, M. M. Masculinity and femininity: A factor analytic study. *Psychological Reports*, 1964, 14, 123–139.

Reed, H. J. An investigation of the relationship between teaching effectiveness and the teacher's attitude of acceptance. *Journal of Experimental Education*, 1953, 21, 277–325.

Rees, M. E., & Goldman, M. Some relationships between creativity and personality. *Journal of General Psychology*, 1961, 65, 145–161.

Reese, H. W. Relationships between self-acceptance and sociometric choices. *Journal of Abnormal and Social Psychology*, 1961, 62, 472–474.

Reeves, T. G., & Shearer, R. A. Differences among campus groups on a measure of self-actualization. *Psychological Reports*, 1973, 32, 135–140.

Rehm, L. P., & Marston, A. R. Reduction of social anxiety through modification of self-reinforcement: An instigation therapy technique. *Journal of Consulting and Clinical Psychology*, 1968, 32, 565–574.

Reichard, S.; Livson, F.; & Petersen, P. G. *Aging and personality—a study of eighty-seven older men*. New York: Wiley, 1962.

Reidy, J. J., & Colvin, R. W. Voice recognition as a measure of self-attitude and relatedness. *A.M.A. Archives of Neurology and Psychiatry*, 1959, 81, 636–638.

Reilly, M. S.; Commins, W. D.; & Stefic, E. C. The complementarity of personality needs in friendship choice. *Journal of Abnormal and Social Psychology*, 1960, 61, 292–294.

Reiss, A. J., Jr., & Rhodes, A. L. Are educational norms and goals of conforming, truant, and delinquent adolescents influenced by group position in American society? *Journal of Negro Education*, 1959, 28, 252–267.

Renzaglia, G. A.; Henry, D. R.; & Rybolt, G. A., Jr. Estimation and measurement of personality characteristics and correlates of their congruence. *Journal of Counseling Psychology*, 1962, 9, 71–78.

Reschly, D. J., & Mittman, A. The relationship of self-esteem status and task ambiguity to the self-reinforcement behavior of children. *Developmental Psychology*, 1973, 9, 16–19.

Rice, L. N. Therapist's style of participation and case outcome. *Journal of Consulting Psychology*, 1965, 29, 155–160.

Richards, H. C., & McCandless, B. R. Socialization dimensions among five-year-old slum children. *Journal of Educational Psychology*, 1972, 63, 44–55.

Richards, J. M., Jr. A factor analytic study of the self-ratings of college freshmen. *Educational and Psychological Measurement*, 1966, 26, 861–870.

Richardson, H. M. Community of values as a factor in friendships of college and adult women. *Journal of Social Psychology*, 1940, 11, 303–312.

Richardson, M. S. Self-concepts and role concepts in the career orientation of college women. *Journal of Counseling Psychology*, 1975, 22, 122–126.

Richmond, B. O., & Dalton, J. L. Teacher ratings and self concept reports of retarded pupils. *Exceptional Children*, 1973, 40, 178–183.

Richmond, B. O.; Mason, R. L.; & Padgett, H. G. Self-concept and perception of others. *Journal of Humanistic Psychology*, 1972, 12, 103–111.

Riley, M. W., & Foner, A. *Aging and society.* Vol. 1. *An inventory of research findings.* New York: Russell Sage Foundation, 1968.

Ringness, T. A. Self concept of children of low, average, and high intelligence. *American Journal of Mental Deficiency*, 1961, 65, 453–461.

Ritter, B. Effect of contact desensitization on avoidance behavior, fear ratings, and self-evaluative statements. *Proceedings of the 76th Annual Convention of the American Psychological Association*, 1968, 3, 527–528.

Rivlin, L. G. Creativity and the self-attitudes and sociability of high school students. *Journal of Educational Psychology*, 1959, 50, 147–152.

Rizzo, R., & Vinacke, E. Self-actualization and the meaning of critical experience. *Journal of Humanistic Psychology*, 1975, 15, 19–30.

Roberts, S. O., & Horton, C. P. Extent of and effects of desegregation. In K. S. Miller & R. M. Dreger (Eds.), *Comparative studies of blacks and whites in the United States.* New York: Seminar Press, 1973.

Roe, A., & Siegelman, M. A parent-child relations questionnaire. *Child Development*, 1963, 34, 355–369.

Roen, S. R. Personality and Negro-White intelligence. *Journal of Abnormal and Social Psychology*, 1960, 61, 148–150.

Rogers, C. R. Client-centered therapy. Boston: Houghton-Mifflin, 1951.

Rogers, C. R. Changes in the maturity of behavior as related to therapy. In C. R. Rogers & R. F. Dymond (Eds.), *Psychotherapy and personality change.* Chicago: University of Chicago Press, 1954. Pp. 215–237.

Rogers, C. R. The necessary and sufficient conditions of therapeutic personality change. *Journal of Consulting Psychology*, 1957, 21, 95–103.

Rogers, C. R. A theory of therapy, personality, and interpersonal relationships, as developed in the client-centered framework. In S. Koch (Ed.), *Psychology: A study of a science.* Vol. 3. New York: McGraw-Hill, 1959. Pp. 184–256.

Rogers, C. R. Psychotherapy today or where do we go from here? *American Journal of Psychotherapy*, 1963, 17, 5-16.

Rogers, C. R., & Dymond, R. F. (Eds.), *Psychotherapy and personality change.* Chicago: University of Chicago Press, 1954.

Rogers, C. R.; Gendlin, E. T.; Kiesler, D. J.; & Truax, C. B. *The therapeutic relationship and its impact: A study of psychotherapy and schizophrenics.* Madison: University of Wisconsin Press, 1967.

Rohrer, J. H., & Edmonson, M. S. *The eighth generation.* New York: Harper & Brothers, 1960.

Rokeach, M. The nature and meaning of dogmatism. *Psychological Review,* 1954, 61, 194-204.

Rokeach, M. *The open and closed mind: Investigations into the nature of belief systems and personality systems.* New York: Basic Books, 1960.

Rokeach, M. The double agreement phenomenon: Three hypotheses. *Psychological Review*, 1963, 70, 304-309.

Rokeach, M. Authoritarianism scales and response bias: Comment on Peabody's paper. *Psychological Bulletin*, 1967, 67, 349-355.

Rokeach, M. *Beliefs, attitudes and values.* San Francisco: Jossey-Bass, 1968.

Rokeach, M. *The nature of human values.* New York: Free Press, 1973.

Rokeach, M., & Fruchter, B. A factorial study of dogmatism and related concepts. *Journal of Abnormal and Social Psychology*, 1956, 53, 356-360.

Rosaldo, M. Z. Woman, culture, and society: A theoretical overview. In M. Z. Rosaldo & L. Lamphere (Eds.), *Woman, culture, and society.* Stanford, Calif.: Stanford University Press, 1974. Pp. 17-42.

Rose, A. M. The subculture of the aging: A framework for research in social gerontology. In A. M. Rose & W. A. Peterson (Eds.), *Older people and their social world.* Philadelphia: Davis, 1965. Pp. 3-16.

Rosen, B. C. Race, ethnicity and the achievement syndrome. *American Sociological Review*, 1959, 24, 47-60.

Rosenbaum, M. E., & deCharms, R. Direct and vicarious reduction of hostility. *Journal of Abnormal and Social Psychology*, 1960, 60, 105-111.

Rosenbaum, M. E., & deCharms, R. Self-esteem and overt expressions of aggression. In N. F. Washburne (Ed.), *Decisions, values, and groups.* New York: Macmillan, 1962. Pp. 291-303.

Rosenbaum, M. E.; Horne, W. C.; & Chalmers, D. K. Level of self-esteem and the learning of imitation and nonimitation. *Journal of Personality*, 1962, 30, 147-156.

Rosenbaum, M. E., & Stanners, R. F. Self-esteem, manifest hostility, and expression of hostility. *Journal of Abnormal and Social Psychology*, 1961, 63, 646-649.

Rosenberg, M. Perceptual obstacles to class consciousness. *Social Forces*, 1953, 32, 22-27.

Rosenberg, M. Parental interest and children's self-conceptions. *Sociometry*, 1963, 26, 35-49.

Rosenberg, M. *Society and the adolescent self image.* Princeton, N.J.: Princeton University Press, 1965.

Rosenberg, M. Which significant others? *American Behavioral Scientist,* 1973, 16, 829-860.

Rosenberg, M. The dissonant context and the adolescent self-concept. In S. Dragastin & G. H. Elder (Eds.), *Adolescence in the life cycle: Psychological change and social context.* Washington, D.C.: Hemisphere Publications, 1975. Pp. 97-116.

Rosenberg, M., & Simmons, R. G. *Black and white self-esteem: The urban school child.* Washington, D.C. American Sociological Association, 1972.

Rosencranz, H., & McNevin, T. A factor analysis of attitudes toward the aged. *Gerontologist,* 1969, 9, 55-59.

Rosenfeld, H. M. Social choice conceived as a level of aspiration. *Journal of Abnormal and Social Psychology,* 1964, 68, 491-499.

Rosenfeld, H. M., & Jackson, J. Temporal mediation of the similarity-attraction hypothesis. *Journal of Personality,* 1965, 33, 649-656.

Rosengren, W. R., & Davids, A. Self-esteem, social perception, and social status in a group of child psychiatric patients. *Perceptual and Motor Skills,* 1961, 13, 63-72.

Rosenkrantz, P.; Vogel, S.; Bee, H.; Broverman, I.; & Broverman, D. Sex-role stereotypes and self-concepts in college students. *Journal of Consulting and Clinical Psychology,* 1968, 32, 287-295.

Rosenman, S. Changes in the representation of self, other, and interrelationship in client-centered therapy. *Journal of Counseling Psychology,* 1955, 2, 271-278.

Rosenthal, J. H. Self-esteem in dyslexic children. *Academic Therapy,* 1973, 9, 27-39.

Rosenthal, R. Interpersonal expectations: Effects of the experimenter's hypothesis. In R. Rosenthal & R. L. Rosnow (Eds.), *Artifact in behavioral research.* New York: Academic Press, 1969. Pp. 181-277.

Rosow, I. *Social integration of the aged.* New York: Free Press, 1967.

Ross, S., & Walters, J. Perceptions of a sample of university men concerning women. *Journal of Genetic Psychology,* 1973, 122, 329-336.

Roth, R. M. The role of self-concept in achievement. *Journal of Experimental Education,* 1959, 27, 265-281.

Roth, R. M. The adjustment of Negro college students at Hampton Institute. *Journal of Negro Education,* 1961, 30, 72-74.

Roth, R. W. The effects of "black studies" on Negro fifth grade students. *Journal of Negro Education,* 1969, 38, 435-439.

Rothbart, M. K., & Maccoby, E. E. Parents' differential reactions to sons and daughters. *Journal of Personality and Social Psychology,* 1966, 4, 237-243.

Rubin, I. M. Increased self-acceptance: A means of reducing prejudice. *Journal of Personality and Social Psychology,* 1967, 5, 233-238. (a)

Rubin, I. M. The reduction of prejudice through laboratory training. *Journal of Applied Behavioral Science,* 1967, 3, 29-50. (b)

Rubin, Z., & Moore, J. C., Jr. Assessment of subjects' suspicions. *Journal of Personality and Social Psychology,* 1971, 17, 163-170.

Rubinstein, E. A., & Lorr, M. A comparison of terminators and remainers in out-patient psychotherapy. *Journal of Clinical Psychology,* 1956, 12, 345-349.

Rubinstein, E. A., & Lorr, M. Self and peer personality ratings of psychotherapists. *Journal of Clinical Psychology,* 1957, 13, 295-298.

Rudikoff, E. C. A comparative study of the changes in the concepts of the self, the ordinary person, and the ideal in eight cases. In C. R. Rogers & R. F. Dymond (Eds.), *Psychotherapy and personality change.* Chicago: University of Chicago Press, 1954. Pp. 85-98.

Rule, B. G., & Hewitt, D. Factor structure of anti-semitism, self-concept, and cognitive structure. *Personality: An International Journal,* 1970, 1, 319-332.

Rule, B. G., & Rehill, D. Distraction and self-esteem effects on attitude change. *Journal of Personality and Social Psychology,* 1970, 15, 359-365.

Rumaldo, Z. J., & Kuvlesky, W. P. Ethnic group identity and orientations toward educational attainment: A comparison of Mexican American and Anglo boys. Paper presented at the annual meeting of the Southwestern Sociological Association, Dallas, Texas, April, 1968.

Russell, D. H. What does research say about self-evaluation? *Journal of Educational Research,* 1953, 46, 561-571.

Rychlak, J. F. The similarity, compatibility, or incompatibility of needs in interpersonal selection. *Journal of Personality and Social Psychology,* 1965, 2, 334-340.

Rychlak, J. F. Personality factors in self- and peer-evaluations of WISC performance intelligence among middle-class children. *Journal of Special Education,* 1970, 4, 269-277.

St. John, N. The effect of segregation on the aspirations of Negro youth. *Harvard Educational Review,* 1966, 36, 284-294.

St. John, N. The elementary classroom as a frog pond: Self-concept, sense of control and social context. *Social Forces,* 1971, 49, 581-595.

Sakowitz, M. L., & Hirschman, R. Self-ideal congruency and therapeutic skill development in nonpaid paraprofessionals. *Journal of Community Psychology,* 1975, 3, 275-280.

Saleh, S. D., & Grygier, T. G. Self-perception of productivity before retirement. *Personnel Administration,* 1966, 29, 35-39.

Sampson, E. E., & Hancock, F. T. An examination of the relationship between ordinal position, personality, and conformity: An extension, replication, and partial verification. *Journal of Personality and Social Psychology,* 1967, 5, 398-407.

Samuels, S. C. An investigation into the self concepts of lower- and middle-class black and white kindergarten children. *Journal of Negro Education,* 1973, 42, 467-472.

Sanders, E. M.; Mefferd, R. B.; & Bown, O. H. Verbal-quantitative ability and certain personality and metabolic characteristics of male college students. *Educational and Psychological Measurement,* 1960, 20, 491-503.

Sanford, F. H. *Authoritarianism and leadership: A study of the follower's orientation to authority.* Philadelphia: Institute for Research in Human Relations, 1950.

Sanford, N. The dynamics of identification. *Psychological Review,* 1955, 62, 106-118.

Sappenfield, B. R., & Balogh, B. Perceived attractiveness of social stimuli as related to their perceived similarity to self. *Journal of Psychology,* 1970, 74, 105-111.

Sarason, I. G., & Koenig, K. P. Relationships of test anxiety and hostility to description of self and parents. *Journal of Personality and Social Psychology,* 1965, 2, 617-621.

Sarason, I. G., & Winkel, G. H. Individual differences among subjects and experimenters and subjects' self-descriptions. *Journal of Personality and Social Psychology,* 1966, 3, 448-457.

Sarbin, T. R., & Rosenberg, B. G. Contributions to role-taking theory: IV. A method for obtaining a qualitative estimate of the self. *Journal of Social Psychology,* 1955, 42, 71-81.

Sarnoff, I. Identification with the aggressor: Some personality correlates of anti-Semitism among Jews. *Journal of Personality,* 1951, 20, 199-218.

Sattler, J. M. Racial "experimenter effects" in experimentation, testing, interviewing, and psychotherapy. *Psychological Bulletin,* 1970, 73, 137-160.

Sattler, J. M. Racial experimenter effects. In K. S. Miller and R. M. Dreger (Eds.), *Comparative studies of blacks and whites in the United States.* New York: Seminar Press, 1973. Pp. 7-32.

Satz, P., & Baraff, A. S. Changes in the relation between self-concepts and ideal-concepts of psychotics consequent upon therapy. *Journal of General Psychology,* 1962, 67, 291-298.

Scandrette, O. C. Classroom choice status related to scores on components of the California Test of Personality. *Journal of Educational Research,* 1953, 47, 291-296.

Schaar, K. Indian self-image "positive" despite social conditions. *American Psychological Association Monitor,* 1974, 5, 4.

Schaefer, C. E. The self-concept of creative adolescents. *Journal of Psychology,* 1969, 72, 233-242.

Schaefer, C. E. Follow-up study of a creativity scale for the Adjective Check List. *Psychological Reports,* 1972, 30, 662.

Schaefer, C. E. A five-year follow-up study of the self-concept of creative adolescents. *Journal of Genetic Psychology,* 1973, 123, 163-170.

Schaefer, C. E., & Anastasi, A. A biographical inventory for identifying creativity in adolescent boys. *Journal of Applied Psychology,* 1968, 52, 42-48.

Schaefer, E. S. A circumplex model for maternal behavior. *Journal of Abnormal and Social Psychology,* 1959, 59, 226-235.

Schaefer, E. S., & Bell, R. Q. Development of a parental attitude research instrument. *Child Development,* 1958, 29, 339-361.

Schaie, K. W. A general model for the study of developmental problems. *Psychological Bulletin,* 1965, 64, 92-107.

Schaie, K. W. Age changes and age differences. *Gerontologist,* 1967, 7, 128-132.

Schaie, K. W., & Strother, C. R. Cognitive and personality variables in college graduates of advanced age. In G. A. Talland (Ed.), *Human aging and behavior.* New York: Academic Press, 1968. Pp. 281-308.

Scheerer, E. T. An analysis of the relationship between acceptance of and respect for self and acceptance of and respect for others in ten counseling cases. *Journal of Consulting Psychology,* 1949, 13, 169-175.

Schlenker, B. R. Self-image maintenance and enhancement: Attitude change following counterattitudinal behavior. *Proceedings of the 81st Annual Convention of the American Psychological Association,* 1973, 8, 271-272.

Schlenker, B. R. Social psychology and science. *Journal of Personality and Social Psychology,* 1974, 29, 1-15.

Schneider, L., & Lysgaard, S. The deferred gratification pattern: A preliminary study. *American Sociological Review,* 1953, 18, 142-149.

Schofield, L. F., & Caple, R. B. Self-concepts of mature and young women students. *Journal of College Student Personnel,* 1971, 12, 297-302.

Schooler, C. Birth order effects: Not here, not now! *Psychological Bulletin,* 1972, 78, 161-175.

Schooley, M. Personality resemblances among married couples. *Journal of Abnormal and Social Psychology,* 1936, 31, 340-347.

Schott, J. F.; Burtness, K. H.; & Wilson, K. W. Breaking down barriers with alcoholics: Marathons. *Proceedings of the 81st Annual Convention of the American Psychological Association,* 1973, 8, 389-390.

Schroeder, C. C. Sex differences and growth toward self-actualization during the freshman year. *Psychological Reports,* 1973, 32, 416-418.

Schurr, K. T.; Towne, R. C.; & Joiner, L. M. Trends in self-concept of ability over 2 years of special-class placement. *Journal of Special Education,* 1972, 6, 161-166.

Schwab, J. J.; Clemmons, R. S.; & Marder, L. The self concept: Psychosomatic applications. *Psychosomatics,* 1966, 7, 1-5.

Schwartz, J. L., & Dubitzky, M. Changes in anxiety, mood, and self-esteem resulting from an attempt to stop smoking. *American Journal of Psychiatry*, 1968, 124, 1580-1584.

Schwendiman, G.; Larsen, K. S., & Dunn, F. Social position, social desirability and self-esteem. *Psychological Reports*, 1970, 27, 117-118.

Sears, R. R. Identification as a form of behavioral development. In D. B. Harris (Ed.), *The concept of development*. Minneapolis: University of Minnesota Press, 1957. Pp. 149-161.

Sears, R. R. Relation of early socialization experiences to self-concepts and gender role in middle childhood. *Child Development*, 1970, 41, 267-289.

Secord, P. F. Consistency theory and self-referent behavior. In R. P. Abelson; E. Aronson; W. J. McGuire; T. M. Newcomb; M. J. Rosenberg; & P. H. Tannenbaum (Eds.), *Theories of cognitive consistency*. Chicago: Rand McNally, 1968. Pp. 349-354.

Secord, P. F., & Backman, C. W. Interpersonal congruency, perceived similarity, and friendship. *Sociometry*, 1964, 27, 115-127.

Seeman, W.; Nidich, S.; & Banta, T. Influence of transcendental meditation on a measure of self-actualization. *Journal of Counseling Psychology*, 1972, 19, 184-187.

Segal, D. R.; Segal, M. W., & Knoke, D. Status inconsistency and self-evaluation. *Sociometry*, 1970, 33, 347-357.

Seitz, F. C. The impact of videotape confrontation and/or discussion on depression. *Psychology*, 1971, 8, 77-81.

Serot, N., & Teevan, R. C. Perception of the parent-child relationship and its relation to child adjustment. *Child Development*, 1961, 32, 373-378.

Seward, G. H. *Psychotherapy and culture conflict*. New York: Ronald Press, 1956.

Seward, G. H. The relation between psychoanalytic school and value problems in therapy. *American Journal of Psychoanalysis*, 1962, 22, 138-152.

Seward, G. H., & Larson, W. R. Adolescent concepts of social sex roles in the United States and the two Germanies. *Human Development*, 1968, 11, 217-248.

Sewell, W. H. Social class and childhood personality. *Sociometry*, 1961, 24, 340-356.

Sewell, W. H.; Haller, A. O.; & Straus, M. A. Social status and educational and occupational aspiration. *American Sociological Review*, 1957, 22, 67-73.

Shanas, E. *The health of older people: A social survey*. Cambridge: Harvard University Press, 1962.

Sharan, M. B. Social change and the self-concept. *Journal of Social Psychology*, 1974, 92, 325-326.

Sharma, S. Self-acceptance and academic achievement—a review of research. *Indian Educational Review*, 1971, 6, 118-125.

Shaw, M. C., & Alves, G. J. The self-concept of bright academic underachievers: Continued. *Personnel and Guidance Journal*, 1963, 42, 401-403.

Shaw, M. C.; Edson, K.; & Bell, H. M. The self-concept of bright underachieving high school students as revealed by an adjective check list. *Personnel and Guidance Journal*, 1960, 39, 193-196.

Shaw, M. E. The self-image of black and white pupils in an integrated school. *Journal of Personality*, 1974, 42, 12-22.

Shen, E. The validity of self estimates. *Journal of Educational Psychology*, 1925, 16, 104-107.

Shepard, L. A., & Glass, G. V. A multitrait-multimethod approach to the construct validation of "acceptance of self" and "acceptance of others." (Project No. 1-H-039) Office of Education, National Center for Educational Research and Development, November, 1972.

Sherman, J. A. *On the psychology of women: A survey of empirical studies.* Springfield, Ill.: Charles C Thomas, 1971.

Sherriffs, A. C., & Jarrett, R. F. Sex differences in attitudes about sex differences. *Journal of Psychology*, 1953, 35, 161-168.

Sherriffs, A. C., & McKee, J. P. Qualitative aspects of beliefs about men and women. *Journal of Personality*, 1957, 25, 452-464.

Sherwood, J. J. Self identity and referent others. *Sociometry*, 1965, 28, 66-81.

Sherwood, J. J. Increased self-evaluation as a function of ambiguous evaluations by referent others. *Sociometry*, 1967, 30, 404-409.

Shlien, J. M. Cross-theoretical criteria for the valuation of psychotherapy. *American Journal of Psychotherapy*, 1966, 20, 125-134.

Shlien, J. M.; Mosak, H. H.; & Dreikurs, R. Effect of time limits: A comparison of two psychotherapies. *Journal of Counseling Psychology*, 1962, 9, 31-34.

Short, J. F., Jr., & Strodtbeck, F. L. *Group process and gang delinquency.* Chicago: University of Chicago Press, 1965.

Shostrom, E. L. An inventory for the measure of self-actualization. *Educational and Psychological Measurement*, 1964, 24, 207-218.

Shostrom, E. L. *EITS Manual for the Personal Orientation Inventory.* San Diego: Calif.: Educational and Industrial Testing Service, 1966.

Shostrom, E. L., & Knapp, R. R. The relationship of a measure of self-actualization (POI) to a measure of pathology (MMPI) and to therapeutic growth. *American Journal of Psychotherapy*, 1966, 20, 193-202.

Shrauger, J. S., & Jones, S. C. Social validation and interpersonal evaluations. *Journal of Experimental Social Psychology*, 1968, 315-323.

Shrauger, J. S., & Lund, A. K. Self-evaluations and reactions to evaluations from others. *Journal of Personality*, 1975, 43, 94-108.

Shuey, A. M. *The testing of Negro intelligence.* (2nd ed.) New York: Social Science Press, 1966.

Shulman, L. S. Negro-white differences in employability, self-concept and related measures among adolescents classified as mentally handicapped. *Journal of Negro Education,* 1968, 37, 227-240.

Siegenthaler, B. M., & Flamm, M. G. Subjects' self-judgments of speech adequacy and judgments by trained observers. *Journal of Speech and Hearing Disorders,* 1961, 26, 244-251.

Sieka, F. L. Facial disfigurement and sex-role esteem. *Rehabilitation Counseling Bullletin,* 1974, 18, 90-98.

Sigall, H., & Aronson, E. Opinion change and the gain-loss model of interpersonal attraction. *Journal of Experimental Social Psychology,* 1967, 3, 178-188.

Silverman, I. Differential effects of ego threat upon persuasibility for high and low self-esteem subjects. *Journal of Abnormal and Social Psychology,* 1964, 69, 567-572.

Silverman, I. Reply to Levonian. *Psychological Reports,* 1970, 27, 545-546.

Silverman, I.; Ford, L.; & Morganti, J. Inter-related effects of social desirability, sex, self-esteem, and complexity of argument on persuasibility. *Journal of Personality,* 1966, 34, 555-568.

Silverman, I.; Shulman, A. D.; & Wiesenthal, D. L. Effects of deceiving and debriefing psychological subjects on performance in later experiments. *Journal of Personality and Social Psychology,* 1970, 14, 203-212.

Simmons, R. G., & Rosenberg, M. Functions of children's perceptions of the stratification system. *American Sociological Review,* 1971, 36, 235-249.

Simmons, R. G.; Rosenberg, F., & Rosenberg, M. Disturbance in the self-image at adolescence. *American Sociological Review,* 1973, 38, 553-568.

Simon, R. J. An assessment of racial awareness, preference, and self identity among white and adopted non-white children. *Social Problems,* 1974, 22, 43-57.

Simon, W. E. Some sociometric evidence for validity of Coopersmith's Self-Esteem Inventory. *Perceptual and Motor Skills,* 1972, 34, 93-94.

Simon, W. E., & Bernstein, E. The relationship between self-esteem and perceived reciprocal liking: A sociometric test of the theory of cognitive balance. *Journal of Psychology,* 1971, 79, 197-201.

Simon, W. E., & Simon, M. G. Self-esteem, intelligence and standardized academic achievement. *Psychology in the Schools,* 1975, 12, 97-100.

Simpson, I. H., Back, K. W.; & McKinney, J. C. Work and retirement. In I. Simpson & J. C. McKinney (Eds.), *Social aspects of aging.* Durham, N.C.: University of North Carolina Press, 1966. Pp. 45-54.

Sims, V. M. *Sims Score Card for Socio-economic Status.* Bloomington, Ill.: Public School Publishing Co., 1927.

Sims, V. M. Some correlates of social-class identification among high-school and college students. *School Review,* 1952, 60, 160-163.

Singer, R. D., & Feshbach, S. Some relationships between manifest anxiety, authoritarian tendencies, and modes of reaction to frustration. *Journal of Abnormal and Social Psychology*, 1959, 59, 404-408.

Singer, S. L., & Stefflre, B. A note on racial differences in job values and desires. *Journal of Social Psychology*, 1956, 43, 333-337.

Singh, U. P., & Prasad, T. Self-esteem, social-esteem, and conformity behaviour. *Psychologia: An International Journal of Psychology in the Orient*, 1973, 16, 61-68.

Sinha, S. N., & Sinha, L. N. Positive and negative self-references in high and low anxious subjects during a free verbalization situation. *Journal of Psychological Researches*, 1968, 12, 71-74.

Skager, R. W., & Braskamp, L. A. *Changes in self-ratings and life goals as related to student accomplishment in college.* (ACT Research Report No. 16). Iowa City, Iowa: American College Testing Program, 1966.

Skolnick, P. Reactions to personal evaluations: A failure to replicate. *Journal of Personality and Social Psychology*, 1971, 18, 62-67.

Smart, M. S., & Smart, R. C. Self-esteem and social-personal orientation of Indian 12- and 18-year-olds. *Psychological Reports*, 1970, 27, 107-115.

Smith, C. R. The relationship between self-concept and success in the freshman year of college. *New Outlook for the Blind*, 1972, 66, 84-89.

Smith, H. P., & Abramson, M. Racial and family experience correlates of mobility aspiration. *Journal of Negro Education*, 1962, 31, 117-124.

Smith, J. The group status of the aged in an urban social structure. In I. H. Simpson & J. C. McKinney (Eds.), *Social aspects of aging.* Durham, N.C.: Duke University Press, 1966. Pp. 210-225. (a)

Smith, J. The narrowing social world of the aged. In I. H. Simpson & J. C. McKinney (Eds.), *Social aspects of aging.* Durham, N.C.: Duke University Press, 1966. Pp. 226-242. (b)

Smith, J., & Turk, H. Considerations bearing on a study of the role of the aged in community integration. In I. H. Simpson & J. C. McKinney (Eds.), *Social aspects of aging.* Durham, N.C.: Duke University Press, 1966. Pp. 195-209.

Smith, J. M., & Schaefer, C. E. Development of a creativity scale for the Adjective Check List. *Psychological Reports*, 1969, 25, 87-92.

Smith, K. H. Ego strength and perceived competence as conformity variables. *Journal of Abnormal and Social Psychology*, 1961, 62, 169-171.

Smith, M. B. The self and cognitive consistency. In R. P. Abelson; E. Aronson; W. J. McGuire; T. M. Newcomb; M. J. Rosenberg; & P. H. Tannenbaum (Eds.), *Theories of cognitive consistency: A sourcebook.* Chicago: Rand McNally, 1968. Pp. 366-372.

Smith, R. B.; Tedeschi, J. T.; Brown, R. C.; & Lindskold, S. Correlations between trust, self-esteem, sociometric choice, and internal-external control. *Psychological Reports*, 1973, 32, 739-743.

Snoek, J. D. Some effects of rejection upon attraction to a group. *Journal of Abnormal and Social Psychology,* 1962, 64, 175-182.

Snyder, R. T. Personality adjustment, self attitudes, and anxiety differences in retarded adolescents. *American Journal of Mental Deficiency,* 1966, 71, 33-41.

Snyder, R.; Jefferson, W.; & Strauss, R. Personality variables as determiners of academic achievement of the mildly retarded. *Mental Retardation,* 1965, 3, 15-18.

Snygg, D., & Combs, A. W. *Individual behavior: A new frame of reference for psychology.* New York: Harper, 1949.

Soares, A. T., & Soares, L. M. Self-perceptions of culturally disadvantaged children. *American Educational Research Journal,* 1969, 6, 31-45.

Soares, A. T., & Soares, L. M. Interpersonal and self-perceptions of disadvantaged and advantaged high school students. *Proceedings of the 78th Annual Convention of the American Psychological Association,* 1970, 5, 457-458. (a)

Soares, A. T., & Soares, L. M. Self-concepts of disadvantaged and advantaged students. *Child Study Journal,* 1970, 1, 69-73. (b)

Soares, A. T., & Soares, L. M. Critique of Soares and Soares' "Self-perceptions of culturally disadvantaged children"—a reply. *American Educational Research Journal,* 1970, 7, 631-635. (c)

Soares, A. T., & Soares, L. M. Expectancy, achievement, and self-concept correlates in disadvantaged and advantaged youths. *Proceedings of the 79th Annual Convention of the American Psychological Association,* 1971, 6, 561-562.

Soares, A. T., & Soares, L. M. Self-concept differential in disadvantaged and advantaged students. *Proceedings of the 80th Annual Convention of the American Psychological Association,* 1972, 7, 195-196.

Soares, L. M., & Soares, A. T. Self concepts of disadvantaged and advantaged students. *Proceedings of the 78th Annual Convention of the American Psychological Association,* 1970, 5, 653-654.

Soares, L. M., & Soares, A. T. Interpersonal perceptions of disadvantaged children. *Proceedings of the 79th Annual Convention of the American Psychological Association,* 1971, 6, 261-262.

Sopchak, A. P. Parental "identification" and "tendency toward disorders" as measured by the Minnesota Multiphasic Personality Inventory. *Journal of Abnormal and Social Psychology,* 1952, 47, 159-165.

Spangler, D. P., & Thomas, C. W. The effects of age, sex, and physical disability upon manifest needs. *Journal of Counseling Psychology,* 1962, 9, 313-319.

Spence, J. T.; Helmreich, R.; & Stapp, J. The personal attributes questionnaire: A measure of sex role stereotype and masculinity-femininity. *JSAS Catalog of Selected Documents in Psychology,* 1974, 4, 43-44.

Spence, J. T.; Helmreich, R.; & Stapp, J. Ratings of self and peers on sex role attributes and their relation to self-esteem and conceptions of masculinity and femininity. *Journal of Personality and Social Psychology*, 1975, 32, 29-39.

Spiegel, D. Psychological health-sickness and the perception of self and others. *Journal of Clinical Psychology*, 1970, 26, 274-276.

Spielberger, C. D., & Gorsuch, R. L. *Mediating processes in verbal conditioning.* Educational Publishing Service, Department of Psychology, Vanderbilt University, 1966.

Sprey, J. Sex differences in occupational choice patterns among Negro adolescents. *Social Problems*, 1962, 10, 11-23.

Springer, D. U. Awareness of racial differences in pre-school children in Hawaii. *Genetic Psychology Monographs*, 1950, 41, 215-270.

Stanley, J. C. Reliability. In R. L. Thorndike (Ed.), *Educational measurement.* (2nd ed.) Washington, D.C.: American Council on Education, 1971. Pp. 356-442.

Star, K. H. Ideal-self response set and Maudsley Personality Inventory scores. *Psychological Reports*, 1962, 11, 708.

Start, K. B. Overestimation of personal abilities and success at first year university examination. *Journal of Social Psychology*, 1963, 59, 337-345.

Steger, J. A.; Simmons, W. L.; & Lavelle, S. Accuracy of prediction of own performance as a function of locus of control. *Psychological Reports*, 1973, 33, 59-62.

Stein, M. I. (Ed.). *Contemporary psychotherapies.* Glencoe, Ill.: Free Press, 1961.

Steinmann, A. A study of the concept of the feminine role of 51 middle-class American families. *Genetic Psychology Monographs*, 1963, 67, 275-352.

Steinmann, A.; Doherty, M. A.; & Fox, D. J. Perceptions of women religious regarding the female role. *National Catholic Guidance Conference Journal,* 1970, 15, 43-54.

Steinmann, A., & Fox, D. J. Male-female perceptions of the female role in the United States. *The Journal of Psychology*, 1966, 64, 265-276.

Steinmann, A., & Fox, D. J. Specific areas of agreement and conflict in women's self-perception and their perception of men's ideal woman in two South American urban communities and an urban community in the United States. *Journal of Marriage and the Family*, 1969, 31, 281-289.

Steinmann, A., & Fox, D. J. Attitudes toward women's family role among black and white undergraduates. *Family Coordinator*, 1970, 19, 363-368.

Steinmann, A.; Levi, J.; & Fox, D. J. Self-concept of college women compared with their concept of ideal woman and men's ideal woman. *Journal of Counseling Psychology*, 1964, 11, 370-374.

Stenner, A. J., & Katzenmeyer, W. G. Self concept, ability and achievement in a sample of sixth grade students. *Journal of Educational Research*, 1976, 69, 270-273.

Stephenson, R. M. Mobility orientation and stratification of 1,000 ninth graders. *American Sociological Review,* 1957, 22, 204-212.

Stevenson, H. W., & Stevenson, N. G. Social interaction in an interracial nursery school. *Genetic Psychology Monographs,* 1960, 61, 37-75.

Stevenson, H. W., & Stewart, E. C. A developmental study of race awareness in young children. *Child Development,* 1958, 29, 399-410.

Stewart, R. A. C. Academic performance and components of self actualization. *Perceptual and Motor Skills,* 1968, 26, 918.

Stimpson, D. V. The influence of commitment and self-esteem on susceptibility to persuasion. *Journal of Social Psychology,* 1970, 80, 189-195.

Stock, D. An investigation into the intercorrelations between the self-concept and feelings directed toward other persons and groups. *Journal of Consulting Psychology,* 1949, 13, 176-180.

Stone, P. J.; Dunphy, D. C.; Smith, M. S.; & Ogilvie, D. M. *The general inquirer: A computer approach to content analysis.* Cambridge, Mass.: M.I.T. Press, 1966.

Stotland, E. Determinants of attraction to groups. *Journal of Social Psychology,* 1959, 49, 71-80.

Strauss, S. The effect of school integration on the self concept of Negro and Puerto Rican children. *Graduate Research in Education and Related Disciplines,* 1967, 3, 63-76.

Streitfeld, J. W. Expressed acceptance of self and others by psychotherapists. *Journal of Consulting Psychology,* 1959, 23, 435-441.

Stricker, L. J.; Messick, S.; & Jackson, D. N. Suspicion of deception: Implications for conformity research. *Journal of Personality and Social Psychology,* 1967, 5, 379-389.

Stricker, L. J.; Messick, S.; & Jackson, D. N. Desirability judgments and self-reports as predictors of social behavior. *Journal of Experimental Research in Personality,* 1968, 3, 151-167.

Stricker, L. J.; Messick, S.; & Jackson, D. N. Evaluating deception in psychological research. *Psychological Bulletin,* 1969, 71, 343-351.

Strupp, H. H., & Bergin, A. E. Some empirical and conceptual bases for coordinated research in psychotherapy: A critical review of issues, trends, and evidence. *International Journal of Psychiatry,* 1969, 7, 18-90.

Strupp, H. H.; Fox, R. E.; & Lessler, K. *Patients view their psychotherapy.* Baltimore, Md.: Johns Hopkins Press, 1969.

Strupp, H. H.; Wallach, M. S.; & Wogan, M. Psychotherapy experience in retrospect: Questionnaire survey of former patients and their therapists. *Psychological Monographs,* 1964, 78 (Whole No. 588).

Subotnik, L. Spontaneous remission: Fact or artifact? *Psychological Bulletin,* 1972, 77, 32-48.

Suchman, E. A.; Phillips, B. S.; & Streib, G. F. An analysis of the validity of health questionnaires. *Social Forces,* 1957-58, 36, 223-232.

Suinn, R. M. The relationship between self-acceptance and acceptance of others: A learning theory analysis. *Journal of Abnormal and Social Psychology,* 1961, 63, 37–42.

Suinn, R. M., & Geiger, J. Stress and the stability of self- and other attitudes. *Journal of General Psychology,* 1965, 73, 177–180.

Suinn, R. M., & Hill, H. Influence of anxiety on the relationship between self-acceptance and acceptance of others. *Journal of Consulting Psychology,* 1964, 28, 116–119.

Sullivan, H. S. *The interpersonal theory of psychiatry.* New York: Norton, 1953.

Sumner, F. C. Marks as estimated by students. *Education,* 1932, 52, 429.

Sweet, J. R., & Thornburg, K. R. Preschoolers' self and social identity within the family structure. *Journal of Negro Education,* 1971, 40, 22–27.

Tamkin, A. S. Selective recall in schizophrenia and its relation to ego strength. *Journal of Abnormal and Social Psychology,* 1957, 55, 345–349.

Tapp, J. T., & Spanier, D. Personal characteristics of volunteer phone counselors. *Journal of Consulting and Clinical Psychology,* 1973, 41, 245–250.

Tarwater, J. W. The adolescent's question: "Who understands who I am?". *Understanding the Child,* 1955, 24, 11–14.

Taylor, A. B. Role perception, empathy and marriage adjustment. *Sociology and Social Research,* 1967, 52, 22–34.

Teichman, M. Ego defense, self-concept and image of self ascribed to parents by delinquent boys. *Perceptual and Motor Skills,* 1971, 32, 819–823.

Teichman, M. Cognitive differentiation between self-concept and image of self ascribed to parents in boys on verge of delinquency. *Perceptual and Motor Skills,* 1972, 34, 573–574.

Terman, L. M., & Tyler, L. E. Psychological sex differences. In L. Carmichael (Ed.), *Manual of child psychology.* (2nd ed.) New York: Wiley, 1954. Pp. 1064–1114.

Thomes, M. M. Children with absent fathers. *Journal of Marriage and the Family,* 1968, 30, 89–96.

Thompson, C. Cultural pressures in the psychology of women. *Psychiatry,* 1942, 5, 331–339.

Thompson, C. "Penis envy" in women. *Psychiatry,* 1943, 6, 123–125.

Thompson, C. Some effects of the derogatory attitude toward female sexuality. *Psychiatry,* 1950, 13, 349–354.

Thompson, W. Correlates of the self concept: Studies on the self concept and rehabilitation. *Dede Wallace Center Monograph No. 6.* Nashville, Tenn.: Counselor Recordings and Tests, 1972.

Thompson, W. R., & Nishimura, R. Some determinants of friendship. *Journal of Personality,* 1952, 20, 305–314.

Thompson, W. R., & Randolph, D. L. A comparison of the relative effectiveness of two different group approaches to counseling with sixth grade pupils. *The Southern Journal of Educational Research*, 1973, 7, 66-79.

Thorndike, R. L. *The concepts of over- and underachievement.* New York: Columbia University, Teachers College, Bureau of Publications, 1963.

Thornton, G. C. The relationship between supervisory and self-appraisals of executive performance. *Personnel Psychology*, 1968, 21, 441-455.

Thorpe, J. G. A study of some factors in friendship formation. *Sociometry*, 1955, 18, 207-214.

Thorpe, L. P.; Clark, W. W.; & Tiegs, E. W. *California Test of Personality Manual.* California Test Bureau/McGraw-Hill, 1953.

Todd, W. B., & Ewing, T. N. Changes in self-reference during counseling. *Journal of Counseling Psychology*, 1961, 8, 112-115.

Tognoli, J., & Keisner, R. Gain and loss of esteem as determinants of interpersonal attraction: A replication and extension. *Journal of Personality and Social Psychology*, 1972, 23, 201-204.

Torrance, E. P. Rationalizations about test performance as a function of self-concepts. *Journal of Social Psychology*, 1954, 39, 211-217. (a)

Torrance, E. P. Some practical uses of a knowledge of self-concepts in counseling and guidance. *Educational and Psychological Measurement,* 1954, 14, 120-127. (b)

Torrance, E. P. *Torrance Tests of Creative Thinking: Directions manual and sorting guide.* Princeton, N.J.: Personnel Press, 1966. (a)

Torrance, E. P. *Technical-norms manual for the Torrance Tests of Creative Thinking: Research edition.* Princeton, N.J.: Personnel Press, 1966. (b)

Torrance, E. P. The Minnesota Studies of Creative Behavior: National and international extensions. *Journal of Creative Behavior*, 1967, 1, 137-154.

Torrance, E. P. *Torrance Tests of Creative Thinking: Norms-Technical Manual.* Lexington, Mass.: Ginn and Company, 1974.

Torrance, E. P., & Khatena, J. *Technical norms manual for "What Kind of Person Are You?".* Mimeographed. Athens, Georgia: University of Georgia, 1970. (a)

Torrance, E. P., & Khatena, J. What Kind of Person Are You? A brief screening device for identifying creatively gifted adolescents and adults. *Gifted Child Quarterly*, 1970, 14, 71-75. (b)

Touhey, J. A symbolic interactionist approach to self-referent behavior. *Psychological Reports*, 1971, 29, 87-90.

Trent, R. D. Sociempathic ability in a group of institutionalized delinquent boys. *Journal of Genetic Psychology*, 1957, 91, 99-108.

Trent, R. D. Anxiety and accuracy of perception of sociometric status among institutionalized delinquent boys. *Journal of Genetic Psychology*, 1959, 94, 85-91.

Treppa, J. A., & Fricke, L. Effects of a marathon group experience. *Journal of Counseling Psychology,* 1972, 19, 466–467.

Trotzer, J. P., & Sease, W. A. The effect of group-centered and topic-centered methods on volunteer college students' self-concepts. *Journal of College Student Personnel,* 1971, 12, 292–296.

Trowbridge, N. T. Effects of socio-economic class on self-concept of children. *Psychology in the Schools,* 1970, 7, 304–306.

Trowbridge, N. T. Self-concept and socio-economic status in elementary school children. *American Educational Research Journal,* 1972, 9, 525–537. (a)

Trowbridge, N. T. Socio-economic status and self-concept of children. *Journal of Teacher Education,* 1972, 23, 63–65. (b)

Trowbridge, N. T. Self concept and IQ in elementary school children. *California Journal of Educational Research,* 1974, 25, 37–49.

Truax, C. B. The meaning and reliability of accurate empathy ratings: A rejoinder. *Psychological Bulletin,* 1972, 77, 397–399.

Truax, C. B.; Schuldt, W. J.; & Wargo, D. G. Self-ideal concept congruence and improvement in group psychotherapy. *Journal of Consulting and Clinical Psychology,* 1968, 32, 47–53.

Truax, C. B., & Wargo, D. G. Effects of vicarious therapy pretraining and alternate sessions on outcome in group psychotherapy with outpatients. *Journal of Consulting and Clinical Psychology,* 1969, 33, 440–447.

Truax, C.; Wargo, D.; & Silber, L. Effects of group psychotherapy with high accurate empathy and nonpossessive warmth upon female institutionalized delinquents. *Journal of Abnormal Psychology,* 1966, 71, 267–274.

Tuckman, J., & Lavell, M. Self-classification as old or not old. *Geriatrics,* 1957, 12, 666–671.

Tuckman, J., & Lorge, I. Attitudes toward old people. *Journal of Social Psychology,* 1953, 37, 249–260.

Tuckman, J., & Lorge, I. Classification of the self as young, middle-aged or old. *Geriatrics,* 1954, 9, 534–536.

Tuckman, J.; Lorge, I.; & Spooner, G. A. The effect of family environment on attitudes toward old people and the older worker. *Journal of Social Psychology,* 1953, 38, 207–218.

Tuddenham, R. D. Correlates of yielding to a distorted norm group. *Journal of Personality,* 1959, 27, 272–284.

Turner, R. H. Is there a quest for identity? *Sociological Quarterly,* 1975, 16, 148–161.

Turner, R. H., & Vanderlippe, R. H. Self-ideal congruence as an index of adjustment. *Journal of Abnormal and Social Psychology,* 1958, 57, 202–206.

Tyler, F. T. Stability of intra-individual patterning of measures of adjustment during adolescence. *Journal of Educational Psychology,* 1957, 48, 217–226.

Uhrbrock, R. S. Personal estimates of character traits. *Pedagogical Seminary,* 1926, 33, 491-496.

Ullman, C. A. Teachers, peers and tests as predictors of adjustment. *Journal of Educational Psychology,* 1957, 48, 257-267.

Underwood, B. J. *Psychological research.* New York: Appleton-Century-Crofts, 1957.

Unger, R. K. *Sex-role stereotypes revisited: Psychological approaches to women's studies.* New York: Harper & Row, 1975.

U.S. Commission on Civil Rights. Racial isolation in the public schools. Vols. 1 and 2. Washington, D.C.: U.S. Government Printing Office, 1967.

University of Massachusetts Counseling Center Staff. Effects of three types of sensitivity groups on changes in measures of self-actualization. *Journal of Counseling Psychology,* 1972, 19, 253-254.

Urban, H. B., & Ford, D. H. Some historical and conceptual perspectives on psychotherapy and behavior change. In A. E. Bergin & S. L. Garfield (Eds.), *Handbook of psychotherapy and behavior change: An empirical analysis.* New York: Wiley, 1971. Pp. 3-35.

Vacchiano, R. B.; Schiffman, D. C.; & Strauss, P. S. Factor structure of the Dogmatism Scale. *Psychological Reports,* 1967, 20, 847-852.

Vacchiano, R. B.; Strauss, P. S.; & Hochman, L. The open and closed mind: A review of dogmatism. *Psychological Bulletin,* 1969, 71, 261-273.

Vacchiano, R. B.; Strauss, P. S.; & Schiffman, D. C. Personality correlates of dogmatism. *Journal of Consulting and Clinical Psychology,* 1968, 32, 83-85.

Vance, J. J., & Richmond, B. O. Cooperative and competitive behavior as a function of self-esteem. *Psychology in the Schools,* 1975, 12, 225-229.

Van den Daele, L. A developmental study of the ego-ideal. *Genetic Psychology Monographs,* 1968, 78, 191-256.

Van Dyne, E. V. Personality traits and friendship formation in adolescent girls. *Journal of Social Psychology,* 1940, 12, 291-303.

Varble, D. L., & Landfield, A. W. Validity of the self-ideal discrepancy as a criterion measure for success in psychotherapy: A replication. *Journal of Counseling Psychology,* 1969, 16, 150-156.

Vargas, M. J. Changes in self-awareness during client-centered therapy. In C. R. Rogers & R. F. Dymond (Eds.), *Psychotherapy and personality change.* Chicago: University of Chicago Press, 1954. Pp. 145-166.

Vavrik, J., & Jurich, A. P. Self-concept and attitude toward acceptance of females: A note. *Family Coordinator,* 1971, 20, 151-152.

Venkatesan, M. Personality and persuasibility in consumer decision making. *Journal of Advertising Research,* 1968, 8, 39-44.

Vicino, F.; Krusell, J.; Bass, B.; Deci, E.; & Landy, D. The impact of PROCESS: Self-administered exercises for personal and interpersonal development. *Journal of Applied Behavioral Science,* 1973, 9, 737-756.

Voss, J. H., & Skinner, D. A. Concepts of self and ideal woman held by college women: A replication. *Journal of College Student Personnel,* 1975, 16, 210-213.

Walberg, H. J. Denominational and socio-economic correlates of professional self-concept. *Theoretische Aspekte der Religionssoziologie II.* [Sociology of Religion: Theoretical Perspectives II.] 1967, 153-164.

Walker, R. N. Some temperament traits in children as viewed by their peers, their teachers, and themselves. *Monographs of the Society for Research in Child Development,* 1967, 32 (Serial No. 114, No. 6).

Walsh, A. M. *Self-concepts of bright boys with learning difficulties.* New York: Bureau of Publications, Teachers College, Columbia University, 1956.

Walsh, W. B., & Osipow, S. H. Career preferences, self-concept, and vocational maturity. *Research in Higher Education,* 1973, 1, 287-295.

Walster, E. The effect of self-esteem on romantic liking. *Journal of Experimental Social Psychology,* 1965, 1, 184-197.

Walster, E. The effect of self-esteem on liking for dates of various social desirabilities. *Journal of Experimental Social Psychology,* 1970, 6, 248-253.

Walton, D. R. Effects of personal growth groups on self-actualization and creative personality. *Journal of College Student Personnel,* 1973, 14, 490-494.

Ward, W. D. Perceived similarity to parents as a function of their secondary reinforcement value. *Perceptual and Motor Skills,* 1971, 33, 203-210.

Ward, W. D., & Day, C. R. Perceived similarity to parents as related to perceived similarity to other adults. *Perceptual and Motor Skills,* 1969, 29, 739-742.

Warner, W. L., & Lunt, P. S. *The social life of a modern community.* New Haven: Yale University Press, 1941.

Warner, W. L.; Meeker, M.; & Eells, K. *Social class in America.* Chicago: Science Research Associates, 1949.

Washburn, W. C. Factors associated with levels of self conceptualization in high school students. *California Journal of Educational Research,* 1961, 12, 200-206, 220.

Washburn, W. C. The effects of physique and intrafamily tension on self-concepts in adolescent males. *Journal of Consulting Psychology,* 1962, 26, 460-466.

Waterman, A. S.; Geary, P. S.; & Waterman, C. K. Longitudinal study of changes in ego identity status from the freshman to the senior year at college. *Developmental Psychology,* 1974, 10, 387-392.

Waterman, A. S., & Waterman, C. K. Relationship between freshman ego identity status and subsequent academic behavior: A test of the predictive validity of Marcia's categorization system for identity status. *Developmental Psychology,* 1972, 6, 179.

Wattenberg, W. W., & Clifford, C. Relation of self-concepts to beginning achievement in reading. *Child Development,* 1964, 35, 461-467.

Wechsler, H., & Funkenstein, D. H. The family as a determinant of conflict in self-perceptions. *Psychological Reports,* 1960, 7, 143-149.

Wegner, E. L. The effects of upward mobility: A study of working status college students. *Sociology of Education,* 1973, 46, 263-279.

Weidman, J. C.; Phelan, W. T.; & Sullivan, M. A. The influence of educational attainment on self-evaluations of competence. *Sociology of Education,* 1972, 45, 303-312.

Weigel, R. D., & Warnath, C. F. The effects of group therapy on reported self-disclosure. *International Journal of Group Psychotherapy,* 1968, 18, 31-41.

Weiner, P. S. Personality correlates of self-appraisal in four-year-old children. *Genetic Psychology Monographs,* 1964, 70, 329-365.

Weinstein, M. S., & Hanson, R. G. Personality trait correlates of verbal interaction levels in an encounter group context. *Canadian Journal of Behavioural Science,* 1975, 7, 192-200.

Weissman, H. N.; Goldschmid, M. L.; Gordon, R.; & Feinberg, H. Changes in self-regard, creativity and interpersonal behavior as a function of audio-tape encounter-group experiences. *Psychological Reports,* 1972, 31, 975-981.

Weissman, H. N.; Seldman, M.; & Ritter, K. Changes in awareness of impact upon others as a function of encounter and marathon group experiences. *Psychological Reports,* 1971, 28, 651-661.

Weitzner, M.; Stallone, F.; & Smith, G. M. Personality profiles of high, middle, and low MAS subjects. *Journal of Psychology,* 1967, 65, 163-168.

Wellman, B. I am a student. *Sociology of Education,* 1971, 44, 422-437.

Welsh, G. S. *Welsh Figure Preference Test: Manual research edition.* Palo Alto, Calif.: Consulting Psychologists Press, 1959.

Wessman, A. E., & Ricks, D. F. *Mood and personality.* New York: Holt, Rinehart, and Winston, 1966.

White, J. The human potential laboratory in the community college. *Journal of College Student Personnel,* 1974, 15, 96-100.

White, K., & Howard, J. L. Failure to be promoted and self-concept among elementary school children. *Elementary School Guidance and Counseling,* 1973, 7, 182-187.

White, K. R. T-groups revisited: Self-concept change and the "fish-bowling" technique. *Small Group Behavior,* 1974, 5, 473-485.

White, W. F.; Anderson, H. E.; & Cryder, H. Allport's theory of the emerging self-concept applied to secondary school students. *Proceedings of the 74th Annual Convention of the American Psychological Association,* 1966, 1, 277-278.

White, W. F.; Anderson, H. E., Jr.; & Cryder, H. The emerging self-concept in relation to select variables of secondary school students. *Journal of Social Psychology,* 1967, 72, 81-88.

White, W. F., & Richmond, B. O. Perception of self and of peers by economically deprived black and advantaged white fifth graders. *Perceptual and Motor Skills,* 1970, 30, 533–534.

Whiteman, M., & Deutsch, M. Social disadvantage as related to intellectual and language development. In M. Deutsch; I. Katz; & A. Jensen (Eds.), *Social class, race, and psychological development.* New York: Holt, Rinehart, and Winston, 1968.

Wiest, W. M. A quantitative extension of Heider's theory of cognitive balance applied to interpersonal perception and self-esteem. *Psychological Monographs: General & Applied,* 1965, 79, 1–20.

Wilcox, A. H., & Fretz, B. R. Actual-ideal discrepancies and adjustment. *Journal of Counseling Psychology,* 1971, 18, 166–169.

Wilkinson, A. E., & Worchel, P. Self-consistency as a function of the parental self. *Psychological Reports,* 1959, 5, 503.

Williams, J. D., & Beebe, J. D. Self-concept and achievement in self-enhancing education. *Psychological Reports,* 1973, 32, 641–642.

Williams, J. E. Acceptance by others and its relationship to acceptance of self and others: A repeat of Fey's study. *Journal of Abnormal and Social Psychology,* 1962, 65, 438–442.

Williams, J. E., & Robertson, J. K. A method for assessing racial attitudes in preschool children. *Educational and Psychological Measurement,* 1967, 27, 671–689.

Williams, J. H. The relationship of self-concept and reading achievement in first grade children. *Journal of Educational Research,* 1973, 66, 378–381.

Williams, M.; McGee, T. F.; Kittleson, S.; & Halperin, L. An evaluation of an intensive group living program with schizophrenic patients. *Psychological Monographs,* 1962, 76 (Whole No. 543).

Williams, R. L., & Byars, H. Negro self-esteem in a transitional society. *Personnel and Guidance Journal,* 1968, 47, 120–125.

Williams, R. L., & Byars, H. The effect of academic integration on the self-esteem of Southern Negro students. *Journal of Social Psychology,* 1970, 80, 183–188.

Williams, R. L., & Cole, S. Self-concept and school adjustment. *Personnel and Guidance Journal,* 1968, 46, 478–481.

Wilson, A. B. Residential segregation of social classes and aspirations of high school boys. *American Sociological Review,* 1959, 24, 836–845.

Wilson, A. B. *The consequences of segregation: Academic achievement in a northern community.* Berkeley, Calif.: Glendessary Press, 1969.

Wilson, D. T. Ability evaluation, postdecision dissonance, and co-worker attractiveness. *Journal of Personality and Social Psychology,* 1965, 1, 486–489.

Wilson, R. C.; Guilford, J. P.; & Christensen, P. R. The measurement of individual differences in originality. *Psychological Bulletin,* 1953, 50, 362–370.

Winch, R. F.; Ktsanes, T.; & Ktsanes, V. Empirical elaboration of the theory of complementary needs in mate-selection. *Journal of Abnormal and Social Psychology*, 1955, 51, 508–513.

Winkler, R. C.; Munger, P. F.; Gust, C. T.; & Teigland, J. J. Changes in the concepts of self and others of NDEA guidance institute members. *Journal of Counseling Psychology*, 1963, 10, 227–231.

Winkler, R. C., & Myers, R. A. Some concomitants of self-ideal discrepancy measures of self-acceptance. *Journal of Counseling Psychology*, 1963, 10, 83–86.

Wise, G. W., & Davis, J. E. The Personal Orientation Inventory: Internal consistency, stability, and sex differences. *Psychological Reports*, 1975, 36, 847–855.

Wolkon, G. H. African identity of the Negro American and achievement. *Journal of Social Issues*, 1971, 27, 199–211.

Woody, R. H. Self-understanding seminars: The effects of group psychotherapy in counselor training. *Counselor Education and Supervision*, 1971, 10, 112–119.

Worchel, P. Adaptability screening of flying personnel: Development of a self-concept inventory for predicting maladjustment. USAF Report No. 56-62, 1957, School of Aviation Medicine.

Worchel, P., & McCormick, B. L. Self-concept and dissonance reduction. *Journal of Personality*, 1963, 31, 588–599.

Works, E. Residence in integrated and segregated housing and improvement in self-concepts of Negroes. *Sociology and Social Research*, 1962, 46, 294–301.

Wright, B., & Tuska, S. The nature and origin of feeling feminine. *British Journal of Social & Clinical Psychology*, 1966, 5, 140–149.

Wright, D. S. A comparative study of the adolescent's concept of his parents and teachers. *Educational Review*, 1962, 14, 226–232.

Wright, R. J.; Fox, M.; & Noppe, L. The interrelationship of creativity, self-esteem, and creative self-concept. *Psychology*, 1975, 12, 11–15.

Wrightsman, L. S., Jr. Authoritarianism and self awareness. *Journal of Social Psychology*, 1962, 56, 179–185.

Wyer, R. S. Self-acceptance, discrepancy between parents' perceptions of their children, and goal-seeking effectiveness. *Journal of Personality and Social Psychology*, 1965, 2, 311–316.

Wylie, R. C. Some relationships between defensiveness and self-concept discrepancies. *Journal of Personality*, 1957, 25, 600–616.

Wylie, R. C. *The self concept: A critical survey of pertinent research literature.* Lincoln: University of Nebraska Press, 1961.

Wylie, R. C. Children's estimates of their schoolwork ability as a function of sex, race, and socioeconomic level. *Journal of Personality*, 1963, 31, 203–224.

Wylie, R. C. Self-ratings, level of ideal-self ratings and defensiveness. *Psychological Reports*, 1965, 16, 135–150.

Wylie, R. C. *The self concept: A review of methodological considerations and measuring instruments.* (Rev. ed.) Vol. 1. Lincoln, Nebraska: University of Nebraska Press, 1974.

Wylie, R. C., & Hutchins, E. B. Schoolwork-ability estimates and aspirations as a function of socioeconomic level, race, and sex. *Psychological Reports,* 1967, 21, 781–808.

Yamamoto, K.; Thomas, E. C.; & Karns, E. A. School-related attitudes in middle-school age students. *American Educational Research Journal,* 1969, 6, 191–206.

Yamamoto, K., & Wiersma, J. Rejection of self and of deviant others among student teachers. *Journal of Special Education,* 1967, 1, 401–408.

Yancey, W. L.; Rigsby, L.; & McCarthy, J. D. Social position and self-evaluation: The relative importance of race. *American Journal of Sociology,* 1972, 78, 338–359.

Yarrow, M. R.; Campbell, J. D., & Yarrow, L. J. Acquisition of new norms: A study of racial desegregation. *Journal of Social Issues,* 1958, 14, 8–28.

Yellott, A. W.; Liem, G. R.; & Cowen, E. L. Relationships among measures of adjustment, sociometric status, and achievement in third graders. *Psychology in the Schools,* 1969, 6, 315–321.

Young, E. R., & Jacobson, L. I. Effects of time-extended marathon group experiences on personality characteristics. *Journal of Counseling Psychology,* 1970, 17, 249–251.

Zelen, S. L. The relationship of peer acceptance, acceptance of others, and self acceptance. *Proceedings of the Iowa Academy of Science,* 1954, 61, 446–449. (a)

Zelen, S. L. Acceptance and acceptability: An examination of social reciprocity. *Journal of Consulting Psychology,* 1954, 18, 316. (b)

Zellner, M. Self-esteem, reception, and influenceability. *Journal of Personality and Social Psychology,* 1970, 15, 87–93.

Zigler, E.; Balla, D.; & Watson, N. Developmental and experiential determinants of self-image disparity in institutionalized and noninstitutionalized retarded and normal children. *Journal of Personality and Social Psychology,* 1972, 23, 81–87.

Ziller, R. C., & Grossman, S. A. A developmental study of the self-social constructs of normals and the neurotic personality. *Journal of Clinical Psychology,* 1967, 23, 15–21.

Ziller, R. C.; Hagey, J.; Smith, M. D.; & Long, B. Self esteem: A self-social construct. *Journal of Consulting and Clinical Psychology,* 1969, 33, 84–95.

Zimmer, H. Motivational factors in dyadic interaction. *Journal of Personality,* 1956, 24, 251–261.

Zirkel, P. A. Self-concept and the "disadvantage" of ethnic group membership and mixture. *Review of Educational Research,* 1971, 41, 211–225.

Zirkel, P. A., & Moses, E. G. Self-concept and ethnic group membership among public school students. *American Educational Research Journal,* 1971, 8, 253–264.

Zola, I. K. Feelings about age among older people. *Journal of Gerontology,* 1962, 17, 65–68.

Zoolalian, C. H. Factors related to differential achievement among boys in ninth-grade algebra. *Journal of Educational Research,* 1965, 58, 205–207.

Zuckerman, M.; Baer, M.; & Monashkin, I. Acceptance of self, parents and people in patients and normals. *Journal of Clinical Psychology,* 1956, 53, 315–320.

Zuckerman, M., & Oltean, M. Some relationships between maternal attitude factors and authoritarianism, personality needs, psychopathology, and self-acceptance. *Child Development,* 1959, 30, 27–36.

Subject Matter Index

789

Anxiety, self-reported
  birth order and, 344–345
  psychotherapy and, 622, 637, 640–644
  self-regard and, 661
    See also in Index of Tests and Measures: Children's Manifest Anxiety Scale, DiLoreto's Interpersonal Anxiety Scale, Spielberger and Gorsuch Trait Anxiety Inventory, S-R Inventory of Anxiousness, Taylor Manifest Anxiety Scale, Welsh A Scale
Approval need. See in Index of Tests and Measures: Marlowe-Crowne Social Desirability Scale
Aspirations for self
  re education, 379
    by race, 218–234
    by racial integration, 235–236
    by socioeconomic class, 106–111, 115
  re occupation, 355, 379
    by race, 218–234
    by socioeconomic class, 106–111, 115
  re task success, 476–477, 498
Attitudes
  similarity and interpersonal attraction, 454, 505, 519–520, 545–547
  toward racial groups, 121, 122, 124, 125–126, 142, 143–145, 148–150, 152–156, 158–161
    by age, 151–152, 153
  toward socioeconomic classes, 80–82
  toward women, 306
Attraction. See under Regard for (evaluation of) others; Regard from (evaluation by) others
Authoritarianism. Chapter 10
  definition of, 603–604
  factor analyses involving, 604
  measurement of, 603–604, 690
  reactions to evaluation and, 476, 495
  regard for others and, 436
  relationships to dogmatism, 604
  relationships to self-concept variables
    method, 606–608, 609
    theory, 604–605, 690
  and self-concept, specific aspects of, 608–610
  self-regard and, 605, 606, 608–610
Autonomy. See in Index of Tests and Measures: Edwards Personal Preference Schedule, Personality Research Form

Balance theory (Heider), 511, 514–515, 517–518, 541, 546–547
  See also Consistency theories

Birth order
  affiliation and, 322
  anxiety, self-reported and, 344–345
  parental treatment and, 344
  self-concept and, 344–345

Career aspirations. See Aspirations
Child-rearing practices. See Parental influences
Children's self-concepts. See under Development; Family Variables; Parental Influences; Racial/Ethnic Status; Socioeconomic level
Cognitive dissonance. See Consistency theory
Complementary need theory, 514, 529
Conformity. See Influenceability
Congruency, 636
  between self and ideal self concepts. See Self-regard
  between self-concept and "reality." See Insightfulness of self-concept; Self-favorability
  within self-concept, 555, 556
  See also Consistency theories
Consistency theories (cognitive)
  achievement and, 355
  effects of others' evaluations and, 468–474, 476, 484–495, 518–519
  influenceability and, 553, 555
  interpersonal similarity and attraction and, 517–518, 547
  vs. self-enhancement, 468–474
Construct validity. See under each substantive heading, relationships with self-concept variables, methodology, measurement
Counseling. See Psychotherapy
Creativity. Chapter 7
  in activities of
    Air Force captains, 413, 415, 423
    architects, 412, 413, 414–415, 416
    art students, 426–429
    business managers, 412, 413, 415, 417
    college seniors (women), 412, 413, 415
    engineers, 418–419, 430
    graduate students, 424
    high school students, 420, 426
    mathematicians, 412, 413, 415, 416, 417
    mathematics students, 426–429
    science majors (college), 421
    science students (high school), 415, 426–429
    scientists, 415, 430
    writers, 412, 413, 415, 416

Index of Proper Names

The Index of Tests and Measures includes proper names of persons associated with particular tests and measures.

Abate, M., 162, 169, 170, 703
Abelson, R. P., 576, 577, 578, 581, 747, 771, 774
Abrams, A. R., 44, 749
Abramson, M., 220, 224, 774
Achord, C. D., 363, 369, 703
Adamczyk, J. S., 637, 737
Adams, H. L., 373, 375, 752
Adank, R., 365, 374, 661, 748
Adesso, V. J., 643, 703
Adler, A., 3, 20, 41, 253, 254, 257, 278, 435, 437, 512, 618, 620, 630, 654, 656, 665, 703
Adler, N. E., 643, 703
Adorno, T. V., 603, 604, 608, 703
Ageton, S. S., 103, 211, 703
Ahammer, I. M., 39, 55, 703
Aisenberg, R., 48, 51, 703
Albrecht, R., 51, 734
Albright, L. E., 418, 430, 756
Alexander, F., 617
Alexander, S., 465, 718
Alexandra, S. M., 464, 703
Alfert, E., 452, 703
Allport, G. W., 3, 9, 703
Alm, G. W., 350, 746
Altrocchi, J., 659, 704
Alves, G. J., 268, 387, 772
Amatora, S. M., 39, 704
Ames, L. B., 13, 704
Amsterdam, B., 12, 704
Anastasi, A., 247, 288, 316, 426, 427, 704, 770
Anastasiow, N. J., 382, 384, 704
Anderson, H. E., 39, 98, 106, 278, 783
Anderson, J. G., 208, 234, 367, 704
Anderson, N. H., 540
Anderson, N. N., 54, 704
Anderson, T. B., 681, 704
Angelino, H., 682, 758
Angyal, A., 3, 704

Annis, H., 445, 717
Ansbacher, H. L., 3, 20, 41, 437, 512, 704
Ansbacher, R. R., 3, 20, 41, 437, 512, 704
Anshen, R., 726
Anthony, J., 343, 708
Antley, M. A., 278, 704
Antley, R. M., 278, 704
Antonovsky, A., 220, 223, 229, 230, 234, 704
Apostal, R. A., 643, 704
Appley, M. H., 575, 576, 578, 590, 591, 704
Applezweig, M. H., 590, 591, 756
Aptowitz, P. H., 142, 150
Arbuckle, D. S., 638, 681, 704, 705
Archambault, F. X., 267, 730
Archibald, W. P., 519, 546, 547, 705
Arkoff, A., 212, 218, 235, 705
Aronson, E., 3, 468, 475, 476, 482, 483, 495, 497, 498, 538, 539, 555, 588, 589, 705, 734, 745, 748, 751, 771, 773, 774
Arrowood, A. J., 451, 474, 483, 484, 490, 705, 721
Arsenian, S., 681, 705
Asch, S., 572, 576, 577, 578, 579, 580, 590, 591, 594, 595, 598
Ashcraft, C., 659, 705
Attenborough, R. E., 26, 101, 106, 218, 705
Auerbach, A. H., 622, 627, 628, 750
Austin, L. J., 164, 288, 290, 708
Ausubel, D. P., 123, 705
Ax, A. F., 660, 744
Axelrod, H. S., 661, 718

Bachman, J. G., 29, 31, 32, 33, 68, 84, 85, 86, 99, 107, 174, 175, 177, 178, 194, 202, 220, 223, 224, 236, 237, 339, 340, 342, 343, 345, 364, 368, 375, 381, 661, 676, 705, 771
Bachrach, H. M., 622, 627, 628, 750

801

Index of Tests and Measures

Only tests and measures cited by proper name in the text are included in this index. Idiosyncratic tests and measures not assigned proper names are omitted.

821